D0456746

Amsterdam

"All you've got to do is decide to go
and the hardest part is over.

So go!"

TONY WHEELER, COFOUNDER – LONELY PLANET

CATHERINE LE NEVEZ,
KATE MORGAN, BARBARA WOOLSEY

Contents

(left) **Noordermarkt p149** One of Amsterdam's many markets.

....

(above) **Vondelpark p159** Great for exploring by bike.

....

(right) **Sticky Fingers p171** Homemade cakes and good coffee.

....

Welcome to Amsterdam

Golden Age canals lined by tilting gabled buildings are the backdrop for Amsterdam's treasure-packed museums, vintage shops and creative drinking, dining and design scenes.

Urban Explorations

Amsterdam's canal-woven core is laced by atmospheric lanes. You never know what you'll find: a hidden garden; a boutique selling Dutch-designed homewares and fashion; a *jenever* distillery; a flower stall with tulips in a rainbow of hues; a monastery-turned-classical-music-venue; an ultra-niche restaurant such as an avocado specialist or one reinventing Dutch classics. Fringing the centre, post-industrial buildings in up-and-coming neighbourhoods now house creative enterprises, from art galleries to craft breweries and cutting-edge tech start-ups, as well as some of Europe's hottest clubs.

Admiring Art

You can't walk a kilometre without bumping into a masterpiece. The Van Gogh Museum hangs the world's largest collection by tortured native son Vincent. A few blocks away, Vermeers, Rembrandts and other Golden Age treasures fill glorious Rijksmuseum. Museum het Rembrandthuis offers more of Rembrandt via his etching-packed studio, while Stedelijk Museum counts Matisses and Mondrians among its modern stock. For blockbuster displays, the Hermitage Amsterdam delivers: the outpost of Russia's State Hermitage Museum uses its three-million-piece home trove to mount mega exhibitions.

Bike & Boat Travel

Two-wheeling is a way of life here. It's how Amsterdammers commute to work, go to the shop, and meet a date for dinner. Abundant bike-hire shops make it easy to gear up and take a spin. If locals aren't on a bike, they may well be on the water. With its canals and massive harbour, this city reclaimed from the sea offers countless opportunities to drift. Hop aboard a canal boat (preferably an open-air one) or one of the free ferries behind Centraal Station, or rent your own for a wind-in-your-hair ride.

Feel Gezellig

Amsterdam is famously *gezellig,* a Dutch quality that translates roughly as 'convivial' or 'cosy'. It's more easily experienced than defined. There's a sense of time stopping, an intimacy of the here-and-now that leaves your troubles behind, at least until tomorrow. The easiest place to encounter this feeling is a *bruin café* (brown cafe; traditional drinking establishment). Named for their wood panelling and walls once stained by smoke, brown cafes have *gezelligheid* (cosiness) on tap, along with good beer. You can also feel *gezellig* lingering after dinner in snug restaurants while the candles burn low.

PAOLO PARADISO/SHUTTERSTOCK ©

Why I Love Amsterdam

By Catherine Le Nevez, Writer

Amsterdam's balancing act between its seeming contradictions constantly inspires me. The city is full of history, with its Golden Age canal houses, Old Masters paintings, *jenever* tasting houses and candlelit *bruin cafés,* yet it's also at the cutting edge of tech innovation, environmental sustainability and break-out design. It's resolutely Dutch but equally a multinational melting pot with an incredible diversity of cultures and cuisines. It's a major European capital yet compact and intimate. And while it famously has a wild side, it also harbours wonderfully low-key, village-like neighbourhoods and creative, repurposed industrial spaces.

For more about our writers, see p320

Above: A street in Amsterdam's Medieval Centre

Amsterdam's
Top 10

Rijksmuseum *(p153)*

1 The Netherlands' top treasure house does not disappoint. The crowds huddle around Rembrandt's humongous *Night Watch* and Vermeer's *Kitchen Maid* in the Gallery of Honour, but that just means the remaining 1.5km of rooms are free for browsing antique ship models, savage-looking swords, crystal goblets and magic lanterns. You could spend days gaping at the beautiful and curious collections tucked into the nooks and crannies. What's more, free sculpture-studded gardens surround the monumental building, which also shelters a Michelin-starred restaurant, Rijks. BOTTOM LEFT: *THE NIGHT WATCH*

👁 *Vondelpark & the South*

Van Gogh Museum *(p156)*

2 Housing the world's largest collection by artist Vincent van Gogh, this museum is as much a tour through the driven painter's troubled mind as it is a tour through his body of work. More than 200 canvases are on display, from his dark, potato-filled early career in the Netherlands through to his later years in sunny France, where he produced his best-known work with its characteristic giddy colour. Also here are 400 of his drawings and 700 letters. Paintings by contemporaries Gauguin, Toulouse-Lautrec, Monet and Bernard round out the retrospective.

👁 *Vondelpark & the South*

MARK READY/LONELY PLANET ©

SARAH COGHILL/LONELY PLANET ©

Brown Cafes (p79)

3 For a quintessential Amsterdam experience, pull up a stool in one of the city's famed *bruin cafés* (brown cafes; traditional Dutch pubs) such as In 't Aepjen (p79). The true specimen has been in business a while and gets its name from centuries' worth of smoke stains on the walls. Brown cafes have candle-topped tables, wooden floors and sometimes an affectionate house cat. Most importantly, brown cafes induce a cosy vibe that prompts friends to linger and chat for hours over drinks – the same enchantment the cafes have cast for centuries.

🍷 *Drinking & Nightlife*

Jordaan (p136)

4 If Amsterdam's neighbourhoods held a 'best personality' contest, the Jordaan would win. The former workers' quarter's intimacy is contagious, with modest old homes, offbeat galleries and vintage shops peppering a grid of tiny lanes. This is the place for jovial bar singalongs and beery brown cafes, the neighbourhood where you could spend a week wandering the narrow streets and still not discover all the hidden courtyards and tucked-away restaurants. The Dutch have a propensity for *gezelligheid* (conviviality) and the Jordaan is a fount of it.

BOTTOM LEFT: CAFÉ PAPENEILAND (P144)

👁 *Jordaan & the West*

Vondelpark (p159)

5 On a sunny day it seems the whole city converges on this sprawling urban oasis. Couples kiss on the grass, friends cradle beers at the outdoor cafes, while others trade songs on beat-up guitars. Street performers work the crowds, joggers and cyclists loop past, and kids romp in the playgrounds. It's all very democratic, and superb for people-watching. The English-style layout incorporates an abundance of ponds, lawns, thickets, sculptures and winding footpaths that encourage visitors to get out and explore the freewheeling scene.

👁 *Vondelpark & the South*

Canal Trips *(p37)*

6 Amsterdam has more canals than Venice and getting on the water is one of the best ways to feel the pulse of the city. You could catch the vibe by sitting canal-side and watching boats glide by: myriad brown cafes seem purpose-built for this sport. Or you could stroll alongside the canals and check out some of the city's 2500-plus houseboats. Better yet, hop on a tour boat and cruise the curved passages. From this angle, you'll understand why Unesco named the waterways a World Heritage site.

🏃 *Canals*

Outdoor Markets *(p57)*

7 Amsterdam is market-mad, and its streets lay out spreads from silks and coins to organic cheeses and bike locks. The Albert Cuypmarkt in De Pijp is king of the lot. Here stalls hawk rice cookers, spices and Dutch snacks, such as sweet *stroopwafels* (syrup-filled waffles). Bulbs fill the Bloemenmarkt, while porcelain teapots and other bric-a-brac tempt at Waterlooplein Flea Market. The Oudemanhuispoort Book Market has been selling tomes for a few centuries. Then there's the antiques market, farmers market, art market...

TOP RIGHT: WATERLOOPLEIN FLEA MARKET (P102)

🔒 *Shopping*

Cycling *(p29)*

8 There are more bicycles in Amsterdam than cars. Everyone rides: young, old, club-goers, police on duty, bankers in suits with ties flapping in the breeze. Pedal power is what moves the masses to work, to shop and to socialise at the city's brown cafes. Hiring a bike not only puts you shoulder to shoulder with locals, it gives you easy access to the city's outer neighbourhoods and their cool architecture and museums, as well as the wind-mill-dotted countryside and its time-warped villages. LEFT: NOORDERPARK IN AMSTERDAM NOORD

🏃 *By Bike*

Anne Frank Huis (p106)

9 Seeing Anne Frank's melancholy bedroom and her diary, preserved alone in its glass case, is a powerful experience that draws over 1¼ million visitors annually. Step behind the bookcase that swings open to reveal the 'Secret Annexe' and go up the steep stairs into the living quarters. It was in this dark and airless space that the Franks hid, observing complete silence during the day, before they were arrested by the Nazis and sent to concentration camps. Anne's father, Otto, was the only survivor.

⊙ *Western Canal Ring*

King's Day (p23)

10 For decades it was Queen's Day, but since the investiture of King Willem-Alexander, it's King's Day, or Koningsdag, now celebrated on his birthday, 27 April (unless it falls on a Sunday, in which case it takes place the day before). It's really just an excuse for a gigantic drinking fest throughout the city's streets and for everyone to wear ridiculous orange outfits, the country's national colour. There's also a *vrijmarkt* (free market) city-wide (where anyone can sell anything) and rollicking free concerts.

🎇 *Month by Month*

What's New

Unearthed Treasures

The decade-and-a-half-long construction of Amsterdam's 2018-opened Noord/Zuidlijn (North–South Metro Line), linking Amsterdam Noord and the World Trade Centre in the south, unearthed over 134,000 archaeological finds from beneath the city's streets and waterways. Some 9500 of them, dating back to 2400 BC, are now displayed in glass cases between the escalators at Rokin metro station. (p69)

Plastic Fishing

The world's first 'plastic-fishing' operator, Plastic Whale, has set sail in Amsterdam: participants are given nets to fish out plastic waste while cruising Amsterdam's waterways, which is then recycled into furniture and even the cruise boats themselves. (p266)

Canal-Bridge Houses

Water views are guaranteed at SWEETS Hotel, an ingenious concept that has transformed 28 canal-bridge houses, where bridge-keepers once lived, into nifty short-stay apartments. (p217)

Eco Sleeping

Inside a monumental brick building at the former gasworks now housing cultural hub Westergasfabriek, the Conscious Hotel Westerpark incorporates wind-powered electricity, recycled materials, and aquaponic walls growing organic vegetables and herbs for its cafe. (p224)

Vegan Dining

Green-minded Amsterdam remains at the forefront of the worldwide vegan dining trend, with a slew of new premises continuing to sprout up. Among them is the Vegan Junk Food Bar, which has several offshoots around town. (p164)

Indonesian Flavours

The city's most feted chef, Ron Blaauw, fires up the spice at 2019-opened Ron Gastrobar Downtown, which serves contemporary Indonesian cuisine and cocktails, and doubles as a DJ-fuelled club. (p75)

Coffee Culture

Amsterdam continues to ride coffee's third wave, with standout roasteries scattered around town such as Drupa, which roasts and brews 'farm to cup' beans to perfection. (p145)

Vondelpark Brewery Outpost

In 2019 beloved Amsterdam craft brewery Brouwerij 't IJ took over the Vondelpark's flying-saucer-shaped Blauwe Theehuis, serving its frothy beers in the city's favourite urban idyll. (p170)

Cocktail Curiosities

Dutch seafarers used to pay their bar tabs with exotic animals and curios collected on their travels. New cocktail bar Rosalia's Menagerie channels their heritage in its decor and its cocktails incorporating Dutch spirits. (p99)

Flight Expansion

Schiphol International Airport will host thousands of additional flights from 2020, with many budget airlines and freight services moving to nearby Lelystad, 50km to Amsterdam's east. (p262)

For more recommendations and reviews, see **lonelyplanet. com/Amsterdam**

Need to Know

For more information, see Survival Guide (p261)

Currency
Euro (€)

Language
Dutch

Visas
Generally not required for stays up to 90 days; from 2021, non-EU nationals will need prior authorisation under the European Travel Information and Authorisation System (ETIAS) system for Schengen area travel.

Money
ATMs widely available. Credit cards accepted in most hotels but not all restaurants. Non-Dutch and/or non-European credit cards are sometimes rejected.

Mobile Phones
Ask your home provider about an international plan. Alternatively, local prepaid SIM cards are widely available and can be used in most unlocked phones.

Time
Central European Time (GMT/ UTC plus one hour).

Tourist Information
The main branch of I Amsterdam Visitor Centre (p271) is located outside Centraal Station.

Daily Costs

Budget:
Less than €130
➡ Dorm bed: €25–60

➡ Supermarkets and lunchtime specials for food: €20

➡ Boom Chicago late-night show ticket: €15

➡ Bike hire per day: €12

Midrange:
€130–300
➡ Double room: from €150

➡ Three-course dinner in casual restaurant: €40

➡ Concertgebouw ticket: €40

➡ Canal Bus day pass: €21

Top end:
More than €300
➡ Four-star hotel double room: from €250

➡ Five-course dinner in top restaurant: from €80

➡ Private canal-boat rental for two hours: from €90

Advance Planning

Four months before Book your accommodation, especially if you're visiting in summer or on a weekend.

Two months before Check club and performing-arts calendars and buy tickets for anything that looks appealing.

Two weeks before Make dinner reservations at your must-eat restaurants, reserve walking or cycling tours, and purchase tickets online to popular attractions like the Van Gogh Museum (p156), Anne Frank Huis (p106) and Rijksmuseum (p153).

Useful Websites

Lonely Planet (www.lonelyplanet.com/amsterdam) Destination information, hotel bookings, traveller forum and more.

I Amsterdam (www.iamsterdam.com) City-run portal packed with sightseeing, accommodation and event info.

Dutch News (www.dutchnews.nl) News titbits and event listings.

Overdose.am (www.overdose.am) Art, music and fashion to-dos.

WHEN TO GO

Summer (June to August) is peak tourist season, with warm weather and lots of daylight for cycling. March to May is tulip time.

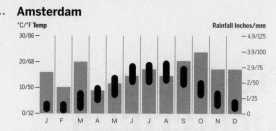

Amsterdam

Arriving in Amsterdam

Schiphol International Airport
Trains to Centraal Station depart every 10 minutes or so from 6am to 12.30am, hourly at other times; the trip takes 15 minutes and costs €4.50. Taxis cost €39.

Centraal Station In central Amsterdam with many tram and metro lines connecting it to the rest of the city; taxis queue near the front entrance (towards the west side).

Bus Stations Eurolines buses use Duivendrecht station, south of the centre, with an easy metro or train link to Centraal Station. FlixBus uses Sloterdijk station, west of the centre, with a six-minute metro or train link to Centraal.

For much more on **arrival** see p262

Getting Around

GVB passes in chip-card form are the most convenient option for public transport. Buy them at GVB ticket offices or visitor centres, or on board (credit/debit cards only, no cash). Always wave your card at the pink machine when entering and departing.

Walking Central Amsterdam is compact and easily covered by foot.

Bicycle Cycling is the locals' main transport mode. Rental companies are all over town; bikes cost about €12 daily.

Tram Fast, frequent and ubiquitous, operating between 6am and 12.30am.

Bus and metro Primarily serve the outer districts; metro 52 links Amsterdam Noord with the World Trade Centre in the south via the city centre and De Pijp.

Ferry Free ferries depart for northern Amsterdam from docks behind Centraal Station.

Taxi Expensive and slow given Amsterdam's maze of streets.

For much more on **getting around** see p264

Sleeping

Rates and crowds peak during festivals, in summer (June to August) and on weekends at any time of the year. Book *well* ahead if you're travelling then. Prices are lowest from October to April (excluding Christmas, New Year and Easter).

Useful Websites

Lonely Planet (lonelyplanet.com/the-netherlands/amsterdam/hotels) Recommendations and bookings.

I Amsterdam (www.iamsterdam.com) Wide range of options including short-stay apartments from the city's official website.

Hotels.nl (www.hotels.nl) For deals on larger properties.

CityMundo (https://amsterdam.citymundo.com) Broker for apartment and houseboat rentals.

For much more on **sleeping** see p217

First Time Amsterdam

For more information, see Survival Guide (p261)

Checklist

➡ Make sure your passport is valid for at least six months after your arrival date

➡ Inform your debit- and credit-card company of your travel

➡ Arrange appropriate travel insurance

➡ Call your mobile phone provider to enquire about roaming charges (abolished within the EU itself) or getting an international plan

What to Pack

➡ Good comfortable shoes – Amsterdam is best appreciated on foot or by bike

➡ Umbrella, because it can be rainy

➡ Electrical adaptor for the Netherlands

➡ A small daypack (the smaller the better to avoid having to check it in when visiting museums)

Top Tips for Your Trip

➡ Plan your time to avoid lengthy queues. Wherever possible, pre-purchase tickets; most can be scanned from a phone.

➡ Make reservations for dinner at midrange and top-end restaurants. Many restaurants are small and customers like to linger. Without a reservation, you might miss out on your favourite spot.

➡ Carry a mix of cash and cards; many establishments take only one or the other.

➡ Walking is one of the best ways to get around this compact city – it's quick, free, and provides the opportunity to wander by hidden lanes and shops you might otherwise miss.

➡ Taking a cruise or renting a boat offers a different perspective of the watery city.

What to Wear

Locals dress stylishly, but practically. Most people wear jeans and hip boots for an evening out.

Pack layers of clothing – Dutch weather is notoriously fickle and there can be chilly spells even in summer. In spring, summer and autumn, a light trench coat or jacket and a small travel umbrella will mean you're prepared for the weather, but will still blend in with the crowd. In winter, bring a proper heavy coat, woolly hat, scarf and gloves to ward off the often-freezing temperatures (and you'll still want that umbrella).

Be Forewarned

Amsterdam is a safe and manageable city and if you use your common sense you should have no problems.

➡ Stay alert for pickpockets in tourist-heavy zones.

➡ Avoid deserted streets in the Red Light District at night.

➡ It is forbidden to take photos of women in the Red Light District windows; this is strictly enforced.

➡ Be careful around the canals. Almost none of them have barriers.

➡ Watch out for bicycles; never walk in bicycle lanes and always look carefully before you cross one.

Exploring Amsterdam

➡ **Bikes** Many bikes for hire are branded; choose a hire company with no signs, such as Black Bikes (p29), to blend in.

➡ **Boats** Rent your own boat to take to the waterways like an Amsterdammer.

➡ **Tours** Get the inside track on the city on a local volunteer-led Mee in Mokum (p266) walking tour.

Taxes & Refunds

Value-added tax (BTW in Dutch) is included in stated prices. It is levied on most goods and services at 6% for restaurants, hotels, books, transport, medicines and museum admissions, and 21% for most other items.

Non-EU residents may be able to claim a refund on a minimum €50 spent per shop per day. Go to the tax office website (www.belastingdienst.nl) for details.

Tipping

In restaurants, tip around 10% for a meal. Tip hotel porters €1 to €2 per bag, and taxi drivers 5% to 10%. See p270 for more information.

Clogs for sale at Albert Cuypmarkt (p178)

Etiquette

➡ **Greetings** Do give a firm handshake and a double or triple cheek kiss.

➡ **Marijuana & alcohol** Don't smoke dope or drink beer on the streets.

➡ **Smoking** Don't smoke (any substance) in bars or restaurants.

➡ **Bluntness** Don't take offence if locals give you a frank, unvarnished opinion. It's not considered impolite, rather it comes from the desire to be direct and honest.

Language

Dutch is the official language, but English is widely spoken. Most restaurants and cafes have menus in Dutch and English; most museums have information posted in both languages.

See Language (p272) for more information.

Top Itineraries

Day One

Vondelpark & the South (p151)

 Begin with the biggies: tram to the Museum Quarter to ogle the masterpieces at the **Van Gogh Museum** and **Rijksmuseum**. They'll be crowded, so make sure you've prebooked tickets. Modern-art buffs might want to swap the **Stedelijk Museum** for one of the others. They're all lined up in a walkable row.

> ✕ **Lunch** Slow food Gartine (p74) grows many ingredients in its garden.

Medieval Centre (p64)

Spend the afternoon in the Medieval Centre. Explore the secret courtyard and gardens at the **Begijnhof**. Walk up the street to the **Dam**, where the **Royal Palace**, **Nieuwe Kerk** and **Nationaal Monument** huddle and provide a dose of Dutch history. Bend over to sip your *jenever* (Dutch gin) like a local at **Wynand Fockink**.

> ✕ **Dinner** Cutting-edge Indonesian food at Ron Gastrobar Downtown (p75).

Red Light District (p64)

 Venture into the Red Light District. A walk down **Warmoesstraat** or nearby Oudezijds Achterburgwal takes in an eye-popping array of fetish-gear shops, live sex shows, smoky coffeeshops and, of course, women in day-glo lingerie beckoning from crimson windows. Then settle in to a brown cafe (traditional Dutch pub), such as **In 't Aepjen**.

Day Two

De Pijp (p175)

 Browse the **Albert Cuypmarkt**, Amsterdam's largest street bazaar, where stalls are piled high with cheeses, fish, *stroopwafels* (syrup-filled waffles) and bargain-priced clothing. Then submit to the **Heineken Experience** to get shaken up, heated up and 'bottled' like the beer you'll drink at the end of the brewery tour.

> ✕ **Lunch** Bakers & Roasters (p184) does brunch best (and all day).

Southern Canal Ring (p118)

Cross into the Southern Canal Ring and stroll along the grand Golden Bend. Visit **Museum Van Loon** for a peek into the opulent canal-house lifestyle, or get a dose of kitty quirk at the **Kattenkabinet**. Browse the **Bloemenmarkt** and behold the wild array of bulbs.

> ✕ **Dinner** Organic dishes and canal views at Buffet van Odette (p125).

Southern Canal Ring (p118)

 When the sun sets, it's time to party at hyperactive, neon-lit **Leidseplein**. **Paradiso** and **Melkweg** host the coolest agendas. Otherwise, the good-time clubs and brown cafes around the square beckon. Try beery **Café de Spuyt** or historic **Eijlders**. For serious all-hours clubbing, head out of the centre to venues like **Warehouse Elementenstraat**.

Het Scheepvaartmuseum (p94)

Heineken Experience (p177)

Day Three

Vondelpark & the South (p151)

 Take a spin around Amsterdam's beloved **Vondelpark**. Elongated and narrow (about 1.5km long and 300m wide), it's easy to explore via a morning jaunt. All the better if you have a bicycle to zip by the ponds, gardens and sculptures.

> **Lunch** Head to Bistro Bij Ons (p110) for timeless Dutch favourites.

Western Canal Ring (p104)

Immerse yourself in the **Negen Straatjes**, a noughts-and-crosses board of speciality shops. The **Anne Frank Huis** is also in the neighbourhood, and it's a must. The claustrophobic rooms, their windows still covered with blackout screens, give an all-too-real feel for Anne's life in hiding. Seeing the diary itself – filled with her sunny writing tempered with quiet despair – is moving, plain and simple.

> **Dinner** Canal views rival exceptional modern cuisine at De Belhamel (p110).

Jordaan (p136)

Spend the evening in the Jordaan, the chummy district embodying the Amsterdam of yore. Hoist a glass on a canal-side terrace at **'t Smalle**, join the houseboat party at **Café P 96**, or quaff beers at heaps of other *gezellig* (cosy) haunts.

Day Four

Nieuwmarkt, Plantage & the Eastern Islands (p87)

 Mosey through **Waterlooplein Flea Market** in Nieuwmarkt. Rembrandt sure loved markets, if his nearby studio is any indication. **Museum het Rembrandthuis** gives a peek at the master's inner sanctum. Neighbouring **Gassan Diamonds** gives free tours. Or check out the intriguing **Verzetsmuseum**, the Resistance Museum, or sea treasures at **Het Scheepvaartmuseum**.

> **Lunch** Try a hot-spiced Surinamese sandwich at Tokoman (p95).

Amsterdam Noord (p198)

Hop on a free ferry to Noord, one of the city's coolest, most up-and-coming neighbourhoods. Check out the cinematic exhibits at the **EYE Film Institute** and the artists' studios in the sprawling **Kunststad** centre at former shipyards **NDSM-werf**. Ascend **A'DAM Tower** for dazzling views across the IJ River to the city centre.

> **Dinner** Views peak at Moon (p202), the revolving restaurant atop A'DAM Tower.

Oosterpark & East of the Amstel (p189)

There are some fantastic nightlife venues in Noord; alternatively, back on the city side of the IJ, an evening spent on the terrace at **De Ysbreeker**, looking out over the bustling, houseboat-strewn Amstel river, is a well-deserved treat.

If You Like...

Art

Van Gogh Museum The world's largest collection of the tortured artist's paintings, from his early work to final pieces. (p156)

Rijksmuseum The Netherlands' mightiest museum displays Rembrandts, Vermeers and more in a dazzling neo-Gothic/Dutch Renaissance building. (p153)

Stedelijk Museum Bountiful modern trove that includes works by Picasso, Chagall, Mondrian, Warhol, Lichtenstein and the CoBrA cohort. (p158)

Museum het Rembrandthuis You almost expect to find the master himself still nipping around his old paint-spattered studio. (p89)

Hermitage Amsterdam This satellite of Russia's Hermitage Museum features one-off exhibitions, from Matisse cut-outs to Byzantine treasures. (p121)

Foam Changing exhibitions showcase world-renowned photographers such as Sir Cecil Beaton, Annie Leibovitz and Henri Cartier-Bresson. (p120)

Kunststad Vast former shipbuilding warehouse now filled with artists' studios. (p200)

Windmills

De Gooyer It's hard to beat drinking freshly made organic beer at the foot of an 18th-century spinner. (p93)

Riekermolen Rembrandt used to sketch by this windmill, south of the city at Amstelpark's edge. (p160)

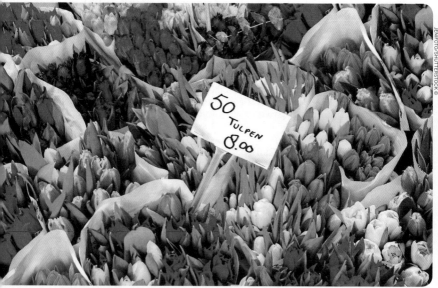

JENIFOTO/SHUTTERSTOCK ©

Tulips for sale at Bloemenmarkt (p121)

Zaanse Schans A whole village of blades turns in the North Sea breeze, a 20-minute train ride from the city. (p216)

National Mill Day Here's your chance to peek inside some of the country's 1200 twirlers, including eight in Amsterdam. (p24)

Parks & Gardens

Vondelpark A mash-up of ponds, lawns, thickets and winding footpaths beloved by Amsterdammers of all ages. (p159)

Museumplein This festive green space draws a crowd for winter ice skating and summer lazing. (p160)

Oosterpark Sweeping park built for nouveau-riche diamond traders a century ago. (p192)

Hortus Botanicus When Dutch ships sailed in the 1600s, the tropical seeds they brought back flourished here. (p93)

Amsterdamse Bos The Amsterdam Forest is criss-crossed with cycling and walking paths, and home to rowing ponds. (p160)

Westerpark Rambling, reedy wilderness abutting a former-gasworks-building-turned-edgy-cultural-centre. (p140)

Park Frankendael Seek out the formal garden that sits behind the Louis XIV–style mansion. (p191)

Sarphatipark De Pijp's fountain-filled park is an urban oasis. (p177)

Flevopark One of Amsterdam's wildest green spaces. (p191)

Active Endeavours

Cycling in Amsterdam Noord Ride into the countryside and spin by time-warp villages and cow-dotted pastures. (p30)

Mee in Mokum Lace up your shoes and see the sights with Mee in Mokum's local volunteer guides. (p266)

Canal Bike Explore the city from a different perspective with a pedal around the canals. (p26)

Ice Skating Museumplein's pond becomes Amsterdam's favourite wintertime rink, resembling the top of a wind-up jewellery box. (p160)

Friday Night Skate Strap on your skates for a 20km jaunt from Vondelpark through the city. (p174)

Sustainable Options

De Ridammerhoeve Feed the kids (both kinds) at the organic goat farm and cafe in Amsterdamse Bos. (p160)

De Kas Sit in a greenhouse and fork into ingredients grown just a few steps away. (p195)

Boerenmarkt This organic farmers market sets up on Saturdays at Noordermarkt and Nieuwmarkt at the Waag. (p103)

Instock This restaurant 'rescues' food about to reach its expiration date, transforming it into three-course meals. (p98)

Lot Sixty One Sniff out the roasting coffee beans from sustainable farms around the globe. (p169)

Marie-Stella-Maris A percentage of this skincare company's profits helps provide clean drinking water worldwide. (p115)

Conscious Hotel Westerpark Wind powers this green hotel, which incorporates recycled materials. (p224)

Moer Restaurant with organic produce and a slow food ethic adjoining the Tire Station hotel. (p164)

For more top Amsterdam spots, see the following:
➡ Canals (p35)
➡ Museums & Galleries (p40)
➡ Eating (p43)
➡ Drinking & Nightlife (p48)
➡ Entertainment (p55)
➡ Shopping (p57)

Architecture

Rijksmuseum Pierre Cuypers' magnificent 1875 design incorporates Renaissance ornaments carved in stone around the facade. (p153)

ARCAM Amsterdam's Centre for Architecture is a one-stop shop for architectural exhibits, guidebooks and maps. (p95)

NEMO Science Museum Renzo Piano's green copper, ship-shaped science museum is a modern classic. (p94)

Scheepvaarthuis This grand 1916 building is the first true Amsterdam School example. (p90)

Beurs van Berlage The 1903 financial exchange building is a temple to capitalism. (p71)

Museum Het Schip In the west, this 1920s housing project is the pinnacle of Amsterdam School style. (p140)

Offbeat Museums

Kattenkabinet Canal house filled with kitty-cat art from the likes of Picasso, Steinlen and Rembrandt. (p122)

Houseboat Museum Get a feel for the compact, watery lifestyle aboard a 23m-long sailing barge. (p138)

PLAN YOUR TRIP IF YOU LIKE...

Tassenmuseum Hendrikje This entire museum is devoted to handbags, from 16th-century pouches to Madonna's modern arm candy. (p122)

Amsterdam Pipe Museum Chinese opium pipes, Turkish water pipes, 1500-year-old Ecuadorian pipes and more cram the cabinets. (p121)

Pianola Museum An extraordinary paean to the player piano, bursting with musical keys from the early 1900s. (p138)

Electric Ladyland The world's first museum of fluorescent art, glowing with psychedelic rocks, rice and rabbits. (p139)

History Lessons

Anne Frank Huis Anne's melancholy bedroom and her actual diary serve as poignant reminders of WWII. (p106)

Oude Kerk The senior citizen of Amsterdam's structures, now more than 700 years old. (p68)

Amsterdam Museum Intriguing multimedia exhibits take you through the twists and turns of Amsterdam's convoluted history. (p70)

Verzetsmuseum Learn about WWII Dutch Resistance fighters during the German occupation. (p94)

Stadsarchief The city's rich archives offer remarkable displays, including Anne Frank's stolen-bike report from 1942. (p121)

Mee in Mokum Local volunteer guides put the city's history into context on these walking tours. (p266)

Food & Drink

Hungry Birds Street Food Tours Work up an appetite on these food-focused walking tours (tastings included). (p266)

Reypenaer Cheese Tasting Guided tastings reveal the intricacies of Dutch cheeses. (p116)

Petit Gâteau Regular pastry-making courses are run by this wonderful patisserie. (p110)

Papabubble Watch sweets being made at this confectioner. (p150)

Baking Lab Baking workshops and a communal bread oven. (p194)

Brouwerij De Prael Tours at this Red Light District brewery are followed by tastings. (p73)

Brouwerij Troost Westergas Tour Troost's Westergas brewery, where it also distils its own gin. (p147)

Brouwerij 't IJ Brewery tours here are made even more memorable by the adjacent 1725-built De Gooyer windmill. (p99)

Heineken Experience Fun interactive tours of Heineken's former brewery. (p177)

Wynand Fockink Distillery tours of this 1679 *jenever* (Dutch gin) distillery are accompanied by half a dozen tastings. (p80)

Markets

Albert Cuypmarkt Iconic street market selling flowers, clothing, food and household goods of every description. (p178)

Lindengracht Market A favourite with local food shoppers. (p149)

Waterlooplein Flea Market Curios, electronic gear, New Age gifts, cheap bicycle parts and more for bargain hunters. (p102)

Oudemanhuispoort Book Market Located in an old, covered alleyway, this place is lined with secondhand booksellers. (p85)

Noordermarkt A market since the early 1600s; antiques and organic fare are the offerings these days. (p149)

Bloemenmarkt Amsterdam's 'floating' flower market (on pilings) teems with beautiful blooming bulbs. (p121)

Sunday Market Superb design stalls at changing locations. (p137)

Romantic Spots

Sarphatipark Roam winding paths past idyllic ponds and fountains in the heart of village-like De Pijp. (p177)

Reguliersgracht The 'canal of seven bridges' enchants at night when its arches glow with tiny gold lights. (p120)

Zuiderkerk Even Claude Monet had to capture the image of this church on the picturesque Groenburgwal canal. (p90)

Vondelpark A hippie haven in the flower power era, this sprawling park still evokes the Summer of Love. (p159)

Schreierstoren The tower where women wept as sailors departed on voyages now houses a cafe. (p71)

Canal Cruise Glide along the city's fairy-tale waterways. (p37)

Month by Month

TOP EVENTS

King's Day, April

Grachtenfestival, August

Amsterdam Dance Event, October

Pride Amsterdam, July/August

Amsterdam Light Festival, early December to mid-January

January

While January is cold and dark, museum queues are nonexistent and there's more time to relax and warm up in a welcoming *café* (bar, pub).

✯✯ National Tulip Day

On the third Saturday in January, Tulpendag (www.tulpentijd.nl) marks the start of the tulip season, which runs to the end of April. Dazzling displays of 200,000 tulips take place on the Dam. In the early afternoon you can walk among them and collect a free tulip.

February

February has few festivities but it's a great time to see the city outside tourist season and experience Amsterdam's *gezellig* (cosy) culture at toasty indoor venues.

✯✯ Chinese New Year

Amsterdam celebrates Chinese New Year (www.iamsterdam.com) with a parade from the Kuan Yin Shrine Buddhist temple in Chinatown to Nieuwmarkt and festivities on the Dam.

March

Early spring weather can be fickle (warm clothes are a must), but if it complies you can get a jump-start on tulip-viewing (and the crowds) at Keukenhof Gardens (p211).

✯✯ DGTL

Three-day techno and house festival DGTL (www.dgtl.nl) takes place Friday to Sunday over the Easter weekend at NDSM-werf, former shipbuilding yards that are now a creative nerve centre in Amsterdam Noord.

April

Days are getting longer, temperatures are rising and flowers are in full bloom in the lead-up to the show-stopping King's Day party, the highlight of Amsterdam's annual calendar.

✯✯ King's Day

One of the biggest – and arguably best – street parties in Europe, King's Day celebrates the birthday of King Willem-Alexander on 27 April (26 April if the 27th is a Sunday). There's uproarious partying, music and *oranjekoorts* (orange fever), as well as a city-wide flea market.

◉ World Press Photo

The internationally renowned World Press Photo (www.worldpressphoto.org) is a gripping exhibition of the year's best photojournalism showcased in the Nieuwe Kerk from mid-April until mid-July.

May

Amsterdam follows Remembrance Day (4 May) observances with Liberation Day (5 May) festivities, and flourishing cafe terraces make this mild month a perfect time to linger in the city.

✨ National Mill Day

During the second weekend in May, many of the 1200 windmills (www.molens.nl) and watermills throughout the country welcome the public into their creaking innards. Look for mills flying a blue pennant.

June

Visitors start flocking to the city in increasing numbers for the peak summer season. It's typically sunny and warm, prime for bicycle rides and drinks on canal-side patios.

☆ Holland Festival

Big-name theatre, dance and opera meet offbeat digital films and experimental music in the Netherlands' biggest performing-arts extravaganza, the Holland Festival (www.hollandfestival.nl). The month-long, highbrow/lowbrow mashup happens at venues citywide.

✨ Open Garden Days

Open Tuinen Dagen (www.opentuinendagen.nl), on the third weekend in June, brings a unique opportunity to view some 25 private gardens along the canals.

July

The days are long, the sun is shining. Crowds clogging Amsterdam's streets and canals add to the city's party atmosphere, while lesser-visited neighbourhoods have plenty of laid-back local hang-outs.

☆ Amsterdam Roots Festival

In early July, the week-long Amsterdam Roots Festival (www.amsterdamroots.nl) programs world music in key venues around town including the Bimhuis and Oosterpark in Amsterdam's east.

☆ Over het IJ Festival

Alternative venues at the NDSM-werf former shipyards in Amsterdam Noord host unconventional performing arts productions for 10 days in mid-July during this festival (www.overhetij.nl).

August

A welter of events takes place during Amsterdam's high summer, yet the city has less sweltering temperatures than many other European cultural capitals and relatively few summer closures.

✨ Pride Amsterdam

The world's only waterborne Pride Parade, taking in the Prinsengracht and Amstel, is a highlight of the Pride Amsterdam (p268) festival, which is celebrated from late July to early August.

☆ Grachtenfestival

Classical musicians pop up in canal-side parks and hidden gardens during mid-August's 10-day Grachtenfestival (www.grachtenfestival.nl), featuring over 250 concerts at 90 locations. Don't miss the free Prinsengracht Concert (www.prinsengrachtconcert.nl) on a floating stage in the Prinsengracht.

☆ Uitmarkt

Over three days in late August, Amsterdam's cultural venues preview their upcoming season on outdoor stages during mega arts event Uitmarkt (www.uitmarkt.nl). It's complemented by big concerts.

September

Summer may technically be over, but September is one of the best months to visit Amsterdam. There are some lively festivals along with fair weather and fewer crowds.

🏃 Amsterdam City Swim

Over 3000 people jump into the canals for the City Swim (www.amsterdamcityswim.nl) in early September to help raise money for charity. Swimmers splash along a route that can change depending on weather and water conditions.

October

Autumnal hues colour Amsterdam's parks and gardens, and while the weather may remain mild, low-season prices start to kick in and queues begin to thin out.

✨ Amsterdam Dance Event

Over five long, sweaty days and nights in mid-October, massive dance-music festival ADE (www.amsterdam-dance-event.nl) sees DJs, artists and clubbers attending over 1000 events at 200-plus venues throughout the city.

(Top) Windmills in Zaanse Schans (p216); many mills open on National Mill Day
(Bottom) A canal during the Amsterdam Light Festival

OLENA Z/SHUTTERSTOCK ©

UNIQUE VISION/SHUTTERSTOCK ©

November

Cultural events and reduced low-season rates make up for the shortening days and chilly nights, while the arrival of Sinterklaas heralds the start of the festive season.

⚜ Sinterklaas Intocht

St Nicholas arrives by boat from Spain (www.sintin amsterdam.nl) in the second half of November, and parades on his white horse to the Dam and Leidseplein to the delight of the city's children.

December

Winter magic blankets the city (as, some years, does snow), ice-skating rinks are set up in open spaces, including the Museumplein, and the city is a vision of twinkling lights.

⚜ Amsterdam Light Festival

During this 53-day festival (www.amsterdamlight festival.com) from late November to mid-January, you can view some 25 'light art' installations reflecting in the waterways' ripples on foot, with a tour or, most spectacularly, on a cruise.

⚜ New Year's Eve

Fireworks light up the skies in a spark-showering spectacle and countless parties take place around the city. Event locations vary annually; check with the I Amsterdam visitor centre (p271) to find out where to ring in the new year.

Travel with Kids

Breathe easy: you've landed in one of Europe's most kid-friendly cities. The famous Dutch tolerance extends to children and Amsterdammers are cheerfully accommodating to them. Virtually all quarters of the city – except the Red Light District, of course – are fair game for the younger set.

KAVALENKAU/SHUTTERSTOCK ©

Outdoor Activities

Green spaces, parks and canals galore provide plenty of fresh-air fun for the little (and not so little) ones.

Parks & Playgrounds

A favourite with kids of all ages is the vast space of Vondelpark (p159), with leafy picnic spots and duck ponds, as well as cool space-age slides at its western end and a playground in the middle. Westerpark (p140) also has a terrific playground, while Sarphatipark (p177) and Oosterpark (p192) shouldn't be overlooked as great open spaces to let the kids run free. Canoeing, a tree-climbing park, paddle boats and a goat farm are among the fun activities in the huge, forested Amsterdamse Bos (p160).

Winter Magic

Kids will love the skating rinks that spring up in public spaces such as the Museumplein (p160). Don't miss uniquely Dutch festive-season treats such as *poffertjes* (small pancakes) and gingery-cinnamon *speculaas* (spiced biscuits), traditionally eaten around Sinterklaas (St Nicholas' Eve; 5 December), and sold at market stalls.

Canals

Take to the canals on a unique pedal-powered ride with **Canal Bike** (www.strom ma.nl; per person per hour €10; ◷ hours vary, last departure usually 4.30pm).

Artis Royal Zoo

The extrovert monkeys, big cats, shimmying fish and dazzling planetarium will keep young eyes shining for hours at Artis Royal Zoo (p93), while teenagers and adults will love the beautifully landscaped grounds. You can also peek inside Micropia, a building on the premises that is a 'zoo' for microbes. It's much more entertaining than it sounds, with exhibits that show how bacteria exchange when you kiss and what microbes live in the poop of anteaters, lions and other animals.

Museum Fun

Amsterdam has plenty of museums that are accessible, educational and, above all, fun.

NEMO Science Museum

A tailor-made, hands-on experience, NEMO Science Museum (p94) is useful for answering all those 'how' and 'why' questions.

Het Scheepvaartmuseum

The life-size ship moored beside the Maritime Museum (p94) lets kids fire a (replica!) cannon, hoist cargo and skedaddle around a reproduction Dutch East India Company vessel from 1749.

Tropenmuseum

The children's section devoted to exotic locations at the Tropenmuseum (p191) is a winner in any language.

Joods Historisch Museum

There is a great kids display on Jewish life in Amsterdam at the Joods Historisch Museum (p91).

Verzetsmuseum

A section at the Verzetsmuseum (p94) known as the Verzetsmuseum Junior puts the Dutch Resistance into context for kids through the experiences of four children: Eva, Jan, Nelly and Henk.

Van Gogh Museum

The Van Gogh Museum (p156) provides a free treasure hunt for kids to search for items in the paintings and displays. A small prize awaits those who complete the hunt.

Beaches & Castles

City Beaches

Urban beaches pop up on Amsterdam's outskirts each summer around the IJ River. While most cater to adults (complete with cocktails and DJs), some are more family-friendly – check with the tourist office for locations. The only one you can swim at is Blijburg (p100), which also has a water-sports centre.

Muiden Castle

Just outside Amsterdam, the Muiderslot (p192) is a 13th-century castle straight out of a fairy tale, with a drawbridge, moat, hulking towers and battlements. It offers special activities (like falconry) for kids on certain days. Combine it with a visit to the atmospheric fort on the nearby island of Pampus (p192).

Rainy-Day Ideas

It's prudent to have a rainy-day plan in your back pocket. In fact, it might be so much fun that kids will hope the sun doesn't come back out all day.

TunFun

Set 'em loose for a romp in the underground, all-round pleasure centre TunFun (p103).

Cinema

Kids can eat popcorn and watch new releases at the art deco Pathé Tuschinskitheater (p132) or the intimate, atmospheric Movies (p148) while adults revel in the historic environs.

Indoor Pool

The recreational Zuiderbad (p174) is a good place to take the kids swimming on a rainy day. Adults will enjoy the palatial vintage interior.

Centrale Bibliotheek Amsterdam

The city's stunning, contemporary OBA: Centrale Bibliotheek Amsterdam (p95) has a whole floor dedicated to children's activities, including comfy reading lounges and the amazing Mouse Mansion, with 100 beautifully detailed rooms, designed by artist Karina Content. Check for weekly story times (some in English) for younger visitors.

NEED TO KNOW

➡ **Admission prices** 'Child' is defined as under 18 years. But at many tourist sites, the cut-off age for free or reduced rates is 12. Some sights may only provide free entry to children under six.

➡ **Bike seats** Most bike-hire shops rent bikes with baby or child seats.

➡ **Babysitting** Many higher-end hotels arrange babysitting services for a fee.

Poffertjes (p44)

Fries

Fries slathered in mayonnaise or other sauces are favourites with all ages. Local institutions include Vleminckx (p74) near the Spui and Wil Graanstra Friteshuis (p110) by the Anne Frank Huis. Frites uit Zuyd (p180) fires up crispy beauties in De Pijp.

Ice Cream

Try the chocolate-dipped waffle cones at Jordino (p141). IJsmolen (p97) has uniquely Dutch flavours such as *stroopwafels* (caramel-syrup-filled wafers) among its line-up. As a bonus, it's located by a windmill.

Cafes & Restaurants

Particularly kid-friendly cafes and restaurants include Het Groot Melkhuis (p171), Café Toussaint (p167) and Café Noorderlicht (p204), which has a big play area outside. At **Kinderkookkafé** (Map p312, D5; ☎020-625 32 57; www.kinderkookkafe.nl; Vondelpark 6b; dishes €1-4; ⏰10am-5pm; 🚼; 🚋1 Overtoom), kids can do the cooking.

Markets

Kids love browsing the markets for both familiar and exotic treats. Try the Albert Cuypmarkt (p178) for *stroopwafels*, *poffertjes* (small pancakes), smoothies, sweets and fresh fruit. Or pick up ingredients here and take a picnic to the nearby Sarphatipark.

Kid-Friendly Cuisine

While Amsterdam's food scene continues to explode with adventurous and sophisticated offerings, you can still find plenty of fare that junior diners will enjoy.

Sandwich Shops

A *broodje* (filled bread roll) or *tosti* (toasted sandwich) always hits the spot. Scores of shops throughout the city specialise in these staples; try Broodje Bert (p75).

Pancakes

The city is full of these kid-pleasing delights. Top choices include Pancakes! (p110) and Pancake Bakery (p111).

For true pancake aficionados, a trip aboard **De Pannenkoekenboot** (Pancake Boat; Map p319; ☎020-626 88 17; www.pannenkoekenboot.nl; Ms van Riemsdijkweg; adult/child from €21.50/16.50; 🚢NDSM-werf) is definitely in order. Brunch and evening cruises depart from the NDSM-werf in Amsterdam Noord, reached by a free ferry.

Burgers

Gourmet burgers made from organic ingredients continue to go gangbusters in Amsterdam. Best burger bets are the Butcher (p179) and Geflipt (p179).

Kid-Friendly Shops

Dozens upon dozens of shops cater for children, who will adore deliberating over toys and sweet treats.

Check out Knuffels (p103) for stuffed-animal toys, Joe's Vliegerwinkel (p103) for kites, Mechanisch Speelgoed (p150) for nostalgic wind-up toys, and De Winkel van Nijntje (p174) for merchandise related to Dutch illustrator Dick Bruna's most famous character – the cute rabbit Miffy (Nijntje in Dutch).

Het Oud-Hollandsch Snoepwinkeltje (p148) has jar after jar of Dutch penny sweets.

By Bike

Bicycles are more common than cars in Amsterdam, and to roll like a local you'll need a two-wheeler. Rent one from the myriad outlets around town or from your accommodation, and the whole city becomes your playground. Cycling is the quintessential activity while visiting.

DUTCHSCENERY/SHUTTERSTOCK ©

Hiring a Bike

Rental shops are everywhere; you'll have to show a passport or European national ID card and leave a credit-card authorisation or pay a deposit (usually €80 to €100). Prices per 24-hour period for basic 'coaster-brake' bikes average €12. Bikes with gears and handbrakes cost more. Electric bikes start from €25 for 24 hours. Theft insurance (from €3 per day) is strongly advised.

Ajax Bike (Map p316; ☑06 1729 4284; www.ajaxbike.nl; Gerard Doustraat 153; bike hire per 4/24hr from €7/9.50, 3hr tours from €20; ⏰10am-5.30pm Mon-Sat, noon-4pm Sun; 🚊4 Stadhouderskade) In De Pijp, with bargain prices on city, kids, tandem and cargo bikes.

Bike City (Map p308; ☑020-626 37 21; www.bikecity.nl; Bloemgracht 68-70; bike rental per day from €14; ⏰9am-5.30pm; 🚊13/17 Westermarkt) Jordaan shop; bikes carry no advertising, so you'll look like a local.

Black Bikes (Map p290; ☑0852 737 454; www.black-bikes.com; Nieuwezijds Voorburgwal 146; bike hire per 3/24hr from €6.50/9, electric bikes €24/37.50; ⏰8am-8pm Mon-Fri, 9am-7pm Sat & Sun; 🚊2/11/12/13/17 Nieuwezijds Kolk) Signless company offering city, kids, tandem and cargo bikes at 10 shops, including this one in the centre.

Damstraat Rent-a-Bike (Map p294; ☑020-625 50 29; www.rentabike.nl; Damstraat 20-22; bike hire per 3/24hr from €7/9.50; ⏰9am-6pm; 🚊4/14/24 Dam) Hires out bikes of all types from its shop near the Dam.

MacBike (Map p290; ☑020-624 83 91; www.macbike.nl; De Ruijterkade 34b; bike hire per 3/24hr from €7.50/9.75, electric bikes €15/25; ⏰9am-6pm; 🚊2/4/11/12/13/14/17/24/26 Centraal Station) Among the most touristy of companies (bikes are bright red, with logos), but has a convenient location at Centraal Station, plus others at **Waterlooplein** (Map p296; ☑020-428 70 05; Waterlooplein 199; ⏰9am-6pm; Ⓜ️Waterlooplein) and **Leidseplein** (Map p304; ☑020-528 76 88; Weteringschans 2; ⏰9am-6pm; 🚊1/2/5/7/11/12/19 Leidseplein). Big assortment of bikes available.

Bike Sharing & Apps

Donkey Republic (www.donkey.bike) Unlock/lock a bike via Bluetooth. Rates per 24 hours are €12. You'll need to return the bike to the same location, or pay €20 extra.

FlickBike (www.flickbike.nl) Locate bikes around town via this app; hire per 30 minutes costs €1. Scan the QR code to unlock/lock the bike. It can be returned to any Amsterdam bike rack.

Spinlister (www.spinlister.com) Like Airbnb for bikes: rent a bike straight from an Amsterdammer. Prices vary.

Bike Tours

A bike tour is an ideal way to get to know Amsterdam. Bike hire is included in prices (tour companies also rent bikes). Be sure to reserve in advance. Great options include the following:

Orangebike (Map p319; ☏06 4684 2083; www.orange-bike.nl; Buiksloterweg 5c; tours €22.50-37.50, hire per hour/day from €5/11; ⊗9am-6pm; 🚢Buiksloterweg) Traditional city and countryside tours (including a beach tour), plus themed options such as food or architectural tours.

Mike's Bike Tours (Map p298; ☏020-622 79 70; www.mikesbiketoursamsterdam.com; Prins Hendrikkade 176a; city tours per adult/child from €28/25, countryside from €32; ⊗office 9am-6pm Mar-Oct, from 10am Nov-Feb; 🚌22/48 Prins Hendrikkade) Fantastic tours cover the city, harbour or windmill-dotted countryside.

Yellow Bike (Map p290; ☏020-620 69 40; www.yellowbike.nl; Nieuwezijds Kolk 29; city tours from €24.50, Waterland tour €34.50; ⊗office 9.30am-6pm; 🚌2/11/12/13/17 Nieuwezijds Kolk) Choose from city jaunts or a spin through the bucolic Waterland region.

Road Rules

➡ Helmets aren't compulsory but are strongly recommended; most bike-hire places rent them for around €2.50 per 24 hours (or bring your own).

➡ Amsterdam has over 500km of bike paths. Use the bicycle lane on the road's right-hand side, marked by white lines and bike symbols.

➡ Cycle in the same direction as traffic and adhere to all traffic lights and signs.

➡ Hand signal when turning.

➡ A bell is mandatory.

➡ After dark, a white or yellow headlight and red tail light are required by law.

➡ Park only in bicycle racks near train and tram stations and in certain public squares (or risk the removal of your bike by the police).

➡ Cycling on footpaths is illegal.

Cycling Tips

➡ Most bikes come with two locks: one for the front wheel (attach it to the bike frame), the other for the back. One of these locks should also be attached to a fixed structure (preferably a bike rack).

➡ Cross tram rails at a sharp angle to avoid getting stuck.

➡ Watch out for vehicles, other bikes and oblivious pedestrians.

➡ Ring your bell as a warning as often as necessary.

Online Journey Planners

➡ **Fietsersbond** (www.routeplanner.fietsersbond.nl) Official route planner of the Dutch Cyclists' Union.

➡ **Holland Cycling** (www.holland-cycling.com) Has a wealth of up-to-date info such as bicycle-repair shops.

➡ **Route You** (www.routeyou.com) Good for scenic routes.

Like a Local

While Amsterdam's popularity as a tourist destination shows no signs of abating (19 million people visited the city in 2018 alone), it's easy to escape the crowds. Hop on a bike, head to the nearest bruin café (brown cafe; traditional Dutch pub) and take a free course in Dutch culture.

MATT MUNRO/LONELY PLANET ©

ynand Fockink (p80)

Delve into Local Neighbourhoods

Beyond the tourist epicentres, Amsterdam's further-flung neighbourhoods are easy to reach and perfect places to engage with local life. Great starting points are the edgy galleries and post-industrial cafes, bars and restaurants of Amsterdam Noord; the backstreets of village-like De Pijp (such as the tucked-away square Van der Helstplein, lined with cafes, pubs and bars); the rapidly gentrifying West, including another post-industrial hub, the former-gasworks-turned-cultural-centre Westergasfabriek (p140); and the multicultural Oost (East).

Embrace the Gezellig Culture

This particularly Dutch quality, which is most widely found in old brown cafes, is one of the best reasons to visit Amsterdam. It's variously translated as 'snug', 'friendly', 'cosy', 'informal' and 'convivial', but *gezelligheid* – the state of being *gezellig* – is more elemental. You'll feel this all-is-right-with-the-world vibe in many places and situations, often while nursing a brew with friends during *borrel* (an informal gathering over drinks). And nearly any low-lit, welcoming establishment qualifies.

Pedal Power

It takes spending all of five minutes in Amsterdam to realise that locals bike everywhere. Literally everywhere. They bike to the dentist, to work, to the opera and to brunch; they bike in snow, rain, sunshine and fog. So don't just rent a bike for a quick spin around the Vondelpark – get on the beaten path by biking everywhere too. Dressing up to bike to dinner and a show, or to drinks and a club, is a typical Dutch pastime that locals shrug off but visitors marvel over. No matter what you wear or where you're going, you'll fit right in.

Navigate the Country

'Holland' is a popular synonym for the Netherlands, yet it only refers to the combined provinces of Noord (North) and Zuid

(South) Holland. (Amsterdam is Noord-Holland's largest city; Haarlem is the provincial capital.) The rest of the country is not Holland, even if locals themselves often make the mistake.

Navigate the City

Amsterdam's concentric canals and similarly named streets make it all too easy to get lost. Some pointers: a *gracht* (canal), such as Egelantiersgracht, is distinct from a *straat* (street) such as Egelantiersstraat. A *dwarsstraat* (cross-street) that intersects a *straat* is often preceded by *eerste, tweede, derde* and *vierde* (first, second, third and fourth; marked 1e, 2e, 3e and 4e on maps). For example Eerste Egelantiersdwarsstraat is the first cross-street of Egelantiersstraat (ie the nearest cross-street to the city centre). Streets preceded by *lange* (long) and *korte* (short) simply mean the longer or shorter street. Be aware, too, that seemingly continuous streets regularly change name along their length.

Soak up Dutch History

On Herdenkingsdag (Remembrance Day; 4 May), King Willem-Alexander lays a wreath for the victims of WWII at the Nationaal Monument (p70) on the Dam. At 8pm sharp, the city solemnly observes a two-minute silence.

The following day, on Bevrijdingsdag (Liberation Day; 5 May), Amsterdammers join together to celebrate the end of Nazi occupation in 1945; it's jubilantly commemorated with speeches, concerts and street parties. The Dam, Vondelpark (p159) and Museumplein (p160) are generally the focus of festivities.

Join in the Festivities

Explore the unique character of Amsterdam's diverse neighbourhoods by partying with the locals at a neighbourhood festival.

Revel in the city's rich Surinamese and African heritage at the food-and-football **Kwaku festival** (www.kwakufestival.nl; ⌨Tulastraat), held in Nelson Mandelapark most weekends from mid-July to early August. Or listen to classic Jordaan ballads during the Jordaan Festival (p142).

Locals party like it's King's Day during the Uitmarkt (p24) festival, which kicks off the cultural season in late August.

Orange Fever

If you've ever attended a sporting event where the Dutch are playing, you'll already be familiar with *oranjegekte* (orange craze), also known as *oranjekoorts* (orange fever). The custom of wearing the traditional colour of the Dutch royal family, the House of Orange-Nassau, was originally limited to celebration days for the monarchy, such as Queen's Day (Koninginnedag), now King's Day (Koningsdag). But particularly since the 1974 FIFA World Cup, when tens of thousands of orange-clad football supporters cheered on every game, the ritual of wearing outlandish orange get-ups – clothes, scarves, wigs, fake-fur top hats, face paint, feather boas, you name it – has become a Dutch phenomenon. To really celebrate like a local, you know what colour to wear.

Local Experiences

The initiative Untourist Guide (www.untouristguide.com) promotes local experiences that encourage visitors to be positive 'changemakers', such as upcycling workshops and weeding an urban farm. Book online or at the **I Amsterdam Store** (Map p290; www.iamsterdam.com; De Ruijterkade 28a, Centraal Station; ⊘8am-7pm Mon-Wed, to 8pm Thu-Sat, 10am-6pm Sun; ⌨2/4/11/12/13/14/17/24/26 Centraal Station).

Socially minded options include Plastic Whale (p266), where you tour Amsterdam's waterways while helping clean them by 'plastic fishing' using nets to fish out plastic waste from the rivers, harbours and canals; materials collected are recycled to make furniture and even the nine-seat electric boats in which the trips take place.

Rederij Lampedusa (p266) sees refugees lead immigration-focused cruises in former refugee boats.

For Free

Although the cost of Amsterdam's accommodation and dining can mount up, there is a bright side. Not only is the entire Canal Ring a Unesco World Heritage site (effectively a free living museum), but there are plenty of things to do and see that are free (or virtually free).

nststad (p200)

Free Sights

Civic Guard Gallery
Stroll through the monumental collection of portraits (p70), from Golden Age to modern.

Rijksmuseum Gardens
Even many locals don't know that the Renaissance and baroque gardens (p154), with rose bushes, hedges and statues, are free and open to the public (including occasional sculpture exhibitions).

Begijnhof
Explore the 14th-century hidden courtyard (p67) and its clandestine churches.

Stadsarchief
You never know what treasures you'll find in the vaults of the city's archives (p121).

Gassan Diamonds
Distinguish your princess from marquise, river from top cape (p91).

Albert Cuypmarkt
Amsterdam's busiest market (p178); it and the city's many other bazaars are all free to browse.

ARCAM
A fascinating look at Amsterdam's architecture (p95) – past, present and future.

Kunststad
Wander through these vast artist studios (p200) in Amsterdam Noord.

NEED TO KNOW
➡ **Discount Cards** Various discount cards (p267) offer savings and freebies at numerous attractions, shops and restaurants.

➡ **Concessions** Students and seniors should bring ID and flash it at every opportunity for reduced admission fees.

➡ **Wi-fi** Visit www.wifi-amsterdam.nl to find free hotspots around town.

The gardens (p154) at Rijksmuseum

NEMO Science Museum Roof Terrace

One of the best views of Amsterdam extends from the roof of this landmark building (p94).

Free Entertainment

For discounted same-day tickets, visit the Last Minute Ticket Shop (www.last minuteticketshop.nl).

Concertgebouw

Sharpen your elbows to get in for Wednesday's lunchtime concert (p171; September to June), often a public rehearsal for the performance later that evening.

Muziektheater

Free classical concerts fill the air during lunch most Tuesdays (p101; September to May).

Bimhuis

Jazz sessions (p102) hot up the revered venue on Tuesday nights.

Openluchttheater

Vondelpark's outdoor theatre (p172) puts on concerts and kids shows throughout summer.

EYE Film Institute

Has pods in the basement where you can watch free films (p201).

Mulligans

Free music sessions and gigs at the city's best-known and loved Irish pub (p132).

King's Day

The ultimate party (p23), this is one of many festivals and events that are totally free. (Well, you might want to bring some euros for beer and a cheap orange wig.)

Free Transport

Ferries

Free ferries depart behind Centraal Station to NDSM-werf, Amsterdam Noord's edgy art community 15 minutes up harbour; to the EYE Film Institute, five minutes across the river; and to IJplein, also a five-minute ride.

Bridge over Leidsegracht

 # Canals

Amsterdammers have always known that their Canal Ring, built during the Golden Age, is extraordinary. Unesco made it official in 2010, when it listed the waterways as a World Heritage site. Today the city has 165 canals spanned by 1753 bridges – more than any other city in the world.

History

Far from being simply decorative or picturesque, or even waterways for transport, the canals were crucial to drain and reclaim the waterlogged land. They solved Amsterdam's essential problem: keeping the land and sea separate.

Names & Layout

In Dutch a canal is a *gracht* (pronounced 'khrakht') and the main canals form the central *grachtengordel* (canal ring). These beauties came to life in the early 1600s, after Amsterdam's population grew beyond its medieval walls and city planners put together an ambitious design for expansion. The concentric waterways they built are the same ones you see today.

CORE CANALS

Starting from the core, the major semicircular canals are the Singel, Herengracht, Keizersgracht and Prinsengracht. An easy way to remember them is that, apart from the singular **Singel** (which originally was a moat that defended Amsterdam's outer limits), these canals are in alphabetical order.

NEED TO KNOW

Canal safety

Virtually none of Amsterdam's canals have fences or barriers. Keep a close eye on young children to ensure they don't take an unexpected plunge.

Ice-skating safety

Drownings periodically occur; stay away from the ice unless you see large groups of people and be very careful at the edges and under bridges – areas with weak ice.

Boating Rules & Advice

➡ Stay on the waterways' right (starboard) side.

➡ Commercial traffic (including tour boats) has right of way, as do boats on your right-hand side.

➡ The speed limit is 7.5km/h (the top speed for many electric rental boats).

➡ Life jackets/vests aren't compulsory (but are strongly recommended).

➡ Drinking alcohol (or taking drugs) while in control of a boat is illegal.

➡ Shouting and amplified music is also illegal on board.

➡ Many bridges have low clearance (less than 2m).

➡ Docking is permitted anywhere in the city except beneath bridges, on narrow waterways, junctions or adjacent to rescue steps, or locations signposted as prohibited.

➡ Switch on your lights at dusk.

The **Herengracht** (p109) is where Amsterdam's wealthiest residents moved once the canals were completed. They built their mansions alongside it (particularly around the Golden Bend), hence its name, which translates to Gentlemen's Canal.

Almost as swanky was the **Keizersgracht** (Emperor's Canal), a nod to Holy Roman Emperor Maximilian I.

The **Prinsengracht** (p111) – named after William the Silent, Prince of Orange and the first Dutch royal – was designed as a slightly cheaper canal with smaller residences and warehouses. It also acted as a barrier against the working-class Jordaan beyond.

RADIAL CANALS

The canals that cut across the core canals like spokes on a bicycle wheel are known as radial canals. From west to east the major radial canals are Brouwersgracht, Leidsegracht and Reguliersgracht, and, like the core canals, they are in alphabetical order.

The **Brouwersgracht** (Brewers Canal) is one of Amsterdam's most beautiful waterways. It takes its name from the many breweries that lined the banks in the 16th and 17th centuries.

The **Leidsegracht** was named after the city of Leiden, to which it was the main water route.

Peaceful **Reguliersgracht** was named after an order of monks whose monastery was located nearby. Today it's often better known as the 'canal of seven bridges' and its iconic scenery isn't lost on canal-boat operators.

Bridges

Some truly striking bridges straddle the city's waterways.

Spanning the Singel, the Torensluis (p113) was built in 1648, making it Amsterdam's oldest bridge (also, at 39m, its widest). The Blauwbrug (p122) crosses the Amstel river, with fish sculptures and imperial-crowned street lamps dotting the way. And you've probably seen the iconic Magere Brug (p120) in photos or appearing in films, stretching over the Amstel, glowing beneath the twinkle of 1200 tiny lights. In the Western Islands, look out for the narrow, charming Drieharingenbrug (p139).

Houseboats

Some 2500 houseboats line Amsterdam's canals. Living on the water became popular after WWII, when a surplus of old cargo ships helped fill the gap of a housing shortage on land. The Prinsengracht displays a particularly diverse mix of houseboats. You can climb aboard one and explore the cosy (ie cramped) interior at the Houseboat Museum (p138), or book to stay overnight on the water yourself in true Amsterdam style.

Greener Canals

While Amsterdam's canals certainly aren't crystal clear (around 12,000 to 15,000 bicycles are pulled from the canals each year), they're cleaner today than ever before in the city's history.

In part this is due to the locks, most of which close three times per week to allow fresh water to be pumped from the IJsselmeer. This creates a current that flushes the stagnant canal water out through open locks on the other side of the city and out to sea – check out the mighty Amstelsluizen (p123) on the Amstel in the Southern Canal Ring. What's more, the canals are regularly patrolled by specialised cleaning boats. And since 2005, houseboats have been required to connect to the city's sewerage system. Virtually all are now connected.

These efforts have made a significant difference, as evidenced by the wildlife the canals now attract. Some 20 fish and crab species live happily below the water's surface. They attract a wide variety of waterbirds such as gulls, herons, ducks, coots and cormorants. You might even see – or more likely, hear – neon-green ring-necked parakeets circling above. These, of course, aren't native; their presence in the city dates from 1976, when a pet-shop owner, tormented by a pair of parakeets screeching in store, hightailed them to the Vondelpark and let them loose. The birds soon bred, and today more than 6000 parakeets shriek around town.

As part of its comprehensive sustainability plan, Amsterdam now only allows electric tour boats on its central canals to keep the waterways as pristine as possible.

Ice Skating

Ice skating was part of the Dutch psyche long before scarfed figures appeared in Golden Age winterscapes. The first skates were made from cow shanks and ribs, had hand-drilled holes and were tied to the feet. When canals and ponds freeze over, everyone takes to the ice.

Boat Tours

Sure they're touristy, but canal cruises are also a delightful way to see the city. Several operators depart from moorings at Centraal Station, Damrak, Rokin and opposite the Rijksmuseum. Prices are similar. To avoid the steamed-up-glass-window effect, look for a boat with an open seating area. On a night tour you'll see the bridges lit up (though these tours usually cost a bit more).

Those Dam Boat Guys (Map p308; ☎020-210 16 69; www.thosedamboatguys.com; tours €25; ⊙by reservation Mar-Sep; ☐13/17 Westermarkt) Small, laid-back local tours.

Ice skating on a canal

Canals by Neighbourhood

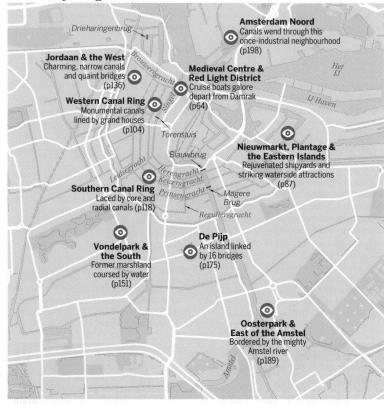

Amsterdam Noord Canals wend through this once-industrial neighbourhood (p198)

Drieharingenbrug

Jordaan & the West Charming, narrow canals and quaint bridges (p136)

Medieval Centre & Red Light District Cruise boats galore depart from Damrak (p64)

Het IJ

IJ Haven

Western Canal Ring Monumental canals lined by grand houses (p104)

Brouwersgracht

Singel

Torensluis

Nieuwmarkt, Plantage & the Eastern Islands Rejuvenated shipyards and striking waterside attractions (p87)

Blauwbrug

Leidsegracht

Herengracht

Keizersgracht

Southern Canal Ring Laced by core and radial canals (p118)

Prinsengracht

Magere Brug

Reguliersgracht

Vondelpark & the South Former marshland coursed by water (p151)

De Pijp An island linked by 16 bridges (p175)

Oosterpark & East of the Amstel Bordered by the mighty Amstel river (p189)

Amstel

Canal Bus (p264) Handy hop-on, hop-off service.

Blue Boat Company (Map p312; 020-679 13 70; www.blueboat.nl; Stadhouderskade 501; 75min tour adult/child €18.50/9; 1/2/5/12 Leidseplein) Day and night-time tours plus various special tours such as a children's pirate-themed tour.

Wetlands Safari (Map p290; 06 5355 2669; www.wetlandssafari.nl; incl transport & picnic adult/child €64/35; 9.30am Mon-Fri, 10am Sat & Sun early Apr-Sep; 2/4/11/12/13/14/17/24/26 Centraal Station) OK, so it's not a canal tour, but it is an exceptional five-hour boat trip canoeing through wetlands and past windmills and 17th-century villages.

Boat Rentals

If you'd like to explore under your own steam, several companies hire out boats; a boat licence isn't required for boats under 15m in length or with a top speed of under 20km/h. Operators provide instruction be-

fore you set sail and usually have waterproof maps of the waterways. Other options for getting out on the water include kayaking.

Canal Bike (p26) Pedal boats for splashing around the canals.

Boaty (p186) Rents cool little electric boats near the Hotel Okura in De Pijp.

Boats4Rent (Map p303; 06 2632 6420; www.bootjehureninamsterdam.com; Polonceau-kade 2; boat hire per 3/10hr from €79/179; by reservation Mar–mid-Oct; Van Limburg Stirumstraat) Electric-powered rental boats next to Westerpark.

Canal Motorboats (Map p303; 020-422 70 07; www.canalmotorboats.com; Zandhoek 10a; rental 1st/2nd/3rd/4th hour €50/40/30/20, subsequent hours €20; 10am-sunset; 48 Westerdoksdijk) Small, electric aluminium boats that carry up to seven passengers.

Lonely Planet's Top Choices

Prinsengracht (p111) The liveliest of Amsterdam's inner canals, with cafes, shops and houseboats lining the quays.

Reguliersgracht (p120) From here you can peer through the arches of seven bridges.

Brouwersgracht (p138) Amsterdammers swear this is the city's most beautiful canal, though it has some seriously tough competition.

Herengracht (p109) Amsterdam's stateliest canal takes in the city's most prestigious real estate along the Golden Bend.

Bloemgracht (p138) This gorgeous canal is home to a large number of fine, gabled houses.

Egelantiersgracht (p138) An elegant and serene canal that feels like you have it (practically) to yourself.

Best Canal Museums

Houseboat Museum (p138) Discover how *gezellig* (convivial, cosy) houseboat living can be aboard this 1914 barge-turned-museum.

Het Grachtenhuis (p108) Inventive multimedia displays explain how the Canal Ring and its amazing houses were built.

Museum Van Loon (p122) Magnificent Golden Age canal house.

Museum Willet-Holthuysen (p123) Sumptuous canal-side property.

Kattenkabinet (p122) Occupies the only canal house on the Golden Bend that's open to the public.

Best Canal Festivals & Events

King's Day (p23) During one of Europe's biggest street parties, plenty of action takes place around the city's famous waterways.

Grachtenfestival (p24) Sees classical musicians play alongside and on the water aboard a barge.

Pride Amsterdam (p24) Amsterdam proudly hosts the only water-borne gay pride festival in the world.

Open Tuinen Dagen (p24) Open Garden Days offer the opportunity to view dozens of private gardens along the canals.

Sinterklaas Intocht (p25) Even St Nicholas sails into town; his arrival by boat heralds the Christmas season.

Amsterdam Light Festival (p25) Walk or take a cruise to see some 25 'light art' installations reflecting in the water.

Amsterdam City Swim (p24) Locals kick and splash through the canals to raise money for charity.

Best Canal Accommodation

SWEETS Hotel (p217) Stay in one of 28 renovated canal-bridge houses.

Houseboat Ms Luctor (p224) A beautiful 1913-built, self-contained boat with mahogany panelling, moored in a quiet location near Centraal Station.

De Dageraad (p221) Eastern Docklands hospitality in an ecofriendly B&B boat that dates from 1929.

Little Amstel (p227) Two-room B&B with a prime position on the Amstel.

Best Canal-Side Dining

De Belhamel (p110) At the head of the Herengracht, this superb restaurant's canal-side tables are an aphrodisiac.

Buffet van Odette (p125) Simple, creative cooking overlooking the Prinsengracht's crooked canal houses.

Gebr Hartering (p98) Exquisitely presented modern Dutch dishes compete with an impossibly romantic canal-side location.

De Prins (p142) This brown cafe (traditional Dutch pub) serves delicious fondue at tables sprinkled along the Prinsengracht.

Best Canal-Side Drinking

't Smalle (p144) Dock right by the stone terrace of the 18th-century former *jenever* (Dutch gin) distillery.

Café P 96 (p145) The summertime terrace of this late-night watering hole is aboard a houseboat.

Café Papeneiland (p144) A 1642 gem on the corner of the Prinsengracht and Brouwersgracht canals.

Café Binnen Buiten (p187) The best canal-side terrace in Amsterdam's 'Latin Quarter', De Pijp.

Edel (p169) Fairy-light-draped charmer at the junction of two canals.

Café de Ceuvel (p202) Canal-side hotspot over the IJ River in Amsterdam Noord.

Tropenmuseum (p191)

54SVISUALS/SHUTTERSTOCK ©

Museums & Galleries

Amsterdam's world-class museums draw millions of visitors each year. The art collections take pride of place – you can't walk a kilometre here without bumping into a masterpiece. Canal-house museums are another local speciality. And, of course, the freewheeling city has a fine assortment of oddball museums dedicated to everything from handbags to houseboats.

All the Art

The Dutch Masters helped spawn the prolific art collections around town. Painters such as Johannes Vermeer, Frans Hals and Rembrandt lived during the Golden Age when a new, bourgeois society of merchants and shopkeepers were spending money to brighten up their homes and workplaces with fresh paintings. The masters were there to meet the need, and their work now fills the city's top museums.

Other Treasures

The Netherlands' maritime prowess during the Golden Age also filled the coffers of local institutions. Silver, porcelain and colonial knickknacks picked up on distant voyages form the basis of collections in the Rijksmuseum (p153), Amsterdam Museum (p70), Het Scheepvaartmuseum (p94) and Tropenmuseum (p191).

Canal-House Museums

There are two kinds: the first preserves the house as a living space, with sumptuous interiors that show how the richest locals lived once upon a time, as at Museum Van Loon (p122). The other type uses the elegant structure as a backdrop for unique collections, such as the Kattenkabinet (p122) for cat art.

Contemporary Galleries

Van Gogh and the Golden Age masters grab the glory, but Amsterdam's art scene goes beyond them. Contemporary galleries dot the city, providing outlets for avant-garde and emerging artists. Many galleries, such as W139 (p73), began as squats and then moved into the mainstream. Gallery-dense neighbourhoods include the Jordaan and the Southern Canal Ring. See contemporary artists at work at Kunststad (p200).

How to Beat the Crowds

Queues at the Van Gogh Museum, Rijksmuseum, Anne Frank Huis and others can easily reach an hour, particularly in summer. Want to avoid the mobs? Here are some strategies:

Take advantage of e-tickets Most sights sell them and there's little to no surcharge. They typically allow you to enter via a separate, faster queue. In some cases, you need to print out the tickets (though scannable mobile-phone tickets are increasingly common).

Go late Queues are shortest during late afternoon and evening. Visit after 3pm for the Rijksmuseum and Van Gogh Museum (also open Friday night plus Saturday night in summer), and after 6pm for the Anne Frank Huis (open late nightly in summer and on Saturday in winter).

Buy a discount card In addition to saving on entrance fees, discount cards commonly provide fast-track entry.

Museums & Galleries by Neighbourhood

➡ **Medieval Centre & Red Light District** (p69) Spans the sacred (several church museums) to the profane (Sexmuseum; Hash, Marijuana & Hemp Museum).

➡ **Nieuwmarkt, Plantage & the Eastern Islands** (p90) Museum het Rembrandthuis, NEMO Science Museum, Het Scheepvaartmuseum and the Verzetsmuseum are scattered around the neighbourhood.

➡ **Western Canal Ring** (p108) Anne Frank Huis draws the mega-crowds; smaller, canal-focused museums pop up too.

➡ **Southern Canal Ring** (p120) Home to the Hermitage Amsterdam plus several quirky museums.

➡ **Jordaan & the West** (p138) Off-the-beaten-path collections from tulips to houseboats to fluorescent art.

NEED TO KNOW

Opening Hours

➡ Most museums open 10am to 5pm, some close on Monday.

➡ The Van Gogh Museum stays open to 9pm on Friday and Saturday mid-June to August, and 9pm Friday September to mid-June.

➡ The Anne Frank Huis opens to 10pm daily from April to October and to 10pm Saturday November to March.

Costs

➡ Tickets are typically €8 to €18.

➡ Kids under 13 often get in for free or half price.

➡ Audioguides are around €5.

Top Tips

➡ Pre-book tickets for the big museums.

➡ Many online tickets only have allocated time slots.

➡ Queues are shortest during late afternoon and evening.

➡ Friday, Saturday and Sunday are the busiest days.

➡ Many hotels sell surcharge-free tickets to the big museums as a service to guests; ask your front-desk staff.

Advance Purchase Recommendations

➡ **Van Gogh Museum & Rijksmuseum** Puts you in a faster queue.

➡ **Anne Frank Huis** E-tickets with set entry times compulsory.

➡ **Stedelijk Museum** Lets you bypass the queue.

➡ **Heineken Experience** E-tickets provide a small discount and faster queue.

➡ **Het Grachtenhuis** E-tickets ensure access to the limited-space tours.

➡ **Vondelpark & the South** (p160) Holds the Museum Quarter and its big three: Van Gogh Museum, Rijksmuseum and Stedelijk Museum.

➡ **De Pijp** (p177) Crowds gather to learn about brewing at the Heineken Experience.

➡ **Oosterpark & East of the Amstel** (p191) Ethnographical displays at Tropenmuseum.

➡ **Amsterdam Noord** (p200) Kunststad has some 250 artists working in its studios.

PLAN YOUR TRIP MUSEUMS & GALLERIES

Lonely Planet's Top Choices

Van Gogh Museum (p156) Hangs the world's largest collection of the tormented artist's vivid swirls.

Rijksmuseum (p153) Rembrandts, Vermeers, crystal goblets and magic lanterns pack the nation's sprawling treasure chest.

Anne Frank Huis (p106) The Secret Annexe and Anne's claustrophobic bedroom provide an unnerving insight into life during WWII.

Pianola Museum (p138) Listen to rare jazz and classic tunes unrolling on vintage player pianos.

Best Art Museums

Museum het Rembrandthuis (p89) Immerse yourself in the old master's paint-spattered studio and handsome home.

Stedelijk Museum (p158) Renowned modern art from Picasso to Mondrian to Warhol fills this museum.

Hermitage Amsterdam (p121) The outpost of Russia's Hermitage Museum picks from its rich home trove to mount mega exhibits.

FOAM (p120) Hip photography museum with changing exhibits by famous shutterbugs.

Best History Museums

Amsterdam Museum (p70) Whizz-bang exhibits take you through seven centuries of the city's intriguing history.

Verzetsmuseum (p94) Find out how the Dutch Resistance operated when the Nazis occupied the country during WWII.

Het Grachtenhuis (p108) Covers the history of Amsterdam's canals.

Best Unusual Museums

Tassenmuseum Hendrikje (p122) A museum of handbags and purses throughout history, with lots of sparkling celebrity clutches.

Sexmuseum Amsterdam (p71) The naughty art and artefacts make for a fun, silly browse.

Electric Ladyland (p139) The world's first museum of fluorescent art offers a trippy glow-in-the-dark experience.

Best Canal-House Museums

Museum Van Loon (p122) This opulent old manor whispers family secrets in its shadowy rooms.

Museum Willet-Holthuysen (p123) Peruse sumptuous paintings, china and a French-style garden with a sundial.

Kattenkabinet (p122) Art devoted to cats (including works by Picasso and Rembrandt) fills a rambling old canal house on the Golden Bend.

Best Underappreciated Museums

Tropenmuseum (p191) Contains a whopping collection of ritual masks, spiky spears and other colonial artefacts.

Het Scheepvaartmuseum (p94) The maritime museum features ancient globes, spooky ship figureheads and a replica schooner to climb.

Museum Ons' Lieve Heer op Solder (p73) Looks like an ordinary canal house, but hides a relic-rich 17th-century church inside.

Best Galleries & Arts Centres

W139 (p73) Ponder political hot-button multimedia works in the thick of the Red Light District.

Civic Guard Gallery (p70) Check out the collection of enormous portraits, from Golden Age to modern day.

Kunststad (p200) Creative studios in former ship-building yards.

Best for Kids

NEMO (p94) Kid-focused, hands-on science labs inside, and a terrace with a splashy summer rooftop water feature.

Joods Historisch Museum (p91) The children's section replicates a Jewish home, with a hands-on music room and a kitchen for baking.

Madame Tussauds Amsterdam (p70) Youngsters get excited to see their favourite celebrities and heroes up close (albeit in wax).

Micropia (p93) The world's first microbe museum has a wall of poop, a 'kiss-o-meter' and other eye-opening exhibits.

Cheese at 't Kaasboertje (p188)

Eating

Amsterdam's sizzling-hot foodie scene boasts a vast array of eating options, such as classic Dutch snacks; reinvented traditional recipes at contemporary restaurants; on-trend establishments pioneering world-first concepts; a wave of new, ultra-healthy eateries, often vegetarian or vegan; and an increasing focus on wine, cocktail and craft-beer pairings. And this multinational city has a cornucopia of cuisines from around the globe.

NEED TO KNOW

Opening Hours

Most restaurants open 11am to 2.30pm for lunch and 6pm to 10pm for dinner.

Price Ranges

Prices are for the cost of a main dish at dinner:

€ less than €12

€€ €12–25

€€€ more than €25

Reservations

Book ahead at places in the middle and upper price brackets. Nearly everyone speaks English. Many places offer online booking options.

Cash & Cards

Many restaurants don't accept credit cards. If they do, there's often a 5% surcharge. Conversely, an increasing number of places accept cards only. Check first.

Saving Money

Dagschotel is dish of the day; heartier appetites might go for a *dagmenu* (a set multicourse menu).

Tipping

Diners do tip, but modestly. Leave 5% to 10% for a cafe snack (if your bill comes to €9.50, you might round up to €10), leave 10% to 15% for a restaurant meal (the higher end for particularly good service).

Best Websites

➡ **Amsterdam Foodie** (www.amsterdamfoodie.nl) Restaurant reviews galore.

➡ **Your Little Black Book** (www.yourlittleblackbook.me) What's new and hot in the city.

➡ **Dutch Review** (www.dutchreview.com) News and reviews of restaurants across the city (and country).

Current Trends

Concept restaurants often see kitchens zeroing in on a single item, such as avocados. Other current trends include gourmet street food (*poké* bowls, ramen, tacos...) as well as all-day brunch. Contemporary Dutch cuisine is also on the rise. Long at the forefront of vegetarian cuisine, Amsterdam led the way with vegan dining and has numerous restaurants citywide.

Amsterdam is a major start-up hub, which extends to its dining landscape. All over the city you'll find expanding minichains of home-grown eateries. Popular ones include Stach (gourmet sandwiches and deli items), SLA (design-your-own salads), De Bakkerswinkel (baked goods), De Pizzabakkers (pizza and Prosecco) and the Butcher (burgers); there are countless others.

Foodhallen (p165), in the De Hallen tram-depot-turned-cultural-complex, has a host of place to eat under one roof, and is a fantastic place to take the city's dining temperature. Festivals, such as food-truck extravaganza **Rollende Keukens** (Rolling Kitchens; www.rollendekeukens.amsterdam; ☉late May/early Jun; 🚋5 Van Hallstraat), are also great for tapping into the zeitgeist.

Specialities

TRADITIONAL DUTCH

Traditional Dutch cuisine revolves around meat, potatoes and vegetables. Typical dishes include *stamppot* (mashed pot), which is potatoes mashed with another vegetable (usually kale or endive) and served with smoked sausage and strips of bacon, and *erwtensoep*, a thick pea soup with smoked sausage and bacon that's usually served in winter.

Pannenkoeken translates to pancakes; the Dutch variety is huge, served one to a plate and topped with sweet or savoury ingredients. The mini version, covered in sugar or syrup, is *poffertjes*. You'll often find these being cooked fresh at markets.

Many snack bars and pubs serve *appeltaart* (apple pie) accompanied by *slagroom* (whipped cream). For breakfast it's common to eat *hagelslag* (chocolate sprinkles) on buttered bread.

CONTEMPORARY DUTCH

Fresh winds are blowing through the Dutch traditional kitchen, breathing new life into centuries-old recipes by giving them a contemporary twist. Creative Dutch chefs are also taking concepts from the rest the world and melding them with locally sourced meats, seafood and vegetables. Amsterdam is ground zero for contemporary Dutch fare.

INDONESIAN & SURINAMESE

The Netherlands' historical ties with Indonesia and Suriname means there are loads of places to try these two cuisines.

The most famous Indonesian dish is a rijsttafel (Indonesian banquet): a dozen or more tiny dishes such as braised beef, pork satay and ribs served with white rice. Other popular dishes are *nasi goreng* – fried rice with onion, pork, shrimp and spices, often topped with a fried egg or shredded omelette – and *bami goreng,* the same thing, but with noodles in place of rice. Indonesian food is usually served mild for Western palates. If you want it hot (*pedis,* pronounced 'p-*dis*'), say so, but be prepared for the ride of a lifetime.

Caribbean-style Surinamese cuisine prominently features curries (chicken, lamb or beef). Roti are burrito-like flatbread wraps stuffed with curried meat or veg; they're delicious, filling and cheap.

Snacks

Vlaamse frites/patat The iconic 'Flemish fries' are cut from whole potatoes and smothered in mayonnaise or myriad other sauces.

Kroketten Croquettes are 'sausages' with various ragu fillings that are crumbed and deep-fried; the ball-shaped variety called *bitterballen* are a popular brown cafe (traditional Dutch pub) snack served with mustard.

Haring Herring is a Dutch institution, sold at stalls around the city. It's salted or pickled, but never cooked, and served with diced onion and sometimes sweet pickles.

Quick Eats

Besides restaurants and *eetcafés* (pub-like places serving affordable meals), there are several quick options.

Broodjeszaken (sandwich shops) are everywhere. Stroll up to the counter and choose your fillings for a fluffy white or wheat roll.

Snack bars are also ubiquitous; FEBO is the most well known, with its long rows of coin-operated yellow windows from which you pluck out a deep-fried treat. Branches are open into the wee hours, and stopping by for a greasy snack after a hard night of drinking is a Dutch tradition.

Cheese

Locals love their *kaas* (cheese). Nearly two-thirds of all cheese sold is Gouda. The tastiest varieties have strong, complex flavours. Try some *oud* (old) Gouda, hard and rich in flavour and a popular bar snack with mustard. Edam is similar to Gouda, but slightly drier and less creamy. Leidse or Leiden cheese is another export hit, laced with cumin seeds and light in flavour.

Sweets

The most famous candy is *drop,* sweet or salty liquorice sold in a bewildering variety of flavours. It's definitely an acquired taste. *Stroopwafels* hide their filling – thick caramel syrup – inside two thin waffles.

Eating by Neighbourhood

➡ **Medieval Centre & Red Light District** (p74) Everything from elegant Dutch to Zeedijk's Asian restaurants to alley-side sandwich shops.

➡ **Nieuwmarkt, Plantage & the Eastern Islands** (p95) Outdoor terraces and dramatic waterfront settings.

➡ **Western Canal Ring** (p109) Cute cafes and small restaurants surround the Negen Straatjes.

➡ **Southern Canal Ring** (p124) Cheap and cheerful around Leidseplein; diverse, quality options on Utrechtsestraat.

➡ **Jordaan & the West** (p140) Convivial little spots are the Jordaan's hallmark; scenester eats dot Westergasfabriek.

➡ **Vondelpark & the South** (p162) From squats serving organic fare to cool-cat international restaurants to the big, airy Foodhallen.

➡ **De Pijp** (p178) Grazing galore in the Albert Cuypmarkt; ethnic places and brunch spots everywhere.

➡ **Oosterpark & East of the Amstel** (p193) Indonesian, Moroccan, Turkish and Surinamese abounds.

➡ **Amsterdam Noord** (p201) Stunning post-industrial and/or waterside settings for creative cuisine.

Local Eat Streets

➡ **Jan Pieter Heijestraat** Sociable spots line this artery between the Vondelpark and De Hallen cultural complex.

➡ **Amstelveenseweg** Loads of international options along the western edge of Vondelpark.

➡ **Utrechtsestraat** Chock-a-block with cafes where cool young Amsterdammers hang out; in the Southern Canal Ring.

➡ **Haarlemmerstraat and Haarlemmerdijk** Adjoining streets spanning the Western Canal Ring and Jordaan with numerous hotspots.

➡ **2e Tuindwarsstraat** Cosy restaurants (many Italian) congregate on and around this narrow Jordaan backstreet.

Lonely Planet's Top Choices

Rijks (p167) Michelin-starred dining in the magnificent Rijksmuseum.

D'Vijff Vlieghen (p75) A treasure rambling through five 17th-century canal houses.

Ron Gastrobar Downtown (p75) Stunning Indonesian cuisine and cocktails from Amsterdam's top chef.

Greetje (p98) Resurrects and re-creates Dutch classics, with mouthwatering results.

De Kas (p195) Dine in the greenhouse that grew your meal's ingredients.

Vleminckx (p74) Phenomenal frites (fries).

Best by Budget

€

Gartine (p74) Slow food sandwiches and a dazzling high tea hide in the Medieval Centre.

Braai BBQ Bar (p162) Street-food-style hotspot barbecuing tangy ribs.

Sterk Staaltje (p95) Greengrocer-like shop filled with ready-to-eat savoury treats.

Avocado Show (p184) Avocados feature in everything from salad bowls to ice cream and cocktails.

€€

Hotel de Goudfazant (p201) French fare in a former garage in Amsterdam Noord.

Mossel en Gin (p143) G&T-battered fish and chips are among the creative gin-infused dishes at this Westergasfabriek stunner.

Balthazar's Keuken (p141) Ever-changing, Mediterranean-tinged dishes served in a revamped blacksmith's forge.

Buffet van Odette (p125) Airy, canal-side terrace for creative pastas and sandwiches.

Wolf Atelier (p143) Ground-breaking gastronomy atop a disused railway bridge.

€€€

De Silveren Spiegel (p76) Refined Dutch cuisine in a romantic step-gabled townhouse.

Greetje (p98) Contemporary Dutch cooking rooted in forgotten Dutch recipes.

Graham's Kitchen (p185) Ingredients at this local secret are sourced from the Amsterdam area.

Marius (p144) The chef whips up a four-course menu from his daily market finds.

Ciel Bleu (p185) Two-Michelin-starred haute cuisine with 23rd-floor views over Amsterdam.

Best by Cuisine

Traditional Dutch

Bistro Bij Ons (p110) Honest-to-goodness Dutch classics.

Pantry (p125) A *gezellig* (cosy, convivial) atmosphere and classic Dutch fare.

Van Dobben (p124) Meaty goodness, diner-style.

Contemporary Dutch

Wilde Zwijnen (p194) The Oost's rustic gem reaps praise for bold, eclectic seasonal fare.

Gebr Hartering (p98) In a seductive canal-side location, the menu changes daily, but is unfailingly delicious.

Hemelse Modder (p96) North Sea fish followed by a heavenly mousse for dessert.

Daalder (p142) Gastronomic contemporary Dutch cuisine.

Indonesian

Dèsa (p180) Hugely popular for its rijsttafel.

Restaurant Blauw (p167) Feted Indonesian fare in contemporary surrounds.

Café Kadijk (p97) Does a mini rijsttafel.

Ron Gastrobar Downtown (p75) Star chef Ron Blaauw's Indonesian cuisine is cutting edge.

Surinamese

Tokoman (p95) Crowds queue for the hot-spiced Surinamese sandwiches.

Spang Makandra (p180) Fabulous array of astonishingly cheap dishes served in cosy surrounds.

Roopram Roti (p193) No-frills spot for flaky roti and fiery hot sauce.

Best Bakeries & Sweets

Patisserie Holtkamp (p126) You're in good company, as the gilded royal coat of arms outside attests.

Baking Lab (p194) A communal oven, baking classes and heavenly breads.

Petit Gâteau (p110) Row upon row of gorgeous minitarts.

Arti Choc (p172) Original and custom-made chocolate creations.

Van Stapele (p75) Insanely addictive dark chocolate cookies.

Best Vegan

Bonboon (p98) Elevated vegan cuisine and a terrace overlooking the water.

Alchemist Garden (p164) Vegan heaven, serving delicious gluten- and lactose-free dishes.

Mastino V (p143) Only serves vegan pizza.

Mr & Mrs Watson (p193) Vegan comfort food including a vegan fondue.

Vegan Junk Food Bar (p164) Plant-based burgers, Dutch *bitterballen* (croquettes) and more.

Best Neighbourhood Gems

Dikke Graaf (p164) Cooking so delicious the aromas lure you in from the street.

Cafe Modern (p202) An Amsterdam Noord favourite.

Éénvistwéévis (p98) Plantage eatery where locals fork into fresh seafood from nearby waters.

Arles (p181) Charming Provençal restaurant in De Pijp.

Best Views

Moon (p202) Take in 360-degree views from A'DAM Tower's revolving restaurant.

REM Eiland (p141) There's nothing like this 22m-high former pirate-radio tower.

Pont 13 (p141) Moored vintage car ferry with a superb Mediterranean-inspired menu.

Cafe-Restaurant Stork (p202) Seafood specialist on the IJ.

Best Brunch

Bakers & Roasters (p184) Banana nutbread French toast and Bloody Marys at Amsterdam's brunch specialist.

Breakfast Club (p163) British, US and Mexican brunch dishes.

Scandinavian Embassy (p184) Goat's milk yoghurt, salmon on Danish rye bread, and more dishes from northern lands.

CT Coffee & Coconuts (p184) Soaring art deco space for coconut-buckwheat pancakes, eggs and avocado toast.

Little Collins (p184) Hip hangout with globe-spanning brunches.

Best Frites

Vleminckx (p74) To slather your golden potatoes in mayonnaise, curry or one of the myriad other sauces?

Wil Graanstra Friteshuis (p110) This family-run stand has served cones of fries near Anne Frank's house for decades.

Frites uit Zuyd (p180) Munch crisp *frites* on the benches out front.

Best Ice Cream

IJsmolen (p97) Try uniquely Dutch flavours near the De Gooyer windmill.

Massimo (p179) Handmade in De Pijp by a fourth-generation gelato maker.

Banketbakkerij Van der Linde (p75) The creamiest vanilla you'll ever taste.

Monte Pelmo (p140) Inventive flavours draw loads of locals.

Best Sandwiches

Vinnies Deli (p110) Inventive all-organic combinations like smoked fish and rhubarb chutney.

Rob Wigboldus Vishandel (p75) Great spot to get your herring on.

Broodje Bert (p75) It's tough to beat house-special lamb meatballs.

Proeflokaal Kef (p202) This cheese specialist makes outstanding sandwiches.

Best Pizza

Pazzi (p141) Perfectly charred crust cradles fresh mozzarella.

Yam Yam (p142) Ever-popular contemporary trattoria.

Lo Stivale d'Oro (p127) The Italian owner fires up a mighty fine disc of goodness.

Sugo (p178) Sublime pizzas by the slice.

PLAN YOUR TRIP EATING

Pllek (p204), Amsterdam Noord

🍷 Drinking & Nightlife

Amsterdam is one of the wildest nightlife cities in Europe and the world. Beyond the Red Light District and hotspots around Leidseplein and Rembrandtplein, the clubbing scene has expanded thanks to 24-hour-licensed venues. Yet you can easily avoid the hardcore party scene: Amsterdam remains a café (pub) society where the pursuit of pleasure focuses on cosiness and charm.

A glass of *jenever* (p51)

Cafés

Cafés When the Dutch say *café*, they mean a pub, and there are more than 1000 throughout Amsterdam. In a city that values socialising and conversation more than the art of drinking itself, *cafés* aren't just about consuming alcohol: they're places to hang out for hours of contemplation or camaraderie. Scores of *cafés* have outside seating on *terrassen* (terraces), which are glorious in summer and sometimes covered and heated in winter. Most serve food as well, ranging from snacks and sandwiches to excellent meals.

Bruin Cafés Amsterdam is famed for its historic *bruin cafés* (brown cafes; traditional drinking establishments). The name comes from the nicotine stains from centuries of use (although recent aspirants slap on brown paint to catch up). Most importantly, the city's brown cafes provide an atmosphere conducive to conversation – and the nirvana of *gezelligheid* (conviviality, cosiness).

Grand Cafés These are spacious, have comfortable furniture and are, well, grand. They all have food menus, some quite elaborate. Despite the name, there's no need to dress up for a visit to a *grand café*.

Theatre Cafés Often similar to *grand cafés,* these are normally attached or adjacent to theatres, serving meals before and drinks after performances. Generally they're good places to catch performers after the show, though they're lovely any time of day.

Drinks

BEER

In stiff competition with a few of their European cohorts – the Belgians, Germans

and Czechs – the Dutch take their beer very seriously (although they drink less per capita than any of them).

Lager is the staple, served cool and topped by a two-finger-thick head of froth to trap the flavour. *Een bier, een pils* or *een vaasje* will get you a normal glass of beer; *een kleintje pils* is a small glass and *een fluitje* is a small, thin, Cologne-style glass. Many places also serve *een grote pils* (a half-litre mug of beer) to please tourists, but it goes flat if you don't drink it quickly.

Local brands include Heineken, Amstel, Grolsch, Oranjeboom, Dommelsch and Bavaria (which, despite its name, isn't German but Dutch). Stronger Belgian beers, such as Duvel and Westmalle Triple, are also very popular. *Witbier* (white beer) is a cloudy wheat beer drunk in summer with a slice of lemon. Dark, sweet *bokbier* comes out in the autumn.

Amsterdam's craft beer scene has exploded in recent years. Alongside long-standing microbreweries like Brouwerij 't IJ and

Above: Outdoor seating at 't Smalle (p144), Jordaan

Left: A coffeeshop menu and marijuana

Brouwerij de Prael, whose beers you'll find around town as well as at the breweries, are innovative brewers such as Brouwerij Troost, Oedipus and Butcher's Tears. You'll also find numerous craft-beer specialist bars and/or shops.

WINE & SPIRITS

It's not just beer here: the Dutch also make the hard stuff. *Jenever* (ye-*nay*-ver; Dutch gin; also spelt *genever*) is made from juniper berries and is drunk chilled. It arrives in a tulip-shaped shot glass filled to the brim – tradition dictates that you bend over the bar, with your hands behind your back, and take a deep sip. Most people prefer *jonge* (young) *jenever,* which is smooth and relatively easy to drink; *oude* (old) *jenever* has a strong juniper flavour and can be an acquired taste.

A common combination, known as a *kopstoot* (head butt), is a glass of *jenever* with a beer chaser – few people can handle more than two or three of these. There are plenty of indigenous liqueurs, including *advocaat* (a kind of eggnog) and the herb-based Beerenburg, a Frisian schnapps.

More Dutch people are drinking wine than ever before, and wine bars are opening all over the city, although almost all wine here is imported from elsewhere in Europe and beyond.

COFFEE

Amsterdam's merchants brought coffee to Europe, and it's still the hot drink of choice. Traditionally, if you simply order *koffie,* you'll get a sizeable cup of java with a small, airline-style container of *koffiemelk,* similar to unsweetened condensed milk.

Caffè-latte-like *koffie verkeerd* ('wrong coffee') comes in a bigger cup or mug with plenty of real milk.

Roasteries and micro-roasteries are springing up around the city, and cafe baristas are increasingly using connoisseur styles of drip coffee.

BORREL

Borrel in Dutch means, quite simply, 'drink' – as in a glass of spirits, traditionally *jenever.* But in social parlance, to be invited to *borrel* means to take part in an informal gathering for drinks, conversation and fun. It usually incorporates food too, especially *borrelhapjes* (bar snacks) like *borrelnootjes* (peanuts covered in a crisp, spicy outer shell), and *kroketten* (croquettes) including *bitterballen* (small, round meat croquettes) – the name comes from the tradition of serving them with bitters, namely *jenever.*

Any occasion can be a reason for *borrel:* a birthday, a beautiful sunset that invites patio sitting or the end of a work day (*vrijdagmiddagborrel,* usually shortened to *vrijmibo* or just *vrimibo,* is specifically Friday-afternoon work drinks with colleagues. When you see a group of locals spilling out of a brown cafe onto the street with a glass of beer in hand? That's *borrel.*

Smoking
MARIJUANA & HASHISH
Despite what you may have heard, cannabis is not *technically* legal in the Netherlands – yet it is widely tolerated. Here's the deal: the purchase and possession of small amounts (5g) of 'soft drugs' (ie marijuana, hashish, space cakes and mushroom-based

COFFEESHOP & SMART SHOP DOS & DON'TS

➡ Do ask coffeeshop staff for advice on what and how to consume, and heed it, even if nothing happens after an hour.

➡ Don't ask for hard (illegal) drugs.

➡ Do ask staff for the menu of products on offer. Most shops offer rolling papers, pipes or bongs to use; you can also buy ready-made joints.

➡ Don't drink alcohol – it's illegal in coffeeshops.

➡ Don't smoke tobacco, whether mixed with marijuana or on its own; it is forbidden inside all establishments, in accordance with Dutch law.

➡ 'Herbal ecstasy' – usually a mix of herbs, vitamins and caffeine – is sold in smart shops; do ask staff what they recommend, as some varieties can have unpleasant side effects.

➡ Psilocybin mushrooms (aka magic mushrooms) are now illegal in the Netherlands, but many smart shops sell mushroom truffles, which have a similar effect.

truffles) is allowed and users won't be prosecuted for smoking or carrying this amount (although authorities do have the right to confiscate it, but this is rare). This means that coffeeshops are actually conducting an illegal business – but again, this is tolerated to a certain extent.

Most cannabis products sold in the Netherlands used to be imported, but today the country has high-grade home produce, so-called *nederwiet*. It's a particularly strong product – the most potent varieties contain 15% tetrahydrocannabinol (THC), the active substance that gets people high (since 2011, anything above 15% is classified as a hard drug and is therefore illegal). In a nutshell, Dutch weed will literally blow your mind – perhaps to an extent that isn't altogether pleasant, which is why many native smokers have sworn off the local product. Newbies to smoking pot and hash should exercise caution; even many regular smokers can't stomach the home-grown stuff.

Space cakes and cookies (baked goods made with hash or marijuana) are sold in a rather low-key fashion, mainly because tourists often have problems with them. If people are unused to the time they can take to kick in and the effects, they could be in for an intense and long-lasting experience.

THE FUTURE OF AMSTERDAM COFFEESHOPS
Since the decriminalisation of soft drugs in 1976, the 'right to smoke' was not threatened in Amsterdam until relatively recently. Amsterdam currently has 167 coffeeshops (31% of the Netherlands' total), which is down from a high of 350 in 1995.

In 2011 the government proposed banning foreigners from cafes selling cannabis and requiring Dutch residents to sign up for a one-year *wietpas* ('weed pass') in order to purchase 'soft drugs' at a coffeeshop. Although the top Dutch court declared that such legislation was unlawful, it indicated that restricting tourists and foreigners from entering coffeeshops would not necessarily be considered unconstitutional. The law was passed in 2012; however, Amsterdam's councillors declared their opposition to it – on the grounds of increased crime, street dealing and antisocial behaviour – and coffeeshops have turned a blind eye. If you're travelling further afield, be aware that elsewhere in the Netherlands, a number of regional councils are using the *wietpas* system, though some coffeeshops in these areas are pursuing this in court, so the outcome is uncertain – ask locally what the situation is when you visit.

Despite the 2014 commencement of the Dutch law dictating that coffeeshops must not operate within 250m of primary schools and 350m of secondary schools in Amsterdam, authorities are also in disagreement, arguing that minors are already forbidden, coffeeshops are monitored and that there are more effective ways to combat youth drug use, such as education. The law has, however, resulted in some 20 coffeeshops closing to date.

For now, Amsterdam's coffeeshops remain accessible to anyone (foreigners or locals) aged 18 and above. Coffeeshops are banned from advertising, and can sell up to 5g of cannabis per day, per customer. But their longer-term future remains a wait-and-see situation.

Clubbing
Amsterdam is banging on Berlin's door to claim the mantle of Europe's clubbing capital. The electronic music extravaganza Amsterdam Dance Event (p24) is a fixture on the city's calendar, and from 2012 Amsterdam has appointed a *nachtburgemeester* (night mayor), representing and encouraging the city's nightlife and economy (the first city in the world to do so).

Inner-city clubs are integrating into the social fabric, and epic venues (including some with 24-hour licences) are occupying repurposed buildings outside the city centre (accessible by public transport) to avoid noise. In addition to club nights, they mount multigenre art exhibitions, markets and other diverse cultural offerings.

Some of the best beats are to the west, at venues such as **Warehouse Elementenstraat** (www.elementenstraat.nl; Elementenstraat 25; usually Fri & Sat; ; 22/281 Contactweg, Isolatorweg), in a vast warehouse; **De School** (020-737 31 97; www.deschoolamsterdam.nl; Dr Jan van Breemenstraat 1; usually Thu-Sat; ; 13 Admiraal Helfrichstraat), in a former technical school; and **De Marktkantine** (020-723 17 60; www.marktkantine.nl; Jan van Galenstraat 6; usually Thu-Sun; ; 18/282 Markthallen), in a market workers' canteen. To the southwest is **Radion** (020-452 47 09; www.radion.amsterdam; Louwesweg 1; hours vary; ; 18/247/288 Louwesweg, 2 Louwesweg), in a former dentistry academy. The post-industrial neighbourhood of Amsterdam Noord is also fertile ground

Drinking & Nightlife by Neighbourhood

Amsterdam Noord
Creative venues in warehouses and shipping containers (p202)

Jordaan & the West
Cosy local *cafés* and post-industrial venues (p144)

Medieval Centre & Red Light District
Jenever tasting rooms meet grand cafes (p77)

Western Canal Ring
Grand hotel bars, historic brown cafes (p112)

Nieuwmarkt, Plantage & the Eastern Islands
Buzzing *cafés* and elegant watering holes (p99)

Southern Canal Ring
Tourists and a fabulous gay scene (p127)

Vondelpark & the South
Serene scene, great local cocktail bars (p167)

De Pijp
Young, hip, ethnic and edgy (p185)

Oosterpark & East of the Amstel
Amstel views and bars in warehouses (p195)

for clubs such as Shelter, buried beneath A'DAM Tower (p200); Tolhuistuin (p205); and Sexyland (p201), with wildly disparate contributions from its 365 members, who each host their own annual event.

Amsterdam's Gay & Lesbian Scene

The Netherlands was the first country to legalise same-sex marriage (in 2001), so it's no surprise that Amsterdam's LGBT+ scene is one the largest in the world. Local gay and lesbian organisations can help you tap into the city's scene.

Five hubs party hardest:

Warmoesstraat In the Red Light District (between the Dam and Centraal Station) hosts the infamous, kink-filled leather and fetish bars.

Zeedijk Near Warmoesstraat, crowds spill onto laid-back bar terraces.

Rembrandtplein In the Southern Canal Ring, this area has traditional pubs and brown cafes, some with a campy bent, and popular lesbian hangouts.

Leidseplein A smattering of trendy venues along Kerkstraat.

Reguliersdwarsstraat Draws the beautiful crowd.

Lonely Planet's Top Choices

't Smalle (p144) Amsterdam's most intimate canal-side drinking, with a gorgeous historic interior.

Warehouse Elementenstraat (p52) One of Europe's hottest 24-hour clubs.

Wynand Fockink (p80) This 1679 tasting house pours glorious *jenevers*.

Pllek (p204) Hip bar made out of old shipping containers with an artificial beach.

SkyLounge (p100) A pinch-yourself, 360-degree city panorama extends from this 11th-floor bar and vast terrace.

Best Brown Cafés

In 't Aepjen (p79) Candles burn all day long in the time-warped, 500-year-old house.

Hoppe (p77) An icon of drinking history beloved by journalists, bums and raconteurs.

De Sluyswacht (p99) Swig in the lock-keeper's quarters across from Rembrandt's house.

Café Pieper (p144) Antique beer mugs hang from the bar at this low-ceilinged gem.

Café de Dokter (p77) Amsterdam's teeniest pub wafts old jazz records and pours whiskeys galore.

Eijlders (p130) Stained-glass artists' favourite with a lingering Resistance spirit.

Best Beer

Brouwerij 't IJ (p99) Wonderful independent brewery at the foot of the De Gooyer windmill.

Brouwerij Troost Westergas (p147) Sip frothy house-made suds and gin.

Brouwerij De Prael (p79) Socially minded brewery that makes strong organic beers.

Oedipus Brewery & Tap Room (p204) Brilliant brewery in Amsterdam Noord.

Bierfabriek (p80) Right in the city centre, this microbrewery also does great food.

Best Coffeeshops

Dampkring (p79) Hollywood made the hobbit-like decor and prize-winning product famous.

Abraxas (p79) A haven of mellow music and comfy sofas spread over three floors.

Greenhouse (p80) Psychedelic mosaics and stained glass plus a big menu for munchies.

La Tertulia (p147) Cool Van Gogh murals mark this quiet spot on the Prinsengracht.

Betty Boop (p130) Gay favourite.

Best Cocktail Bars

Rosalia's Menagerie (p99) Dutch heritage–themed cocktails in vintage surrounds.

Tales & Spirits (p77) House infusions and vintage glasses.

Canvas (p195) Edgy, artsy bar with great views atop the *Volkskrant* newspaper building (now a flash hotel).

Twenty Third Bar (p186) Aerial 23rd-floor views, sublime champagne cocktails and two-Michelin-star bar snacks.

Door 74 (p129) Speakeasy-style bar mixing some of Amsterdam's wildest cocktails.

Best Gay & Lesbian Hangouts

't Mandje (p80) Amsterdam's oldest gay bar is a trinket-covered beauty.

Getto (p81) A younger crowd piles in for cheap food and Red Light District people-watching.

Montmartre (p133) Legendary bar where Dutch ballads and old top-40 hits tear the roof off.

De Trut (p147) A Sunday fixture on the scene.

Best Coffee

Monks Coffee Roasters (p147) Unmissable house blend.

Lot Sixty One (p169) Red-hot Amsterdam roastery.

Scandinavian Embassy (p184) Coffee sourced from Scandinavian microroasteries.

Espressofabriek (p147) Aromatic roastery at Westergasfabriek.

Koffiehuis De Hoek (p112) Charming, old-fashioned coffeehouse experience.

Best Wine Bars

Worst Wijncafe (p142) Chequerboard-tiled wine bar with superb sausage tapas dishes.

Glouglou (p187) All-natural, by-the-glass wines.

Pata Negra (p131) Wonderfully rustic Spanish-style bodega.

Rayleigh & Ramsay (p186) Has a unique self-dispensary system.

Entertainment

Amsterdam supports a flourishing arts scene, with loads of big concert halls, theatres, cinemas, comedy clubs and other performance venues filled on a regular basis. Music fans are superbly catered for here, and there is a fervent subculture for just about every genre, especially jazz, classical, rock and avant-garde beats.

Music

JAZZ

Jazz is extremely popular, from far-out, improvisational stylings to more traditional notes. The grand Bimhuis (p102) is the big game in town, drawing visiting musicians from around the globe, though its vibe is more that of a funky little club. Smaller jazz venues abound and it's easy to find a live combo.

CLASSICAL

Amsterdam's classical music scene, with top international orchestras, conductors and soloists crowding the agenda, is the envy of many European cities. Choose between the flawless Concertgebouw (p171) or dramatic Muziekgebouw aan 't IJ (p101) for the main shows.

ROCK

Many of the city's clubs also host rock bands. Huge touring names often play smallish venues such as the Melkweg (p134) and Paradiso (p133); it's a real treat to catch one of your favourites here.

Comedy & Theatre

Given that the Dutch are fine linguists and have a keen sense of humour, English-language comedy thrives in Amsterdam, especially around the Jordaan. Local theatre tends towards the edgy and experimental.

Cinema

Amsterdam's weather is fickle and, let's face it, even art lovers can overdose on museums. Luckily this town is a cinephile's heaven, with oodles of art-house cinemas. Numerous screenings are in English.

Entertainment by Neighbourhood

→ **Medieval Centre & Red Light District** (p81) Several young rock/DJ clubs thrash throughout the 'hood, while avant-garde theatres line Nes.

→ **Nieuwmarkt, Plantage & the Eastern Islands** (p101) Classical venues include the Muziekgebouw aan 't IJ, Bimhuis and Conservatorium.

→ **Western Canal Ring** (p114) Limited options until the Felix Meritis cultural centre reopens in 2020.

→ **Southern Canal Ring** (p132) Clubs and live-music venues fan out around Leidseplein.

→ **Jordaan & the West** (p148) Venues for comedy, blues and cult films, plus the Westergasfabriek complex.

→ **Vondelpark & the South** (p171) Home to the world-renowned Concertgebouw, free theatre in the park and squats-turned-culture-centres.

→ **De Pijp** (p187) Great cinema, a smattering of jazz and buskers.

→ **Oosterpark & East of the Amstel** (p196) Mega-venues and Amsterdam's beloved football team entertain here.

→ **Amsterdam Noord** (p205) Live music plays regularly at venues like Café Noorderlicht and Pllek.

NEED TO KNOW

Opening Hours

Entertainment in Amsterdam can range from afternoon matinees to three-day-long raves, so opening hours are as sporadic and diverse as the delights on offer. Check individual venues for full details.

Discounted Tickets

Last Minute Ticket Shop (www.lastminuteticket shop.nl) sells same-day half-price tickets for concerts, performances and even club nights online. Events are handily marked 'LNP' (language no problem) if understanding Dutch isn't vital.

Resources

➡ **I Amsterdam** (www. iamsterdam.com) Events listings.

➡ **I Amsterdam Magazine** Magazine covering the local scene, published four times per year and available at the visitor centre, local newsagents and various hotels.

➡ **Film Ladder** (www. filmladder.nl/amster dam) Movie listings.

Lonely Planet's Top Choices

Melkweg (p134) A galaxy of diverse music, cinema and theatre in a former dairy.

Muziekgebouw aan 't IJ (p101) Acoustically and visually stunning performing-arts venue on the IJ River.

Westergasfabriek (p140) Options abound in this post-industrial former-gasworks-turned-cultural-complex.

Paradiso (p133) One-time church that now preaches a gospel of rock and roll.

Studio K (p196) Diverse venue in Oost.

Best Classical & Opera

Concertgebouw (p171) World-renowned concert hall with superb acoustics.

Orgelpark (p172) Listen to organ music in a lovely restored church on the edge of the Vondelpark.

Best Jazz & Blues

Bimhuis (p102) The beating jazz heart of the Netherlands, inside the Muziekgebouw aan 't IJ.

Jazz Café Alto (p134) Excellent little club where you're practically on stage with the musicians.

Maloe Melo (p149) All subgenres of blues get a run at this good-time venue.

Bourbon Street Jazz & Blues Club (p133) Jam sessions regularly take place here.

Best Rock

Pacific (p148) Westergasfabriek venue with regular gigs and a rock-and-roll spirit.

De Nieuwe Anita (p148) Rock out by the stage behind the bookcase-concealed door.

Cave (p134) Basement venue hosting live hard rock and metal.

Best Cinemas

EYE Film Institute (p201) New, old, foreign, domestic: the Netherlands' uber-mod film centre shows quality films of all kinds.

Pathé Tuschinskitheater (p132) Amsterdam's most famous cinema, with a sumptuous art deco/Amsterdam School interior.

Movies (p148) Amsterdam's oldest cinema dates from 1912.

Best Theatre & Comedy

Boom Chicago (p148) Laugh-out-loud improv-style comedy in the Jordaan.

Internationaal Theater Amsterdam (p133) Large-scale plays, operettas and festivals right on Leidseplein.

Theater Amsterdam (p148) Gleaming glass theatre with a multilingual translation system.

Best Free or Low Cost

Openluchttheater (p172) Open-air summertime performances in the Vondelpark.

Muziektheater (p101) Free lunchtime classical concerts most Tuesdays from September to June.

Concertgebouw (p171) Wednesday's free lunchtime concerts from September to June are often rehearsals for the evening's performance.

Best for Kids

Amsterdams Marionetten Theater (p102) Fairy-tale stage sets and stringed puppets bring operas to life.

Kriterion (p102) Lots of films for kids.

Filmhallen (p165) New-release children's films and a retro caravan selling popcorn.

Shopping

During the Golden Age, Amsterdam was the world's warehouse, stuffed with riches from the far corners of the earth. The capital's cupboards are still stocked with all kinds of exotica (just look at that red-light gear!), as well as antiques, but you'll also find cutting-edge Dutch fashion and design.

Specialities

Dutch fashion Locals have mastered the art of casual style, and it streams right out of the no-nonsense side of the national character. The result is hip, practical designs – such as floaty, layered separates and tailored denim – that don't get caught in bike chains.

Dutch-designed homewares Dutch designers have shown a singular knack for bringing a creative, stylish touch to everyday objects.

Antiques and art Stores selling gorgeous antiques pop up all around the city. They're not cheap, but the quality is usually excellent. The Spiegel Quarter offers a long line of shops along Spiegelgracht and Nieuwe Spiegelstraat that attract moneyed browsers.

Delftware The Dutch have been firing up the iconic blue-and-white pottery since the 1600s. A few shops in Amsterdam sell the real deal, but it's much more common (and affordable) to buy replica pottery.

Flower bulbs Exotic tulip bulbs and other flower seeds are popular gifts to take home. Check customs regulations, since bringing bulbs into your home country can be prohibited.

Cheese Dutch *kaas* is justifiably famous and makes a great economical souvenir. Gouda and Edam are the most common varieties. Check customs (and packaging) regulations.

Alcohol *Jenever* (Dutch gin) is a distinctive souvenir.

Bongs, pot-leaf-logoed T-shirts and sex toys This is Amsterdam after all, so it's no surprise that these items are legion in Red Light District shops.

Boutiques & Shopping Streets

Stumbling across offbeat little boutiques is one of the great joys of shopping in Amsterdam. Teeny stores selling only juggling supplies or gifts for cats (and their owners)? They're here. The best areas for such finds are the nexus of the Western Canal Ring and Jordaan, along Haarlemmerstraat and Haarlemmerdijk, which are lined with boutiques. To the south the Negen Straatjes (p115) offers a satisfying browse among its pint-sized, one-of-a-kind shops. Staalstraat in Nieuwmarkt is another bountiful vein.

The busiest shopping streets are Kalverstraat by the Dam and Leidsestraat, which leads into Leidseplein. Both are lined with clothing and department stores.

Near Vondelpark, stylish fashion boutiques line Cornelis Schuytstraat and Willemsparkweg. Close by, PC Hooftstraat queues up Chanel, Diesel, Gucci and other luxury brands along its length.

Markets

No visit to Amsterdam is complete if you haven't experienced one of its lively outdoor markets.

Check dates for the design-oriented Sunday Market (p137), at various locations, and the IJ Hallen (p205) flea market, in Amsterdam Noord.

DAILY MARKETS

Amsterdam's daily markets are open every day except Sunday. Albert Cuypmarkt (p178) in De Pijp is the largest, busiest market, offering food, clothing and everything else.

NEED TO KNOW

Opening Hours

➡ Department stores and large shops: 9am or 10am to 6pm Monday to Saturday, noon to 6pm Sunday.

➡ Smaller shops: 10am or noon to 6pm Tuesday to Friday; 10am to 5pm Saturday (and Sunday if open at all); from noon or 1pm to 5pm or 6pm Monday (if open at all).

➡ Many shops stay open late (to 9pm) Thursday.

Taxes

➡ Non-EU residents are entitled to a tax refund on purchases over €50 if the store has the proper paperwork (request it when paying).

➡ At the airport, present your goods, receipts and passport, get your refund cheque stamped and take it to the Global Refund office. Allow ample time.

Cash & Cards

Some smaller stores do not accept credit cards. Conversely, some shops only accept Dutch PIN debit cards, not credit cards or cash (there will be a sign on the window or door).

Shopping App

The nifty app AMS NXT (www.amsterdamnext.com) guides you from long-standing classics to hot new design stores and temporary pop-up concept stores.

Multi-product Dappermarkt (p192), near Oosterpark, is similar but smaller.

There's bric-a-brac galore at Waterlooplein Flea Market (p102) in Nieuwmarkt. Ten Katemarkt (p165) adjoins the cultural and design complex De Hallen, with fresh food, flowers and more. The Flower Market, Bloemenmarkt (p121), specialises in bulbs (and kitsch souvenirs); it's located in the Southern Canal Ring and open every day, *including* Sunday. Old tomes, maps and

sheet music are the speciality at Oudemanhuispoort Book Market (p85) in the centre.

WEEKLY MARKETS

Hit Westermarkt (p149) in the Jordaan on Monday for clothing. Also on Monday in the Jordaan, Noordermarkt (p149) has flea-market wares. On Wednesdays and Saturdays a small group of vendors sells stamps and coins at Postzegelmarkt (p85) in the centre. On Saturday, head to Lindengracht Market (p149) in the Jordaan for food, arts, crafts and trinkets, Boerenmarkt (p103) farmers market in Nieuwmarkt or Noordermarkt (p149) in the Jordaan. On Sunday in summer there's the Antiques Market (p103) on Nieuwmarkt, and the Art Market (p86) on the Spui in the centre.

Shopping by Neighbourhood

➡ **Medieval Centre & Red Light District** (p84) From adult shops to bookshops and design emporiums.

➡ **Nieuwmarkt, Plantage & the Eastern Islands** (p102) Waterlooplein Flea Market is a key draw, along with eccentric local shops on Staalstraat.

➡ **Western Canal Ring** (p114) The Negen Straatjes hold the mother lode of teensy, quirky speciality shops.

➡ **Southern Canal Ring** (p134) Hunt for art and antiques in the Spiegel Quarter, and fashion, music and homewares nearby.

➡ **Jordaan & the West** (p149) Jordaan shops are artsy and eclectic; Haarlemmerdijk has the newest, coolest boutiques.

➡ **Vondelpark & the South** (p172) Stylish boutiques on Cornelis Schuytstraat and Willemsparkweg and ultra-luxe labels on PC Hooftstraat.

➡ **De Pijp** (p187) Beyond Albert Cuypmarkt are quirky shops, galleries, and vintage and designer fashion boutiques.

➡ **Oosterpark & East of the Amstel** (p197) Trawl the ethnically diverse Dappermarkt.

➡ **Amsterdam Noord** (p205) Vintage finds and cool homewares in industrial surrounds.

Lonely Planet's Top Choices

X Bank (p84) Stunning Dutch design showcase.

Pied à Terre (p172) Europe's largest travel bookshop will make anyone's feet itch.

De Kaaskamer (p115) This 'cheese room' is stacked to the rafters with goodness.

Kramer Kunst & Antiek (p134) Antique treasures here include beautiful Delftware tiles.

Concerto (p134) The city's best music shop has recordings in all genres.

Best Markets

Albert Cuypmarkt (p178) Vibrant street market spilling over with food, fashion and bargain finds.

Waterlooplein Flea Market (p102) Piles of curios for treasure hunters.

Westermarkt (p149) Bargain-priced clothing and fabrics at scores of stalls.

Lindengracht Market (p149) Wonderfully authentic local affair, with bushels of fresh produce.

IJ Hallen (p205) Enormous monthly flea market at NDSM-werf.

Dappermarkt (p192) Multi-ethnic food, clothing and homewares.

Best Books

Mendo (p117) Sleek bookshop specialising in art, design, architecture, fashion and photography.

Oudemanhuispoort Book Market (p85) Covered alleyway lined with second-hand book stalls.

American Book Center (p86) English-language books of all kinds sprawl across three floors.

Best Fashion

Locals (p84) Locally designed fashion and accessories for men and women.

Love Stories (p115) Stunning swimsuits and lingerie by Amsterdam designer Marloes Hoedeman.

VLVT (p174) Up-and-coming Dutch-designed women's fashion on chic Cornelis Schuytstraat.

Vanilia (p115) Dutch label making limited-edition womenswear.

Best Souvenirs

Bloemenmarkt (p121) Bulbs, bulbs and more bulbs fill Amsterdam's 'floating' flower market.

Galleria d'Arte Rinascimento (p150) Royal Delftware ceramics (both antique and new).

Mark Raven Grafiek (p84) Artsy, beyond-the-norm T-shirts and prints of the city.

Best Dutch Design

Hôtel Droog (p102) The famed collective is known for sly, playful, repurposed and reinvented homewares.

Frozen Fountain (p115) Amsterdam's best-known showcase of Dutch-designed furniture and homewares.

Memento (p149) Contemporary Delftware to Dutch flower-scented perfumes.

Hutspot (p187) Funky store giving emerging designers an opportunity to sell their work.

Mobilia (p135) Dutch design is stunningly showcased at this three-storey 'lifestyle studio'.

X Bank (p84) Dazzling, monthly-changing displays.

Best Food & Drink

Hart's Wijnhandel (p135) Historic shop selling tipples, including *jenever*.

Het Oud-Hollandsch Snoepwinkeltje (p148) All kinds of Dutch candies, including sweet and salty *drop* (Dutch liquorice).

Papabubble (p150) Sweet, sugary, made-in-front-of-you creations.

Bier Baum (p188) Craft beers from Amsterdam and the world.

't Kaasboertje (p188) Cheeses galore.

Best Antiques & Vintage

Antiekcentrum Amsterdam (p150) Quirky indoor mall with stalls offering anything from 1940s dresses to 1970s Swedish porn.

Zipper (p117) Vintage fashion finds.

Gastronomie Nostalgie (p85) Beautiful old china, goblets, candlesticks and other tableware from far-flung auctions.

360 Volt (p115) Reconditioned industrial light fittings.

Explore Amsterdam

AMSTERDAM'S TOP SIGHTS

Neighbourhoods at a Glance

1 Medieval Centre & Red Light District p64

Amsterdam's oldest quarter is remarkably preserved, looking much as it did in its Golden Age heyday. It's the busiest part of town for visitors. While some come to see the Royal Palace and Oude Kerk, others make a beeline for the coffeeshops and Red Light District.

2 Nieuwmarkt, Plantage & the Eastern Islands p87

Buzzing Nieuwmarkt is sewn through with rich seams of history. Leafy Plantage takes it down a gear, with the sprawling zoo and botanical gardens. It segues into the Eastern Islands, with a completely different atmosphere, combining maritime history, flagship modern architecture and bars in ex-warehouses.

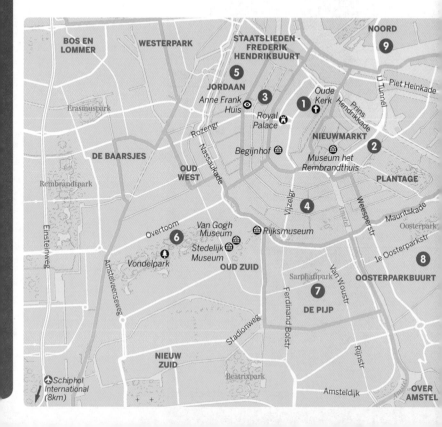

❸ Western Canal Ring p104

Grand old mansions and tiny, charming speciality shops line the glinting waterways of the Western Canal Ring, one of Amsterdam's most gorgeous areas. Roaming around them can cause days to vanish. But most people come here for a singular reason: to visit Anne Frank's house and see her famous diary.

❹ Southern Canal Ring p118

The Southern Canal Ring is a horseshoe-shaped loop of parallel canals. It's home to the nightlife hubs of Leidseplein and Rembrandtplein, where bars, clubs and restaurants cluster around large squares. Between these two districts, the canals are lined by some of the city's most elegant houses; the area also encompasses many fine museums, a flower market and waterside restaurants and bars.

❺ Jordaan & the West p136

The Jordaan teems with cosy pubs, galleries and markets crammed into a grid of tiny lanes. It's short on conventional sights, but it's a wonderfully atmospheric place for an aimless stroll. It abuts the West, industrial badlands that have been transformed into an innovative cultural hub.

❻ Vondelpark & the South p151

Vondelpark has a special place in Amsterdam's heart, a lush green egalitarian space where everyone hangs out at some point. Close to the park, the wealth-laden Old South holds the Van Gogh, Stedelijk and Rijksmuseum collections. Further south still is the lush Amsterdamse Bos (Amsterdam Forest) and the Cobra Museum.

❼ De Pijp p175

A hotbed of creativity, multicultural De Pijp preserves its village-like atmosphere. The neighbourhood's centrepiece is Amsterdam's largest street market, the colourful Albert Cuypmarkt, and the fashion boutiques, vintage shops, experimental restaurants and free-spirited *cafés* (pubs) that surround it.

❽ Oosterpark & East of the Amstel p189

Oost (East) is one of Amsterdam's most culturally diverse neighbourhoods. It grew up in the 19th century, with grand buildings and wide boulevards. Large, English-style Oosterpark was laid out in 1861, while lush Flevopark dates from when this area was a country retreat. Beyond this is Amsterdam's newest neighbourhood, IJburg, built across several islands, with the city beach.

❾ Amsterdam Noord p198

Amsterdam Noord encompasses cutting-edge architecture, ex-industrial areas and hangars-turned-hipster-hangouts with walls covered in street art, all minutes away from fields, horses and the odd windmill. It is perfect for exploring by bike, and escaping the crowds of central Amsterdam.

Medieval Centre & Red Light District

MEDIEVAL CENTRE | RED LIGHT DISTRICT

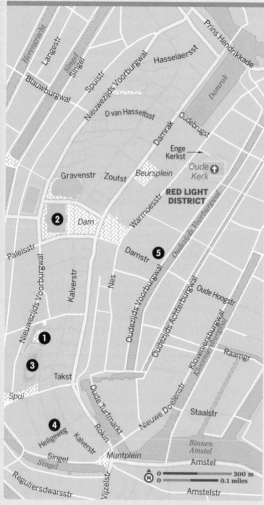

Neighbourhood Top Five

1 **Amsterdam Museum** (p70) Discovering what makes Amsterdam the city it is today on a voyage through seven pivotal periods across a millennium of history at this high-tech museum.

2 **Royal Palace** (p66) Marvelling at the chandeliered opulence and taking a Dutch history lesson at the city's landmark palace.

3 **Begijnhof** (p67) Pushing open the door to find this tranquil courtyard's hidden gardens and churches.

4 **Vleminckx** (p74) Biting into crisp golden *frites* (fries) slathered in mayonnaise, curry or peanut sauce from Amsterdam's best *frites* stand.

5 **Wynand Fockink** (p80) Bowling up to this 17th-century tasting house to knock back a *jenever* (Dutch gin) or taking a pre-booked weekend tour.

For more detail of this area see Map p290 and p294 ➡

Explore Medieval Centre & Red Light District

Amsterdam's heart beats in its medieval core and centuries-old Red Light District. All visitors end up here at some point. Centraal Station (p69) is the main landmark; Damrak slices south from the station to the Dam – Amsterdam's central square and home to the Royal Palace (p66).

There are several intriguing sights, but the big-ticket museums lie elsewhere. The main activity here is wandering. The compact area is laced with atmospheric lanes, and 17th-century tasting rooms, brown cafes, hidden courtyards and tiny speciality shops are the prizes for those who venture off the main drags.

While the infamous Red Light District can get rowdy at night, it has some beautiful historical bars, as well as the stunning Oude Kerk (p68), the city's oldest church.

The area's layout has changed little since the 17th century and some vistas look like they belong in a Golden Age landscape. You could easily spend your entire trip here, so remember: there are more neighbourhoods beyond.

Local Life

➡ **Bikes** The multistorey bike-parking station to the west of Centraal Station (p69), jam-packed with 3500-plus bikes, demonstrates how integral cycling is to Amsterdam life. A 7000-capacity bike station beneath the IJ opens in 2021. Plans are also underway for two floating bike-parking stations with a combined capacity of 4000.

➡ **Beers & books** Inviting *cafés* (pubs) and bookshops ring the Spui (p71), a favoured haunt of academics and journalists.

➡ **Dam** A fair, a protest, a speech by the monarch – there's always something drawing people to Amsterdam's main square (p69).

Getting There & Away

➡ **Tram** The majority of the city's 15 tram lines go through the neighbourhood en route to Centraal Station. Useful lines include trams 2, 11, 12, 13 and 17, which travel to the station's west side, and trams 4, 14 and 24, which travel to the east side.

➡ **Metro** Metros travel from Centraal to Amsterdam's outer neighbourhoods, and to Amsterdam Noord and Station Zuid via a stop in the Medieval Centre at Rokin.

➡ **Boat** Free ferries run to NDSM-werf and elsewhere in Amsterdam Noord, departing from the **piers** (Map p290; De Ruijterkade) behind Centraal Station.

Lonely Planet's Top Tip

If you're after somewhere to drink or dine around Centraal Station (p69), Chinatown is just 550m southeast along Zeedijk. There are also a couple of casual places on the station's revitalised northern side alongside the IJ River near the docks for the free ferries to Amsterdam Noord.

✖ Best Places to Eat

➡ D'Vijff Vlieghen (p75)
➡ De Silveren Spiegel (p76)
➡ Vleminckx (p74)
➡ Ron Gastrobar Downtown (p75)
➡ Gartine (p74)

For reviews, see p74.➡

🍷 Best Places to Drink

➡ In 't Aepjen (p79)
➡ Cut Throat (p77)
➡ Wynand Fockink (p80)
➡ Tales & Spirits (p77)
➡ Proeflokaal de Ooievaar (p80)
➡ Café de Dokter (p77)

For reviews, see p77.➡

🛍 Best Places to Shop

➡ X Bank (p84)
➡ Locals (p84)
➡ Mark Raven Grafiek (p84)
➡ Oudemanhuispoort Book Market (p85)
➡ Posthumus (p84)
➡ Hempstory (p86)

For reviews, see p84.➡

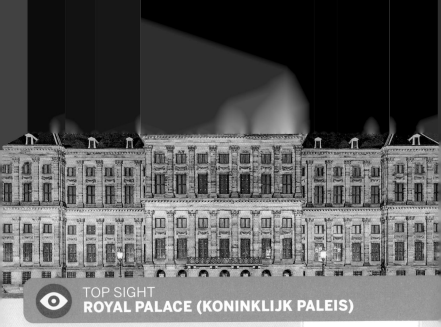

TOP SIGHT
ROYAL PALACE (KONINKLIJK PALEIS)

Today's Royal Palace began life as a glorified town hall and was completed in 1665. Its architect, Jacob van Campen, spared no expense to display Amsterdam's wealth in a way that rivalled the grandest European buildings of the day. The result is opulence on a big scale. It's worth seeing the exterior at night, when the palace is dramatically floodlit.

Officially, the Dutch king, King Willem-Alexander, lives in this landmark palace and pays a symbolic rent, though his actual residence is in Den Haag. If he's not here in Amsterdam, visitors have the opportunity to come in and wander around the monumental building.

Most of the rooms spread over the 1st floor, which is awash in chandeliers (51 shiners in total), along with damasks, gilded clocks, and some spectacular paintings by artists including Ferdinand Bol and Jacob de Wit. The great *burgerzaal* (citizens' hall) that occupies the heart of the building was envisioned as a schematic of the world, with Amsterdam as its centre. Check out the maps inlaid in the floor; they show the eastern and western hemispheres, with a 1654 celestial map in the middle.

In 1808 the building became the palace of King Louis, Napoleon Bonaparte's brother. In a classic slip-up in the new lingo, French-born Louis told his subjects here that he was the 'rabbit' (*konijn*) of Holland, when he actually meant 'king' (*koning,* which had the old spelling variation *konink*). Napoleon dismissed him two years later. Louis left behind about 1000 pieces of Empire-style furniture and decorative artworks. As a result, the palace now holds one of the world's largest collections from the period.

DON'T MISS

➡ Chandeliers (all 51 of them)
➡ The *burgerzaal*
➡ Paintings by Ferdinand Bol and Jacob de Wit
➡ Empire-style decor

PRACTICALITIES

➡ Map p294, C1
➡ ☏020-522 61 61
➡ www.paleisamster dam.nl
➡ Dam
➡ adult/child €10/free
➡ ◷10am-5pm
➡ ▣4/14/24 Dam

TOP SIGHT
BEGIJNHOF

It feels like something out of a story book. You walk up to the unassuming door, push it open and voila – a hidden courtyard of tiny houses and gardens opens up before you. The 14th-century Begijnhof is not a secret these days, but somehow it remains a surreal oasis of peace in the city's midst.

The Beguines were a Catholic order of unmarried or widowed women who lived a religious life without taking monastic vows. The Begijnhof was their convent of sorts. The last true Beguine died in 1971.

One of two churches hidden in the *hof* (courtyard), the 1671 **Begijnhof Kapel** (Map p294; www.begijnhofkapelamsterdam.nl; Begijnhof 30; ☺1-6.30pm Mon, 9am-6.30pm Tue-Fri, 9am-6pm Sat & Sun) is a 'clandestine' chapel where the Beguines were forced to worship after the Calvinists took away their Gothic church. Go through the dog-leg entrance to find marble columns, stained-glass windows and murals commemorating the Miracle of Amsterdam. (In short: in 1345 the final sacrament was administered to a dying man, but he was unable to keep down the communion wafer and brought it back up. Here's the miracle part: when the vomit was thrown on the fire, the wafer would not burn. Yes, it's all depicted in wall paintings.)

The other church is known as the **Engelse Kerk** (English Church; Map p294; www.ercadam.nl; Begijnhof 48; ☺9am-5pm), built around 1392. It was eventually rented out to the local community of English and Scottish Presbyterian refugees – including the Pilgrim Fathers – and it still serves as the city's Presbyterian church. Look for pulpit panels by Piet Mondrian, in a figurative phase. Note that as this church is still in frequent use, it's sometimes closed to visitors.

Look out, too, for the **Houten Huis** (Wooden House; Map p294) at No 34. It dates from around 1465, making it the oldest preserved wooden house in the Netherlands.

DON'T MISS

→ Begijnhof Kapel
→ Engelse Kerk
→ Houten Huis
→ Miracle of Amsterdam paintings

PRACTICALITIES

→ Map p294, B5
→ www.nicolaas-parochie.nl
→ admission free
→ ☺9am-5pm
→ 🚋2/11/12 Spui

TOP SIGHT
OUDE KERK (OLD CHURCH)

Amsterdam's oldest building, Oude Kerk dates to 1306. First Catholic and now Protestant, the Gothic-style structure holds the city's oldest church bell (1450), a stunning Vater-Müller organ (1726/1742) and 15th-century choir stalls with surprisingly naughty carvings. The church was built to honour the city's patron saint, St Nicholas (the inspiration for red-suited St Nick).

Many famous Amsterdammers are buried under the worn **tombstones** set in the floor, including Rembrandt's wife, Saskia van Uylenburgh. Each year on 9 March at 8.39am, a beam of light touches her grave and special events take place. Other notable graves are those of diamond dealer Killiaen van Rensselaer, naval hero Jacob van Heemskerck, organist Jan Pieterszoon Sweelinck, and the family tomb of Cornelis de Graeff. Some 10,000 citizens in all lie beneath the church. Ask for a map when you enter.

Art exhibitions regularly take place here, along with concerts and services featuring the church's four organs. As well as the Vater-Müller organ, the Oude Kerk has a 1965 transept organ, an Italian organ and a cabinet organ, all of which can be heard during concerts and church services.

Those who don't mind climbing narrow stairs can go on a half-hour tour of the 67m-high **tower** (Oudekerkstoren; www.westertorenamsterdam.nl; tour €9; ⊙1-7pm Mon-Sat Apr-Oct) for a sweeping view of the city's gabled rooflines. Tower tours depart every half hour.

The church is situated in the Red Light District, with sex workers in windows a stone's throw from the holy walls. Outside is the **statue of Belle**, erected as a nod to sex-industry workers worldwide. The cobblestones by the church's main entrance contain another bold statement: a **golden torso** of a naked woman held by a padlocked hand. It mysteriously appeared one day, was removed by police and then put back as most people seemed to like it.

DON'T MISS

➡ Floor tombstones, including Rembrandt's wife Saskia

➡ Choir-stall carvings

➡ Golden torso

➡ Surrounding Red Light ambience

➡ Tower tour

PRACTICALITIES

➡ Map p290, E7

➡ ☎020-625 82 84

➡ www.oudekerk.nl

➡ Oudekerksplein

➡ adult/child €12/free

➡ ⊙10am-6pm Mon-Sat, 1-5.30pm Sun

➡ ⎇4/14/24 Dam

SIGHTS

A handful of museums are tucked in the Medieval Centre, including city-history museum the Amsterdam Museum (p70), along with landmarks such as the Royal Palace (p66) and charming surprises such as the Begijnhof (p67) courtyard. Racier sights in the Red Light District include sex museums, prostitution museums and marijuana museums, contrasting with the 15th-century Nieuwe Kerk (p71) and the Kuan Yin Shrine (p72) Buddhist temple.

Medieval Centre

ROYAL PALACE
PALACE

See p66.

BEGIJNHOF
COURTYARD

See p67.

BELOW THE SURFACE
GALLERY

Map p294 (www.belowthesurface.amsterdam; Rokin metro station; MRokin) During the construction of Amsterdam's 2018-opened Noord/Zuidlijn (North–South metro line), more than 134,000 archaeological finds were unearthed from beneath the streets and waterways. Now 9500 of them dating as far back as 2400 BC are stunningly displayed in glass cases between Rokin metro station's escalators (visitors need a valid public transport ticket). Transport, craft and industry, buildings and interiors feature at the southern entrance. Objects at the northern entrance span science, communications, weapons, armour, recreation, personal items and clothing.

Collection highlights include coins (from as early as 1371), ice-skating blades from the Middle Ages, 15th-century padlocks, 17th-century pottery, an 18th-century piggy bank, 19th-century pocket watches and military uniform buttons, a 1922 car radiator cap, 1935 toy car replica of the Bluebird that broke the world land-speed record the same year, and 1980s mobile phones.

DAM
SQUARE

Map p294 (☐4/14/24 Dam) This square is the very spot where Amsterdam was founded around 1270. Today pigeons, tourists, buskers and the occasional funfair (complete with Ferris wheel) take over the grounds. It's still

a national gathering spot, and if there's a major speech or demonstration it's held here.

Long before it hosted fun and games, the square was split into two sections: Vissersdam, a fish market where the Bijenkorf (p85) department store now stands, and Vijgendam, probably named for the figs and other exotic fruits unloaded from ships. Various markets and events have been held here through the ages, including executions – you can still see holes on the front of the Royal Palace (p66) where the wooden gallows were affixed.

FASHION FOR GOOD
MUSEUM

Map p294 (☐020-261 96 80; www.fashionfor good.com; Rokin 102; ⊙11am-7pm Mon-Fri, to 6pm Sat & Sun; MRokin, ☐4/14/24 Rokin) 🗲**FREE** The world's first sustainable fashion museum delves into the history of fashion, the latest industry technology and innovation, and the stories behind day-to-day clothing, such as the T-shirt. The colourful and interactive exhibition may make you think twice about your own consumer behaviour, highlighting, for example, that garments travel an average of 14,000km and are handled by 100 people before you buy them. Visitors leave with a personalised 'sustainable fashion action plan', encouraging you to make environmentally conscious fashion choices.

CENTRAAL STATION
NOTABLE BUILDING

Map p290 (Stationsplein; ☐2/4/11/12/13/14/17/24/26 Centraal Station) Beyond being a transport hub, Centraal Station is a sight in itself. The turreted marvel dates from 1889. One of the architects, PJ Cuypers, also designed the Rijksmuseum, and you can see the similarities in the faux-Gothic towers, the fine red brick and the abundant reliefs (for sailing, trade and industry).

Built on an artificial island, the station was designed as a neo-Renaissance 'curtain', a controversial plan that effectively cut off Amsterdam from the IJ River. The garage in the right-hand wing was built to shelter the Dutch royal carriage, but it's rarely there (read: never).

ST NICOLAASKERK
CHURCH

Map p290 (www.nicolaas-parochie.nl; Prins Hendrikkade 73; ⊙11am-4pm Tue-Fri, noon-3pm Mon & Sat; ☐2/4/11/12/13/14/17/24/26 Centraal Station) In plain view from Centraal Station, the neo-Renaissance towers and magnificent cupola belong to the city's main Catholic church, the first to be built (between

1884 and 1887) after Catholic worship became legal again in the 19th century. As St Nicholas is the patron saint of seafarers, the church became an important symbol for Amsterdam.

The interior is notable for its high altar, the theatrical crown of Emperor Maximilian I and depictions of the Stations of the Cross, on which tireless painter Jan Dunselman laboured for 40 years.

ALLARD PIERSON MUSEUM
MUSEUM

Map p294 (📞020-525 25 56; www.allardpierson museum.nl; Oude Turfmarkt 127; adult/child €10/5; ⏰10am-5pm Tue-Fri, 1-5pm Sat & Sun; Ⓜ Rokin, 🚊4/14/24 Rokin) Run by the University of Amsterdam and named for its first professor of archaeology, Allard Pierson (1831–96), this museum contains a rich archaeological collection made accessible by its manageable scale. You'll find an actual mummy, vases from ancient Greece and Mesopotamia, a very cool wagon from the royal tombs at Salamis (Cyprus), and galleries full of other items providing insight into daily life in ancient times. There are detailed descriptions in Dutch and English.

NATIONAAL MONUMENT
MONUMENT

Map p294 (Dam; 🚊4/14/24 Dam) The obelisk on the Dam's eastern side was built in 1956 to commemorate WWII's fallen. Fronted by two lions, its pedestal has a number of symbolic statues: four males (war), a woman with child (peace) and men with dogs (resistance). The 12 urns at the rear hold earth from war cemeteries of the 11 provinces and the Dutch East Indies. The war dead are still honoured here at a ceremony every 4 May.

MADAME TUSSAUDS AMSTERDAM
MUSEUM

Map p294 (www.madametussauds.com/am sterdam; Dam 20; adult/child €24.50/20.50; ⏰9.30am-9.30pm Aug, from 10am Sep-Jul; 🚊4/14/24 Dam) Sure, Madame Tussauds wax museum is overpriced and cheesy, but its focus on local culture makes it fun: 'meet' the Dutch royals, politicians, painters and pop stars, along with global icons (Rafael Nadal, George Clooney, Barack Obama, Marvel superheros et al). Kids love it. Buying tickets online will save you a few euros and get you into the fast-track queue. Hours can vary; check the calendar online.

⊙ TOP SIGHT
AMSTERDAM MUSEUM

Amsterdam's history museum is a spiffy place to learn about what makes the city tick. Start with the multimedia DNA exhibit, which breaks down Amsterdam's 1000-year history across entrepreneurship, free thinking, citizenship and creativity into seven whiz-bang time periods. At the Revolt Against the King and Church display, you can even dress as a civic guard (ruffled collar!) and have a photo taken; it goes to the museum's Flickr page.

Afterwards, plunge into the maze-like lower floors to see troves of religious artefacts, porcelains and paintings. There are also displays on the world wars and the spread of bicycle use, and a recreation of the original Café 't Mandje, a touchstone in the gay-rights movement.

The museum building used to be Amsterdam's civic orphanage. While you're in the courtyard, note the cupboards (now filled with art) in which the orphans stored their possessions. An exhibition specifically for children covers 17th-century orphanage life, with displays of dormitories, classrooms, bathrooms and kitchens.

Grand Golden Age paintings line the free **Civic Guard Gallery** (Map p294; Kalverstraat 92; ⏰10am-5pm) FREE in the arcade next door.

DON'T MISS

➔ Café 't Mandje recreation
➔ Civic Guard Gallery paintings
➔ Orphans' cupboards

PRACTICALITIES

➔ Map p294, B4
➔ 📞020-523 18 22
➔ www.amsterdam museum.nl
➔ Gedempte Begijnensloot
➔ adult/child €15/free
➔ ⏰10am-5pm
➔ 🚊2/11/12 Spui

BEURS VAN BERLAGE   HISTORIC BUILDING

Map p290 (020-530 41 41; www.beursvanber
lage.com; Damrak 243; 4/14/24 Dam) Master
architect and ardent socialist HP Berlage
(1856–1934) built Amsterdam's financial exchange in 1903. He filled the temple of capitalism with decorations that venerate labour,
including tile murals of the well-muscled
proletariat of the past, present and future.
Within two decades trading had outgrown
the building and relocated. The building
now hosts conferences and art exhibitions.

On Open Monumenten Dag (Open Monuments Day; held the second weekend in
September), you can access the bell tower
for panoramic views.

SEXMUSEUM AMSTERDAM   MUSEUM

Map p290 (www.sexmuseumamsterdam.nl;
Damrak 18; €5; 9.30am-11.30pm; 2/4/11/
12/13/14/17/24/26 Centraal Station) The Sexmuseum is good for a giggle. You'll find
replicas of pornographic Pompeian plates,
erotic 14th-century Viennese bronzes, some
of the world's earliest nude photographs,
an automated farting flasher in a trench
coat, and a music box that plays 'Edelweiss'
and purports to show a couple in flagrante

delicto. It's sillier and more fun than other
erotic museums in the Red Light District.
Minimum age for entry is 16.

PAPEGAAI   CHURCH

Map p294 (www.nicolaas-parochie.nl; Kalverstraat
58; 10am-4pm Mon-Sat, 9.45am-2pm Sun;
4/14/24 Dam) An unexpected oasis in the
sea of consumerism on Kalverstraat, the curious Petrus en Pauluskerk, aka Papegaai, is
a Catholic church from the 17th century that
was a clandestine house of worship. Note the
papegaai (parrot) over the door that gave
the church its name. The slogan you'll see
upon entering: '15 minutes for God'.

SPUI   SQUARE

Map p294 (2/11/12 Spui) Inviting *cafés* and
high-brow bookshops ring the Spui, a favoured haunt of academics, students and
journalists. On Friday (weather permitting)
a small book market sets up on the square;
on Sunday it's an art market (p85). And
just so you know, it's pronounced 'spow'
(rhymes with 'now').

SCHREIERSTOREN   HISTORIC BUILDING

Map p290 (www.schreierstoren.nl; Prins Hendrikkade 95; 2/4/11/12/13/14/17/24/26

TOP SIGHT
NIEUWE KERK

Don't let the 'New Church' name fool you – the structure dates from 1408 (though it *is* a good century
fresher than the Oude Kerk). Located right on the Dam,
this basilica is the historic stage for royal weddings and
the investiture of Dutch monarchs. The stained glass
over the main entrance recalls Queen Wilhelmina, who
ascended the throne in 1898, aged 18. Most recently,
the investiture of King Willem-Alexander took place here
in 2013. Other than for such ceremonies, the building no
longer functions as a church but rather a hall for multimedia exhibitions and organ concerts.

The interior is plain, but several key furnishings – the
magnificent oak chancel, the bronze choir screen and
the massive gilded organ (1645) – justify a look. Naval
hero Admiral Michiel de Ruyter and poets Joost van den
Vondel and Pieter Corneliszoon Hooft are among the
luminaries buried here.

It's possible to walk in and take a free peek, but you'll
have to pay the admission fee to get up close. Pick up a
'welcome' brochure, which maps out the highlights, at
the entrance. Opening times and admission fees can
vary depending on what's going on.

DON'T MISS

➡ Window for
Queen Wilhelmina's
investiture

➡ Organ

➡ Monuments to
De Ruyter, Van den
Vondel and Hooft

➡ Chancel

PRACTICALITIES

➡ Map p290, B7

➡ 020-626 81 68

➡ www.nieuwekerk.nl

➡ Dam

➡ adult/child €12.50/
free

➡ 10am-6pm

➡ 2/11/12/13/17
Dam

RED LIGHT DISTRICT NITTY-GRITTY

➡ Taking photos of the windows is strictly *verboten*. Your first instinct might be to take a quick snap, but don't do it – out of simple respect, and to avoid having your camera or phone tossed in a canal by the sex workers' enforcers.

➡ For their own safety, sex workers' quarters are equipped with a button that, when pressed, activates a light outside. The police or other protectors show up in a hurry.

➡ The red lights of the Red Light District have been around for a long time; even as early as the 1300s, women carrying red lanterns met sailors near the port. Red light is flattering and, especially when used in combination with black light, it makes teeth sparkle.

Centraal Station) Built around 1480 as part of the city's defences, this tower is where Henry Hudson set sail for the New World in 1609; a plaque outside marks the spot. It's called the 'weeping tower' in lore – it was where women waved farewell to sailors' ships – but the name actually comes from the word 'sharp' (for the way the corner jutted into the bay). Step into the **VOC Café** (Map p290; ☎020-428 82 91; ⊘10am-1am Sun-Thu, to 2.30am Fri & Sat) to see inside the tower.

RONDE LUTHERSE KERK   HISTORIC BUILDING
Map p290 (Round Lutheran Church; ☎020-551 20 60; www.koepelkerk.com; Singel 11; ⊘by appointment; ☒2/11/12/13/17 Nieuwezijds Kolk) Built between 1668 and 1671, this domed church has the curious distinction of being the only round Protestant church in the country. Falling attendance forced its closure in 1936. Although it's not open to the public (other than for conferences, trade fairs and events), it's connected by a tunnel to the neighbouring Amsterdam Renaissance Hotel, which you can contact about visiting if the church is not in use.

Ironically, the old church on the Spui, which the Ronde Lutherse Kerk was designed to replace, is still in use.

👁 Red Light District

OUDE KERK   CHURCH
See p68.

KUAN YIN SHRINE   BUDDHIST TEMPLE
Map p290 (Fo Guang Shan He Hua Temple; www.ibps.nl; Zeedijk 106-118; ⊘noon-5pm Tue-Sat, 10am-5pm Sun; Ⓜ Nieuwmarkt) Europe's largest Chinese Imperial–style Buddhist temple, built in 2000, is dedicated to Kuan Yin, the Buddhist goddess of mercy. Enter through the side gates (as is customary; the main gates are reserved for monks and nuns), make a donation, light an incense stick and ponder the thousand eyes and hands of the Bodhisattva statue.

The ornate 'mountain gate' – an intriguing concept in the narrow confines of the Zeedijk – refers to the traditional setting of Buddhist monasteries. The middle section set back from the street was designed along principles of feng shui.

CANNABIS COLLEGE   CULTURAL CENTRE
Map p294 (☎020-423 44 20; www.cannabiscollege.com; Oudezijds Achterburgwal 124; ⊘11am-7pm; ☒4/14/24 Dam) This nonprofit centre offers visitors tips and tricks for having a positive smoking experience and provides the low-down on local cannabis laws. There are educational displays and a library. Staff can provide maps and advice on where to find coffeeshops that sell organic weed and shops that are good for newbies. T-shirts, stickers, postcards and a few other trinkets with the logo are for sale, too.

HASH, MARIJUANA & HEMP MUSEUM   MUSEUM
Map p294 (☎020-624 89 26; www.hashmuseum.com; Oudezijds Achterburgwal 148; €9; ⊘10am-10pm; ☒4/14/24 Dam) Simple exhibits here cover dope botany and the relationship between cannabis and religion. Highlights include an impressive pipe collection, an interactive vaporiser and a kiosk where you can create an e-card of yourself in a marijuana field. Admission also includes the **Hemp Gallery** (Map p294; Oudezijds Achterburgwal 130; ⊘10am-10pm), filled with hemp art and historical items, in a building 30m north.

The Sensi Seeds company (conveniently attached to the museum) owns the whole thing, so it's no surprise you get to peek at a roomful of growing plants as part of the deal.

RED LIGHT SECRETS   MUSEUM

Map p290 (Museum of Prostitution; ☏020-846 70 20; www.redlightsecrets.com; Oudezijds Achterburgwal 60h; €12.50; ⊙10am-midnight; 🚊4/14/24 Dam) Inside a former brothel in a 17th-century canal house, this museum fills a gap by showing curious visitors what a Red Light room looks like and answering basic questions about the industry. There's a short film as well as photo opportunities aplenty (ahem, dominatrix room). The venue takes less than an hour to tour. Tickets are €2 cheaper online.

BROUWERIJ DE PRAEL   BREWERY

Map p290 (☏020-408 44 70; www.deprael.nl; Oudezijds Voorburgwal 30; tour with 1/4 beers €8.50/17.50; ⊙tours hourly 1-6pm Mon-Fri, 1-5pm Sat, 2-5pm Sun; 🚊2/4/11/12/13/14/17/24/26 Centraal Station) Brouwerij De Prael offers engaging behind-the-scenes tours of its brewery. Tours depart on the hour and last 40 minutes, followed by a sample (or four). The neighbouring taproom (p79) is a great place to try more of its wares. De Prael also makes liqueurs that you can buy at the brewery's attached shop.

An outpost (p147) is located in Amsterdam's rapidly growing Houthavens neighbourhood in the West.

PROSTITUTION
INFORMATION CENTRE   LIBRARY

Map p290 (PIC; ☏020-420 73 28; www.pic-amsterdam.com; Enge Kerksteeg 3; ⊙noon-5pm Wed-Fri, to 7pm Sat; 🚊4/14/24 Dam) Established by a former sex worker, the PIC provides frank information about the industry to those in the trade, their customers and curious tourists. It has a small on-site shop selling enlightening reading material and souvenirs.

TROMPETTERSTEEG   STREET

Map p290 (🚊4/14/24 Dam) An intriguing place to view the Red Light action is Trompettersteeg, a teeny alley where the women in the windows charge some of the highest prices. Claustrophobes, beware: the alley is only 1m wide and always busy. Look for the entrance in the block south of the Oude Kerk.

W139   GALLERY

Map p290 (☏020-622 94 34; www.w139.nl; Warmoesstraat 139; ⊙noon-6pm; 🚊4/14/24 Dam) **FREE** Duck into this contemporary arts centre and ponder the multimedia exhibits, which often have an edgy political angle. Check the website for frequent artist talks.

TOP SIGHT
MUSEUM ONS' LIEVE HEER OP SOLDER

The Museum Ons' Lieve Heer op Solder is one of those 'secret' Amsterdam places. What looks like an ordinary canal house in the Red Light District turns out to have an entire Catholic church stashed inside, with room for 150 worshippers. Ons' Lieve Heer op Solder (Our Dear Lord in the Attic) was founded in the mid-1600s, when local merchant Jan Hartman decided to build a covert church in his house so his son could study to be a priest. At the time, the country's Calvinist rulers had outlawed public worship of Catholicism.

As you wander through the church, you get to see not only the city's richest collection of Catholic art but also period pieces from 17th-century canal-house life. There's a fantastic labyrinth of staircases, cubby-hole quarters, heavy oak furniture and a porcelain-tiled kitchen. Once you're upstairs – in the attic, so to speak – you'll see that the church itself is unexpectedly grand, with a marble-columned altar and a painting by Jacob de Wit, a steep gallery and an impressive organ.

DON'T MISS

➡ Altar
➡ Jacob de Wit painting
➡ Kitchen and other restored 17th-century rooms

PRACTICALITIES

➡ Map p290, F6
➡ ☏020-624 66 04
➡ www.opsolder.nl
➡ Oudezijds Voorburgwal 38
➡ adult/child €12.50/6
➡ ⊙10am-6pm Mon-Sat, from 1pm Sun
➡ 🚊4/14/24 Dam

MEDIEVAL CENTRE & RED LIGHT DISTRICT SIGHTS

MEDIEVAL CENTRE & RED LIGHT DISTRICT EATING

PROSTITUTION FACTS & FIGURES

➡ Year prostitution officially legalised in the Netherlands: 2000

➡ Number of sex workers in Amsterdam: approximately 7000, though estimates range between 6000 and 9500

➡ Minimum legal age to work as a sex worker in the Netherlands: 21

EATING

Snack stands and cafes abound for quick, inexpensive dishes, and numerous pubs serve food. Amsterdam's small Chinatown, with pan-Asian restaurants, centres on Zeedijk. Throughout the neighbourhood, an increasing number of places offering refined, often highly creative dining are flourishing.

Medieval Centre

⭐ VLEMINCKX   FAST FOOD €
Map p294 (www.vleminckxdesausmeester.nl; Voetboogstraat 33; fries €3-5, sauces €0.70; ⊙noon-7pm Mon, 11am-7pm Tue-Wed & Fri-Sun, 11am-8pm Thu; ᗕ2/11/12 Koningsplein) Frying up *frites* since 1887, Amsterdam's best *friterie* has been based at this hole-in-the-wall takeaway shack near the Spui since 1957. The standard order of perfectly cooked crispy, fluffy *frites* is smothered in mayonnaise, though its 28 sauces also include apple, green pepper, ketchup, peanut, sambal and mustard. Queues almost always stretch down the block, but they move fast.

⭐ GARTINE   CAFE €
Map p294 (☎020-320 41 32; www.gartine.nl; Taksteeg 7; dishes €6.50-15, high tea €18-25.50; ⊙10am-6pm Wed-Sat; ᗕ; Ⓜ Rokin, ᗕ4/14/24 Rokin) ⏺ Gartine is magical, from its covert location in an alley off busy Kalverstraat to its mismatched antique tableware and its sublime breakfast pastries (including a dark-chocolate, honey and raspberry soufflé), sandwiches and salads (made from produce grown in its garden plot and eggs from its chickens). The sweet-and-savoury high tea, from 2pm to 5pm, is a treat.

DE LAATSTE KRUIMEL   CAFE €
Map p294 (☎020-423 04 99; www.delaatste kruimel.nl; Langebrugsteeg 4; dishes €3-10.50; ⊙8am-8pm Mon-Sat, from 9am Sun; Ⓜ Rokin, ᗕ4/14/24 Rokin) Opening to a tiny canalside terrace and decorated with vintage finds from the Noordermarkt and wooden pallets upcycled as furniture, the 'Last Crumb' has glass display cases filled with pies, quiches, breads, cakes and lemon-and-poppy-seed scones. Grandmothers, children, couples on dates and just about everyone else crowd in for sweet treats and fantastic organic sandwiches.

CRÊPERIE BRETONNE COCOTTE   CRÊPES €
Map p290 (☎020-737 20 15; www.cocotte-hex agone.com; Spuistraat 127; crêpes €6-8, galettes €10.50-13.50; ⊙9am-6pm Sun-Thu, to 9pm Fri & Sat; ᗕ2/11/12/13/17 Dam) Inside a charming gabled canal house, this split-level space has soaring brick walls, recycled timbers and mezzanine seating. Savoury galettes (made with organic, gluten-free buckwheat flour from Brittany's oldest mill) come with scrumptious fillings such as Breton sardines and sautéed sliced apples, or an Amsterdam version with smoked herring, potatoes and crème fraîche. Sweet crêpes include salted caramel with almonds.

DE SOEPBAR   SOUP €
Map p290 (www.desoepbaramsterdam.nl; Spuistraat 106; soup small/medium/large/extra-large €4.35/5.95/7.25/12.50; ⊙11am-8pm; ᗕᗕ; ᗕ2/11/12/13/17 Nieuwezijds Kolk) Four to five organic soups made daily at 'the soup bar' always include vegetarian and vegan options. Choices might include goat's cheese, thyme and cauliflower; baked onion, peanut and bean sprouts; spicy watermelon and feta gazpacho; pumpkin and mustard; or pea, smoked sausage and sour cream. All are served with bread; you can dine on-site or take away.

GEBR NIEMEIJER   CAFE €
Map p290 (www.gebroedersniemeijer.nl; Nieuwendijk 35; dishes €5-10.50, pastries €1.50-4.50; ⊙8.15am-5.30pm Tue-Fri, to 4.30pm Sat, 9am-4.30pm Sun; ᗕ; ᗕ2/4/11/12/13/14/17/24/26 Centraal Station) This French bakery is a real find near Centraal Station. Take a seat at one of the sturdy wooden tables beneath the art deco ceiling to linger over flaky croissants at breakfast or sandwiches made with breads including house-speciality

sourdough or walnut bread, with fillings such as lamb sausage, Gruyère cheese and fig jam at lunch.

LANSKROON
BAKERY €

Map p294 (www.lanskroon.nl; Singel 385; dishes €2-6; ☺8am-7pm Mon-Fri, 9am-7pm Sat, 10am-7pm Sun Apr-Sep, to 5.30pm Oct-Mar; 🚊2/11/12 Spui) The fourth-generation-run Lanskroon is famed for its *stroopwafels* – crispy, big as a dessert plate and slathered with caramel, honey or fig paste. In winter, locals come for spiced *speculaas* cookies and other Christmas treats; in summer the thick nut- or fruit-swirled ice cream is a favourite with kids.

PANNENKOEKENHUIS UPSTAIRS
DUTCH €

Map p294 (🖉020-626 56 03; www.upstairs pannenkoeken.nl; Grimburgwal 2; mains €7-13; ☺noon-6pm Mon-Sat, to 5pm Sun; 🇲Rokin, 🚊4/14/24) Climb some of Amsterdam's steepest stairs inside a 1539 building to reach this small-as-a-postage-stamp restaurant with 100-plus teapots hanging from the ceiling, portraits of the Dutch royals and paintings of old Amsterdam. Traditional Dutch pancakes here include bacon, cheese and ginger. It's a two-person show, so things happen at their own pace; opening hours can be erratic. Cash only.

BANKETBAKKERIJ VAN DER LINDE
ICE CREAM €

Map p290 (Nieuwendijk 183; ice creams small/medium/large from €1/1.20/1.60; ☺1-5pm Mon, 11am-5.45pm Tue-Thu, 9am-5.45pm Fri, 9am-5pm Sat, noon-5pm Sun; 🚊4/14/24 Dam) A long line regularly snakes out the door of this narrow, generations-old shop where everyone is queuing for – wait for it – vanilla ice cream. That's the only flavour! Only this vanilla is unlike any other: a soft, velvety sugar cloud almost like whipped cream in texture. Choose from cones, cups or waffle ice-cream sandwiches, each in three sizes.

BROODJE BERT
SANDWICHES €

Map p294 (Singel 321; sandwiches €5-8; ☺8am-5pm; 🚊2/11/12 Spui) Join the locals sitting on wooden chairs in the sun (or at the window seats inside) at this fabulous little sandwich shop in a winning canal-side location. In addition to huge sandwiches, such as marinated grilled chicken or the eponymous house special 'Broodje Bert' (lamb meatballs on Turkish bread), there are burgers and omelettes made to order. Cash only.

VAN STAPELE
BAKERY €

Map p294 (www.vanstapele.com; Heisteeg 4; 1/6 cookies €2/10; ☺10am-6.30pm; 🚊2/11/12 Spui) Teensy Van Stapele is a true specialist, baking just one thing and baking it well: chocolate cookies. Specifically, it's a Valrhona dark chocolate cookie on the outside, filled with melted white chocolate inside. The super-sweet disc is served soft and warm straight from the oven (it makes 46 every 10 minutes). Arrive early as the day's bake often sells out.

ROB WIGBOLDUS VISHANDEL
SANDWICHES €

Map p290 (Zoutsteeg 6; sandwiches €3-6.50; ☺9am-5pm Tue-Sat; 🚊4/14/24 Dam) A wee three-table oasis in a narrow alleyway just off the touristy Damrak, this fish shop serves excellent herring sandwiches on a choice of white or brown rolls. Other sandwich fillings include smoked eel, Dutch prawns and fried whitefish.

DUTCH DELICACY
DELI €

Map p294 (De Mannen Van Kaas; www.demannen vankaas.nl; Spuistraat 330; cheese tasting board €15; ☺8am-10pm; 🖉; 🚊2/11/12 Spui) Dutch cheeses are the speciality of this split-level deli; taste them on cheese boards at its handful of tables, or get them vacuum packed to take home. Cheeses also fill sandwiches (eg truffled Gouda, chicken, rocket and mayo), and are baked into loaves (eg blue cheese, pesto and tomato). Sweet treats include cinnamon scrolls and towering Dutch apple pie.

★D'VIJFF VLIEGHEN
DUTCH €€

Map p294 (🖉020-530 40 60; www.vijffvlieghen. nl; Spuistraat 294-302; mains €19.50-26.50; ☺6-10pm; 🚊2/11/12 Spui) Spread across five 17th-century canal houses, the 'Five Flies' is a jewel. Old-wood dining rooms overflow with character, featuring Delft Blue tiles and original works by Rembrandt; chairs have copper plates inscribed with the names of famous guests (Walt Disney, Mick Jagger...). Exquisite dishes range from smoked goose breast with apple to roast veal with turnips with Dutch crab mayonnaise.

★RON GASTROBAR DOWNTOWN
INDONESIAN €€

Map p294 (🖉020-790 03 22; www.rongastrobar indonesia.nl; Rokin 49; mains €17.50-27, rijsttafel per person €39.50; ☺noon-10pm Tue-Thu, to 11pm Fri-Sun; 🖈; 🇲Rokin, 🚊4/14/24 Rokin)

Beneath a striking curved glass-and-metal ceiling, superstar chef Ron Blaauw showcases cutting-edge Indonesian cuisine: *saté kambing* (grilled goat skewers with peanut sauce), *udang peteh* (shrimp with bitter beans in coconut sauce) and *bebek mendoan* (slow-cooked duck with tempeh and green-sambal mayo). Downstairs, the lush jungle-themed bar serves Indonesian-inspired cocktails and morphs into a club on Fridays and Saturday nights.

The entrance is hidden down a small alleyway just off Rokin.

TOMAZ   DUTCH €€

Map p294 (☑020-320 64 89; www.tomaz.nl; Begijnensteeg 6-8; mains lunch €8-17, dinner €15-32; ☺noon-10pm; ⓐ2/11/12 Spui) Charming little Tomaz hides near the Begijnhof and is a fine spot for a light lunch or an informal dinner. Staples include a daily *stamppot* (potato mashed with other vegetables), veal croquettes, IJsselmeer mussels and Dutch sausages. A vegetarian special is always available. Linger for a while over a game of chess.

★DE SILVEREN SPIEGEL   DUTCH €€€

Map p290 (☑020-624 65 89; www.desilveren spiegel.com; Kattengat 4-6; mains €28-36.50, 4-/5-/7-/8-course menus €54.50/75.50/86/ 96.50; ☺6-9pm Mon-Sat; ⓐ2/11/12/13/17 Nieuwezijds Kolk) Hung with replicas of Old Masters, the 'Silver Mirror' is an exceedingly elegant space inside a 1614-built, step-gabled red-brick townhouse. Exquisite dishes served on handcrafted porcelain might include lobster stuffed with North Sea crab with vintage Gouda foam or Texel lamb crown with asparagus mousse and cinnamon jus (set menus only on weekends). Book ahead and dress for the occasion.

🍴 Red Light District

IVY & BROS   CAFE €

Map p290 (www.facebook.com/ivyandbros; Oudezijds Voorburgwal 96; dishes €4.50-13.50; ☺10am-7pm; 🐾🖉; Ⓜ Nieuwmarkt) Except for the life-size replica megalodon shark jaws suspended above the open kitchen, all of the artwork at this hip cafe is for sale, as is the furniture and crockery. Most of its hot dishes, sandwiches and salads (such as homemade cottage cheese and pome-

granate) are vegetarian, with some vegan options. Coffees come etched with extraordinarily intricate designs.

HOFJE VAN WIJS   CAFE €€

Map p290 (☑020-624 04 36; www.cafewijs.nl; Zeedijk 43; mains €18.50, 2-/3-course menus €24/28.50; ☺4-10pm Thu, noon-10pm Fri & Sat, noon-8pm Sun; ⓐ2/4/11/12/13/14/17/24/26 Centraal Station) Two-century-old coffee and tea vendor Wijs & Zonen (the monarch's purveyor) maintains this pretty courtyard restaurant. It serves Dutch stews, a couple of fish dishes (plus a vegetarian option), and fondue on Thursday evenings, along with *jenevers* (Dutch gins) and its own-brewed beers. Live acoustic sets take place on Saturday nights.

BIRD SNACKBAR   THAI €€

Map p290 (☑020-420 62 89; www.thaibird.nl; Zeedijk 77; mains €10-16; ☺1-10pm Mon-Wed, to 10.30pm Thu-Sun; ⓐ2/4/11/12/13/14/17/24/26 Centraal Station) Bird has some of the best Asian food on the Zeedijk – the chefs, wedged in a tiny kitchen, don't skimp on lemongrass, fish sauce or chilli. The resulting curries and basil-laden meat and seafood dishes will knock your socks off. There's a bit more room to spread out in its (slightly pricier) restaurant across the street (No 72).

NAM KEE   CANTONESE €€

Map p290 (☑020-624 34 70; www.namkee.nl; Zeedijk 111-113; mains €12.50-23; ☺11.30am-10.30pm; Ⓜ Nieuwmarkt) It won't win any design awards, but year in, year out, Nam Kee, serving Cantonese classics, is the most popular Chinese spot in town. The steamed oysters and black-bean sauce are legendary. If you want to avoid the fluorescent-light ambience, try Nam Kee's nearby Nieuwmarkt **branch** (Map p296; ☑020-639 28 48; Geldersekade 117; mains €12.50-23; ☺4pm-midnight Mon-Fri, 2.30pm-midnight Sat, 2.30-11pm Sun; 🖉; Ⓜ Nieuwmarkt), which is fancier.

NEW KING   CHINESE €€

Map p290 (☑020-625 21 80; www.newking.nl; Zeedijk 115-117; mains €12-26; ☺11am-10.30pm; 🖉; Ⓜ Nieuwmarkt) Spread over several levels and adjoining buildings, this classy, low-lit restaurant is one of Chinatown's most beloved; book ahead or plan to wait at busy times. Its signature dish is its black-bean steamed oysters; other standouts include salt-and-pepper prawns, whole Peking duck and numerous vegetarian choices including a delectable tofu and aubergine hotpot. Welcoming staff are ultra-efficient.

WHITE ROOM
GASTRONOMY €€€

Map p294 (☑020-554 61 14; www.restaurant thewhiteroom.com; Dam 9; 2-/3-course lunch menu €32.50/57.50, 5-/7-/9-course dinner menu €79/99/119; ⊙6.30-10pm Tue & Wed, noon-1.30pm & 6.30-10pm Thu-Sat; ☐4/14/24 Dam) Inside the opulent NH Grand Hotel Krasnapolsky (a listed historical monument), this ivory-white dining room with columns, mirrors, gilding and crystal chandeliers is believed to be Amsterdam's oldest restaurant, dating from 1885. Its Michelin-starred cuisine might incorporate smoked sea bass and avocado macarons; rosehip-marinated oysters; langoustine, pork belly and pumpkin millefeuille; and roast pigeon breast with hazelnut foam.

 DRINKING & NIGHTLIFE

This area is renowned for its wild pubs and bars as well as its coffeeshops (cannabis cafes), but choices here are surprisingly diverse, taking in genteel *jenever* distillery tasting houses, unchanged-in-decades *bruin cafés* (brown cafes), breweries, and on-trend addresses such as a combined craft beer bar and barber shop. Zeedijk and Warmoesstraat are the twin hubs of the area's gay scene.

 Medieval Centre

★TALES & SPIRITS
COCKTAIL BAR

Map p290 (www.talesandspirits.com; Lijnbaanssteeg 5-7; ⊙5.30pm-1am Tue-Thu & Sun, to 3am Fri & Sat; ☐2/11/12/13/17 Nieuwezijds Kolk) Chandeliers glitter beneath wooden beams at Tales & Spirits, which creates its own house infusions, syrups and vinegar-based shrubs. Cocktails such as Any Port in a Storm (Porter's gin, Sailor Jerry spiced rum, sherbet and jalapeño bitters) and the Van Gogh–inspired Drop of Art (with *oude jenever* and absinthe) are served in vintage and one-of-a-kind glasses.

Minimum age is 21.

★HOPPE
BROWN CAFE

Map p294 (www.cafehoppe.com; Spui 18-20; ⊙8am-1am Sun-Thu, to 2am Fri & Sat; ☐2/11/12 Spui) An Amsterdam institution, Hoppe has been filling glasses since 1670. Barflies and raconteurs toss back brews amid the ancient wood panelling of the *bruin café* at No 18 and the more modern, early-20th-century pub at No 20. In all but the iciest weather, the energetic crowd spills out from the dark interior and onto the Spui.

★CUT THROAT
BAR

Map p290 (☑06 2534 3769; www.cutthroatbar ber.nl; Beursplein 5; ⊙bar noon-11pm Mon-Thu, 11am-2am Fri, 10am-2pm Sat, noon-7pm Sun, barber to 8pm Mon-Fri, to 6pm Sat & Sun; 🛜; ☐4/14/24 Dam) Beneath 1930s arched brick ceilings, Cut Throat ingeniously combines a men's barbering service (book ahead) with a happening bar serving international craft beers, cocktails including infused G&Ts (such as blueberry and thyme or mandarin and rosemary), 'spiked' milkshakes and coffee from Amsterdam roastery De Wasserette. Brunch stretches to 4pm daily; all-day dishes span fried chicken and waffles to burgers.

CAFÉ BELGIQUE
BEER CAFE

Map p290 (www.cafe-belgique.nl; Gravenstraat 2; ⊙3pm-1am Mon-Wed, 1pm-1am Thu & Sun, 1pm-3am Fri & Sat; ☐2/11/12/13/17 Dam) Pull up a stool at the carved wooden bar and choose from the glinting brass taps. It's all about Belgian beers here: eight flow from the spouts, and another 50 or so are available in bottles. The ambience is quintessentially *gezellig* (convivial, cosy) and draws lots of chilled-out locals. Live music or DJs play some nights.

CAFÉ DE DOKTER
BROWN CAFE

Map p294 (Rozenboomsteeg 4; ⊙4pm-1am Wed-Sat; ☐2/11/12 Spui) Candles flicker on the tables, old jazz records play in the background, and chandeliers and a birdcage hang from the ceiling at atmospheric de Dokter, which at 18 sq metres is allegedly Amsterdam's smallest pub. Whiskeys and smoked beef sausage are specialities. A surgeon opened it in 1798, hence the name. The sixth generation of his family still runs it.

DE BLAUWE PARADE
BAR

Map p290 (www.deblauweparade.com; Nieuwezijds Voorburgwal 178; ⊙4pm-midnight; 🛜; ☐2/11/12/13/17 Dam) A frieze of Delft blue-and-white tiles – the world's largest

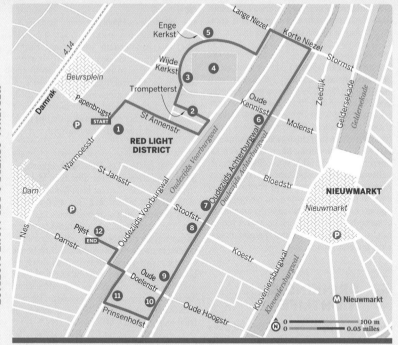

🏃 Neighbourhood Walk
Red-Light Stroll

START CONDOMERIE HET GULDEN VLIES
END GREENHOUSE
LENGTH 1.1KM; ONE HOUR

For a glimpse of the sinful side of the city, take a short walk on the wild side through Amsterdam's oldest quarter.

1 Condomerie het Gulden Vlies (p86) is a shrine to condom art, selling all designs, sizes and colours.

Turn left onto Oudezijds Voorburgwal from St Annenstraat. **2 Trompettersteeg** (p73) is the second street en route to Oude Kerk. The medieval alley is only 1m wide, and the red-light windows keep it busy.

On Oudekerksplein, you'll see the **3 statue of Belle** (p68), which embodies sex workers and their rights. A contradiction if ever there was one, 14th-century **4 Oude Kerk** (p68) is the city's oldest building, but the surrounding square has long been ground zero for prostitution. Look near the entrance for the **5 golden torso** pavement plaque (p68).

Just northwest of the church, the **6 Prostitution Information Centre** (p73) nforms sex workers and visitors alike.

Cross the canal onto Korte Niezel and turn right down Oudezijds Achterburgwal, where the **7 Red Light Secrets** (p73) museum recreates a Red Light room while providing information on the world's oldest profession.

It's rapid-fire vice from here: live sex shows at **8 Casa Rosso** (p81), smoky vaporisers at the **9 Cannabis College** (p72), botany lessons at the **10 Hash, Marijuana & Hemp Museum** (p72), and legendary cannabis strain 'Big Bud' at the attached Sensi Seeds shop.

Turn right along Prinsenhofstraat towards Oudezijds Voorburgwal. On the corner, popular coffeeshop **11 Greenhouse** (p80) is renowned for its high-quality cannabis and serves good food and music.

Cross to the western side of Oudezijds Voorburgwal and urn into Pijlsteeg to end at **12 Wynand Fockink** (p80), a *jenever* distillery dating from 1679.

Delft-tile tableau – wraps around the walls above beautiful wood panelling at this exquisite bar (a listed monument) within the **Die Port van Cleve** (Map p290; ☎020-714 20 00; www.dieportvancleve.com) hotel. Regular events include tasting sessions of liqueurs on Monday and *jenevers* on Wednesday (both from 7pm), where you pay by the glass.

HUMMINGBIRD — COFFEE

Map p294 (www.hummingbird.amsterdam; Spuistraat 217; ⏲8am-6pm Mon-Fri, 9am-6pm Sat, 10am-6pm Sun; 📶; 🚋2/11/12/13/17 Dam) A hummingbird by Brazilian street artist L7matrix covers one wall of this hip cafe, with local art also for sale. Small-batch roasts (London's Kiss the Hippo; Ecuador's Filipe Abade) are brewed to perfection on a state-of-the-art Modbar espresso machine. There's a handful of seats inside and out front. Discounts for lidless coffees and reusable cups aim to achieve zero waste.

DAMPKRING — COFFEESHOP

Map p294 (www.dampkring-coffeeshop-amsterdam.nl; Handboogstraat 29; ⏲8am-1am; 📶; 🚋2/11/12 Koningsplein) With an interior that resembles a larger-than-life lava lamp, Dampkring is famed for having one of Amsterdam's most comprehensive cannabis menus, with details about aroma, taste and effect. Its name references the ring of the earth's atmosphere where smaller items combust.

ABRAXAS — COFFEESHOP

Map p294 (www.abraxas.amsterdam; Jonge Roelensteeg 12; ⏲8am-1am; 📶; 🚋2/11/12/13/17 Dam) Mellow music, comfy sofas, thick milkshakes and rooms with different energy levels spread across Abraxas' floors, connected by a spindly spiral staircase. The considerate staff make it a great place for coffeeshop newbies (though the fairy-tale artwork can get a bit intense).

PRIK — GAY

Map p290 (www.prikamsterdam.nl; Spuistraat 109; ⏲4pm-1am Mon-Thu, to 3am Fri, 3pm-3am Sat, to 1am Sun; 🚋2/11/12/13/17 Dam) 'Lovely liquids, sexy snacks and twisted tunes' is the siren call of this hyper-retro bar with cocktails galore and Prosecco on tap. DJs spin pop, house and dance tunes on Friday and Saturday.

Red Light District

★IN 'T AEPJEN — BROWN CAFE

Map p290 (Zeedijk 1; ⏲noon-1am Mon-Thu, to 3am Fri & Sat; 🚋2/4/11/12/13/14/17/24/26 Centraal Station) Candles burn even during the day in this 15th-century building – one of two remaining wooden buildings in the city – which has been a tavern since 1519. In the 16th and 17th centuries it was an inn for sailors from the Far East, who often brought *aapjes* (monkeys) to trade for lodging. Vintage jazz on the stereo enhances the time-warp feel.

The inn became so overrun with monkeys that they were given to a customer, who kept them in his garden; this evolved into the Artis Royal Zoo (p93).

★BROUWERIJ DE PRAEL — BREWERY

Map p290 (www.deprael.nl; Oudezijds Armsteeg 26; ⏲noon-midnight Mon-Wed, to 1am Thu-Sat, to 11pm Sun; 📶; 🚋2/4/11/12/13/14/17/24/26 Centraal Station) Sample organic beers (Scotch ale, IPA, barley wine and many more varieties) from the socially minded De Prael brewery (p73), known for employing people with a history of mental illness. Its multilevel taproom has comfy couches and big wooden tables strewn about. There's often live music. A four-beer tasting flight costs €10.

TAILOR BAR — COCKTAIL BAR

Map p294 (www.barthetailor.com; Dam 9; ⏲5pm-1am; 📶; 🚋4/14/24 Dam) The drinks list at this elegant bar in the NH Grand Hotel Krasnapolsky pays homage to AW Krasnapolsky, a tailor who moved from Germany to Amsterdam in 1856 and worked at this site before then founding the hotel. Cocktails include the Tailor's Cut (*oude jenever,* vermouth and smoky bitters) and Felt Pockets (Irish whiskey and Ceylon and green teas).

LOW-KEY COFFEESHOPS

If loud music, trippy decor and big crowds aren't your thing, smaller, more relaxed coffeeshops worth considering include the living-room-like **Tweede Kamer** (Map p294; www.tweedekamercoffeeshop.nl; Heisteeg 6; ⏲10am-1am; 🚋2/11/12 Spui) and mellow **Coffeeshop Rusland** (Map p294; www.coffeeshop-rusland-amsterdam.com; Rusland 16; ⏲8am-12.30am; Ⓜ Rokin, 🚋4/14/24 Rokin).

TASTING HOUSES

Tasting houses hide among the Centre's streets, offering a prime opportunity to try *jenever* and other local liqueurs. Most have been pouring their wares for two to three centuries. Look out for the following:

Wynand Fockink (Map p294; 020-639 26 95; www.wynand-fockink.nl; Pijlsteeg 31; tours €17.50; tasting tavern 2-9pm daily, tours 3pm, 4.30pm, 6pm & 7.30pm Sat & Sun; 4/14/24 Dam) Dating from 1679, this small tasting house in an arcade behind NH Grand Hotel Krasnapolsky serves scores of *jenevers* and liqueurs. Although there's no seating, it's an intimate place to knock back a shot glass or two. At weekends, guides give 45-minute distillery tours (in English) that are followed by six tastings; reserve online.

Proeflokaal de Ooievaar (Map p290; www.proeflokaaldeooievaar.nl; St Olofspoort 1; noon-midnight; 2/4/11/12/13/14/17/24/26 Centraal Station) Not much bigger than a vat of *jenever*, this magnificent little tasting house has been going strong since 1782. On offer are 14 *jenevers* and liqueurs (such as Bride's Tears with gold and silver leaf) from the De Ooievaar distillery, still located in the Jordaan. Despite appearances, the house has not subsided but was built leaning over.

De Drie Fleschjes (Map p290; www.dedriefleschjes.nl; Gravenstraat 18; 2-8.30pm Mon-Sat, 3-7pm Sun; 2/11/12/13/17 Dam) A treasure dating from 1650, with a wall of barrels made by master shipbuilders, the tasting room of distiller Bootz specialises in liqueurs, including its signature almond-flavoured *bitterkoekje* (Dutch-style macaroon) liqueur, as well as superb *jenever*. Take a peek at the collection of *kalkoentjes* (small bottles with hand-painted portraits of former mayors).

BIERFABRIEK
MICROBREWERY

Map p294 (020-528 99 10; www.bierfabriek. com; Nes 67; 3pm-1am Mon-Thu, to 2am Fri, 1pm-2am Sat, to 1am Sun; Rokin, 4/14/24 Rokin) Bierfabriek's Pure pilsner, Nero porter and Rosso ruby ale (plus a seasonally changing variety) are brewed in these raw-concrete surrounds and best accompanied by its signature grilled chicken served with a hefty portion of fries and mayonnaise (or just help yourself to the in-shell peanuts that abound on the tables). Reserve to guarantee a table at busy times.

'T MANDJE
GAY & LESBIAN

Map p290 (www.cafetmandje.amsterdam; Zeedijk 63; 4pm-1am Tue-Thu, 3pm-3am Fri & Sat, 3pm-1am Sun; 2/4/11/12/13/14/17/24/26 Centraal Station) Amsterdam's oldest gay bar opened in 1927, then shut in 1982 when the Zeedijk grew too seedy. But its trinket-covered interior was lovingly dusted every week until it reopened in 2008. Devoted bartenders can tell you about the bar's brassy lesbian founder Bet van Beeren. It's one of the most *gezellig* places in the centre, gay or straight.

GREENHOUSE
COFFEESHOP

Map p294 (www.greenhouse.org; Oudezijds Voorburgwal 191; 9am-1am; ; 4/14/24 Dam) This is one of the most popular coffeeshops in town, with a mostly young, backpacking crowd partaking of the wares. Smokers love the funky music, multicoloured mosaics and high-quality weed and hash. It also serves breakfast, lunch and dinner to suit all levels of the munchies.

WINSTON KINGDOM
CLUB

Map p290 (www.winston.nl; St Christopher's at the Winston, Warmoesstraat 131; 9pm-4am Sun-Thu, to 5am Fri & Sat; ; 4/14/24 Dam) Even non-clubbers will love Winston Kingdom for its indie-alternative music beats, great DJs and live bands. No matter what's on – from 'dubstep mayhem' to Thailand-style full-moon parties – the scene can get pretty wild in this good-time little space inside St Christopher's at the Winston (p220). Check its agenda for events.

MOLLY MALONE'S
IRISH PUB

Map p290 (www.mollyinamsterdam.com; Oudezijds Kolk 9; 11.30am-1am Mon-Thu, to 3am Fri, 11am-3am Sat, to 1am Sun; ; 2/4/11/12/13/14/17/24/26 Centraal Station) Dark, woody Molly's holds spontaneous trad-music sessions (bring your own instrument and let loose) as well as various live music gigs. Irish beverages include ciders and fabulous Galway Hooker craft beers in addition to stout and 70-plus whiskeys. Live sports screen on big HD TVs; pub grub ranges from burgers to ribs and roasts.

EAGLE
GAY

Map p290 (www.eagleamsterdam.com; Warmoesstraat 90; ⊘11pm-4am Sun-Thu, to 5am Fri & Sat; 🚊2/4/11/12/13/14/17/24/26 Centraal Station) Around since 1979, the Eagle is a classic. This men-only, leather-denim bar offers three levels of action, including basement darkrooms and a house-music-thumping, laser-light-swirling dance floor. Queues can be lengthy at weekends. Regular events range from DJs to naked nights and bondage play parties.

KAPITEIN ZEPPO'S
BAR

Map p294 (www.zeppos.nl; Gebed Zonder End 5; ⊘11am-1am Mon-Thu, to 3am Fri & Sat, noon-1am Sun; Ⓜ Rokin, 🚊4/14/24 Rokin) Tucked down an alleyway off Grimburgwal, this site has assumed many guises throughout the centuries: a cloister during the 14th, a horse-carriage storehouse in the 17th and a cigar factory in the 19th. The soulful little *café* has a timeless bohemian feel, whether you're at the tile-topped, candlelit tables or in the garden with its twinkling lights.

GETTO
GAY & LESBIAN

Map p290 (www.getto.nl; Warmoesstraat 51; ⊘4pm-1am Mon-Thu, to 2am Fri & Sat, to midnight Sun; 🚊2/4/11/12/13/14/17/24/26 Centraal Station) This long restaurant-bar is loved for its open, welcoming attitude, great people-watching from the front, and rear lounge where you can chill. It's a haven for the gay and lesbian crowd and anyone who wants a little bohemian subculture in the Red Light District's midst. Food includes 'diva burgers'; happy hour is from 4pm to 10pm.

☆ ENTERTAINMENT

Many bars in the Medieval Centre have live music; the area's best dedicated venue is Bitterzoet. Nes is lined with theatres, including the spectacularly renovated Tobacco Theater, hosting plays, concerts and cabarets in a former tobacco auction house. In the Red Light District, Oudezijds Achterburgwal has theatres of an entirely different sort (yes, live sex shows).

BITTERZOET
LIVE MUSIC

Map p290 (⌨020-421 23 18; www.bitterzoet.com; Spuistraat 2; ⊘8pm-late; 🚊2/11/

12/13/17 Nieuwezijds Kolk) Always full, always changing, this venue with a capacity of just 350 people is one of the friendliest places in town, with a diverse crowd. Music (sometimes live, sometimes courtesy of a DJ) can be funk, roots, drum 'n' bass, Latin, Afro-beat, old-school jazz or hip-hop groove.

TOBACCO THEATER
THEATRE

Map p294 (⌨020-242 06 99; www.tobacco.nl; Nes 75-87; Ⓜ Rokin, 🚊4/14/24 Rokin) A 1900-built tobacco auction house now contains this architecturally designed theatre, which stages dinner-and-cabaret shows in English, Dutch and German, and presents theatre productions and concerts. In addition to the 300-capacity theatre, it has an experimental art and concept room in the cellar, along with several lounge areas including a cocktail bar overlooking the stage, and an old bank vault.

FRASCATI
THEATRE

Map p294 (⌨020-626 68 66; www.frascatitheater.nl; Nes 63; ⊘closed Aug; Ⓜ Rokin, 🚊4/14/24 Rokin) This experimental theatre is a draw for young Dutch directors, choreographers and producers. Expect multicultural dance and music performances, as well as hip-hop, rap and breakdancing. Check the website for upcoming events.

DE BRAKKE GROND
THEATRE

Map p294 (⌨020-622 90 14; www.brakkegrond.nl; Flemish Cultural Centre, Nes 45; 🕾; Ⓜ Rokin, 🚊4/14//24 Rokin) De Brakke Grond sponsors a fantastic array of music, experimental video, modern dance and exciting young theatre at its nifty performance hall in the Flemish Cultural Centre. Upcoming events are listed on its website.

CASA ROSSO
LIVE PERFORMANCE

Map p294 (www.casarosso.nl; Oudezijds Achterburgwal 106-108; admission with/without drinks €62/47; ⊘7pm-2am Sun-Thu, to 3am Fri & Sat; 🚊4/14/24 Dam) It might be stretching it to describe a live sex show as 'classy', but this theatre is clean and comfortable and always packed with couples and hen parties. Acts can be male, female, both or lesbian (although not gay – sorry, boys!). Performers demonstrate everything from positions of the Kama Sutra to pole dances and incredible tricks with lit candles.

EIVAISLAV/SHUTTERSTOCK ©

1. Bike hire (p29)
Ride around Amsterdam like a local.

2. Brouwerij 't IJ (p99)
Ride to this brewery at the foot of a windmill.

3. Bikes everywhere
One of Amsterdam's many bikes, tied to a bridge.

4. Zaanse Schans (p216)
Just a 90-minute bike ride from Amsterdam.

PUT OUT THE RED LIGHT?

Since 2007 city officials have reduced the number of Red Light windows in an effort to clean up the Red Light District. They claim it's not about morals but about crime: pimps, traffickers and money launderers have entered the scene and set the neighbourhood on a downward spiral. Opponents point to a growing conservatism and say the government is using crime as an excuse because it doesn't like Amsterdam's reputation for sin.

To date, some 300 windows remain, down from 482. Scores of sex workers and their supporters have protested against the closures: the concern is that closing the windows simply forces sex workers to relocate to less safe environments. A buy-back project to replace windows with studios and local shops was largely unsuccessful, resulting in tourist-driven businesses (eg cheap souvenir shops) filling the gaps. However, from 2020, the city will ban guided tours along the Red Light District's windows (guided tours in the rest of the city centre are still allowed to operate, but require tour guides to have a special permit and abide by relevant rules).

Other initiatives for changing the face of the area include the introduction of festivals such as the **Red Light Jazz Festival** (www.redlightjazz.com; ☉early Jun).

SHOPPING

Kalverstraat and its surrounds are filled with high-street chains and get crammed with shoppers, while Damrak is awash with souvenir shops. More esoteric shops, selling everything from Dutch-designed homewares, fashion and art to reconditioned retro computer games, can be found in the backstreets. The Red Light District is home to a wild assortment of adult and fetish shops, as well as 'smart shops' selling magic truffles.

🔒 Medieval Centre

★ X BANK   DESIGN
Map p294 (www.xbank.amsterdam; Spuistraat 172; ☉10am-8pm Fri-Wed, to 9pm Thu; 🚊2/11/12/13/17 Dam) More than just a concept store showcasing Dutch-designed haute couture and ready-to-wear fashion, furniture, art, gadgets and homewares, the 700-sq-metre X Bank – in a former bank that's now part of the striking W Amsterdam (p221) hotel – also hosts exhibitions, workshops, launches and lectures. Interior displays change every month; check the website for upcoming events.

LOCALS   FASHION & ACCESSORIES
Map p294 (www.localsamsterdam.com; Spuistraat 272; ☉1-6pm Mon, 11.30am-6pm Tue-Sat, noon-6pm Sun; 🚊2/11/12 Spui) Jeweller Suzanne Hof set up this boutique to showcase designs from her own label, Sugarz, but also to provide a platform for small-scale designers from the Netherlands and especially from Amsterdam. Along with men's and women's fashion (T-shirts, jeans, dresses), you'll find scarves, hats, gloves, handbags and homewares (vases, cushions, crockery, paintings and contemporary twists on hand-painted Delftware tiles).

MARK RAVEN GRAFIEK   GIFTS & SOUVENIRS
Map p290 (www.markraven.nl; Nieuwezijds Voorburgwal 174; ☉10.30am-6pm; 🚊1/2/5/13/14/17 Dam) Artist Mark Raven's distinctive vision of Amsterdam is available on posters, coasters and well-cut T-shirts that make great souvenirs. Prices are impressively reasonable and there's often a sale rack out front.

POSTHUMUS   STATIONERY
Map p294 (www.posthumuswinkel.nl; St Luciënsteeg 25; ☉10am-5.30pm Tue-Fri, 11am-5.30pm Sat; 🚊2/11/12/13/17 Dam) Established in 1865, this wonderfully preserved shop with original timber cabinetry produces lacquer stamps for wax seals (and sells sealing wax), brass branding stamps, shutter stamps for embossing, and rubber hobby stamps (with ink pads) in Dutch-themed designs such as gabled canal houses. Stamps can be made to order. It also has feathered, quill-like fountain pens and fine papers.

BONBON BOUTIQUE   JEWELLERY
Map p294 (www.bonbonboutique.nl; Rosmarijnsteeg 8; ☉11am-6pm Mon-Sat, noon-6pm Sun; 🚊2/11/12 Spui) A white-on-white space is the backdrop for Amsterdam-designed jewellery

(rings, earrings, bracelets, necklaces and pendants) crafted from gold, sterling silver, brass, precious stones and coloured crystal. Jewellery-making workshops in English and Dutch (from €60 for two hours) teach you hammering, bending, cutting and filing techniques on creations you get to keep.

ANDRIES DE JONG BV
GIFTS & SOUVENIRS

Map p294 (www.andriesdejong.nl; Muntplein 8; ⊙10am-6pm Mon-Sat; 🚋24 Muntplein) Since 1787, when seafarers have needed ship fittings, rope or brass lamps, they've come to Andries de Jong. Traditional clocks, bells, boats in bottles and other quaint maritime gifts weigh down the crowded shelves among the workers' items, along with strong, brightly coloured flags.

OUDEMANHUISPOORT BOOK MARKET
BOOKS

Map p294 (Oudemanhuispoort; ⊙11am-4pm Mon-Sat; MRokin, 🚋4/14/24 Rokin) Second-hand books weigh down the tables in the atmospheric covered alleyway between Oudezijds Achterburgwal and Kloveniersburgwal, where you'll rub tweed-patched elbows with University of Amsterdam professors thumbing through volumes of Marx, Aristotle et al. Old posters, maps and sheet music are for sale too. Most titles are in Dutch, though you'll find a few in English mixed in. Cash only.

PGC HAJENIUS
GIFTS & SOUVENIRS

Map p294 (www.hajenius.com; Rokin 96; ⊙noon-6pm Mon, 9.30am-6pm Tue-Sat, noon-5pm Sun; MRokin, 🚋4/14/24 Rokin) With its century-old stained glass, gilt trim, Italian marble and soaring leather ceilings, this tobacco emporium is worth checking out even if you're not a cigar connoisseur. Regular customers, including members of the Dutch royal family, have private humidors here. You can sample Cuban and other exotic cigars in the handsome smoking lounge.

DE BIJENKORF
DEPARTMENT STORE

Map p294 (www.debijenkorf.nl; Dam 1; ⊙10am-9pm Tue-Sat, 11am-9pm Sun & Mon; 🚋4/14/24 Dam) Amsterdam's most fashionable department store has a grander exterior than interior, but it occupies the city's highest-profile location, facing the Royal Palace. Shoppers will enjoy the well-chosen clothing, cosmetics, accessories, toys, homewares and books. The snazzy cafe on the 5th floor has a terrace with steeple views.

GASTRONOMIE NOSTALGIE
HOMEWARES

Map p294 (www.gastronomienostalgie.nl; Nieuwezijds Voorburgwal 304; ⊙11am-5pm; 🚋2/11/12 Spui) The owner scours international auctions for the gorgeous china plates, crystal goblets, silver candlesticks and other antique homewares spilling out of this jam-packed shop. Ring the brass bell to get in, then prepare to browse for a good long while.

MAGNA PLAZA
MALL

Map p290 (www.magnaplaza.nl; Nieuwezijds Voorburgwal 182; ⊙10am-10pm; 🚋1/2/5/13/14/17 Dam) This grand 19th-century landmark building, once the main post office, is now home to an upmarket shopping mall with more than 40 boutiques stocking fashion, gifts and jewellery – everything from Mango and Sissy Boy to a cashmere specialist. After browsing, stop for refreshments at its 1100 sq metre food hall, where choices include Amsterdam burger specialist the **Butcher** (Map p294; www.the-butcher.com; Paleisstraat 14; burgers €6.50-12.50; ⊙11am-1am Sun-Thu, to 3am Fri & Sat).

LAUNDRY INDUSTRY
CLOTHING

Map p294 (www.laundryindustry.com; St Luciënsteeg 18; ⊙11am-6pm Tue-Sat, noon-6pm Sun & Mon; 🚋2/11/12 Spui) Hip urban shoppers head here for well-cut, well-designed women's and men's clothes by this Dutch design house. Shoes, jewellery and designer knick-knacks are also for sale. A coffee bar provides a caffeine fix.

POSTZEGELMARKT
MARKET

Map p294 (Stamp & Coin Market; Nieuwezijds Voorburgwal 280; ⊙10am-4pm Wed & Sat; 🚋2/11/12 Spui) This little street-side market sells rare, highly collectable postage stamps, coins and medals.

RUSH HOUR RECORDS
MUSIC

Map p290 (www.rushhour.nl; Spuistraat 116; ⊙1-7pm Mon, 11am-7pm Tue, Wed, Fri & Sat, 11am-9pm Thu, 1-6pm Sun; 🚋4/14/24 Dam) House and techno are the main genres on offer in this vast space, but funk, jazz, dubstep, electronica and disco fill the bins too. A favourite with DJs and multimedia artists, it's an excellent spot to find out what's going on in the underground dance-music scene.

ART MARKET
MARKET

Map p294 (www.artamsterdam-spui.com; Spui; ⊙11am-6pm Sun Mar-Dec; 🚋2/11/12 Spui) Save on gallery fees by buying direct from the artists at Amsterdam's art market. Some 60 Dutch and contemporary artists set up on the square every week.

AMERICAN BOOK CENTER   BOOKS

Map p294 (ABC; www.abc.nl; Spui 12; ☉noon-8pm Mon, 10am-8pm Tue-Sat, 11am-6.30pm Sun; 🚊2/11/12 Spui) Rambling over three storeys, this excellent bookshop is the biggest source of English-language books in Amsterdam. Its greatest strengths are in the artsy ground-floor department, but on the upper floors there's fiction and oodles of special-interest titles, plus a good travel section. It also stocks foreign publications such as the *New York Times* and top-notch postcards.

DE BIERKONING   DRINKS

Map p294 (www.bierkoning.nl; Paleisstraat 125; ☉11am-7pm Mon-Sat, noon-7pm Sun; 🚊2/11/12/13/17 Dam) Not only does De Bierkoning stock more than 2000 varieties of beer (with an emphasis on Belgian, German, British and, of course, Dutch brews) but it also has a vast beer glass selection, T-shirts with beer logos, and beer guidebooks to the region. It also carries a small array of ciders.

🏠 Red Light District

MARY GO WILD   MUSIC

Map p290 (www.marygowild.nl; Zeedijk 44; ☉1-7pm Wed & Sun, noon-8pm Thu, noon-7pm Fri & Sat; 🚊2/4/11/12/13/14/17/24/26 Centraal Station) House and techno are the specialities of this vinyl shop on Zeedijk. DJs often play in-store; it also has its own online radio station, and hosts occasional raves in its basement. It's one of the best sources of information for clubbing events around town.

CONDOMERIE HET GULDEN VLIES   ADULT

Map p290 (www.condomerie.com; Warmoesstraat 141; ☉11am-9pm Mon & Wed-Sat, to 6pm Tue, 1-6pm Sun; 🚊4/14/24 Dam) In the heart of the Red Light District, this brightly lit boutique sells condoms in every imaginable size, colour, flavour and design (horned devils, marijuana leaves, Delftware tiles...), along with lubricants and saucy gifts. Photos aren't allowed inside the shop.

HEMPSTORY   CONCEPT STORE

Map p294 (www.hempstory.nl; Oudezijds Achterburgwal 142; ☉11am-7pm Tue-Wed, Fri-Sat, to 9pm Thu, noon-7pm Sun & Mon; 🚊4/14/24 Dam) Everything at this light-filled contemporary boutique is made from hemp: skincare ranges (soaps, moisturisers, and body washes such as hemp and ginseng), insect repellent, homewares (blankets, throws, cushions, botanical prints on hemp paper), men's and women's clothing (shirts, jackets, scarves, hats), and hemp-cord jewellery. Its tiny cafe serves (non-active) hemp tea, hemp-seed cakes and hemp-seed smoothies.

RED LIGHT RECORDS   MUSIC

Map p290 (www.redlightrecordsamsterdam.com; Oudekerksplein 26; ☉noon-7pm Mon-Fri, to 6pm Sat & Sun; 🚊4/14/24 Dam) Tucked in a courtyard off the street, this shop sits in a former Red Light window. Ring the doorbell to get buzzed in and join the DJs flicking through stacks of spacey Euro-disco, house and funk music. Headphone stations let you listen before you buy. The underground Red Light Radio station (www.redlightradio.net) operates from a window across the way.

KOKOPELLI   ADULT

Map p290 (www.kokopelli.nl; Warmoesstraat 12; ☉11am-10pm; 🚊2/4/11/12/13/14/17/24/26 Centraal Station) Were it not for its trade in 'magic truffles' (similar to the now-outlawed psilocybin mushrooms, aka 'magic mushrooms'), you might swear this large, beautiful space was a fashionable clothing or homewares store. There's a coffee and juice bar and a chill-out lounge area overlooking Damrak.

WONDERWOOD   HOMEWARES

Map p294 (📞020-625 37 38; www.wonderwood.nl; Rusland 3; ☉noon-6pm Wed-Sat & by appointment; Ⓜ Nieuwmarkt) As much a museum as a shop (look up to see the 1565-built timber ceiling), WonderWood specialises in the moulded-plywood creations of George Nelson, Marcel Breuer and others. Some of the vintage furniture pieces are for sale and some are available in reissue (ie old designs remade). It ships worldwide; smaller wooden objects are also available.

Nieuwmarkt, Plantage & the Eastern Islands

NIEUWMARKT | PLANTAGE | EASTERN ISLANDS

Neighbourhood Top Five

❶ Museum het Rembrandthuis (p89) Viewing Rembrandt's former home and studio, where you can see his brushes, wonderful etchings and cabinet stuffed with seashells and Roman busts.

❷ Het Scheepvaartmuseum (p94) Fathoming the history of Dutch seafar-ing through this extensive state-of-the-art maritime collection.

❸ Muziekgebouw aan 't IJ (p101) Catching live classical music or jazz at this acoustically and visu-ally stunning venue.

❹ Verzetsmuseum (p94) Gaining an insight through letters, photos, films and more into the personal stories of the Dutch Resist-ance to the horrific WWII occupation.

❺ Rederij Lampedusa (p266) Taking a fascinat-ing tour with storytelling, theatre or music co-run by migrants, on a former refugee boat.

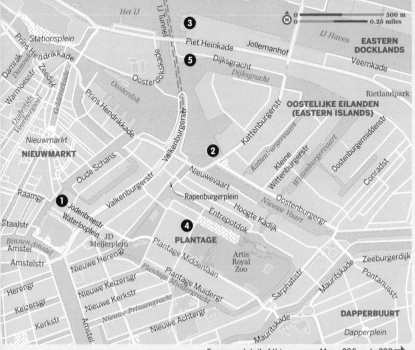

For more detail of this area see Map p296 and p298 ➡

Lonely Planet's Top Tip

Nieuwmarkt and the Eastern Islands have an eclectic mix of architecture, from the fantastical Scheepvaarthuis (a classic example of the Amsterdam School) to Renzo Piano's green-tinged NEMO Science Museum. Several unique buildings cluster near where Kloveniersburgwal and Oude Hoogstraat intersect, while on the Eastern Islands there are some seminal modern buildings, including the 'Whale'.

✕ Best Places to Eat

➡ Greetje (p98)

➡ Sterk Staaltje (p95)

➡ Tokoman (p95)

➡ Frank's Smokehouse (p97)

➡ De Plantage (p97)

For reviews, see p95. ➡

♀ Best Places to Drink

➡ Rosalia's Menagerie (p99)

➡ Brouwerij 't IJ (p99)

➡ SkyLounge (p100)

➡ Hannekes Boom (p101)

➡ De Nieuwe KHL (p101)

For reviews, see p99. ➡

🔒 Best Places to Shop

➡ Puccini Bomboni (p103)

➡ Hôtel Droog (p102)

➡ Waterlooplein Flea Market (p102)

➡ Jacob Hooy & Co (p103)

➡ Pols Potten (p103)

For reviews, see p102. ➡

Explore Nieuwmarkt, Plantage & the Eastern Islands

Centred on its namesake square, busy Nieuwmarkt (New Market) bursts with historic reminders of its glorious past, even if it's more about nightlife and shopping these days. Rembrandt painted canalscapes here, and Jewish merchants built up thriving businesses until the community's decimation during WWII occupation.

The neighbourhood's most entrancing sight is Museum het Rembrandthuis, the master's impressive home and studio. In the old Jewish quarter is an excellent collection of museums housed in historic synagogues.

East of Nieuwmarkt is the city's leafiest neighbourhood, Plantage (Plantation). It was developed from a former swamp in the 17th century, but an economic crisis led to many plots of land remaining unsold. The authorities developed these into parks, resulting in a lovely place to stroll and laze. Beside its splendid 19th-century architecture, there is the historic Artis Royal Zoo (p93), and the verdantly exotic Hortus Botanicus (p93).

Further east, there's another completely contrasting area of the city, the former shipyard and warehouse district of the Eastern Islands (Oostelijke Eilanden) and their Eastern Docklands (Oostelijk Havengebied).

Local Life

➡ **Street Life** The *cafés* (pubs and bars) ringing Nieuwmarkt square buzz in the afternoon and evening.

➡ **Waterside Life** Head to the houseboats and riverside cafes such as Kanis & Meiland (p101) off the beaten track on the Eastern Islands to enjoy a laid-back drink.

➡ **Snack Life** Join the queues to fit in a fiery bite of Suriname at Tokoman (p95).

➡ **Brewery Life** You can't get more classically Dutch than sitting in the shadow of a windmill, sampling the fragrant beers of organic Brouwerij 't IJ (p99).

Getting There & Away

➡ **Tram** Tram 14 goes to Waterlooplein, the Jewish sights and Plantage. Tram 7 goes to the Eastern Islands and Eastern Docklands. Tram 26 travels along the IJ River.

➡ **Metro** Stops at Waterlooplein and Nieuwmarkt.

➡ **Bus** Buses 22 and 48 are useful for areas of the Eastern Islands and Eastern Docklands that the tram doesn't reach.

➡ **Boat** Canal Bus stops are at NEMO/Het Scheepvaartmuseum (Map p298) and near Amstel and Waterlooplein (Map p296). The Passenger Terminal Amsterdam (Map p298; Piet Heinkade) is near Bimhuis.

TOP SIGHT
MUSEUM HET REMBRANDTHUIS

This museum provides an unparalleled insight into one of the Netherlands' greatest artistic geniuses, Rembrandt van Rijn. The museum occupies the three-storey canal house where the artist lived at the height of his success, and the interiors have been reconstructed according to a detailed inventory made when he had to leave the house after his fortunes took a dive.

The house dates from 1606. Rembrandt ran the Netherlands' largest painting studio here between 1639 and 1658. However, the house was ultimately Rembrandt's financial undoing. As his work fell out of fashion, he was unable to pay off the mortgage, and in 1656 the house and its effects were sold to compensate his creditors. It's thanks to the debt collector's itemised list that the museum has been able to reproduce the interior so authentically. Rembrandt lived the rest of his years in cheaper digs in the Jordaan.

On the ground floor you'll see Rembrandt's living room and bedroom, furnished with the type of box bed fashionable at the time; it was believed that sleeping sitting up prevented death during the night. An anteroom where he received clients is covered in paintings: wares for sale. The house gives an insight into art as a trade, with the showroom downstairs and, upstairs, the cubicles for Rembrandt's pupils.

Upstairs is the master's light-filled studio, laid out as though he's just nipped out for a snack. Facing north, offering ideal light, this is where he painted masterpieces such as *The Night Watch*. The room is recognisable from an etching on display, and artists give demonstrations on how Rembrandt mixed paints. Across the hall is his 'Cabinet', a room crammed with curiosities like those he collected: seashells, glassware, Roman busts and stuffed alligators.

A small room is devoted to Rembrandt's famous etchings. The museum has a near-complete collection of them (about 250), although they're not all on display at once. Demonstrators crank up an oak press to show etching techniques several times daily.

DON'T MISS

➡ The paint-filled studio
➡ The seated box beds
➡ Etching demos
➡ Rembrandt's recreated collection 'Cabinet'
➡ The audioguide

PRACTICALITIES

➡ Map p296, C5
➡ ☏ 020-520 04 00
➡ www.rembrandthuis.nl
➡ Jodenbreestraat 4
➡ adult/child €14/5
➡ ⏰ 10am-6pm
➡ Ⓜ Waterlooplein

⊙ SIGHTS

Historic buildings and Rembrandt's former home lie close to Nieuwmarkt, while to the south south is the vast square of Waterlooplein and the former Jewish quarter, with its stately synagogues containing the Joods Historisch Museum. To the east are the airy green spaces of Plantage, including parks, the botanical gardens and lush Artis Royal Zoo (p93), edged by two other great small museums: Micropia (p93), exposing the invisible world of bacteria and viruses, and Verzetsmuseum (p94), where personal stories bring existence under Nazi occupation to life.

⊙ Nieuwmarkt

MUSEUM HET REMBRANDTHUIS   MUSEUM
See p89.

SCHEEPVAARTHUIS   ARCHITECTURE
Map p296 (Shipping House; www.amrathamster dam.com; Prins Hendrikkade 108; ⊡22/34/35 Prins Hendrikkade) Now the five-star Grand Hotel Amrath, the grand 1916 Scheepvaarthuis is a neo-Gothic art deco beauty, the first and finest example of the expressionist Amsterdam School of architecture. The exterior resembles a ship's bow, awash with nautical detailing; look for figures of Neptune, his wife and four females who represent the compass points. Staff are happy for tourists to look around: head up to the 3rd floor to see the Great Hall with its leaded glass designed by Willem Bogtman.

WAAG   HISTORIC BUILDING
Map p296 (www.indewaag.nl; Nieuwmarkt 4; ⊙bar-restaurant 11am-11pm Mon-Wed, from 9am Thu-Sat; ⓂNieuwmarkt) The multi-turreted Waag was built as a gate in the city walls in 1488. In 1601 the walls were destroyed to allow the city to expand, and the building was turned into Amsterdam's main weigh house, and later a spot for public executions. A bar-restaurant occupies it today. Out the front, Nieuwmarkt hosts a variety of events, including a Saturday farmers market and a Sunday antiques market.

In its early days the Waag looked more like a castle, fronted by a moat-like canal. By the 17th century it was home to various guilds. The surgeons' guild, which occupied the upper floor, commissioned Rembrandt's famous *The Anatomy Lesson of Dr Tulp* (displayed in the Mauritshuis museum in Den Haag). The masons' guild was based in the tower facing the Zeedijk; note the superfine brickwork.

ZUIDERKERK   CHURCH
Map p296 (☑020-308 03 99, tower tours 020-689 25 65; www.zuiderkerkamsterdam.nl; Zuiderkerkhof 72; ⓂNieuwmarkt) Famed Dutch Renaissance architect Hendrick de Keyser built the 'Southern Church' in 1611. This was the first custom-built Protestant church in Amsterdam – Catholic in design but with no choir. The final church service was held here in 1929. During the 1944–45 'Hunger Winter' of WWII it served as a morgue.

Telephone or visit www.westertoren amsterdam.nl to arrange climbing the tower for a sky-high city view. At the time of research, the church was undergoing restorations and tours were not happening, but there were plans to start running them again from April 2020.

PINTOHUIS   ARCHITECTURE
Map p296 (Openbare Bibliotheek; ☑020-370 02 10; www.huisdepinto.nl; St Antoniesbreestraat 69; ⊙10.30am-5.30pm Tue-Fri, 1-5pm Sat; ⓂNieuwmarkt) St Antoniesbreestraat was once a busy street, but it lost many of its old buildings during the metro's construction. The Pintohuis remains, however. It was once owned by wealthy Sephardic Jew Isaac de Pinto, who had it remodelled with Italianate pilasters in the 1680s. It's now a library – pop inside to admire the beautiful ceiling frescoes, featuring gold and soaring birds.

PORTUGUESE-ISRAELITE SYNAGOGUE   SYNAGOGUE
Map p296 (www.jck.nl; Mr Visserplein 3; adult/child 13-17yr/child 6-12yr/under 6yr €17/8.50/4.25/free; ⊙10am-5pm Sun-Fri May-Aug, 10am-5pm Sun-Thu, to 4pm Fri Mar, Apr, Sep & Oct, reduced hours Nov-Feb; ⓂWaterlooplein) With dizzying wooden barrel-vaulted ceilings, this was the largest synagogue in Europe when it was completed in 1675. It's still in use today, and has no electric lights – after dark the candles in the vast chandeliers are lit for services. The large library belonging to the Ets Haim seminary is one of Europe's oldest and most important Jewish book collections. Outside (near the entrance) stairs lead underground to the treasure chambers with displays of 16th-century manuscripts and gold-threaded tapestries.

The synagogue's architect, Elias Bouman, was inspired by the Temple of Solomon, but the building's classical lines are typical of the Dutch capital. It was restored after WWII. Candlelight concerts are held here roughly once a month. Admission also provides entry to the Joods Cultureel Kwartier (Jewish Cultural Quarter) sites, including the Joods Historisch Museum.

STOPERA   NOTABLE BUILDING

Map p296 (📞020-625 54 55; www.operaballet.nl/; Waterlooplein 22; guided tour adult/child €9.50/7.50; ⊙tours 1.15pm Tue & 12.15pm Sat; 🚊14 Waterlooplein) This 1986, curved waterside building is called Stopera because it houses both the *stadhuis* (city hall) and the opera and ballet hall, aka Muziektheater (p101). For a peek behind the scenes, take a guided tour on Saturday or Tuesday. Tours are in Dutch but there is an English brochure, and usually English explanations by the guide. Free lunchtime concerts usually take place from 12.30pm to 1pm on Tuesdays from September to June; doors open at 12.15pm.

MONTELBAANSTOREN   HISTORIC BUILDING

Map p296 (Montelbaan Tower; Oude Schans 2; 🚊4/12/14/24/26 Centraal Station) This graceful tower looks monumental rather than functional, but it was originally built to strengthen Amsterdam's eastern defences in 1512. Positioned on the old city wall, it gave sentries a good view of suspicious characters on the wharves along Oude Schans. The decorative topping, octagonal base and open wooden steeple were added in 1606 to dampen the bells on the clock after neighbours complained. A few years later, it began to list under the weight, but residents attached cables and pulled it upright.

GASSAN DIAMONDS   FACTORY

Map p296 (www.gassan.com; Nieuwe Uilenburgerstraat 173-175; ⊙9am-5pm; Ⓜ Waterlooplein) **FREE** If you're interested in diamonds, join a 40-minute free guided tour to see diamond cutters and polishers in action at this workshop. It will prime you on assessing diamonds, then land you in the shop with a chance to own your own sparklers, at a price.

The factory is on Uilenburg, one of the islands reclaimed in the 1580s during a sudden influx of Sephardic Jews from Spain and Portugal. In the 1880s Gassan became the first diamond factory to use steam power.

OOST-INDISCH HUIS   ARCHITECTURE

Map p296 (East Indies House; Oude Hoogstraat 24; Ⓜ Nieuwmarkt) The mighty Dutch East

---

TOP SIGHT
JOODS HISTORISCH MUSEUM

In an impressive complex of four beautiful Ashkenazic synagogues dating from the 17th and 18th centuries, the Jewish Historical Museum is full of fascinating insights into Amsterdam's Jewish past. The enormous **Great Synagogue** is home to displays showing the rise of Jewish enterprise and its role in the Dutch economy, and the history of Jews in the Netherlands, from when they first fled to the country in the 1600s. The horror of their treatment during the German occupation of WWII is evoked by interviews with those who lived through it. The exhibition also covers how 25,000 Dutch Jews went into hiding (18,000 survived) and what life was like after the war as they tried to repatriate.

The complex always has two temporary exhibitions on and there is a **Children's Museum** set up as the home of a Jewish family, the Hollanders. There are regular activities, whereby kids can bake challah bread in the kitchen and play tunes in the music room.

The free, English-language audioguide that talks you through the collection is excellent, as is the bright cafe serving kosher dishes.

DON'T MISS
→ Beautiful early illustrated books
→ WWII interviews
→ Children's Museum
→ Free audioguide

PRACTICALITIES
→ Map p296, D7
→ 📞020-531 03 10
→ www.jck.nl
→ Nieuwe Amstelstraat 1
→ adult/child 13-17yr/child 6-12yr/under 6yr €17/8.50/4.25/free
→ ⊙11am-5pm
→ Ⓜ Waterlooplein

SKINNY HOUSES

Amsterdam is full of slender homes because property used to be taxed on frontage. So the narrower your facade, the less you paid.

Witness the narrow house at **Oude Hoogstraat 22** (Map p296; ⓂNieuwmarkt). It's 2.02m wide, 5m deep and several storeys tall, occupying a mere 12 sq metres per storey. This could well be the tiniest (self-contained) house in Europe.

Nearby, the **Kleine Trippenhuis** (Map p296; Kloveniersburgwal 26; ⓂNieuwmarkt) is 2.44m wide. It stands opposite the **mansion** (Map p296; Kloveniersburgwal 29; ⓂNieuwmarkt) once owned by the wealthy Trip brothers and, so the story goes, their coachman exclaimed: 'If only I could have a house as wide as my masters' door!' Webers fetish shop (p102) now occupies the skinny building.

India Company (Verenigde Oost-Indische Compagnie; VOC), founded in 1602, was one of the earliest multinational companies, trading spices, opium and more with Asia. This imposing red-and-white edifice is the company's former office, built between 1551 and 1643 and attributed in part to Hendrick de Keyser, the busy city architect. The VOC sailed into rough waters and was dissolved in 1798. The building is now owned by the University of Amsterdam.

DOCKWORKER STATUE   STATUE

Map p296 (JD Meijerplein; ⓂWaterlooplein) Mari Andriessen's *Dockworker* statue (1952), a monumental, aghast-looking figure, was commissioned to commemorate the general strike that began among dockworkers on 25 February 1941 to protest against the treatment of Jews. The first deportation roundup had occurred here a few days earlier.

The anniversary of the strike is still an occasion for wreath-laying, but has become a low-key affair with the demise of the Dutch Communist Party.

⊙ Plantage

With expanses of green that are a pleasing contrast to the canal house-lined city centre,

Plantage contains parks, botanical gardens and the Artis Royal Zoo. It wasn't intended this way: city planners reclaimed the land east of the Amstel with a view to adding new housing developments. However, the boom was already over, and in 1682, the area was converted into garden plots. The area also contains the Jewish quarter, and when construction boomed during the 19th century, it became an entertainment district. Its darkest hour came during WWII, when its large Jewish community was detained and deported from here.

HOLLANDSCHE SCHOUWBURG   MEMORIAL

Map p298 (National Holocaust Museum, Holland Theatre; ☏020-531 03 10; www.jck.nl; Plantage Middenlaan 24; adult/child 13-17yr/child 6-12yr/under 6yr €17/8.50/4.25/free; Ⓣ11am-5pm; ◻14 Artis) Few theatres have had a history of such highs and lows. It was opened as the Artis Theatre in 1892 and became a hub of cultural life in Amsterdam, staging major dramas and operettas. In WWII the occupying Germans turned it into a Jew-only theatre, and later, horrifyingly, a detention centre for Jews held for deportation.

Tickets cover admission to all of the Joods Cultureel Kwartier (Jewish Cultural Quarter) sites, including the Joods Historisch Museum (p91) and the Portuguese-Israelite Synagogue (p90).

The occupiers processed up to 80,000 Jews here on their way to the death camps. Glass panels are engraved with the names of all Jewish families deported, there is a memorial garden, and upstairs is a modest exhibit hall with photos and personal video stories of Jewish life during the war.

WERTHEIMPARK   PARK

Map p298 (Plantage Parklaan; ◻14 Artis) Adding to the lush greenness of the Plantage area, the city's oldest park is a small, lovely, willow-shaded spot for lazing by the Nieuwe Herengracht. It contains the **Auschwitz Memorial**, designed by Dutch writer and artist Jan Wolkers: a panel of cracked mirrors installed in the ground reflects the sky, and an inscription reads 'Nooit Meer' (Never Again). Buried beneath the monument lies an urn with ashes of those who died at Auschwitz.

ENTREPOTDOK   ARCHITECTURE

Map p298 (◻14 Plantage Kerklaan) In an area northeast of the Plantage, there is a 500m row of warehouses that once belonged to the Dutch East India Company (VOC). This powerful organisation, the Amazon of its day, grew rich on sea trade in the 17th century. This was the largest storage depot in Europe at the time – located in a customs-free zone.

Some of the original facades have been preserved, and the warehouses are now used as hip offices, apartments and dockside cafes, with tables perfect for lazing away an afternoon at the water's edge.

HORTUS BOTANICUS GARDENS
Map p298 (Botanical Garden; 020-625 90 21; www.dehortus.nl; Plantage Middenlaan 2a; adult/child/under 5yr €9.75/5.50/free; ⊙10am-5pm; ⬚14 Mr Visserplein) A botanical garden since 1638, it bloomed as tropical seeds and plants were brought in by Dutch trading ships. From here, coffee, pineapple, cinnamon and palm-oil plants were distributed throughout the world. The 4000-plus species are kept in wonderful structures, including the colonial-era seed house and a three-climate glasshouse.

The butterfly house is a hit with kids in particular. Free one-hour guided tours take place at fixed times or on request; check the schedule on the website.

DE GOOYER WINDMILL WINDMILL
Map p298 (Funenkade 5; ⬚7 Hoogte Kadijk) This 18th-century grain mill is the sole survivor of five windmills that once stood in this part of town. It was moved to its current spot in 1814, fully renovated in 1925 and is now a private home.

The public baths alongside the windmill were converted into Brouwerij 't IJ (p99) in 1985.

MUIDERPOORT GATE
Map p298 (Alexanderplein; ⬚14 Alexanderplein) A dome tops this neoclassical arch, which was built in 1770 as a gateway to the city. On the south side you'll see the Amsterdam emblem of three St Andreas' crosses, while on the other side there's a cog ship emblem, which appeared on Amsterdam's coat of arms in medieval times.

In 1811 Napoleon rode triumphantly through the gate with his royal entourage, and promptly demanded food for his ragged troops.

◉ TOP SIGHT
ARTIS ROYAL ZOO

Rambling, leafy and full of interesting historic architecture, this is mainland Europe's oldest zoo. The diverse wildlife occupies extensive habitats, including African savannah and tropical rainforest, and there are 900 different animal species, 200 tree species and an aquarium with coral reefs, as well as a planetarium and kids petting zoo. There are also lots of opportunities to see the feeding times of various animals: check the daily schedule.

Adjoining the zoo is the marvellous **Micropia** (Map p298; ☑020-523 36 71; www.micropia.nl; adult/child €15/13; ⊙9am-6pm Sun-Wed, to 8pm Thu-Sat), which will leave you feeling uncomfortably aware of the invisible world of the microbe. Hands-on exhibits and microscopes enable you to peer through and witness fascinating, if unsettling, facts about how many living organisms there are on everyday objects: discard your toothbrush before three months or it'll be host to seven million bacteria. There are also glass models of and information on viruses from ebola to smallpox. It's aimed at those aged eight and over.

Locals visit the zoo to stroll the paths laid out through the former Plantage gardens. The grounds are packed with heritage-listed 19th-century buildings and monuments, and there are several cafes on-site.

DON'T MISS
➜ Micropia museum
➜ The aquarium
➜ The lion habitat
➜ The African savannah

PRACTICALITIES
➜ Map p298, B4
➜ ☑020-523 34 00
➜ www.artis.nl
➜ Plantage Kerklaan 38-40
➜ adult/child €24/20.50, incl Micropia €30.50/26.50
➜ ⊙9am-6pm Mar-Oct, to 5pm Nov-Feb
➜ ⬚14 Artis

◉ Eastern Islands

Visitors often overlook the Eastern Islands, but they're a great place to escape the crowds of the city centre, despite being just next door (about 10 minutes by bike or tram). There are lots of waterside choices for lunch or a drink, plus plenty of boats, maritime history and modern architecture.

★HET SCHEEPVAARTMUSEUM   MUSEUM
Map p298 (Maritime Museum; ☑020-523 22 22; www.hetscheepvaartmuseum.nl; Kattenburgerplein 1; adult/child €16.50/8; ⊙9am-5pm; ☐22/48 Kattenburgerplein) A waterfront 17th-century admiralty building houses this state-of-the-art presentation of maritime memorabilia. Highlights include imaginatively presented Golden Age maps, fascinating 19th-century photos of early voyages and an audiovisual, immersive journey evoking a voyage by ship. There's plenty to keep the kids interested, too. Outside, you can clamber over the full-scale replica of the 700-tonne *Amsterdam* – one of the largest ships in the Dutch East India Company fleet – with its tiny bunks and sailors' hammocks, and admire the **Royal Barge** in the boathouse.

★NEMO SCIENCE MUSEUM   SCIENCE CENTRE
Map p298 (☑020-244 01 81; www.nemoscience museum.nl; Oosterdok 2; €17.50, roof terrace free; ⊙10am-5.30pm, closed Mon early Sep-early Feb, roof terrace to 9pm Jul & Aug; ⚐; ☐22/48 Kadijksplein) Perched atop the entrance to the IJ Tunnel is this unmissable green-copper building with a slanted roof, designed by Italian architect Renzo Piano and almost surrounded by water. Its rooftop square has great views and water- and wind-operated hands-on exhibits. Inside, everything is interactive, with four floors of investigative mayhem kids of all ages will enjoy. Experiment with lifting yourself up via a pulley, making bubbles, building structures, dividing light into colours, racing your shadow, watching a chain-reaction display and discovering the teenage mind.

Piano conceived the design as the inverse of the IJ Tunnel below. Inside, his design reflects a 'noble factory', with exposed wiring and pipes.

TOP SIGHT
VERZETSMUSEUM

The Dutch Resistance Museum illuminates the reality of German occupation in WWII, using personal stories, films, letters and photographs. To see the museum properly will take at least a couple of hours.

Beginning with the build-up to WWII in the 1930s, the chronologically arranged exhibits give a powerful insight into the difficulties of this most painful period of Dutch history. Details about attempts to resist the Nazis – such as regular strikes, which resulted in harsh punishments and murders – have particular resonance. There is also unflinching evidence of the minority of locals who fell in with the Nazis. The museum uncovers the kinds of active and passive resistance that took place, how the illegal Resistance press operated, how 300,000 people were kept in hiding and how all this was funded. Beneath the mezzanine, an exhibit covers the Dutch role in the Pacific War, particularly in relation to Indonesian independence from the Netherlands. Labels are in Dutch and English.

Included in admission, the Verzetsmuseum Junior relates the stories of four Dutch children with engaging hands-on exhibits, as interesting for adults as it is for kids.

DON'T MISS
➡ The Resistance press exhibits
➡ The Pacific War exhibit
➡ Letters and personal stories

PRACTICALITIES
➡ Map p298, B4
➡ ☑020-620 25 35
➡ www.verzets museum.org
➡ Plantage Kerklaan 61
➡ adult/child €11/6
➡ ⊙10am-5pm Mon-Fri, 11am-5pm Sat & Sun
➡ ☐14 Plantage Kerklaan

OBA: CENTRALE BIBLIOTHEEK AMSTERDAM
LIBRARY

Map p298 (Amsterdam Central Library; ☑020-523 09 00; www.oba.nl; Oosterdokskade 143; ⊘8am-10pm Mon-Fri, 10am-10pm Sat & Sun; ♿; ☒4/12/14/24/26 Centraal Station) **FREE** This being Amsterdam, it has one of the coolest libraries you can imagine, built in 2007 and spread over multiple light, bright floors. The basement is devoted to kids, and has a wigwam, a huge polar bear and the magical, marvellous Mouse Mansion, with 100 beautifully detailed rooms, the work of artist Karina Content. On the 7th floor is the reasonably priced food court, where an outdoor terrace offers thrilling panoramic views across the water to Amsterdam's old town.

ARCAM
ARCHITECTURE

Map p298 (Stichting Architectuurcentrum Amsterdam; ☑020-620 48 78; www.arcam.nl; Prins Hendrikkade 600; ⊘1-5pm Tue-Sun; ☒22/48 Kadijksplein) **FREE** The curved Amsterdam Architecture Foundation, a striking waterside building designed by Dutch architect René van Zuuk, hosts changing architectural exhibitions plus Architecture Talk & Walk tours (€24.50). The tours consist of a 45-minute lecture followed by a guided two-hour walk, and run on Fridays at 1.30pm from April to October.

VERENIGING MUSEUMHAVEN
MUSEUM

Map p298 (Harbour Society Museum; www.museumwerf.nl/museumhaven; Prins Hendriklaan; ☒22/48 Kadijksplein) **FREE** In the port area between the NEMO Science Museum and the Het Scheepvaartmuseum, you'll find an open-air museum of around 20 historical ships docked, complete with information plaques on each of them.

 EATING

You've got lots of eating-out choices in Nieuwmarkt, with some gems amid this central Amsterdam hub. Plantage is only a short bike ride away, but a different world in atmosphere. Head to this leafy district for laid-back neighbourhood restaurants and cafes, while you can expect excellent dining with spectacular river views on the Eastern Islands and Eastern Docklands.

✖ Nieuwmarkt

STERK STAALTJE
DELI €

Map p296 (www.sterkstaaltje.com; Staalstraat 12; dishes €4-10; ⊘8.30am-7pm Mon-Fri, 8.30am-6pm Sat, 10am-7pm Sun; ☒24 Muntplein) With pristine fruit and veg stacked up outside, Sterk Staaltje is worth entering just to breathe in the scent of the foodstuffs, with a fine range of ready-to-eat treats: teriyaki meatballs, spinach and pumpkin quiche, filling salads and hearty soups. The sandwiches are particularly fantastic – roast beef, horseradish and rucola (arugula/rocket) or marinated chicken with guacamole and sour cream.

TOKOMAN
SURINAMESE €

Map p296 (www.tokoman.nl; Waterlooplein 327; sandwiches €3.75-5.50, dishes €6.50-12.50; ⊘11am-7pm Mon-Sat; Ⓜ Waterlooplein) Queue with the folks getting their Surinamese spice on at Tokoman. It makes a sensational *broodje pom*, a sandwich filled with a tasty mash of chicken and a starchy Surinamese tuber. You'll want the *zuur* (pickled cabbage relish) and *peper* (chilli) on it, plus a cold can of coconut water to wash it down. There's another **branch** (Map p296; Zeedijk 136; ⊘11.30am-9.30pm; Ⓜ Nieuwmarkt) close by.

SOUP EN ZO
SOUP €

Map p296 (☑020-422 22 43; www.soupenzo.nl; Jodenbreestraat 94; soup €5-8; ⊘11am-8pm Mon-Fri, noon-7pm Sat & Sun; Ⓜ Waterlooplein) Great when you need your cockles warmed, this is part of a chain that serves delicious fresh soups of the day, which may include a creamy sweet potato with coconut or a hearty lentil beef, as well as salads (*en zo* means 'and so on' in Dutch). There are some outside tables as well as bar stools inside.

OCHA THAI
THAI €

Map p296 (☑020-625 99 58; Binnen Bantammerstraat 1; mains €9-18; ⊘4-10.30pm Tue-Sun; Ⓜ Nieuwmarkt) Nothing fancy, this simple cafe serves up authentic and tasty Thai cuisine – great green and red curries, pad thai and papaya salad – at excellent prices. It's small and it fills up quickly, so expect to share your table. Note: there's no alcohol.

TISFRIS
CAFE €

Map p296 (www.tisfris.nl; St Antoniebreestraat 142; dishes €4.50-14; ⊘9am-8pm; ☒14 Waterlooplein) High-ceilinged TisFris floods with light through huge plate-glass windows, has outdoor seating for sunny days, and is handily located near Rembrandthuis (p89). It's ideal for a drink or a light lunch, such as warm goat's cheese and walnut salad, pumpkin lasagne, a beef or veggie burger, or an open sandwich topped with avocado, creamy paprika hummus and olive tapenade.

TOKO JOYCE INDONESIAN €
Map p296 (www.tokojoyce.nl; Nieuwmarkt 38; dishes €8.50-17; ⏰11am-8pm Tue-Sat, from 1pm Mon & Sun; Ⓜ Nieuwmarkt) With a few bar-stool seats, this cheap and cheerful choice is great for a quick bite. You choose from a selection of Indonesian-Surinamese food; the 'lunch box' (you choose noodles or rice, plus two spicy, coconutty toppings) is great value. There's *spekkoek* (layered gingerbread) to finish and, if you don't fancy eating in, canal-side benches beckon a few steps from the door.

FRENZI MEDITERRANEAN €€
Map p296 (☎020-423 51 12; www.frenzi-restaurant.nl; Zwanenburgwal 232; mains lunch €8-16, mains dinner €17.50-22.50, tapas €5.50-7; ⏰10am-11pm; 🚊24 Muntplein) Frenzi has lots of atmosphere, with its scrubbed wood tables lit with candles and its decorative tiled floor, and serves delicious tapas at dinner – Manchego cheese and fig compote; portobello mushrooms with melted Spanish Cabrales cheese – but save room for mains such as homemade gnocchi or fresh codfish with an almond crust. Sandwiches and salads are on the lunch menu.

POCO LOCO CAFE €€
Map p296 (☎020-624 29 37; www.diningcity.net/pocoloco; Nieuwmarkt 24; mains lunch €4.50-12, dinner €12-18; ⏰9am-1am Sun-Thu, to 3am Fri & Sat; 🍴🖥; Ⓜ Nieuwmarkt) Poco Loco is a good spot for people-watching on Nieuwmarkt, while tucking into filling salads and sandwiches for lunch, or pan-European tapas for dinner, such as prawns fried in garlic oil and *patatas bravas* (potatoes in a spicy sauce). Grab a terrace seat or head into the 1970s-styled interior. The kitchen usually closes around 11pm.

NYONYA ASIAN €€
Map p296 (www.nyonyamalaysiarest.nl; Kloveniersburgwal 38; mains €10-19; ⏰1-9pm; Ⓜ Nieuwmarkt) This little place, a simple cafe with a black and white tiled floor, makes a mean bowl of laksa (spicy noodle soup), a complex beef, chicken or prawn rendang curry (spicy and coconutty), and several other Malaysian specialities, including *nasi goreng* (fried rice). There's no alcohol, but you can sip milky tea or Sarsae, a Chinese root beer. Cash only.

LATEI CAFE €€
Map p296 (www.latei.net; Zeedijk 143; lunch dishes €4-11, dinner mains €9-17; ⏰8am-6pm Mon-Wed, 8am-10pm Thu & Fri, 9am-10pm Sat, 10am-6pm Sun; 🍴🖥; Ⓜ Nieuwmarkt) If you like any of the vintage furnishings at Latei, you can take them home: they're for sale. This laid-back split-level cafe, one of the hipper spots around Nieuwmarkt, serves dinner from Thursday through Saturday, often an Asian dish by the local 'cooking collective'. Otherwise, it's sandwiches, apple pie and *koffie verkeerd* (milky coffee).

HEMELSE MODDER DUTCH €€€
Map p296 (☎020-624 32 03; www.hemelsemodder.nl; Oude Waal 11; 3-/4-/5-course menu €39/49/57; ⏰6-11pm; Ⓜ Nieuwmarkt) 'Heavenly Mud', named after its signature dark and white chocolate mousse, has a stylish mid-century-style interior and a Dutch-meets-global menu that emphasises North Sea fish and farm-fresh produce. Dishes include pan-fried North Sea cod fillet with lemongrass sauce and rack of lamb with white wine gravy. There's a lovely terrace for when the sun comes out.

LASTAGE FRENCH €€€
Map p296 (☎020-737 08 11; www.restaurantlastage.nl; Geldersekade 29; 3-/4-/5-/6-course menus from €49/55/65/75; ⏰6.30-10pm Wed-Sun; 🚊4/12/14/24/26 Centraal Station) Classy Lastage is a gastronomic oasis at the edge of the Red Light District. Step inside and you're a world away from the sleaze nearby, and the creative cooking is equally sophisticated. Black pudding with white asparagus and sea lavender may be followed by lamb with sweetbread and a roasted garlic jus.

✗ Plantage

IJSCUYPJE ICE CREAM €
Map p298 (www.ijscuypje.nl; Plantage Kerklaan 35; ⏰noon-7pm; 🚊14 Plantage Kerklaan) Great ice-cream shop with locations across Amsterdam, including this one close to the zoo. Scoops of dairy-free sorbets or creamy

NAP: AMSTERDAM'S SEA LEVEL MEASUREMENT

It is widely known that Amsterdam (and indeed more than half of the Netherlands) lies a couple of metres below sea level, but when's the last time you heard anyone ask 'which sea level'? In fact, sea levels vary around the globe and even around the Netherlands. The average level of the former Zuiderzee, in the lee of Friesland, was slightly lower than that of the North Sea along the Netherlands' exposed west coast.

The Normaal Amsterdams Peil (NAP; Normal Amsterdam Level) was established in the 17th century as the average high-water mark of the Zuiderzee and it still forms the zero reference for elevation countrywide. It is now used throughout the EU as the European Vertical Reference System (EVRS). The **NAP Visitors Centre** (Map p296; www.normaalamsterdamspeil.nl; Amstel 1; €1; ⊘9am-6pm Mon-Fri; ᰔ14 Waterlooplein) shows the ins and outs of the NAP, with information sheets and a touchscreen to explain the details. Water columns represent different sea levels, as well as disastrous flood levels in 1953 (4.55m above NAP). The centre was closed for repairs at the time of the research.

treats, such as salted caramel and strawberry, are satisfyingly large.

IJSMOLEN
ICE CREAM €

Map p298 (Zeeburgerstraat 2; 1/2/3/4 scoops €1.60/2.90/3.90/4.90; ⊘noon-9pm; ᰔ7 Hoogte Kadijk) Homemade ice cream at this spot near the De Gooyer Windmill (p93) comes in Dutch flavours, such as *stroopwafel* (classic caramel-syrup-filled wafers), plus *stracciatella* (vanilla with shredded chocolate) and strawberry cheesecake. Pure fruity flavours include mango, mint and passionfruit. Cash only.

CAFÉ SMIT EN VOOGT
CAFE €€

Map p298 (http://cafesmitenvoogt.nl; Plantage Parklaan 10; lunch mains €6-10, dinner mains €14-20; ⊘kitchen 10am-9.30pm, bar to 1am; 🛜; ᰔ14 Plantage Kerklaan) On a leafy corner, with high ceilings and a relaxed vibe, this cool and laid-back cafe is ideal for a salad or sandwich for lunch, or a coffee and slice of apple pie when visiting Museum het Rembrandthuis (p89) or the adjacent Wertheimpark (p92). There's also a more substantial dinner menu.

BOX SOCIAAL
INTERNATIONAL €€

Map p298 (☑020-280 55 78; www.boxsociaal.com; Plantage Middenlaan 30a; dishes €8-23; ⊘9am-11pm; 🛜; ᰔ14 Artis) Set up by two Aussies, this stylish neighbourhood cafe opposite the zoo (p93) has you covered any time of the day. Brunch on smashed avo on toast, enjoy all-day pub grub, including an Aussie-style chicken parma, or settle in for a more upmarket dinner of caramelised four-hour-braised beef cheek with Asian slaw, paired with a *stroopwafel* espresso martini.

CAFÉ KADIJK
INDONESIAN €€

Map p298 (☑06 1774 4441; www.cafekadijk.nl; Kadijksplein 5; mains €15-20; ⊘4pm-1am Sun-Thu, to 3am Fri & Sat, kitchen 4-10pm; ᰔ22/48 Kadijksplein) This snug split-level cafe with leaf-print wallpaper is popular for its excellent, good-value Indonesian food, including a mini €20 version of the normally gigantic rijsttafel (Indonesian banquet). There's a big terrace with views across the water in summer. No credit cards.

✖ Eastern Islands

★FRANK'S SMOKEHOUSE
SEAFOOD €€

Map p298 (☑020-585 71 07; www.smokehouse.nl; Oostenburgervoorstraat 1; platters from €16, mains €15-24, sandwiches from €3.50; ⊘deli 10am-7pm Tue-Fri, 9am-6pm Sat, 10am-6pm Sun, restaurant 11.30am-10pm Tue-Sat, to 6pm Sun; ᰔ22 Wittenburgergracht) Frank is a prime supplier to Amsterdam's restaurants, and you can try his renowned smoked fish and meats at this smart deli-restaurant. Delicious takeaway sandwiches (smoked halibut, truffle cheese or warm smoked ham with relish) are available from the deli, or dine in on smoked fish platters, king crab or smoked brisket, along with their excellent beer featuring smoked malt.

You can also pick up some smoked olive oil or smoked chocolate, and have some Alaskan salmon vacuum-packed for travelling (customs regulations permitting).

DE PLANTAGE
EUROPEAN €€

Map p298 (☑020-760 68 00; www.caferestaurantdeplantage.nl; Plantage Kerklaan 36; lunch mains €7.50-21.50, dinner mains €19.50-23.50;

⊙kitchen 9am-10pm Mon-Fri, 10am-10pm Sat & Sun, bar to 1am; ⊟14 Plantage Kerklaan) Huge and graceful, this is an impressive space in an 1870s-built, 1900-expanded former greenhouse decked with blond wood and black chairs, and offering views of the Artis Royal Zoo (p93) aviary. Food is creative and tasty, including ravioli filled with wild boar ragu, and Iberian pork belly with carrot cream and roasted celeriac. Unfortunately the service can be a letdown.

Tables scatter beneath trees strung with fairy lights in summer.

BONBOON   VEGAN €€

Map p298 (☑06 1809 8855; www.bonboon.nl; Piraeusplein 59; mains €19, 3-course menu €35; ⊙6-10pm Wed & Thu, from 1-10pm Fri-Sun; ☑; ⊟7 Azartplein) A sign on the wall reads 'eat beans, not beings' at this creative vegan restaurant opposite the water, with so much more than beans on the menu. Start with beluga lentil and cauliflower cream with truffle oil, then move on to mains such as portobello pie. Dishes are superbly presented and there's a great terrace next to bobbing houseboats.

INSTOCK   INTERNATIONAL €€

Map p298 (☑020-363 57 65; www.instock.nl; Czaar Peterstraat 21; lunch dishes €6-11, dinner dishes €8.90 or 4-course menu €31; ⊙8.30am-10pm Mon-Fri, from 10am Sat & Sun; ☑; ⊟7 Eerste Coehoornstraat) ✔ Instock's food is extremely tasty, with some surprising combinations – like a talented chef has conjured up a great meal from leftovers! This is precisely the raison d'être of Instock: reducing food waste by using products that are still in date but would otherwise be thrown out. It also offers fine Pieper beer, made from some of the Netherlands' 340 million annually discarded potatoes.

There's a terrace on the quiet street, the interior is light and bright, and there's live music on Saturday nights. Cards only – no cash.

HAPPYHAPPYJOYJOY   ASIAN €€

Map p298 (☑020-344 64 24; www.happyhappy joyjoy.asia; Oostelijke Handelskade 4; dishes €6-13; ⊙noon-1am; ☎; ⊟26 Rietlandpark) Happy happy joy joy is how you'll feel after digging into some tasty Asian fusion. Sit under hanging red lanterns out front or take in the eye-catching interior of vintage Chinese posters and bright paper umbrellas. The kitchen (in a Chinese shipping crate) turns out everything from a Peking duck bao to a fresh, spicy green prawn curry.

There are a few branches around town.

ÉÉNVISTWÉÉVIS   SEAFOOD €€

Map p298 (☑020-623 28 94; www.eenvistwee vis.nl; Schippersgracht 6; mains €18.50-25.50, 3-/4-course menu €34.50/41.50; ⊙6-10pm Tue-Sat; ⊟22/48 Kadijksplein) With a chandelier interior, this small, unassuming yet classy Amsterdam favourite is the type of place locals put on their best shirt to go to. The short menu revels in simplicity and utilises whatever is in season, such as oysters, prawns and white asparagus.

KOMPASZAAL   CAFE €€

Map p298 (☑020-419 95 96; www.kompaszaal.nl; KNSM-laan 311; lunch dishes €6-10, dinner mains €15.50-18.50; ⊙10am-5pm Wed, 10am-1am Thu & Fri, 11am-1am Sat & Sun; ☎; ⊟7 Azartplein) Set in the century-old Royal Dutch Steamboat Company (KNSM in Dutch) arrivals hall, this huge, airy cafe has kept some vintage fittings and there's a long balcony overlooking the river. Light lunches include *croque monsieurs* and tuna melts, while for dinner you can tuck into more substantial dishes, or drop in for high tea (Wednesday to Sunday, 1pm to 3.30pm).

Regular 1950s swing, jazz, tango and salsa events take place on Friday nights.

★GEBR HARTERING   DUTCH €€€

Map p296 (☑020-421 06 99; www.gebr-harter ing.nl; Peperstraat 10; mains €27.50, 5-/7-course menus €55/80; ⊙6-10.30pm; ⊟22/48 Prins Hendrikkade) Lined in pale rustic wood, this gem was founded by two food-loving brothers, who offer either à la carte or a multi-course menu that changes daily according to the best seasonal produce available. A meal here is always a delight to linger over, so settle in and enjoy the accompanying wines and peaceful canal-side location.

★GREETJE   DUTCH €€€

Map p298 (☑020-779 74 50; www.restaurant greetje.nl; Peperstraat 23-25; mains €24-29; ⊙6-10pm; ⊟22/48 Prins Hendrikkade) ✔ This is Amsterdam's most creative Dutch restaurant, using the best seasonal produce to resurrect and re-create traditional recipes, such as slow-cooked veal with Dutch-brandy-marinated apricots and suckling pork in apple syrup with mustard sauce. The tasting menu (€55) starts with the Big Beginning, a selection of six starters served high-tea style.

DRINKING & NIGHTLIFE

There are plenty of bars and coffeeshops around Nieuwmarkt, whose pavement cafes are perfect for watching the world go by. For something a bit more quirky, head to the Brouwerij 't IJ microbrewery adjacent to the De Gooyer Windmill. To hang with the city's cool crowd, make your way to the Eastern Islands' fabulous shack-like hangouts, including Hannekes Boom (p101), a hipster beer garden with a waterfront location.

Nieuwmarkt

⭐ROSALIA'S MENAGERIE   COCKTAIL BAR
Map p296 (☎020-330 62 41; www.rosalias.amsterdam; Kloveniersburgwal 20; ◷6pm-late; MNieuwmarkt) Named after the owner's grandmother, this charming bar in the canal-side boutique hotel, Misc EatDrinkSleep (p221), feels like your grandma's living room with its rich floral wallpaper, knick-knacks and baroque armchairs. It serves expertly made tipples focusing on Dutch heritage, including *jenever*-based cocktails and organic wines, and a small menu of tasty snacks. Best to book a table ahead on weekends.

⭐DE SLUYSWACHT   BROWN CAFE
Map p296 (☎020-625 76 11; www.sluyswacht.nl; Jodenbreestraat 1; ◷12.30pm-1am Mon-Thu, to 3am Fri & Sat, to 7pm Sun; MWaterlooplein, ⓣ14 Waterlooplein) Out on a limb by the canal and listing like a ship in high winds, this tiny black building dating to 1695 was once a lock-keeper's house on the Oude Schans. The canal-side terrace with views of the Montelbaanstoren is a charming spot to relax with a Dutch or Belgian beer and bar snacks, including *bitterballen* (deep-fried meatballs), chips and toasties.

BLUEBIRD   COFFEESHOP
Map p296 (Sint Antoniesbreestraat 71; ◷9.30am-1am; 🛜; MNieuwmarkt) Away from Niewmarkt's main cluster of coffeeshops, Bluebird does attract tourists but it has a more local vibe. The multiroom space has murals and local artists' paintings, a non-alcoholic bar with organic herbal teas and a kitchen serving snacks, such as pancakes and pizza. It's especially well known for its hash, including varieties not available elsewhere in Amsterdam. Cash only.

CAFE DE ENGELBEWAARDER   BROWN CAFE
Map p296 (☎020-625 37 72; www.cafe-de-engelbewaarder.nl; Kloveniersburgwal 59; ◷10am-1am Mon-Thu, 10am-3am Fri & Sat, 11am-1am Sun; MNieuwmarkt) A cafe for literature and music lovers, with regular photographic exhibitions, this is a peaceful canal-side haven, renowned for its in-house live jazz band on Sunday afternoon from 4.30pm to 7pm September to June. It specialises in Belgian brews from the Palm brewery, and there are around 20 beers on tap.

LOKAAL 'T LOOSJE   BROWN CAFE
Map p296 (☎020-627 26 35; www.loosje.nl; Nieuwmarkt 32-34; ◷8.30am-1am Sun-Thu, to 3am Fri & Sat; MNieuwmarkt) A colourful mix of locals and tourists throng the tables to sip drinks – including beers by local breweries Oedipus (p204) and 2 Chefs – at this venerable cafe on Nieuwmarkt. Inside are fine pictorial tiling walls, mosaic floor and stencilled glass, and wicker chairs spill onto the herringbone pavement terrace out front in fine weather.

CAFE CUBA   COCKTAIL BAR
Map p296 (www.cafecuba.nl; Nieuwmarkt 3; ◷1pm-1am Mon-Thu, 11am-3am Fri & Sat, 11am-1am Sun; MNieuwmarkt) This is where the classic Dutch brown cafe (pub) meets the Caribbean: there's a background of faded decadence, palm-leaf-print walls, rattan lightshades and photos of Hemingway. It's an ideal Nieuwmarkt spot for slouching behind a table, preparing for the night ahead with cocktails such as mai tais and mojitos.

Plantage

⭐BROUWERIJ 'T IJ   BREWERY
Map p298 (www.brouwerijhetij.nl; Funenkade 7; ◷brewery 2-8pm, English tour 3.30pm Fri-Sun; 🚍7 Hoogte Kadijk) 🍺 Can you get more Dutch than drinking a craft beer beneath the creaking sails of the 1725-built De Gooyer Windmill? Amsterdam's leading microbrewery makes delicious standard, seasonal and limited-edition brews; try the smooth, fruity 'tripel' Zatte, which was their first creation back in 1985. Enjoy yours in the tiled tasting room, lined by an amazing bottle collection, or the plane-tree-shaded terrace.

WORTH A DETOUR

IJBURG

Amsterdam's newest neighbourhood, IJburg, feels like an architectural vision of a model city. Construction by the city of Amsterdam first started on these three artificial islands – Steigereiland, Haveneiland and Rieteilanden – in the IJmeer lake in 1996 to ease Amsterdam's housing shortage, and the first IJburg residents arrived in 2002. It's a 15-minute tram ride (26) from Centraal Station, or less than 10 minutes from the Eastern Islands.

It's best visited on a warm sunny day, when you can take advantage of Amsterdam's (artificial) beach, **Blijburg** (🚋IJburg), a lovely swathe of white imported sand at the eastern end of IJburg. You can go windsurfing or paddle boarding here; **Surfcenter IJburg** (www.surfcenterijburg.nl; Pampuslaan 497; windsurfer/SUP rental per hour €20/10; ⊙11am-6.30pm Sat & Sun May-Oct, 3-9.30pm Wed-Fri Jun-Sep) rents windsurfers from its shipping container.

The area is also home to some great restaurants, cafes and bars. **Espressofabriek** (www.espressofabriek.nl; IJburglaan 1489; ⊙8am-6pm Mon-Fri, from 10am Sat & Sun; 🛜) is a modern neighbourhood cafe with loads of natural light and well-made coffee using single-origin beans roasted locally at their Westerpark branch. You can also snack on delicious homemade vegan cakes and muffins.

Organic produce is prioritised by the passionate Italian chefs at **Restaurant Bloem** (📞020-416 06 77; www.bloemopijburg.nl; IJburglaan 1289; mains €16-24; ⊙5.30-10pm), where the breezy beach-style decor belies the exceptional food. The menu changes daily but might include house-made linguine with clams, chilli and parsley, or fresh tuna grilled with white asparagus and served with green-bean salsa, as well as authentic wood-fired pizzas. Cash only.

Fittingly named for the Normaal Amsterdams Peil (NAP, p97), Amsterdam's sea-level benchmark, harbourside restaurant **NAP** (📞020-416 40 00; www.napamsterdam.nl; Krijn Taconiskade 124; mains €14-22, tapas €4-13.50; ⊙8.30am-midnight Mon-Thu, 8.30am-3am Fri, 10am-1am Sat, 10am-midnight Sun; 🚼) has a terrace overlooking IJburg's boat-filled marina and a chic semi-industrial interior. Tapas dishes include spicy prawns and oysters with vinaigrette, while mains might include ravioli with pumpkin and truffle or steak with red-wine gravy and fries.

There are also ferries from IJburg to Muiden (p192), the most scenic way to visit its medieval castle, the Muiderslot, and fortress island, Pampus. The **boat** (📞020-427 88 88; www.amsterdamtouristferry.com; Bert Haanstrakade 1051, IJburg; adult/child ferry & admission to either Pampus or Muiderslot €21/16; ⊙11am Tue-Sun Apr-Oct) leaves mid-morning, allowing a couple of hours' exploration before the return journey.

Tasting flights of five beers go for €10.50. A beer is included in the 30-minute brewery tour that runs in English at 3.30pm Friday to Sunday (€6.50).

⭐**SKYLOUNGE** COCKTAIL BAR
Map p298 (📞020-530 08 75; www.skyloungeamsterdam.com; Oosterdoksstraat 4; ⊙11am-1am Sun-Tue, to 2am Wed & Thu, to 3am Fri & Sat; 🛜; 🚋4/12/14/24/26 Centraal Station) With wow-factor views whatever the weather, this bar offers a 360-degree panorama of Amsterdam from the 11th floor of the DoubleTree Amsterdam Centraal Station hotel – and it gets better when you head out to its vast SkyTerrace, with an outdoor bar. Toast the view with a huge range of cocktails, craft beers and spirits. DJs regularly hit the decks from 9pm.

CAFÉ KOOSJE BROWN CAFE
Map p298 (www.koosjeamsterdam.nl; Plantage Middenlaan 37; ⊙8am-1am Mon-Thu, to 3am Fri, to 2am Sat; 🚋14 Plantage Kerklaan) Between the Artis Royal Zoo and the Hollandsche Schouwburg, Koosje has a lovely location, where you can perch at the window or on the terrace and sup wine or Dutch draft or bottled beers. Snaffle sandwiches for lunch, such as cheese, pickle and mustard, and choose between dishes from chicken satay to vegetarian lasagne for dinner.

DE GROENE OLIFANT
BROWN CAFE

Map p298 (www.degroeneolifant.nl; Sarphatistraat 510; ⊙11am-1am Sun-Thu, to 3am Fri & Sat; 🛈; 🚋9/14 Alexanderplein) A local favourite for generations, the Green Elephant is 19th-century elegance meets modern bohemian, with tiled floors, dark bentwood chairs and leaf-print wallpaper. Sit at the wood-panelled circa-1880 bar and admire the art deco stained glass, retreat to the lofted dining room for dinner or catch some rays on the popular outdoor terrace.

🍺 Eastern Islands

★HANNEKES BOOM
BEER GARDEN

Map p298 (📞020-419 98 20; www.hannekes boom.nl; Dijksgracht 4; ⊙11am-1am Sun-Thu, to 3am Fri & Sat; 🚋26 Muziekgebouw) Reachable via a couple of pedestrian/bike bridges from the NEMO Science Museum (p94), this cool, laid-back waterside cafe is built from recycled materials and has a fantastic leafy beer garden. Join the arty crowd enjoying the sunshine at brightly coloured picnic tables under the trees. If the weather's no good, cosy into a vintage armchair by the fire inside.

The site dates back to 1662, when it was a guard post monitoring maritime traffic into the city.

DE NIEUWE KHL
BAR

Map p298 (📞020-779 15 75; www.khl.nl; Oostelijke Handelskade 44; ⊙4pm-midnight; 🛈; 🚋26 Rietlandpark) Set in a historic 1917 brick building with stunning tilework and a retro colour scheme of pale green and pink, KHL's bar opens to a vine-shaded terrace that makes a superb spot for a glass of wine sourced from small vineyards. Regular live events range from Dutch folk bands to cabaret matinees on Sundays.

KANIS & MEILAND
CAFE

Map p298 (📞020-737 06 74; www.kanisenmei land.nl; Levantkade 127; ⊙10am-1am; 🛈; 🚋7 Azartplein) 'Islanders' love this hidden-away waterfront place, a lovely spot for Dutch and Belgian beers, cocktails or a glass of wine. There's a fab terrace overlooking houseboats on the water, and the interior is large but cosy with wooden tables and tall windows facing the 'mainland'. It serves tasty sandwiches and soup for lunch, and sophisticated dinner mains.

HPS
COCKTAIL BAR

Map p298 (📞06 2528 3620; www.hpsamster dam.com; Rapenburg 18; ⊙6pm-1am Sun-Thu, to 3am Fri & Sat; 🚋32/33 Prins Hendrikkade) Art deco lights, floral wallpaper, chesterfields and waistcoated mixologists-as-alchemists behind the bar set the scene at the sophisticated yet cosy HPS (Hiding in Plain Sight). The maestro mixers produce concoctions such as Dillicious (dill-infused vodka, pickled lemon and ginger beer) and Beetlejuice (tequila, jalapeno-infused Cointreau, fresh beetroot juice and balsamic vinegar), and the service is warm and friendly.

DE DRUIF
BROWN CAFE

Map p298 (Rapenburgerplein 83; ⊙3pm-1am Sun-Thu, to 3am Fri & Sat; 🚋22 Kadijksplein) A jovial canal-side watering hole, 'The Grape' is one of Amsterdam's oldest pubs and was once a distillery, evident in its gas chandeliers, carpet-lined tables and spirit barrels lining the wall behind the bar. Sample the range of beers and *jenever* while soaking up the sun on its terrace, or stay cosy indoors with a window seat and canal views.

ENTERTAINMENT

Head to the IJ waterfront for jazz and classical concerts at the striking Muziekgebouw aan 't IJ and Bimhuis (p102), catch an opera or ballet performance at the Muziektheater, or settle in for an art-house flick at the Kriterion (p102) cinema. Kids will love the puppetry at the Amsterdams Marionetten Theater (p102).

MUZIEKTHEATER
CLASSICAL MUSIC

Map p296 (📞020-625 54 55; www.operaballet. nl; Waterlooplein 22; ⊙box office noon-6pm Mon-Fri, to 3pm Sat & Sun or until performance Sep-Jul; Ⓜ️Waterlooplein, 🚋14 Waterlooplein) The Muziektheater is home to the Netherlands Opera and the National Ballet, with some spectacular performances. Big-name performers and international dance troupes also take the stage here. Free classical concerts (12.30pm to 1pm) are held most Tuesdays from September to June in its Boekmanzaal; doors open at 12.15pm.

MUZIEKGEBOUW AAN 'T IJ
CONCERT VENUE

Map p298 (📞tickets 020-788 20 00; www.muziek gebouw.nl; Piet Heinkade 1; ⊙box office 2-6pm Mon-Sat; 🚋26 Muziekgebouw) A dramatic glass-and-steel box on the IJ waterfront, this multidisciplinary performing-arts venue has a state-of-the-art main hall with flexible stage layout and great acoustics. Its jazz stage, Bimhuis, is more intimate. Try the Last Minute Ticket Shop (www.last minuteticketshop.nl) for discounts.

MEZRAB –
HOUSE OF STORIES   PERFORMING ARTS

Map p298 (www.mezrab.nl; Veemkade 576; ☺8pm-1am Sun-Thu, to 3am Fri & Sat; ☐26 Kattenburgerstraat) This wonderfully eclectic harbourside cultural centre hosts storytelling sessions in English and Dutch, Iranian rock bands, hip-swinging Latin American bands, European folk dances, comedy nights and much more. Hours can vary.

KRITERION   CINEMA

Map p298 (☎020-623 17 08; www.kriterion.nl; Roetersstraat 170; tickets from €5; ☐7 Weesperplein) Kriterion was originally a student organisation involved in hiding and protecting Jews from the Nazis during WWII. In 1945 the group opened this cinema to provide employment for students unable to complete their studies. Today it's still going strong, with a great array of art-house premieres, classics and kids flicks, plus there's a cafe-bar. Check the website for English-language screenings.

AMSTERDAMS
MARIONETTEN THEATER   PUPPETRY

Map p296 (☎020-620 80 27; www.marionetten theater.nl; Nieuwe Jonkerstraat 8; adult/child €16/7.50, 90-min tour €15; Ⓜ️Nieuwmarkt) An enchanting enterprise that seems to exist in another era, this marionette theatre presents fairy tales and Mozart operas, such as *The Magic Flute,* in a former blacksmith's shop. Kids and adults alike are enthralled by the magical stage sets, period costumes and beautiful singing voices that bring the diminutive cast to life.

BIMHUIS   JAZZ

Map p298 (☎020-788 21 88; www.bimhuis.nl; Piet Heinkade 3; ☐26 Muziekgebouw) On the IJ riverbank, Bimhuis is the Netherlands' most important jazz venue. Its stylish digs are at the Muziekgebouw aan 't IJ (p101) and it draws international jazz greats, along with hosting world music, electronica and other genres.

 # SHOPPING

Nieuwmarkt has lots of small boutiques and a few interesting independent shops, selling everything from fetish-wear to haberdashery, while Waterlooplein hosts a pretty decent flea market. There is a cluster of the city's chicest homeware shops on the Eastern Islands.

🔒 Nieuwmarkt

★HÔTEL DROOG   DESIGN

Map p296 (www.droog.com; Staalstraat 7; ☺9am-7pm; ☐24 Muntplein) Not a hotel, but a local design house. Droog means 'dry' in Dutch, and these products are full of dry wit. You'll find all kinds of stylish versions of useful things – a clothes-hanger lamp or streamlined hot water bottle – as well as the kind of clothing that should probably by law only be worn by a designer or an architect.

Also here is a gallery space, a delightful fairy-tale garden and a high-beamed all-white cafe, overlooked by a tapestry of Rembrandt's *The Night Watch.* To live the life, rent the top-floor apartment (double €300, book well in advance).

WATERLOOPLEIN FLEA MARKET   MARKET

Map p296 (www.waterlooplein.amsterdam; Waterlooplein; ☺9.30am-6pm Mon-Sat; Ⓜ️Waterlooplein; ☐14 Waterlooplein) Covering the square once known as Vlooienburg (Flea Town), this flea market isn't huge but there are some good finds (and a bit of tourist tat, too) including handicrafts, antiques, records and vintage leather coats. The street market started in 1880, when Jewish traders living in the neighbourhood began selling their wares here.

WEBERS   ADULT

Map p296 (☎020-638 17 77; www.webershol land.nl; Kloveniersburgwal 26; ☺1-7pm; Ⓜ️Nieuwmarkt) Housed in the historic Kleine Trippenhuis (p92), this is where to get your kinky boots, and all other forms of top-end sauce, with every kind of fetish-wear imaginable (and unimaginable).

ANTIQUES MARKET   MARKET

Map p296 (Nieuwmarkt; ☺9am-5pm Sun; Ⓜ️Nieuwmarkt) Treasure hunters will find lots of old books and bric-a-brac to peruse.

JACOB HOOY & CO
COSMETICS

Map p296 (www.jacobhooy.nl; Kloveniersburgwal 12; ⊙10am-6pm Mon-Fri, to 5pm Sat; MNieuwmarkt) A proper apothecary shop, lined by wooden drawers and rounded barrels with their contents inscribed in flowing font, Jacob Hooy & Co has been selling medicinal herbs, homeopathic remedies and natural cosmetics since 1743. It also now sells a range of body lotion, herbal tea, cosmetics and organic wine.

PUCCINI BOMBONI
CHOCOLATE

Map p296 (www.puccinibomboni.com; Staalstraat 17; ⊙9am-7pm Mon-Fri, 11am-7pm Sat & Sun; ⊡24 Muntplein) 🍫 Chocolate bonbons are piled up in pyramids that are works of art here, full of rich and distinctive flavours such as tamarind, lemongrass, sour cherry and calvados, and the beans are sourced from sustainable farms. Note: the shop has been known to close in warm weather – for the sake of the chocolates, of course.

RETRO & CHIC
VINTAGE

Map p296 (Staalstraat 21; ⊙11am-6.30pm Tue-Sat, from noon Mon & Sun; MWaterlooplein) One of Amsterdam's many vintage shops, this stands out for the hand-picked feel and quality of its retro collection. There's some super jewellery as well as silk gowns and splendid hats.

BOERENMARKT
MARKET

Map p296 (Farmers Market; Nieuwmarkt; ⊙9am-4pm Sat; MNieuwmarkt) 🍎 Stalls selling organic foods and produce draw crowds on Saturdays.

KNUFFELS
TOYS

Map p296 (www.knuffels.nl; St Antoniesbreestraat 39-51; ⊙10am-6pm; ♿; MNieuwmarkt) Bobbing mobiles and suspended toys have a motor and strings keeping them in fascinating constant motion in the window of this busy toyshop. There are plenty of *knuffels* (soft cuddly toys), puppets, teddies and jigsaw puzzles.

JOE'S VLIEGERWINKEL
TOYS

Map p296 (Nieuwe Hoogstraat 19; ⊙noon-6pm Tue-Fri, to 5pm Sat; MNieuwmarkt) Kids and grown-ups will appreciate this specialised kite shop, which also sells lots of other random stuff, from solar-powered hula dancers to lantern fairy lights. You can also buy build-it-yourself kits.

HENXS
CLOTHING

Map p296 (www.henxs.com; St Antoniesbreestraat 136-138; ⊙11am-7pm Mon-Sat, noon-6pm Sun; MNieuwmarkt) This store is skater and graffiti-artist heaven with clothing, graffiti supplies and edgy accessories.

🏛 Eastern Islands

POLS POTTEN
HOMEWARES

Map p298 (☏020-419 35 41; www.polspotten.nl; Loods 6, KNSM-laan 39; ⊙10am-6pm Tue-Sat, noon-5pm Sun; ⊡7 Azartplein) The Eastern Islands are particularly style conscious, and the go-to shop for local residents, as well as stylish Amsterdammers from all over, is this large interior-design store. With plenty of hip colourful furniture, as well as fabulous ceramics and hand-blown glassware, it's a good spot to pick up a gift or souvenir.

🏃 SPORTS & ACTIVITIES

TUNFUN
PLAYGROUND

Map p296 (www.tunfun.nl; Mr Visserplein 7; adult/child €3/8.50; ⊙10am-6pm, last entry 5pm; ♿; ⊡14 Mr Visserplein) A great way to entertain kids on a rainy day (although this is when it's busiest), this indoor playground occupies a former traffic underpass. Kids can clamber over soft play equipment, jump on trampolines, try to escape the 'black box' and play on a soccer pitch. There's a cafe serving kids favourites, such as *poffertjes* (small pancakes) and Nutella sandwiches.

Kids must be accompanied by an adult. The entrance is located opposite the Portuguese-Israelite Synagogue; look for the two green arches and stairs leading down. Adult entry price includes tea or coffee.

GLOWGOLF
MINIGOLF

Map p298 (☏020-737 18 09; www.glowgolf.nl/en/amsterdam; Prins Hendrikkade 194; adult/child €10/9; ⊙11am-9pm Sun-Wed, to 11pm Thu, to midnight Fri & Sat; ⊡22 Kadijksplein) From the street Noah's Arq looks like a normal pub, but down in the basement it harbours this trippy mini-golf course. The 15 psychedelically coloured holes are played under black light, making them glow luridly in the dark (and making you feel like you're inside a giant pinball machine). The 3D glasses really max out the surreal experience.

Western Canal Ring

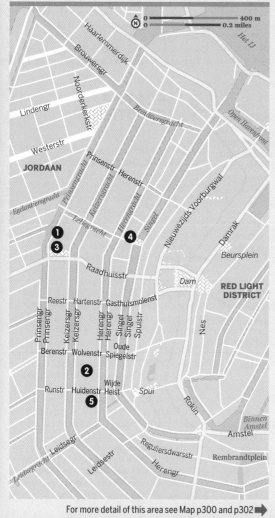

Neighbourhood Top Five

1 **Anne Frank Huis** (p106) Contemplating the brave life and tragic death of the most famous Dutch girl in history in the poignant 'Secret Annexe' of the house where she and her family hid from the Nazis.

2 **Negen Straatjes** (p115) Browsing the speciality shops along these compact and captivating 'nine streets' criss-crossed by picturesque canals.

3 **Westerkerk** (p108) Scaling the bell tower, seeing the Netherlands' largest nave and catching a carillon recital.

4 **Reypenaer Cheese Tasting** (p116) Learning to distinguish an aged Gouda from a young *boerenkaas* (farmer's cheese).

5 **Bijbels Museum** (p108) Viewing rare bibles, a scale model of the Jewish Tabernacle and biblical plants in the garden of this canal-house-turned-museum.

For more detail of this area see Map p300 and p302 ➡

Explore Western Canal Ring

This whole area is a Unesco World Heritage site and you could spend countless hours admiring the architecture along its canals. And while the neighbourhood is loaded with high-profile sights, much of the charm here is simply soaking up the atmosphere: from the street, from a boat, from a backyard garden, from a rooftop balcony or from the terrace of a canal-side cafe.

Begin your first day at the neighbourhood's northern end around the hip Haarlemmerbuurt shopping district and work your way south, weaving in and out of the lanes and canals to visit the Multatuli Museum (p109), admire the architecture of the Huis Met de Hoofden (p109) and pay homage to the Homomonument (p109) and the Westerkerk (p108) until you wind up (having prebooked!) at the Anne Frank Huis (p106) in the early evening, when it's least crowded.

On your second day, start with some of Amsterdam's most enjoyable shopping along the Negen Straatjes (p115; Nine Streets). This tic-tac-toe board of *straatjes* (small streets) is full of one-off speciality shops and quirky little boutiques stocking antiques, fashion and homewares. The area is dotted with drinking and dining venues whose clientele spills out into the streets in warmer weather.

Make time to check out the Bijbels Museum (p108), canal-house museum Het Grachtenhuis (p108) and the Huis Marseille (p108) photography museum, before finishing up at the Prinsengracht's bars and restaurants.

Local Life

→ **Borrel** Brown cafes (pubs) such as Café de Vergulde Gaper (p114) are especially popular for the time-honoured Dutch tradition of *borrel* (p51).

→ **Snacks** Join locals queuing for fries slathered in mayonnaise or spicier sauces at Wil Graanstra Friteshuis (p110).

→ **Canals** The Prinsengracht (p111) is a perennial favourite, whatever the weather.

→ **Food and fashion** The Haarlemmerbuurt (p114), incorporating Haarlemmerstraat, is a hotspot for restaurants, gourmet provisions and kitchen shops, interspersed with edgy fashion boutiques.

Getting There & Away

→ **Trams** Trams 13 and 17 stop near the main attractions. Any tram that stops near the Dam or Spui is convenient for the area's south, while Centraal Station is handy for the northern end.

→ **Boat** The Canal Bus stop (Map p300) near Westermarkt is handy for the Anne Frank Huis.

Lonely Planet's Top Tip

Thursday is an ideal time to discover this neighbourhood, when many businesses – including numerous shops in the jewel-box-like Negen Straatjes (p115) (Nine Streets) – are open extended hours.

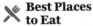
Best Places to Eat

→ De Belhamel (p110)
→ Bistro Bij ons (p110)
→ Petit Gâteau (p110)
→ Vinnies Deli (p110)

For reviews, see p109.➡

Best Places to Drink

→ 't Arendsnest (p112)
→ Café de Vergulde Gaper (p114)
→ Café het Molenpad (p112)
→ Café Tabac (p112)
→ De Doffer (p114)

For reviews, see p112.➡

Best Places to Shop

→ Frozen Fountain (p115)
→ 360 Volt (p115)
→ De Kaaskamer (p115)
→ Love Stories (p115)
→ Denham the Jeanmaker (p115)
→ Vanilia (p115)

For reviews, see p114.➡

WESTERN CANAL RING

◉ TOP SIGHT
ANNE FRANK HUIS

It is one of the 20th century's most compelling stories: a young Jewish girl forced into hiding with her family and their friends to escape deportation by the Nazis. The house they used as a hideaway should be a highlight of any visit to Amsterdam; indeed, it attracts some 1¼ million visitors a year.

Background

Stepping through the bookcase that swings open to reveal the 'Secret Annexe' and going up the steep stairs into the living quarters – where the Frank family lived for more than two years – is to step back into a time that seems both distant and tragically real.

It took the German army just five days to occupy all of the Netherlands, along with Belgium and much of France. And once Hitler's forces had swept across the country, many Jews – including Anne Frank and her family – went into hiding. Anne's diary describes how restrictions were gradually imposed on Dutch Jews: from being forbidden to ride streetcars to being forced to hand over their bicycles and not being allowed to visit Christian friends.

The Franks moved into the upper floors of the specially prepared rear of the building, along with another couple, the Van Pels (called the Van Daans in Anne's diary), and their son, Peter. Four months later Fritz Pfeffer (called Mr Dussel in the diary) joined the household. Here they survived until they were betrayed to the Gestapo in August 1944.

Ground Floor

Entered from Westermarkt, the house is contained within a modern, square shell that retains the original feel of the building (it was used during WWII as offices and a warehouse).

DON'T MISS

➡ Anne's red plaid diary
➡ Anne's bedroom
➡ WWII newsreels
➡ Peter van Pels' room
➡ Video of Anne's schoolmate Hanneli Goslar

PRACTICALITIES

➡ Map p300, A6
➡ ☎020-556 71 05
➡ www.annefrank.org
➡ Prinsengracht 263-267
➡ adult/child €10.50/5.50
➡ ⊙9am-10pm Apr-Oct, 9am-7pm Sun-Fri, to 10pm Sat Nov-Mar
➡ 🚊13/17 Westermarkt

Its expanded museum shows multilingual news reels of WWII footage narrated using segments of Anne's diary: it inextricably links the rise of Hitler with the Frank family's personal saga.

Offices

View the former offices of Victor Kugler, Otto Frank's business partner; his identity card and the film magazines he bought for Anne are on display. The other office area belonged to Miep Gies, Bep Voskuijl and Johannes Kleiman, two women and a man who worked in the office by day and provided food, clothing, school supplies and other goods – often purchased on the black market or with ration cards – for the eight members of the Secret Annexe. You can see some of their personal documents here.

Secret Annexe

While the lower levels present history with interactive modern technology, the former living quarters of the Frank family in the *achterhuis* (rear house) retain their stark, haunting austerity. It's as if visitors are stepping back into 1942. Notice how windows of the annexe were blacked out to avoid arousing suspicion among people who might see it from surrounding houses (blackouts were common practice to disorient bombers at night).

Take a moment to observe the ingenious set-up of the Secret Annexe as you walk through. You then enter two floors of the dark and airless space where the Franks and their friends observed complete silence during the daytime until they were betrayed, arrested by the Nazis and sent to concentration camps. Otto Frank, Anne's father, was the only survivor.

Anne's Bedroom

As you enter Anne's small, simple bedroom, which she shared with Fritz Pfeffer, you can still sense the remnants of a young girl's dreams: the physical evidence of her interests and longings is on the wall with her photos of Hollywood stars and postcards of the Dutch royal family.

The Diary

More haunting exhibits and videos await after you return to the front house – including Anne's red plaid diary itself, sitting alone in its glass case. Watch the video of Anne's old schoolmate Hanneli Goslar, who describes encountering Anne at Bergen-Belsen.

AFTER THE WAR

The Franks were among the last Jews to be deported and Anne died in the Bergen-Belsen concentration camp in March 1945, only weeks before it was liberated. After the war, Otto published Anne's diary, which was found among the litter in the annexe (the furniture had been carted away by the Nazis).

TICKETS

It's compulsory to prepurchase tickets (€0.50 surcharge) via the website, when you must also choose a time slot. While 80% of tickets are released two months ahead, 20% are made available online on the day. You'll need to preprint tickets or show them on your phone.

WESTE.
Map p300 (l
amsterdam.nl;
⊙9am-8pm Mon-
als

◉ SIGHTS

The Anne Frank Huis (p106) is the neighbourhood's number-one drawcard, but other engaging museums include the fascinating canal-house museum Het Grachtenhuis. Climbing the striking Westerkerk bell tower rewards with spectacular views over the canals.

ANNE FRANK HUIS   MUSEUM
See p106.

HET GRACHTENHUIS   MUSEUM
Map p302 (Canal House; ☎020-421 16 56; www.hetgrachtenhuis.nl; Herengracht 386; adult/child €15/7.50; ⊙10am-5pm Tue-Sun; ☒2/11/12 Koningsplein) Learn about the remarkable feats of engineering behind the Canal Ring through this museum's holograms, videos, models, cartoons, scale model of Amsterdam and other innovative exhibits, which explain how the canals and the houses that line them were built. Unlike at most Amsterdam museums, you can't simply wander through: small groups go in together to experience the multimedia exhibits. It takes about 45 minutes, and you'll come out knowing why Amsterdam's houses tilt. Admission includes an audioguide.

WESTERKERK   CHURCH
Map p300 (Western Church; ☎020-624 77 66; www.westerkerk.nl; Prinsengracht 281; ⊙10am-3pm Mon-Sat early May-Oct, 10am-3pm Mon-Fri Nov-early May; ☒13/17 Westermarkt) The main gathering place for Amsterdam's Dutch Reformed community, this church was built for rich Protestants to a 1620 design by Hendrick de Keyser. The nave is the largest in the Netherlands and is covered by a wooden barrel vault. The huge main organ dates from 1686, with panels decorated with instruments and biblical scenes. Rembrandt, who died bankrupt at nearby Rozengracht, was buried in a pauper's grave somewhere in the church. Its bell tower can be climbed.

Look out for free 30-minute lunchtime concerts in the summer months. Year-round, carillon recitals are held from noon to 1pm on Tuesday; the best place to listen ⸮ from the nearby Bloemgracht. The bells ⸮ chime mechanically every 15 minutes.

⸮KERK BELL TOWER   TOWER
⸮020-689 25 65; www.westertoren
⸮rinsengracht 281; tours €9;
⸮at Apr-Sep, 9am-5.30pm

Oct; ☒13/17 Westermarkt) The bell tower of the Westerkerk is famously topped by the blue imperial crown that Habsburg emperor Maximilian I bestowed on the city for its coat of arms in 1489. The climb up the stairs of the 85m tower can be strenuous and claustrophobic, but the guide takes breaks on the landings while describing the bells, and the panoramic views are worth it. Tours depart every half hour. Children under six aren't permitted.

WEST-INDISCH HUIS   HISTORIC BUILDING
Map p300 (West Indies House; Herenmarkt 97; ☒18/21/22 Buiten Brouwersstraat) Built in 1617 as a meat market and militia barracks, this historical building was rented by the Dutch West India Company (Geoctroyeerde West-Indische Compagnie; GWC) as its headquarters in 1623. It was here that the GWC's governors signed off on the construction of a fort on the island of Manhattan in 1625, establishing New Amsterdam (now New York City).

BIJBELS MUSEUM   MUSEUM
Map p302 (Bible Museum; ☎020-624 24 36; www.bijbelsmuseum.nl; Herengracht 366-368; adult/child €12.50/free; ⊙10am-5pm; ☒2/11/12 Spui) A scale model of the Jewish Tabernacle described in Exodus – built by dedicated minister Leendert Schouten and drawing thousands of visitors even before it was completed in 1851 – is the star attraction at this bible museum. Inside a 1622 canal house, the museum has an extraordinary collection of bibles, including the Netherlands' oldest, a 1477-printed Delft Bible, and a 1st edition of the 1637 Dutch authorised version. Trees and plants mentioned in the Good Book feature in the garden.

HUIS MARSEILLE   MUSEUM
Map p302 (☎020-531 89 89; www.huismarseille.nl; Keizersgracht 401; adult/child €9/free; ⊙11am-6pm Tue-Sun; ☒2/11/12 Keizersgracht) Large-scale temporary exhibitions from its own collection are staged at this well-curated photography museum, which also hosts travelling shows. Themes include portraiture, nature or regional photography. Exhibitions are spread out over several floors and in a summer house behind the main house.

French merchant Isaac Focquier built Huis Marseille in 1665, installing a map of the French port Marseille on the facade. The original structure remains largely intact.

MULTATULI MUSEUM   MUSEUM

Map p300 (☎020-638 19 38; www.multatuli-museum.nl; Korsjespoortsteeg 20; ☺10am-5pm Tue, from noon Wed-Sun; ☐2/11/12/13/17 Nieuwezijds Kolk) **FREE** Better known by the pen name Multatuli (Latin for 'I have suffered greatly'), writer Eduard Douwes Dekker is most recognised for *Max Havelaar* (1860), his novel about corrupt colonialists in the Dutch East Indies. This small but fascinating house-museum chronicles his life and work, and shows furniture and artefacts from his time in Indonesia.

POEZENBOOT   ANIMAL SANCTUARY

Map p300 (Cat Boat; ☎020-625 87 94; www.de poezenboot.nl; Singel 38; by donation; ☺1-3pm Mon, Tue & Thu-Sat; ☐2/11/12/13/17 Nieuwezijds Kolk) Cat-lovers may want to check out this quirky boat on the Singel. It was founded in 1966 by a local woman who became legendary for looking after several hundred stray cats at a time. The boat has since been taken over by a foundation and can hold some 50 kitties in proper pens. Some are permanent residents, and the rest are ready to be adopted (after being neutered and implanted with an identifying computer chip, in line with Dutch law).

HUIS MET DE HOOFDEN   HISTORIC BUILDING

Map p300 (House with the Heads; www.embassy ofthefreemind.com; Keizersgracht 123; admission adult/child €12.50/free, guided tour per person €7.50; ☺10am-5pm Wed-Sat; ☐13/17 Westermarkt) A whimsical example of Dutch Renaissance style, this 1622 canal house designed by Hendrick de Keyser and his son Pieter has a beautiful step gable with six heads at door level representing the classical muses: Apollo, Diana, Ceres, Bacchus, Minerva and Mercury.

Today it houses the Embassy of the Free Mind museum, celebrating two millennia of free thinkers, and the Ritman Library (Bibliotheca Philosophica Hermetica), whose ancient spiritual and philosophical titles are being digitised thanks to author Dan Brown's donation. Guided tours lasting 30 minutes (English available) take place at 10.30am and 2.30pm. Look out for occasional free lunchtime classial concerts.

HOMOMONUMENT   MONUMENT

Map p300 (www.homomonument.nl; cnr Keizersgracht & Raadhuisstraat; ☐13/17 Westermarkt) Behind the Westerkerk, this 1987-installed cluster of three 10m granite triangles re-calls persecution by the Nazis, who forced gay men to wear a pink triangle patch. One of the triangles steps down into the Keizersgracht and is said to represent a jetty from which gay men were sent to the concentration camps. Others interpret the step up from the canal as a symbol of rising hope.

DE RODE HOED   CULTURAL CENTRE

Map p300 (The Red Hat; ☎020-589 16 80; www. rodehoed.nl; Keizersgracht 102; tickets free-€13-15; ☐13/17 Westermarkt) Occupying three glorious 17th-century canal houses – which once sheltered the Vrijburg, the largest clandestine church in the Netherlands – this cultural centre offers lectures, sometimes in English, by world-renowned authors and debates on the topics of the day, as well as concerts; check the agenda online. The centre was named for the former milliner located here (spot the identifying tile on the facade). Cards only, no cash.

EATING

The Western Canal Ring may not have the multicultural dining diversity of other parts of town, but the Negen Straatjes (p115) are filled with cute cafes and small restaurants to match their lovely boutiques, and the Jordaan neighbourhood is only a hop, skip and jump away.

> ## HERENGRACHT
>
> Dug out during the 17th-century Golden Age, the Herengracht (Gentlemen's Canal) takes its name from the wealthy landowners who built properties here. Some buildings lean forward and have hoists in the gables: given the narrowness of the interior staircases, people used these hoists to haul large goods to upper floors.
>
> Just north of the Herengracht, near its intersection with the Brouwersgracht, you'll find the Herenmarkt, a small square that's home to the historical 17th-century West-Indisch Huis, the former headquarters of the Dutch West India Company.
>
> The Herengracht is at its grandest along the Golden Bend (p120) in the Southern Canal Ring.

VINNIES DELI
CAFE €

Map p300 (www.vinnieshomepage.com; Haarlem-merstraat 46; mains €6-14.50; ⊘7.30am-5pm Mon-Fri, 9am-5pm Sat, 9.30am-5pm Sun; ✍; 🚋2/4/11/12/13/14/17/24/26 Centraal Station) 🍃 Only organic, locally sourced produce is used in Vinnes' extensive all-day break-fasts, gourmet sandwiches, lush salads, creative cakes and hot specials such as kale-and-mushroom frittata or roasted miso-marinated aubergine. Coffee is from Amsterdam roastery Bocca. Vegan op-tions abound. If you're imagining the cafe's designer furniture in your lounge room, you're in luck: all the pieces are for sale.

PETIT GÂTEAU
PASTRIES €

Map p300 (☏020-737 15 85; www.petitgateau. nl; Haarlemmerstraat 80; pastries €2.50-5.50; ⊘10am-6pm; 🚋18/21/22 Buiten Brouwersstraat) Paris-trained pastry chef Meike Scaling and her team create exquisite French pas-tries on-site: intricate 'miniminis' (tiny tarts topped with jewel-like fruits), glazed éclairs, macarons made from ground al-mond flour, shell-shaped madeleine cakes, and 15 savoury quiches. Regular two-hour pastry-making classes (in English and Dutch) cost €50; check the online agenda for dates.

STUBBE'S HARING
SEAFOOD €

Map p300 (Singel Haarlingersluis; dishes €3.30-7; ⊘noon-7pm Tue-Sat; 🚋2/4/11/12/ 13/14/17/24/26 Centraal Station) Overlooking the Singel, footsteps from Centraal Station, Stubbe's open-air fish stall has been provid-ing pickled herring to Amsterdammers for more than a century. You can eat it straight up or on a bread roll; just be sure to sprin-kle it with diced onion first. Hours can vary.

SINGEL 404
CAFE €

Map p302 (Singel 404; dishes €4.50-8.50; ⊘10.30am-6pm; ✍; 🚋2/11/12 Spui) It's easy to miss this tucked-away spot, despite its location near the bustling Spui (look for the cobalt-blue awning). The menu is as simple as can be – smoked-salmon sandwiches, pumpkin soup, honey-mint lemonade – but the prices are rock bottom, the portions are generous and the quality is superb. There's a handful of tables inside and out.

WIL GRAANSTRA FRITESHUIS
FAST FOOD €

Map p300 (Westermarkt 11; frites €3-4.50; sauce €0.30-0.50; ⊘noon-7pm Mon-Sat; 🚋13/17 Westermarkt) Legions of Amsterdammers swear by the crispy chips at Wil Graan-stra Friteshuis. The family-run business has been frying on the square by the Westerkerk since 1956. Most locals top their cones with mayonnaise, though *oor-log* ('war', a peanut sauce–mayo combo), curry sauce and piccalilli (relish) rock the taste buds too. Cash only.

PANCAKES!
DUTCH €

Map p302 (☏020-528 97 97; www.pancakes.am sterdam; Berenstraat 38; mains €6-13; ⊘8am-6pm; 🀫✍🀫; 🚋13/17 Westermarkt) The blue-tile tables at snug little Pancakes! are always packed with diners tucking into the signature dish, whether sweet (apple, nuts and cinnamon) or savoury (ham, chicory and camembert cheese). Gluten-free varie-ties are available. Smiley-face pancakes are a favourite with kids.

★DE BELHAMEL
EUROPEAN €€

Map p300 (☏020-622 10 95; www.belhamel.nl; Brouwersgracht 60; mains €24-26, 3-/4-course menus €38/48; ⊘noon-4pm & 5.30-10pm; 🚋18/21/22 Buiten Brouwersstraat) In warm weather the canal-side tables here at the head of the Herengracht are enchanting, and the richly wallpapered art nouveau interior set over two levels provides the perfect backdrop for exquisitely presented dishes such as poached sole with wild-spinach bisque, veal sweetbreads with po-lenta and spring onion jus, or a half lobster with velvety truffle mayonnaise.

BISTRO BIJ ONS
DUTCH €€

Map p300 (☏020-627 90 16; www.bistrobijons. nl; Prinsengracht 287; mains €12.50-21.50; ⊘11am-10pm Tue-Sun; 🀫; 🚋13/17 Westermarkt) If you're not in town visiting your Dutch *oma* (grandma), try the honest-to-goodness cooking at this charming retro bistro in-stead. Classics include *stamppot* (potatoes mashed with another vegetable) with sau-sage, *raasdonders* (split peas with bacon, onion and pickles) and *poffertjes* (small pancakes with butter and powdered sugar). House-made liqueurs include plum and *drop* (liquorice) varieties.

LE CŒUR
FRENCH €€

Map p300 (☏020-625 85 00; www.lecoeur. nl; Hartenstraat 24; breakfast dishes €3.50-14, mains lunch €8.50-22.50, dinner 18.50-28.50; ⊘8am-10pm; 🀫; 🚋13/17 Westermarkt) Framed by a black facade, 'the Heart' is a chic spot for breakfast (brioche with smoked salmon; truffled eggs) and lunch (grilled croque-madame or croque-monsieur ham-and-cheese sandwiches; snails with garlic butter; steak tartare). Dinner ups the ante with superbly executed classics including rabbit, hazelnut and cognac terrine or confit duck deg with duck-fat-cooked dauphinoise potatoes.

BLACK & BLUE   STEAK €€

Map p300 (☑020-625 08 07; www.steakrestaurantamsterdam.nl; Leliegracht 46; mains lunch €9-18.50, dinner €17-34.50; ☺11am-10pm; ☎; 🚊13/17 Westermarkt) Black & Blue's Josper (super-hot Spanish charcoal oven) char-grills succulent Black Angus steaks, accompanied by Béarnaise sauce, herb butter or pepper relish, and generous sides of *frites* (fries) and salads, with a half-lobster option. The split-level, parquet-floored space opens to a canal-side terrace overlooking the picturesque Leliegracht. Caramelised pineapple, also cooked on the Josper, is the pick of the desserts.

BISTROT NEUF   FRENCH €€

Map p300 (☑020-400 32 10; www.bistrotneuf.nl; Haarlemmerstraat 9; mains lunch €10-18.50, dinner €22.50-26, 3-course lunch/dinner menu €29/36.50; ☺noon-11pm; 🚊2/4/11/12/13/14/17/24/26 Centraal Station) The cooking at this wine-cork-adorned bistro covers all the classics – bouillabaisse (traditional Provençal fish stew), steak tartar with *frites* (fries), snails with garlic and parsley butter, *cassoulet* (slow-cooked casserole with pork and white beans), lemon-thyme-stuffed quail and *côte de bœuf* (rib steak) for two or three people – and is accompanied by a wine list spanning 60 French vintages.

DE LUWTE   EUROPEAN €€

Map p300 (☑020-625 85 48; www.restaurantdeluwte.nl; Leliegracht 26-28; mains €17.50-25.50; ☺6-10pm Sun-Thu, to 10.30pm Fri & Sat; 🚊13/17 Westermarkt) Strikingly designed with recycled timbers and interior plants, De Luwte also has artfully presented cooking. Seared scallops with fried lotus root and parsnip purée, and venison with roast quince are among the highlights, alongside the house-speciality Black Angus tomahawk steak for two. Great cocktails include Het Bruin (*oude jenever,* advocaat, hazelnut liqueur and cream sherry).

PRINSENGRACHT

The Herengracht and Keizersgracht might be grander, but locals love to hang out on the Prinsengracht, the liveliest of Amsterdam's inner canals. In summertime you could spend a whole weekend just enjoying its warm-weather charms – exploring the shops and kicking back on its cafe terraces – as boats glide by and houseboats bob against the quays in the breeze. During the chillier months, it's a winter wonderland where (conditions permitting) you might see skaters take to the iced-over canal.

CAFÉ RESTAURANT
VAN PUFFELEN   CAFE €€

Map p302 (☑020-624 62 70; www.restaurantvanpuffelen.com; Prinsengracht 375-377; mains €9.50-19.50, 2-/3-course menus €27.50/35; ☺kitchen 4-9.30pm Mon-Thu, 1-10pm Fri, noon-10pm Sat & Sun, bar to midnight; 🚊13/17 Westermarkt) This large cafe-restaurant stretches across two canal houses beautifully decorated with ruby-coloured light fittings and dark timber furniture, with enticing nooks and crannies for a cosy drink. Changing dishes made from local organic produce might include grilled octopus with parsley-lemon dressing or herb-crusted pork with mustard sauce. Meals can be served aboard your boat at the landing stage out front.

PANCAKE BAKERY   DUTCH €€

Map p300 (☑020-625 13 33; www.pancake.nl; Prinsengracht 191; mains €9-16.25; ☺9am-9.30pm; ☎🡥🡥; 🚊13/17 Westermarkt) In a restored 17th-century warehouse that once belonged to the Dutch East India Company, this basement restaurant offers a dizzying 78 varieties of pancake, from sweet (such as Hollandse, with caramel *stroopwafel* shards, chocolate flakes and cinnamon ice cream) to savoury (eg Thaise, with chicken, red curry, bamboo shoots and broccoli). Kids varieties include Pirate, Fireman and Princess pancakes.

STOUT   PERUVIAN €€

Map p300 (☑020-616 36 64; www.restaurantstout.nl; Haarlemmerstraat 73; mains lunch €8-15, dinner €12-21, evening tapas €6-12; ☺11am-10pm Sun-Thu, to 11pm Fri & Sat; 🚊18/21/22 Buiten Brouwersstraat) *Pan chapla* (Peruvian sandwiches) and egg dishes such as *huevos de codorniz con patatas* (quail eggs and potatoes) are among the lunch choices at this contemporary restaurant. Evening dishes might include Pisco-marinated scallops or chimichurri-marinated lamb chops grilled over charcoal. In warm weather, sit at the outdoor tables to watch the world go by.

BREDA
BISTRO €€€

Map p300 (☑020-622 52 33; www.bredagroup-amsterdam.com; Singel 210; menus €32.50-48.50 dinner €62.50-86.50; ⊘noon-2pm & 6-10pm; ☒2/ 12/13/17 Dam) Southern Dutch city Breda inspired this contemporary canal-side bistro, which combines sustainable ingredients, adventurous flavours and refined techniques in dishes such as smoked eel-skin broth; ribeye with charred corn, a mini potato soufflé and blood-sausage sauce; and beetroot sorbet with white chocolate and black-olive dust. Multicourse 'surprise menus' are zero-choice, but dietary requirements can be accommodated with advance notice.

DE STRUISVOGEL
BISTRO €€€

Map p302 (☑020-423 38 17; www.restaurant destruisvogel.nl; Keizersgracht 312; 3-course menu €29.50; ⊘5.30-10pm Sun-Fri, 5-10pm Sat; ☒13/17 Westermarkt) This former basement kitchen to some large canal houses offers great value. The bird (*struisvogel* means 'ostrich'), served with butter-poached pear and port, regularly stars on the menu alongside a nightly rotating menu of local, mostly organic, produce such as hazelnut-crusted Jerusalem artichoke, goat's cheese and white-truffle pie, and lemon-and-raspberry cheesecake with lavender sauce.

🍷 DRINKING & 🍸 NIGHTLIFE

Cafés (pubs) in this refined district tend to have stylish interiors and elaborate drinking (and dining) menus. There are a few down-to-earth brown cafes, and more in the nearby Jordaan.

★ 'T ARENDSNEST
BROWN CAFE

Map p300 (www.arendsnest.nl; Herengracht 90; ⊘noon-midnight Sun-Thu, to 2am Fri & Sat; ☒2/11/12/13/17 Nieuwezijds Kolk) This gorgeous restyled *bruin café*, with glowing copper *jenever* (Dutch gin) boilers behind the bar, only serves Dutch beer – but with more than 100 varieties (many from small

breweries), including 52 rotating on tap, you'll need to move here to try them all. It also has more than 40 gins, ciders, whiskies and liqueurs, all of which are Dutch too.

PLUK
CAFE

Map p302 (www.pluk-amsterdam.com; Reestraat 19; ⊘9am-6pm; ☎; ☒13/17 Westermarkt) Fresh-squeezed juices, smoothies and 'warm shakes' (such as pumpkin spice syrup, espresso, *stroopwafel*, cinnamon and whipped cream) are the standout reasons to drop by Pluk's mezzanine cafe. While you're here, snack on Dutch favourites such as pancakes or apple pie, and browse the ground floor's baskets of fruit and veggies, and homewares from chopping boards to contemporary ceramics.

KOFFIEHUIS DE HOEK
COFFEE

Map p302 (www.facebook.com/Koffiehuisde hoek; Prinsengracht 341; ⊘8am-4pm Mon-Fri, to 4.30pm Sat, 9am-4.30pm Sun; ☎; ☒13/17 Westermarkt) This *koffiehuis* (espresso bar; not to be confused with a coffeeshop selling cannabis) is one of the best places in the city to get an old-fashioned coffee-house experience in Amsterdam. Come for a coffee and a slice of its famous apple pie (baked throughout the day) in a charming, chequered-tablecloth atmosphere.

CAFÉ HET MOLENPAD
BAR

Map p302 (www.cafehetmolenpad.nl; Prinsengracht 653; ⊘noon-1am Sun-Thu, to 3am Fri & Sat; ☎; ☒2/11/12 Prinsengracht) By day, this updated brown cafe is full of people catching the afternoon sun on the terrace. By night the atmosphere turns quietly romantic, with low lamps and candlelight illuminating little tables beneath pressed-tin ceilings. The meat-filled *bitterballen* (deep-fried meatballs) and cheese croquettes are outstanding and justify a stop in their own right.

CAFÉ TABAC
BAR

Map p300 (www.cafetabac.eu; Brouwersgracht 101; ⊘noon-1am Mon-Thu, noon-3am Fri, 11am-3am Sat, 11am-1am Sun; ☎; ☒18/21/22 Buiten Brouwersstraat) Is Café Tabac a *bruin café*, a designer bar, a fantastic place for Indonesian dishes or simply an idyllic place to while away a few blissful hours at the intersection of two of Amsterdam's most stunning canals? The regulars don't seem concerned about definitions but simply enjoy the views and kicking back beneath the beamed ceilings.

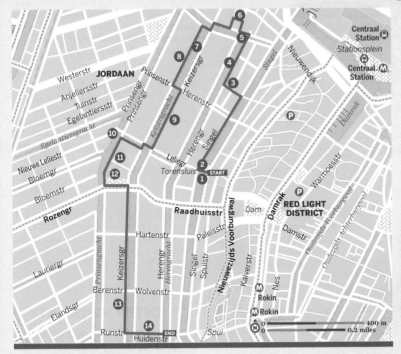

🚶 Neighbourhood Walk
Western Canal Ring

START SINGEL, TORENSLUIS
END NEGEN STRAATJES
LENGTH 3KM; 2½ HOURS

Discover the Western Canal Ring's 17th-century waterways during this walk.

Originally a moat that defended Amsterdam's outer limits, the **1 Singel** is the first canal west of the centre. **2 Torensluis**, Amsterdam's oldest bridge, crosses it. Stop to admire the statue of author Eduard Douwes Dekker, or Multatuli. Continue to the **3 Multatuli Museum** (p109).

Next up is the **4 Herengracht** (p109) (Gentlemen's Canal), with some of Amsterdam's most sought-after real estate.

The Herengracht soon intersects with the pretty **5 Brouwersgracht** (Brewer's Canal; p138), which took its name from the many suds-makers located here in the 16th and 17th centuries. To the north is Herenmarkt, home to the 17th-century **6 West-Indisch Huis** (p108), where the Dutch West India Company authorised the establishment of New Amsterdam (now New York City).

Turning south, cross the canal into the **7 Keizersgracht** (Emperor's Canal). You'll soon spot the imposing, red-shuttered **8 Greenland Warehouses**, which used to store whale oil. Cross the Keizersgracht and continue to the **9 Huis Met de Hoofden** (p109), with its carvings of Apollo, Ceres and Diana, the work of noted architect Hendrick de Keyser and his son Pieter.

Turn west at peaceful Leliegracht and then south onto **10 Prinsengracht** (p111). The **11 Anne Frank Huis** (p106) is on your left. Just south are the soaring towers of the **12 Westerkerk** (p108).

Back on Keizersgracht, south of Berenstraat is the **13 Felix Meritis** (p114), a one-time Enlightenment society venue that's now an alternative theatre; the building's colonnaded facade served as a model for Amsterdam's Concertgebouw.

Since you're probably hungry, thirsty or both by this point, head to one of the cafes lining the nearby **14 Negen Straatjes** (p115) before browsing the boutiques of these nine little streets.

LOCAL KNOWLEDGE

HAARLEMMERBUURT

Amsterdam's coolest neighbourhood-within-a-neighbourhood (or two – it straddles the Western Canal Ring and the Jordaan), the Haarlemmerbuurt (www.haarlemmerbuurt-amsterdam.nl) stretches along Haarlemmerstraat and its western extension, Haarlemmerdijk, and is lined with restaurants, food shops, designer workshops and boutiques. Its website (in Dutch, but easy to navigate) has details of one-off events.

PÂTISSERIE POMPADOUR TEAHOUSE

Map p302 (www.pompadour.amsterdam; Huidenstraat 12; ⊙10am-6pm Mon-Fri, 9am-6pm Sat, noon-6pm Sun, closed mid–late Jul; 🚊2/11/12 Spui) Sip top-notch tea and Spanish-roasted coffee while nibbling homemade Valrhona-chocolate pralines and pastries at this beautiful little Negen Straatjes tearoom with wood panelling dating from 1795.

GREENHOUSE COFFEESHOP

Map p300 (www.greenhouse.org; Haarlemmerstraat 64; ⊙9am-1am; 🛜; 🚊18/21/22 Buiten Brouwersstraat) Yes, that stretch of the floor is glass and there really are koi swimming underfoot in this contemporary coffeeshop lounge. Once you tire of the fish, peer into the microscope to see THC crystals or contemplate one of the pies spinning in the display case.

CAFÉ DE VERGULDE GAPER BROWN CAFE

Map p300 (www.deverguldegaper.nl; Prinsenstraat 30; ⊙10am-1am Mon, 11am-1am Tue-Thu & Sun, 11am-3am Fri, 10am-3am Sat; 🛜; 🚊13/17 Westermarkt) Decorated with old chemists' bottles and vintage posters, this former pharmacy has a canal-side terrace with afternoon sun and occasional live jazz. It's popular with locals, especially for after-work drinks. The name translates to the 'Golden Gaper', for the open-mouthed bust of a Moor traditionally posted at Dutch apothecaries.

SIBERIË COFFEESHOP

Map p300 (Brouwersgracht 11; ⊙11am-11pm Sun-Thu, to midnight Fri & Sat; 🛜; 🚊2/11/12/13/17 Nieuwezijds Kolk) Popular among locals, Siberië has offerings beyond marijuana – its owners regularly schedule cultural events such as art exhibits, poetry slams, acoustic concerts, DJ nights and even horoscope readings. It's one of the better places for an actual coffee too.

DE DOFFER BROWN CAFE

Map p302 (www.cafededoffer.nl; Runstraat 12-14; ⊙11am-3am; 🚊2/11/12 Spui) Writers, artists and students frequent this popular brown cafe for affordable food and good conversation. The dining room, with its old Heineken posters, large wooden tables and, occasionally, fresh flowers, is particularly atmospheric at night.

PROEFLOKAAL A VAN WEES DISTILLERY

Map p302 (De Admiraal; www.proeflokaalvanwees.nl; Herengracht 319; ⊙noon-midnight Sun-Wed, to 1am Thu, to 2am Fri & Sat; 🚊2/11/12 Spui) The grandest and largest of Amsterdam's tasting houses only pours its Jordaan-produced house brands: 17 *jenevers* and 60 liqueurs.

☆ ENTERTAINMENT

Entertainment options in the Western Canal Ring are limited to church concerts and occasional live music at bars and restaurants; the only dedicated entertainment venue is the Felix Meritis. The neighbouring Jordaan and the West, Medieval Centre and Red Light District, and Southern Canal Ring brim with venues.

FELIX MERITIS THEATRE

Map p302 (☎020-627 94 77; www.felixmeritis.nl; Keizersgracht 324; 🛜; 🚊2/11/12 Spui) Amsterdam's centre for arts, culture and science is renowned for staging innovative modern theatre, music and dance, as well as talks on politics, diversity, art, technology and literature. It was closed for renovations at the time of writing, and expected to reopen in spring 2020.

SHOPPING

You could easily spend all of your shopping time in the Negen Straatjes, with its abundance of small, specialist boutiques, but be sure to check out the hip shops in the Haarlemmerbuurt too.

★ NEGEN STRAATJES   AREA

Map p302 (Nine Streets; www.de9straatjes.nl;
🚊2/11/12 Spui) In a city packed with countless shopping opportunities, each seemingly more alluring than the last, the Negen
Straatjes represent the very densest concentration of consumer pleasures. These 'nine
little streets' are indeed small, each just
a block long. The shops are tiny too, and
many are highly specialised. Eyeglasses?
Cheese? Single-edition art books? Each has
its own dedicated boutique.

The streets – from west to east, and
north to south: Reestraat, Hartenstraat,
Gasthuismolensteeg, Berenstraat, Wolvenstraat, Oude Spiegelstraat, Runstraat,
Huidenstraat, Wijde Heisteeg – form a grid
bounded by Prinsengracht to the west and
Singel to the east.

To help navigate the welter of shops here,
pick up a copy of *The Nine Streets* shopping
guide, available at many tourist offices and
in many of the shops themselves, as well as
online at www.theninestreets.com.

★ FROZEN FOUNTAIN   HOMEWARES

Map p302 (www.frozenfountain.com; Prinsengracht 645; ⊙1-6pm Mon, 10am-6pm Tue-Sat,
noon-5pm Sun; 🚊2/11/12 Prinsengracht) Frozen Fountain is Amsterdam's best-known
showcase of furniture and interior design.
Prices are not cheap, but the daring designs
are offbeat and very memorable (designer
penknives, kitchen gadgets and that birthday gift for the impossible-to-wow friend).
Best of all, it's an unpretentious place where
you can browse at length without feeling
uncomfortable.

LOVE STORIES   FASHION & ACCESSORIES

Map p302 (www.lovestoriesintimates.com; Herengracht 298; ⊙noon-7pm Mon, 11am-7pm Tue-Fri,
11am-6pm Sat, noon-6pm Sun; 🚊2/11/12 Spui)
On the Herengracht, this boutique is the
flagship store of lingerie brand Love Stories,
which was set up by Amsterdam interior designer and stylist-turned-fashion-designer
Marloes Hoedeman. Her comfortable, affordable lingerie comes in a range of playful,
unexpected colour combinations and prints,
and is designed to work with outerwear;
there's also a stunning line of swimwear.

360 VOLT   HOMEWARES

Map p302 (📞020-810 01 01; www.360volt.com;
Prinsengracht 397; ⊙11am-6pm Thu-Sat; 🚊13/17
Westermarkt) One of the keys to creating a
quintessentially *gezellig* (cosy, convivial)

atmosphere is ambient lighting, making
this shop stocking vintage industrial lighting (restored to meet energy-efficient international standards) a real find. Its lights
grace some of the world's hottest bars, restaurants, hotels and film sets, such as the
James Bond instalment *Spectre*. Worldwide
shipping can be arranged.

MARIE-STELLA-MARIS   COSMETICS

Map p302 (www.marie-stella-maris.com; Keizersgracht 357; ⊙10am-6pm Tue-Sat, noon-6pm Sun
& Mon; 🚊2/11/12 Keizersgracht) 🌿 Marie-
Stella-Maris was set up as a social enterprise to provide clean drinking water
worldwide. It donates a percentage from
every purchase of its locally bottled min-
eral waters and its aromatic plant-based
skincare products (body lotions, hand
soaps, shea butter) and home fragrances
(travel pillow sprays, scented candles) to
support its cause. Its basement cafe–water
bar opens at weekends.

DENHAM THE JEANMAKER
MEN'S STORE   CLOTHING

Map p302 (www.denhamthejeanmaker.com;
Prinsengracht 495; ⊙noon-6pm Sun & Mon,
10am-6pm Tue, Wed, Fri & Sat, 10am-8pm Thu;
🚊2/11/12 Spui) Next door to its studio,
where jeans are produced, this flagship,
'zoned' boutique carries the cutting-edge
jeanmaker's menswear lines. Jeans aside,
you'll find jackets, knitwear and accessories. Cool vintage touches in-store include
an antique haberdashery display case and a
vintage scissor collection.

Other nearby boutiques include its **wom-
en's store** (Map p302; Runstraat 17; ⊙noon-
6pm Sun & Mon, 10am-6pm Tue, Wed, Fri & Sat,
10am-8pm Thu) around the corner.

DE KAASKAMER   FOOD

Map p302 (www.kaaskamer.nl; Runstraat 7;
⊙noon-6pm Mon, 9am-6pm Tue-Fri, 9am-5pm
Sat, noon-5pm Sun; 🚊2/11/12 Spui) The name
means 'the cheese room' and De Kaaskamer
is indeed stacked to the rafters with Dutch
and organic varieties, as well as olives,
tapenades, salads and other picnic ingredients. You can try before you buy or pick
up a cheese-filled baguette to go. Vacuum-
packing is available to take cheeses home.

VANILIA   FASHION & ACCESSORIES

Map p302 (www.vanilia.com; Runstraat 9;
⊙10am-6pm Tue, Wed, Fri & Sat, to 7pm Thu,
noon-6pm Sun & Mon; 🚊2/12 Keizersgracht) 🌿

CHEESE TASTING

Here's your chance to become a *kaas* (cheese) connoisseur: century-old Dutch cheesemaker **Reypenaer** (Map p300; ☑020-320 63 33; www.reypenaer cheese.com; Singel 182; tastings from €17.50; ⊙tastings by reservation; 🚊2/11/12/13/17 Dam) offers tastings in a rustic classroom beneath its shop. The hour-long session includes six cheeses – four cow's milk, two goat's milk – from young to old, with wine and port pairings. Expert staff members guide you through them, helping you appreciate the cheeses' look, aroma and taste.

Other options include cheese-and-*jenever* tastings at the House of Bols (p162), or cheese tastings combined with a canal boat tour; check the agenda online.

Dutch label Vanilia only designs limited editions, so you're unlikely to find the same styles here twice. Along with women's clothing (tops, trousers, dresses, skirts and jumpsuits), it also has lingerie, hats, belts, shoes, sunglasses, bags and jewellery, many made from salvaged offcuts of materials to reduce its environmental footprint.

EDDY VAREKAMP   ART
Map p300 (www.eddyvarekamp.nl; Hartenstraat 30; ⊙1-5pm Thu-Sun; 🚊13/17 Westermarkt) Amsterdam-born artist Eddy Varekamp showcases his paintings, prints and ceramics incorporating stylished streetscapes and scenes from Amsterdam life at his Negen Straatjes gallery (other themes include animals, music and love). Posters, cards and prints made with stencils and lino by fellow Amsterdammer Rosa Herzberg also depict the city.

ANECDOTE   FASHION & ACCESSORIES
Map p302 (www.anecdote.nl; Wolvenstraat 15; ⊙10am-6pm Tue, Wed, Fri & Sat, to 8pm Thu, noon-6pm Sun & Mon; 🚊1317 Westermarkt) A former garage now houses this flagship boutique of Amsterdam designer Jetteke van Beuningen, whose biennial collections of women's skirts, shorts, trousers, skirts and coats (and accessories such as bags), in classical colours and prints, are inspired by her love of travel and nature.

PROPERTY OF   FASHION & ACCESSORIES
Map p300 (www.thepropertyof.com; Herenstraat 2; ⊙11am-6.30pm Mon-Sat, noon-6pm Sun; 🚊2/12/13/17 Nieuwezijds Kolk) Black-and-white chequerboard floor tiles and black-painted timber cabinetry create a dramatic backdrop for the leather goods on display at this Dutch manufacturer's flagship boutique. Premium materials are crafted into handbags, backpacks, laptop and tablet bags, luggage tags, key chains, watchbands and wallets.

WAXWELL RECORDS   MUSIC
Map p300 (www.waxwell.com; Gasthuismolensteeg 8; ⊙noon-7pm Mon-Sat, to 6pm Sun; 🚊2/12/13/17 Dam) New and secondhand vinyl is restocked weekly at this light, bright and well-organised shop, which specialises in jazz, soul, blues, reggae and pop. You can listen to tracks on two turntables in store.

TENUE DE NÎMES   CLOTHING
Map p300 (www.tenuedenimes.com; Haarlemmerstraat 92-94; ⊙noon-7pm Mon, 11am-7pm Tue-Fri, 10am-6pm Sat, noon-6pm Sun; 🚊18/21/22 Buiten Brouwersstraat) Denim clothing for men and women by legendary brands such as Levi's, Rogue Territory, Pure Blue Japan, Edwin, Naked & Famous, Acne and Rag & Bone are the speciality of this hip boutique.

L'ÉTOILE DE SAINT HONORÉ   VINTAGE
Map p302 (www.etoile-luxuryvintage.com; Reestraat 24; ⊙noon-6pm Mon-Thu, 11am-6pm Fri & Sat, noon-5pm Sun; 🚊13/18 Westermarkt) Dior, Louis Vuitton, Gucci and Valentino are among the designer brands of handbags, purses, luggage, belts, shoes, scarves and coats at this luxury vintage boutique. Prices reflect the stringent quality control.

CONCRETE MATTER   GIFTS & SOUVENIRS
Map p300 (www.concrete-matter.com; Gasthuismolensteeg 12; ⊙1-6pm Mon, 11am-6pm Tue-Fri, 10am-6pm Sat, noon-6pm Sun; 🚊13/17 Dam) At this concept store with a difference, everything is specifically curated for men, from casual clothing to classic car books to shaving kits, referee whistles, aviator sunglasses, flask and shot-glass sets, pocketknives and other items that make great gifts.

DARLING   CLOTHING
Map p302 (www.thedarlingamsterdam.com; Runstraat 4; ⊙1-6pm Mon, 11am-6pm Tue-Sat, noon-6pm Sun; ☎; 🚊2/11/12 Spui) Original,

affordable, locally designed clothes, whimsical accessories and some great homewares at the Darling are why the Negen Straatjes continue to delight and surprise.

MARLIES DEKKERS   CLOTHING
Map p302 (www.marliesdekkers.com; Berenstraat 18; ☺1-6pm Mon, 11am-6pm Tue-Sat, noon-5pm Sun; 🚊13/17 Westermarkt) Preeminent Dutch lingerie designer Marlies Dekkers is known for her subtle hints of bondage, detailed on exquisite undergarments. Summer sees an equally seductive range of swimwear. The shop itself has a sultry air with handpainted wallpaper and a lounge area with a fireplace.

GAMEKEEPER   TOYS
Map p300 (www.gamekeeper.nl; Hartenstraat 14; ☺10am-6pm Mon & Sat, 10am-6.30pm Tue, Wed & Fri, 10am-8.30pm Thu, 11am-6pm Sun; 🚊13/17 Westermarkt) The selection of board games here is dizzying. Start with checkers, chess and mah-jong, and move on to Cathedral (build a city in the style of the Great Wall of China or the souk in Marrakesh) or Rush Hour (help a car get out of traffic). Popular card games include the strategic, Russian Roulette–style Exploding Kittens.

'Cooperative' games encourage players to play with, not against, each other.

HESTER VAN EEGHEN   SHOES
Map p300 (www.hestervaneeghen.com; Hartenstraat 1; ☺1-6pm Mon, 11am-6pm Tue-Sat, noon-5pm Sun; 🚊13/17 Westermarkt) Designed in Amsterdam and handcrafted in Italy from fine leather, internationally renowned Hester van Eeghen's unique shoes are for those who dare to dress their feet dramatically in bright colours, fur, suede, and geometric patterns and prints. Her handbags (available down the street at Hartenstraat 37) are just as attention grabbing.

AMSTERDAM
WATCH COMPANY   FASHION & ACCESSORIES
Map p300 (www.awco.nl; Reestraat 3; ☺11am-6pm Tue-Fri, to 5pm Sat; 🚊13/17 Westermarkt)

The small, passionate and highly skilled team here restores old watches (postwar to mid-1970s). The company is also the exclusive Amsterdam dealer of Dutch watchmakers including Van der Gang, Roland Oostwegel, and Christiaan van der Klaauw, who makes fewer than 200 watches a year.

ZIPPER   VINTAGE
Map p302 (www.zippervintageclothing.com; Huidenstraat 7; ☺noon-6.30pm Mon, 11am-6.30pm Tue, Wed, Fri & Sat, 11am-8pm Thu, 1-6.30pm Sun; 🚊2/11/12 Spui) Seriously nostalgic, retro secondhand gear here might include wacky printed shirts, stovepipe jeans, '40s zoot suits and pork-pie hats. The shop is restocked twice weekly.

EXOTA   CLOTHING
Map p300 (www.kinglouie.nl; Hartenstraat 13; ☺10.30am-6.30pm Mon-Fri, 10am-6pm Sat, noon-6pm Sun; 🚊13/17 Westermarkt) Exota sells its own hip King Louie label plus global brands such as Kookai and French Connection, with chic designs for both men and women. Across the street at Hartenstraat 10, its sister shop stocks sportier women's clothes and kids threads.

LAURA DOLS   VINTAGE
Map p302 (✆020-624 90 66; www.lauradols.nl; Wolvenstraat 7; ☺11am-6pm Mon-Wed & Sat, 11am-7pm Thu & Fri, noon-6pm Sun; 🚊2/11/12 Spui) Compulsive style-watchers head to this vintage-clothing store for fur coats, 1920s beaded dresses, lace blouses and '40s movie-star accessories such as handstitched leather gloves. Vintage wedding dresses are available to view by appointment.

MENDO   BOOKS
Map p302 (www.mendo.nl; Berenstraat 11; ☺10.30am-6pm Mon-Sat, noon-5pm Sun; 🚊13/17 Westermarkt) Graphic-design agency Mendo runs this smart black-walled bookshop specialising in books in the creative realm: art, design, architecture, fashion and photography.

Southern Canal Ring

Neighbourhood Top Five

❶ Hermitage Amsterdam (p121) Goggling at blockbuster exhibitions drawn from the wealth of treasures at the original St Petersburg museum.

❷ Golden Bend (p120) Ambling along the stretch of canal-side property that practically purrs with Golden Age elegance, and imagining which house you would choose if you could.

❸ Reguliersgracht (p120) Enjoying romantic 'ahhs' on the so-called 'canal of seven bridges', and seeing how many of them you can spot at once.

❹ Museum van Loon (p122) Getting an insight into the lavish lifestyle of Amsterdam's top rung from the Golden Age up to the 19th century in this gracious canal-side abode.

❺ Museum Willet-Holthuysen (p123) Exploring the lavishness of patrician canal-house life in this historic former family home.

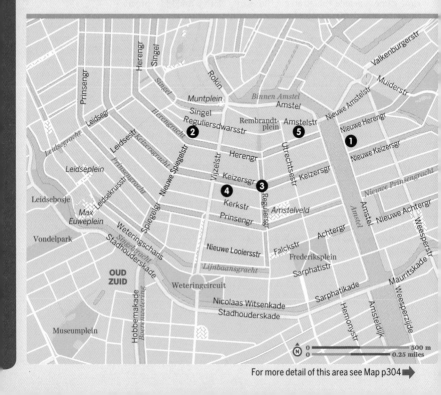

For more detail of this area see Map p304 ➡

Explore Southern Canal Ring

The graceful arc of the Southern Canal Ring spans the area from the radial Leidsegracht in the west to the Amstel in the east. Packed with museums, restaurants, cafes, shops and miles of gorgeous canals, the district deserves at least a day to explore. Anchored by the nightlife centres of Leidseplein (p120) and Rembrandtplein (p120) (including the gay hub of Reguliersdwarsstraat), the neighbourhood offers plenty to occupy you after dark.

Highlights include the cacophonous, touristy and flower-filled Bloemenmarkt (p121), the grand and exquisite houses of the Golden Bend (p120), and the splendid interior decoration of Museum Van Loon (p122).

Check out the big-name exhibitions at the Hermitage Amsterdam (p121), then stroll past the Amstelsluizen (p123) and the Gijsbert Dommer Huis (p124; House with the Blood Stains!). Around the corner, canal house Museum Willet-Holthuysen (p123) offers a look at the lifestyle of the 19th-century A-list.

There are tons of eating options around Utrechtsestraat; to feed your soul, take in the view of the seven bridges along Reguliersgracht (p120). End your night on lively Rembrandtplein.

Local Life

➔ **Cakes** Feast like the Dutch royals on beautiful baked goods from Patisserie Holtkamp (p126), given the seal of approval with the royal coat of arms.

➔ **Cafes** Off Prinsengracht, tiny Weteringstraat feels like a secret passage; look out for local *bruin café* (brown cafe; traditional Dutch pub) Café de Wetering (p130).

➔ **Cocktails** The door is unmarked and you're best to reserve ahead to get in, but the cocktails at speakeasy Door 74 (p129) are worth it.

➔ **Music** Locals scan the manifold riches of Concerto (p134), a rambling vinyl shop with regular live gigs and a cafe for hanging out with musos all day.

Getting There & Away

➔ **Tram** This area is well-served by trams. For the Leidseplein area, take tram 1, 2, 5, 7, 11, 12 or 19. To reach Rembrandtplein, take tram 4, which travels down Utrechtsestraat, or tram 14. Tram 24 cuts through the centre of the neighbourhood down busy Vijzelstraat.

Lonely Planet's Top Tip

At first glance, Leidseplein and Rembrandtplein may look like nothing more than tourist traps for the stag and hen or travel-in-a-pack brigades. But they're serious (or not-so-serious) fun, with plenty of authentic bars and cafes just waiting to be discovered. To escape the hullabaloo and hang out with the locals, head to happening Utrechtsestraat.

Best Places to Eat

➔ Van Dobben (p124)

➔ Pantry (p125)

➔ Buffet van Odette (p125)

➔ Guts (p127)

➔ Ron Gastrobar Oriental (p125)

For reviews, see p124. ➡

🍷 Best Places to Drink

➔ Back to Black (p129)

➔ Bakhuys Amsterdam (p129)

➔ Café Langereis (p129)

➔ Door 74 (p129)

➔ Lion Noir (p130)

For reviews, see p127. ➡

☆ Best Entertainment

➔ Melkweg (p134)

➔ Paradiso (p133)

➔ Koninklijk Theater Carré (p133)

➔ Pathé Tuschinskitheater (p132)

For reviews, see p132. ➡

SOUTHERN CANAL RING

⊙ SIGHTS

The semicircular grid of the Southern Canal Ring packs in glorious sights particularly evocative of Amsterdam's Golden Age, such as the illustrious art of the Hermitage, the gracious architecture of the Golden Bend, and the canal house museums of Van Loon (p122) and Willet-Holthuysen (p123), plus a scattering of other charming stops, such as the Amsterdam Pipe Museum and Kattenkabinet (p122).

★FOAM   GALLERY
Map p304 (Fotografiemuseum Amsterdam; www. foam.org; Keizersgracht 609; adult/child €12.50/ free; ☺10am-6pm Sat-Wed, to 9pm Thu & Fri; 🚊4 Keizersgracht) From the outside, it looks like a grand canal house, but this is the city's most important photography gallery. Its simple, spacious galleries, some with skylights or large windows for natural light, host four major exhibitions annually, featuring world-renowned photographers such as William Eggleston and Helmut Newton. There's a **cafe** in the basement.

LEIDSEPLEIN   SQUARE
Map p304 (🚊1/2/5/7/11/12/19 Leidseplein) Historic architecture, beer, clubs and steakhouses – welcome to Leidseplein. The square is always busy, but after dark it gets thronged by a mainstream crowd of party lovers (more tourists than locals). A major hub for nightlife and trams, it has countless pubs and clubs, masses of restaurants and an aroma of roasted meat. Pavement cafes at the northern end are perfect for people-watching. Entertainment venues line the streets around the square; nearby Kerkstraat has a cluster of gay venues.

On the square's eastern side, farmers would once leave their horses and carts at the Leidsepoort (Leiden Gate) before entering town; it was demolished in 1870. The strip of greenery with large chestnut trees on the other side of the Singelgracht is called Leidsebosje (Leiden Wood).

GOLDEN BEND   ARCHITECTURE
Map p304 (Gouden Bocht; Herengracht, btwn Leidsestraat & Vijzelstraat; 🚊2/11/12 Koningsplein) The Golden Bend is Amsterdam's swankiest stretch of property. Its handsome mansions are a monument to the Golden Age, when precious goods swelled the cellars of homes already stuffed with valu-

ables. The richest Amsterdammers ruled their affairs from here. The earliest mansions date from the 1660s, when the Canal Ring was expanded south. Thanks to some city-hall lobbying, the gables here were built twice as wide as the standard Amsterdam model, and the rear gardens deeper.

Apart from the Kattenkabinet (p122) museum, the homes are only open to the public on Open Monuments Day (Open Monumentendag; a weekend in mid-September).

REGULIERSGRACHT   CANAL
Map p304 (🚊4/14 Rembrandtplein) Crossing Herengracht, Keizersgracht and Prinsengracht canals, this waterway was dug in 1658 to link the Herengracht with the canals further south. The prettiest of Amsterdam's canals, it is famous for its seven bridges, though if you stand where it crosses Herengracht, you can count 15 bridges in all directions. The houses lining the canal are a decorative feast of gables and adornments. Reguliersgracht was named after an order of monks whose monastery was located nearby.

Where Prinsengracht crosses Reguliersgracht, there is a house with a **stork statue** above the door – the dwelling once belonged to a midwife.

REMBRANDTPLEIN   SQUARE
Map p304 (🚊4/14 Rembrandtplein) First called Reguliersplein, then Botermarkt for the butter markets held here until the mid-19th century, this somewhat brash square now takes its name from the **statue** of the painter erected in 1876. Beneath Rembrandt is a photo-op favourite: imposing life-sized bronze **statues** re-creating his famous painting, *The Night Watch* (see the original in the Rijksmuseum, p153).

Rembrandtplein evolved into a nightlife hub as cafes, restaurants and clubs opened their doors, and remains a cornerstone of Amsterdam nightlife.

MAGERE BRUG   BRIDGE
Map p304 (Skinny Bridge; btwn Kerkstraat & Nieuwe Kerkstraat; 🚊4 Prinsengracht) Dating from the 1670s, the nine-arched 'Skinny Bridge' has had several incarnations, first in timber and later in concrete. It has a hand-operated central section that can be raised to let boats through. The bridge is especially pretty at night, when it glows with 1200 tiny lights. It has appeared in several films, including the 1971 James Bond thriller *Diamonds Are*

Forever. Stand in the middle and feel it sway under the passing traffic.

AMSTERDAM PIPE MUSEUM   MUSEUM
Map p304 (📞020-421 17 79; www.pipemuseum.nl; Prinsengracht 488; adult/child €10/5; ⊙noon-6pm Wed-Sat; 🚊2/11/12 Prinsengracht) This museum is in the grand 17th-century canal house of the marvellously single-minded pipe collector who gathered this unexpectedly fascinating collection from around 60 different countries over 40 years. Knowledgeable guides take you through the exhibits, from the earliest South American pipes, dating from 500 BC, to 15th-century Dutch pipes, Chinese opium pipes, African ceremonial pipes and much more. A peek into the house is worth the price of admission alone.

KRIJTBERG   CHURCH
Map p304 (📞020-623 19 23; www.krijtberg.nl; Singel 446; ⊙1-5pm Tue-Thu, Sat & Sun; 🚊1/2/5 Koningsplein) The spiky spires of this neo-Gothic church are an unmissable landmark amid rows of handsome Singel homes. Officially known as the St Franciscus Xaveriuskerk, Krijtberg (Chalk Hill) replaced a clandestine Jesuit chapel on the same site in 1883; it's remained Jesuit to this day. If you get the chance, have a peek inside: the interior is typically, lavishly Jesuit, covered with paintings and statuary.

English mass is held on Saturdays at 5.15pm, and on some religious holidays.

BLOEMENMARKT   MARKET
Map p304 (Flower Market; Singel, btwn Muntplein & Koningsplein; ⊙9am-5pm; 🚊2/11/12 Koningsplein) Flowers are not treats, but essentials in Amsterdam. Ever since 1860, this famous flower market has been located at the spot where nurserymen and women, having sailed up the Amstel from their smallholdings, would moor their barges to sell their wares directly to customers. No longer floating (it's now perched on piles), the market has plenty of high-kitsch miniature clogs, fridge magnets and wooden tulips; it's also a good place to buy (real) tulips in season and bulbs year-round.

STADSARCHIEF   MUSEUM
Map p304 (Municipal Archives; 📞tour reservations 020-251 15 11; www.amsterdam.nl/stadsarchief; Vijzelstraat 32; ⊙10am-5pm Tue-Fri, noon-5pm Sat & Sun; 🚊24 Muntplein) **FREE** A

TOP SIGHT
HERMITAGE AMSTERDAM

On the Amstel riverbank, this grand 17th-century almshouse is home to an impressive branch of the State Hermitage Museum of St Petersburg. Why is this bastion of Russian culture here? It's all down to long-standing ties between Russia and the Netherlands: Tsar Peter the Great learned shipbuilding here in 1697.

The **Portrait Gallery of the Golden Age** is a long-running exhibit, with 30 group portraits that are contemporaries of Rembrandt's *The Night Watch*. The works are startlingly large, showing the importance of the associations they depict; paintings include Rembrandt's *Anatomy Lesson of Dr Deijman*. The museum usually hosts a few **temporary exhibitions**, often drawing from the Russian museum's amazing cache of art objects, covering themes such as the Romanovs or Dutch masterpieces. These temporary exhibitions change about twice a year.

Outside is the Outsider Art Museum, a collaboration between the Hermitage, Haarlem's Dolhuys Museum of the Mind and health-care facility Cordaan. It features changing exhibitions of work produced by artists whilst in psychiatric institutions. Admission is usually free; enter from the garden.

DON'T MISS
➡ Temporary exhibitions
➡ Portrait Gallery of the Golden Age
➡ Outsider Art Museum
➡ Guided tours

PRACTICALITIES
➡ Map p304, G3
➡ 📞020-530 87 55
➡ www.hermitage.nl
➡ Amstel 51
➡ single exhibitions adult/child €18/free, all exhibitions €25/free
➡ ⊙10am-5pm; ♿
➡ Ⓜ Waterlooplein, 🚊14 Waterlooplein

SOUTHERN CANAL RING SIGHTS

distinctive striped building dating from 1923, this former bank now houses 23km of shelving storing Amsterdam archives. Fascinating displays of archive gems, such as the 1942 police report on the theft of Anne Frank's bike and a letter from Charles Darwin to Artis Royal Zoo in 1868, can be viewed in the enormous tiled basement vault.

Tours (adult/child €7.50/free, 1¼ hours) run at 2pm on Sundays, and must be booked in advance.

Upstairs, a **gallery space** mounts temporary exhibits (adult/child €7.50/5).

TASSENMUSEUM HENDRIKJE   MUSEUM

Map p304 (Museum of Bags & Purses; ☎020-524 64 52; www.tassenmuseum.nl; Herengracht 573; adult/child €13/4; ☉10am-5pm; ☒4/14 Rembrandtplein) This grand 17th-century canal-house museum has a covetable collection of arm candy. More than 5000 bags can be found here, including a medieval pouch, Perspex 1960s containers, design classics by Chanel, Gucci and Versace, an '80s touchtone phone bag and Madonna's ivy-strewn 'Evita' bag from the film's premiere. The **cafe** has pricey-but-nice high teas and cakes.

BLAUWBRUG   BRIDGE

Map p304 (Blue Bridge; btwn Waterlooplein & Amstelstraat; Ⓜ Waterlooplein, ☒14 Waterlooplein) Built in 1884, this highly decorated stone bridge replaced an old, blue (hence the name) wooden crossing that had connected these shores of the Amstel since the 17th century. The current version was modelled on the Alexander III bridge in Paris, and features tall, ornate street lamps topped by the imperial crown of Amsterdam, fish sculptures and foundations shaped like the prow of a medieval ship.

KATTENKABINET   MUSEUM

Map p304 (Cat Cabinet; ☎020-626 90 40; www.kattenkabinet.nl; Herengracht 497; adult/child €7/free; ☉10am-5pm Mon-Fri, noon-5pm Sat & Sun; ☒; ☒24 Muntplein) When kitties go to the great sofa in the sky, most doting owners comfort themselves with a photo on the mantel; wealthy financier Bob Meijer founded an entire museum in memory of his red tomcat John Pierpont Morgan III. The collection includes artworks by Tsuguharu Foujita, Théophile Alexandre Steinlen and Amsterdam's chief sculptor, Hildo Krop. A visit here also gives you the opportunity

◉ TOP SIGHT
MUSEUM VAN LOON

This beautiful house-turned-museum plunges you into the lavish lifestyle of the wealthy in 19th-century Amsterdam. Built in 1672, it was first home to acclaimed painter Ferdinand Bol. By the late 1800s, the Van Loons, a prominent patrician family, had moved in and have lived here ever since; they still occupy the building's upper floors.

The house is filled with opulent furniture and portraits that seem to whisper secrets as you go from room to gorgeous room. Among the 150 portraits of the Van Loon family are important paintings such as *The Marriage of Willem van Loon and Margaretha Bas* by Jan Miense Molenaer. But the main exhibit is the house itself. It's full of set-piece interior decoration, with intricate stucco on the ceilings, a garden room overlooking the garden's formal hedges, and the glorious decoration of the guest bedroom. It's the only such mansion where you can still see a rear coach house, which once housed horse-drawn carriages at the end of the pristine formal courtyard garden.

The powerhouse below is the basement kitchen, where cook Leida presided for almost 40 years. Over the next few years, the family intends to open the wine cellar, the pantry and the storage to visitors.

DON'T MISS
➡ The interior details
➡ The 19th-century basement kitchen
➡ The dramatic bedrooms
➡ The formal garden
➡ The coach house

PRACTICALITIES
➡ Map p304, E4
➡ ☎020-624 52 55
➡ www.museumvanloon.nl
➡ Keizersgracht 672
➡ adult/child €10/5.50, free with Museum & I Amsterdam cards
➡ ☉10am-5pm
➡ ☒4 Keizersgracht

to explore one of the Golden Bend's grand houses; it's the only one open to the public.

You may get the chance to admire the cats that live in the building along with the art collection.

AMSTELSLUIZEN ARCHITECTURE

Map p304 (Amstel Locks; 🚋4 Prinsengracht) These impressive sluices on the Amstel river, near Koninklijk Theater Carré, date from 1674 and are still in use to today. They allow the canals to be flushed with fresh water from lakes north of the city, rather than salt water from the IJ River, an innovation that made the city more livable. The locks are shut while fresh water flows in, while the sluices on the western side of the city are left open as the stagnant water is pumped out to sea.

AMSTELKERK CHURCH

Map p304 (☏020-520 00 60; www.amstelkerk. net; Amstelveld 10; ⊙9am-5pm Mon-Fri; 🚋4 Prinsengracht) Looking more like a country house than a church, the pinewood Amstelkerk was erected in 1668 as a *noodkerk* (makeshift church) under the direction of the city architect, Daniël Stalpaert, who also designed the town hall on the Dam. The idea was that a permanent church would be built next to it, but plans for this were abandoned in the 1840s.

During the French occupation, Napoleon used the building to keep his horses. Later, in 1840, the square-shaped interior was updated with a neo-Gothic look and the addition of a pipe organ. Van Gogh heard his uncle's sermon here in 1877.

DE DUIF CHURCH

Map p304 (The Dove; ☏020-520 00 90; www. deduif.net; Prinsengracht 756; ⊙hours vary; 🚋4 Prinsengracht) In 1796, following the French-installed government's proclamation of religious freedom, De Duif became the Netherlands' first Catholic church to be built with a public entrance in more than two centuries. The original church was demolished due to unstable construction; its replacement was built in 1857. Today, De Duif is an ecumenical church, and is also used as a venue for concerts, opera and private events.

If you're able to go inside, check out the clay friezes of the Stations of the Cross on the right wall, the pulpit carvings of St

TOP SIGHT
MUSEUM WILLET-HOLTHUYSEN

Built in 1687 for mayor Jacob Hop and redesigned in 1739, this house-turned-museum offers insight into the 19th-century lives of the merchant class' super-rich. It's named after Louisa Willet-Holthuysen, who lived a lavish, bohemian life here with her husband Abraham from 1861. She bequeathed the property to the city in 1895.

As you stroll through the patrician house, you'll find out plenty about the lifestyle and interests of Abraham and Louisa. They were keen art collectors, and the rich selection of furniture and art includes notable paintings by Jacob de Wit. Also look for the *place de milieu* (centrepiece) that was part of the family's 275-piece Meissen table service in the Louis XVI–style ground-floor dining room, and the original 17th-century stained-glass windows upstairs. Downstairs, the kitchen and scullery provide a glimpse of the work required to keep the house running, with simple decoration and lovely original tiling on the walls.

The intimate garden with a sundial is a reconstruction dating from 1972, created in the French classical style. It was originally smaller than it is today, as a coach house occupied some of the space. You can also peek at the garden through the iron fence at the Amstelstraat end.

DON'T MISS

➡ Jacob de Wit paintings
➡ The French garden
➡ The Louis XVI–style ground floor
➡ 17th-century glass painting

PRACTICALITIES

➡ Map p304, F3
➡ ☏020-523 18 70
➡ www.willet holthuysen.nl
➡ Herengracht 605
➡ adult/child €12.50/free
➡ ⊙10am-5pm
➡ 🚋4/14 Rembrandtplein

PHOTOGRAPHING THE SEVEN BRIDGES

It's easy to get swept away in the raucous local nightlife and forget that one of Amsterdam's most romantic canals flows through this neighbourhood. The Reguliersgracht (p120), aka the 'canal of seven bridges', is especially enchanting by night, when its humpbacked arches glow with tiny gold lights.

Though the best views are from aboard a boat, you can still get great vistas from land. Stand with your back to the Thorbeckeplein and with the Herengracht flowing directly in front of you to the left and right. Lean over the bridge and look straight ahead down the Reguliersgracht. Ahhh. Now kiss your sweetie.

Willibrordus of Utrecht, and the organ reaching up to the vaulted ceiling, a sight in its own right.

GIJSBERT DOMMER HUIS HISTORIC BUILDING
Map p304 (Amstel 216; 🚊4 Keizersgracht) This handsome greystone house is known dramatically as the 'House with the Blood Stains'. Six-time mayor and diplomat Coenraad van Beuningen lost his fortune, then his mind, and scribbled graffiti on the facade, allegedly in his own blood. His mysterious 17th-century writing – which includes Hebrew letters and obscure Kabbalah symbols – is still faintly visible.

Wealthy businessman Gijsbert Dommer commissioned the house in 1671, hence the name.

✗ EATING

Leidseplein has steakhouses cheek by jowl, though there are more interesting gems to be found that are not just about slabs of beef. For more scenic and singular eateries, your best bet is on the nearby side streets or canals. Rembrandtplein has a somewhat brash feel; for a better meal, walk a few steps to Utrechtsestraat, one of the finest restaurant rows in town.

★**VAN DOBBEN** DUTCH €
Map p304 (🖉020-624 42 00; www.eetsalonvan dobben.nl; Korte Reguliersdwarsstraat 5-9; dishes €3-8; ⏰10am-9pm Mon-Thu, to 2am Fri & Sat, 10.30am-8pm Sun; 🕾; 🚊4/14 Rembrandtplein) Open since the 1940s, Van Dobben has a cool diner feel, with white tiles and a siren-red ceiling. Traditional meaty Dutch fare is its forte: low-priced, finely sliced roast-beef sandwiches with mustard are an old-fashioned joy, or try the *pekelvlees* (akin to corned beef) or *halfom* (if you're keen on *pekelvlees* mixed with liver).

SALSA SHOP MEXICAN €
Map p304 (🖉020-2051040; www.salsashop.com; Amstelstraat 32; mains around €10; ⏰11.30am-10pm Sun-Thu, to 11pm Fri & Sat; 🚊4/14 Rembrandtplein) Salsa Shop lets you create your own burritos, bowls and taco salads. The interiors are modern and simple; good for an easy stop near Rembrandtplein.

DE CARROUSEL DUTCH €
Map p304 (🖉020-625 80 02; www.decarrousel pannenkoeken.nl; HM van Randwijkplantsoen 1; dishes €6-12; ⏰10am-8pm; 🕾; Ⓜ️Vijzelgracht, 🚊1/7/19/24 Vijzelgracht) De Carrousel serves some of Amsterdam's best pancakes, but its decor also takes the cake. The wooden building is covered in neon lights and red-leather armchairs, and in the middle is an old carousel, hence the name. A large wooden deck also provides plentiful outdoor seating.

As well as the larger thin pancakes, you can also try Dutch *poffertjes* here – tiny pancakes topped with powdered sugar.

SOUP EN ZO SOUP €
Map p304 (www.soupenzo.nl; Nieuwe Spiegel-straat 54; soup €4.50-8; ⏰11am-8pm Mon-Fri, noon-7pm Sat & Sun; 🖉; 🚊1/7/19 Spiegelgracht) On a chilly Amsterdam day, you can't beat a steaming cup of soup from this little specialist. Daily choices might include potato with Roquefort; lentil and minced beef, prunes and pumpkin; or spicy spinach and coconut. Takeaway only.

STACH DELI €
Map p304 (www.stach-food.nl; Nieuwe Spiegel-straat 52; dishes €7.50-15; ⏰8am-10pm Mon-Sat, 9am-9pm Sun; 🖉; 🚊1/7/19 Spiegelgracht) This branch of popular deli Stach gets crowded but is a great option for takeaway meals like pastas, including spinach and ricotta ravioli, and sandwiches such

as carpaccio, truffle mayonnaise and ruccola; or buffalo mozzarella and sun-dried tomato. Grab your goodies to eat on a canal-side bench.

POKÉ PERFECT
HAWAIIAN €

Map p304 (www.pokeperfect.com; Prinsengracht 502; mains around €10; ⊘11.30am-9pm; 🍴; 🚊1/2/5/7/11/12/19 Leidseplein) Exercise lovers on the run flock to this pale, gleaming place, which offers fast food that is as healthy as takeaway gets. The poké (pronounced *poh*-kay) consists of sushi rice and several different toppings, like raw fish, tofu, and edamame beans, served in a bowl: it's fresh, light and tasty. There's counter service and just a couple of tables.

★ VEGAN JUNK FOOD BAR
VEGAN €€

Map p304 (www.veganjunkfoodbar.com; Reguliersdwarsstraat 57; mains €9-15; ⊘11am-1am Sun-Thu, to 3am Fri & Sat; 🍴🍴; 🚊24 Muntplein) This flashy restaurant, vaunting pink graffiti walls and neon lights, serves healthy 'junk' food. Plant-based burgers are the best-known fare, but you can also order sashimi made from tapioca, fruity cocktails and CBD-infused juice.

★ BUFFET VAN ODETTE
CAFE €€

Map p304 (☏020-423 60 34; www.buffet-am sterdam.nl; Prinsengracht 598; mains €9-18.50; ⊘noon-midnight Wed-Mon; 🍴; 🚊1/7/19 Spiegelgracht) This white-tiled cafe with an enchanting canal-side location serves delicious dishes made with great ingredients and a dash of creativity. Try the splendid platter of cured meats, or mains such as ravioli with pumpkin, sage and hazelnut, or smoked salmon, lentils and poached egg.

DIGNITA HOFTUIN
CAFE €€

Map p304 (www.eatwelldogood.nl; Nieuwe Herengracht 18a; dishes €8-14; ⊘9am-6pm; 🍴🚼; Ⓜ️Waterlooplein, 🚊14 Waterlooplein) Set in the garden behind the Hermitage (p121), this cafe serves a brunchy menu of Ottolenghi-style salads, sandwiches and light snacks. Its walls are glass, and the place is flooded with light; there are also chairs and tables outside. It's a dreamy spot on a sunny summer's day.

This is a good choice for families: children can play on the enclosed grass area and there are toys inside. The cafe is part of the Not for Sale social-enterprise model, providing training and employment for vulnerable people.

RON GASTROBAR ORIENTAL
ASIAN €€

Map p304 (☏020-223 53 52; www.rongastrobar oriental.nl; Kerkstraat 23; dim sum €8.50, mains €17.50; ⊘5.30-11pm; 🍴; 🚊2/11/12 Prinsengracht) Michelin-starred chef Ron Blaauw began his food revolution at Ron Gastrobar (p167) near Vondelpark, introducing a one-price menu of tapas-style dishes so diners could eat fine cuisine without settling down for a long formal meal. This is his Asian version. The menu includes delicacies such as dim sum of steamed scallop with Chinese mushroom and crispy prawns with wasabi mayo.

PANTRY
DUTCH €€

Map p304 (☏020-620 09 22; www.thepantry. nl; Leidsekruisstraat 21; mains €13.75-20, 3-course menus €21.50-31.25; ⊘11am-10.30pm; 🚊1/2/5/7/11/12/19 Leidseplein) With wood-panelled walls and sepia lighting, this little restaurant is *gezellig* (cosy, convivial) indeed. Tuck into classic Dutch dishes such

SOUTHERN CANAL RING EATING

AMSTERDAM AMERICAN HOTEL

This **building** (Map p304; ☏020-556 30 00; www.amsterdamamericanhotel.com; Leidsekade 97; d from €250; 🚊1/2/5/7/11/12/19 Leidseplein) is a magnificent art nouveau beast. The founder of the original hotel, Cornelis Alidus Anne (CAA) Steinigeweg had helped establish a Dutch settlement on Grand Island, New York, hence the 'American' in the name. Designed by architect Willem Kromhout, today's hotel is an expansion of the original 1880s Viennese Renaissance-style building, which was covered in symbols of Americana. Life-sized statues on the facade represent the five continents.

You can, of course, stay at the luxury hotel. Its restaurant **Café Americain** (Map p304; ☏020-556 30 10; www.cafeamericain.nl; Amsterdam American Hotel, Leidsekade 97; ⊘6.30am-midnight; 🍴; 🚊1/2/5/7/11/12/19 Leidseplein) is a heritage-listed showpiece, with a beautifully restored art nouveau interior featuring stained glass, exquisite light fittings and murals. It has long been affectionately dubbed 'Amsterdam's living room', and is open to non-guests.

as *zuurkool stamppot* (sauerkraut and potato mash served with a smoked sausage or meatball) or *hutspot* ('hotchpotch', with stewed beef, potatoes, carrots and onions).

GOLDEN TEMPLE
VEGETARIAN €€

Map p304 (☑020-626 85 60; www.restaurant goldentemple.com/en; Utrechtsestraat 126; €15-22; ⊙5-11pm; ☑; ☐4 Prinsengracht) You can't miss this vegetarian restaurant thanks to a bold shopfront painted to resemble temple carvings. Inside, psychedelic paintings and colourful cushions surround guests feasting on no-meat meals ranging from curry to pizza and corn tortillas. Last order is at 9.30pm.

CAFÉ GEORGE
BRASSERIE €€

Map p304 (☑020-626 08 02; www.cafegeorge. nl; Leidsegracht 84; mains €7.50-27; ⊙11am-midnight; ☎; ☐2/11/12 Prinsengracht) This canal-side brasserie will likely lure you in with cool Amsterdammers congregating on white chairs outside, but the inside is just as charming – skylights bathe a long row of tables against a grand wooden bar. Several wines are available by the glass.

Fancy comfort dishes include lobster linguini and steak frites, but you can also order sandwiches, salads and eggs.

CAFÉ VAN LEEUWEN
BRASSERIE €€

Map p304 (www.cafevanleeuwen.nl; Keizersgracht 711; mains €7-17; ⊙8am-10pm Mon-Sat, to 9pm Sun; ☐4 Keizersgracht) Brown cafe in style,

---

ROYAL PASTRIES

Patisserie Holtkamp (Map p304; www.patisserieholtkamp.nl; Vijzelgracht 15; baked goods €3-7; ⊙8.30am-6pm Mon-Fri, to 5pm Sat; Ⓜ Vijzelgracht, ☐1/7/19/24 Vijzelgracht) is where the Dutch royals stock up on baked goods. It was founded in 1886; the gorgeous art deco interior was added in 1928 by architect Piet Kramer. There's a lavish fit-for-a-queen spread inside, with delicacies including creamy cakes and its famous *kroketten* (croquettes).

The *kroketten*, with fillings such as lobster and veal, are on the menus of some of the city's top restaurants. Its prawn versions are reputedly Amsterdam's finest.

Check out the gilded royal coat of arms, topped by a crown, on the building's facade.

---

with lots of dark-wooded charm, dangling light bulbs and an exposed brick wall, this spot offers fine brasserie-style dishes such as succulent hamburgers and open sandwiches. It's a great place for breakfast or brunch, and the canal-side setting is fabulous.

The bar stays open until 1am Sunday to Thursday, and 3am Friday and Saturday.

ROSE'S CANTINA
LATIN AMERICAN €€

Map p304 (☑020-625 97 97; www.roses-amsterdam.nl; Reguliersdwarsstraat 40; mains €18-28.50; ⊙kitchen 5.30-10pm Tue-Thu, bar to 1am, to 3am Fri & Sat; ☐2/11/12 Koningsplein) Rose's is a great addition to Amsterdam's gay street with a grass-green interior topped by massive glitter balls and a greenery-fringed courtyard. Enjoy pisco sours and dishes like ceviche (raw fish cured in lime juice), Argentinian steak and grilled octopus in either setting. On the weekends, DJs spin pop, house and Latin beats, leading to impromptu dance parties.

IN DE BUURT
INTERNATIONAL €€

Map p304 (www.indebuurt-amsterdam.nl; Lijnbaansgracht 246; mains €12.50-16; ⊙kitchen 5-10pm, bar to 1am Sun-Thu, to 3am Fri & Sat; ☐1/2/5/7/11/12/19 Leidseplein) It may be in the Leidseplein, but In de Buurt keeps it classy, serving up spare ribs glazed with apple and ginger and steak tartare with truffle mayo, as well as delicious gin and tonics. It has a canal-side summer terrace and a cosy interior with exposed-brick walls, beams and bottles.

DE BLAUWE HOLLANDER
DUTCH €€

Map p304 (☑020-627 05 21; www.deblauwehollander.nl; Leidsekruisstraat 28; mains €15.50-19.75; ⊙noon-11pm; ☐1/2/5/7/11/12/19 Leidseplein) It's all cosiness and comfort food at this red-lamp-lit place, with a menu including Dutch staples such as pea soup with bacon, and *stamppot* (veggie mash) with pork sausage. Look for the Dutch flag flying out front.

BOUCHON DU CENTRE
FRENCH €€

Map p304 (☑020-330 11 28; www.bouchonducentre.nl; Falckstraat 3; mains €15-20; ⊙noon-3pm & 5-8pm Wed-Fri, noon-5pm Sat; ☐4/7 Frederiksplein) Classic red-and-white gingham tablecloths set the scene at this authentic-feeling Lyonnais *bouchon* (informal rustic bistro). The menu changes daily but revolves around *bouchon* staples such as *andouillette* (offal sausage) and *quenelles de brochet* (pike dumplings). Don't miss a round of wonderfully gooey St Marcellin cheese and Rhône Valley wines such as Beaujolais.

LO STIVALE D'ORO
ITALIAN €€

Map p304 (📞020-638 73 07; www.lostivaledoro.nl; Amstelstraat 49; pizzas €9.50-15, mains €8-22; ⏰5-10.30pm Wed-Sun; 🚊4/14 Rembrandtplein) Conviviality is the name of the game at the 'Golden Boot', which offers a textbook gregarious Italian welcome, plus awesome pizzas and pastas. Italian owner Mario occasionally pulls out his guitar and strums for the crowd.

PIET DE LEEUW
STEAK €€

Map p304 (📞020-623 71 81; www.pietdeleeuw.nl; Noorderstraat 11; mains €13-25; ⏰noon-10.30pm Mon-Fri, 5-10.30pm Sat & Sun; 🚊4 Prinsengracht) With dark-wood furniture and wood-panelled walls hung with pictures, this feels like an old-school pub. The building dates from 1900, but it's been a steakhouse and a hang-out since the 1940s. Sit down at individual or communal tables and tuck into good-value steaks served with a choice of sauces, salad and piping-hot fries.

BOJO
INDONESIAN €€

Map p304 (📞020-622 74 34; www.bojo.nl; Lange Leidsedwarsstraat 49-51; mains €12-18; ⏰4pm-midnight; 🚊2/11/12 Prinsengracht) Bojo was started by two cousins who'd worked on a cruise ship together more than 40 years ago, and is a good choice for some late-night, stomach-lining Indonesian food. It's surprisingly peaceful, given the location. Clubbers come for sizzling satay, filling fried rice and steaming bowls of noodle soup.

EATMOSFERA
ITALIAN €€

Map p304 (📞020-737 23 18; Korte Reguliersdwarsstraat 8; dishes €15-27.50; ⏰5.30-10.30pm Sun-Thu, to 11pm Fri, noon-4pm & 6-11pm Sat; 📞📶; 🚊4/14 Rembrandtplein) Hidden behind an orange door down a quiet alley, Eatmosfera is an Italian eatery that's comfy and modern. Exposed brick, dim lights and ample artwork set the mood for wining and dining. Wood-fired pizzas and pasta are served from an open kitchen.

BO NAM
VIETNAMESE €€

Map p304 (📞020-370 21 78; www.bo-nam.nl; Lange Leidsedwarsstraat 57; mains €10-24; ⏰noon-10pm Mon-Thu, to 11pm Fri & Sat; 🚊1/2/5/7/11/12/19 Leidseplein) This sleekly modern Vietnamese eatery is a cut-above

affair with low lighting and an arty 'camouflage' mural. Try the *bánh mì* (Vietnamese baguette) for lunch, or plump for delicately prepared *pho* (Vietnamese noodle soup) and rice noodles at dinner.

The bar stays open until 1am Monday to Thursday, and to 3am Friday and Saturday.

HERENGRACHT RESTAURANT & BAR
EUROPEAN €€

Map p304 (📞020-616 24 82; www.deherengracht.com; Herengracht 435; mains lunch €6-24, dinner €17.50-23.50; ⏰kitchen 11am-10.30pm, bar to 1am Sun-Thu, to 3am Fri & Sat; 📶; 🚊2/11/12 Koningsplein) With canal-side seats on a busy corner, Herengracht has a sleek interior and a rear courtyard for dining al fresco. Choose from signature dishes like steak tartare, and a brioche burger with fried onions, bacon and mature Dutch cheese.

★GUTS
EUROPEAN €€€

Map p304 (📞020-362 00 30; www.bredagroup-amsterdam.com/guts; Utrechtsestraat 6; menu €42.50, extra dishes €5-18; ⏰noon-3pm & 6-10pm; 🚊4/14 Rembrandtplein) Guts' four-course menu is constantly changing and customisable with add-on à la carte options, like razor clams and charcuterie. The focus is on sustainable, regional products with little flourishes, and for lunch you can even share a whole turbot. Exposed bulbs and white-brick walls keep things sophisticated.

VAN VLAANDEREN
FRENCH €€€

Map p304 (📞020-622 82 92; www.restaurant-vanvlaanderen.nl; Weteringschans 175; mains €16-35; ⏰6-10pm Tue-Thu & Sat, noon-10pm Fri; Ⓜ Vijzelgracht, 🚊1/7/19/24 Vijzelgracht) One of the best French restaurants in town, Van Vlaanderen purrs with class, with white tablecloths, sophisticated French cooking (how about some spring chicken with duck liver, Cajun herbs and vermouth?) and lovely canal views from a raised deck.

🍷 DRINKING & NIGHTLIFE

There's something for everyone in this nightlife zone. Choose from the more laid-back, if often heaving, theatre *cafés* (bars) and brown cafes (traditional Dutch pubs), frenetic gay bars, smoky coffeeshops and pumping house clubs. The bars and clubs of Leidseplein

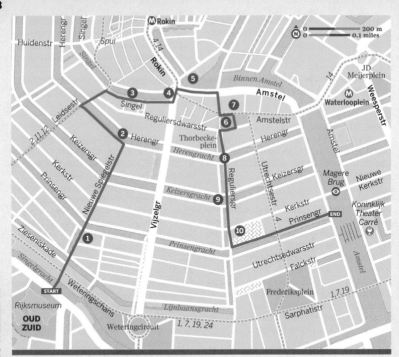

Neighbourhood Walk
Southern Canal Ring

START SINGELGRACHT
END AMSTEL RIVER
LENGTH 4KM; TWO HOURS

Set off at the Singelgracht and head north into the ❶ **Spiegel Quarter**, a nexus of canalside art and antique shops, the main stretch of which is Nieuwe Spiegelstraat. On Herengracht, Amsterdam's swankiest patch of real estate – the ❷ **Golden Bend** (p120) – has a row of double-fronted houses (rare in Amsterdam) awash with classical French flourishes.

Stop by the bustling ❸ **Bloemenmarkt** (p121); at the eastern end, you'll see one of Amsterdam's most enduring emblems, the striking ❹ **Munttoren** (Mint Tower), built in 1480 as part of Amsterdam's wall and fortifications. From here, head east along the Amstel river to take in the grand ❺ **Hotel de l'Europe** facade, and the terrace restaurant where polished skiffs moor. At the bridge, turn south into tiny Halvemaansteeg and the beating heart of the entertainment

district around ❻ **Rembrandtplein** (p120). Pose with the life-sized figures re-creating Rembrandt's *The Night Watch*, before making your way up the stairs to ❼ **De Kroon** (p131), one of the square's most stylish *grand cafés* with a great view of all the action.

Pass through shady Thorbeckeplein to the Herengracht, lean on the bridge and do your Insta-thing on ❽ **Reguliersgracht** (p120), the 'canal of seven bridges'. Where Prinsengracht crosses Reguliersgracht, there is a red-painted home with a statue of a stork over the door – the dwelling once belonged to a midwife.

Where Keizersgracht and Reguliersgracht join up, you can count a whopping ❾ **15 bridges** as you peer east-west and north-south. Further south you'll come to the ❿ **Amstelkerk** (p123), a curious wooden church with a belfry that still looks makeshift despite being built more than 300 years ago.

Head east down Prinsengracht until you reach the Amstel river. From here, you can admire the petite **Magere Brug** (p120) and **Koninklijk Theater Carré** (p133).

feel more full of tourists than locals, but there is a mix of options in the area, and they're always fun if you're up for it. If you're looking for more serious club action, Rembrandtplein's the ticket. Utrechtsestraat is great for more sophisticated local haunts, while rainbow flags abound on Reguliersdwarsstraat, Amsterdam's major gay street.

★BAKHUYS AMSTERDAM   CAFE

(✆020-370 48 61; www.bakhuys-amsterdam.nl; Sarphatistraat 61; ⊙7am-7pm Mon-Sat, 8am-5pm Sun; ☜; Ⓜ Weesperplein, 🚊Weesperplein) In this large industrial space, watch from up close as bakers knead dough and work the wood-fired oven. Benches provide ample space for coffee dates or laptop work fuelled by pastries and sweets.

★BACK TO BLACK   CAFE

Map p304 (✆020-304 49 88; www.backtoblack coffee.nl; Weteringstraat 48; ⊙8am-6pm Mon-Fri, from 9am Sat & Sun; ☜; 🚊1/7/19 Spiegelgracht) It's easy to lose track of time in this ultra-cool neighbourhood cafe with teal walls and exposed light bulbs and wood shelves hanging on ropes. Back to Black chooses its beans with care and roasts them locally in Amsterdam. It also serves a small but stellar selection of cakes and pastries.

★DOOR 74   COCKTAIL BAR

Map p304 (✆020-634 04 51 22; www.door-74.nl; Reguliersdwarsstraat 74; ⊙8pm-3am Sun-Thu, to 4am Fri & Sat; 🚊4/14 Rembrandtplein) You'll need to send a text or WhatsApp for a reservation to gain entry to this speakeasy behind an unmarked door. Some of Amsterdam's most amazing cocktails are served in a classy, dark-timbered Prohibition-era atmosphere beneath pressed-tin ceilings. Themed cocktail lists change regularly. Very cool.

★CAFÉ LANGEREIS   CAFE

Map p304 (✆020-785 06 41; www.cafelangereis. nl; Amstel 202; ⊙10am-3am Sun-Thu, to 4am Fri & Sat; ☜; 🚊4/14 Rembrandtplein) By the Amstel, Café Langereis is a recreation of a brown cafe, a look the friendly young owner so admires that she scoured the city for antique fixtures and furniture to evoke the lived-in vintage feel. Freshly ground coffee, fresh flowers on the tables, an upright piano and a classic-rock soundtrack keep things vibrant.

OTHERSIDE   COFFEESHOP

Map p304 (www.theotherside.nl; Reguliersdwarsstraat 6; ⊙10am-midnight; ☜; 🚊2/11/12 Koningsplein) This buzzing choice has designer chandeliers and a lively, laid-back vibe. It's on the neighbourhood's main gay street and is favoured by a mixed crowd.

A BAR   COCKTAIL BAR

Map p304 (✆020-520 32 45; www.a-bar.nl; Professor Tulpplein 1, InterContinental Amstel Amsterdam; ⊙5pm-1am Mon-Thu, noon-1am Fri & Sat; ☜; Ⓜ Weesperplein, 🚊1/7/19 Weesperplein) The InterContinental Amstel Amsterdam is an impressive 19th-century building right on the riverside, and its A Bar opens on to a huge sofa-lined terrace. Inky-blue walls are a stylish backdrop for cocktails such as an Albert Cuyp Markt with *stroopwafel*-infused vodka. It also serves bar snacks. There are regular chilled DJ sessions and live music.

DUKE OF TOKYO   KARAOKE

Map p304 (✆020-777 93 32; www.dukeoftokyo. com; Reguliersdwarsstraat 37; ⊙5pm-1am Mon, Wed & Thu, to 3am Fri, 2pm-3am Sat, to 1am Sun; 🚊2/11/12 Konigsplein) From front to back, Duke of Tokyo is packed with trendy designs. Each of the bar's eight karaoke booths has a different look inspired by districts like Harajuku. Reserve online for two hours starting from €10 per person. A wide variety of cocktails, wine and sake are sure to reveal your inner starlet.

BAR LEMPICKA   CAFE

Map p304 (✆020-622 02 09; www.barlempicka. com/en; Sarphatistraat 23; ⊙9am-1am Sun-Thu, to 3am Fri & Sat; ☜; Ⓜ1/7/19 Weesperplein, 🚊1/7/19 Weesperplein) This spacious art deco haven opens early for breakfast. As the day progresses, the leather booths and bar stools fill up with coffee- and cocktail-drinkers. You can also sit on the terrace for a nice Amstel view.

BAR DÓ   BAR

Map p304 (✆020-240 22 39; Vijzelgracht 35; 10am-1am Sun-Thu, to 3am Fri & Sat; ☜; Ⓜ Vijzelgracht, 🚊1/7/19/24 Vijzelgracht) Tropical decor and refreshing cocktails make Bar Dó a lovely escape. If the weather agrees, the outdoor street seating opposite a set of leaning houses is an excellent spot for people-watching.

SOUTHERN CANAL RING DRINKING & NIGHTLIFE

BOEREJONGENS — COFFEESHOP

Map p304 (☑020-447 35 57; www.boerejongens.com; Utrechtsestraat 21; ☺7am-12.45am; ☐4 Keizersgracht) At Boerejongens, a takeaway cannabis dispensary, good style is as important as good product. Employees wear white aprons, suspenders and bowties, while 'bouncers' in bowler hats coordinate the queue out front.

GREENWOODS — TEAHOUSE

Map p304 (☑020-420 43 30; www.greenwoods.eu; Keizersgracht 465; mains €12-15; ☺9.30am-4pm Mon-Thu, to 5pm Fri-Sun; ☎; ☐2/11/12 Keizersgracht) Greenwoods' cosy basement is perfect for escaping the canal bustle for scones and a cuppa. Breakfast and lunch are also available, including eggs prepared many ways and burgers. There is also an outdoor seating area overlooking Keizersgracht.

BETTY BOOP — COFFEESHOP

Map p304 (Reguliersdwarsstraat 29; ☺9am-1am; ☎; ☐4/14 Rembrandtplein) The 2nd floor of this cool gay-friendly coffeeshop is a great vantage point over the Reguliersdwarsstraat nightlife strip, and a popular place to hang out and sample some quality smokes. Its now-closed sister branch was where Quentin Tarantino wrote some of *Pulp Fiction*. It's uncertain whether the brand's infamous space cakes contributed to his creative flow.

DE BALIE — CAFE

Map p304 (☑020-553 51 30; www.debalie.nl; Kleine Gartmanplantsoen 10; ☺9am-1am Mon-Thu, to 3am Fri, 10am-3am Sat, to 1am Sun; ☎; ☐1/2/5/7/11/12/19 Leidseplein) In the former district courthouse, this appealingly gracious hang-out has triple-height ceilings, stained glass and chandeliers. It's a cafe, bar and arts centre that hosts events with a socio-political bent. De Balie offers a good choice of beers, cocktails, juices, teas and coffees, and food such as burgers, salads and sandwiches.

BOCCA COFFEE — COFFEE

Map p304 (www.bocca.nl; Kerkstraat 96; ☺8am-6pm Mon-Fri, from 9am Sat & Sun; ☎; ☐2/11/12 Prinsengracht) The team behind Bocca Coffee knows its stuff, having sourced beans from Ethiopia to sell to cafes across the city for more than 15 years. It's now serving some seriously good caffeine hits in this light, spacious coffeehouse. Take a seat at the large wooden bar or get comfy in a vintage armchair. Cash only.

LION NOIR — COCKTAIL BAR

Map p304 (☑020-627 66 03; www.lionnoir.nl; Reguliersdwarsstraat 28; ☺6pm-1am Sun-Thu, to 3am Fri & Sat; ☐2/11/12 Koningsplein) Lion Noir hosts a glamorous crowd, here for excellent cocktails as well as superlative dining on creative French-inspired dishes with an Asian twist. Interior artist Thijs Murré designed the eclectic, satisfyingly out-there interior of green walls, plants, birdcages and taxidermied birds; the greenery-shaded terrace is equally lovely.

CLUB UP — CLUB

Map p304 (☑020-623 69 85; www.clubup.nl; Korte Leidsedwarsstraat 26; ☺11pm-4am Thu, to 5am Fri & Sat; ☐1/2/5/7/11/12/19 Leidseplein) Garage, house, funk, soul, hip-hop, techno, live bands and performance art keep the punters happy at this small, quirky club. Entrance is occasionally through social club De Kring, at Kleine Gartmanplantsoen 7–9; check the Club Up website for details.

EIJLDERS — BROWN CAFE

Map p304 (☑020-624 27 04; www.cafeeijlders.com; Korte Leidsedwarsstraat 47; ☺4.30pm-1am Mon-Thu, noon-2am Fri & Sat, to 1am Sun; ☐1/2/5/7/11/12/19 Leidseplein) During WWII, this stained-glass-trimmed *bruin café* was a meeting place for artists who refused to toe the cultural line imposed by the Nazis, and the spirit lingers on. It's still an artists' cafe, with waistcoated waiters and a low-key feel by day, but it gets noisier at night, in keeping with its Leidseplein surrounds. Events range from pub quizzes to poetry slams.

CAFÉ DE WETERING — BROWN CAFE

Map p304 (☑020-622 96 76; Weteringstraat 37; ☺4pm-1am Mon-Thu, to 3am Fri, 3pm-2am Sat, 3pm-1am Sun; ☐1/7/19 Spiegelgracht) With a cascade of greenery draped over the outside, Café de Wetering is a cosy charmer for a drink or a snack, with a large fireplace and a gloriously faded interior that wouldn't look out of place in a Vermeer painting. It's always packed with locals, and isn't far from the antiques corridor of Nieuwe Spiegelstraat.

CAFÉ BRECHT — BAR

Map p304 (☑020-627 22 11; www.cafebrecht.nl; Weteringschans 157; 11am-1am Sun-Thu, to 3am Fri & Sat; Ⓜ Vijzelgracht, ☐1/7/19/24 Vijzelgracht) Café Brecht is one of Amsterdam's loveliest bars, with mismatched armchairs, vintage furniture, books and board games; all are a hit with a young and gorgeously boho crowd – it gets absolutely crammed in here. It's named after seminal German dramatist and poet Bertolt Brecht, hence the German poetry inscribed on the walls.

PATA NEGRA
BAR

Map p304 (☎020-422 62 50; www.pata-negra.nl; Utrechtsestraat 124; ⊗noon-1am Sun-Thu, to 3am Fri & Sat; 🚊4 Prinsengracht) Ablaze with tiling the colour of sunshine, this Spanish tapas bar has an agreeably battered interior and its margaritas are the business. It gets busy with a lively crowd downing sangria with garlic-fried shrimps and grilled sardines (tapas €6 to €12.50).

FREDERIX
CAFE

Map p304 (☎020-223 18 03; www.frederixcof fee.com; Frederiksplein 29; ⊗8am-6pm Mon-Sat, from 9am Sun; 🛜; 🚊4 Prinsengracht) This tucked-away, skylit place on lush Frederiksplein specialises in roasting beans from international coffee specialists; as you'd expect, the coffee is damn fine. It offers exceedingly good poached eggs and other brunch staples.

COFFEESHOP FREE
COFFEESHOP

Map p304 (Reguliersdwarsstraat 70; ⊗10am-1am; 🛜; 🚊24 Muntplein) Pocket-sized Coffeeshop Free has sported its bamboo-heavy tiki-bar vibe for decades. The South Seas mural provides a nicely faded, balmy-days setting, though there's a TV screen showing sport too.

CAFÉ DE SPUYT
BROWN CAFE

Map p304 (☎020-624 89 01; www.cafedespuyt. nl; Korte Leidsedwarsstraat 86; ⊗4pm-3am Mon-Thu, 3pm-4am Fri & Sat, 3pm-3am Sun; 🚊1/2/5/7/11/12/19 Leidseplein) Amid the hubbub off busy Leidseplein, this is a mellow, friendly brown cafe with yellow walls and mismatched decorations. The main attraction here is the massive chalkboard menu of more than 150 Dutch and Belgian speciality beers, including abbey and Trappist brews and seasonal tipples.

BULLDOG PALACE
COFFEESHOP

Map p304 (www.thebulldog.com; Leidseplein 15; ⊗coffeeshop 8am-1am, bar 10am-1am Mon-Wed, to 2am Thu & Sun, to 3am Fri & Sat; 🛜; 🚊1/2/5/7/11/12/19 Leidseplein) Bulldog's as corporate as a coffeeshop gets, with a chain of outlets, a hotel and merchandise, but it's

one of the oldest and most famous in Amsterdam. Housed in a former police station, it has two sides: one for smoking, one for drinking. Both crowds are pretty much the same: stags and hens, backpackers and corporate travellers blowing off steam.

DE KROON
BAR

Map p304 (☎020-625 20 11; www.dekroon.nl; Rembrandtplein 17; ⊗4pm-1am Sun-Thu, to 3am Fri, 3pm-4am Sat; 🚊4/14 Rembrandtplein) Up winding sets of stairs, Rembrandtplein's renovated *grand café* dates from 1898. It has dizzyingly high ceilings, armchairs to sink into and glittering chandeliers. De Kroon offers a long list of cocktails, wine and beers, plus a barbecue-oriented menu of grilled fish and meat. It converts into a club on Friday and Saturday nights.

BRASSERIE NEL
BAR

Map p304 (☎020-626 11 99; www.brasserienel. nl; Amstelveld 12; ⊗10am-1am Sun-Thu, to 3am Fri & Sat; 🛜; 🚊4 Prinsengracht) NeL, a stately white house on a hidden-away square, is a contender for having the best terrace in Amsterdam. Outside, mature trees provide a canopy that dapples the sunshine on a good day. Inside, there's a mellow brasserie on one side and a stylish bar on the other.

OOSTERLING
BROWN CAFE

Map p304 (☎020-623 41 40; www.cafeooster ling.nl; Utrechtsestraat 140; ⊗8.30am-9pm Mon & Tue, to 1am Wed-Sat, to 8pm Sun; 🚊4 Prinsengracht) Opened in the 1700s as a tea and coffee outlet for the Dutch East India Company, Oosterling is now run by friendly brothers Oscar and Marcel, the fourth generation of Oosterlings at the helm since 1877. It's one of the very few *cafés* with an off-licence bottle-shop permit.

SUZY WONG
BAR

Map p304 (www.suzy-wong.nl; Korte Leidsedwarsstraat 45; ⊗6pm-1am Sun-Thu, to 3am Fri & Sat; 🚊1/2/5/7/11/12/19 Leidseplein) A knowingly fabulous crowd frequents Suzy Wong, a celeb magnet for its exclusive feel and louche drawing room interior featuring red-velveteen wallpaper and a faux bamboo garden. Fresh fruit mojitos are the tipple of choice; on Thursday's Mojito Night, they cost just €6.50.

CAFÉ SCHILLER
CAFE

Map p304 (☎020-624 98 46; www.cafeschil ler.nl; Rembrandtplein 24a; ⊗3pm-1am Mon-Thu, 12.30pm-3am Fri & Sat, to 1am Sun; 🛜; 🚊4/14

SOUTHERN CANAL RING DRINKING & NIGHTLIFE

Rembrandtplein) Schiller has fabulous original art deco fittings such as funky chandeliers and lamps shaped like thorny roses. Portraits of Dutch actors and cabaret artists from the 1920s and '30s line the walls, painted by the eponymous former owner himself.

CAFE MANKIND BAR

Map p304 (☎020-638 47 55; www.mankind.nl; Weteringstraat 60; ⏱noon-midnight Mon-Sat; ☏; 🚊1/7/19 Spiegelgracht) This tucked-away gay-friendly cafe-bar is conveniently close to the Rijksmuseum and has an appealing narrow terrace right alongside the canal. There is also a kitchen (noon to 4pm and 5pm to 8.30pm) serving sandwiches, salads and small snacks.

DOLPHINS COFFEESHOP COFFEESHOP

Map p304 (☎020-774 33 36; Kerkstraat 39; ⏱10am-1am; ☏; 🚊2/11/12 Prinsengracht) Painted with huge fishtank-style murals and decorated with fake rocks and other underwater ephemera, this trippy space makes it seem like you're smoking underwater (if you squint). You can also get toasties, pastries, tea and juices.

CHICAGO SOCIAL CLUB BAR

Map p304 (☎020-760 11 71; www.chicagosocialclub.nl; Leidseplein 12; ⏱bar 8pm-4am Sun-Thu, to 5am Fri & Sat, club from 11pm Thu-Sat; 🚊1/2/5/7/11/12/19 Leidseplein) Founded in 1923, this intimate bar and club on Leidseplein is still going strong, though the music policy has somewhat changed: these days, the sonic menu is filled with house and techno. Nights here attract a laid-back, cool crowd. The minimum age is 21.

ITA BRASSERIE CAFE

Map p304 (☎020-795 99 95; www.ita.nl/nl/café-brasserie; Leidseplein 26, Internationaal Theater Amsterdam; ⏱10am-1am Sun-Thu, to 2am Fri & Sat; ☏; 🚊1/2/5/7/11/12/19 Leidseplein) Hung with chandeliers, this curved and columned space looks like a wedding cake. The brasserie brims with actors and chattering culture hounds deconstructing the avant-garde play they just watched in the attached Internationaal Theater Amsterdam.

WHISKEY CAFÉ L&B BAR

Map p304 (☎020-625 23 87; www.lbwhiskyproeverijen.nl; Korte Leidsedwarsstraat 92; ⏱8pm-3am Mon-Thu, to 4am Fri & Sat, 5pm-3am Sun; 🚊1/2/5/7/11/12/19 Leidseplein) If amber spirits are your thing, you're in luck: this friendly, busy bar has 1350 (yes, 1350!) different varieties from Scotland, Ireland, America and Japan. The knowledgeable bar staff will help you navigate the list.

JIMMY WOO CLUB

Map p304 (☎020-626 31 50; www.jimmywoo.com; Korte Leidsedwarsstraat 18; ⏱11pm-3am Thu, to 4am Fri & Sat; 🚊1/2/5/7/11/12/19 Leidseplein) It's been around a while, but superluxe Jimmy Woo is still the go-to place for a crowd of beautiful young things. Its sultry look is by designer Thijs Murré, and the lower floor has a ceiling covered in tiny lights that pulsate to the music. Queues are extremely long, and the door policy strict – you have to look the part. Arrive early or call ahead to try to get on the list.

MULLIGANS IRISH PUB

Map p304 (☎020-622 13 30; www.mulligans.nl; Amstel 100; ⏱4pm-1am Mon-Thu, to 3am Fri, 2pm-3am Sat, to 1am Sun; ☏; 🚊4/14 Rembrandtplein) Foremost among Amsterdam's Irish pubs, Mulligans has properly poured Guinness and Magners cider on tap. It's great fun, with live Irish trad music most nights from around 9pm (no cover charge).

☆ ENTERTAINMENT

On either side of the Southern Canal Ring, the nightlife centres of Leidseplein and Rembrandtplein throng with people and buzz with a party atmosphere. You'll be spoilt for choice with live-music venues and nightclubs featuring big-name DJs. On Leidseplein, the grand Internationaal Theater Amsterdam stages major plays and festivals; smaller theatres and cinemas are scattered throughout the neighbourhood.

★PATHÉ TUSCHINSKITHEATER CINEMA

Map p304 (www.pathe.nl; Reguliersbreestraat 26-34; €11; ⏱9.30am-12.30am; 🚊4/14 Rembrandtplein) This fantastical cinema, with a facade that's a prime example of the Amsterdam School of architecture, is worth visiting for its sumptuous art deco interior alone. The *grote zaal* (main auditorium) is the most stunning; it generally screens blockbusters, while the smaller theatres play art-house and indie films. Visit the interior on an audio tour (€10) when films aren't playing.

SOUTHERN CANAL RING GAY & LESBIAN NIGHTLIFE VENUES

Taboo Bar (Map p304; www.taboobar.nl; Reguliersdwarsstraat 45; ⊗5pm-3am Mon-Thu, to 4am Fri, 4pm-4am Sat, to 3am Sun; 🕾; 🚊2/11/12 Koningsplein) Gay favourite Taboo has plentiful two-for-one happy hours (6pm to 8pm and 1am to 2am). It's snug inside, though on warmer days everyone spills out onto the street. On Wednesdays, cocktails cost €6 and a drag show and competitions like 'pin the tail on the sailor' take place.

Church (Map p304; www.clubchurch.nl; Kerkstraat 52; ⊗8pm-1am Tue & Wed, 10pm-4am Thu, 10pm-5am Fri & Sat, 4-8pm Sun; 🚊2/11/12 Keizersgracht) There are no sermons or psalms at this church: this is a hardcore gay cruise club that holds themed events. Unless you come dressed appropriately (check the website for details) or with super-hot boys (or are one yourself), you probably won't get in.

Montmartre (Map p304; www.cafemontmartre.nl; Halvemaansteeg 17; ⊗5pm-3am Sun-Thu, to 4am Fri & Sat; 🚊4/14 Rembrandtplein) A crammed gay bar that's long been a local favourite. It's known for its Dutch music, and patrons sing (or scream) along to recordings of Dutch ballads and old top-40 hits. There's also a lively programme of karaoke, drag, and '80s and '90s hits.

Lellebel (Map p304; www.lellebel.nl; Utrechtsestraat 4; ⊗9pm-3am Mon-Thu, 3pm-5am Fri & Sat, to 3am Sun; 🚊4/14 Rembrandtplein) This dandy place with pink leopard-print walls is just off Rembrandtplein and specialises in drag queen fabulousness. Themed nights including karaoke, singing drag queens and bingo.

The cinema was built by Abraham Tuschinski, a Polish Jewish immigrant. He and most of his family were murdered in Nazi concentration camps, and the cinema was renamed 'Tivoli'. After WWII it returned to its original name.

KONINKLIJK
THEATER CARRÉ
PERFORMING ARTS

Map p304 (☑0900 25 25 255; www.carre.nl; Amstel 115-125; admission varies; ⊗box office 4-6pm; Ⓜ Weesperplein, 🚊1/7/19 Weesperplein) The Carré family started their career with a horse act at the annual fair, progressing to this circus theatre in 1887. The classical facade is richly decorated with faces of jesters, dancers and theatre folk. It hosts a great programme of quality music and theatre; the Christmas circus is a seasonal highlight.

INTERNATIONAAL
THEATER AMSTERDAM
THEATRE

Map p304 (☑020-624 23 11; www.ita.nl; Leideplein 26; ⊗box office noon-6pm Mon-Sat & 2hr before performances; 🚊1/2/5/7/11/12/19 Leidseplein) When this theatre with the grand balcony arcade was completed in 1894, public criticism of the design was so fierce that the exterior decorations were never completed; architect Jan Springer was so upset, he retired. The horseshoe auditorium seats 1200 spectators and is used for large-scale plays, operettas and festi-vals. Don't miss the chandeliered splendour of its ITA Brasserie theatre cafe.

Be sure to check out its shop **International Theatre & Film Books** (Map p304; ☑020-622 64 89; www.theatreandfilmbooks. com; ⊗noon-6pm Mon, from 11am Tue-Sat).

PARADISO
LIVE MUSIC

Map p304 (☑020-622 45 21; www.paradiso. nl; Weteringschans 6-8; admission varies; 🕾; 🚊1/2/5/7/11/12/19 Leidseplein) In 1968 a beautiful old church turned into the 'Cosmic Relaxation Center Paradiso'. Today, the vibe is less hippy than funked-up odyssey, with big all-nighters, themed events and indie nights. The smaller hall hosts up-and-coming bands, but there's something special about the Main Hall, where it seems the stained-glass windows might shatter under the force of the fat beats.

BOURBON STREET
JAZZ & BLUES CLUB
LIVE MUSIC

Map p304 (www.bourbonstreet.nl; Leidsekruisstraat 6-8; admission varies; ⊗11pm-4am Sun-Thu, to 5am Fri & Sat; 🚊2/11/12 Prinsengracht) This intimate venue has a full and eclectic weekly music programme. Take part in open jam sessions on Mondays, or come by on Tuesdays for soul and reggae. It offers blues and rock on Wednesdays; funk on Thursdays; rock, pop and Latin on Fridays; pre-rock on Saturdays; and world, folk and samba on Sundays.

SOUTHERN CANAL RING ENTERTAINMENT

Entry is free before 11pm (10.30pm on Friday and Saturday) when most concerts start.

MELKWEG
LIVE MUSIC

Map p304 (020-531 81 81; www.melkweg. nl; Lijnbaansgracht 234a; admission varies; 1/2/5/7/11/12/19 Leidseplein) In a former dairy, the nonprofit 'Milky Way' offers a dazzling galaxy of diverse gigs, featuring both DJs and live bands. One night it's electronica, the next reggae or punk, and the next heavy metal. Roots, rock and mellow singer-songwriters all get stage time too. Check out the website for information on its cutting-edge cinema, theatre and multimedia offerings.

JAZZ CAFÉ ALTO
JAZZ

Map p304 (www.jazz-cafe-alto.nl; Korte Leidsedwarsstraat 115; 9pm-3am Sun-Thu, to 4am Fri & Sat; 1/2/5/7/11/12/19 Leidseplein) This is an intimate, atmospheric *bruin café*–style venue for serious jazz and (occasionally) blues. There are live gigs nightly. Doors open at 9pm, but music starts around 10pm – get here early if you want to snag a seat.

CAVE
LIVE MUSIC

Map p304 (020-626 89 39; www.thecave.nl; Prinsengracht 472; live-music tickets from €3; 8pm-3am Sun-Thu, to 4am Fri & Sat; 2/11/12 Prinsengracht) This grunge-fest is buried in a basement. Metalheads rejoice: there are live hard rock and metal gigs Thursday to Saturday, and DJs spin the same the rest of the week. For those about to rock, we salute you.

DE UITKIJK
CINEMA

Map p304 (www.uitkijk.nl; Prinsengracht 452; €11; hours vary; 2/11/12 Prinsengracht) Located in a 1913 canal house, this fun arthouse stalwart is the city's oldest surviving cinema and has a great programme that mixes classic oldies with more recent and foreign films.

DE HEEREN VAN AEMSTEL
LIVE MUSIC

Map p304 (www.deheerenvanaemstel.nl; Thorbeckeplein 5; noon-3am Mon-Thu, to 4am Fri & Sat; 4/14 Rembrandtplein) A student and expat favourite, this is a *grand café*–style club, with a roster of live bands and themed nights, all oiled by cheap drinks, especially midweek.

 # SHOPPING

Whether you're after tulip bulbs, quirky Dutch fashion and design, or rare *jenever* (Dutch gin), you'll find it on the Southern Canal Ring. The Nieuwe Spiegelstraat (the spine of the Spiegel Quarter) is renowned for its antique stores, bric-a-brac, collectables, tribal and oriental art, and commercial art galleries.

★CONCERTO
MUSIC

Map p304 (020-261 26 10; www.concerto. amsterdam/en; Utrechtsestraat 52-60; 10am-6pm Mon, Wed, Fri & Sat, to 7pm Thu, noon-6pm Sun; 4 Keizersgracht) This rambling shop is muso heaven, with a fabulous selection of new and secondhand vinyl and CDs encompassing every imaginable genre, including rockabilly, classical and more. It's good value and has listening facilities, plus a sofa-strewn, living-room-style cafe and regular live sessions (see the website for details).

★VLIEGER
STATIONERY

Map p304 (020-623 58 34; www.vliegerpapier. nl; Amstel 34; noon-6pm Mon, 9am-6pm Tue-Fri, 11am-5.30pm Sat; 4/14 Rembrandtplein) Love stationery and paper? Make a beeline for Vlieger. Since 1869, this two-storey shop has been supplying it all: Egyptian papyrus, beautiful handmade papers from Asia and Central America, papers inlaid with flower petals or bamboo, and paper textured like snakeskin.

★KRAMER KUNST & ANTIEK
ANTIQUES

Map p304 (020-626 11 16; www.antique-tile shop.nl; Prinsengracht 807; 10am-6pm Mon-Fri, to 7pm Sat, 1-6pm Sun; 1/7/19 Spiegelgracht) Specialising in antique blue-and-white Dutch tiles, this engrossing, crammed-to-the-rafters shop is chock-a-block with fascinating antiques, silver candlesticks, crystal decanters, jewellery and pocket watches. It's now run by the third-generation of Kramers, brothers Sebastian and Eduard.

HOOGKAMP ANTIQUARIAAT
ANTIQUES

Map p304 (020-625 88 52; www.prenten.net; Spiegelgracht 27; 1-6pm; 1/7/19 Spiegelgracht) On quaint Spiegelgracht, this antiques shop sells prints that make for great souvenirs. You'll find old maps and landscapes of Amsterdam, artworks, and quirky surprises like nature photography and scientific diagrams – just shuffle through the display stacks.

MAISONNL   HOMEWARES

Map p304 (www.maisonnl.com; Utrechtsestraat 118; ◉1-6pm Mon, 10am-6pm Tue-Sat, 1-5pm Sun; 🚋4 Prinsengracht) This little concept store sells all sorts of beautiful things you didn't realise you needed, such as Christian Lacroix notebooks and cute-as-a-button mouse toys in matchboxes by Maileg. There's a clothing rack down the back.

SHIRT SHOP   CLOTHING

Map p304 (🕿020-423 20 88; www.shirtshopam sterdam.com; Reguliersdwarsstraat 64; ◉1-7pm; 🚋24 Muntplein) On Amsterdam's main gay street, this shop has a kaleidoscopic array of the go-to going-out garb for many local men: nicely patterned smart shirts, as well as some funky T-shirts featuring Mexican skulls and more.

TINKERBELL   TOYS

Map p304 (🕿020-625 88 30; www.tinkerbelltoys. nl; Spiegelgracht 10; ◉1-6pm Mon, 10am-6pm Tue-Sat, noon-5pm Sun; 🚋1/7/19 Spiegelgracht) The mechanical bear blowing bubbles outside this shop fascinates kids, as do the intriguing technical and scientific toys inside. You'll also find historical costumes, plush toys and a section for babies.

ATELIER ANNA + NINA   JEWELLERY

Map p304 (🕿020-261 57 17; www.anna-nina.nl; Reguliersgracht 85h; ◉noon-6pm Mon, 10am-6pm Tue-Fri, 11am-5pm Sat, 11am-5pm Sun; 🚋4 Prinsengracht) Inside a beautiful brick building, this shop from local jewellery designer Anna + Nina sells dainty and minimalistic pieces.

SKATEBOARDS
AMSTERDAM   SPORTS & OUTDOORS

Map p304 (🕿020-421 20 96; www.skateboards-amsterdam.nl; Vijzelstraat 77; ◉1-6pm Sun & Mon, 11am-6pm Tue-Sat; 🚋24 Muntplein) Skater-dude heaven, with everything required for the freewheeling lifestyle: cruisers, longboards, shoes, laces, caps, beanies, bags, backpacks, and clothing including Spitfire and Thrasher T-shirts and a fantastic selection of band T-shirts.

MOBILIA   HOMEWARES

Map p304 (🕿020-622 90 75; www.mobilia.nl; Utrechtsestraat 62; ◉9.30am-6pm Mon-Sat; 🚋4 Prinsengracht) Dutch and international design is stunningly showcased at this three-storey 'lifestyle studio', with sofas, workstations, bookshelves, lighting, cushions, rugs and much more.

HART'S WIJNHANDEL   ALCOHOL

Map p304 (www.hartswijn.nl; Vijzelgracht 27; ◉10am-6pm Mon, 9.30am-6pm Tue-Fri, 10am-5pm Sat; Ⓜ Vijzelgracht, 🚋1/7/19/24 Vijzelgracht) Browsing for *jenever* and French and Italian wines at this genteel, galleried shop with a pedigree stretching back to 1880 is an absolute pleasure. Classical music plays in the background and knowledgeable staff are on hand to help.

JASKI   ART

Map p304 (🕿20-620 39 39; www.jaski.nl; Nieuwe Spiegelstraat 29; ◉noon-6pm; 🚋2/11/12 Keizersgracht) A large commercial gallery selling paintings, prints, ceramics and sculptures by some of the most famous members of the CoBrA (Copenhagen, Brussels, Amsterdam) movement.

LIEVE HEMEL   ART

Map p304 (🕿062-903 90 95; www.lievehemel. nl; Nieuwe Spiegelstraat 3; ◉noon-6pm Tue-Sat; 🚋16/24 Keizersgracht) This small, fine gallery specialises in magnificent contemporary Dutch realist paintings and sculptures.

LOOK OUT   CLOTHING

Map p304 (🕿020-625 50 32; www.lookoutmode. nl; Utrechtsestraat 91-93; ◉noon-6pm Mon, 10am-6pm Tue-Sat; 🚋4 Prinsengracht) Look Out has been peddling funky threads since 1972, and is run by the daughter of the original founder. Catering to men and women, it sells notably colourful clothes and stocks super-stylish labels such as Zenggi, Xirena and Missoni.

REFLEX MODERN ART GALLERY   ART

Map p304 (www.reflexamsterdam.com; Weteringschans 79a; ◉11am-6pm Tue-Sun; 🚋1/7/19 Spiegelgracht) This stylish and prominent gallery shows and sells contemporary art, prints, photography, and books from international artists.

SOUTHERN CANAL RING SHOPPING

Jordaan & the West

JORDAAN | THE WEST

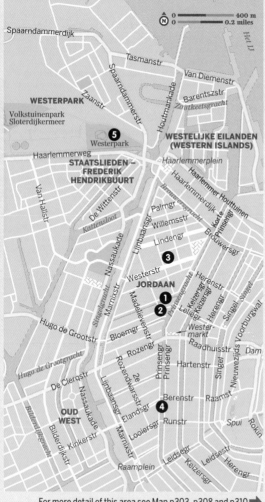

Neighbourhood Top Five

❶ De Twee Zwaantjes (p145) Losing yourself in the labyrinth of narrow streets and charming canals before spending the evening in the neighbourhood's *bruin cafés* (brown cafes; traditional Dutch pubs) such as this one – nothing is more quintessentially Amsterdam.

❷ Amsterdam Tulip Museum (p138) Learning about the fascinating history and production of the country's favourite bloom.

❸ Pianola Museum (p138) Listening to rare jazz and classical tunes play on vintage pianolas.

❹ Houseboat Museum (p138) Discovering what it's like to live on the city's waterways aboard this barge dating from 1914.

❺ Westerpark (p140) Cycling around the unique mash-up of reedy wilderness and old gasworks buildings turned into design studios, cafes, restaurants and theatres.

For more detail of this area see Map p303, p308 and p310 ➡

Explore Jordaan & the West

Though gentrified today, the Jordaan was a rough, densely populated *volksbuurt* (district for the common people) until the mid-20th century, and that history still shows. You'll discover that this neighbourhood is a curiously enchanting mix of its traditional gritty, hard-drinking, leftist character and its revitalised, trend-conscious sheen.

Start the day at the northern end of the Jordaan and criss-cross towards the neighbourhood's south, catching the area's museums, architecture and, if you time it right, markets along the way. Take a coffee break at one of the many canal-side cafes along the Prinsengracht.

On day two, go west. Hop on a bike and wend through the Western Islands before a spin around verdant Westerpark (p140). In the evening, revel in the possibilities that any night in the Westergasfabriek (p140) presents, from an art-house film to jazz or rock 'n' roll.

Local Life

⇒ **Markets** Join the area's residents browsing the weekly outdoor markets – Noordermarkt (p149), Lindengracht Market (p149) and Westermarkt (p149) – for mouthwatering food, bargain clothes and flea-market treasures.

⇒ **Cultural hang-outs** Locals flock to former gasworks and now cutting-edge cultural complex Westergasfabriek (p140) to enjoy its festivals, bars and restaurants...and more markets (www.sundaymarket.nl) too.

⇒ **Docklands dining** Two of Amsterdam's most extraordinary bar-restaurants – in a former offshore pirate radio and TV rig, and aboard a moored 1927-built ferry – are just north of the Western Islands in the Houthavens (p141) area.

Getting There & Away

⇒ **Tram** Trams 3, 5, 7, 17 and 19 skirt the neighbourhood's western edge; trams 13 and 17 go through its centre.

⇒ **Bus** Buses 18, 21, 22 and 48 provide the quickest access from Centraal Station to the neighbourhood's north and west, and the Western Islands.

⇒ **Car** Whatever you do, don't try to drive through the Jordaan's narrow streets. Seriously.

Lonely Planet's Top Tip

Be aware that trams 3 and 5 don't pass by Centraal Station (p262) but take ring routes around the centre instead. If you're heading to areas such as Westerpark (p140) and Westergasfabriek (p140) from Centraal, a bus is by far your best bet.

 Best Places to Eat

⇒ Mossel en Gin (p143)
⇒ Daalder (p142)
⇒ Wolf Atelier (p143)
⇒ REM Eiland (p141)
⇒ Marius (p144)
⇒ Balthazar's Keuken (p141)

For reviews, see p140.

 Best Places to Drink

⇒ 't Smalle (p144)
⇒ Monks Coffee Roasters (p147)
⇒ Brouwerij Troost Westergas (p147)
⇒ Westergasterras (p147)
⇒ Café Papeneiland (p144)
⇒ Cafe Soundgarden (p144)

For reviews, see p144.

Best Places to Shop

⇒ Moooi Gallery (p149)
⇒ Het Oud-Hollandsch Snoepwinkeltje (p148)
⇒ Lindengracht Market (p149)
⇒ Memento (p149)
⇒ Robins Hood (p150)

For reviews, see p149.

JORDAAN & THE WEST

◉ SIGHTS

The area doesn't have any big-hitting sights, but that's not the point. In the Jordaan it's the little things that are appealing – the narrow lanes, the old facades, the funny little shops and taking your time wandering without worrying if you get lost. Likewise in the West, the key attractions are wandering, eating and nightlife (not necessarily in that order).

◉ Jordaan

BROUWERSGRACHT   CANAL

Map p308 (Brewers Canal; 🚋3 Haarlemmerplein) Pretty as a Golden Age painting, the Brewers Canal took its name from the many breweries located here in the 16th and 17th centuries. Goods such as leather, coffee, whale oil and spices were also stored and processed here in giant warehouses, such as those with the row of spout gables that still stand at Brouwersgracht 188–194.

It's a great place to stroll and to see the waterborne action on King's Day (p12).

AMSTERDAM TULIP MUSEUM   MUSEUM

Map p308 (🕿020-421 00 95; www.amsterdam tulipmuseum.com; Prinsengracht 116; adult/child €5/3; ⏰10am-6pm; 🚋13/17 Westermarkt) Allow around half an hour at this diminutive museum, which offers an overview of the history of the country's favourite bloom. Through exhibits, timelines and two short films (in English), you'll learn how Ottoman merchants encountered the flowers in the Himalayan steppes and began commercial production in Turkey, how fortunes were made and lost during Dutch 'Tulipmania' in the 17th century, and how bulbs were used as food during WWII. You'll also discover present-day growing and harvesting techniques.

There's a great collection of tulip vases designed to accommodate separate stems, and a gift shop overflowing with floral souvenirs.

PIANOLA MUSEUM   MUSEUM

Map p308 (🕿020-627 96 24; www.pianola.nl; Westerstraat 106; museum adult/child €9/5, concert tickets from €12.50; ⏰11am-5pm Fri & Sat, to 4pm Sun year-round, concerts Sep-Jun; 🚋3/5 Marnixplein) This is a very special place, crammed with pianolas from the early 1900s. The museum has around 50,

although only a dozen are on display at any given time, as well as some 30,000 music rolls and a player pipe organ. The curator gives an hour-long guided tour and music demonstrations with great zest. Regular concerts are held on the player pianos, featuring anything from Mozart to Fats Waller and rare classical or jazz tunes composed specially for the instrument.

More eclectic musical offerings include a popular tango series.

HOUSEBOAT MUSEUM   MUSEUM

Map p310 (🕿020-427 07 50; www.houseboat museum.nl; Prinsengracht 296k; adult/child €4.50/3.50; ⏰10am-5pm daily Jul & Aug, Tue-Sun Sep-Jun; 🚋13/17 Westermarkt) This quirky museum, a 23m-long sailing barge from 1914, offers a good sense of how *gezellig* (cosy) life can be on the water. The actual displays are minimal, but you can watch a presentation on houseboats (some pretty and some ghastly) and inspect the sleeping, living, cooking and dining quarters with all the mod cons. Cash only.

AMSTERDAM CHEESE MUSEUM   MUSEUM

Map p308 (🕿020-331 66 05; www.cheesemu seumamsterdam.com; Prinsengracht 112; ⏰9am-7pm; 🚋13/17 Westermarkt) **FREE** It's a tourist ploy, but a good-humoured one. The main floor is a cheese shop with abundant free samples. The basement floor contains a small 'museum' with a handful of exhibits, clothes you can don to look like a Dutch cheesemaker and snap a photo, and the world's most expensive cheese slicer (encrusted with diamonds).

BLOEMGRACHT   CANAL

Map p308 (Flower Canal; 🚋13/17 Westermarkt) In the 17th century the 'Herengracht of the Jordaan', as the Bloemgracht was called, was home to paint and sugar factories, and a large number of fine gabled houses, such as the Renaissance-style **De Drie Hendricken** (Map p308; Bloemgracht 87-91). Many artists also lived on Bloemgracht, including Jurriaan Andriessen, whose work is displayed in the Rijksmuseum.

EGELANTIERSGRACHT   CANAL

Map p308 (🚋13/17 Westermarkt) Many parts of the Jordaan are named after trees and flowers, and this canal, lined by lovely houses built for artisans and skilled traders, takes its name from the eglantine rose (sweet briar).

JOHNNY JORDAANPLEIN SQUARE

Map p310 (cnr Prinsengracht & Elandsgracht; ⬚13/17 Westermarkt) This shady little square is named for Johnny Jordaan (the pseudonym of Johannes Hendricus van Musscher), a popular musician in the mid-1900s who sang the romantic music known as *levenslied* (tears-in-your-beer-style ballads). The colourfully painted hut – a municipal transformer station – proudly displays one of his song lyrics, which waxes lyrical about the beauty of the city. Behind the hut you'll find Johnny, and members of the Jordaan musical hall of fame, cast in bronze.

On King's Day (p12), this is where many Jordaanians head to rock out to live music.

ELECTRIC LADYLAND MUSEUM

Map p308 (📞020-420 37 76; www.electric-lady-land.com; 2e Leliedwarsstraat 5; adult/child €5/free; ⊙by reservation 2-6pm Wed-Sat; ⬚13/17 Westermarkt) The world's first museum of fluorescent art features owner Nick Padalino's psychedelic sculpture work on one side and cases of naturally luminescent rocks and manufactured glowing objects (money, government ID cards etc) on the other. Jimi Hendrix, the Beatles and other trippy artists play on the stereo while Nick describes each item in the collection. His gallery-shop is upstairs.

NOORDERKERK CHURCH

Map p308 (Northern Church; www.noorderkerk. org; Noordermarkt 48; ⊙10.30am-12.30pm Mon, 11am-1pm Sat; ⬚3/5 Marnixplein) Near the Prinsengracht's northern end, this imposing Calvinist church was completed in 1623 for the 'common' people in the Jordaan. (The upper classes attended the Westerkerk further south.) It was built in the shape of a broad Greek cross (four arms of equal length) around a central pulpit, giving the entire congregation unimpeded access. Hendrick de Keyser's design, unusual at the time, would become common for Protestant churches throughout the country. It hosts the well-regarded Saturday-afternoon **Noorderkerkconcerten** (Map p308; www. noorderkerkconcerten.nl; tickets from €16.50; ⊙2pm Sat; ⬚3/5 Marnixplein) concert series. Sunday services take place at 10am and 6.30pm.

HAARLEMMERPOORT GATE

Map p308 (Haarlemmerplein; ⬚3 Haarlemmerplein) Once a defensive gateway to the city, the Haarlemmerpoort marked the start of the journey to Haarlem, which was a major trading route. The neoclassical structure, with Roman-temple-styled Corinthian pillars, was finished just in time for King William II's staged entry for his 1840 investiture, hence

WESTERN ISLANDS

In the early 17th century, the wharves and warehouses of the Western Islands, north of the Jordaan, were abuzz with activity. The Golden Age was taking off, the Dutch still dominated the sea trade and money flowed into this old harbour like beer from a barrel. The wealthy Bicker brothers, both mayors of Amsterdam, even built their own Bickerseiland here to cater for their ships.

Few tourists visit here today, partly because the district is shielded from view by the railway line. Yet it's roughly a 10-minute walk (or five-minute bike ride) from Centraal Station and a wonderful area to wander, with cute drawbridges and handsome old warehouses nestled in quiet lanes. Many addresses have been converted to charming homes as well a few artists studios. Most are closed to the public, but the **Ravestijn Gallery** (Map p303; 📞020-530 60 05; www.theravestijngallery.com; Westerdoksdijk 824; ⊙noon-5pm Mon-Sat; ⬚48 Westerdoksdijk) FREE hosts photography exhibitions.

The Prinseneiland (named in honour of the first three Princes of Orange) and Realeneiland (named after the 17th-century merchant Reynier Reael) are the two prettiest isles. The narrow bridge linking them, the **Drieharingenbrug** (Three Herrings Bridge; Map p303; Realengracht; ⬚3 Zoutketsgracht), is a quaint replacement for the pontoon that used to be pulled aside to let ships through.

Now a modern yacht harbour, the **Zandhoek** (Map p303; ⬚48 Barentszplein), on Realeneiland's eastern shore, is a picturesque stretch of waterfront. In the 17th century this area was a 'sand market', where ships purchased sand by the bagful for ballast. Galgenstraat (Gallows St), the street south of the Zandhoek, is so named as it was once possible to see the executions in Amsterdam Noord from here.

its little-known official name of Willemspoort (see the plaque inside). Traffic stopped running through the gate when a bypass was built over the Westerkanaal.

◎ The West

WESTERGASFABRIEK CULTURAL CENTRE
Map p303 (☎020-586 07 10; www.westergasfabriek.nl; Pazzanistraat; ᘓ5 Van Limburg Stirumstraat/Van Hallstraat) Adjacent to the Westerpark, this late-19th-century Dutch Renaissance complex was the city's western gasworks until gas production ceased in 1967. The formerly polluted site underwent a major clean-up before it re-emerged as a cultural and recreational park, with lush lawns, a long wading pool and cycleways. Its post-industrial buildings now house creative spaces including advertising agencies and TV production studios, as well as regular festivals and events, plus a slew of dining, drinking and entertainment options.

WESTERPARK PARK
Map p303 (Spaarndammerstraat; ᘓ3 Haarlemmerplein) Eco-urban Westerpark – with grassy expanses of lawns (packed in summer with picnickers, sun worshippers and families), tree-shaded walkways and cycleways, ponds, fountains and abundant bird life – adjoins the post-industrial Westergasfabriek cultural centre.

MUSEUM HET SCHIP MUSEUM
Map p303 (☎020-686 85 95; www.hetschip.nl; Oostzaanstraat 45; tour adult/child €15/5; ☉11am-5pm Tue-Sun, English tour 3pm; ᘓ22 Spaarndammerstraat) Just north of Westerpark over the train tracks, this remarkable 1921-completed housing project is a flagship of the Amsterdam School of architecture. Designed by Michel de Klerk for railway employees and loosely resembling a ship, the triangular block has a rocket-like tower linking the wings of the complex. Admission includes a 45-minute guided tour; English tours run at 3pm but may be available at other times.

✖ EATING

Restaurants in the Jordaan exude the conviviality that is a hallmark of the neighbourhood. Many people gravitate to the restaurants along Westerstraat, while the Haarlemmerbuurt also has numerous options. Or simply wander the narrow backstreets where the next hotspot may be opening up. Self-caterers shouldn't miss the neighbourhood's markets (p149). Those looking for nouveau scenester eats will strike it rich in the West, particularly in and around Westergasfabriek. For off-the-radar dining in a unique setting, head to the Houthavens district.

✖ Jordaan

WINKEL CAFE €
Map p308 (www.winkel43.nl; Noordermarkt 43; dishes €4-9; ☉kitchen 7am-10pm Mon & Sat, 8am-10pm Tue-Fri, 10am-10pm Sun, bar to 1am Sun-Thu, to 3am Fri & Sat; ☎; ᘓ3/5 Marnixplein) This sprawling, indoor-outdoor space is great for people-watching, popular for breakfast (organic muesli, omelettes), coffees and small meals such as wild-boar stew with sauerkraut and cranberry sauce. Its tall, cakey apple pie, served with clouds of whipped cream, hits it out of the park. On market days (Monday and Saturday) there's almost always a queue out the door.

MR HAZ TACOS €
Map p308 (☎020-891 55 11; www.mrhaztacobar.nl; Egelantiersstraat 24; tacos €9.75; ☉5-10pm Tue-Thu, to 11pm Fri, noon-11pm Sat, noon-10pm Sun; ᘓ13/17 Westermarkt) Named for Madrid street artist Mr Hazelnut, whose striking murals cover the walls, this taco bar also goes bold with flavours, from fiery jerk chicken to Yucatan spiced pulled pork; shrimp, chorizo and tomatillo; and Reuben (pastrami, sauerkraut and grilled jalapeños). Mezcal and tequila cocktails and Mexican beers are served for another 90 minutes after the kitchen closes.

MONTE PELMO ICE CREAM €
Map p308 (www.montepelmo.nl; 2e Anjeliersdwarsstraat 17; 1/2/3/4/5 scoops €1.70/3/4.10/5/6; ☉1-10pm; ᘓ3/5 Marnixplein) Apple pie, *stroopwafel* (traditional caramel-filled waffle), cinnamon, and white chocolate with hazelnut are just some of the intense flavours concocted by this 1957-founded ice cream maker. Queues twist out the door in the evening.

PAZZI   PIZZA €

Map p310 (☑020-320 28 00; www.pazziamster
dam.nl; 1e Looiersdwarsstraat 4; pizzas €8.50-
15.50; ⊙5-10pm; ☐7/17 Elandsgracht) At this
parquet-floored place with marble-topped
tables, wood-fired pizzas are made with
serious care. Perfectly charred crusts come
topped with fresh buffalo mozzarella, Parma ham, spicy salami, black truffles and
other quality ingredients. Italian beers are
the ideal accompaniment. It doesn't take
reservations, so arrive early or late.

JORDINO   SWEETS €

Map p308 (www.jordino.nl; Haarlemmerdijk 25a;
ice cream €3.50; ⊙1-6.30pm Mon, 10am-6.30pm
Tue-Sat, noon-6.30pm Sun; ☐18/21/22 Buiten
Oranjestraat) It's the best of both worlds: Jordino makes rich chocolates and velvety ice
cream and combines the two by scooping the
ice cream atop ice cones dipped in chocolate or
caramel. Of its 100-plus flavours, 24 (including fruit-based sorbets) are available at any
one time. Other creations include chocolate
tulips and famous Dutch paintings.

BALTHAZAR'S KEUKEN   MEDITERRANEAN €€

Map p310 (☑020-420 21 14; www.balthazars
keuken.nl; Elandsgracht 108; 3-course menu
€34.50; ⊙6-10.30pm Tue-Sun; ☐5/7/19 Elandsgracht) In a former blacksmith's forge, with
a modern-rustic look and an open kitchen,
this is consistently one of Amsterdam's
top-rated restaurants. Don't expect a wide-
ranging menu: the philosophy is basically
'whatever we have on hand', which might
mean sea bass and crab gnocchi or rabbit
with sauerkraut jelly and pear sauce, but
it's invariably delectable. Reservations
recommended.

TRATTORIA DI DONNA SOFIA   ITALIAN €€

Map p308 (☑020-623 41 04; www.trattoriadi
donnasofia.com; Anjeliersstraat 300; mains €14-
29.50; ⊙5-11pm; ☐3/5 Marnixplein) With rustic decor and white-clothed tables, Donna
Sofia – named for the owner's grandmother
– has a daily-changing blackboard menu of
Neapolitan dishes chalked in Italian. Pastas are made in-house and risottos are a
speciality; fresh herbs enhance the flavours
of the fish, meat and vegetarian dishes. All-
Italian vintages feature on the small but
well-chosen wine list.

MANTOE   AFGHANI €€

Map p308 (☑020-421 63 74; http://restaurant
mantoe.nl; 2e Liedwarsstraat 13; mains €19.50,

**DESTINATION DINING IN
HOUTHAVENS**

Just north of the Western Islands,
Amsterdam's rapidly emerging
Houthavens district – long-time docklands now being turned into a residential neighbourhood – is home to two
incredible restaurants: **REM Eiland**
(☑020-688 55 01; www.remeiland.
com; Haparandadam 45; mains lunch
€8.50-13, dinner €18.50-29.50; ⊙kitchen
noon-4pm & 5.30-10pm, bar to 11pm;
☐48 Koivistokade), in a former sea rig
that previously housed a pirate radio
station, and **Pont 13** (☑020-770 27
22; www.pont13.nl; Haparandadam 50;
mains lunch €7.50-11, dinner €17-22.50;
⊙kitchen noon-4pm & 5.30-10pm Tue-
Sun, bar noon-midnight Tue-Sun; ☎; ☐48
Koivistokade), on a 1927-built former
car ferry. From Centraal Station, take a
bus or a taxi (around €15), or hop on a
bike (15 minutes).

2-/3-course menus €24.50/28.50; ⊙5-10.30pm
Wed-Sun; ☑; ☐13/17 Westermarkt) An Afghan
family runs this small restaurant, which is
so cosy it feels like you're dining in someone's home. There's no menu: it's just whatever they cook that day, perhaps *mantu*
(steamed dumplings) stuffed with minced
meat and herbs, or *qormah e nadroo* (a
spicy lamb dish), served with *palaw* (baked
rice). A good wine list tops it off.

A mini three-course menu for kids costs
€12.50.

Don't be in a hurry, as the multiple courses take a while.

BOCA'S   TAPAS €€

Map p308 (☑020-820 37 27; www.bar-bocas.
nl; Westerstraat 30; bar snacks €3.50-7, platters
€21-58.50; ⊙kitchen 9am-9pm Mon & Sat, 10am-
9pm Tue-Fri, 11am-9pm Sun, bar to 1am Sun-Thu,
to 3am Fri & Sat; ☎; ☐3/5 Marnixplein) Fronted
by a red awning and white-timber facade,
this hip little bar is the perfect place for a
drink accompanied by bar snacks. Try the
mini lasagnes, burgers, bruschetta and
steak tartar, or bigger selections on wooden
boards: cheese platters, veggie platters, seafood platters, meat platters, sweet platters.
If you can't decide, go for Boca's combination platter.

JORDAAN & THE WEST EATING

JORDAAN FESTIVAL

Practitioners of the nostalgic, tears-in-your-beer folk music called *levenslied* – a speciality of the tight-knit Jordaan – take to the stage in early September for this three-day festival (www.jordaan festival.nl).

YAM YAM
ITALIAN €€

Map p310 (☑020-681 50 97; www.yamyam.nl; Frederik Hendrikstraat 88-90; pizzas €8-15, mains €13.50-17.50; ⊙5.30-10pm Wed-Sun; ☐3 Hugo de Grootplein) The wood-fired oven at this contemporary trattoria turns out thin-crust varieties such as salami and fennel seed, and the signature Yam Yam (organic smoked ham, mascarpone and truffle sauce). There are also great pastas and creative desserts such as salted-pecan caramel tart.

SEMHAR
ETHIOPIAN €€

Map p308 (☑020-638 16 34; www.semhar.nl; Marnixstraat 259-261; mains €16-20; ⊙4-10pm Tue-Sun; ☑; ☐5 Bloemgracht) Owner Yohannes gives his customers a warm welcome (as do the heavenly aromas wafting from the kitchen) and is passionate about the quality of his *injera* (slightly sour, spongy pancakes), used to scoop up richly spiced stews and vegetable combos. The most romantic tables are the handful at the back overlooking the canal.

TOSCANINI
ITALIAN €€

Map p308 (☑020-623 28 13; www.restau ranttoscanini.nl; Lindengracht 75; mains lunch €8.50-17.50, dinner €18-23; ⊙noon-2.30pm & 6-10.30pm Mon-Sat; ☑; ☐3/5 Marnixplein) Classy Toscanini bakes its own bread, rolls its own pasta and pours Italian wines. The weekly-changing dishes that grace the white tablecloths might include crêpes stuffed with ricotta and nettle, or veal with sweetbread and mushroom sauce. Desserts such as layered Palermo chocolate cake promise to weaken even the fiercest of dietary resolves. Book ahead, even on weeknights.

MOEDERS
DUTCH €€

Map p310 (www.moeders.com; Rozengracht 251; mains €16-21.50; ⊙5-10.30pm Mon-Fri, noon-10.30pm Sat & Sun; ☐5/13/17/19 Marnixstraat/Rozengracht) Mum's the word at 'Mothers'. When this welcoming place opened in 1990 customers were asked to bring their own plates and photos of their mums as donations and the decor remains a delightful hotchpotch. So does the food, from traditional pumpkin *stamppot* (potato mash) to calf's liver with bacon and onion, stews and fish dishes. Reservations (online only) are recommended.

DE PRINS
CAFE €€

Map p308 (☑020-624 93 82; www.deprins.nl; Prinsengracht 124; mains €7-18.50; ⊙kitchen 10am-10pm, bar to 1am Sun-Thu, to 2am Fri & Sat; ☐13/17 Westermarkt) On a picturesque stretch of the Prinsengracht, this brown cafe is an idyllic spot for a drink on the canal-side terrace or in the cosy bar. But it's best known for its excellent kitchen. Breakfast is served until 3pm; lunch specialities include prawn or meat *bitterballen* (croquettes). The pick of the dinner menu is a rich four-cheese fondue.

★ DAALDER
GASTRONOMY €€€

Map p308 (☑020-624 88 64; www.daalderam sterdam.nl; Lindengracht 90; 3-/4-course lunch menu €37.50/45, 5-/7-course dinner menus €69/89; ⊙6.30-9.30pm Thu, noon-2pm & 6.30-9.30pm Fri-Mon; ☐3 Nieuwe Willemsstraat) An unassuming black facade conceals a spectacular interior with terrazzo floors, a marble bar and designer lighting. Daalder serves unforgettable contemporary Dutch cuisine. Surprise menus might span a lobster meringue amuse-bouche with red seaweed foam, to scallop carpaccio with coriander-infused gin gel, lamb neck with black-garlic mousse and caramel-centred *stroopwafel* cake with *speculaas* (spiced biscuit) crumb and white-pepper ice cream. Menus are zero choice but dietary requirements can be accommodated with advance notice.

✗ The West

WORST WIJNCAFE
TAPAS €

Map p303 (☑020-625 61 67; www.deworst.nl; Barentszstraat 171; tapas €9-17, brunch mains €9-13; ⊙noon-midnight Mon-Sat, 10am-10pm Sun; ☐3 Zoutkeetsgracht) Named for its sausage-skewed tapas dishes (veal-tongue white sausage, chorizo, lobster sausage with spinach and asparagus), this chequerboard-tiled wine bar is the more casual sibling of esteemed restaurant Marius (p144) next door. Other dishes include pigs' trotters or grilled octopus. There's a fantastic range of mostly French wines by the glass. Sunday brunch is a local event.

DE BAKKERSWINKEL CAFE €

Map p303 (020-688 06 32; www.debakkers winkel.nl; Polonceaukade 1, Westergasfabriek; snacks €4-7, dishes €8-16; 8.30am-5pm Mon-Thu, 8.30am-6pm Fri, 10am-6pm Sat & Sun; 5 Van Limburg Stirumstraat) The wonderful 'Bakery' has numerous branches throughout the city (and country), but this one is uniquely situated by the drawbridge in the old regulator's house at the former gasworks (p140), with mezzanine seating, comfy sofas and a sunny terrace. Quiches, fish terrines, soups and sourdough sandwiches are excellent, and the carrot cake unmissable. There's an adjacent takeaway kiosk for Westerpark (p140) picnics.

★ WOLF ATELIER GASTRONOMY €€

Map p303 (020-344 64 28; www.wolfatelier.nl; Westerdoksplein 20; mains €25, 4-/5-/15-course menus €46/52/78; noon-5pm & 6-10pm Mon-Sat; 18/21/22 Buiten Brouwersstraat) Atop a 1920 railway swing bridge, a glass box with pivoting windows is the showcase for experimental chef Michael Wolf's wild flavour combinations: hazelnut-crusted foie gras, langoustine tartare with hollandaise, oxtail velouté with daikon, and blueberry crème brûlée with blackberry Chantilly cream and raspberry dust. The 360-degree views are magical at night; diners can linger for a drink until 1am.

★ MOSSEL EN GIN SEAFOOD €€

Map p303 (020-486 58 69; www.mosselengin. nl; Gosschalklaan 12, Westergasfabriek; mains €16-22; kitchen 4-10.30pm Tue-Thu, 2-10.30pm Fri, 1-10.30pm Sat & Sun, bar to midnight Tue-Thu & Sun, to 1am Fri & Sat; 5 Van Hallstraat) *Mosselen* (mussels) and gin are the twin specialities of this spectacular double-height mezzanine space within Westergasfabriek (p140), opening onto two sun-soaked beer gardens. Mussels-and-fries come in seven styles, including with crème fraîche and gin; it also serves inspired gin-and-tonic-battered fish and chips, and lobster or shrimp croquettes with gin mayo. Alongside seven gins, six house infusions include beetroot and basil.

MASTINO V VEGAN €€

Map p310 (www.mastinovegan.nl; Bilderdijkstraat 192; pizza €13-19; 5-10pm Tue-Sun; 3/17 Bilderdijkstraat/Kinkerstraat) Pizzas are 100% vegan and gluten-free at Mastino V, behind a timber facade in a split-level, bare-brick space on up-and-coming Bilderdijkstraat. Rice, almond and corn are used to create the bases; toppings include several vegan cheeses (mozzarella, Parmesan, brie and smoked cheese among them). Desserts, such as blueberry-and-orange cake or chocolate brownies, are gluten-free and vegan too.

LITTLE COLLINS CAFE €€

Map p310 (020-370 23 97; www.littlecollins. nl; Bilderdijkstraat 140; dishes €8-19; 9am-4pm Mon, Wed & Sun, to 10pm Thu-Sat; 3/7/17 Bilderdijkstraat/Kinkerstraat) Bilderdijkstraat's brunch scene was boosted by the 2019 opening of this light, bright cafe. Lemon curd and goat's cheese 'cigars', salted cod on walnut sourdough, and lamb merguez sausages with smoked yoghurt on dukkah-dusted flatbread are among the all-day options. At night, sharing dishes might include seared mackerel with miso-pickled sea cabbage, or sweet-potato-stuffed squid with saffron mayo.

DE REIGER DUTCH €€

Map p308 (www.dereigeramsterdam.nl; Nieuwe Leliestraat 34; mains €18.50-24.50; 5-9.30pm Tue-Fri, noon-4pm & 6-10.30pm Sat, 4-10.30pm Sun, bar to 11.30pm Tue-Fri, to 10.30pm Sat & Sun; 13/17 Westermarkt) Assiduously local and very atmospheric, this corner *café* (pub) – one of the Jordaan's oldest, with high beamed ceilings and art nouveau and art deco fittings – has a quiet front bar and a noisy, more spacious dining section at the back serving a short but stellar menu (venison and stewed pear with honey-cinnamon sauce, for instance). No reservations or credit cards.

RAÏNARAÏ ALGERIAN €€

Map p303 (020-486 71 09; www.rainarai.nl; Polonceaukade 40, Westergasfabriek; mains €19.50-23.50, 2-/3-course menus €32.50/36; noon-10pm Tue-Sun; 5 Van Hallstraat) Brightly coloured cushions and copper fixtures adorn this old industrial building in the Westergasfabriek (p140). The Algerian menu changes constantly but might offer grilled sardines with asparagus, broad beans and tomatoes, or a chicken and apricot tajine. There's usually a vegetarian dish of the day, such as aubergine stuffed with cauliflower and spiced chickpeas.

MEATLESS DISTRICT
VEGAN €€

Map p310 (☑020-722 08 04; www.meatless district.com; Bilderdijkstraat 65-67; dishes €9-16.50; ☺noon-10pm Mon-Fri, 10am-10pm Sat & Sun; 🚇🅿; 🚊3/13/19 Bilderdijkstraat/De Clercqstraat) Inspired by New York's Meatpacking District, with a whitewashed and exposed brick open-plan interior and outdoor tables with timber benches, this vegan cafe is a favourite for brunch (*speculaas* granola with coconut-milk yoghurt; chia pudding with gingerbread; spinach- and potato-stuffed roast tomatoes), served to 4pm. Tempeh burgers, spicy carrot-stuffed aubergine, and pulled jackfruit and black-rice salad are typical evening choices.

⭐MARIUS
EUROPEAN €€€

Map p303 (☑020-422 78 80; www.restaurant marius.nl; Barentszstraat 173; 4-course menu €49; ☺6.30-10pm Mon-Sat; 🚊3 Zoutkeetsgracht) Foodies swoon over pocket-sized Marius, tucked amid artists studios in the Western Islands. Chef Kees Elfring shops at local markets, then creates his daily four-course, no-choice menu from what he finds. The result might be grilled prawns with fava-bean purée or beef rib with polenta and ratatouille. Marius also runs the fabulous wine and tapas bar Worst Wijncafe (p142) next door.

APOSTROF
EUROPEAN €€€

Map p303 (☑06 2491 8611; www.apostrofam sterdam.nl; Planciusstraat 49; 3-/4-/5-/6-course menus €35/43/50/56; ☺6-10pm Wed-Sun; 🚊3 Zoutkeetsgracht) Well-priced European wines pair perfectly with chef Sjoerd Visser's mix-and-match multicourse menus (no à la carte) of monthly changing dishes. Choices might include shiitake-stuffed quail, Parma-ham-wrapped rabbit with sage-and-truffle crème, and rhubarb with white chocolate and star anise. Inside a curved corner building, the contemporary dining room is dominated by a vivid forest mural along one wall.

🍷 DRINKING & NIGHTLIFE

Anyone who seeks an authentic *café* (pub) experience 'with the locals' will love the Jordaan. Off the tourist radar, the West attracts an artsy crowd.

🍸 Jordaan

⭐'T SMALLE
BROWN CAFE

Map p308 (Egelantiersgracht 12; ☺10am-1am Sun-Thu, to 2am Fri & Sat; 🚊13/17 Westermarkt) Dating back to 1786 as a *jenever* (Dutch gin) distillery and tasting house, and restored during the 1970s with antique porcelain beer pumps and lead-framed windows, this locals' favourite is one of Amsterdam's most charming *bruin cafés* (brown cafes; pubs). Dock your boat right by the pretty stone terrace, which is wonderfully convivial by day and impossibly romantic at night.

VESPER BAR
COCKTAIL BAR

Map p308 (www.vesperbar.nl; Vinkenstraat 57; ☺6pm-1am Tue-Thu, 5pm-3am Fri & Sat; 🚇; 🚊18/21/22 Buiten Oranjestraat) This luxe bar's location on a low-key stretch of Jordaan shops and businesses gives it a certain mystique. Its martinis will coax out your inner James Bond – or Vesper Lynd (the lead female character in *Casino Royale*). Other cocktails include Q's Old Fashioned (rye whiskey, cherry-leaf syrup, bitters and cracked coffee beans).

CAFE SOUNDGARDEN
BAR

Map p310 (www.cafesoundgarden.nl; Marnixstraat 164-166; ☺1pm-1am Mon-Thu, to 3am Fri, 3pm-3am Sat, to 1am Sun; 🚇; 🚊5/13/17/19 Marnixstraat) In this grungy all-ages dive bar, the 'Old Masters' are the Ramones and Black Sabbath. Somehow a handful of pool tables, 1980s and '90s pinball machines, unkempt DJs and lovably surly bartenders add up to an ineffable magic. Bands occasionally make an appearance, and the waterfront terrace scene is more like an impromptu party in someone's backyard.

CAFÉ PAPENEILAND
BROWN CAFE

Map p308 (Prinsengracht 2; ☺10am-1am Sun-Thu, to 3am Fri & Sat; 🚊3/5 Marnixplein) With Delft Blue tiles and a central stove, this *bruin café* is a 1642 gem. The name, 'Papists' Island', goes back to the Reformation, when there was a clandestine Catholic church on the canal's northern side. Papeneiland was reached via a secret tunnel from the top of the stairs – ask bar staff to show you the entrance.

CAFÉ PIEPER
BROWN CAFE

Map p310 (www.facebook.com/CafePieper; Prinsengracht 424; ☺4pm-midnight Mon & Tue, noon-1am Wed & Thu, noon-2am Fri & Sat, 1pm-midnight

Sun; 2/12 Prinsengracht) Small, unassuming and unmistakably old (1665), Café Pieper features stained-glass windows, antique beer mugs hanging from the bar and a working Belgian beer pump (1875). Sip an Amsterdam-brewed Brouwerij 't IJ beer or a terrific cappuccino as you marvel at the claustrophobia of the low-ceilinged bar (people were shorter back in the 17th century – even the Dutch, it seems).

DRUPA
COFFEE

Map p308 (www.drupacoffee.com; 1e Anjeliersdwarsstraat 16a; ⏰9am-5.30pm Tue-Fri, 10am-5.30pm Sat & Sun; 🛜; 3/5 Marnixplein) 'Farm to cup' coffee here focuses on Colombian beans, which Drupa roasts, grinds and brews utilising methods including V60, Chemex and Kyoto-style cold-brew towers. The white-painted interior has a handful of seats at tiny tables, or you can pick up a coffee (and bags of beans) to go.

CAFÉ CHRIS
BROWN CAFE

Map p308 (www.cafechris.nl; Bloemstraat 42; ⏰3pm-1am Mon-Thu, to 2am Fri & Sat, to 9pm Sun; 13/17 Westermarkt) The Jordaan's oldest *bruin café* dates from 1624: workers constructing the Westerkerk's bell tower collected their pay here. The interior has scarcely changed since, retaining leadlight windows, dark-timber panelling and bare floorboards. Antique ceramic beer mugs hang above the bar, and there's a vintage silver cash register. The most recent addition is a 1980s pool table.

WATERKANT
BAR

Map p310 (www.waterkantamsterdam.nl; Marnixstraat 246; ⏰11am-1am Sun-Thu, to 3am Fri & Sat; 🛜; 7/17 Elandsgracht) Tucked under an oddball circular parking garage on the Jordaan's outskirts, this rollicking canal-side pub serves good brews (many local); for something different, try a watermelon gin and tonic. You can also order Surinamese dishes such as *rotis* (flat breads) and *puntjes* (filled bread rolls). The terrace is heated in chilly weather. DJs spin on weekends.

CAFÉ P 96
BROWN CAFE

Map p308 (www.p96.nl; Prinsengracht 96; ⏰11am-3am Sun-Thu, to 4am Fri & Sat; 🛜; 13/17 Westermarkt) If you don't want the night to end, P 96 is an amiable hang-out. When most other *cafés* in the Jordaan shut down for the night, this is where everyone ends up, rehashing their evening and striking up conversations with strangers. In summertime head to the terrace across the street aboard a houseboat.

CAFÉ DE JORDAAN
BROWN CAFE

Map p310 (☎020-627 58 63; Elandsgracht 45; ⏰10am-1am Mon-Thu, to 3am Fri, noon-3am Sat, 1pm-1am Sun; 7/17 Elandsgracht) A relaxed spot for a *biertje* (glass of beer), this old-style Jordaan *café* comes into its own at 5pm on Sunday, when crooners link arms and sing along to classic Dutch tunes.

DE TWEE ZWAANTJES
BROWN CAFE

Map p308 (☎020-625 27 29; www.cafedetweezwaantjes.nl; Prinsengracht 114; ⏰3pm-1am Sun-Thu, noon-3am Fri & Sat; 13/17 Westermarkt) The small, authentic 'Two Swans' is at its hilarious best on Wednesday nights, when patrons and staff belt out classic Dutch tunes, and Thursday nights, when cabaret meets karaoke. The fact that singers are often fuelled by the liquid courage of the Trappist beers on tap only adds to the spirited fun. Don't be afraid to join in.

There's a live pianist on Sunday nights; Tuesday is Motown night.

WESTERGASFABRIEK

A stone's throw northwest of the Jordaan, former gasworks site Westergasfabriek (p140) is now a cultural and recreational area. Its slew of drinking and entertainment options includes the following:

Mossel En Gin (p143) Gins are used in creative cooking and cocktails.

Espressofabriek (p148) Cavernous coffee roastery.

Westergasterras (p147) Bar opening to one of Amsterdam's best terraces.

Brouwerij Troost Westergas (p147) Brewery for hop heads and cool cats.

Pacific (p148) Indie gigs and DJ sets.

Westerunie (p148) Pumpin' post-industrial club.

JORDAAN & THE WEST DRINKING & NIGHTLIFE

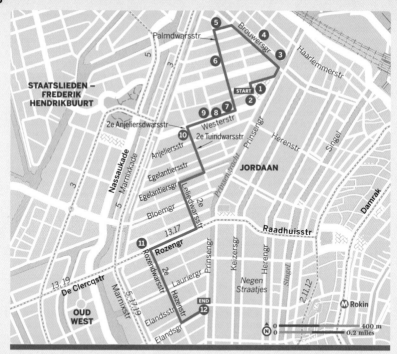

🏃 Neighbourhood Walk
Lost in the Jordaan

START NOORDERKERK
END JOHNNY JORDAANPLEIN
LENGTH 2.7KM; ONE HOUR

Begin at the **1 Noorderkerk** (p139). This cross-shaped church was revolutionary at the time, providing the working-class congregation with altar views from four transepts. Out front is the **2 Noordermarkt**, site of Amsterdam's most attractive farmers market (p149), and a flea market.

Make your way north to **3 Brouwersgracht** (p138). As you move west along 'Brewers Canal', you'll see the old warehouses **4 Groene & Grauwe Valk**. At the second drawbridge, go left into Palmgracht and look out for the red door to **5 Rapenhofje** (at 28–38). This courtyard was home to one of Amsterdam's oldest almshouses (1648).

South along Palmdwarsstraat you'll pass tiny food shops and restaurants. Note the stone tablet of the **6 white fat pig** over the butcher-deli at 2e Goudsbloemdwarsstraat 26. Soon you'll reach Westerstraat, a main

drag of the Jordaan, with the **7 Pianola Museum** (p138), a weekly **8 clothing market** and alluring places for a bite or drink, such as **9 Café 't Monumentje**. At 2e Anjeliersdwarsstraat, turn left to enter what locals call the **10 garden quarter** of ivy-clad lanes and diminutive squares.

Zigzag your way down to Leliedwarsstraat and continue until you hit Rozengracht. Speciality shops sell silk pillows and colourful kitchenware, among other stock. **11 Rembrandt's sterfhuis** (death house) is at 184; he died here in 1669 (look for the plaque). The part of the Jordaan on 2e Rozendwarsstraat and around is a mad jumble of styles. Secondhand stores, fancy boutiques and art shops pop up along the way.

Cross over Lauriergracht, turning left into Elandsgracht. You will find **12 Johnny Jordaanplein** (p139), a square dedicated to local hero and singer of schmaltzy tunes such as 'Bij ons in de Jordaan' (With Us in the Jordaan). There are bronze busts of Johnny and his band, and a colourful utility hut splashed with nostalgic lyrics.

DE TRUT
GAY & LESBIAN

Map p310 (www.trutfonds.nl; Bilderdijkstraat 165e; ⊙10pm-4am Sun; ⊒3/7/13/19 Bilderdijkstraat/Kinkerstraat) In the basement of a former squat, this Sunday-night club is a gay and lesbian institution. It's run by volunteers and comes with an attitude; arrive well before 11pm (the space is fairly small). No cameras are allowed inside; phones must be turned off.

LA TERTULIA
COFFEESHOP

Map p310 (www.coffeeshoptertulia.com; Prinsengracht 312; ⊙11am-7pm Tue-Sat; ⊒7/17 Elandsgracht) A long-standing favourite, this mother-and-daughter-run coffeeshop has a greenhouse feel. You can sit outside by the Van Gogh–inspired murals, play some board games or contemplate the Jurassic-sized crystals by the counter. Bonus: Tertulia actually has good coffee, along with *stroopwafels*.

SAAREIN
GAY & LESBIAN

Map p310 (www.saarein2.nl; Elandsstraat 119; ⊙4pm-1am Tue-Thu & Sun, to 2am Fri, 1pm-2am Sat; ⊒7/17 Elandsgracht) A rainbow flag flies above this canal house dating from the 1600s. A one-time feminist stronghold, it's still a meeting place for lesbians, although these days gay men are welcome too. There's a small menu with tapas, soups and specials, as well as a pool table with purple baize.

CAFÉ 'T MONUMENTJE
BROWN CAFE

Map p308 (www.monumentje.nl; Westerstraat 120; ⊙8.30am-1am Mon-Thu, to 3am Fri, 9am-3am Sat, 11am-1am Sun; ⊒3/5 Marnixplein) This slightly scruffy yet lovable *café* is always heaving with local barflies. It's a fun spot for a beer and a snack after shopping at the Westermarkt. Singalongs take place on the first Monday of the month; it also hosts occasional live music.

🍷 The West

★ MONKS COFFEE ROASTERS
COFFEE

Map p310 (www.monkscoffee.nl; Bilderdijkstraat 46; ⊙8am-5pm Tue-Sun; 🐾; ⊒3/13/19 Bilderdijkstraat/De Clercqstraat) Monks' phenomenal house blend, prepared with a variety of brewing methods, is outstanding; it also serves superb coffee from small-scale specialists such as Amsterdam's Lot Sixty One and White Label Coffee, and Paris' Café

Lomi. The cavernous space is brilliant for brunch (try the avocado toast with feta, chilli and lime, or banana bread with mascarpone and caramelised pineapple).

★ BROUWERIJ TROOST WESTERGAS
BREWERY

Map p303 (☎020-737 10 28; www.brouwerijtroost.nl; Pazzanistraat 27, Westergasfabriek; ⊙4pm-midnight Mon-Thu, to 3am Fri, noon-3am Sat, to midnight Sun; 🐾; ⊒5 Van Limburg Stirumstraat) Troost's cavernous, industrial Westergasfabriek (p140) space is punctuated by big silver tanks cooking up saison, blond ale and smoked porter varieties. The brewery also uses the tanks to distil its own gin, and makes its own hard lemonade. Live jazz plays on Wednesday from 8pm; 45-minute brewery tours (€8) run at 4pm Saturday. Credit cards only (no cash).

Takeaway beers and gins are sold at its shop.

★ WESTERGASTERRAS
BAR

Map p303 (www.westergasterras.nl; Klönneplein 4-6, Westergasfabriek; ⊙11am-1am Mon-Thu, to 3am Fri, 10am-3am Sat, to 1am Sun; 🐾; ⊒5 Van Limburg Stirumstraat) Overlooking reed-filled ponds and a weir, the massive decked terrace here is hotly contested on sunny afternoons, but the soaring brick-and-steel post-industrial interior is also crammed every day of the week. Sophisticated pub food (the likes of beef carpaccio) is served until 10pm. Its popular dance club lets loose on Thursdays in summer.

BROUWERIJ DE PRAEL HOUTHAVENS
BREWERY

Map p303 (www.deprael.nl; Nieuwe Hemweg 2; ⊙11am-10pm Tue & Wed, to 11pm Thu & Sat, to midnight Fri, noon-10pm Sun; ⊒22 Zaanstraat) The plain industrial exterior doesn't give much away but the Houthavens location (opened 2019) of the socially minded Brouwerij De Prael has a stunning, contemporary interior of polished concrete floors, and tables made from recycled timbers. Beers include Bitter Blonde (German-style session beer), DIPA (double India Pale Ale) and Dortmunder (lager).

ESPRESSOFABRIEK
COFFEE

Map p303 (www.espressofabriek.nl; Pazzanistraat 39, Westergasfabriek; ⊙9am-6pm Mon-Fri, 10am-6pm Sat & Sun; 🐾; ⊒5 Van Limburg Stirumstraat) Heady aromas of roasting coffee waft from inside this monumental brick building at the Westergasfabriek (p140) former gasworks. Try its brews with cookies, cupcakes, muffins and traditional Dutch apple pie.

WESTERUNIE CLUB

Map p303 (☑020-684 84 96; www.westerunie.nl; Klönneplein 6, Westergasfabriek; ⊙hours vary; ☜; 🚊5 Van Limburg Stirumstraat) House, techno and acid dominate at this club in a concrete, steel and brick building with exposed pipes and great acoustics for the state-of-the-art sound system in the post-industrial Westergasfabriek (p140) complex. Mega events often spill over into neighbouring spaces.

 # ENTERTAINMENT

Good entertainment options in this neighbourhood span art-house cinemas, venues hosting live music in a diverse range of genres and comedy venues Boom Chicago and Comedy Café, with performances in English.

THEATER AMSTERDAM PERFORMING ARTS

(☑020-705 50 55; www.theateramsterdam.nl; Danzigerkade 5; 🚊48 Koivistokade) Surrounded by the construction of docklands-turned-neighbourhood Houthavens, this gleaming theatre has a glass facade providing views over the IJ River. Its 15,000-sq-metre auditorium means it can accommodate huge

---

LIQUORICE

....

The Dutch love their sweets, the most famous of which is *drop,* the word for all varieties of liquorice. It may be gummy-soft or tough as leather, and shaped like coins or miniature cars, but the most important distinction is between *zoete* (sweet) and *zoute* (salty). The latter is often an alarming surprise, even for avowed fans of the black stuff. But with such a range of textures and additional flavours – mint, honey, laurel – even liquorice sceptics might be converted. **Het Oud-Hollandsch Snoepwinkeltje** (Map p308; www.snoepwinkeltje.com; 2e Egelantiersdwarsstraat 2; ⊙11am-6.30pm Tue-Sat; 🚊3/5 Marnixplein) is a good place to do a taste test.

---

sets for large-scale theatre and music productions. A cutting-edge system translates the on-stage works into eight languages. If you're arriving by boat, you can pull up at its dock.

BOOM CHICAGO COMEDY

Map p310 (☑020-217 04 00; www.boomchicago. nl; Rozengracht 117; ☜; 🚊5/13/17/19 Marnixstraat/Rozengracht) Boom Chicago stages seriously funny improv-style comedy shows in English that make fun of Dutch culture, American culture and everything that gets in the cross-hairs. Edgier shows happen in the smaller upstairs theatre. The on-site bar helps fuel the festivities with buckets of ice and beer.

COMEDY CAFÉ COMEDY

Map p303 (☑020-722 08 27; www.comedycafe. nl; IJdok 89; tickets from €15, open mic nights €5; ⊙6.30-11pm; 🚊48 Westerdoksdijk) Comedy acts perform every night of the week at this dockside venue. Open mic nights in English take place on Wednesday; shows in Dutch typically take place on Friday and Saturday, with comedians performing in English on other nights – check the agenda and book tickets online.

PACIFIC LIVE MUSIC

Map p303 (www.pacificamsterdam.nl; Polonceaukade 23, Westergasfabriek; ⊙bar 11am-1am Sun-Wed, to 3am Thu, to 4am Fri & Sat, DJs & live music from 11pm Thu-Sat; 🚊5 Van Limburg Stirumstraat) Pacific is home to live music, DJ sets and plenty of rock-and-roll spirit to go along with the potent drinks and hearty food. The sprawling terrace is strewn with picnic tables.

DE NIEUWE ANITA ARTS CENTRE

Map p310 (www.denieuweanita.nl; Frederik Hendrikstraat 111; 🚊3 Hugo de Grootplein) This living-room venue expanded for noise rockers has a great *café.* In the back, behind the bookcase-concealed door, the main room has a stage and screens cult movies (in English) on Monday. DJs, vaudeville-type acts and comedy shows are also on the eclectic agenda.

MOVIES CINEMA

Map p308 (☑020-638 60 16; www.themovies.nl; Haarlemmerdijk 161; tickets €11.50; 🚊3 Haarlemmerplein) Amsterdam's oldest cinema, dating from 1912, is a *gezellig* gem screening indie films alongside mainstream flicks. Tickets

JORDAAN MARKETS

Lindengracht Market (Map p308; www.jordaanmarkten.nl; Lindengracht; ⊙9am-4pm Sat; ⛢3 Nieuwe Willemsstraat) Dating from 1895, Saturday's Lindengracht Market is a wonderfully local affair, with 232 stalls selling fresh produce, including fish and a magnificent array of cheese, as well as Dutch delicacies including *stroopwafels*, flowers, clothing and homewares. Arrive as early as possible to beat the crowds.

Noordermarkt (Northern Market; Map p308; www.jordaanmarkten.nl; Noordermarkt; ⊙flea market 9am-1pm Mon, farmers market 9am-3pm Sat; ⛢3/5 Marnixplein) A market square since the early 1600s, the plaza in front of the Noorderkerk (p139) hosts a couple of lively markets each week. Monday morning's **flea market** has some amazing bargains, while Saturday morning sees local shoppers flock to the lush **boerenmarkt** (farmers market), overflowing with organic produce.

Westermarkt (Map p308; www.jordaanmarkten.nl; Westerstraat; ⊙9am-1pm Mon; ⛢3/5 Marnixplein) Bargain-priced clothing and fabrics are sold at 170 stalls at the Westermarkt (which isn't in fact on Westermarkt but on Westerstraat, just near the Noordermarkt).

are €1 cheaper online. You can dine in the pan-Asian restaurant (open 5.30pm to 10pm) or have a pre-film tipple at the inviting *café*.

MALOE MELO — BLUES
Map p310 (☎020-420 45 92; www.maloemelo.com; Lijnbaansgracht 163; ⊙9pm-3am Sun-Thu, to 4am Fri & Sat; ⛢5/17/19 Elandsgracht) This is the freewheeling, fun-loving altar of Amsterdam's tiny blues scene. Music ranges from funk and soul to Texas blues and rockabilly. The cover charge is usually around €5.

 SHOPPING

Shops here have an artsy, eclectic, homemade feel. The area around Elandsgracht is the place for antiques and art, as well as speciality shops covering everything from hats to cats (p150). Straddling the Jordaan and Western Canal Ring, the Haarlemmerbuurt (p114), incorporating hip Haarlemmerdijk in the northern Jordaan, teems with trendy food and fashion boutiques. The Jordaan also has some fabulous food and flea markets.

⭐**MEMENTO** — DESIGN
Map p310 (www.memento.amsterdam; Prinsengracht 238; ⊙3-7pm Wed-Sun; ⛢13/17 Westermarkt) Levitating lamps and vases (using magnets), retro flipping clocks, Delft-style porcelain with contemporary designs such as cyclists and tilting canal houses, gable-shaped chopping boards, wine coolers made from leather offcuts, Dutch

flower-scented perfumes, tulip- and green parrot-printed boxer shorts, and Van Gogh–printed scarves are just some of the ingenious items by Amsterdam designers at this original boutique.

⭐**MOOOI GALLERY** — DESIGN
Map p308 (☎020-528 77 60; www.moooi.com; Westerstraat 187; ⊙10am-6pm Tue-Sat; ⛢3/5 Marnixplein) Founded by Dutch designer Marcel Wanders, this gallery-shop features Dutch design at its most over-the-top, from the life-size black horse lamp to the 'blow away vase' (a whimsical twist on the classic Delft vase) and the 'killing of the piggy bank' ceramic pig (with a gold hammer).

DISTORTION RECORDS — MUSIC
Map p308 (www.distortion.nl; Westerstraat 244; ⊙11am-6pm Tue, Wed, Fri & Sat, to 9pm Thu; ⛢3/5 Marnixplein) Squeeze into this small jam-packed shop to browse for vinyl from the 1970s onwards in genres ranging from punk and funk to alternative, indie, garage, grunge, industrial, electro, hip-hop, acid jazz and neo-folk. The Ramones, Buzzcocks, Psychedelic Furs, Kraftwerk, Incognito and Dr Dre are among the artists you might unearth.

URBAN CACAO — CHOCOLATE
Map p310 (www.facebook.com/UrbanCacao; Rozengracht 200; ⊙10am-6.30pm Tue-Sat, noon-6.30pm Sun & Mon; ⛢5/13/17/19 Marnixstraat/Rozengracht) Chocolatier, patissier and glacier Hans Mekking is the mastermind behind Urban Cacao. Filled with his chocolate bars, truffles and pralines using fair-trade beans (with sugar-free varieties), the stylish

space also has colourful macarons (such as passion fruit and chocolate, mandarin and basil, and orange and gold dust for King's Day), plus ice cream in summer and hot chocolate in winter.

ROBINS HOOD
DESIGN

Map p308 (www.robinshood.nl; 2e Tuindwars-straat 7; ☺noon-5pm Mon-Sat; ☐3/5 Marnix-plein) Whitewashed walls and floorboards create a blank canvas for the upcycled vintage and Dutch-designed products here. Browse for unique items including vases, bags, scarves, jewellery, sunglasses, lamps, art, stationery and some truly only-in-the-Netherlands items such as *stroopwafel* coasters.

BACK BEAT RECORDS
MUSIC

Map p308 (☎020-627 16 57; www.backbeat.nl; Egelantiersstraat 19; ☺11am-6pm Tue-Sat; ☐13/17 Westermarkt) Back Beat has been selling jazz, soul and funk music since 1988. Whether you're looking for Sly and the Family Stone on vinyl, a Chet Baker box set or Charles Earland playing Hammond-organ on CD, this little shop has it covered. The owner is a font of local jazz lore; you can find out about concerts around town and buy tickets here.

PAPABUBBLE
FOOD

Map p308 (☎020-626 26 62; www.papabubble.nl; Haarlemmerdijk 70; ☺noon-6pm Wed, 10am-6pm Sat; ☐3 Haarlemmerplein) This hip sweet-shop looks more like a gallery. Pull up a cushion and perch on the stairs to watch the mesmerising process of transforming sugar into sweets with flavours such as pomelo and lavender.

CELLARRICH
FASHION & ACCESSORIES

Map p308 (www.cellarrichretail.nl; Haarlemmerdi-jk 98; ☺11am-6pm Tue-Fri, to 5.30pm Sat; ☐3 Haarlemmerplein) Accessorise with colourful, creative leather wallets, bags and jewellery at Cellarrich (named for the designers' original Prinsengracht cellar workshop). There are beautiful leather-bound notebooks too.

CATS & THINGS
GIFTS & SOUVENIRS

Map p310 (☎020-428 30 28; www.catsandthings.nl; Hazenstraat 26; ☺11.30am-6pm Tue-Fri, to 5pm Sat; ☐7/17 Elandsgracht) If you're a cat lover, or shopping for someone who is, this quirky shop – with its own resident cats – is a must. It stocks every feline-themed

gift imaginable (statues, artworks, cat-adorned homewares) as well as presents for kitty (baskets, food, collars and climbers).

ARNOLD CORNELIS
FOOD

Map p310 (☎020-625 85 85; www.cornelis.nl; Elandsgracht 78; ☺8.30am-6pm Mon-Fri, to 5pm Sat; ☐7/17 Elandsgracht) Your dinner hosts will be impressed if you present them with something from this long-standing shop, such as fruitcake, cheesecake or biscuits made with Malaga wine. At lunchtime grab a flaky pastry filled with cheese, meat or vegetables.

MECHANISCH SPEELGOED
TOYS

Map p308 (www.mechanisch-speelgoed.nl; Wes-terstraat 67; ☺10am-6pm Mon-Fri, to 5pm Sat; ☐3/5 Marnixplein) This adorable shop is crammed full of nostalgic toys, including snow domes, glow lamps, masks, finger puppets and wind-up toys. And who doesn't need a good rubber chicken every once in a while? Hours can vary.

GALLERIA D'ARTE RINASCIMENTO
CERAMICS

Map p308 (☎020-622 75 09; www.delft-art-gallery.com; Prinsengracht 170; ☺9am-6pm; ☐13/17 Westermarkt) Royal Delftware ceramics (both antique and new) at this pretty shop span all manner of vases, platters, brooches, Christmas ornaments and intriguing 19th-century wall tiles and plaques.

'T ZONNETJE
DRINKS

Map p308 (☎020-623 00 58; www.t-zonnetje.com; Haarlemmerdijk 45; ☺9am-6pm Mon-Fri, to 5pm Sat; ☐18/21/22 Buiten Oranjestraat) At this charming shop within a 1642 building, you can find teas from all over the world, as well as coffees, spices and accoutrements.

ANTIEKCENTRUM AMSTERDAM
ANTIQUES

Map p310 (Amsterdam Antique Centre; www.antiekcentrumamsterdam.nl; Elandsgracht 109; ☺11am-6pm Mon & Wed-Fri, to 5pm Sat & Sun; ☐5/7/17/19 Elandsgracht) Anyone with an affinity for odd antiques and bric-a-brac may enter this knick-knack mini-mall and never come out. Spanning 1750 sq metres, there are 55 stalls and larger shops, and a market on Wednesday, Saturday and Sunday. You're just as likely to find 1940s silk dresses as you are 1970s Swedish porn.

Vondelpark & the South

Neighbourhood Top Five

❶ Rijksmuseum (p153) Getting happily lost amid the riches of one of the world's finest museums: Rembrandt, Vermeer, gilded dollhouses, Delftware and magic lanterns.

❷ Van Gogh Museum (p156) Seeing the world's best collection of Van Gogh's work up close, from vibrant yellow sunflowers to purple-blue irises.

❸ Amsterdamse Bos (p160) Cycling, boating or communing with goats in Amsterdam's surprisingly vast forest.

❹ Stedelijk Museum (p158) Discovering works by Mondrian, Matisse, Warhol, Appel, De Kooning, Yayoi Kusama and more at Amsterdam's fabulous modern art museum.

❺ Vondelpark (p159) Free-wheeling through the green heart of the city, packing a picnic, taking it easy, spotting a Picasso sculpture and catching a play at its open-air theatre.

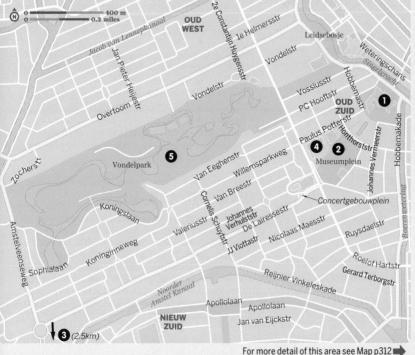

For more detail of this area see Map p312 ➡

Lonely Planet's Top Tip

Getting peckish after an afternoon in Vondelpark? Amstelveenseweg, running along the western edge of the park, is a fabulous place to eat, with restaurants ranging from vegan to Chinese, Indonesian, Indian, Dutch and Italian, interspersed with stylish wine bars and cosy *cafés* (pubs). Wander along and see what you find.

✕ Best Places to Eat

➡ Ron Gastrobar (p167)

➡ Foodhallen (p165)

➡ Adam (p167)

➡ Moer (p164)

➡ Rijks (p167)

➡ Vegan Junk Food Bar (p164)

For reviews, see p162.➡

☐ Best Places to Drink

➡ Labyrinth (p169)

➡ Lot Sixty One (p169)

➡ Edel (p169)

➡ Wildschut (p171)

➡ Welling (p170)

For reviews, see p167.➡

🔒 Best Places to Shop

➡ J&B Craft Drinks (p172)

➡ Goochem Speelgoed (p172)

➡ Pied à Terre (p172)

➡ Maker Store (p165)

For reviews, see p172.➡

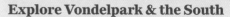

Explore Vondelpark & the South

Amsterdam's big three museums – Rijksmuseum, Van Gogh Museum (p156) and Stedelijk Museum (p158) – are all lined up on Museumplein (p160). You could easily spend a couple of days visiting them, each a splendid treasure trove of art. In the evening, the action shifts to the Concertgebouw (p171), the grand music hall, and genteel *cafés* and buzzing bars spring to life in the streets around the Vondelpark (p159).

Amsterdam's favourite green hangout is not particularly large, but repays after some exploration, and is perfect for lingering over a drink or picnic. Further south, you can explore Amsterdamse Bos (p160), which feels almost like countryside, and is a great place to go running, biking, riding or boating. For something more cultural, take the metro to the Cobra Museum (p162).

North, around Overtoom, the streets burst with eateries and shops for all budgets, while those along Cornelis Schuytstraat to the south are more exclusive. You'll find plenty of dining options around Amstelveenseweg at the park's western end, and around the city's food hall, Foodhallen (p165), inside the De Hallen (p165).

Local Life

➡ **Cycling** If you want to gain confidence on two wheels away from traffic-filled streets, Vondelpark (p159) is the perfect place to practise whirring around like a local.

➡ **Skating** Join local in-line skaters setting off from Vondelpark for a two-hour mass skate (p174) every Friday night. In winter, the pond at Museumplein (p160) becomes a popular ice-skating rink.

➡ **Bunker Life** Buried inside the 1e Constantijn Huygensstraat bridge, the Vondelbunker (p170) hosts underground entertainment and activist activities.

➡ **Boating Life** Take a canoe out on the 'Amsterdam Amazon' down south in Amsterdamse Bos (p160).

➡ **Take a Dip** The grand 1912 Zuiderbad (p174) building is a lovely public swimming pool.

Getting There & Away

➡ **Tram** Trams 12 and 5 from Centraal Station stop at Museumplein and the main entrance to Vondelpark; tram 2 travels along the southern side of the park on Willemsparkweg. Trams 3 and 12 cross the 1e Constantijn Huygensstraat bridge near the park's main entrance, and cross Kinkerstraat near De Hallen. Tram 1 from Centraal travels along Overtoom near the park's western edge.

➡ **Bus** Bus 397 zips to Museumplein from the airport in about 30 minutes.

TOP SIGHT
RIJKSMUSEUM

The **Rijksmuseum is a magnificent repository of art,** its restaurant (p167) has a Michelin star *and* it's the only museum with a cycle lane through its centre. Beautifully presented, it includes masterpieces by homegrown geniuses, such as Rembrandt, Vermeer and Van Gogh. It was conceived to hold several national and royal collections, which occupy 1.5km of gallery space.

The Layout

The museum is spread over four levels, from Floor 0 (where the main atrium is) to Floor 3. The collection is huge. You can see the highlights in a couple of hours, but you may want to allocate much longer. Pick up a floor plan from the information desk by the entrance. Galleries are well marked; each room displays the gallery's number and theme, which are easy to match to the floor plan. The 1st floor is split into two sides by the atrium, with separate access on either side.

Floor 2 Highlights: 1600–1700

It's best to start your visit on the 2nd floor, which contains the highlights of the collection, with its Golden Age masterpieces, in the **Gallery of Honour**. It's a bit convoluted to reach, but well signposted.

Jan Vermeer & Dutch interiors

This floor hosts beautiful works by Vermeer, with intimate domestic scenes, glimpses into private life, rendered in almost photographic detail. Check out the dreamy *Milkmaid* (1660, also called *The Kitchen Maid*). Notice the holes in the wall? The nail with shadow? In *Woman in Blue Reading a Letter* (1663) Vermeer shows only parts of objects, such as the tables, chairs and map, leaving the viewer to figure out the rest. Pieter de Hooch, Vermeer's contemporary, also depicts everyday life, with subjects such as the intimate *A Mother Delousing her Child* (1658), also called *A Mother's Duty*.

Jan Steen

Jan Steen became renowned for painting chaotic households to convey moral teachings, such as *The Merry Family* (1668). None of the drunken adults notice the little boy sneaking a taste of wine, and an inscription translates as 'As the old sing, so shall the young twitter'. Steen's images made quite an impression: in the 18th century the expression 'a Jan Steen household' entered the local lexicon to mean a crazy state of affairs.

Rembrandt

You'll find several wonderful works by Rembrandt, including his resigned, unflinching self-portrait as the Apostle Paul. *The Jewish Bride* (1665), showing a couple's intimate caress, impressed Van Gogh, who declared he would give up a decade of his life just to sit before the painting for a fortnight with only a crust of bread to eat.

The Night Watch & Civic Guards

Rembrandt's gigantic *The Night Watch* (1642) is the rock star of the museum, with perennial crowds in front of it. The work is titled *Archers under the Command of Captain Frans Banning Cocq,* and *The Night Watch* name was bestowed years later, thanks to a layer of grime that gave the impression it was a nocturnal scene. It's since been restored to its original colours, complete with sunbeams through the windows. It was once larger,

DON'T MISS

➡ Rembrandt's *The Night Watch*

➡ Vermeer's *Milkmaid* (also called *The Kitchen Maid*)

➡ De Hooch's *A Mother's Duty*

➡ Delftware pottery

➡ Dollhouses

➡ Michelin-starred restaurant

PRACTICALITIES

➡ National Museum

➡ Map p312, H4

➡ ☏020-674 70 00

➡ www.rijksmuseum.nl

➡ Museumstraat 1

➡ adult/child €20/free

➡ ⊘9am-5pm

➡ 🚊2/5/12 Rijksmuseum

QUEUES & TICKETS

Entrance queues can be long. Friday, Saturday and Sunday are the busiest days. It's least crowded before 10am and after 3pm. Buy your ticket online to save time; while you must still wait in the outdoor queue, once inside you can proceed straight into the museum (otherwise you must stand in another queue to pay). Museumkaart and I Amsterdam cardholders (p267) get the same privilege.

AIRPORT ART

The Rijksmuseum has a free minibranch at Schiphol airport that hangs eight to 10 stellar Golden Age paintings. It's located after passport control between lounges 2 and 3.

but was cut down to fit a previous location. Several other huge civic guard paintings surround it. Fun fact: Captain Cocq, the central figure in *The Night Watch,* once lived in the house at Singel 140–142.

Delftware & Dollhouses

Intriguing Golden Age swag fills the rooms on either side of the Gallery of Honour. Delftware was the Dutch attempt to reproduce Chinese porcelain in the late 1600s; Gallery 2.22 displays lots of the delicate pottery. Gallery 2.20 is devoted to mind-blowing dollhouses. Merchant's wife Petronella Oortman employed carpenters, glassblowers and silversmiths to make the 700 items inside her dollhouse.

Cuypers Library

There's something Escher-like about this towering book-lined space, one of the world's finest art libraries: view it from the balcony on Floor 2.

Floor 1 Highlights: 1700–1900

Highlights on Floor 1 include the *Battle of Waterloo,* the Rijksmuseum's largest painting (in Gallery 1.12), taking up almost an entire wall. Three Van Gogh paintings hang in Gallery 1.18. Gallery 1.16 recreates a gilded, 18th-century canal house room.

Floor 0 Highlights: 1100–1600

This floor is packed with fascinating curiosities. The **Special Collections** have sections including magic lanterns, armoury, ship models, musical instruments and silver miniatures. Early gems include works by Dürer, and Charles V's cutlery. The serene **Asian Pavilion**, a separate structure often devoid of crowds, holds first-rate artworks from China, Indonesia, Japan, India, Thailand and Vietnam.

Floor 3 Highlights: 1900–2000

This floor has a limited, but interesting, collection. It includes paintings by Karel Appel, Constant Nieuwenhuys and their CoBrA compadres (a post-WWII movement) and cool furnishings by Dutch designers, such as Gerrit Rietveld and Michel de Klerk. There's also a Nazi chess set, and an unsettling wall of Nias islanders' facial casts, dating from 1910.

Facade & Gardens

Pierre Cuypers designed the 1885 building. Check out the exterior, which mixes neo-Gothic and Dutch Renaissance styles. The museum's gardens – aka the 'outdoor gallery' – host big-name sculpture exhibitions at least once a year. You can stroll for free amid the roses, hedges, fountains and a cool greenhouse.

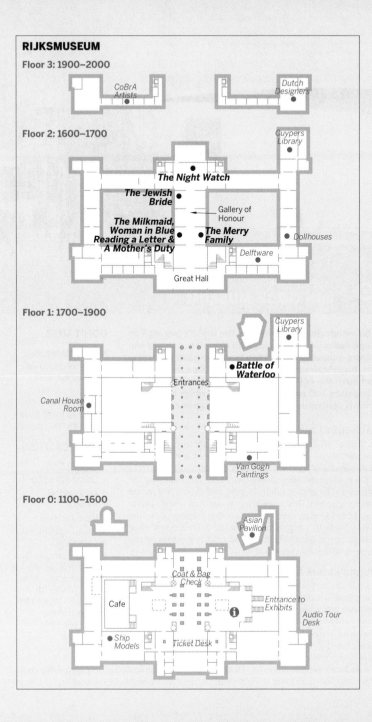

RIJKSMUSEUM

Floor 3: 1900–2000

CoBrA Artists

Dutch Designers

Floor 2: 1600–1700

Cuypers Library

The Night Watch

The Jewish Bride

Gallery of Honour

The Milkmaid, Woman in Blue Reading a Letter & A Mother's Duty

The Merry Family

Dollhouses

Delftware

Great Hall

Floor 1: 1700–1900

Cuypers Library

Battle of Waterloo

Entrances

Canal House Room

Van Gogh Paintings

Floor 0: 1100–1600

Asian Pavilion

Coat & Bag Check

Cafe

Entrance to Exhibits

Audio Tour Desk

Ship Models

Ticket Desk

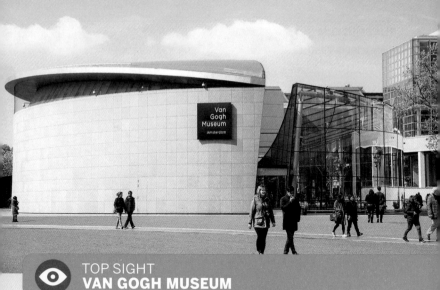

YURY DMITRIENKO/SHUTTERSTOCK ©

◉ TOP SIGHT
VAN GOGH MUSEUM

This wonderful museum holds the world's largest Van Gogh collection. It's a poignant experience to see the perma-queues outside, then trace the painter's tragic yet breathtakingly productive life. Opened in 1973 to house the collection of Vincent's brother, Theo, it comprises 200 paintings and 500 drawings by Vincent and his contemporaries, including Gauguin and Monet.

Museum Layout & Highlights

In 2015 a swish extension added 800 sq metres of space to the museum, which now spreads over four levels, moving chronologically from Floor 0 (ground floor) to Floor 3. It's still a manageable size; allow a couple of hours to browse the galleries. The audioguide is helpful and there's a separate one for children. It's fascinating to see Van Gogh's evolution from his early depictions of sombre countryfolk in the Netherlands to his pulsating, swirling French landscapes. The paintings tend to be moved around, depending on the current exhibition theme (say, Van Gogh's images of nature).

Potato Eaters & Skeleton with Burning Cigarette

Van Gogh's earliest works – showing raw, if unrefined, talent – are from his time in the Dutch countryside and Antwerp between 1883 and 1885. He painted peasant life, exalting their existence in works such as *The Potato Eaters* (1885). The symbolic *Still Life with Bible* (1885), painted after his father's death, shows a burnt-out candle, his Protestant minister father's bible and a much-thumbed smaller book, *La Joi de Vivre,* representing Van Gogh's more secular philosophy. He painted *Skeleton with Burning Cigarette* (1886) when he was a student at Antwerp's Royal Academy of Fine Arts.

DON'T MISS

➡ *The Potato Eaters*
➡ *The Yellow House*
➡ *Wheatfield with Crows*
➡ *Sunflowers*
➡ *Skeleton with Burning Cigarette*

PRACTICALITIES

➡ Map p312, G5
➡ ☎020-570 52 00
➡ www.vangogh museum.nl
➡ Museumplein 6
➡ adult/child €19/free, audioguide €5/3
➡ ⊙9am-7pm Sun-Thu, to 9pm Fri & Sat late Jun-Aug, 9am-6pm Sat-Thu, to 9pm Fri May-late Jun & Sep-late Oct, shorter hours rest of year
➡ 🚊2/3/5/12 Van Baerlestraat

Self-Portraits

In 1886 Van Gogh moved to Paris, where Theo worked as an art dealer. Vincent began to paint self-portraits as a way of improving his portraiture without paying for models, which he couldn't afford. He met some of the Impressionists, and his palette began to brighten.

Sunflowers & The Yellow House

In 1888 Van Gogh left for Arles in Provence to paint its colourful landscapes and try to achieve his dream of creating an artists colony. *Sunflowers* (1889) and other blossoms that shimmer with intense Mediterranean light are from this period. So is *The Yellow House* (1888), a rendering of the abode Van Gogh rented in Arles. The artist Paul Gauguin came to stay, but they quarrelled terribly. *The Bedroom* (1888) depicts Van Gogh's sleeping quarters at the house. In 1888 he sliced off part of his ear during a bout of psychosis.

Wheatfield with Crows

Van Gogh had himself committed to an asylum in Saint-Rémy in 1889. While there, his work became ever more extraordinary. His wildly expressive, yet tightly controlled landscapes are based on the surrounding countryside, with its cypress and olive trees. This period includes the sinuous, pulsating *Irises*. In 1890 he went north to Auvers-sur-Oise. One of his last paintings, *Wheatfield with Crows* (1890), is particularly menacing and ominous, and was finished shortly before his suicide, though it wasn't his final work.

Extras

The museum has multiple **listening stations** for diverse recordings of Van Gogh's letters, mainly to and from Theo, who championed his work. The museum has categorised all of Van Gogh's letters at www.vangoghletters.org. There are daily workshops (for adults and kids) where you can create your own works of art.

Other Artists

Thanks to Theo van Gogh's prescient collecting, you'll also see works by Vincent's contemporaries, including Gauguin, Monet and Toulouse-Lautrec. Paintings by Van Gogh's precursors, such as Jean-François Millet and Gustave Courbet, also pepper the galleries, as do works by artists Van Gogh influenced.

Exhibition Wing

Gerrit Rietveld, the influential Dutch architect, designed the museum's main building. Behind it, reaching towards Museumplein, is a separate wing (opened in 1999) designed by Kisho Kurokawa and commonly referred to as 'the Mussel'. It hosts temporary exhibitions by big-name artists.

RED VINEYARD AT ARLES

Van Gogh sold only one painting during his lifetime *(Red Vineyard at Arles)*. It hangs at Moscow's Pushkin Museum.

LIBRARY

The museum's **library** (Map p312; ✆020-570 59 78; Gabriël Metsustraat 8; ◷10am-12.30pm & 1.30-5pm Mon-Fri; ☐3/5/12 Museumplein) FREE has a wealth of reference material – some 35,000 books and articles – for serious study.

FRIDAY NIGHTS

The museum stays open to 9pm on Friday, when it hosts special cultural events and opens a bar downstairs. There's usually live music or a DJ.

TOP SIGHT
STEDELIJK MUSEUM

This is an impressive, light, bright modern art museum, displaying artworks from its 90,000-strong collection dating from 1870 to the present day. The permanent collection rotates, but you're likely to see works by Monet, Picasso, Kandinsky, Matisse, Chagall, Warhol, Rothko, De Kooning and more. Temporary installations of the latest in contemporary art show in its newer wing.

AM Weissman designed the 1895 main building. In the ground-floor **Stedelijk Base** exhibition, the works on display do change but you're likely to see all sorts of modern masterpieces: Henri Matisse cut-outs, Yayoi Kusama soft sculptures, Picasso abstracts, and a vivid collection of paintings by Dutch homeboys Piet Mondrian, Willem de Kooning and Karel Appel. There's also usually an exhibition devoted to the art and design of De Stijl, with works by Mondrian and Lichtenstein.

Head upstairs, and the works become more modern, ranging from 1950 to the present. Here you might view anything from avant-garde short films to a photography exhibition. Exhibits change regularly, so you never know what will be on hand, but count on it being offbeat and provocative.

DON'T MISS

➡ Appel murals
➡ De Stijl exhibits
➡ Excellent temporary exhibitions
➡ Modern art masterpieces

PRACTICALITIES

➡ Map p312, G5
➡ 020-573 29 11
➡ www.stedelijk.nl
➡ Museumplein 10
➡ adult/child €18.50/free
➡ ⊙10am-6pm Sat-Thu, to 10pm Fri
➡ 2/3/5/12 Van Baerlestraat

The newer wing, designed by Benthem Crouwel Architects, opened in 2012. It is also known as 'the Bathtub' and you'll know why when you see it. It houses temporary contemporary exhibitions.

That smooth, white tub material, by the way, is called Twaron, a synthetic fibre that's five times as strong as steel and typically used in yacht hulls.

Kids will find inventive hands-on installations and other activities in the **Family Lab**.

The Stedelijk's **library** (open Tuesday to Saturday from noon to 5pm) is a great resource, with catalogues, books, archive material, art magazines, and art and design documentaries, as well as wi-fi. Admission is free (no museum entrance ticket required).

TOP SIGHT
VONDELPARK

Amsterdam's favourite playground is the green expanse of Vondelpark, with its 47 hectares of lawns, ponds and winding paths receiving around 12 million visitors a year: tourists, roller skaters, dog walkers, kids and stoners. There's a constant parade of bikes, and on sunny days you can hardly move for picnics all around the grass.

Originally this was a private park, only open to the rich. Its sprawling, English-style gardens, with ponds, lawns, bridges and footpaths, were laid out on marshland by architect Jan David Zocher and opened in 1865. Between 1875 and 1877, Zocher's son, Louis Paul, expanded the park to its current size.

It was known as Nieuwe Park (New Park), but in 1867 a **statue** (Map p312) of poet and playwright Joost van den Vondel (1587–1679) was created by sculptor Louis Royer. Amsterdammers began referring to the park as Vondelspark, which led to it being formally renamed. The **rose garden** (Map p312) was added in 1936. Vondelpark was bought by the City Council in 1953, and finally opened to the public.

About a century after opening, the swampy location meant the park had actually sunk by 2–3m. After it was listed as a national monument in the mid-1990s, major renovations incorporated an extensive drainage system and refurbished walking and cycling paths, while retaining its historic appearance.

Near the eastern end, the 19th-century Italian Renaissance-style pavilion is now a cafe-bar, Vondelpark3 (p169). The park also has several other cafes, playgrounds and a wonderful open-air theatre, Openluchttheater (p172). For something a bit more alternative, check out what's on at Vondelbunker (p170). Art is strewn throughout the park, with 69 sculptures all up. Among them is Picasso's huge abstract work *Figure découpée l'Oiseau* (The Bird; 1965), known locally as **The Fish** (Map p312), which he donated for the park's centenary.

Catch the park's highlights on a self-guided walking tour. For bicycle rentals, MacBike (p29) is fairly close to the park's main entrance.

DON'T MISS
* Rose garden
* Proeflokaal 't Blauwe Theehuis
* Picasso's *The Fish*
* Open-air theatre

PRACTICALITIES
* Map p312, D5
* www.hetvondelpark.net
* 12 Van Baerlstraat, 5 Museumplein

⊙ SIGHTS

Vondelpark is Amsterdam's green soul, and a few paces away lie the city's greatest museums, all conveniently close together around Museumplein, including the Rijksmuseum, Van Gogh Museum and the Stedelijk Museum. Further south, you can explore the vast parklands of Amsterdamse Bos, and the Cobra Museum (p162), devoted to the De Stijl art movement. North of Vondelpark, there is the arts and food hall De Hallen (p165), created from former tram sheds.

RIJKSMUSEUM	MUSEUM

See p153.

VAN GOGH MUSEUM	MUSEUM

See p156.

VONDELPARK	PARK

See p159.

STEDELIJK MUSEUM	MUSEUM

See p158.

MUSEUMPLEIN	SQUARE

Map p312 (🚊2/3/5/12 Van Baerlestraat) Amsterdam's most famous museums cluster around this public square, which has that Amsterdam essential: a skateboard ramp, as well as a playground and ice-skating pond (in winter). Locals and tourists mill around, everyone picnics here when the weather warms up, and there are food and craft stalls on the third Sunday of the month. The space is also used for public concerts and special events.

Museumplein was laid out to host the World Exhibition in 1883, but gained its lasting title only when the Rijksmuseum opened two years later.

One of many facelifts raised a triangle of turf at the southern end, dubbed the 'ass's ear' for its shape; it's now a popular spot for sun worshippers. There's a large supermarket concealed below.

AMSTERDAMSE BOS	PARK

(Amsterdam Forest; www.amsterdamsebos. nl; Bosbaanweg 5; ☉24hr; 🚊347, 357, Ⓜ️Van Boshuizenstraat) Amsterdam's forest is a vast swathe (roughly 1000 hectares) of almost countryside, 20 minutes by bike south of Vondelpark. Planted in 1934 to provide employment during the Great Depression, its lakes, woods and meadows are crisscrossed by paths and dotted with cafes. You can rent bicycles, feed baby goats in spring, take a horse-riding lesson, boat the rural-feeling waterways, see a play at the open-air theatre and ascend to the treetops in the climbing park.

It's a glorious place to go with kids, though best if you explore by bike due to its size. There's a **bike rental** (www.amsterdamse bosfietsverhuur.nl; rental per hour/day €5/10; ☉10am-6pm) kiosk across from the forest entrance and a **visitor centre** (📞020-545 61 00; www.amsterdamsebos.nl; Bosbaanweg 5, ☉10am-5pm Tue-Sun) with information. In the densest thickets you forget you're near a city at all (though you're right by Schiphol airport). A lot of locals use the park, but it rarely feels crowded.

MOCO MUSEUM	MUSEUM

Map p312 (www.mocomuseum.com; Honthorst-straat 20; adult/child 16-17yr/child 10-15yr/under 10yr €14.50/12/9.50/free; ☉9am-7pm; 🚊2/3/5/12 Van Baerlestraat) A private house, the 1904 Villa Alsberg has been converted into the 'Modern Contemporary' (Moco) museum by a couple who are private collectors and curators. The cramped rooms are not an ideal gallery space, but big-name exhibitions by artists such as Banksy, Yayoi Kusama and Salvador Dalí haul in the crowds, and it's interesting to explore the building.

RIEKERMOLEN	WINDMILL

(www.molens.nl; Ⓜ️RAI, 🚊4 RAI) Like a scene from another century, just outside Amstelpark's south edge, on the west bank of the Amstel River, stands this 1636 windmill. In a field southwest of the mill, you'll find a statue of a sitting Rembrandt, who sketched the windmill here along the riverbank.

DE RIDAMMERHOEVE	FARM

(www.geitenboerderij.nl; Nieuwe Meerlaan 4; ☉10am-5pm Wed-Mon Apr-Oct, Wed-Sun Nov-Mar; 🚊347, 357) FREE A remarkable place in Amsterdamse Bos is this organic working goat farm, where kids can feed bottles of milk to, well, kids (€1 for a bottle) in season. There are goat's cheese-making workshops, and you can even do goat yoga (€26 including coffee and cake). The cafeteria sells goat's-milk smoothies and ice cream, as well as cheeses made on the premises.

AMSTELPARK
PARK

(Europaboulevard; ⊙8am-dusk; 🚻; MRAI, 🚈4 RAI) Pastoral haven Amstelpark has particularly creative garden layouts and many different species of flowers – it was originally created in 1972 for the bloom-buster flower show, Floriade, which takes place all over the Netherlands every 10 years. The park has rose and rhododendron gardens that blaze with colour in season. As well as flower lovers, the park is sure-fire family territory, with a petting zoo, mini-golf and a playground. In summer a miniature train chugs its way around the park.

Art exhibitions are held in the Glazen Huis (Glass House), the Orangerie and the Papillon Gallery.

HOLLANDSCHE MANEGE
NOTABLE BUILDING

Map p312 (☎020-618 09 42; www.dehollandsche manege.nl; Vondelstraat 140; adult/child €8/4; ⊙10am-5pm; 🚈1/11 1e Constantijn Huygensstraat) The neoclassical Hollandsche Manege is a surprise to discover just outside Vondelpark. Entering is like stepping back in time, into a grandiose indoor riding school inspired by the famous Spanish Riding School in Vienna. Designed by AL van Gendt and built in 1882, it retains its charming horse-head facade and has a large riding arena inside.

Visit the stables and/or watch the instructors put the horses through their paces from the elevated cafe. Entry includes a cup of tea or coffee. At the time of research, there were plans to renovate the building.

DIAMOND MUSEUM
MUSEUM

Map p312 (www.diamantmuseumamsterdam. nl; Paulus Potterstraat 8; adult/child €10/7.50; ⊙9am-5pm; 🚈2/5/12 Rijksmuseum) The extensive bling on display at the small, low-tech Diamond Museum is all clever recreations. You get a lot of background on the history of the trade and various historic sparkly crowns and jewels. Here you'll learn how Amsterdam was the globe's diamond trade epicentre for many centuries, where local Jews dominated the cutting and polishing business, and how the business moved to Antwerp after WWII following the decimation of the Jewish population here.

Those so inclined can save money by going next door to the attached Coster Diamonds (p174) – the company owns the museum – and taking a free workshop tour, where you can see gem cutters and polishers doing their thing.

OLYMPIC STADIUM
STADIUM

(☎020-305 44 00; www.olympischstadion. nl; Olympisch Stadion 21; tours per person €10; 🚈16/24 Olympisch Stadion) Built for the 1928 Olympic Games, this elegant stadium was

Riekermolen

VONDELPARK & THE SOUTH SIGHTS

WORTH A DETOUR

COBRA MUSEUM

It's well worth making the effort to visit this out-of-the-way canal-side **museum** (☎020-547 50 50; www.cobra-museum.nl; Sandbergplein 1; adult/child €12.50/8; ☺11am-5pm Tue-Sun; ⓂAmstelveen Centrum) in the town of Amstelveen. The building, designed by Dutch architect Wim Quist, makes a light-flooded setting for work from the post-WWII CoBrA movement (the name is taken from the city initials where the group's founders lived – Copenhagen, Brussels and Amsterdam). Its members produced highly expressionist works known for their primitive, childlike qualities, and the museum's boldly coloured, avant-garde paintings, ceramics and statues include many by Karel Appel, the style's most famous practitioner.

The charmingly surreal fountain outside the front entrance is Appel's work. Asger Jorn, Anton Rooskens, Corneille and Constant were among the other members. The CoBrA movement was active for just three years (1948–51). The art is less of a unified whole than a philosophy, inspired by Marxism, of using materials at hand to create paintings, sculpture and even poetry. Changing exhibits by contemporary artists are on show as well.

The metro stop is 1km southeast of the museum; follow the 'CoBrA' signs. You can easily pair a trip here with a visit to Amsterdamse Bos (p160) nearby. Buses 347 and 357 run up and down the main street from the museum to the forest; otherwise it's a 35-minute walk to the forest visitor centre.

designed by Jan Wils, a protégé of famous architect HP Berlage, and is functionalist in style. It has a soaring tower from which the Olympic flame burned for the first time during competition. Guided one-hour tours are available for groups of a minimum of five people, but must be arranged in advance. It hosts occasional big-name gigs as well as sporting events.

Athletics Phanos organises a free long-distance run practice on the second Friday of the month.

ELECTRISCHE MUSEUMTRAMLIJN
AMSTERDAM   MUSEUM

(Tram Museum Amsterdam; ☎020-673 75 38; www.museumtramlijn.org; Amstelveenseweg 264; return adult/child €5.50/3.50; ☺11am-5pm Sun Apr-Oct; ♿; ☐170, 172, ☐16 Haarlemmermeer Station) A handsome red-brick building, the former Haarlemmermeer Station is now the starting point for the tram museum, which is not a static experience but a chance to ride on a gleaming selection of historic European trams that run between here and Amstelveen. A return trip takes about 1¼ hours and skirts the large Amsterdamse Bos recreational area. The tram departs two to three times per hour; see the website for details.

Haarlemmermeer Station is southwest of Vondelpark and just north of the Olympic Stadium.

HOUSE OF BOLS   MUSEUM

Map p312 (www.houseofbols.com; Paulus Potterstraat 14; admission incl 1 cocktail €16, over 18yr only; ☺1-6.30pm Sun-Thu, to 9pm Fri & Sat; ☐2/5/12 Van Baerlestraat) Cheesy but fun: here you undertake an hour's self-guided tour through this *jenever* (Dutch gin) museum. In the 'Hall of Taste' you'll try to differentiate between scents and flavours, while in the 'Distillery Room' you'll learn about the process of extraction. You'll learn more about the history of gin than you would think possible, and get to try shaking your own cocktail, plus drink a Bols confection of your choice at the end.

🍴 EATING

International options abound around Amstelveenseweg and inside De Hallen's Foodhallen (p165). Head to Vondelpark's squats (p170) for organic vegan fare, and to the diverse restaurants along Overtoom and Jan Pieter Heijestraat. Treat yourself at Michelin-starred Rijks (p167).

★BRAAI BBQ BAR   BARBECUE €

Map p312 (☎020-221 13 76; www.braaiamsterdam.nl; Schinkelhavenkade 1; dishes €6.50-15.50; ☺4-9.30pm; ☐1/11/17 Surinameplein) Once a *haringhuis* (herring stand), this tiny place is now a street-food-style barbecue bar, with a great canal-side setting. Braai's speciality is marinated, barbecued ribs (half or full rack), biltong and roasted sausages, but there is a veggie burger, too. Tables scatter under the trees alongside the water. No alcohol is served.

IJSCUYPJE
ICE CREAM €

(www.ijscuypje.nl; Amstelveenseweg 218; 1 scoop €1.70; ⊙noon-7pm; ☐2 Amstelveenseweg) This branch of IJscuypje is well located for a post-dinner treat after dining at one of Amstelveenseweg's many restaurants. Choose from a range of dairy-free sorbets and ice cream flavours such as spiced cookie and *stroopwafel*.

DUTCH WEED BURGER JOINT
VEGAN €

Map p312 (☑020-331 29 30; www.dutchweed burger.com; Nicolaas Beetsstraat 47; mains €10-13; ⊙1-9pm Wed-Fri, noon-9pm Sat & Sun; ☎☑; ☐753, ☐7/17 Ten Katestraat) This intimate vegan restaurant specialises in tasty burgers and 'fish' bites made from seaweed, not the other type of 'weed' common here. Don't be put off by the green bread bun – it contains the Dutch Weed Burger Joint's signature ingredient: winterweed, grown on home turf in the Oosterschelde National Park in the south of the Netherlands.

HAP HMM
DUTCH €

Map p312 (☑020-618 18 84; www.hap-hmm.nl; Eerste Helmersstraat 33; mains €10-14; ⊙5-9.15pm Mon-Fri; ☑; ☐1 1e Constantijn Huygensstraat) With old family photos adorning the walls, an evening at this homely eatery almost feels like dining in someone's home. The menu offers an array of classic Dutch comfort foods, from rich beefs stews to chicken casseroles, and a good selection of vegetarian options. Just like any home-cooked meal, dishes are served with a selection of boiled vegetables.

The schnitzel was crowned the best in Amsterdam by Dutch newspaper *Het Parool*. Note: credit cards are not accepted.

DIGNITA VONDELPARK
CAFE €

Map p312 (☑020-221 44 58; www.eatwell dogood.nl; Koninginneweg 218; mains €7-15; ⊙8.30am-5pm; ☎; ☐Amstelveenseweg) This light, airy cafe looks like many other hipster brunch spots, but Dignita has socially worthwhile credentials too, pumping its profits into helping vulnerable individu-

als. The all-day brunch dishes are delicious, from the Dutch breakfast board of breads, croissants, avocado, free-range ham and cheese to a slow-cooked Black Angus beef burger, and there's plenty of tempting homemade cakes.

TOKO KOK KITA
INDONESIAN €

Map p312 (☑020-670 29 33; www.kokkita.nl; Amstelveenseweg 166; mains €5-9; ⊙noon-8.30pm Tue-Sat, from 5pm Sun; ☐2 Amstelveenseweg) A humble Indonesian *toko* (shop) attracting queues for its authentic Indonesian dishes. Diners choose either rice or noodles and then select their vegetables and meat from a pick-and-mix serving counter. Locals often top their meals off with a traditional spicy boiled egg.

HOLY RAVIOLI
ITALIAN €

Map p312 (☑06 1118 7122; www.holyravioli.nl; Jan Pieter Heijestraat 88; mains €7-13; ⊙1-9pm Sun-Wed, from 11am Thu-Sat; ☐7/17 Jan Pieter Heijestraat) Pasta maker Holy Ravioli supplies restaurants around town, but you can get ready-to-eat takeaway meals here (or, if you're lucky, snag a seat at its few tables). Delicious ravioli varieties include veal and sage with anchovy butter and wild spinach salad, and a vegan option with sweet potato, coconut and cavolo nero; or try the confit duck, truffle and forest-mushroom lasagne.

BREAKFAST CLUB
CAFE €

Map p312 (www.thebreakfastclub.nl; Bellamystraat 2; dishes €6-13; ⊙8am-4pm Mon-Fri, to 5pm Sat & Sun; ☐7/17 Ten Katestraat) If you're hankering for breakfast any time of day, this bright corner cafe is perfect: Mexican breakfasts with huevos rancheros (spicy eggs); English-style, with homemade baked beans, bacon, eggs, mushrooms and sausages; or New York buttermilk pancakes with berries and honeycomb butter. There are other tantalising pancake options too, plus muesli, avocado toast and eggs Benedict.

IJSBOUTIQUE
ICE CREAM €

Map p312 (☑020-664 08 09; www.ijsboutique.nl; Johannes Verhulststraat 107; ice cream 1/2/3/4 scoops €1.65/3.10/4.20/5.20; ⊙noon-10pm; ☐2 Cornelis Schuytstraat) In the upmarket shopping area around Cornelis Schuytstraat and Willemsparkweg, IJsboutique has fittingly sophisticated, seasonal ice cream flavours, such as passionfruit sorbet and lime pie.

BOERDERIJ MEERZICHT
DUTCH €

(www.boerderijmeerzicht.nl; Koenenkade 56; pancakes €6-12.50; ☺10am-7pm Wed-Sun Mar-Oct, to 6pm Fri-Sun Nov-Feb; ♿; ☒170/172 Van Nijenrodeweg) In Amsterdamse Bos, on the northwest side of the Bosbaan (the long lake used for sculling), this old farmhouse is a marvellously family-friendly restaurant. There's an enclosure for peacocks and *Bambi*-esque deer – you can buy seeds to feed them – plus a playground with sand-pits and diggers. Pancakes on the menu complete the child-heaven vibe (available from 11am).

ALCHEMIST GARDEN
VEGAN €

Map p312 (☒020-334 33 35; www.facebook.com/AlchemistGarden; Overtoom 409; dishes €4-13; ☺9am-10pm Mon-Sat, noon-9pm Sun; ♿; ☒1/11 Rhijnvis Feithstraat) 🌱 This bright, high-ceilinged cafe's food may be gluten-, lactose- and glucose-free, but it's certainly tasty. There's a health-rich, vitamin-filled organic menu (raw 'hot dog', pumpkin burger and pesto-stuffed portobello mushrooms), plus smoothies, juices, a huge range of herbal teas, organic wine by the bottle and guilt-free treats such as raw chocolate cake. Many ingredients are from the owner's own garden.

Ask about wild-food foraging walks in the Vondelpark in spring. The cafe also hosts regular events from meditation and holistic massage to chai ceremonies; check the Facebook page for the schedule.

LUNCHROOM WILHELMINA
CAFE €

Map p312 (☒020-618 97 78; www.lunchroomwilhelmina.nl; 1e Helmersstraat 83a; mains €5-10; ☺9am-5pm Wed-Mon; ☒1 1e Constantijn Huygensstraat) On a quiet street, facing a flower shop, this charmingly serene neighbourhood cafe is a pleasant escape for a simple breakfast of egg dishes, lunch (quiches, sandwiches, soups, salads) or a coffee and cake pit stop.

RENZO'S
DELI €

Map p312 (☒020-673 16 73; www.renzos.nl; Van Baerlestraat 67; dishes per 100g €2-3.50, sandwiches €7-8; ☺9am-9pm Mon-Fri, 10am-9pm Sat & Sun; ☒3/5/12/16/24 Museumplein) Renzo's deli resembles an Italian *tavola calda* (hot table), where you can select hot and cold ready-made dishes, such as meatballs, pasta and salads, plus stuffed sandwiches and delicious cannoli (Sicilian 'little tubes', filled with ricotta cream). There are a few tables crammed into the space, or it's perfect to take away to nearby Museumplein (p160).

★DIKKE GRAAF
MEDITERRANEAN €€

Map p312 (☒020-223 77 56; www.dikkegraaf.nl; Wilhelminastraat 153; small plates €7.50-14.50; ☺3pm-1am Wed-Sun; ☒1/11 Rhijnvis Feithstraat) This local favourite features industrial-styled copper lamps and scrubbed-wood tables, and opens to an olive-tree-ringed terrace. It's a truly fabulous spot for *borrel* (drinks), with by-the-glass wines and small sharing plates such as bruschetta, charcuterie and Manchego sheep's cheese.

VEGAN JUNK FOOD BAR
VEGAN €€

Map p312 (www.veganjunkfoodbar.com; Staringplein 22; burgers from €9.50; ☺noon-10pm; 🌱♿; ☒1 Jan Pieter Heijestraat) 🌱 Not your average plant-based eatery, the Vegan Junk Food Bar serves up cruelty-free fast-food favourites in a casual setting with bright graffiti-strewn walls. Comfort-food offerings include non-meat 'beef' burgers bulging with 'cheese', pickles, special sauce and a fried onion mix; vegan takes on seafood dishes such as crispy shrimp or sashimi; and loaded fries. Don't miss the meat-free take on Dutch classic *bitterballen* (croquette balls).

MOER
INTERNATIONAL €€

Map p312 (☒020-820 33 30; Amstelveenseweg 7; lunch mains €9-12.50, dinner mains €18.50-27; ☺noon-10pm; ♿; ☒1 Rhijnvis Feithstraat) 🌱 Attached to the Tire Station (p226) hotel, Moer has a plate-glass wall onto the street, artful moss and green credentials – the ceiling is insulated by plants and heating is channelled from the kitchen. Chef Dirk Mooren cooks up a storm in the open kitchen, serving organic and sustainable food with lots of vegetarian choices, along with natural wines.

DE ITALIAAN
ITALIAN €€

Map p312 (☒020-683 68 54; www.deitaliaan.com; Bosboom Toussaintstraat 29; pizza €10-19.50, pasta & mains €14.50-23; ☺5.30-10pm Mon-Fri, noon-10pm Sat & Sun; ☒1 1e Constantijn Huygensstraat) With outdoor seating on leafy Bosboom Toussaintstraat, and a warm pop-art-orange interior, this contemporary restaurant serves sophisticated Italian dishes, such as prosciutto crudo–filled tortellini in broth, and grilled rib eye with rocket, parmesan and balsamic vinegar. The mag-

DE HALLEN

A spectacular food hall and cultural complex, **De Hallen** (Map p312; www.dehallen-amsterdam.nl; Bellamyplein 51; 7/17 Ten Katestraat) has galvanised the whole surrounding district north of Vondelpark. It was converted from vast red-brick 1902-built tram sheds in 2014 to incorporate a skylit food hall, a restaurant, library, design shops, boutiques, a bike seller-repairer, a cinema and a hotel. Regular events held inside include themed **weekend markets** (such as organic produce or Dutch design); check the website to find out what's happening. A vibrant street market, Ten Katemarkt, is right outside.

Foodhallen (Map p312; www.foodhallen.nl; Hannie Dankbaar Passage 3; dishes €3-20; 11am-11.30pm Sun-Thu, to 1am Fri & Sat) A buzzing ex-tram shed full of eclectic food stalls and bars, including many international offerings, such as Viet View Vietnamese street food and Jabugo Iberico Bar ham; there's also the Beer Bar serving local tipples from Oedipus and 2 Chefs.

Kanarie Club (Map p312; 020-218 17 76; www.kanarieclub.nl; Hannie Dankbaar Passage 3; breakfast & lunch mains €10-15, dinner mains €20-21; 8.30am-11pm Mon-Thu, 9.30am-2.30am Fri & Sat, 9.30am-11pm Sun;) Framed by a soaring floor-to-ceiling glass wall looking through to the Foodhallen inside De Hallen, this restaurant serves all-day breakfasts and a brasserie-style menu, such as pancakes, Caesar salad and *bitterballen*.

ReCycle (Map p312; 020-489 70 29; www.recyclefietsen.nl; Hannie Dankbaar Passage 27; noon-6pm Mon, 11am-7pm Tue-Fri, 11am-6pm Sat & Sun) The clue is in the name: this warehouse space sells new and secondhand bikes, and offers repairs and restoration. As to be bike-less in Amsterdam could be more than a local could bear, you can borrow a bike while you wait for yours to become available.

Filmhallen (Map p312; www.filmhallen.nl; Hannie Dankbaar Passage 12; tickets adult/child from €11.50/8) A cool, hip film venue within De Hallen, this screens art-house films and new mainstream releases in both Dutch and English.

Ten Katemarkt (Map p312; Ten Katestraat; 9am-5pm Mon-Sat) Right outside De Hallen, this buzzing daily (except Sunday) street market has everything you'll find at Amsterdam's bigger, better-known markets – fresh fish, fruit and vegetables, fabulous Dutch cheeses, antipasti, nuts, spices, ready-to-eat snacks such as steaming-hot *frites* (fries), fashion, fabrics, homewares and bike locks – but a much more local crowd.

Maker Store (Map p312; 020-261 76 67; www.themakerstore.nl; Hannie Dankbaar Passage 39; noon-7pm Tue-Fri & Sun, from 11am Sat) This large bright store stocks a fantastic selection of quirky gifts, books, clothing and homeware made by local artists.

nificent wood-fired pizzas, including the house-speciality 'De Italiaan' – Gorgonzola, mushrooms, rocket and black truffle – can all be made gluten-free.

SEAFOOD BAR
SEAFOOD €€

Map p312 (020-670 83 55; www.theseafoodbar.com; Van Baerlestraat 5; mains €13-36; 11am-11pm; 2/5 Van Baerlestraat) White-tiled and exposed-brick walls give this popular seafood specialist a fresh, urban feel, while counter as well as table seating makes it a good choice for solo diners. Plates heaving with oysters and platters with king crab legs sticking out are delivered to tables and the kitchen turns out a mean, crispy fish and chips.

WG CAFE
CAFE €€

Map p312 (020-689 56 00; Marius van Bouwdijk Bastiaansestraat 55; dishes €6-17.50; 10am-1am Sun-Thu, to 3am Fri & Sat; 1 Overtoom) On a little square and attached to the fringe Amsterdam Theater House just off Overtoom, this is a laid-back local favourite for a drink or a bite to eat. The quiet off-road location and board games make it a good choice with kids, and the menu offers everything from a tuna melt and homemade pasta to burgers and salads.

VAN 'T SPIT
ROTISSERIE €€

Map p312 (www.vantspit.nl; De Clercqstraat 95; half/whole chicken €11.90/23; ☺kitchen 5-10pm, bar to 1am; 🚊13/19 Willem de Zwijgerlaan) At stripped-back Van 't Spit it's all about roast chicken, with piles of wood ready for the rotisserie. Choices are simple – select from a half or whole chicken (there are no other mains), and decide if you want sides (corn on the cob, fries, salad and homemade coleslaw).

GEORGE BISTRO BISTRO
BISTRO €€

Map p312 (☎020-303 30 76; www.george. amsterdam; Valeriusplein 2; mains €9.50-17; ☺11am-late; 🚊2 Valeriusplein) So good they named it twice, this French-style bistro has large windows, wooden chairs and a buzzy atmosphere. George's menu includes lobster cooked on the Josper charcoal grill with parsley butter and lemon, and eight different types of burger (including halloumi, grilled tuna with wasabi mayo, and the classic bistro burger with smoked bacon and aged cheese) on toasted brioche buns.

L'ENTRECÔTE ET LES DAMES
FRENCH €€

Map p312 (☎020-679 88 88; www.entrecote-et-les-dames.nl; Van Baerlestraat 47-49; lunch mains €14.50, 2-course dinner menu €25.75; ☺noon-3pm & 5.30-10pm; 🚊3/5/12 Museumplein) Black-and-white awnings, a wall made from wooden drawers and a wrought-iron balcony set the scene at this restaurant, which has a simple menu of steak or fish. Go for the *entrecôte* (premium beef steak) at dinner or a steak sandwich for lunch, and save room for scrumptious desserts: perhaps chocolate mousse, *tarte au citron* (lemon tart) or *crêpes au Grand Marnier*.

CARTER
BISTRO €€

Map p312 (☎020-752 68 55; www.barcarter.nl; Valeriusstraat 85; mains lunch €6-14, dinner €17-21; ☺noon-midnight; 🖬; 🚊16 Emmastraat) In the swanky residential neighbourhood the Old South, this split-level dining space has art and photography covering the walls, and a lovely street-side terrace. Lunch includes sandwiches and salads while the dinner menu is impressive, with dishes such as Black Angus burger and steak tartare. Its kids menu (€15) comes with hot dog, fries, salad and Smarties ice cream.

NARBONNE
BISTRO €€

Map p312 (☎020-618 42 63; www.narbonne. nl; Bosboom Toussaintstraat 28; dishes €5-15; ☺5.30-11pm Tue-Sat; 🗷; 🚊1 1e Constantijn Huygensstraat) Neighbourhood favourite Narbonne offers a mix of well-executed Mediterranean tapas, with dishes to share including smoked mozzarella tortellini, baked mushrooms, marinated artichokes, skewered scallops, fresh oysters with lime and chive dressing and grilled beef skewers. Book ahead.

RESTAURANT DE KNIJP
FRENCH €€

Map p312 (☎020-671 42 48; www.deknijp.nl; Van Baerlestraat 134; mains €18-27; ☺4pm-12.30am; 🚊3/5/12/16/24 Museumplein) A dark-wood eatery close to Amsterdam's museum district, this evening-only French-influenced place offers meaty classics, such as snails in creamy garlic sauce, as well as more out-there choices, including guinea fowl breast with plum sauce. The tables on two levels tend to fill up when there's a show at the nearby Concertgebouw, and it's one of the few local places to serve food late.

DE BOSBAAN CAFE
CAFE €€

(www.debosbaan.nl; Bosbaan 4; lunch dishes €6.50-15, dinner mains €17-23.50; ☺10am-10pm; 🗻; 🚊347, 357) Located in Amsterdamse Bos (p160) near the forest's entrance, De Bosbaan Cafe is a grand lodge-like refuge for coffee or meals. Its terrace overlooks the lake, so it's a perfect viewpoint for watching the rowers on a sunny afternoon.

BRASSERIE DE JOFFERS
BRASSERIE €€

Map p312 (☎020-673 03 60; www.brasseriede joffers.nl; Willemsparkweg 163; mains €13-22; ☺8am-8pm Mon-Sat, from 9am Sun; 🗷; 🚊2 Cornelis Schuytstraat) Near the Vondelpark, this restaurant has a shaded terrace that entices you to sit nursing a drink in the sunshine, as well as a timber and curved-glass shopfront and an interior that's all upholstered banquettes and old-school art deco charm. The menu includes salads, burgers and a great range of sandwiches stuffed with fillings.

PASTIS
FRENCH €€

Map p312 (☎020-616 61 66; www.pastisam sterdam.nl; 1e Constantijn Huygensstraat 15; mains €13.50-24; ☺5-10pm Mon-Fri, 3-10.30pm Sat & Sun; 🚊1 1e Constantijn Huygensstraat) Red awning, pavement tables, rustic interior, bottle-lined walls and charcuterie: immerse yourself in a corner of France, with a regularly changing menu that might include house-made pâté, steak tartare, confit of chicken, and *entrecôte* (beefsteak) with tarragon aioli and *frites* – and, of course, some of that namesake anise-flavoured spirit.

CAFÉ TOUSSAINT
BISTRO €€

Map p312 (📞020-685 07 37; www.cafe-tous saint.nl; Bosboom Toussaintstraat 26; dishes lunch €5-14, dinner €12-21; ⏱10am-5pm Mon, 10am-midnight Tue-Thu & Sun, 9am-1am Fri & Sat; 🖤; 🚊1 1e Constantijn Huygensstraat) An enchantingly pretty place to stop for a bite, this casual neighbourhood gem feels like it's straight out of an Edith Piaf song. Come for a croissant and cappuccino under the trees, or in the candlelit evenings for delicious meat and fish of the day creations and tasty quiches, followed by warm apple pie with ice cream.

LALIBELA
ETHIOPIAN €€

Map p312 (📞020-683 83 32; www.lalibela.nl; 1e Helmersstraat 249; mains €11-17; ⏱5-11pm; 🖍🖤; 🚊1 Jan Pieter Heijestraat) Named after the ancient African city, this small and colourful restaurant feels like you're in another country. It was the Netherlands' first Ethiopian restaurant and it's still a cracker. Sip Ethiopian beer from a half-gourd and eat rich stews, egg and vegetable dishes served with *injera* (slightly sour, spongy pancakes) instead of utensils to a soundtrack of African music.

★RIJKS
INTERNATIONAL €€€

Map p312 (📞020-674 75 55; www.rijksrestau rant.nl; Rijksmuseum; mains €24-32, 3-/4-course lunch menus €42/52, 6-course dinner menu €79; ⏱11.30am-3pm & 5-10pm Mon-Sat, 11.30-3pm Sun; 🚊2/5/12 Rijksmuseum) In a beautiful space with huge windows and high ceilings in part of the Rijksmuseum (p153), Rijks was awarded a Michelin star in 2016. Chef Joris Bijdendijk uses locally sourced ingredients, adheres to slow food ethics and draws on historic Dutch influences for his creative, highly imaginative cuisine. For lunch or dinner you can choose a set menu or à la carte.

★ADAM
GASTRONOMY €€€

Map p312 (📞020-233 98 52; www.restaurant adam.nl; Overtoom 515; 3-/4-/5-/6-course menus €38.50/46.50/52.50/62; ⏱6-10.30pm Tue-Sat; 🖍; 🚊1/11/17 Surinameplein) This seriously gourmet, chic and intimate restaurant serves exquisitely presented food. The surprise menu changes on a monthly basis; choose from one of the course menus of vegetarian or meat and fish dishes. Dessert is either a cheese platter or a chef's surprise, and paired wines are available for €7.50 per glass.

★RON GASTROBAR
INTERNATIONAL €€€

Map p312 (📞020-496 19 43; www.rongastrobar. nl; Sophialaan 55; dishes €17.50, steak & seafood €42.50-92.50; ⏱noon-2.30pm & 5.30-10.30pm; 🖤; 🚊2 Amstelveenseweg) Ron Blaauw ran his two-Michelin-star restaurant in these pared-down, spacious designer premises before turning it into a more affordable 'gastrobar' (still Michelin-starred), whereby you get the quality without the formality. He serves gourmet tapas-style dishes, dry-aged rib steaks and stellar seafood sharing dishes, or you can choose the 'best of Gastrobar' six-course menu for €69.50 per person.

RESTAURANT BLAUW
INDONESIAN €€€

Map p312 (📞020-675 50 00; www.restau rantblauw.nl; Amstelveenseweg 158; mains €22.50-27.50, rijsttafel per person €30-35; ⏱6-10pm Mon-Fri, 5pm-10pm Sat & Sun; 🚊2 Amstelveenseweg) The *New York Times* voted Blauw the 'best Indonesian restaurant in the Netherlands' and legions agree. The rijsttafel (Indonesian banquet) is a feast with a choice of meat and veg, seafood and veg, or veg only; otherwise you can opt for à la carte. Menu standouts include *ikan kembung* (mackerel with candlenut sauce) and *gulai domba* (braised lamb with coconut curry and cinnamon). Reserve ahead.

BLUE PEPPER
INDONESIAN €€€

Map p312 (📞020-489 70 39; www.restaurant bluepepper.com; Nassaukade 366; mains €18-20, rijsttafel per person from €44.50; ⏱5.30-10pm; 🖍; 🚊7/10 Raamplein) This is one of Amsterdam's finest gourmet Indonesian restaurants, where Chef Sonja Pereira serves beautifully presented work-of-art Indonesian cuisine in an intimate dining room. The rijsttafel includes specialities from across the islands, such as wild scallops with saffron, orange, sea greens and macadamia nuts, and wild guinea fowl in a sweet, sour and spicy *rudjak* sauce.

Vegetarian and vegan rijsttafel menus are also options.

🍺 DRINKING & NIGHTLIFE

There are plenty of cool bars and beer specialists around Vondelpark, plus club nights at former squats and even an old school.

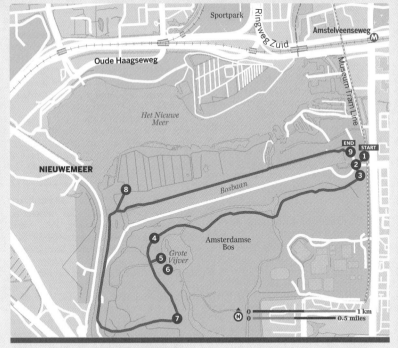

Neighbourhood Walk
Amsterdamse Bos

START AMSTERDAMSE BOS BIKE RENTAL
END DE BOSBAAN CAFE
LENGTH 3.5KM; TWO HOURS

An easy-to-reach escape from the city, Amsterdamse Bos is a huge swathe of countryside, combining thick trees, meadows and waterways.

The best way to explore the park is by bike. If you don't have wheels, you can hire from the ❶ **bicycle rental kiosk** (p160) by the main entrance, which also has a child-friendly cafe, with hammocks and toys galore, plus sandwiches. A good place to start is the ❷ **visitors centre** (p160) close to the main entrance. It has some information on the park and, more importantly, you can pick up a map to get your bearings. Also by the entrance is ❸ **Fun Forest** (p174), a treetop climbing park for kids or adults, which uses ropes, ladders and bridges.

Head west for 2.5km and you'll come to the ❹ **open-air theatre** (p172). It stages classic plays (in Dutch) and big-name gigs throughout summer. Nearby at ❺ **Grote Vijver** you can rent ❻ **kayaks** (p174) and pedal boats to explore what the owner calls the 'Amsterdam Amazon'. It may be an exaggeration but the waterway is surrounded by greenery on all sides and you'd never imagine that you're in the city.

About 750m south is the park's most delightful attraction, ❼ **De Ridammerhoeve** (p160), a working goat farm. The cafe sells goat's-milk ice cream and other dairy products. There are cheese-making workshops as well as goat yoga.

There are a couple of options for a meal after your park activities. A short distance from the theatre, on the northwest side of the Bosbaan (the long lake used for sculling), is ❽ **Boerderij Meerzicht** (p164). Kids will adore this old farmhouse, with its deer and peacock enclosure, plus diggers and climbing frames in the playground. Back by the park entrance, ❾ **De Bosbaan Cafe** (p166) is a lodge-like refuge with a great terrace overlooking the lake.

★ **LABYRINTH** COCKTAIL BAR

Map p312 (☏020-845 09 72; www.labyrinth amsterdam.nl; Amstelveenseweg 53; ☺4.30pm–midnight Mon, Wed, Thu & Sun, to 2am Fri & Sat) Mixologist Sam Kingue Ebelle concocts impressively inventive cocktails (€10.50 to €13) at this moody bar on Amstelveenseweg. For theatrical drama, try the Full Severity of Compassion (rye whisky, spiced rum, cherry brandy, vermouth infused with cocoa nibs, absinthe and bitters), delivered in a box and wafting gum-arabic smoke when opened.

The bar is kitted out with African art, hosts regular poetry readings and the excellent African-Caribbean-inspired menu includes jerk chicken wings and codfish croquettes.

★ **LOT SIXTY ONE** COFFEE

Map p312 (www.lotsixtyonecoffee.com; Kinkerstraat 112; ☺8am-6pm Mon-Fri, 9am-6pm Sat & Sun; ☎; ☐3/7/17 Bilderdijkstraat) ✐ Look downstairs to the open cellar to see (and, better still, smell) fresh coffee beans being roasted on the Probat at this streetwise spot. Beans are sourced through distributors from individual ecofriendly farms in Brazil, Kenya and Rwanda, to name a few. All coffees are double shots (unless you specify otherwise); watch Kinkerstraat's passing parade from a window seat.

Soy and oat milk are available. You can also buy bags of beans to take away.

KOFFIE ACADEMIE COFFEE

Map p312 (☏020-370 79 81; www.koffie-acad emie.nl; Overtoom 95; ☺8.30am-5pm Mon-Fri, 9am-5pm Sat & Sun; ☎; ☐1 1e Constantijn Huygensstraat) Join creative types with laptops, locals having business chats and tourists looking to recharge their batteries at this small, hip cafe decked out in moody industrial tones and with a soundtrack of cool tunes. Beans are locally roasted, staff are super friendly and there's breakfast granola and toasted sandwiches if you're in need of a bite.

VONDELPARK3 CAFE

Map p312 (☏020-639 25 89; www.vondelpark3.nl; Vondelpark 3; ☺10am-midnight; ☐3 Overtoom) Located in the former Vondelpark pavilion at the northeastern end of the park (p159), this stylish and comfortable cafe has a large terrace overlooking the pond – perfect for a morning coffee or sunset drink. It also does food from breakfast through to dinner and snacks in between, including charcuterie and cheese platters.

DE VONDELTUIN BAR

Map p312 (☏06 2756 5576; www.vondeltuin.nl; Vondelpark 7; ☺from 10am, closing hours vary; ☒; ☐2 Amstelveenseweg) Inside the Vondelpark, at its western edge, is this laid-back, hippyish-feeling bar-cafe and beer garden. Drink amid greenery in this cheery corner, with beer, burgers, salads and snacks on the menu, and space for kids to play.

EDEL BAR

Map p312 (☏020-799 50 00; www.lokaaledel.nl; Postjesweg 1; ☺noon-midnight; ☐7/17 Witte de Withstraat) On Het Sieraard's waterfront, Edel has lots of waterside seating as it's at the sweet spot where two canals cross. Inside and out it's filled with creative types who work in the local buildings. With hipster staff and creative food on offer, it really comes into its own in summer, lit by a canopy of twinkling fairy lights after dark.

BUTCHER'S TEARS BREWERY

(www.butchers-tears.com; Karperweg 45; ☺4-9pm Wed-Sun; ☐24 Haarlemmermeerstation) In-the-know hop heads like to go straight to the source of cult brewers Butcher's Tears. The brewery's all-white clinical-feeling taproom is tucked at the end of an out-of-the-way industrial alley and offers a rotating line-up of beers on tap, drawing inspiration from historical brewing techniques. You can pull up a chair in the front car park on sunny days.

CRAFT & DRAFT CRAFT BEER

Map p312 (www.craftanddraft.nl; Overtoom 417; ☺4pm-midnight Mon-Thu, 4pm-2am Fri, 2pm-2am Sat, noon-midnight Sun; ☐1/11 Rhijnvis Feithstraat) Craft beer fans are spoilt for choice, with no fewer than 40 beers from around the world on rotating taps and hundreds more by the bottle. Try one of the four house beers from the Netherlands including the Dutch Eagle West Coast IPA, a smooth Belgian tripel, or an experimental seasonal such as a kiwi and cucumber cider.

You can have a drink in the bar, or take a tap beer parkwards in a 1L growler. The beer shop opens when the bar opens and closes at 10pm for takeaways.

CAFÉ BÉDIER BROWN CAFE

Map p312 (☏020-662 44 15; Sophialaan 36; ☺noon-1am Mon-Thu, to 3am Fri, 11am-3am Sat, to 1am Sun; ☐2 Amstelveenseweg) Café Bédier is a post-work favourite with a terrace out the front that is often so crowded on a summer

VONDELPARK & THE SOUTH DRINKING & NIGHTLIFE

VONDELPARK SQUATS

The Vondelpark and its surrounds have strong links to the cultural revolution, when Amsterdam became the *magisch centrum* (magic centre) of Europe. Hippies flocked to Amsterdam during the 1960s and '70s, a housing shortage saw speculators leaving buildings empty and squatting became widespread. The Dutch authorities turned the park into a temporary open-air dormitory. Although the sleeping bags are long gone today, an indie spirit persists.

Buried beneath the park's 1e Constantijn Huygensstraat bridge (you could take the tram straight over it or walk right past it and never know it was there) is the **Vondelbunker** (Map p312; www.vondelbunker.nl; Vondelpark 8a; ⊙hours vary; ▤1 1e Constantijn Huygensstraat). A fallout shelter dating from 1947, it became Amsterdam's first youth centre in 1968 and a hotbed of countercultural creativity and activism. If the unmarked black metal doors are open, you might catch an underground gig, film or 'activist salon'.

Fringing the Vondelpark are several squats that have gone legit and been turned into alternative cultural centres. In the former Netherlands Film Academy, graffiti-covered ex-squat **OT301** (Map p312; www.ot301.nl; Overtoom 301; ▤1 Jan Pieter Heijestraat) hosts an eclectic line-up of bands and DJs. There are bars as well as the friendly vegan restaurant **De Peper** (Map p312; ☏020-412 29 54; www.depeper.org; mains €7-10; ⊙dinner 7-8.30pm Tue, Thu & Fri, bar 6pm-1am Tue & Thu, to 3am Fri; ✍), serving cheap, organic meals in a loveable dive-bar atmosphere. Sit at the communal table to connect with like-minded folk. Same-day reservations are required; call between 4pm and 7pm.

Another former squat, **OCCII** (Map p312; ☏020-671 77 78; www.occii.org; Amstelveenseweg 134; ⊙hours vary; ▤2 Amstelveenseweg) maintains a thriving alternative scene, and books underground bands, many from Amsterdam. It has a collectively run, no-frills restaurant **Eetcafé MKZ** (Map p312; ☏020-679 07 12; www.veganamsterdam.org/mkz; 1e Schinkelstraat 16; mains from €5; ⊙from 7pm Tue & Thu-Sat; ✍; ▤2 Amstelveenseweg) serving vegan food. Call between 2.30pm and 6pm to reserve your spot.

evening that it looks like a street party in full swing. Inside it also gets rammed; the leather-upholstered wall panels and hardwood floors put a 21st-century twist on classic brown cafe decor. Top-notch bar food, too.

CAFÉ SCHINKELHAVEN
BROWN CAFE

Map p312 (www.cafeschinkelhaven.nl; Amstelveenseweg 126; ⊙11am-1am Sun-Thu, to 3am Fri & Sat; 🛜; ▤2 Amstelveenseweg) Close to the Vondelpark, Café Schinkelhaven's hugely popular candle-topped terrace tables make an irresistible pit stop before heading along Amstelveenseweg in search of dinner. Friendly staff make you feel like a regular from the moment you arrive.

GOLDEN BROWN BAR
BAR

Map p312 (www.goldenbrownbar.nl; Jan Pieter Heijestraat 146; ⊙11am-1am Sun-Thu, to 3am Fri & Sat; 🛜; ▤1 Jan Pieter Heijestraat) This perennially hip, two-level bar attracts a young professional crowd that spills out onto the pavement. It does great cocktails and doubles as a Thai restaurant.

WELLING
BROWN CAFE

Map p312 (☏020-662 01 55; www.cafewelling.nl; Jan Willem Brouwersstraat 32; ⊙4pm-1am Mon-Thu, to 2am Fri, 3pm-2am Sat, to 1am Sun; ▤2/3/5/12 Museumplein) Tucked away behind the Concertgebouw (Concert Hall), this wood-panelled well-worn lovely is a relaxed spot to sip a frothy, cold *biertje* (glass of beer) and mingle with intellectuals and artists. There's often live music, such as by jazz musicians after their gigs at the Concertgebouw; check the website for upcoming events. Note: cash only.

PROEFLOKAAL 'T BLAUWE THEEHUIS
BAR

Map p312 (www.brouwerijhetij.nl; Vondelpark 5; ⊙9am-midnight; 🛜; ▤2 Jacob Obreachstraat) No, it's not a blue and white UFO cake stand landed in the park, this is the Vondelpark outpost of local brewery heroes

Brouwerij 't IJ (p99). Opened in late 2019, it is the perfect place to while away a sunny afternoon with excellent craft beer on the large circular terrace.

HET GROOT MELKHUIS   CAFE

Map p312 (☎020-612 96 74; www.grootmelk huis.nl; Vondelpark 2; ⏱10am-5pm; 🕾🚼; 🚋1 Jan Pieter Heijestraat) This rambling Swiss-chalet-style timber house has a gingerbread look about it, at the edge of the Vondelpark forest. It's actually a regular cafe with coffees, beers, wine and light snacks, as well as the go-to hangout for families with kids. It encompasses a playground with sandpits, diggers and so on, but there's deck seating by a swan-gliding pond as well.

WILDSCHUT   GRAND CAFE

Map p312 (www.cafewildschut.nl; Roelof Hartplein 1; ⏱9am-midnight Mon, to 1am Tue-Fri, 10am-1am Sat, to midnight Sun; 🚋3/5/12/24 Roelof Hartplein) A fabulously old-school vintage bar, this *grand café* is a real gathering place for the Old South neighbourhood. When the weather's warm, everyone heads to the terrace for views of the Amsterdam School. When the weather's not great, soak up the atmosphere in the art deco interior with its marbled walls and stained glass.

STICKY FINGERS   COFFEE

Map p312 (☎020-820 33 33; www.stickyfingers. nl; Amstelveenseweg 3; ⏱7.30am-5pm Mon-Fri, to 6pm Sat & Sun; 🚋Rhijnvis Feithstraat) With its photogenic powder-pink tiled wall, this light, bright cafe adjoining the Tire Station hotel (p226) has a tempting cabinet of rich tarts and homemade cakes, some vegan and gluten-free, plus a quality cup of coffee. Its large windows let in plenty of natural light and are perfectly positioned for watching the world pass by.

COLD PRESSED JUICERY   JUICE BAR

Map p312 (www.thecoldpressedjuicery.com; Willemsparkweg 8; ⏱7.30am-7pm Mon-Fri, 9am-6pm Sat, 10am-6pm Sun; 🚋2 Cornelis Schuytstraat) 🌿 You'll be bursting with health after a cold-pressed, all-natural juice, such as the Pro (apple, fennel, lemon and probiotic) or a shot of turmeric, orange and black pepper. Smoothies are made with fresh coconut and homemade hemp or nut milks, or try a charcoal and black sesame or golden turmeric latte. All ingredients are 100% certified organic.

GOLLEM'S PROEFLOKAAL   BROWN CAFE

Map p312 (☎020-612 94 44; www.cafegollem.nl; Overtoom 160-161; ⏱1pm-1am Mon-Thu, noon-3am Fri & Sat, to 1am Sun; 🚋1 1e Constantijn Huygensstraat) Hugely popular with locals and tourists for its long list of Belgian beers, this longstanding favourite (literally, 'Gollem Tasting') is where you can settle down to sip a Kriek (cherry beer) or a Trappist ale amid vintage beer signs and paintings of tippling monks. Soak it up with dishes such as Trappist cheese fondue, croquettes and Flemish stew.

TUNES BAR   COCKTAIL BAR

Map p312 (☎020-570 00 00; www.conservatori umhotel.com; Conservatorium Hotel, Van Baerlestraat 27; ⏱4pm-1am Mon-Thu, 12.30pm-2am Fri & Sat, to midnight Sun; 🚋2/3/5/12/16 Van Baerlestraat) A small but exceedingly sleek bar inside the stunning Conservatorium Hotel, Tunes has a long transparent bar and wow-factor flower displays. Admire them while you sample one of its speciality G&Ts, such as a Gin Mare, with orange, basil and fevertree tonic, or Monkey 47, with elderflower and blackberries. There's also a fine cocktail list, with all drinks around the €20 mark.

☆ ENTERTAINMENT

For alternative entertainment, including great DJs and live music, check out Vondelpark's squats.

★CONCERTGEBOUW   CLASSICAL MUSIC

Map p312 (Concert Hall; ☎020-671 83 45; www.concertgebouw.nl; Concertgebouwplein 10; ⏱box office 1-7pm Mon-Fri, 10am-7pm Sat & Sun; 🚋3/5/12 Museumplein) The Concert Hall was built in 1888 by AL van Gendt, who managed to engineer its near-perfect acoustics. Bernard Haitink, former conductor of the Royal Concertgebouw Orchestra, once remarked that the world-famous hall was the orchestra's best instrument. Free half-hour concerts take place every Wednesday at 12.30pm from September to June; arrive early. Try the Last Minute Ticket Shop (www.last minuteticketshop.nl) for half-price seats to selected performances.

Those aged 29 or younger (ID required) can queue at the box office for €16 'Sprint' tickets one hour prior to shows. Guided tours in English (€11, 75 minutes) show that, in spite of Van Gendt's limited musical knowledge, he gave the two-tiered Grote Zaal (Main Hall) acoustics that are the envy of sound designers worldwide, along with a baroque trim, panels inscribed with the names of classical composers, a massive pipe organ and a grand staircase via which conductors and soloists descend to the stage.

OPENLUCHTTHEATER   THEATRE

Map p312 (Open-Air Theatre; 020-428 33 60; www.openluchttheater.nl; Vondelpark 5a; ☉early May-early Sep; 1/3/11 1e Constantijn Huygensstraat) The Vondelpark's marvellous open-air theatre hosts free concerts in summer, with a laid-back, festival feel. The program includes world music, dance, theatre, stand-up comedy and more.

ORGELPARK   CONCERT VENUE

Map p312 (020-515 81 11; www.orgelpark.nl; Gerard Brandtstraat 26; tickets €12.50-20; 1/11 Jan Pieter Heijestraat) A unique performance space for organ music, with four big organs in a lovely restored church on the edge of the Vondelpark. Around 80 events take place each year, including concerts of classical, jazz and improvised music.

AMSTERDAMSE BOS THEATRE   THEATRE

(www.bostheater.nl; De Duizendmeterweg 7; ☉Jun-early Sep) This large, open-air amphitheatre stages plays from Shakespeare to *The Gruffalo* in Dutch, as well as regular gigs. It's close to Schipol airport, and so actors pause for planes passing overhead.

🛍 SHOPPING

The Old South, south of Vondelpark, is one of Amsterdam's most exclusive areas, with shops to match. Stylish shops line Cornelis Schuytstraat and Willemsparkweg; check www.cornelisschuytstraat.com for new openings. Nearby, ultraluxe shopping avenue PC Hooftstraat teems with designer brands. There are several unique boutiques at the De Hallen complex.

★ PIED À TERRE   BOOKS

Map p312 (020-627 44 55; www.piedaterre. nl; Overtoom 135-137; ☉1-6pm Mon, 10am-6pm Tue, Wed & Sat, to 7pm Thu & Fri; 1/3/11 1e Constantijn Huygensstraat) Travel lovers will be in heaven in the galleried, skylit interior of Europe's largest travel bookshop. If it's

travel- or outdoor-related, you can dream over it here: gorgeous globes, travel guides in multiple languages and over 600,000 maps. Order a coffee, pull up a chair and plan your next trip.

J&B CRAFT DRINKS   DRINKS

Map p312 (020-244 01 77; www.facebook.com/ jbcraftdrinks; Jan Pieter Heijestraat 148; ☉2-8pm Tue-Thu & Sun, noon-10pm Fri, to 9pm Sat; 1/11 Jan Pieter Heijestraat) J&B Craft Drinks offers a huge range of craft beers, ciders and tasty soda from all over the globe, which are available cold from the fridge, making them perfect to take to the nearby Vondelpark on a hot day.

THINGS I LIKE
THINGS I LOVE   FASHION & ACCESSORIES

Map p312 (020-779 34 23; www.thingsi likethingsilove.com; Eerste Constantijn Huygensstraat 25-27; ☉1-6pm Mon & Sun, 11am-6pm Tue, Wed, Fri & Sat, to 8pm Thu; 1 1e Constantijn Huygensstraat) Browse for hip threads, unique homewares and must-have accessories at this stylish store with a few branches around town.

ARTI CHOC   CHOCOLATE

Map p312 (www.artichoc.nl; Koninginneweg 141; ☉9.30am-6pm Tue-Fri, to 5pm Sat; 2 Valeriusplein) Chocolate is almost too beautiful to eat at this luxury choc stop, with homemade pralines and truffles ready to melt in the mouth. There are over 50 kinds, including gluten-free, cocoa-free and lactose-free varieties with inventive flavours. If you'd like something really unique, it also designs and makes custom chocolates, including clogs, tulips and Delft-blue tiles.

GOOCHEM SPEELGOED   TOYS

Map p312 (020-612 47 04; www.goochem.nl; 1e Constantijn Huygensstraat 80; ☉1-6pm Mon, 9.30am-6pm Tue-Sat; 1 1e Constantijn Huygensstraat) This large toy shop spread over two floors has been putting grins on small faces for over three decades. Overlooked by a huge stuffed giraffe, there's a fine range of board games, musical instruments, cute wooden pull-along toys, dolls, costumes, tea sets, books, puzzles and super-soft cuddly toys.

JOHNNY
AT THE SPOT   FASHION & ACCESSORIES

Map p312 (www.johnnyatthespot.com; Jan Pieter Heijestraat 94; ☉1-6pm Mon, 11am-6pm Tue, Wed & Sat, to 7pm Thu & Fri, 1-5pm Sun; 7/17 Jan

A film screening at Vondelpark's Openluchttheater

Pieter Heijestraat) Cool concept store Johnny at the Spot fills several interconnected buildings with uber-hip men's and women's clothing, shoes and raincoats from Amsterdam designers and all over the globe. Homewares include everything from plants and soaps to ceramics and furniture.

VAN AVEZAATH BEUNE   FOOD & DRINKS
Map p312 (www.vanavezaath-beune.nl; Johannes Verhulststraat 98; ⊙8am-6pm Mon-Fri, to 5pm Sat; ◉2 Cornelis Schuytstraat) Try not to drool over the cabinet of chocolates and delectable pastries here as you agonise over your selection. Otherwise opt for a box of chocolate *amsterdammertjes* (the bollards along city pavements) – a great gift, assuming you can keep from eating them yourself.

BEVER
WOMEN'S STORE   SPORTS & OUTDOORS
Map p312 (www.bever.nl; Overtoom 51-53; ⊙11am-7pm Mon, 10am-7pm Tue, Wed, Fri & Sat, to 9pm Thu, noon-6pm Sun; ◉1/2/5 Leidseplein) This branch of one of the Netherlands' leading outdoors stores stocks a good range of women's clothing and accessories. It's just around the corner from the main store (p174).

SCHWUNG
AMSTERDAM   FASHION & ACCESSORIES
Map p312 (☑020-334 30 35; www.schwungamsterdam.nl; Jan Pieter Heijestraat 166; ⊙1-6pm Mon, 11am-6pm Tue & Sat, 11am-7pm Wed-Fri, 1-5pm Sun; ◉1 Jan Pieter Heijestraat) Sells women's clothing and menswear from labels such as American Vintage, Kings of Indigo and Notes du Nord.

DENIM CITY STORE   CLOTHING
Map p312 (☑020-820 86 14; www.denimcity.org; De Hallen, Hannie Dankbaar Passage 22; ⊙11am-6pm Mon-Fri, 10am-6pm Sat, noon-5pm Sun; ◉7/17 Ten Katestraat) A huge store devoted to the blue stuff, with jeans by Levi, Nudie, Lee, Pepe, Kings of Indigo and many more. It also recycles denim into original pieces.

GATHERSHOP   DESIGN
Map p312 (www.gathershop.nl; Hannie Dankbaar Passage 19; ⊙noon-6pm Tue-Sun; ◉17 Ten Katestraat) The beautifully curated Gathershop is a gift buyer's dream, stocking handmade and fair-trade items from clothing to homewares. Between the carefully arranged plants and cacti, which are also for sale, you'll discover delicate jewellery, simple glazed ceramic cups, minimalist stationery and natural skincare products.

NIKKIE   FASHION & ACCESSORIES
Map p312 (☑020-358 51 85; www.nikkie.com; Willemsparkweg 175; ⊙noon-5.30pm Mon & Sun, 10am-6pm Tue-Fri, to 5.30pm Sat; ◉2 Cornelis Schuytstraat) Amsterdam-based Nikkie Plessen was a familiar face on Dutch TV as an actress and presenter, but she's

now swapped the screen for women's fashion design, establishing two boutiques in town and several others in the Netherlands. Street-smart collections run from red-white-and-black 'activewear' and silk blouses to hole-punch dresses.

VLVT
FASHION & ACCESSORIES

Map p312 (www.vlvt.nl; Cornelis Schuytstraat 22; ⊙10am-6pm Tue-Sat, noon-6pm Sun & Mon; ☐2 Cornelis Schuytstraat) Up-and-coming Dutch-designed fashion for women is stocked at this chic, light-filled boutique, featuring carefully curated Dutch and international designers, including labels such as Elisabetta Franchi, Notes du Nord, Pierre Balmain and Zoe Karssen.

BEVER
SPORTS & OUTDOORS

Map p312 (www.bever.nl; Stadhouderskade 4; ⊙11am-7pm Mon, 10am-7pm Tue, Wed, Fri & Sat, to 9pm Thu, noon-6pm Sun; ☐1/2/5 Leidseplein) One of the Netherlands' leading outdoor-equipment retailers, Bever is a great place to dream of adventures, browsing tents, backpacks, sleeping bags et al. This store also has a large range of men's clothing and accessories. The women's store can be found around the corner on Overtoom.

BUISE
FASHION & ACCESSORIES

Map p312 (www.buise.nl; Cornelis Schuytstraat 12; ⊙1-6pm Mon, 10am-6pm Tue-Fri, to 5.30pm Sat; ☐2 Cornelis Schuytstraat) A chic boutique selling cool fashion-pack favourites, such as pieces by Isabel Marant and other labels, including Paul & Joe and Ganni.

COSTER DIAMONDS
JEWELLERY

Map p312 (☎020-305 55 55; www.costerdiamonds.com; Paulus Potterstraat 2; ⊙9am-5pm; ☐2/5/12 Rijksmuseum) Founded in 1840, Coster is Europe's oldest working diamond factory. Watch the polishers at work on a free guided tour – more interesting than the nearby Diamond Museum (p161).

DE WINKEL VAN NIJNTJE
TOYS

(www.dewinkelvannijntje.nl; Scheldestraat 61; ⊙1-6pm Mon, 10am-6pm Tue-Fri, to 5pm Sat, noon-5pm Sun; ☐; ☐12 Scheldestraat) A Miffy (Nijntje in Dutch) emporium, devoted entirely to the much-adored character of Dutch illustrator Dick Bruna. The mouthless one is celebrated in all sorts of enticing merchandise, from crocheted dolls to Royal Delftware plates.

SPORTS & ACTIVITIES

ZUIDERBAD
SWIMMING

Map p312 (☎020-252 13 90; Hobbemastraat 26; €4.60; ⊙hours vary; ☐; ☐2/5 Hobbemastraat) Once the Velox cycling school, this was converted into a beguilingly splendid public pool. It's a grand 1912 edifice behind the Rijksmuseum, restored to its original glory, full of tiles, character and appreciative paddlers. The schedule for swimming *(recreatiezwemmen in diep water)* varies daily; check it online at www.amsterdam.nl/zuiderbad/openingstijden.

KANOVERHUUR
AMSTERDAMSE BOS
KAYAKING

(☎020-645 78 31; www.kanoverhuur-adam.nl; Grote Speelweide 5; 1-/2-person kayak per hr €7/12, 2-/4-person pedal boat per hr €12/20) Rents out kayaks and pedal boats in Amsterdamse Bos.

FRIDAY NIGHT SKATE
SKATING

Map p312 (www.fridaynightskate.com; Vondelpark; ⊙8.30pm Fri; ☐2/5 Hobbemastraat) Every Friday night (except in rain and snow), the Vondelpark is the start of a 20km, two-hour-long mass rollerblade skate through Amsterdam. It's open to anyone with reasonable skating proficiency (ie knowing how to brake!). Arrive at the meeting point, adjacent to the Vondelpark3 (p169) restaurant by 8pm (8.15pm in winter). Check the website for details of skate (and safety gear) rental outlets.

FUN FOREST
ADVENTURE SPORTS

(www.funforest.nl; Bosbaanweg 3; adult/child €25/20; ⊙10am-6pm early Jul-early Sep, hours vary Sep-Jun; ☐347, 357) Next to the entrance to Amsterdamse Bos is Fun Forest, a tree-top climbing park for children or adults that uses ropes, ladders and bridges. Admission provides three hours of activities. Check the website for opening hours as they vary.

De Pijp

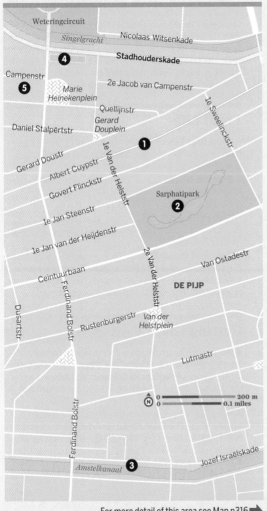

Neighbourhood Top Five

❶ Albert Cuypmarkt (p178) Feasting your senses on the fresh produce, cheeses, fish, colourful plants and cut flowers, inexpensive clothing, accessories, homewares, bike parts and quirky Dutch souvenirs at this six-day-a-week street market.

❷ Sarphatipark (p177) Strolling through an urban oasis of lawns, statues, ponds and fountains in De Pijp's picturesque central park.

❸ Boaty (p186) Setting sail in an electric boat to cruise Amsterdam's canals at your own pace.

❹ Heineken Experience (p177) Touring the boisterously fun brewery before boarding its canal boat for a cruise across town to A'DAM Tower.

❺ Bakers & Roasters (p184) Delving into De Pijp's thriving brunch scene at specialists such as this neighbourhood favourite.

Lonely Planet's Top Tip

Many successful Amsterdam businesses put down their first roots in De Pijp, and this innovative neighbourhood has a constant turnover of pop-ups, start-ups and new openings. Backstreets to watch include Frans Halsstraat, 1e Van der Helststraat, 2e Van der Helststraat, Cornelis Troostplein and Ruysdaelkade.

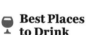

Best Places to Eat

➡ Ciel Bleu (p185)
➡ Bakers & Roasters (p184)
➡ Graham's Kitchen (p185)
➡ Avocado Show (p184)
➡ Restaurant Sinne (p185)

For reviews, see p178.➡

Best Places to Drink

➡ Brouwerij Troost (p186)
➡ Twenty Third Bar (p186)
➡ Glouglou (p187)
➡ Café Sarphaat (p187)

For reviews, see p185.➡

Best Places to Shop

➡ Albert Cuypmarkt (p178)
➡ Hutspot (p187)
➡ Cottoncake (p187)
➡ Tiller Galerie (p188)
➡ Record Mania (p188)

For reviews, see p187.➡

Explore De Pijp

De Pijp's village character is partly due to the fact that it's an island, connected to the rest of the city by 16 bridges. Its name, 'the Pipe', is thought to reflect its straight, narrow streets that resemble the stems of old clay pipes.

The district's feel is more attributable to its history. The area's 1860s tenement blocks provided cheap housing for newly arrived industrial-revolution workers. In the 1960s and '70s many working-class residents left for greener pastures and the government refurbished the tenement blocks for immigrants. Inhabited today by all walks of life, with gentrification continuing apace, this arty, foodie neighbourhood retains a strong community-oriented spirit.

Start your day trawling the Albert Cuypmarkt (p178) before strolling through peaceful Sarphatipark. Explore the streets' boutiques and speciality shops – and choose your dinner destination from the overwhelming options – before heading to the Heineken Experience. If you time it for the late afternoon, the tasting at the end provides a built-in happy hour (though of course in fun-loving De Pijp it almost always feels like happy hour).

Local Life

➡ **Local beer** Heineken might not brew in De Pijp any more, but the 'hood has a fantastic craft brewery that does, Brouwerij Troost (p186).

➡ **Seafood snacks** Locals love to hit up De Pijp's herring stands (p181) on and around the Albert Cuypmarkt (p178); Volendammer Vishandel (p179) is a favourite.

➡ **Hidden hangout** Tucked-away square Van der Helstplein is lined with low-key local *cafés* (pubs) such as Café Ruis (p186).

➡ **Red Light District** On De Pijp's western border, along Ruysdaelkade, opposite Hobbemakade, there's a little red-light district (minus the stag parties and drunken crowds that frequent its city-centre counterpart).

Getting There & Away

➡ **Metro** The Noord/Zuidlijn (north–south metro line; M52) serves De Pijp station. There are entrances at the corner of Ferdinand Bolstraat and Albert Cuypstraat, and at the corner of Ferdinand Bolstraat and Ceintuurbaan.

➡ **Tram** Tram 24 rolls north–south from Centraal Station along Ferdinand Bolstraat right by De Pijp's main sights. Tram 4 travels from Centraal Station via Rembrandtplein to De Pijp, while tram 3 traverses De Pijp between the Vondelpark and Oost. Tram 12 cuts through De Pijp en route from Leidseplein to the south.

SIGHTS

Apart from the Albert Cuypmarkt (p178) and the Heineken Experience, sights in De Pijp are few. What's really enjoyable here is wandering through the neighbourhood and soaking up the bohemian atmosphere in the bars, restaurants and boutiques.

SARPHATIPARK   PARK
Map p316 (🚋3 2e Van der Helststraat) While Vondelpark is bigger in size and reputation, this tranquil English-style park delivers an equally potent shot of pastoral summertime relaxation, with far fewer crowds. Named after Samuel Sarphati (1813–66), a Jewish doctor, businessman and urban innovator, the grounds incorporate ponds, gently rolling meadows and wooded fringes. In the centre is the 1886-built Sarphati Memorial, a bombastic temple with a fountain, gargoyles and a bust of the great man himself.

HUIS MET DE KABOUTERS   ARCHITECTURE
Map p316 (House with the Goblins; Ceintuurbaan 251; 🚋3 Van Woustraat) Look up as you pass Ceintuurbaan 251: on the elaborately carved wooden gables of the 1884 neo-Gothic mansion here you'll see two cheeky lime-green goblin sculptures dressed in red hats and shorts; one is holding a red ball and the other is reaching to catch it. The building was designed by architect AC Boerma; it's thought the sculptures symbolise his client's surname, Van Ballegooijen, which translates in part to 'throwing a ball'. It's been a listed national monument since 1984.

SARPHATI MEMORIAL   MEMORIAL
Map p316 (Sarphatipark; 🚋3 2e Van der Helststraat) In the Sarphatipark, this 1886 temple incorporates a fountain, gargoyles and a bust of Samuel Sarphati (1813–66), after whom the park is named.

DE DAGERAAD   ARCHITECTURE
Map p316 (Dawn Housing Project; Pieter Lodewijk Takstraat; 🚋4 Amstelkade) The Housing Act of 1901 forced the city to rethink neighbourhood planning and condemn slums. De Dageraad housing estate was developed between 1918 and 1923 for poorer families. One of the most original architects of the expressionist Amsterdam School, Piet Kramer, drew up plans for this idiosyncratic complex in collaboration with Michel de Klerk.

◉ TOP SIGHT
HEINEKEN EXPERIENCE

Heineken has been going strong since 1864 and this multisensory 'Experience' is an appropriately immodest (read: commercial) celebration of its place in Dutch brewing history.

On the site of the company's old De Pijp brewery, which closed in 1988, the 'Experience' is a rollicking self-guided tour. Allow at least 90 minutes to learn the storied history of the Heineken family, find out how the logo has evolved, and follow the brewing process from water and hops through to bottling. Along the way you can watch Heineken commercials from around the world, sniff the mash in copper tanks, visit the horse stables and make your own music video. The crowning glory is Brew You – a 4D multimedia exhibit where you 'become' a beer as you get shaken up, heated up, sprayed with water and 'bottled'. True beer connoisseurs will shudder, but it's a lot of fun.

Self-guided tours conclude with two tastings; there are also 2½-hour VIP guided tours (€55) incorporating a five-beer tasting with cheese pairings, and Rock the City tickets (€32.50) that include a canal cruise across town to A'DAM Tower (p200).

DON'T MISS
➜ 'Becoming' a beer with Brew You
➜ Learning to pour a frothy Dutch pint
➜ Sampling Heineken's wares

PRACTICALITIES
➜ Map p316, C1
➜ ☎020-523 94 35
➜ https://tickets.heine kenexperience.com
➜ Stadhouderskade 78
➜ adult/child self-guided tour €21/14.50
➜ ⏰10.30am-9pm daily Jul & Aug, shorter hours rest of year
➜ Ⓜ Vijzelgracht, 🚋24 Marie Heinekenplein

EATING

De Pijp's thriving foodie scene is adventurous and international yet also quintessentially Dutch. Choices include street-food stalls, salad bars, cheap, filling Surinamese and Asian spots, on-trend addresses including the world's first all-avocado cafe (p184), gastronomic standouts and atmospheric *bruin cafés* (pubs) serving food. Brunch is especially good in this neighbourhood, with many cafes specialising in exceptional mid-morning menus. Albert Cuypstraat, Ferdinand Bolstraat and Ceintuurbaan are ideal starting points.

LE SALONARD
DELI €

Map p316 (www.lesalonard.com; 1e Van der Helststraat 21; dishes €4.50-9.50; ⊙10am-4pm Mon, to 6pm Tue-Sat; 🚊24 Marie Heinekenplein) Piled high with pastries (both savoury – such as quiches and gourmet sandwiches and sausage rolls – and sweet, including custard tarts and moelleux chocolate cakes), cheeses, charcuterie, breads and a floor-to-ceiling wall of wines, this enticing deli also makes up *borrel* (drinks) platters to snack on over vintages by the bottle or glass on the pavement terrace out front.

SIR HUMMUS
MIDDLE EASTERN €

Map p316 (www.sirhummus.nl; Van der Helstplein 2; dishes €7-13; ⊙noon-9pm Wed-Sun; 🞧; 🚊3/4 2e Van der Helststraat) This is the brainchild of three young Israelis whose passion for the chickpea dip led to a London street-market stall and then this hummus-dedicated cafe. Creamy, all-natural, preservative- and additive-free hummus is served with pillowy pita bread and salad; SH also makes fantastic falafels. You can eat in or take away, but arrive early before it sells out.

SUGO
PIZZA €

Map p316 (www.sugopizza.nl; Ferdinand Bolstraat 107; pizza slice €4-5.50; ⊙11am-9pm Sun-Thu, to 10pm Fri & Sat; 🞧; Ⓜ De Pijp, 🚊3/12/24 De Pijp) 🍃 Spectacular pizza slices at this two-storey restaurant are cooked daily, displayed beneath glass and warmed in ovens. Its 20 different topping combinations include caramelised onion, mascarpone, walnut and black olive, or potato, mushroom and truffles. Veggies are locally sourced; meats and cheeses are from small farms in Italy. Take-

---

◉ TOP SIGHT
ALBERT CUYPMARKT

Want to experience Amsterdam at its wonderfully chaotic, multicultural best? Head to this sprawling street market, which sets up daily except Sunday.

Named after landscape painter Albert Cuyp (1620–91) and going strong since 1905, the Albert Cuypmarkt is Amsterdam's largest and busiest market, and it's legendary for its huge variety. Scores of aromatic stalls sell Dutch cheeses – from a four-year-old Gouda to a creamy *boerenkaas* (farmer's cheese) – fish, crustaceans, olives, oils, herbs and spices, and bushels of fresh fruit and veggies. Need some Saturday-night bling or a new phone cover? How about a bike lock, a hair-curling iron or some flowers to brighten your hotel room? There's also a staggering array of (mostly funky, sometimes junky) men's and women's clothing and accessories, as well as ceramics, fabrics and a host of other homewares.

Don't miss the shops hidden behind the stalls, selling everything from kitchen gadgets to luggage, bolts of fabric, soaps, shampoos and much more.

Classic Dutch snacks to eat as you wander range from herring to *frites* (fries), *poffertjes* (icing-sugar-dusted mini pancakes) and piping-hot *stroopwafels* (caramel-syrup-filled waffles).

DON'T MISS

➡ Cheeses galore
➡ Only-in-the-Netherlands gifts such as fluffy clog slippers
➡ On-the-go snacks

PRACTICALITIES

➡ Map p316, D3
➡ www.albertcuypmarkt.amsterdam
➡ Albert Cuypstraat, btwn Ferdinand Bolstraat & Van Woustraat
➡ ⊙9am-5pm Mon-Sat
➡ Ⓜ De Pijp, 🚊24 Marie Heinekenplein

away packaging is made from recycled paper and energy is 100% sustainable.

There are numerous vegetarian, vegan and gluten-free options.

MASSIMO
GELATO €

Map p316 (Van Ostadestraat 147; 1/2/3/4 scoops €1.60/3.20/4.50/6; ⊙1-10pm; 🚊3/4 2e Van der Helststraat) Gelato is made daily on-site from family recipes using local, organic milk, butter and yoghurt, along with imported Italian ingredients such as lemons from the passionate fourth-generation gelato maker's native Liguria. Scrumptious flavours including cinnamon and fig; honey, yoghurt and cherry; coffee and hazelnut; and pear and walnut are scooped with a spatula into hand-rolled waffle cones or tubs. Cards only.

GEFLIPT
BURGERS €

Map p316 (www.gefliptburgers.nl; Van Woustraat 15; dishes €9-13; ⊙11.30am-9.30pm Sun-Thu, to 10.30pm Fri & Sat; 🛜; 🚊4 Stadhouderskade) Competition is fierce for the best burgers in this food-driven neighbourhood, but Geflipt is a serious contender. In a stripped-back, industrial-chic interior, it serves luscious combinations (such as Gasconne beef, bacon, golden cheddar, red-onion compote and fried egg) on brioche buns with sauces cooked daily on the premises from locally sourced ingredients.

BUTCHER
BURGERS €

Map p316 (📞020-470 78 75; www.the-butcher.com; Albert Cuypstraat 129; burgers €7-13.50; ⊙11am-midnight; Ⓜ De Pijp, 🚊24 Marie Heinekenplein) Burgers at this sizzling spot are cooked right in front of you (behind a glass screen, so you won't get splattered). Mouthwatering choices include Silence of the Lamb (with spices and tahini), the Codfather (beer-battered blue cod and homemade tartar sauce), an Angus-beef truffle burger and a veggie version. Ask about its 'secret kitchen' cocktail bar.

TACO CARTEL
MEXICAN €

Map p316 (📞020-737 21 11; www.taco-cartel.com; Van Woustraat 29; dishes €10-12.50; ⊙noon-9.30pm Mon-Wed, 11am-9pm Thu-Sun; 🛜🍷; 🚊4 Stadhouderskade) Fronted by a sky-blue facade, this cheap, cheerful restaurant serves nine varieties of its namesake tacos and another nine different burritos with fillings such as roast sweet potato, tomatillo (Mexican husk tomato), grilled corn, mango, black beans, pico de gallo (tomato,

onion and cilantro salsa), pickled carrots and radishes, smoky ancho chillies, spicy ground beef and pulled pork.

BAKKEN MET PASSIE
BAKERY €

Map p316 (www.bakkenmetpassie.nl; Albert Cuypstraat 53; dishes €2-9; ⊙7.30am-6pm Tue-Sat; Ⓜ De Pijp, 🚊3/12/24 De Pijp) Spicy carrot cake, flourless chocolate-and-raspberry cake, a zesty lemon cake, classic Dutch apple pie and cookies such as oatmeal, cranberry and coconut are among the sweet treats at 'Baking with Passion'; there are also quiches, filled croissants and sandwiches on its own artisan breads. It's a handy early opener for breakfast, which is served until noon.

SEA SALT & CHOCOLATE
CAFE €

Map p316 (www.seasaltandchocolate.nl; Sint Willibrordusstraat 58; dishes €2.75-5; ⊙11am-11pm Mon-Fri, noon-11pm Sat & Sun; 🛜; 🚊3/4 Van Woustraat) Tucked away in a quiet side street, this little cafe serves cakes (including spicy *speculaas* (spiced biscuit) cheesecake and signature sea-salt chocolate cupcakes with caramel icing) and cookies (walnut, oatmeal and raisin, or lemon shortbread), baked on the premises each day. Pick up treats to take away; there's also a bench with stool seating. Cards only, no cash.

VOLENDAMMER VISHANDEL
SEAFOOD €

Map p316 (1e Van der Helststraat; dishes €2-6; ⊙8am-5pm Mon-Sat; Ⓜ De Pijp, 🚊24 24 Marie Heinekenplein) Dutch flags fly from this traditional *haringhuis* ('herring house', ie takeaway fish shop), which has its own fishing fleet at the seaside resort of Volendam, 20km northeast. Along with herring served chopped with diced onion on a fluffy bread roll, classic deep-fried snacks include *kibbeling* (fried whitefish pieces), *lekkerbekje* (whole fried whitefish) and *gerookte paling* (smoked eel).

VENKEL
CAFE €

Map p316 (www.venkelsalades.nl; Albert Cuypstraat 22; mains €8-12; ⊙11am-9pm; 🛜🍷; Ⓜ De Pijp, 🚊3/12/24 De Pijp) 🍷 Timber tables at this light-filled salad bar are made from a fallen Vondelpark tree, as are planks on which dishes such as homemade hummus, housebaked breads and vegetable chips are served. Salads come in bamboo bowls. Ingredients – red quinoa, hazelnuts, aubergine, goat's cheese, beetroot, lentils, spinach, micro herbs, edible flowers, fruits and berries – are organic; virtually everything is vegetarian.

STROOM
CAFE €

Map p316 (www.stroomindepijp.nl; Ferdinand Bolstraat 151; dishes €6-14.50; ⏰8.30am-6pm; ☎📶; 🚊4/12 Cornelis Troostplein) A charming timber-framed corner building with large windows houses this split-level cafe with mezzanine seating, which opens onto one of De Pijp's sunniest terraces. Breakfast options include organic yoghurt with muesli, or a Dutch breakfast with ham, cheese and eggs; lunch dishes range from elaborate open-faced sandwiches, toasties and salads to burgers (including veggie varieties).

FRITES UIT ZUYD
FAST FOOD €

Map p316 (www.cafeparhasard.nl; Ceintuurbaan 113-115; frites small/medium/large €2.50/3/3.50, sauce €0.50-1.50; ⏰2-11pm Mon-Thu, 1-11pm Fri-Sun; ☎; 🚇De Pijp, 🚊3/12/24 De Pijp) De Pijp's best *frites* by far are at takeaway shop Frites uit Zuyd, with black-and-white chequerboard tiling on the walls and floors, and at its sleek sit-down restaurant **Friterie par Hasard** (Map p316; mains €10.50-23.50; ⏰noon-10pm Mon-Thu, to 11pm Fri-Sun; ☎) next door. Crispy, fluffy *frites* are accompanied by traditional pickles, mustard, or sauces such as satay, mayo or chilli-spiced sambal. Wooden benches line the pavement out front.

OMELEGG
CAFE €

Map p316 (www.omelegg.com; Ferdinand Bolstraat 143; dishes €6-12; ⏰7am-4pm Mon-Fri, 8am-4pm Sat & Sun; ☎; 🚊4/12 Cornelis Troostplein) In sparing surrounds with polished-concrete floors, wooden furniture and a mural of traditional Dutch windmills on the back wall, this omelette specialist serves a weekly changing option, plus menu regulars such as Mariachi (spicy jalapeños, mushrooms and sun-dried tomatoes), Viking Fisherman (smoked salmon, dill, crème fraîche and lemon zest) and Chilli Hernandez (homemade chilli con carne and cheese). No reservations.

SLA
CAFE €

Map p316 (www.ilovesla.com; Ceintuurbaan 149; dishes €8-12; ⏰11am-9pm; 📶; 🚊3/4 2e Van der Helststraat) Amsterdam's fashionistas flock to this super-stylish salad bar for its soups, its juices and especially its extensive array of fresh, healthy salads you design yourself. All of the meat, poultry and dairy products, 90% of the vegetables, and the wines are organic. Cards only.

SPANG MAKANDRA
SURINAMESE €

Map p316 (☎020-670 50 81; www.spangmakandra.nl; Gerard Doustraat 39; mains €6-12; ⏰11am-10pm Mon-Sat, 1-10pm Sun; 🚇De Pijp, 🚊24 Marie Heinekenplein) There are just 26 seats at this cosy restaurant, and it's a red-hot favourite with students and Surinamese and Indonesian expats; you'll need to book for dinner. The reward is a fabulous array of dishes including fish soups and satay with spicy sauces at astonishingly cheap prices. All the food is halal; no alcohol is served.

STACH
DELI €

Map p316 (☎020-754 26 72; www.stach-food.nl; Van Woustraat 154; dishes €4-10.50; ⏰8am-10pm Mon-Sat, 9am-10pm Sun; 🚊3/4 Van Woustraat) An Aladdin's cave of fresh produce, jams, preserves, teas, coffees, juices and chocolates, this food emporium also makes some of the best (and best-value) sandwiches around, loaded with gourmet ingredients. If it's not picnic weather, there's a mezzanine dining area inside.

TAART VAN M'N TANTE
BAKERY €

Map p316 (☎020-776 46 00; www.detaart.com; Ferdinand Bolstraat 10; dishes €5-9.50; ⏰10am-6pm Wed-Sun; 🚊24 Marie Heinekenplein) One of Amsterdam's best-loved cake shops operates from this ultra-kitsch parlour, turning out apple pies (Dutch, French or 'tipsy'), pecan pie and wish-you-could-bake-like-this cakes. Hot-pink walls accent cakes dressed like Barbie dolls – or are they Barbies dressed as cakes?

WARUNG MINI CEINTUURBAAN
SURINAMESE €

Map p316 (☎020-334 28 50; www.warungminiamsterdam.com; Ceintuurbaan 205; mains €6.50-10; ⏰11am-10pm Mon-Sat, 1-10pm Sun; 🚊3/4 Van Woustraat) This unassuming little restaurant has forged a loyal client base thanks to its affordable Surinamese specialities, including *saoto* soup. This steaming broth comes loaded with shredded chicken, bean sprouts and a boiled egg, and is accompanied by a side of rice. Other staples include generous portions of roti and spicy deep-fried *bara* (lentil dumplings).

DÈSA
INDONESIAN €€

Map p316 (☎020-671 09 79; www.restaurantdesa.com; Ceintuurbaan 103; mains €13-22, rijsttafel €18.50-35; ⏰5-10pm; 📶; 🚇De Pijp, 🚊3/12/24 De Pijp) Named for the Indonesian word for 'village' (apt for this city, but especially this 'hood), Dèsa is wildly popular for its rijsttafel (Indonesian banquet). À la carte options include *serundeng* (spiced fried coconut), *ayam besengek* (chicken cooked in saffron and coconut milk), *sambal goreng telor* (stewed eggs in spicy Balinese sauce), and *pisang goreng* (fried banana) for dessert.

FOU FOW RAMEN
RAMEN €€

Map p316 (www.foufow.nl; Van Woustraat 3; mains €11-16; ⊘noon-3pm & 5-9pm Tue-Sun; 🚃4 Stadhouderskade) Paper lanterns sway from the ceiling of this restaurant, which opens to a covered, plant-filled courtyard out back – an idyllic spot for a bowl of chilled ramen in summer. Year round you can also get steaming-hot, aromatic ramen dishes, and various sides such as spicy tofu with chilli sauce and crispy chicken wings.

SPAGHETTERIA
ITALIAN €€

Map p316 (www.spaghetteria-pastabar.nl; Van Woustraat 123; pasta €9-16.50; ⊘5-10pm; 🚃3/4 Van Woustraat) Freshly made pastas at this hip Italian-run 'pasta bar' come in six daily options that might include beetroot ravioli with goat's cheese; basil fettuccini with clams; squid-ink spaghetti with pesto and sun-dried tomatoes; and ham tortellini in creamy truffle sauce. The huge wooden communal table (and well-priced Italian wines) adds to the electric atmosphere.

ESCOBAR
LATIN AMERICAN €€

Map p316 (☑020-845 56 40; www.escobar.nu; 1e Sweelinckstraat 10; mains €16-25, tapas €4.50-12; ⊘kitchen 4-11pm Mon-Wed, noon-11pm Thu-Sun, bar to 1am Sun-Thu, to 3am Fri & Sat; 🛜; 🚃4 Stadhouderskade) An Amsterdam School–style former municipal bathhouse (1931), today this split-level space with a wrought-iron-framed mezzanine is a vibrant spot for tapas such as *arepita* (Venezuelan corn bread) with spicy tomatoes and sour cream, or larger meals such as barbecued celeriac with smoked Manchego cream, or sea bass ceviche, accompanied by house sangria and mostly Argentinian and Spanish wines.

MANGIANCORA
PIZZA €€

Map p316 (☑020-471 43 11; www.mangian coraamsterdam.nl; Ferdinand Bolstraat 170; pizza €8.50-16.50; ⊘5-10pm Tue-Sun; 🖋; Ⓜ De Pijp, 🚃3/12/24 De Pijp) Everything at Mangiancora is imported from Italy's Naples region – not only ingredients and wines but even the sand and stone from Mount Vesuvius that the owners, twin brothers Andrea and En-

HOW TO EAT A HERRING

'Hollandse Nieuwe' isn't a fashion trend – it's the fresh catch of super-tasty herring, raked in every June. The Dutch love it, and you'll see vendors selling the salty fish all over town. Although Dutch tradition calls for dangling the herring above your mouth, this isn't the way it's done in Amsterdam. Here it is served in bite-size chunks and eaten with a toothpick, topped with *uitjes* (diced onions) and *zuur* (sweet pickles). A *broodje haring* (herring roll) is even handier, as the fluffy white roll holds on the toppings and keeps your fingers free of fish fat – think of it as an edible napkin.

rico, used to build their pizza oven. There are occasional pasta dishes such as black truffle and cream gnocchi, and Naples-style *saltimboccas* ('pizza sandwiches').

BAR FISK
SEAFOOD €€

Map p316 (☑020-235 21 17; www.barfisk.nl; 1e Sweelinckstraat 23; mains lunch €8-12, dinner €12.50-18.50; ⊘kitchen 6-10pm Mon-Wed, 5-10pm Thu & Fri, noon-10pm Sat & Sun, bar to 1am; 🛜; 🚃3/4 Van Woustraat) 🖋 Fish-scale tiles in marine blues and greens clad the bar at switched-on seafood bar Fisk. Small lunchtime sharing plates (oysters with limoncello dressing; Zeeland mussels steamed in vanilla and white wine) precede more substantial dinner mains such as barbecued whole sea bass with fennel pesto.

Superb cocktails include the New Amsterdam, made from *oude jenever* (old jenever, ie Dutch gin), Amaro Montenegro, cherry liqueur and chocolate bitters.

ARLES
PROVENCAL €€

Map p316 (☑020-679 82 40; www.arles-amster dam.nl; Govert Flinckstraat 251; mains €22, 3-/4-/5-course menus €37/45/52; ⊘6-10pm Tue-Sat; 🚃4 Stadhouderskade) Named for the town famously painted by Van Gogh, this charming spot evokes the sunny southern French region in its sage-hued dining room, cosy cellar, vine-draped courtyard and greenhouse-style conservatory. Provençal classics are given innovative twists, such as veal tartare marinated in house-distilled gin with miso and lime powder, or lamb's tongue with parsnip-and-thyme panna cotta with wasabi-and-watercress sauce.

DE PIJP EATING

WILL SALTER/LONELY PLANET ©

1. Huis met de Kabouters (p177)
A neo-Gothic mansion featuring two goblins.

2. Hotel de Goudfazant (p201)
An industrial-looking restaurant in a former garage.

3. Rembrandt and *Night Watch* statues (p120)
Be part of the famous painting on Rembrandtplein.

4. Condomerie Het Gulden Vlies (p86)
For condoms in all kinds of designs.

5. NDSM Werf (p200)
A former shipyard turned edgy arts community.

DE PIJP'S TOP FIVE BRUNCH SPOTS

Bakers & Roasters (Map p316; www.bakersandroasters.com; 1e Jacob van Campenstraat 54; dishes €9-16.50; ☺8.30am-4pm; ☏; ☒24 Marie Heinekenplein) Sumptuous brunch dishes served up at the Brazilian–Kiwi-owned Bakers & Roasters include banana-nutbread French toast with homemade banana marmalade and crispy bacon; Navajo eggs with pulled pork, avocado, mango salsa and chipotle cream; and a smoked-salmon stack with poached eggs, potato cakes and hollandaise. Wash your choice down with a fiery Bloody Mary. Fantastic pies, cakes and slices, too.

Avocado Show (Map p316; www.theavocadoshow.com; Daniël Stalpertstraat 61; mains €10-16; ☺9am-5pm; ☏⚲; Ⓜ De Pijp, ☒24 Marie Heinekenplein) A world first, this cafe uses avocado in *every* dish, often in ingeniously functional ways (burgers with avocado halves instead of buns, salad 'bowls' made from avocado slices). Finish with avocado ice cream or sorbet. Avocado cocktails include a spicy Guaco Mary and an avocado daiquiri. It doesn't take reservations, so prepare to queue. Cards only; no cash.

CT Coffee & Coconuts (Map p316; ☏020-354 11 04; www.coffeeandcoconuts.com; Ceintuurbaan 282-284; mains lunch €8-15.50, dinner €15-19; ☺8am-11pm; ☏; Ⓜ De Pijp, ☒3/12/24 De Pijp) A 1920s art deco cinema has been stunningly transformed into this open-plan, triple-level, cathedral-like space (with a giant print of John Lennon at the top). Brunch dishes – including coconut, almond and buckwheat pancakes; French-toast brioche with apricots; avocado-slathered toast with dukkah and lemon dressing; and scrambled eggs on sourdough with crumbled feta – are served to 1pm.

Scandinavian Embassy (Map p316; www.scandinavianembassy.nl; Sarphatipark 34; dishes €5-14; ☺8am-6pm Mon-Fri, 9am-6pm Sat & Sun; ☒3/4 2e Van der Helststraat) Oat-meal porridge with blueberries, honey and coconut, served with goat's-milk yoghurt; salt-cured salmon on Danish rye with sheep's-milk yoghurt; muesli with strawberries; and freshly baked pastries (including cinnamon buns) make this blond-wood-panelled spot a perfect place to start the day – as does its phenomenal coffee, sourced from Scandinavian microroasteries (including a refreshing cold brew with tonic water).

Little Collins (Map p316; ☏020-753 96 36; www.littlecollins.nl; 1e Sweelinckstraat 19; tapas €4-16, brunch €8-16; ☺9am-4pm Mon & Tue, to 10pm Wed-Sun; ☏; ☒3/4 Van Woustraat) On a side street near Albert Cuypmarkt, this hip hang-out is hopping during brunch, when dishes might include toasted brioche with grilled halloumi, homemade plum jam, crème fraîche, hazelnuts, basil and mint (plus four different Bloody Marys). The evening tapas menu is equally inspired: seared calamari with green-mango salsa, for instance, or crispy duck with cucumber and chilli.

THRILL GRILL   AMERICAN €€

Map p316 (☏020-760 67 50; www.thrillgrill.nl; Gerard Doustraat 98; mains €9-18.50; ☺noon-10pm Sun-Wed, to 11pm Thu-Sat; ☏⚲; Ⓜ De Pijp, ☒24 Marie Heinekenplein) Burgers are the big deal at Thrill Grill (including its signature double-beef Thrill Burger with Gouda and bacon), accompanied by truffle-Parmesan fries, but it also offers lighter lunchtime dishes (open sandwiches, salads), while evening alternatives span grilled chicken, hot dogs and nachos. Milkshakes include boozy options such as bourbon and chocolate. There are mini burgers and hot dogs for kids.

BRASSERIE SENT   BARBECUE €€

Map p316 (☏020-676 24 95; www.restaurantsent. nl; Saenredamstraat 39; mains €17-29; ☺kitchen 6-10.30pm, bar to 1am Sun-Thu, to 3am Fri & Sat; Ⓜ De Pijp, ☒24 Marie Heinekenplein) Smoke-infused meats at this barbecue specialist are cooked in a Big Green Egg (ceramic Japanese-*kamado*-style grill and charcoal smoker), including veal rib-eye, lamb leg, pork rib and Chateaubriand steak for two. There's also the option of sea bass with clams; for non-carnivores, choices (cooked separately) include mushroom-and-truffle ravioli. Book ahead, especially at weekends.

SURYA   INDIAN €€

Map p316 (☏020-676 79 85; www.suryarestau rant.nl; Ceintuurbaan 147; mains €15-23.50; ☺5-11pm Tue-Sun; ☒3/4 2e Van der Helststraat) Indian restaurants can be surprisingly hit and miss in this multicultural city, making classy Surya an invaluable address for fans of Subcontinental cuisine. Menu standouts include a feisty madras, a fire-breathing vindaloo, tandoori tikka dishes and silky tomato-based *paneer makhni* with soft cottage cheese made fresh on the premises each day. Mains come with pappadams, rice and salad.

VOLT
BISTRO €€

Map p316 (☑020-471 55 44; www.restaurant volt.nl; Ferdinand Bolstraat 178; mains lunch €8-15, dinner €15-22; ◷kitchen 5.30-10pm Mon-Fri, noon-3.30pm & 5.30-10pm Sat & Sun, bar to 1am Sun-Thu, to 3am Fri & Sat; ☑4/12 Cornelis Troostplein) Strung with coloured light bulbs, Volt is a neighbourhood fixture for daily changing, market-sourced dishes such as turbot-and-prawn ravioli with cauliflower cream, Thai-style steak tartare, or crab *gyoza* (Japanese dumplings). Its bar stays open until late, or head across the street to its *bruin café* sibling, **Gambrinus** (Map p316; www.gambrinus.nl; Ferdinand Bolstraat 180; ◷11am-1am Sun-Thu, to 3am Fri & Sat; ☎).

MAMOUCHE
MOROCCAN €€

Map p316 (☑020-670 07 36; www.restaurant mamouche.nl; Quellijnstraat 104; mains €15.50-23.50; ◷5-11pm Tue-Sun; ☑24 Marie Heinekenplein) Refined Mamouche's minimalist dining room, with mottled raw-plaster walls and slat-beam ceilings, complements its French-accented North African cuisine, which includes tajines (Moroccan stews), couscous (with spicy sea bass and saffron butter, for example), and other mainstays including duck confit with sweet-potato mash and cinnamon.

★ GRAHAM'S KITCHEN
GASTRONOMY €€€

Map p316 (☑020-364 25 60; www.grahams kitchen.amsterdam; Hemonystraat 38; 3-/4-/5-/6-course menus €39/49/59/68; ◷6-10pm Tue-Sat; ☑4 Stadhouderskade) A veteran of Michelin-starred kitchens, chef Graham Mee now crafts intricate dishes at his own premises. Multicourse menus (no à la carte) might include a venison and crispy smoked-beetroot macaron, cucumber and gin-cured salmon, veal with wasabi and ghost crab, and deconstructed summer-berry crumble with wood-calamint ice cream. Mee personally explains each dish to diners.

Most produce is organic and sourced from the Amsterdam area. The intimate space is small, so reserve well ahead. Tables are set up on the pavement in summer.

★ CIEL BLEU
GASTRONOMY €€€

Map p316 (☑020-678 74 50; www.cielbleu.nl; Hotel Okura Amsterdam, Ferdinand Bolstraat 333; tasting menus from €195; ◷6.30-10pm Mon-Sat; ☑4/12 Cornelius Troostplein) Mind-blowing two-Michelin-star creations at this pinnacle of gastronomy change with the seasons; spring might see scallops and oysters with vanilla sea salt and gin-and-tonic foam, king crab with salted lemon, beurre blanc ice cream and caviar, or salt-crusted pigeon with pomegranate jelly and pistachio dust. Also incomparable is the 23rd-floor setting with aerial views north across the city.

RESTAURANT SINNE
GASTRONOMY €€€

Map p316 (☑020-682 72 90; www.restaurant sinne.nl; Ceintuurbaan 342; 3–8-course menus €39-89, with paired wines €63-153; ◷6-9pm Wed-Sat, noon-3pm & 6-9pm Sun; ☑3/4 2e Van der Helststraat) Watching the chefs work their magic in an open kitchen at the back of Michelin-starred Sinne is almost as thrilling as dining on the results. Multicourse menus (no à la carte) might start with a carrot-and-cumin macaron, move on to foie gras mousse, then red mullet with monk's beard, finishing with roast banana with caramel-miso sauce and micro basil leaves.

MISS KOREA BBQ
KOREAN €€€

Map p316 (☑020-679 06 06; www.misskorea.nl; Albert Cuypstraat 66-70; adult/child €29.90/12.50; ◷5-11pm Tue-Sun; ☑; Ⓜ De Pijp, ☑24 Marie Heinekenplein) Tables at this wildly popular restaurant have inset barbecue plates to sizzle up pork belly, seasoned beef, squid, prawns and vegetables yourself. You can order three ingredients per round for an unlimited number of rounds; there's a penalty for uneaten food to minimise wastage. Ice-cream flavours include green tea and black sesame; there are Korean spirits, rice wine and beers. On Tuesdays and Wednesdays, adult prices are slightly cheaper at €27.90.

DRINKING & NIGHTLIFE

The neighbourhood that houses the old Heineken brewery (p177) is chock-full of places to drink. The area also has a wonderful craft brewery (p186), and some superb wine bars and cocktail bars. In particular, the streets around Gerard Douplein heave with high-spirited local crowds that spill onto *café* (pub) terraces.

DE PIJP DRINKING & NIGHTLIFE

DE PIJP DRINKING & NIGHTLIFE

BOAT HIRE

Its location on peaceful Amstelkanaal makes **Boaty** (Map p316; ☑06 2714 9493; www.amsterdamrentaboat.com; Jozef Israëlskade; boat rental per 3hr/full day from €79/179; ☺9am-30min before sunset early Mar-Oct; ᠗4/12 Scheldestraat) ⬩ an ideal launching pad for exploring the waterways. You don't need a boat licence or experience. Book ahead online, or phone for same-day reservations. Its ecofriendly electric boats carry up to six people. The season can run longer or shorter depending on weather conditions.

★BROUWERIJ TROOST   BREWERY
Map p316 (☑020-760 58 20; www.brouwerij troost.nl; Cornelis Troostplein 21; ☺4pm-midnight Mon-Thu, 4pm-3am Fri, 2pm-3am Sat, 2pm-midnight Sun; ☎; ᠗4/12 Cornelis Troostplein) ⬩ Watch beer being brewed in copper vats behind a glass wall at this outstanding craft brewery. Its dozen beers include a summery blonde, a smoked porter, a strong tripel and a deep-red Imperial IPA; it also distils cucumber and juniper gin from its beer, and serves fantastic bar food, including crispy prawn tacos and humongous burgers. Book on weekend evenings.

RAYLEIGH & RAMSAY   WINE BAR
Map p316 (www.rr.wine; Van Woustraat 97; ☺3pm-1am Mon-Thu, noon-2am Fri & Sat, noon-1am Sun; ᠗3/4 Van Woustraat) Wine is a serious business at this vintage-style bar named for the two Scottish chemists who discovered that oxygen is lighter than argon gas, which R&R uses to prevent oxidisation. Its top-up-card payment system lets you dispense wines yourself by the 'sip', half or full glass. Alongside cheese and charcuterie, sharing platters feature shucked oysters, tinned sardines and shrimp croquettes.

TWENTY THIRD BAR   COCKTAIL BAR
Map p316 (www.okura.nl; Hotel Okura Amsterdam, Ferdinand Bolstraat 333; ☺6pm-1am Sun-Thu, to 2am Fri & Sat; ᠗4/12 Cornelius Troostplein) High up in the skyscraping Hotel Okura Amsterdam (p227), Twenty Third Bar has sweeping views to the west and south. The adjacent twin-Michelin-starred kitchen of Ciel Bleu (p185) also creates stunning bar snacks (€9 to €15) such as tuna sashimi cornets or goose liver and mango macarons, as well as syrups, purées and infusions for its cocktails; champagne cocktails are a speciality.

JACOB'S JUICE   JUICE BAR
Map p316 (www.jacobs-juice.com; 1e Jacob Van Campenstraat 34; ☺9am-5pm Mon & Wed-Sat, 10am-5pm Sun; ᠗24 Marie Heinekenplein) ⬩ Reducing food waste was the inspiration behind Jacob's Juice. Its owners collect imperfect fruit and vegetables each day from the Albert Cuypmarkt that stallholders would otherwise discard (an average of 500kg per month). They then transform them into super-healthy juices (such as cucumber, celery and lemon), smoothies (eg pineapple, raspberry and passion fruit) and pickled veggies in recycled jam jars.

JONES BROTHERS COFFEE   COFFEE
Map p316 (www.jonesbrotherscoffee.com; Sint Willibrordusstraat 54; ☺9am-6pm Mon-Fri; ᠗3/4 Van Woustraat) ⬩ Jones Brothers roasts organic and UTZ (certified sustainable) beans in Amsterdam and brews them here; you can stop for a coffee at its clutch of tables, or get a coffee to go (cups and lids are 100% plant based). Beans are sold whole, ground or as capsules for coffee machines.

CAFÉ RUIS   BAR
Map p316 (www.cafe-ruis.nl; Van der Helstplein 9; ☺3pm-1am Mon-Thu, to 3am Fri, noon-3am Sat, to 1am Sun; ☎; ᠗3/4 2e Van der Helststraat) Opening to one of the liveliest terraces on plane-tree-shaded square Van der Helstplein, Café Ruis has a lounge-room-like interior with mismatched furniture, board games and a resident dog, Moe. Craft beers on tap include Amsterdam Brewboys' Amsterdam Pale Ale. Texelse Bierbrouwerij's Tripel, brewed on the island of Texel, is among the bottled options.

BOCA'S   BAR
Map p316 (www.bar-bocas.nl; Sarphatipark 4; ☺noon-1am Mon-Thu, 10am-3am Fri & Sat, 11am-1am Sun; ☎; ᠗3/4 2e Van der Helststraat) Boca's (inspired by the Italian word for 'mouth') is the ultimate spot for *borrel*. Mezzanine seating overlooks the cushion-strewn interior, but in summer the best seats are on the terrace facing leafy Sarphatipark. Its pared-down wine list (seven by-the-glass choices) goes perfectly with sharing platters (fish, cheese, meat or vegetarian).

GLOUGLOU WINE BAR

Map p316 (www.glouglou.nl; 2e Van der Helst-straat 3; ☺4pm-midnight Mon-Wed, noon-midnight Thu & Sun, noon-1am Fri & Sat; 🕾; 🚊3/4 2e Van der Helststraat) Natural, all-organic, additive-free wines are the stock-in-trade of this convivial neighbourhood wine bar in a rustic stained-glass-framed shop, where the party often spills out into the street. More than 40 well-priced French wines are available by the glass; it also sells bottles to drink on-site or take away.

CAFÉ SARPHAAT BROWN CAFE

Map p316 (☏020-675 15 65; Ceintuurbaan 157; ☺9am-1am Sun-Thu, to 3am Fri & Sat; 🕾; 🚊3/4 Van Woustraat) Grab an outdoor table along Sarphatipark, order a frothy beer and see if you don't feel like a local. This is one of the neighbourhood's most genial spots, with a lovely old bar that makes sipping a *jenever* in broad daylight seem like a good idea. Free live jazz takes place most Sunday afternoons.

CAFÉ BINNEN BUITEN BROWN CAFE

Map p316 (www.cafebinnenbuiten.nl; Ruysdael-kade 115; ☺10am-1am Sun-Thu, to 3am Fri & Sat; 🕾; Ⓜ️De Pijp, 🚊3/12/24 De Pijp) The minute there's a sliver of sunshine, this place gets packed. Sure, the food's good and the bar's candlelit and cosy. But what really draws the crowds is simply the best canal-side terrace in De Pijp – an idyllic spot to while away an afternoon.

KATSU COFFEESHOP

Map p316 (www.katsu.nl; 1e Van der Helststraat 70; ☺10am-midnight Mon-Thu, to 1am Fri & Sat, 11am-midnight Sun; Ⓜ️De Pijp, 🚊3 2e Van der Helststraat) Like De Pijp itself, this relaxed coffeeshop brims with colourful characters of all ages and dispositions.

CAFÉ BERKHOUT BROWN CAFE

Map p316 (www.cafeberkhout.nl; Stadhouderskade 77; ☺10am-1am Mon-Thu, to 3am Fri & Sat, 11am-1am Sun; 🕾; 🚊24 Marie Heinekenplein) With its dark wood, mirror-and-chandelier splendour and shabby elegance, this brown cafe is a natural post–Heineken Experience wind-down spot. (It's right across the street.) Great food includes house-speciality burgers.

BARÇA BAR

Map p316 (www.barca.nl; Marie Heinekenplein 30-31; ☺11am-midnight Sun-Thu, to 2am Fri & Sat; 🕾; 🚊24 Marie Heinekenplein) One of the hottest

hang-outs in the 'hood, this 'Barcelona in Amsterdam'–themed bar is the heartbeat of Marie Heinekenplein. Tapas and Catalan mains are served alongside an extensive choice of Spanish wines and sparkling *cava*. Cosy up in the plush gold and dark-timber interior or spread out on the terrace.

☆ ENTERTAINMENT

Due to its residential make-up, De Pijp doesn't have much in the way of entertainment. A few bars, such as Café Sarphaat, host mellow live music, and there's a central cinema screening art-house films. Otherwise, you'll find plenty of options in the nearby Southern Canal Ring, and Vondelpark and the South neighbourhoods.

RIALTO CINEMA CINEMA

Map p316 (☏020-676 87 00; www.rialtofilm.nl; Ceintuurbaan 338; adult/child from €11/7; ☺noon-midnight; 🚊3/4 2e Van der Helststraat) Opened in 1920, this art deco cinema near Sarphatipark shows eclectic art-house fare from around the world (foreign films have Dutch subtitles). Tickets can be purchased online or at the box office. There are three screens and a stylish on-site cafe.

🔒 SHOPPING

After you've hit the Albert Cuypmarkt (p178), head to the surrounding streets, which are less crowded and are dotted with boutiques and galleries.

★HUTSPOT DESIGN

Map p316 (www.hutspot.com; Van Woustraat 4; ☺10am-7pm Mon-Sat, noon-6pm Sun; 🕾; 🚊4 Stadhouderskade) Named after the Dutch dish of boiled and mashed veggies, 'Hotchpotch' was founded with a mission to give young entrepreneurs the chance to sell their work. As a result, this concept store is an inspired mishmash of Dutch-designed furniture, furnishings, art, homewares and clothing as well as an in-house cafe, a barber, a photo booth and various pop-ups.

★COTTONCAKE CONCEPT STORE

Map p316 (www.cottoncake.nl; 1e Van der Helststraat 76; ☺10am-6.30pm Mon-Fri, to 6pm Sat, 11am-6pm Sun; 🚊3/4 2e Van der Helststraat)

Painted cotton-white inside and out, this chic little shop makes and sells its own scented candles and perfumes, and stocks fashion, jewellery and homewares from Dutch designers Yaya and Mimi et Toi as well as international labels. It has a small cafe on its mezzanine where you can stop for homemade cakes, waffles, fresh-squeezed juices and Amsterdam White Label coffee.

BIER BAUM
DRINKS

Map p316 (www.bier-baum.nl; Sarphatipark 1; ⊙2-10pm Sun-Fri, noon-10pm Sat; 🚊3/4 2e Van der Helststraat) Perfect for Sarphatipark picnic supplies, Bier Baum has fridges keeping many of its craft beers cold, and growlers that you can fill by the litre. Look out for Dutch brews such as Amsterdam's Brouwerij 't IJ, Haarlem's Uitje Brewing Co and Nijmegen's Oersoep, and international beers from as far afield as New Zealand and Hawaii.

BRICK LANE
FASHION & ACCESSORIES

Map p316 (www.bricklane-amsterdam.nl; Gerard Doustraat 80; ⊙1-6pm Mon, 10.30am-6pm Tue-Sat, 12.30-5.30pm Sun; MDe Pijp, 🚊24 Marie Heinekenplein) Individual, affordable designs for women arrive at this London-inspired boutique every couple of weeks, keeping the selection up-to-the-minute.

RECORD MANIA
MUSIC

Map p316 (www.recordmania.nl; Ferdinand Bolstraat 30; ⊙10am-6pm Mon-Sat, noon-6pm Sun; 🚊24 Marie Heinekenplein) Fantastically old-school, Record Mania stocks vinyl (singles and LPs) and CDs, including rare recordings by artists including Johnny Cash, JJ Kale, Eric Clapton, Def Leppard, the Beatles and the Wailers. The shop, with old posters, stained-glass windows, and records and CDs embedded in the floor, is a treasure in itself.

'T KAASBOERTJE
FOOD & DRINKS

Map p316 (Gerard Doustraat 60; ⊙1-5.30pm Mon, 9am-5.30pm Tue-Fri, to 4pm Sat; MDe Pijp, 🚊24 Marie Heinekenplein) Enormous wheels of Gouda line the walls of this enticing cheese shop, and more cheeses fill the glass display cabinet. Crispbreads and crackers are on hand, as well as reds, whites and rosés from the Netherlands, Belgium and Germany.

VAN BEEK
ART

Map p316 (www.vanbeekart.nl; Stadhouderskade 63-65; ⊙1-6pm Mon, 9am-6pm Tue-Fri, 10am-5pm Sat; 🚊24 Marie Heinekenplein) If you're inspired by Amsterdam's masterpiece-filled galleries, street art and picturesque canalscapes, the De Pijp branch of this venerable Dutch art-supply shop is a great place to pick up canvases, brushes, oils, watercolours, pastels, charcoals and more.

RAAK
FASHION & ACCESSORIES

Map p316 (www.raakamsterdam.nl; 1e Van der Helststraat 46; ⊙10am-6pm Tue-Sat, noon-6pm Sun & Mon; 🚊24 Marie Heinekenplein) Unique casual clothing, bags, jewellery and homewares by Dutch and Scandinavian designers fill Raak's shelves and racks.

TILLER GALERIE
ART

Map p316 (www.facebook.com/tillergalerie.amsterdam; 1e Jacob van Campenstraat 1; ⊙noon-6pm Wed-Sat; 🚊24 Marie Heinekenplein) This intimate, friendly gallery has works by George Heidweiller (check out the surreal Amsterdam skyscapes), Peter Donkersloot's portraits of animals and iconic actors such as Marlon Brando, and Herman Brood prints.

STENELUX
GIFTS & SOUVENIRS

Map p316 (📞020-662 14 90; 1e Jacob van Campenstraat 2; ⊙11am-5pm Thu-Sat; 🚊24 Marie Heinekenplein) Browse Stenelux' delightful collection of gems, minerals, stones and fossils. The fascinating collection from this world and beyond includes meteorites.

BLOND
GIFTS & SOUVENIRS

Map p316 (www.blond-amsterdam.nl; Ferdinand Bolstraat 44; ⊙9am-6pm Mon-Fri, to 5pm Sat, 10am-5pm Sun; MDe Pijp, 🚊24 Marie Heinekenplein) In a Barbie-pink shop that doubles as a tearoom, the blonde owners sell plates and dishes that they glaze in colourful, often hilarious designs – ladies lunching, beach scenes, cakes and chocolates – that make great gifts for anyone who likes modern kitsch with a sense of humour. Sweet treats such as lemon meringue tarts are served on Blond's own crockery.

Oosterpark & East of the Amstel

Neighbourhood Top Five

1 Tropenmuseum (p191) Browsing the Museum of the Tropics' impressive and creatively displayed ethnographic collection, plus imaginative temporary exhibitions and a children's museum.

2 Dappermarkt (p192) Experiencing a slice of local life while sniffing out Turkish pide, kebabs and olives at food stalls amid multipack sock vendors.

3 Oosterpark (p192) Relaxing with the locals, seeking out the political monuments and watching wild parakeets and heron.

4 Canvas (p195) Clinking glasses to the sweeping city views from the city's coolest rooftop bar.

5 Distilleerderij 't Nieuwe Diep (p195) Sampling some of the 100 or so gins at this divine little lakeside distillery, tucked away in Flevopark like the gingerbread house from *Hansel and Gretel*.

For more detail of this area see Map p318 ➡

Lonely Planet's Top Tip

Oosterpark plays host to a number of lively events during the summer and it's a great place to get a feel for the multicultural makeup of the neighbourhood. A highlight is the global music performed on an open-air stage as part of the week-long Roots Festival (www.amsterdamroots.nl), which usually takes place in late June to early July at various venues around town.

Best Places to Eat

➡ De Kas (p195)

➡ Marits Eetkamer (p193)

➡ Wilde Zwijnen (p194)

➡ Roopram Roti (p193)

➡ Mr & Mrs Watson (p193)

For reviews, see p193.

Best Places to Drink

➡ De Ysbreeker (p195)

➡ Distilleerderij 't Nieuwe Diep (p195)

➡ Canvas (p195)

➡ De Biertuin (p196)

➡ Walter Woodbury Bar (p195)

For reviews, see p195.

Best Places to Shop

➡ Dappermarkt (p192)

➡ Het Faire Oosten (p197)

➡ De Pure Markt (p197)

➡ All the Luck in the World (p197)

➡ Linnaeus Bookstore (p197)

For reviews, see p197.

OOSTERPARK & EAST OF THE AMSTEL

Explore Oosterpark & East of the Amstel

Oost is gradually seeing the tendrils of gentrification winding through the neighbourhood, with cafes, boutiques, bread makers, restaurants and hip hotels sprouting up. However, this is still an area with lots of local life and vitality, where many different communities live side by side, a fact that's most obvious at Dappermarkt (p192), where knickers for sale flap in the breeze as women in headscarves push buggies through the throng, and you can feast on kebabs, piled-high dried fruit or fried fish.

The Tropenmuseum (Tropics Museum) offers another rich cultural mix. The endlessly intriguing artefacts offer insights into Dutch colonial activities in the East Indies.

The green expanse of Oosterpark (p192) makes a fine diversion, with its large pond, several monuments and increasing numbers of fun bars with terraces. The lively main strip, Javastraat, is a fantastic mix of multicultural shops and restaurants, alongside cool bars and boutiques. Another buzzing area for bars and restaurants is the pretty neighbourhood around Transvaalkade. Further east you hit Park Frankendael, a romantic former country estate, and a little further on is leafy Flevopark with its enchanting waterside gin distillery (p195).

Local Life

➡ **Cool bars and multicultural delights** On Javastraat (which 1e van Swindenstraat turns into) old Dutch fish shops and the latest hip bars, such as Walter Woodbury (p195), sit adjacent to Moroccan and Turkish grocers.

➡ **Arts centre** Join local arty types catching independent flicks, local bands and theatre performances or just stopping by for vegetarian fare at Studio K (p196).

➡ **Market finds** If you're looking for an authentic place to shop, Dappermarkt (p192) is it. If gourmet burgers and artisanal cheeses are your (organic) jam, the monthly De Pure Markt (p197) in Park Frankendael is the place.

Getting There & Away

➡ **Tram** Tram 14 goes from Amsterdam Centraal Station to Alexanderplein for the Tropenmuseum, or tram 19 from Leidseplein to 1e van Swindenstraat. Tram 14 swings through the Oosterpark area on its east–west route, and tram 3 services the area via Museumplein.

➡ **Bus** No 757 starts at Amsterdam Centraal Station and stops near Oosterpark.

➡ **Metro** The Wibautstraat stop is a stone's throw from the cool bars and hotels at the Oost's southwest edge.

➡ **Train** Muiderpoort station is handy for Javastraat.

⊙ SIGHTS

There are few major sights in the Oost area, but it is home to the fascinating ethnographical Tropenmuseum and local multicultural Dappermarkt (p192), as well as lovely Oosterpark (p192), Park Frankendael and Flevopark, sites of several interesting memorials. Further east still, you can relax on Amsterdam's city beach at IJburg (p100) or take a trip to the fortifications of Muiden (p192).

FLEVOPARK   PARK
(⊙24hr; 🚃7/14 Flevopark) Formerly a Jewish cemetery, this area was bought by the city in 1956, when it was turned into a park. It has a wilder, more rambling feel than Amsterdam's more central green spaces. There's a large pond, the Distilleerderij 't Nieuwe Diep (p195) gin distillery and a large outdoor swimming pool in summer.

PARK FRANKENDAEL   PARK
Map p318 (www.huizefrankendael.nl; Middenweg; ⊙dawn-dusk; 🚃19 Hogeweg) These lovely, landscaped gardens are the grounds of a former country estate; the mansion, Frankendael House, is still standing and there are walking paths, flapping storks, decorative bridges and the remains of follies. The excellent De Pure Markt (p197) is held here on the last Sunday of each month.

FRANKENDAEL HOUSE   HISTORIC BUILDING
Map p318 (www.huizefrankendael.nl; Middenweg 72; ⊙gardens dawn-dusk, house noon-5pm Sun; 🚃19 Hugo de Vrieslaan) FREE This area was rolling countryside several centuries ago. In the 18th century, wealthy Amsterdammers would pass their summers and weekends in large country retreats on a tract of drained land called Watergraafsmeer. There were once around 40 such mansions, but the last survivor is Frankendael, an elegant, restored Louis XIV–style mansion. Its formal gardens are open to the public daily.

Staff hold a free open house every Sunday from noon to 5pm when you can explore the building on your own, or go on a guided tour (in Dutch; it departs at noon). Often there's an art exhibition going on as well. The Merkelbach cafe (p195) sits in the adjoining coach house and its patio overlooks the gardens. Be sure to view the house's forecourt with its gushing fountain and statues of Bacchus and Ceres.

OOSTERPARK & EAST OF THE AMSTEL SIGHTS

⊙ TOP SIGHT
TROPENMUSEUM

The gloriously quirky Tropenmuseum (Tropics Museum) has a whopping collection of ethnographic artefacts from all over the world. Galleries surround a huge central hall across three floors and present exhibits with insight, imagination and lots of multimedia. The impressive arched building was built in 1926 to house the Royal Institute of the Tropics, and is still a leading research institute for tropical hygiene and agriculture.

The Tropenmuseum's permanent collection, **Things That Matter**, addresses the social issues of what might happen to culture if a country disappears due to environmental issues. There are also excellent **temporary exhibits**, which can range from the Hajj pilgrimage to Mecca and photographs of Aleppo to pop art and robots of Japan.

The museum has a kids section, **Tropenmuseum Junior**, the first children's museum in the Netherlands, aimed at children from six to 13 years of age. It's great for hands-on fun, with loads of interactive exhibits.

The **gift shop** stocks enticing and unusual arts and crafts, and the on-site restaurant, De Tropen (p193), has a lovely terrace and serves global cuisine.

DON'T MISS
➡ Cafe and terrace
➡ Special exhibits

PRACTICALITIES
➡ Map p318, C1
➡ ☎0880 042 800
➡ www.tropenmuseum.nl
➡ Linnaeusstraat 2
➡ adult/child €16/8
➡ ⊙10am-5pm Jul-Sep, closed Mon Oct-Jun
➡ 👶
➡ 🚃19 1e van Swindenstraat

WORTH A DETOUR

MUIDEN

Only 20 to 30 minutes from Amsterdam Centraal by train, or a more leisurely ferry ride from IJburg (p100), Muiden is an unhurried historic town renowned for its fairy-tale red-brick castle, the Muiderslot. Life otherwise focuses on the busy central lock that funnels scores of pleasure boats out into the vast IJsselmeer.

Built in 1280 by Count Floris V, son of Willem II, the exceptionally preserved moated fortress **Muiderslot** (Muiden Castle; ☑0294-256 262; www.muiderslot.nl; Herengracht 1; adult/child €15.50/9; ☺10am-5pm Mon-Fri, from noon Sat & Sun Apr-Oct, 10am-5pm Tue-Sun Nov-Mar) is equipped with round towers, a French innovation. The count was a champion of the poor and a French sympathiser, two factors that were bound to spell trouble; Floris was imprisoned in 1296 and murdered while trying to flee. Today it's the Netherlands' most visited castle. Free entry for I Amsterdam cardholders.

Off the coast lies a derelict fort on the island of **Pampus** (www.pampus.nl; adult/child ferry & admission €18/14; ☺10.30am-5pm Tue-Sun May-Oct). This massive 19th-century bunker was a key member of a ring of 42 fortresses built to defend Amsterdam and is great fun to explore. The huge defences were designed to be flooded if the city came under attack. Unfortunately, aeroplanes came into the picture and the fortifications were never used. Rescued from disrepair by Unesco, Pampas is now a World Heritage site. Ferries to Pampus depart from Muiderslot port on a varying schedule in season. Usually there's at least one morning departure, which allows a couple of hours to prowl the fort before a mid-afternoon return.

In warm weather, the clientele of little bar **Café Ome Ko** (www.omekomuiden. nl; Herengracht 71; ☺8am-1am Sun-Wed, to 2am Thu-Sat), with its large green-striped awnings, turns the street outside into one big party. When there's no party on, it's a perfect spot to watch the comings and goings through the busy lock right outside. It serves lunchtime sandwiches and classic Dutch bar snacks (croquettes et al).

Muiden is easily reached from IJburg: it's a pleasant signposted 7km cycle route (you can also walk it in around 1½ hours). Alternatively, ferry is the best way to reach either Muiden or Pampas from IJburg. Ferries (p100) depart from the marina and include admission to either site. Bicycles travel for free.

Buses 320, 322 and 327 link Amsterdam's Amstel station (20 minutes, twice hourly) with Muiden. The castle is then a 1km walk or you can take bus 110 to Brandweer-kazerne Muiden, from where it's a 10-minute walk.

DAPPERMARKT   MARKET

Map p318 (www.dappermarkt.nl; Dapperstraat; ☺9am-5pm Mon-Sat; 🚊1/3 Dapperstraat) The busy, untouristy Dappermarkt is a swirl of life and colour, with around 250 stalls. It reflects the Oost's diverse immigrant population, and is full of people, foods (apricots, olives, fish, Turkish kebabs) and goods from costume jewellery to cheap clothes, all sold from stalls lining the street.

Dapperstraat is named after Olfert Dapper, a 17th-century doctor and writer. His book *Description of Africa* was a seminal text of its time, which he wrote despite never having travelled outside the Netherlands.

OOSTERPARK   PARK

Map p318 (☺dawn-dusk; 🚻; 🚊19 1e van Swindenstraat) The lush greenery of Oosterpark, with wild parakeets in the trees and herons stalking the large ponds, brings an almost tropical richness to this varied neighbourhood, despite being laid out in English style. It was established in 1891 as a pleasure park for the diamond traders who found their fortunes in the South African mines, and it still has an elegant, rambling feel.

On the south side, look for two monuments: one commemorates the **abolition of slavery** (Map p318; 🚊1/3 Beukenweg) in the Dutch colonies in 1863; the other, **De Schreeuw** (The Scream, Theo van Gogh Memorial; Map p318; 🚊1/3 Beukenweg), is a metal profile shouting into the sky, celebrating free speech and, more specifically, filmmaker Theo van Gogh, who was murdered nearby in 2004. Another (living) monument to Van Gogh is the **Spreeksteen** (Map p318; 🚊1/3 Linnaeusstraat), a rock podium marking a 'speakers' corner' established in 2005.

Families will enjoy the playground with a wading pool in summer on the park's north side.

EATING

There are some great eating choices – especially global and creative cuisine – in Oost. They may take a little more time to reach, but they are well worth the effort. You'll find a few eating options in the parks – Oosterpark and Park Frankendael – and the neighbourhood is home to a couple of excellent vegan restaurants.

BETER & LEUK
CAFE €

Map p318 (www.beterenleuk.nl; 1e Oosterparkstraat 91; dishes €5-13; ⏱8.30am-5pm Mon-Fri, 9.30am-5pm Sat & Sun; 🔌📷; 🚊3 Wibautstraat/Ruyschstraat) 🌱 Bright prints and artwork adorn the whitewashed walls at cute, pocket-sized Beter & Leuk, a haven for those looking for organic, vegan and gluten-free food. It's well known for its delicious breakfasts, along with tempting homemade cakes and muffins.

WORLD OF FOOD
STREET FOOD €

(www.worldoffoodamsterdam.nl; Develstein 100; dishes around €10; ⏱noon-9pm Mon-Thu, to 10pm Fri, 1-10pm Sat, 1-9pm Sun; 📷🚻; 🚇Diemen-Zuid) This parking-garage-turned-street-food-venue is a popular spot in the Bijlmer neighbourhood. Stalls serve up good, honest food at excellent prices from a range of cuisines, including Peruvian, Mexican, Indonesian, Thai and North Indian.

DE TROPEN
INTERNATIONAL €

Map p318 (📞020-568 20 00; www.amsterdamdetropen.nl; Linnaeusstraat 2; dishes €6.50-16; ⏱10am-6pm; 🚻; 🚊19 1e van Swindenstraat) This grand cafe has a superb terrace overlooking Oosterpark, and suitably for its setting in the Tropenmuseum (p191), offers a global menu. The food receives mixed reports, but it's nonetheless a wonderfully laid-back place to take some time out. Also has a kids menu.

HET IJSBOEFJE
ICE CREAM €

Map p318 (Beukenplein 5; 1/2/3 scoops €1.70/3.20/4; ⏱noon-8pm, to 10pm Jun-Aug; 🚊3/7 Beukenweg) A popular ice-cream stop close to Oosterpark, with benches outside and tons of delicious flavours inside. There

are always happy punters around, tucking into satisfyingly big portions of flavours such as *stroopwafel*, limoncello gelato and bright blue bubblegum Smurf – a winner with kids.

ROOPRAM ROTI
SOUTH AMERICAN €

Map p318 (1e Van Swindenstraat 4; mains €5.50-13.50; ⏱2-9pm Tue-Sun; 🚊19 1e van Swindenstraat) This simple canteen-style Surinamese cafe often has a queue out the door, but it moves fairly fast. Place your order at the bar – the scrumptiously punchy and flaky lamb roti 'extra' (with egg) and the *barra* (lentil doughnut) are winners – and don't forget the fiery hot sauce.

It's super-delicious for takeaway or to eat at one of the half-dozen tables.

★ LOUIE LOUIE
INTERNATIONAL €€

Map p318 (📞020-370 29 81; www.louielouie.nl; Linnaeusstraat 11; dishes €7-15; ⏱9am-1am Sun-Thu, to 3am Fri & Sat; 📷; 🚊Muiderpoort) With its rough wooden floorboards, big windows, fur-backed bar, model stags, squashy leather sofas and covered terrace, this relaxed brasserie-style place is perfect for a chilled-out meal. The menu is a fusion of Asian and Mexican dishes, from huevos rancheros in the morning to Asian salads, tacos, pork belly, burritos and wonton soup later in the day. Vegan options, too.

MR & MRS WATSON
VEGAN €€

Map p318 (📞020-261 93 60; www.watsonsfood.com; Linnaeuskade 3h; lunch dishes €9-16, dinner mains €17-19; ⏱11.30am-11.30pm; 📷; 🚊19 Hogeweg) 🌱 Named after the couple who coined the term 'veganism', this intimate, popular restaurant delivers wonderful plant-based comfort food. The seasonal menu might include sloppy joe chilli burgers of sliced seitan steak or vegan *bitterballen* 'better balls' with a Thai coconut curry filling. Don't miss the signature cheese platters and fondue – hard to believe it's not the real thing.

MARITS EETKAMER
VEGAN €€

Map p318 (📞020-776 38 64; www.maritseetkamer.nl; Andreas Bonnstraat 34h; 3-/4-/5-course dinner €31/38/43; ⏱6pm-midnight Thu-Sat; 📷; 🚇Weesperplein) Dining at Marits is like eating in a friend's extremely elegant living room, with adjoining conservatory. Marits and Gino cook up a storm with a plant-based set menu that changes every month. Everything is sourced locally where possible, so beer comes from Brouwerij 't IJ (p99) and organic eau de vie and liqueur from Distilleerderij 't Nieuwe Diep.

WILDE ZWIJNEN
DUTCH €€

(☑020-463 30 43; www.wildezwijnen.com; Javaplein 23; mains €20-27, 3-/4-course menus €34/40; ⊙6-10pm Mon-Thu, noon-late Fri-Sun; ☎; ☒14 Javaplein) ✒ The name means 'wild boar' and there's usually game on the menu in season at this modern Dutch restaurant. With pale walls and wood tables, the restaurant has a pared-down, rustic-industrial feel, and serves locally sourced, seasonal dishes with a creative twist. It's a meat-eater's paradise, but there's usually a vegetarian choice as well.

The chevron-floored Wilde Zwijnen Eetbar next door (open 5pm to late Tuesday to Saturday) is more of a tapas-style eatery, with delicious small plates for €7 to €12.

EDDY SPAGHETTI
ITALIAN €€

Map p318 (☑020-370 93 88; www.eddyspaghetti.nl; Krugerplein 23; mains €11-18; ⊙5-10pm; Ⓜ️Wibautstraat) Eddy's is an intimate neighbourhood spot that does fantastic pizzas and pastas from its short and sweet menu, including *linguine vongole* (clams, chilli, white wine and garlic) and a delicious ravioli filled with duck rillettes. Finish off with an espresso martini.

CAFE-RESTAURANT DAUPHINE
INTERNATIONAL €€

Map p318 (☑020-462 16 46; www.caferestaurantdauphine.nl; Prins Bernhardplein 175; lunch mains €10-24, dinner mains €16-30; ⊙9am-1am Mon-Fri, 11am-1am Sat & Sun; Ⓜ️Amstel) This ginormous, stylish, converted Renault car showroom serves up a range of international dishes, from steak tartare and Iberico pork cutlets to grilled sea bass with saffron couscous and a classic hamburger with fries. It's named after a type of car produced by Renault in the 1950s, and is fronted by a huge neon sign.

COTTAGE
BRITISH €€

Map p318 (☑020-223 08 35; www.thecottage.amsterdam; Linnaeusstraat 88; dishes €5-17.50; ⊙8.30am-10pm Wed-Mon; ☎; ☒Muiderpoort) A superb, popular and friendly neighbourhood cafe-bar, where the quirky decor features lots of foxes, stuffed and pictorial, and the menu focuses on that most underrated of cuisines: British comfort food! There's the full Cottage breakfast (sausage, bacon,

eggs and homemade baked beans) and Sunday roasts, plus scones with clotted cream and jam. There are also outside tables for sunny days with a Pimm's.

JACOBZ
INTERNATIONAL €€

Map p318 (☑06 4245 4677; www.jacobsz.amsterdam; Ringdijk 1a; 3-/4-/5-course menu €37/47/55; ⊙6pm-midnight Mon-Sat; Ⓡ️Muiderpoort) Named after the building's 18th-century architect, Caspar Philips Jacobsz, this restaurant is housed in a grand old inn (a former courthouse, then turned into 'the courthouse inn' before its current incarnation) on the corner of a canal. It offers fine gastronomy and fresh seasonal ingredients at reasonable prices complemented by superior service.

CAFE MOJO
INTERNATIONAL €€

Map p318 (☑020-233 13 67; www.mojo-amsterdam.nl; Ringdijk 3; lunch dishes €3-9.50, dinner mains €14-22; ⊙11am-1am Sun-Thu, to 3am Fri & Sat; Ⓜ️Wibautstraat) A lovely open-fronted bar right by the canal, with a superb terrace that's just perfect for a summer drink. Quaff beers by local Amsterdam breweries Brouwerij 't IJ, Oedipus and Two Chefs, while you chow down on sandwiches and soups at lunch, or burgers, pastas and steaks for dinner.

EETCAFE IBIS
ETHIOPIAN €€

Map p318 (☑06 5764 2122; www.eetcafeibis.com; Weesperzijde 43; mains €15-18; ⊙5-11pm Tue-Sun; ☑; ☒3 Wibautstraat/Ruysschstraat) Bright with African art and brilliant-hued textiles, Ibis is a cosy and delightful spot to get your

---

BAKING LAB

Breathe in the scent of fresh baking in this open **bakery** (Map p318; ☑020-240 01 58; www.bakinglab.nl; Linnaeusstraat 99; 3hr basic bread-making workshop €45, 1½hr kids workshop €20; ⊙8am-6pm Wed-Sat, to 5pm Sun; ☒3/7 Linnaeusstraat), where workshops are offered for both adults and children. You can make your own bread here in the spirit of the old communal bakery, where people used to bring dough to knead and put in the shared oven, as few houses had ovens of their own. You can also snack on hummus, sandwiches, vegan cakes or tarts (dishes €3.50 to €9.50).

hands on (literally, using the spongy Ethiopian *injera* bread) herb-laced vegetable stews and spicy lamb and beef dishes; try the Ibis Special (meat or veg version), which combines five dishes and bread. Ibis sells African beers to go with the authentic food.

MERKELBACH
CAFE €€

Map p318 (☑020-665 08 80; http://restaurant merkelbach.nl; Middenweg 72; dishes €7-14, lunch menu €32; ☺8.30am-10.30pm Tue-Sat, to 6pm Sun & Mon; ☐19 Hugo de Vrieslaan) The Merkelbach cafe sits in the coach house adjoining Frankendael House (p191), and proffers dishes such as soups, salads and pastas with slow food credentials. Its patio is perfect for summer alfresco dining overlooking Frankendael's formal gardens (open to the public).

★DE KAS
INTERNATIONAL €€€

Map p318 (☑020-462 45 62; www.restaurantde kas.nl; Park Frankendael, Kamerlingh Onneslaan 3; 3-/4-course lunch menu €35/45, 5-/6-course dinner menu €57/65; ☺noon-2pm & 6.30-10pm Mon-Fri, 6.30-10pm Sat; ☑; ☐19 Hogeweg) 🌿 In a row of stately greenhouses dating to 1926, De Kas has an organic attitude to match its chic glass setting. It grows most of its own herbs and produce right here and the result is incredibly pure flavours and innovative combinations. There's one set menu daily, based on whatever has been freshly harvested. Reserve in advance.

🍷 DRINKING & NIGHTLIFE

Oost has some of Amsterdam's best and most varied drinking options, including rooftop bars with stupendous views, a gin distillery hidden in a park and a brewery beneath a windmill. Javastraat is a great strip to explore, with a string of bars.

★DISTILLEERDERIJ 'T NIEUWE DIEP
DISTILLERY

(☑06 2537 8104; www.nwediep.nl; Flevopark 13a; ☺3-8pm Tue-Sun Apr-Oct, to 6pm Nov-Mar; ☐3/14 Soembawastraat) Appearing out of the woods like a *Hansel and Gretel* cottage, the quaint architecture and rural setting of this old pumping station are enchanting and it feels like you've escaped to a magical countryside retreat, though it's just leafy Flevopark. The little distillery makes

around 100 small-batch *jenevers* (Dutch gin), herbal bitters, liqueurs and fruit distillates from organic ingredients according to age-old Dutch recipes.

The outdoor terrace is on a little lake next to an orchard. To get here by public transport, walk east from the tram stop; it's about a 10-minute walk into the park. Cash only.

★DE YSBREEKER
BROWN CAFE

Map p318 (☑020-468 18 08; www.deysbreeker. nl; Weesperzijde 23; ☺8am-1am Sun-Thu, to 2am Fri & Sat; ☑; ☐3 Wibautstraat/Ruyschstraat) This gloriously historic but updated *bruin café* (traditional Dutch pub) first opened its doors in 1702. It's named after an icebreaker that used to dock in front to break the ice on the river during the winter months (stained-glass windows illustrate the scene). Inside, stylish drinkers hoist beverages in the plush booths and along the marble bar.

It's great for organic and local beers (such as De Prael) and bar snacks such as homemade meatballs and shrimp croquettes, and there's a wonderful canal-side terrace for watching the riverboats glide by.

★CANVAS
BAR

Map p318 (www.volkshotel.nl; Wibautstraat 150; ☺7am-1am Mon-Thu, 7am-2am Fri, 8am-2am Sat, 8am-1am Sun; ☑; ⓂWibautstraat) Zoom up to the Volkshotel's (p228) 7th-floor bar for some of the best views in town, either through its large windows or on the open terrace. A creative-folk and hipster magnet, there are few better places for a drink in Amsterdam. On Sundays in winter, non-guests can head up to the rooftop for a dip in one of the hot tubs.

The Wibautstraat metro stop is a stone's throw away; follow signs saying 'Gijsbrecht van Aemstelstraat' as you exit the station.

WALTER WOODBURY BAR
BAR

Map p318 (☑020-233 30 21; www.walterwood burybar.nl; Javastraat 42; ☺11am-1am Sun-Thu, to 3am Fri & Sat; ☐Muiderpoort) On rapidly gentrifying Javastraat, Walter Woodbury's Javanese-inspired, plant-filled and wooden interior has chesterfield lounges perfect for cosying into for expertly made classic cocktails and tasty bar snacks, including vegan *bitterballen* (deep-fried meatballs). Local beers on tap include Oedipus, Brouwerij 't IJ and Two Chefs, or sample one of the speciality G&Ts.

The bar is named after the English explorer who first documented the Indonesian island of Java.

RUM BARREL   COCKTAIL BAR

(📞06 3838 2052; www.rumbarrel.nl; Javastraat 143; ⏰6pm-1am Wed & Thu, 5pm-3am Fri & Sat, 5pm-1am Sun; 🚊14 Javaplein) Transport yourself to the tropics with a Caribbean negroni and spicy watermelon punch at this Caribbean tiki bar. It mixes up a menu of over 200 Spanish-, English- and French-style rums, along with classic tropical cocktails with a twist. Snack on fried coconut chicken, spicy voodoo shrimp and chorizo croquettes.

RUM BABA CAFE   COFFEE

Map p318 (📞020-846 94 98; www.rumbaba.nl; Pretoriusstraat 33; ⏰8am-6pm Mon-Fri, 9am-6pm Sat & Sun; 📶; 🚊Muiderpoort) A light-filled corner cafe that fills with creatives on laptops and hip mums catching up over expertly made brew, Rum Baba does its own roasting just a few doors up at its roastery and bakery. Pair your coffee with a delicious slice of home-baked salted caramel apple pie or banana bread.

4850   COFFEE

Map p318 (www.4850.nl; Camperstraat 48-50; ⏰9am-11pm Mon, Tue & Thu, 9am-midnight Fri, 10am-midnight Sat, 10am-11pm Sun; 📶; 🚊3 Camperstraat) From your morning caffeine fix to an evening tipple, hip cafe-bar 4850 has you covered. It turns out a great coffee along with an impressive selection of wines displayed across the rear wall. Natural light floods the industrial-meets-mid-century interior, while the outdoor pavement area is the ideal spot for sunny days.

BAR BASQUIAT   BAR

Map p318 (📞020-370 83 34; www.barbasquiat.nl; Javastraat; ⏰9am-1am Sun-Thu, to 3am Fri & Sat; 🚊Muiderpoort) A cool neighbourhood bar with outside tables and a lively buzz on ever livelier Javastraat, serving up local beers and cocktails, as well as excellent Indonesian street food.

BAR BUKOWSKI   BAR

Map p318 (📞020-370 16 85; www.barbukowski. nl; Oosterpark 10; ⏰8am-1am Mon-Thu, 8am-3am Fri, 9am-3am Sat, 9am-1am Sun; 🚊3/7 Beukenweg) This stylish cafe-bar is not exactly the kind of dive Bukowski might have favoured, but it's a fine spot paying homage to the writer and the perfect place to linger under a cascade of greenery outside on sunny days, or to sink into a dark leather chair indoors when the rain sets in. Supplement your tipples with a *flammkuchen* (Alsatian thin-crust pizza).

DE BIERTUIN   BEER GARDEN

Map p318 (📞020-665 09 56; www.debiertuin. nl; Linnaeusstraat 29; ⏰11am-1am Sun-Thu, to 3am Fri & Sat; 📶; 🚊19 1e van Swindenstraat) With a covered terrace and heaters for chillier weather, 'the beer garden' attracts a young and beautiful crowd of locals with its lengthy beer list (around 16 on tap and over 50 more Dutch and Belgian varieties in bottles) and tasty pub food, such as burgers, burritos and fried chicken waffles (mains €11 to €14).

COFFEE BRU   COFFEE

Map p318 (📞020-751 99 56; www.coffeebru.nl; Beukenplein 14; ⏰8am-6pm Mon-Fri, 9am-6pm Sat & Sun; 📶; 🚊3 Camperstraat) This popular neighbourhood hangout has comfy chairs and benches, loads of light and excellent coffee, along with tasty freshly made sandwiches, plus a tempting selection of cakes, including some vegan-friendly treats.

☆ ENTERTAINMENT

At the far southern end of the neighbourhood you'll find a couple of arenas hosting big-name music acts, along with the Johan Cruijff ArenA, home of the Netherland's famous football team, Ajax. To tap into the Oost arts scene, check out what's on at Studio K.

STUDIO K   ARTS CENTRE

Map p318 (📞020-692 04 22; www.studio-k.nu; Timorplein 62; ⏰11am-1am Sun-Thu, to 3am Fri & Sat; 📶; 🚊14 Zeeburgerdijk) This hip Oost arts centre always has something going on, with a cinema, a nightclub, a stage for bands and a theatre. There's also an eclectic restaurant, serving sandwiches and salads for lunch and vegetarian-friendly, international-flavoured dishes for dinner, and a huge terrace.

Stop in for a coffee and you might wind up dancing all night.

ZIGGO DOME
CONCERT VENUE

(www.ziggodome.nl; De Passage 100; 🚇; Ⓜ Bijlmer ArenA) The 17,000-seat, indoor Ziggo Dome hosts big-name concerts: Metallica, Katy Perry, Nick Cave and Elton John have tramped these boards.

JOHAN CRUIJFF ARENA
FOOTBALL

(www.johancruijffarena.nl; Arena Blvd 1; 🚇; Ⓜ Bijlmer ArenA) This high-tech complex with a retractable roof was formerly known as Amsterdam ArenA, but is now named after the Netherlands' best ever football player. It is the home of four-time European champions Ajax, the country's most famous football team. Games usually take place on Saturday evenings and Sunday afternoons from August to May. The arena also hosts big-name live-music shows. It's about 7km southeast of central Amsterdam, easily accessible by metro.

Fans can also take a one-hour guided tour of the stadium (adult/child €16.50/11). See the website for the schedule.

AFAS LIVE
CONCERT VENUE

(www.afaslive.nl; Arena Blvd 590; Ⓜ Bijlmer ArenA) This mid-sized venue has excellent acoustics and lighting, plus an on-site restaurant. Expect rock and pop acts from medium to big names.

 ## SHOPPING

You can shop all over the globe at the Tropenmuseum (p191) gift shop, while in the surrounding streets there is a smattering of interesting independent boutiques. Perhaps the best places to shop in Oost are the markets, with the multicultural Dappermarkt (p192) for street food, cheap clothes, toys, electronics and more, and the excellent monthly organic and crafts De Pure Markt.

★ DE PURE MARKT
MARKET

Map p318 (www.puremarkt.nl; Park Frankendael; ⊙11am-6pm last Sun of month Mar-Dec; 🚊19 Hogeweg) 🌿 On the last Sunday of the month De Pure Markt sets up in Park Frankendael (p191), with artisanal and organic producers selling delicious gourmet foodstuffs. Peruse the market with a coffee

or craft beer in hand, then grab a bite from the food stalls. Quality arts and crafts for sale include handwoven rugs, wooden chopping boards and fashion made from recycled materials.

HET FAIRE OOSTEN
GIFTS & SOUVENIRS

Map p318 (www.hetfaireoosten.nl; Waldenlaan 208; ⊙noon-6pm Mon, 10.30am-6pm Tue-Sat, noon-5pm Sun; 🚉Muiderpoort) 🌿 The perfect place to pick up an interesting gift or souvenir, Het Faire Oosten is stocked with beautiful homewares, quirky books, accessories and clothing by designers with an emphasis on sustainability. Check out the cool raincoats made from recycled plastic bottles, fair trade wooden kitchen utensils, vegan leather-look bags and eco-conscious yet still fashionable clothing made from organic cotton.

LINNAEUS BOOKSTORE
BOOKS

Map p318 (📞020-468 71 92; www.linnaeus boekhandel.nl; Middenweg 29; ⊙11am-6pm Mon, 9am-6pm Tue-Fri, 9am-5pm Sat, 1-5pm Sun; 🚉Muiderpoort) Lovely neighbourhood bookstore with a well-curated selection of English novels, travel guides and children's books.

THINGS I LIKE
THINGS I LOVE
FASHION & ACCESSORIES

Map p318 (📞020-846 69 95; www.thingsi likethingsilove.com; Javastraat 75a; ⊙1-6pm Mon, 11am-6pm Tue, Wed & Fri, 11am-8pm Thu, noon-6pm Sat & Sun; 🚉Muiderpoort) Stocks clothing for hip, young women along with accessories and quirky, cool homewares. There are a few branches around town.

ALL THE LUCK IN THE WORLD
HOMEWARES

Map p318 (www.alltheluckintheworld.nl; Linnaeusstraat 20; ⊙10am-6pm; 🚊7 Linnaeusstraat) A charming little concept store selling chic accessories, jewellery and offbeat yet classy homewares and gifts. It also has an on-site cafe.

WE ARE VINTAGE
VINTAGE

Map p318 (www.facebook.com/WeAreVintage. eu; 1e Van Swindenstraat 43; ⊙11am-7pm; 🚊19 1e van Swindenstraat) This packed-to-the-gills shop has a great range of good-quality secondhand threads, from 1990s shirts to '70s maxi dresses.

Amsterdam Noord

Neighbourhood Top Five

1 **A'DAM Tower** (p200) Taking in the view from this skyscraper of fantastical fun, complete with a daredevil swing over the edge, plus a revolving restaurant, a hotel and nightclub.

2 **Nieuwendammerdijk** (p200) Meandering along this enchantingly pretty narrow dyke of wooden houses, surrounded by flowers, greenery and birdsong.

3 **EYE Film Institute** (p201) Admiring the angular, gleaming white architecture of the IJ-side Eye, with its exhibitions on all things cinema and a great cafe with waterside terrace.

4 **Kunststad (Art City)** (p200) Exploring the artist studios in this massive former warehouse, with artworks dangling from the ceiling and enough room to cycle around.

5 **Bars, cafes & restaurants** (p204) Hanging out at one of Noord's ultra-cool bar-cafe-restaurants, such as Pllek, with its waterside location and artificial beach.

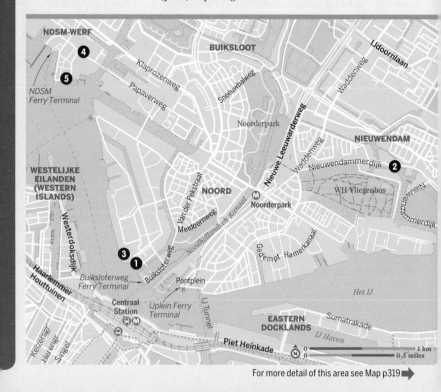

For more detail of this area see Map p319 ➡

Explore Amsterdam Noord

The NDSM (p200) former shipbuilding yard was an important industrial area that fell into disuse from the 1980s, before being taken over by squatters who filled the void. Today it has numerous cool waterside restaurants, striking architecture, a hangar full of artists studios, the huge monthly IJ Hallen (p205) flea market and an ex-USSR submarine (p201) in the harbour. From here it's a five- to 10-minute bike ride to the A'DAM Tower (p200) and the EYE Film Institute (p201), both also accessible from Centraal Station via direct ferry.

Further along the riverbank to the east are more waterside bars and restaurants, and the enchantingly pretty dyke, Nieuwendammerdijk (p200). The nearest ferry stop for this area from Centraal is IJplein. There are plenty of cycle routes into the countryside from Amsterdam Noord, and from here you can explore the lakes and *polder* (area of drained land) that lie to the north.

Local Life

→ **Bike rides** Take a bike ride (p30) into the countryside north of Amsterdam past sights such as the Krijtmolen d'Admiraal windmill and out into the fresh green of the *polder*.

→ **Coffee with a view** Have some proper Italian coffee at the Caffé Italiano Al Ponte (p204) kiosk by the IJplein ferry stop.

→ **Apple tart** Dig into this delicious Dutch favourite at charming old cafe Café 't Sluisje (p204), overlooking the lock.

→ **Treasure hunt** Rummage for vintage furniture finds at Neef Louis Design (p205) or IJ Hallen (p205) flea market.

→ **Catch a film** Head to ultra-hip FC Hyena (p205) for art-house flicks with natural wine and delicious snacks.

Getting There & Away

→ **Boat** There are free 24-hour ferries between Amsterdam Centraal Station, Buiksloterweg, NDSM and IJplein.

→ **Bike** You can take bikes over on the ferry, or hire bikes locally.

→ **Metro** The North–South line 52 links Amsterdam Zuid in the south with Noorderpark and Noord stations via Amsterdam Centraal Station. Noorderpark is the more convenient stop out of the two for most Noord attractions, though in most cases the ferry is the best option.

Lonely Planet's Top Tip

The best way to explore Noord is via bike. Places are spread out, there isn't much traffic and there are lots of cycle routes. You can take bikes on the free ferries, or hire one on the Noord side of the river through **Orange-bike** (p30).

 ## Best Places to Eat

→ Hotel de Goudfazant (p201)

→ Cafe-Restaurant Stork (p202)

→ Proeflokaal Kef (p202)

→ Coba (p202)

→ Moon (p202)

For reviews, see p201.

Best Places to Drink

→ Café de Ceuvel (p202)

→ Café Noorderlicht (p204)

→ Oedipus Brewery & Tap Room (p204)

→ Pllek (p204)

→ Walhalla Taproom (p204)

For reviews, see p202.

 ## Best Places to Shop

→ IJ Hallen (p205)

→ Neef Louis Design (p205)

→ Van Dijk and Ko (p205)

For reviews, see p205.

AMSTERDAM NOORD

◉ SIGHTS

The major sights in the Noord are just across the water from the city centre, with the A'DAM Tower offering panoramic views over the city, and the EYE Film Institute showing exhibitions on cinema. Look out also for cutting-edge architecture, including the EYE and Kraanspoor. Seek out the arty enclave of NDSM-werf, with its artists studios at Kunststad, street-art-covered buildings and regular IJ Hallen flea market, and take a stroll to admire the endearingly pretty dyke houses of Nieuwendammerdijk.

★NIEUWENDAMMERDIJK   STREET

Map p319 (🚌32 Buikslotermeerplein) Enchanting chocolate-box prettiness characterises this long, narrow street of wooden Dutch houses, now prime real estate, with hollyhocks nodding beside every porch. Many houses date from the 1500s, and numbers 202 to 204 were where the shipbuilding family De Vries Lentsch lived. Numbers 301 to 309 were once captains' houses.

★NDSM-WERF   AREA

Map p319 (www.ndsm.nl; NDSM-plein; 🚢NDSM-werf) This derelict shipyard turned edgy arts community, 15 minutes upriver from the city centre, wafts a post-apocalyptic vibe. An old submarine slumps in the harbour, abandoned trams rust by the water's edge, and street art is splashed on most surfaces. Young creatives hang out at the smattering of cool cafes, and hip businesses such as MTV and Red Bull have their European headquarters here. The area is also a centre for underground culture and events, including the Over het IJ Festival (p24).

A new street-art museum, billed as the world's largest, is due to open here in late 2019; check www.streetart.today for updates.

KUNSTSTAD   ART STUDIO

Map p319 (Art City NDSM; www.ndsmloods.nl; NDSM-plein; ⊙8am-6pm; 🚢NDSM-werf) **FREE** This former shipbuilding warehouse is filled with over 80 artists studios, with some 250 artists working in the NDSM *broedplaats* (breeding ground). It's a big enough space that you can cycle or walk around the area, with huge artworks hang-

◉ TOP SIGHT
A'DAM TOWER

This imposing tower on the waterfront was built in 1971 and named the 'Overhoeks' (Diagonal) because of its angle to the rest of the building. Used as the Royal Dutch Shell oil company offices, it's now a multivenue extravaganza, with a 360-degree **viewing platform** on its 100m-high rooftop, complete with telescopes, where you can lounge on super-sized cushions in fine weather.

There's also a giant **six-person swing** that kicks out right over the edge for adrenaline junkies (you're well secured and strapped in; €5 per person).

The lift that whisks you up has a mesmerising light show overhead and, as well as the rooftop panorama, on the 20th floor there's the **Ma'dam bar**, with stunning views through its floor-to-ceiling windows. A floor below is the **Moon** (p202) revolving restaurant, for which you need to book ahead. Note: your ticket allows admission to the bar but not the Moon restaurant.

There is also the **Shelter** basement nightclub in the tower, open Friday and Saturday nights, and a suave hotel, **Sir Adam** (p228).

DON'T MISS

➡ The 360-degree viewing platform
➡ The giant swing over the tower's edge
➡ Drinks in the bar
➡ Moon revolving restaurant

PRACTICALITIES

➡ Map p319, B4
➡ www.adamlookout.com
➡ Overhoeksplein 1
➡ lookout adult/child/family €13.50/7.50/32
➡ ⊙lookout 10am-10pm, last admission 9pm
➡ 🚢Buiksloterweg

ing from the ceiling, and structures within the hangar. There is a visitor centre for information and to buy artworks, and the exhibition space NDSM Fuse (both open noon to 6pm Friday to Sunday).

EYE FILM INSTITUTE MUSEUM, CINEMA

Map p319 (☑020-589 14 00; www.eyefilm.nl; IJpromenade 1; adult/child exhibitions €11/free, films €11/7.50; ⊗exhibitions 10am-7pm; ☑Buiksloterweg) At this modernist architectural triumph that seems to balance on its edge on the banks of the IJ (also pronounced 'eye') River, the institute screens movies from its 40,000-title archive in four theatres, sometimes with live music. Exhibitions of costumes, digital art and other cinephile amusements run in conjunction with what's playing. A view-tastic bar-restaurant with a fabulously sunny terrace (when the sun makes an appearance) is a popular hangout on this side of the river.

The attached gift shop sells vintage film posters and a great selection of books for movie lovers.

SUBMARINE B-80 LANDMARK

Map p319 (NDSM Haven; ☑NDSM-werf) Soviet Project 611 submarine B-80, dating from 1952, was built in Severodvinsk, Russia, and previously moored in the Dutch Navy port of Den Helder in North Holland. It was brought to Amsterdam and had its interior stripped, as the owners hoped to rent it as a party venue, but it now lies as an empty, if visually arresting, shell in the harbour.

SEXYLAND ARTS CENTRE

Map p319 (www.sexyland.amsterdam; Ms van Riemsdijkweg 39; monthly membership €2.50, admission dependent on event; ⊗hours vary; ☑NDSM-werf) See the neon sign and you'll be forgiven for thinking this is an outpost of the Red Light District. But Sexyland is a members' club that has 365 co-owners, each of whom puts on an annual event. These can range from roller disco and book presentations to club nights and stoner metal bands; the public can attend any of the activities by buying a month-long membership.

The initiative came from the pop-up Eddie the Eagle Museum. The founders were originally planning to open in a former porn cinema in central Amsterdam, hence the name, but instead found these premises – a long, low hut that once served as barracks.

KRAANSPOOR ARCHITECTURE

Map p319 (☑NDSM-werf) 'Craneway' is an extraordinary piece of architecture, built above a repurposed (you've guessed it) craneway, by OTH Architecten in 2007. The glass box above the stilts of the industrial base looks almost weightless, and houses offices with amazing waterfront views.

EATING

Noord has some spectacular places to eat, with superlative cooking, often sourcing fresh local ingredients, in striking waterfront spaces. You'll find everything from authentic Italian pizza and creative Mexican to French gastronomy and fresh seafood.

WAARGENOEGEN CAFE €

Map p319 (Papaverweg 46; snacks €3-8; ⊗10am-4pm Mon-Fri, 9am-5pm Sat, noon-5pm Sun; ☑NDSM-werf) This hippie-like cafe in a container behind two large vintage stores, Neef Louis (p205) and Van Dijk & Ko (p205), serves deliciously good toasties with fillings such as cheese, chorizo and red onion, and a particularly fantastic apple tart.

LANDMARKT INTERNATIONAL €

(☑restaurant 020-490 43 33; www.landmarkt.nl; Schellingwouderdijk 339; ⊗9am-8pm Mon-Sat, 11am-7pm Sun, restaurant 10am-10pm Mon-Sat, 11am-7pm Sun; ☑) This large covered food market has fresh fruit, vegetables, an onsite bakery, gourmet foodstuffs, and a fine selection of cheese, wine and beers. There's also an in-house restaurant with well-priced snacks and dishes. It's a great place to go with kids on a sunny day, as there's a field and swings, as well as outdoor seating that feels immersed in countryside.

★HOTEL DE GOUDFAZANT FRENCH €€

Map p319 (☑020-636 51 70; www.hotelde goudfazant.nl; Aambeeldstraat 10h; 3-course menu €32; ⊗6pm-midnight Tue-Sun; ☑IJplein; ⓂNoorderpark) With a name taken from lyrics of the Jacques Brel song 'Les Bourgeois', this extraordinary gourmet hipster restaurant spreads through a cavernous former garage, still raw and industrial, and sticks to the theme by having cars parked inside. Rockstar-looking chefs cook up a French-influenced storm in the open kitchen. There is no hotel, FYI, except in name.

Staff roll up the garage's big doors in warm weather and you can watch the passing barge traffic while you eat.

★PROEFLOKAAL KEF   CHEESE €€

Map p319 (☑020-737 08 17; www.abrahamkef.nl; Van der Pekplein 1b; platters from €12; ⊙noon-7pm Wed, Thu & Sun, to 9pm Fri & Sat; ⊛Buiksloterweg) Specialising in Dutch and French cheese since 1953, Fromagerie Kef has a few shops around town, and here, at their canalside tasting room/cafe, you can sample the goods. Book ahead for cheese tastings (€25 per person) or opt for a sandwich filled with Dutch aged sheep's cheese with fig compote or a cheese platter, paired with a craft beer from local brewery Walhalla (p204).

COBA   MEXICAN €€

Map p319 (☑06 4084 8875; www.coba-taqueria. com; Schaafstraat 4; small plates €9.50; ⊙6pm-midnight Thu-Sun; ☑; ⓂNoorderpark) This cool taqueria serves a small but inspiring menu of tacos, tostadas and quesadillas, alongside tequila-based cocktails, natural wines and fresh juices. The interior features bare concrete with subtle Mexican-inspired touches. You'll need to order around two plates per person, but what they lack in size they make up for in flavour. Dishes change weekly and are served with homemade salsas.

CAFE MODERN   GASTRONOMY €€

Map p319 (☑020-494 06 84; www.modernam sterdam.nl; Meidoornweg 2; lunch 2-/3-course menu €19.50/25, dinner 5-course menu €48; ⊙noon-3pm & 6-10pm Mon-Sat; ⊛Buiksloterweg) Amid artful yet simple decor with a subtle designer feel, Cafe Modern is serious about its gastronomy yet without any stuffiness. There's a choice of a two- or three-course set lunch and a five-course set dinner, incorporating fresh seasonal ingredients on the 'surprise' menu.

It has a few hotel rooms above the restaurant.

CAFE-RESTAURANT STORK   SEAFOOD €€

Map p319 (☑020-634 40 00; www.restaurant stork.nl; Gedempt Hamerkanaal 201; mains €13-27; ⊙11am-midnight, closed Mon Oct-Mar; ⊛IJ-plein, ⓂNoorderpark) A sometime factory on the IJ River, this huge place has a dramatically soaring interior and a cool waterfront terrace shaded with sails. It feels right that Stork should specialise in fish and seafood (though there are a few veggie and meat dishes too), serving especially good crab

legs as well as other crustaceans and fish of the day.

IL PECORINO   ITALIAN €€

Map p319 (☑020-737 15 11; www.ilpecorino.nl; Van der Pekplein 11; mains €16.50-19.50, pizza €8.50-17; ⊙5-11pm Mon-Thu, 3-11pm Fri-Sun; ☑; ⊛Buiksloterweg) Vintage Italian prints on the wall and a black-and-white tiled floor give this smart Italian restaurant a '60s-inspired trattoria feel. Authentic thin-crust wood-fired pizza and pasta dishes such as pappardelle ragù with wild boar are on offer, and there's a kids menu, too.

HANGAR   INTERNATIONAL €€

Map p319 (☑020-363 86 57; www.hangar.am sterdam; Aambeeldstraat 36; lunch mains €9-21, dinner mains €21-24; ⊙10am-1am; ⊛IJplein, ⓂNoorderpark) Going by the name, it should come as no surprise that this restaurant is in a hangar. It's a relaxing choice on the water's edge, with a great deck and laid-back music, providing a beachy vibe. Dishes include crunchy and filling Ottolenghi-style salads, charcuterie platters, lamb with artichoke and garlic, and steak tartare.

MOON   INTERNATIONAL €€€

Map p319 (☑020-237 63 11; www.restaurant moon.nl; A'DAM Tower, Overhoeksplein 1; lunch 3-/4-/5-course menu €40/50/60, dinner 5-/6-/7-course menu €65/75/85; ⊙noon-2pm & 6-9pm; ⊛Buiksloterweg) The rather swanky revolving restaurant at the top of the A'DAM Tower (p200) is an undoubtedly cheesy but nevertheless enjoyable novelty experience. There's one revolution an hour, and the food is fairly fussy but good quality, with moon-themed dishes on the menu. Book ahead.

▼ DRINKING & NIGHTLIFE

Amsterdam Noord has some of the city's most fabulous bars on the waterfront, built from shipping containers, on boats, or with their own beaches and gardens. There are also some top craft beer breweries to check out.

★CAFÉ DE CEUVEL   CAFE

Map p319 (☑020-229 62 10; www.deceuvel.nl; Korte Papaverweg 4; ⊙11am-midnight Tue-Thu & Sun, to 2am Fri & Sat; ☑34/35 Mosplein, ⓂNoorderpark) Tucked in a former shipyard and

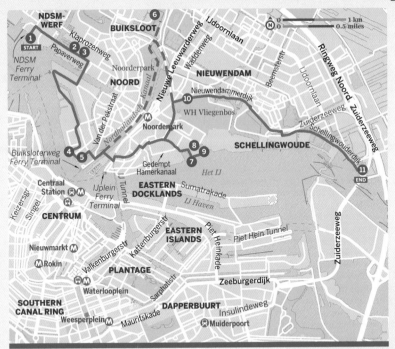

Neighbourhood Cycle
Amsterdam Noord

START NDSM-WERF
END LANDMARKT
LENGTH 12KM; 40 MINUTES TO TWO HOURS

As Amsterdam Noord is a large area and fairly spread out, it's a great idea to take a bike ride to some of the further flung parts, rather than pounding the pavement. You can rent bikes on this side of the river and there's a wide choice of cycle ways, too.

For a bike ride that takes in some of the highlights, catch a free ferry to ❶ **NDSM-werf** (p200), which was a booming ship-building area from 1870 until bankruptcy beckoned in 1984. Now it has a somewhat post-apocalyptic vibe and is a centre for counterculture and street art. Here you can explore the artists studios of Kunststad, see the Russian-built submarine B-80 lying empty in the harbour, and have a drink at one of the hip cafes in the area.

Next stop, visit the vintage shops on Papaverweg, including ❷ **Neef Louis Design** (p205) and ❸ **Van Dijk & Ko** (p205) to pick up a retro souvenir to take home. From here,

it's only around a five-minute cycle to reach the angular ❹ **EYE Film Institute** (p201) and the 1971 ❺ **A'DAM Tower** (p200). Check out the exhibitions at the film institute, whiz up to the top of the tower or continue along the river. You can either cycle inland along Noordhollandsch Kanaal to see the windmill ❻ **Krijtmolen d'Admiraal**, or stay on the riverbank, in which case you'll need to take your bike along the top of a lock gate (there's a narrow path) to continue. Beyond here, it's a few minutes' cycling to ❼ **FC Hyena** (p205), ❽ **Hotel de Goudfazant** (p201) and ❾ **Hangar**.

Next, the route goes a little inland, heading towards a wooded area, from where you turn right onto the top of a dyke. This leads you along the Noord's prettiest street, ❿ **Nieuwendammerdijk** (p200). Continue along the road that hugs the riverfront, until you reach the food emporium of ⓫ **Landmarkt** (p201), a superb halt for a drink or a snack, before backtracking or heading to eastern Amsterdam over Zuiderzeeweg bridge.

designed by architect Wouter Valkenier, built from recycled materials and with a focus on sustainability, this waterside spot is built out onto an island. With drinks including homemade lemongrass and ginger soda, plus bottled beer from local heroes Oedipus Brewery and Brouwerij 't IJ (p99), it's a surprising oasis alongside the canal.

The largely vegan menu (mains €6 to €12) is all about organic, homegrown and locally sourced food, with an ever-changing selection of daily specials.

★PLLEK   BAR

Map p319 (www.pllek.nl; TT Neveritaweg 59; ◷9.30am-1am Sun-Thu, to 3am Fri & Sat; ⊠NDSM-werf) Uber-cool Pllek is a Noord magnet, with hip things of all ages streaming over to hang out in its interior made of old shipping containers and, when the weather allows, lounge on its artificial sandy beach. It's a terrific spot for a waterfront beer or glass of wine.

Locals flock here for events, too: alfresco film screenings on Tuesday nights from June to August, Sunday morning yoga classes, and dance parties under the giant disco ball on Friday and Saturday nights. Organic vegetarian and certified-wild fish dishes do the job when hunger strikes (lunch dishes €8.50 to €13.50, evening mains €18 to €21.50). In colder weather, the indoor fireplace invites lingering.

CAFÉ NOORDERLICHT   CAFE

Map p319 (www.noorderlichtcafe.nl; NDSM-plein 102; ◷11am-midnight; ⊞; ⊠NDSM-werf) The original Café Noorderlicht was in a boat, which burned down. Safely ensconced in a soaring greenhouse, with grassy waterside lawns outside and a ministage, it now has a pub-garden-meets-festival vibe. There's a big play area outside so it's good for families. Tasty food with lots of veg options, craft beers, cocktails and coffee are all on the menu.

WALHALLA TAPROOM   BREWERY

Map p319 (www.walhallacraftbeer.nl; Spijkerkade 10; ◷4-11pm Fri, 2-11pm Sat, 2-8pm Sun; ⊠IJplein, ⓂNoorderpark) In an out-of-the-way industrial area, tiny Walhalla is a relaxed microbrewery that has quickly gained a reputation for its excellent beer. There are a few tables out front and the taproom has around 13 beers on tap, all named after gods, from the Loki golden ale to the Osiris

farmhouse ale. Try a tasting paddle of four beers from €10.

It was set up after a successful crowd-funding campaign to get it up and running. You can combine a trip here with a stop at Oedipus Brewery nearby.

COFFEE VIRUS A-LAB   COFFEE

Map p319 (☑020-244 23 41; www.thecoffeevirus.nl; Overhoeksplein 2; ◷9am-4.30pm Mon-Fri; ⊠; ⊠Buiksloterweg) Sharing a co-working start-up space called A-Lab with the University of Arts, this cool cafe made from mostly recycled materials is a convenient coffee stop next to A'DAM Tower. Coffee is divided into three flavour profiles – sweet, sour and bitter – and beans are sourced from local roasters. Pastries, banana bread, sandwiches, soups and salads are also on offer.

GARAGE NOORD   BAR

Map p319 (☑06 4210 8720; www.facebook.com/garagenrd; Gedempt Hamerkanaal 40; ◷6pm-5am Thu-Sat; ⓂNoorderpark) With its industrial setting, this small, laid-back venue has a rough-around-the-edges feel, very much in keeping with its neighbours on the up-and-coming Gedempt Hamerkanaal. Around midnight the space transforms from a casual cafe, restaurant and bar into a club playing host to a changing line-up of DJs.

CAFFÈ ITALIANO AL PONTE   CAFE

Map p319 (☑06 4208 7482; www.alponte.nl; Pontplein 1; ◷8am-5pm Mon-Fri, 10am-5pm Sat & Sun, reduced hrs Oct-Mar; ⊠IJplein) This little kiosk next to the IJplein ferry stop serves wonderful authentic Italian coffee. The friendly Italian owners also make excellent panino sandwiches, and there are a few tables so you can drink your coffee with a fabulous waterside view.

CAFÉ 'T SLUISJE   BROWN CAFE

Map p319 (☑020-636 17 12; www.cafehetsluisje.nl; Nieuwendammerdijk 297; ◷11am-1am Tue-Sun; ⊠; ⓂNoorderpark) The historic 'cafe of the lock' overlooks the *sluis* (lock) of its name in a very pretty spot with an inviting terrace. It serves a delicious apple tart and is a great place for a break.

OEDIPUS BREWERY & TAP ROOM BREWERY

Map p319 (www.oedipus.com; Gedempt Hamerkanaal 85; ◷5-10pm Thu, 2-11pm Fri & Sat, 2-10pm Sun; ⊠IJplein, ⓂNoorderpark) Oedipus began with four friends trying out some experimental brewing methods, and its brightly labelled bottles are now an Amsterdam institution. This converted warehouse space is a key Noord hangout, with outdoor seating lit by coloured fairy lights. Immerse yourself in some Oedipus history by sampling Mannenliefde ('Men Love'), its first-ever beer, flavoured with lemongrass, Szechuan pepper and Sorachi Ace hops.

Sensational burgers by the Beef Chief, including veggie options, are a perfect pairing (€10-13).

⭐ ENTERTAINMENT

FC HYENA
CINEMA

Map p319 (www.fchyena.nl; Aambeeldstraat 24; ⏲kitchen 6-9pm; 🚢IJplein, Ⓜ Noorderpark) Join Amsterdam's ocol crowd sipping natural wine on the waterfront terrace and dining on sophisticated snacks cooked in the wood-fired oven, before catching a film at this hot spot in a converted warehouse. All films, which are mainly art-house flicks, are shown in English, and lounges are spacious and comfy. Food and drink can be taken into the movie.

DE RUIMTE
ARTS CENTRE

Map p319 (www.cafederuimte.nl; Distelweg 83; tickets €5-10; ⏲5pm-1am Thu, 5pm-3am Fri, 4pm-1am Sun; 🚢IJplein, Ⓜ Noorderpark) This arts centre and cafe hosts a changing roster of events from jazz and poetry to experimental electronica. Friday nights usually offer live music you can put your dancin' shoes on for – Ethiopian jazz, rock 'n' roll, brass bands. The cafe serves a weekly changing menu of mostly vegan global dishes.

TOLHUISTUIN
LIVE PERFORMANCE

Map p319 (☎020-763 06 50; www.tolhuistuin.nl; IJpromenade 2; ⏲cafe 11am-late, restaurant 10am-10pm; 🚢Buiksloterweg) In what was the Shell workers' canteen for 70 years from 1941, the nifty Tolhuistuin arts centre hosts African dance troupes, spoken word, visual art and much more on its garden stage under twinkling lights. It also houses club nights and big-name gigs in the Paradiso venue.

On sunny days, the brightly coloured trestle tables at the venue's cafe are perfectly placed for a pre- or post-ferry drink. The 1st-floor THT restaurant offers share-plate-style dining, though the price-to-portion-size ratio is not always as satisfying as the arts and views in the rest of the venue.

 SHOPPING

Especially good for hunting down vintage or creative finds, Amsterdam Noord has increasing numbers of independent vendors hawking unusual stuff, as well as the city's best flea market. For a more local vibe, head to Van der Pekstraat, which hosts a number of weekly markets, including a Saturday market and an organic farmers market on Fridays.

IJ HALLEN
MARKET

Map p319 (www.ij-hallen.nl; NDSM-plein; ⏲9am-4.30pm Sat & Sun monthly; 🚢NDSM-werf) This whopping flea market takes place once a month, with 750 stalls outside in a huge area at NDSM-werf. It goes indoors into two NDSM warehouses from October to March, when there are a mere 500 stands. Check the website for the schedule. Admission is €5 for adults, €2 for children.

NEEF LOUIS DESIGN
VINTAGE

Map p319 (www.neeflouis.nl; Papaverweg 46; ⏲10am-6pm Tue-Sat; 🚢NDSM-werf) A huge warehouse full of vintage, designer and industrial furniture, this is a treasure trove of antique luggage, mid-century bookcases, retro radios, neon signs and much, much more.

VAN DIJK & KO
VINTAGE

Map p319 (www.vandijkenko.nl; Papaverweg 46; ⏲10am-6pm Tue-Sat, noon-6pm Sun; 🚢NDSM-werf) A warehouse full of interesting antiques and vintage furniture, wardrobes, glassware, prints and more for sale.

BLOM & BLOM
HOMEWARES

Map p319 (☎020-737 26 91; www.blomandblom.com; Chrysantenstraat 20; ⏲9am-5pm Mon-Fri; 🚢NDSM-werf) Repurposed German industrial lamps are on sale at this one-of-a-kind workshop, run by two brothers (hence, Blom & Blom). Each lamp has a description of where the fixture was found, the state it was in, its condition and its original purpose. They're costly, but glorious. It's best to call ahead as opening hours vary.

Day Trips from Amsterdam

Haarlem p207
Alleys wind among grand 17th-century buildings in this lively city, just a 15-minute hop from Amsterdam.

Leiden p210
Rembrandt's picturesque, canal-woven birthplace is home to the country's oldest and most prestigious university.

Keukenhof Gardens p211
See the world's largest, loveliest flower gardens in bloom during spring.

Delft p213
Delft's Gothic and Renaissance architecture rivals its beautiful Delftware pottery.

Zaanse Schans p216
Watch windmills twirl and meet the millers at this delightful open-air museum.

Haarlem

Explore

As you stroll from glorious art nouveau Haarlem Centraal train station (a national monument) to the old centre along Kruisweg and Kruisstraat, past exclusive boutiques, art galleries and antiques shops, the city's wealth and elegance soon become apparent. Stop off at the Corrie ten Boom House to pay homage to one of the Netherlands' most admired Renaissance figures before heading to the lively Grote Markt. Just a few blocks south is the Frans Hals Museum. Haarlem was once more important in the art world than Amsterdam, and this incomparable museum possesses one of the country's finest assemblies of Dutch paintings.

Given Haarlem's quick and easy access to Amsterdam, you can easily stay on for sunset drinks, catch live music and enjoy the city's buzzing nightlife.

The Best...

➡ **Sight** Frans Hals Museum
➡ **Place to Eat** Restaurant Mr & Mrs (p209)
➡ **Place to Drink** Jopenkerk (p209)

Top Tip

Try to visit on a Saturday when Haarlem's lively market is in full swing. There's also a market on Monday, but the Frans Hals Museum is closed.

Getting There & Away

Train Services from Amsterdam Centraal Station to Haarlem Centraal are frequent (€4.50, 15 minutes, up to eight per hour); the Grote Markt is an 850m walk south of the station. When the trains stop running at night, the N30 night bus links Haarlem Centraal Station to Schiphol Airport, Amsterdam.

Car From the ring road west of Amsterdam, take the N200, which becomes the A200.

Need to Know

➡ **Location** 20km west of Amsterdam
➡ **Rent a Bike Haarlem** (www.rentabikehaarlem.nl)
➡ **Tourist office** (VVV; ☎023-531 73 25; www.

◉ SIGHTS

★**GROTE KERK VAN ST BAVO** CHURCH
(www.bavo.nl; Oude Groenmarkt 22; adult/child €2.50/1.25; ☺10am-5pm Mon-Sat yr-round, noon-5pm Sun Jul & Aug) Topped by a towering 50m-high steeple, the Gothic Grote Kerk van St Bavo contains some fine Renaissance artworks, but the star attraction is its stunning Müller organ – one of the most magnificent in the world, standing 30m high and with about 5000 pipes, dating from 1738. It was played by Handel and a 10-year-old Mozart. Free hour-long **organ recitals** take place at 8.15pm Tuesday, 1.15pm Saturday and occasionally 4pm Thursday and 2.30pm Sunday from May to early October.

★**FRANS HALS MUSEUM – HOF** MUSEUM
(☎023-511 57 75; www.franshalsmuseum.nl; Groot Heiligland 62; adult/child incl Frans Hals Museum – Hal €16/free; ☺11am-5pm Tue-Sat, noon-5pm Sun) A must for anyone interested in the Dutch Masters, this superb museum is located in the poorhouse where Hals spent his final years. It focuses on the 17th-century Haarlem School; its pride and joy are eight group portraits of the Civic Guard that reveal Hals' exceptional attention to mood and psychological tone. Other greats represented here include Pieter Bruegel the Younger and Jacob van Ruisdael. Tickets include admission to the modern- and contemporary-art **Frans Hals Museum – Hal** (Grote Markt 16; ☺11am-5pm Tue-Sat, from noon Sun).

STADHUIS HISTORIC BUILDING
(Town Hall; Grote Markt 2) At the western end of the Grote Markt is the florid 14th-century town hall, which sprouted many extensions, including a balcony where judgements from the high court were pronounced. It only opens to the public on Open Monuments Day (the second weekend of September).

LAURENS COSTER STATUE STATUE
(Grote Markt) On the main square north of the Grote Kerk is the bronze Laurens Coster statue, installed in 1856. Haarlemmers believe that Coster has a claim, along with Gutenberg, to be called the inventor of movable type.

Haarlem

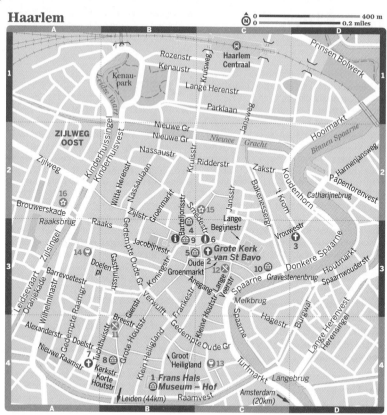

PROVENIERSHUIS HISTORIC BUILDING

(www.hofjesinhaarlem.nl; Grote Houtstraat 142d; ⏰10am-5pm Mon-Sat) **FREE** Off Grote Houtstraat southwest of the Grote Markt is one of Haarlem's prettiest buildings, the Proveniershuis. It started life as a *hofje* (almshouse) and for a time became the headquarters of St Joris Doelen (the Civic Guard of St George).

TEYLERS MUSEUM MUSEUM

(☑023-516 09 60; www.teylersmuseum.nl; Spaarne 16; adult/child €14/2; ⏰10am-5pm Tue-Fri, 11am-5pm Sat & Sun) Teylers (1778) is the country's oldest continuously operating museum. Its array of whizz-bang inventions includes an 18th-century electrostatic machine that conjures up visions of mad scientists. The eclectic collection also has paintings from the Dutch and French schools, and a magnificent, sky-lighted Oval Room displays natural-history specimens in elegant glass cases. Temporary exhibitions regularly take place. Admission includes an audioguide.

BAKENESSERKERK CHURCH

(www.stadsherstel.nl; cnr Vrouwestraat & Bakenesserstraat; ⏰1-4.30pm Mon-Fri, noon-4pm 3rd Sun of month) The striking Bakenesserkerk is a late-15th-century church with a lamplit tower of sandstone. The stone was employed here when the Grote Kerk proved too weak to support a heavy steeple – hence the wooden tower. Small art exhibitions take place here.

CORRIE TEN BOOM HOUSE HISTORIC BUILDING

(☑023-531 08 23; www.corrietenboom.com; Barteljorisstraat 19; by donation; ⏰10am-3.30pm Tue-Sat Apr-Oct, 11am-3pm Tue-Sat Nov-Mar) Known as 'the hiding place', the Corrie ten Boom House is named for the matriarch of a family who lived here during WWII. She hid hundreds of Jews and Dutch resistors in a secret compartment in her bedroom until they could be spirited to safety. In 1944 the family was betrayed and sent to concentration camps, where three died. Reserve hour-long tours at least five days ahead.

Haarlem

NIEUWE KERK   CHURCH
(www.bavo.nl; Nieuwe Kerksplein; ⊘10am-5pm Mon-Sat, noon-5pm Sun Jul & Aug, noon-5pm Mon-Sat Sep-Jun) Walk down charming Korte Houtstraat to Nieuwe Kerk; the ornate tower by Lieven de Key is supported by a rather boxy design by Jacob van Campen.

✕ EATING & DRINKING

DE HAERLEMSCHE VLAAMSE   FAST FOOD €
(www.dehaerlemschevlaamse.nl; Spekstraat 3; frites €1.80-5.20, sauces €0.80; ⊘11am-6.30pm Mon-Wed & Fri, to 9pm Thu, to 6pm Sat, noon-5pm Sun) Line up at this local institution for a cone of crispy, golden fries made from fresh potatoes, with one of a dozen sauces, including three kinds of mayonnaise.

★RESTAURANT MR & MRS   BISTRO €€
(☎023-531 59 35; www.restaurantmrandmrs.nl; Lange Veerstraat 4; small plates €11-13, 4-/5-/6-course menu €40/48/56; ⊘5.30-10pm Tue-Sun) Unexpectedly gastronomic cooking at this tiny restaurant is artfully conceived and presented. Small hot and cold plates designed for sharing, such as whiskey-poached

oysters with candied sea vegetables, sea bass and olive mille-feuille, and walnut-, pumpkin- and Gorgonzola-stuffed guinea fowl are followed by desserts like raspberry and pineapple tarte tatin. Book ahead.

BRICK   EUROPEAN €€
(☎023-551 18 70; www.restaurantbrick.nl; Breestraat 24-26; mains €15.50-21.50, 3-/4-/5-course menus €29.50/37.50/45; ⊘6-10pm) You can watch Brick's chefs preparing spectacular burgers, steaks and multicourse pan-European menus (wine pairings available) from the street-level dining room as well as the 1st-floor space, which has a glass floor directly above the open kitchen. There are pavement tables out front, but in summer the best seats are on the roof terrace.

★JOPENKERK   BREWERY
(www.jopenkerk.nl; Gedempte Voldersgracht 2; ⊘bar 10am-1am, cafe 10am-11pm, restaurant 5.30-9.30pm Tue-Sat) Haarlem's most atmospheric place to drink is this independent brewery in a stained-glass-windowed church. Enjoy brews such as citrusy Hopen, fruity Lente Bier and chocolatey Koyt along with bar snacks – *bitterballen* (meat-filled croquettes) and cheeses – beneath the gleaming copper vats. Head to the restaurant for dishes made from local, seasonal ingredients.

★DEDAKKAS   ROOFTOP BAR
(www.dedakkas.nl; 6th fl, Parkeergarage de Kamp, De Witstraat; ⊘9am-11pm Tue, Wed & Sun, to midnight Thu-Sat; 🛜) It looks like any other multistorey car park, but taking the lift to the 6th floor brings you out at this fabulous rooftop with a greenhouse-style glass cafe and timber terrace with views over Haarlem. Regular events include barbecues, cinema screenings, yoga, DJs and live-music gigs.

☆ ENTERTAINMENT

CAFÉ STIELS   LIVE MUSIC
(☎023-531 69 40; www.stiels.nl; Smedestraat 21; ⊘8pm-2am Sun-Wed, to 4am Thu-Sat) Bands play jazz and rhythm and blues on Café Stiels' back stage most nights from 10pm.

PATRONAAT   LIVE MUSIC
(☎023-517 58 58; www.patronaat.nl; Zijlsingel 2; ⊘hours vary) Haarlem's top music and dance club attracts bands, from country to punk. Events usually start around 10pm.

Leiden

Explore

As you walk south from Leiden's striking hyper-modern Centraal Station, the city's traditional character unfolds. A five-minute stroll takes you to Leiden's historic waterways, the most notable of which are the Oude Rijn and the Nieuwe Rijn.

Leiden is renowned for being Rembrandt's birthplace; the home of the Netherlands' illustrious university (Einstein was a regular professor) with a lively near-27,000-strong student population; and the place where America's Pilgrims raised money to lease the leaky Mayflower that took them to the New World in 1620.

The city's museums, all within walking distance of each other, are a key draw, as is wandering along the pretty canals.

The Best...

➡ **Sight** Museum De Lakenhal

➡ **Place to Eat** In den Doofpot (p213)

➡ **Place to Drink** Borgman & Borgman (p213)

Top Tip

Explore the university precinct, where one of Europe's oldest botanical gardens coexists with Leiden's buzzing student life.

Getting There & Away

Train Trains run from Amsterdam Centraal Station (€9.60, 35 minutes, five per hour).

Car Take the A4 from the southwest point of Amsterdam's A10 ring road.

Need to Know

➡ **Location** 45km southwest of Amsterdam

➡ **Oldenburger bike hire** (www.olden-burger.nl)

➡ **Tourist office** (☏071-516 60 00; www.visitleiden.nl; Stationsweg 26; ⊗7am-7pm Mon-Fri, 10am-4pm Sat, 11am-3pm Sun; ☏)

◉ SIGHTS

★**MUSEUM DE LAKENHAL**   MUSEUM
(☏071-516 53 60; www.lakenhal.nl; Oude Singel 32; adult/child €12.50/free; ⊗10am-5pm Tue-Sun)

Leiden's foremost museum reopened in 2019 following a lengthy renovation. Its 1640-built premises (a former cloth warehouse) displays its exceptional permanent art and history collection. Adjoining it, a striking new building hosts temporary exhibitions. The museum's masterpieces include *The Spectacles Pedlar* by the city's native son Rembrandt, *The Astronomer* by Gerrit Dou (Rembrandt's first student), *Playing Couple* by Jan Steen, and *The Last Judgement* by Lucas van Leyden,

★**RIJKSMUSEUM VAN OUDHEDEN**   MUSEUM
(National Museum of Antiquities; ☏071-516 31 63; www.rmo.nl; Rapenburg 28; adult/child €12.50/4; ⊗10am-5pm Tue-Sun) Home to the Rijksmuseum's collection of Greek, Etruscan, Roman and Egyptian artefacts, this museum is best known for its Egyptian halls, which include the reconstructed **Temple of Taffeh**, a gift from Anwar Sadat for helping to save ancient Egyptian monuments from flood. Other Egyptian exhibits include mastabas from Saqqara and a room of mummy cases. First-floor galleries are replete with Greek, Etruscan and Roman statuary and vases, as well as treasures from the ancient Near East.

★**RIJKSMUSEUM BOERHAAVE**   MUSEUM
(☏071-751 99 99; www.rijksmuseumboerhaave.nl; Lange St Agnietenstraat 10; adult/child €13/5.50; ⊗10am-5pm Tue-Sun, daily during school holidays) Named in honour of physician, botanist, chemist and University of Leiden teacher Herman Boerhaave (1668–1738), this impressive museum of science and medicine has exhibits profiling major scientific discoveries in the Netherlands, and the doctors and scientists behind them. The museum is housed in a 15th-century convent that later became the first academic hospital in Northern Europe, and a multimedia introduction is presented in a recreated anatomical theatre.

★**MUSEUM VOLKENKUNDE**   MUSEUM
(National Museum of Ethnology; www.volkenkunde.nl; Steenstraat 1; adult/child €15/6; ⊗10am-5pm Tue-Sun, daily during school holidays) Cultural achievements by civilisations worldwide are showcased here, with a collection of more than 300,000 artefacts from across the globe. Permanent galleries are dedicated to the cultures of Africa, the Arctic and North America, Asia, Central and South America, China, Indonesia, Japan and Korea, and Oceania. Highlights include the atmospherically lit Buddha Room next to the Japan

KEUKENHOF GARDENS

The 32-hectare **Keukenhof** (☑0252-465 555; www.keukenhof.nl; Stationsweg 166; adult/child €18/8, canal cruise €8/4; ⊙8am-7.30pm mid-Mar–mid-May) is the world's largest bulb-flower garden, with over seven million bulbs and a total of 800 varieties of tulips. It attracts around 1.5 million visitors during its eight-week season, when its fields and planted displays of multicoloured tulips, daffodils and hyacinths are in bloom. You can hire bikes outside the gardens (per day €15), or take a cruise from Keukenhof's windmill to view the floral kaleidoscope. Online tickets are slightly cheaper. It's 1km west of Lisse.

Keukenhof Express buses run from destinations including Europaplein at RAI in Amsterdam's south during the season; combination tickets are available.

and Korea section and the 'Mountain of the Immortals' carving in the China section. Temporary exhibitions are also impressive.

HORTUS BOTANICUS LEIDEN GARDENS

(☑071-527 51 44; www.hortusleiden.nl; Rapenburg 73; adult/child €7.50/3; ⊙10am-6pm Apr-Oct, to 4pm Tue-Sun Nov-Mar) Founded by the University of Leiden in 1590, this is one of Europe's oldest botanical gardens (the oldest was created in Padua, Italy, in 1545). The majority of its collections originate from Southeast and East Asia. Built structures include an 18th-century orangery and a tropical glasshouse constructed in 1938; more recent additions include a winter garden and Chinese herb garden. Its orchid greenhouses are closed on weekends.

PIETERSKERK CHURCH

(☑071-512 43 19; www.pieterskerk.com; Kloksteeg 16; adult/child €4/free; ⊙11am-6pm) Crowned by its huge steeple, this now deconsecrated church is often under restoration – a good thing, as it has been prone to collapse since it was built in 1121. Its most distinctive feature is an unusual marble and stone floor.

The precinct includes the gabled **Latin School** (Lokhorststraat 16), which was attended by a pupil named Rembrandt from 1616 to 1620. Across the plaza, look for the **Gravensteen** (Pieterskerkhof 6), which dates from the 13th century and was once a prison. The gallery facing the plaza was where judges watched executions.

LEIDEN AMERICAN PILGRIM MUSEUM MUSEUM

(☑071-512 24 13; www.leidenamericanpilgrimmuseum.org; Beschuitsteeg 9; adult/child €5/free; ⊙1-5pm Thu-Sat) This museum is a fascinating restoration of a one-room house occupied around 1610 by the soon-to-be Pilgrims. The house itself dates from 1365–70 (check out the original 14th-century floor tiles), but

the furnishings are from the Pilgrims' period. Curator Jeremy Bangs is an author who has written extensively on the Pilgrims and has a vast knowledge of their Leiden links.

BURCHT VAN LEIDEN PARK

(⊙sunrise-sunset) **FREE** This 11th-century citadel on a *motte* (raised earthwork) surrendered its protective function as the city grew around it and subsequently fell into disrepair. Now a shell, it has been transformed into a park commanding views over Leiden.

LEIDEN UNIVERSITY UNIVERSITY

(www.universiteitleiden.nl; Rapenburg) The country's oldest university was a gift to Leiden from Willem the Silent in 1575 for withstanding two Spanish sieges in 1573 and 1574. The campus comprises an interesting mix of modern and antique buildings that are scattered around town.

DE VALK MUSEUM

(The Falcon; ☑071-516 53 53; www.molenmuseumdevalk.nl; 2e Binnenvestgracht 1; adult/child €5/2.50; ⊙10am-5pm Tue-Sat, 1-5pm Sun) Leiden's landmark tower windmill – built in 1743 and now a museum – is considered one of the best examples of its kind. Its arms still occasionally rotate, but the last grain was ground here in 1965. Upstairs, an audiovisual presentation imparts plenty of information about windmills in the Netherlands.

NATURALIS BIODIVERSITY CENTRE MUSEUM

(☑071-751 96 00; www.naturalis.nl; Darwinweg 2; €16; ⊙10am-5pm) This museum's sections span botany, geology, entomology (insects), invertebrates, vertebrates and palaeontology (fossils and more) collected all over the globe by Dutch explorers, archaeologists and scientists. It also houses a T-Rex skeleton.

Leiden

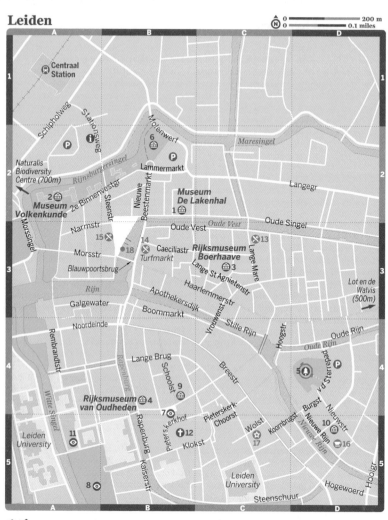

⚔ EATING & DRINKING

OUDT LEYDEN
CRÊPES €

(☑071-513 31 44; www.oudtleyden.nl; Steenstraat 49; pancakes €7-16; ⊙11.30am-9.30pm; 🚲🚻) The giant Dutch-style pancakes here widen the eyes of kids and adults alike. Whether you're after something savoury (marinated salmon, sour cream and capers), sweet (apple, ginger and powdered sugar) or simply adventurous (ginger and bacon), this welcoming place hits the spot every time. Vegetarian options are plentiful; children's pancakes cost €4 to €6.25.

BRASSERIE DE ENGELENBAK
EUROPEAN €€

(☑071-512 54 40; www.deengelenbak.nl; Lange Mare 38; dishes €7-13, dinner mains €17-22; ⊙restaurant 11am-10pm Tue-Sun, bar 11am-midnight) In the shadow of the 17th-century Marekerk, this elegant brasserie's menu changes seasonally, and might feature smoked duck with stout sauce or baked halibut with chorizo. Tables outside enjoy views of the passing crowds. Its adjoining *café* (pub) serves salads (such as roast beetroot and goat's cheese), sandwiches (eg avocado, tempeh and roast cauliflower) and light dishes like quiches.

Leiden

LOT EN DE WALVIS   INTERNATIONAL €€

(☏071-763 03 83; www.lotendewalvis.nl; Haven 1; dishes €8.50-10.50, mains €14.50-20.50; ☺9am-10pm Mon-Fri, to 1am Sat & Sun; ☎) The sun-drenched terrace at the water's edge, friendly staff and excellent food (such as quinoa and pomegranate salad or garlic-and lime-marinated cod burgers,) make this cafe in the handsome 1889 De Volharding warehouse a Leiden hotspot.

★IN DEN DOOFPOT   EUROPEAN €€€

(☏071-512 24 34; www.indendoofpot.nl; Turfmarkt 9; mains €35, 3-/4-course lunch menu €45/55, 4-/5-/6-course dinner menu €60/70/80; ☺12.30-3pm & 5-10pm Mon-Fri, 5-10pm Sat; ☏) Given the sky-high calibre of chef Patrick Brugman's food, advance reservations here are essential. This is extremely creative cooking, with monthly changing menus featuring dishes such as smoked tzatziki with green apple, sesame-crusted ox tail with ginger and shallot sauce, or sea bass with razor-clam vinaigrette. Vegetarian menus are available on request, as are by-the-glass wine pairings.

★BORGMAN & BORGMAN   CAFE

(☏071-566 55 37; www.borgmanborgman.nl; Nieuwe Rijn 41; ☺9am-5pm Mon, 8am-6pm Tue-Sat,10.30am-5pm Sun; ☎) The Giesen W6 roaster in the window signals that this hip cafe is serious about its coffee, and its baristas deliver on this promise. There's also a small menu of breakfast dishes, sandwiches (€4.50 to €7.50) and toasties. The music on the sound system is excellent and the canal-side terrace catches the sun all day.

 ENTERTAINMENT

DRANKLOKAAL DE WW   LIVE MUSIC

(www.deww.nl; Wolsteeg 4; ☺2pm-2am Sun-Wed, to 3am Thu, to 4am Fri & Sat; ☎) On Friday and Saturday, live rock in this bar can expand to a stage in the alley, with crowds trailing up to the main street. On other nights DJs play. Though the emphasis is on music, there's a great beer selection. Cash only.

🏃 SPORTS & ACTIVITIES

REDERIJ REMBRANDT   CRUISE

(☏071-513 49 38; www.rederijrembrandt.nl; Blauwpoortshaven 5; adult/child 4-12yr/child under 4yr €10/6.50/2.50; ☺11.30am-4pm Mar-Oct) One-hour cruises of the canals around the old-town centre are accompanied by multilingual commentary (including English).

Delft

Explore

Compact and charming, Delft is synonymous with its blue-and-white-painted porcelain. It's very popular with visitors strolling its narrow canals, gazing at the remarkable old buildings and meditating on the career of Golden Age painter Johannes Vermeer, who was born and lived here, so getting an early start helps beat the crowds.

Delft

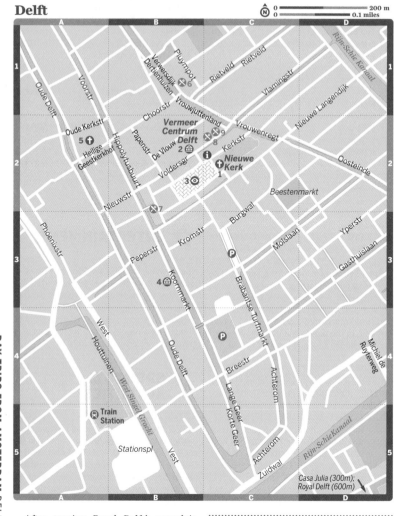

N
0 ————————— 200 m
0 ————————— 0.1 miles

After touring Royal Delft's porcelain factory, Koninklijke Porceleyne Fles, pick up a walking tour brochure from the tourist office and explore the city's riches at your own pace. Be sure to allow time for shopping, eating and drinking around the Markt.

Excellent-value hotels cater to visitors who want to linger.

The Best

➡ **Sight** Vermeer Centrum Delft
➡ **Place to Eat** Kek
➡ **Place to Drink** De Waag (p216)

Top Tip

It's not all Delftware and Vermeer: take time to wander the streets of one of the Netherlands' most exquisite cities, a treasure trove of Gothic and Renaissance architecture.

Getting There & Away

Train Services between Amsterdam Centraal Station and Delft are frequent (€13.80, one hour, four per hour).

Car From the A4 take A13/E19, which passes through Delft en route to Rotterdam.

Delft

Need to Know

➡ **Location** 55km southwest of Amsterdam

➡ **Delft by Cycle** (www.delftbycycle.nl)

➡ **Tourist office** (☎015-215 40 52; www.delft. com; Kerkstraat 3; ☺10am-5pm Tue-Sat, to 4pm Sun & Mon Apr-Sep, 10am-4pm Tue-Sat, 11am-3pm Sun & Mon Oct-Mar)

◉ SIGHTS

★**VERMEER CENTRUM DELFT**   MUSEUM
(☎015-213 85 88; www.vermeerdelft.nl; Voldersgracht 21; adult/child €9/5; ☺10am-5pm) Vermeer was born in Delft in 1632 and lived here until his death in 1675. Although none of his works remain in Delft, this centre exhibits reproductions of his paintings, screens a short film about his life, and has displays on 17th-century painting techniques and materials. Audioguides and guided tours at 10.30am on Sunday are free. The centre sells maps for the Vermeer Cube Walk, which guides you to Vermeer information points around town.

★**NIEUWE KERK**   CHURCH
(New Church; www.oudeennieuwekerkdelft.nl; Markt 80; adult/child incl Oude Kerk €5.50/1.50, tower €4.50/2.50, incl Oude Kerk & tower €8.50/3.50; ☺9am-6pm Mon-Sat Apr-Oct, 11am-4pm Mon-Fri, 10am-5pm Sat Nov-Jan, 10am-5pm Mon-Sat Feb & Mar) Construction of Nieuwe Kerk lasted from 1381 to 1655. The church has been the final resting place of almost every member of the House of Orange since 1584, including William of Orange (Willem the Silent), who lies in a marble mausoleum. Children under five are not permitted to climb the 109m-high tower, whose 376 narrow, spiralling steps lead to panoramic views.

OUDE KERK   CHURCH
(Old Church; www.oudeennieuwekerkdelft.nl; Heilige Geestkerkhof 25; adult/child incl Nieuwe Kerk €5.50/1.50, incl Nieuwe Kerk & Nieuwe Kerk tower €8.50/3.50; ☺9am-6pm Mon-Sat Apr-Oct, 11am-4pm Mon-Fri, 10am-5pm Sat Nov-Jan, 10am-5pm Mon-Sat Feb & Mar) Founded c 1246, Oude Kerk is a surreal sight: its 75m-high tower leans nearly 2m due to subsidence due to its canal location, hence its nickname Scheve Jan ('Leaning John'). The older section features an austere barrel vault; the newer northern transept has a Gothic vaulted ceiling. One of the tombs in the church is that of Vermeer.

MARKT   SQUARE
One of the largest historic market squares in Europe, rectangular Markt was first paved in the late 15th century. It is edged by the town hall, Nieuwe Kerk, cafes, boutiques and souvenir shops. A market is held on Thursday.

ROYAL DELFT   FACTORY
(Koninklijke Porceleyne Fles; ☎015-760 08 00; www.royaldelft.com; Rotterdamseweg 196; adult/child €14/8.75; ☺9am-5pm mid-Mar–Oct, 9am-5pm Mon-Sat, noon-5pm Sun Nov–mid-Mar) The town's most famous earthenware factory has been handcrafting its blue-and-white porcelain since 1653. Admission includes an audioguide that leads you through a painting demonstration, the museum and the factory's production process. For many the tour highlight is the gift shop. It's 1.5km south of the Markt.

MUSEUM PAUL TETAR VAN ELVEN   MUSEUM
(☎015-212 42 06; www.tetar.nl; Koornmarkt 67; adult/child €5/free; ☺1-5pm Tue-Sun) This is the former studio and home of 19th-century artist Paul Tetar van Elven, who lived and worked here from 1864 until 1894. The museum features his reproductions of notable paintings (his speciality), along with antique furniture, oriental porcelain and Delftware he collected. The evocative interior retains its original furnishings and lived-in feel.

✖ EATING & DRINKING

★**KEK**   CAFE €
(www.kekdelft.nl; Voldersgracht 27; dishes €4-10.50; ☺8.30am-6pm; 🛜🍴) On this stylish cafe's menu you will find fresh juices, fruit smoothies and a tempting array of cakes,

muffins and sandwiches made with local seasonal produce (vegan, sugar-free and gluten-free options available). It also offers all-day breakfasts and coffee made using Rotterdam-roasted Giraffe beans.

PURO CUCINA   CAFE €

(www.purocucina.nl; Voldersgracht 28; dishes €5.50-14; ☺9am-6pm Wed-Mon; 🤶) A sleek, modern interior is arranged around an open kitchen. The menu includes breakfast favourites (pancakes with ricotta and honey, granola with yoghurt and fruit), simple yet tasty lunch dishes such as salads and a daily pasta dish, and cake with coffee.

DE WAAG   CAFE €€

(📞015-213 03 93; www.de-waag.nl; Markt 11; cafe mains €7.50-20, restaurant mains €24; ☺kitchen 10am-10pm, bar to 1am; 🤶) With a sprawling terrace behind the town hall and housed in an atmospheric 16th-century *waag* (weighing house), this is perfect for a post-sightseeing beer. The food is well above average – either in the upmarket 1st-floor restaurant (dinner only) or in the casual cafe downstairs.

BRASSERIE 'T CRABBETJE   SEAFOOD €€

(📞015-213 88 50; www.crabbetjedelft.nl; Verwersdijk 14; mains €19.50-35.50, 3-/4-course menu €36.50/45.50; ☺5.30-10pm Wed-Sun; 🤶🍴) Sustainably sourced seafood is given the gourmet treatment at this unassuming restaurant. A kids menu costs €14.50.

🛏 SLEEPING

CASA JULIA   B&B €€

(📞015-256 76 12; www.casajulia.nl; Maerten Trompstraat 33; s/d/ste/f from €65/75/115/155; 🤶) This boutique B&B in a 1920s building is the most stylish and comfortable accommodation in Delft, offering 24 rooms with TV, work desk and tea. Most are small, so opt for a 'comfort' option if possible. It also has a suite with a balcony and kitchenette, and two family rooms. Breakfast costs €12.

Zaanse Schans

Explore

People come for an hour and stay for several. It's a prime place to see windmills operating, though only a few of the 1000 or so windmills

formerly in the area have been restored. One of the six working windmills sells fat jars of its freshly ground mustard, while the others turn out oils, flour and sawn planks. Most are open for inspection, and it's a delight to clamber about the creaking works.

Top Tip

Hire a bike and pedal from Amsterdam to Zaanse Schans. The 90-minute picturesque journey is a highlight of many a holiday.

Getting There & Away

Train From Amsterdam Centraal Station (€3.30, 18 minutes, four per hour) take the train towards Alkmaar and get off at Zaandijk Zaanse Schans – it's a well-signposted 1.5km walk to Zaanse Schans.

Car Travel to the northwestern side of Amsterdam on the A10 ring road and take the A8 turn-off. Exit at Zaandijk.

Need to Know

➡ **Location** 22km northwest of Amsterdam

➡ **Fietsverhuur Zaanse Schans bike rental** (www.zaanseschansbikerent.nl)

➡ **Tourist office** (📞075-681 00 00; www.zaanseschans.nl; Zaans Museum, Schansend 7; ☺9am-5pm Apr-Sep, 10am-5pm Oct-Mar)

👁 SIGHTS

⭐ZAANSE SCHANS
WINDMILLS   WINDMILLS

(📞075-681 00 00; www.dezaanseschans.nl; Kalverringdijk; per windmill adult/child €5/2.50; ☺most windmills 9am-5pm Apr-Oct, hours vary Nov-Mar) The working, inhabited village Zaanse Schans functions as a windmill gallery on the Zaan river. You can explore the authentic windmills at your own pace, seeing the vast moving parts firsthand. Individual windmill opening hours vary.

One mill has paint pigments for sale – you can see the materials used in Renaissance masterpieces turned into powders.

The other buildings have been brought here from all over the country to recreate a 17th-century community. There's a cheese maker, early Albert Heijn market, and a clog factory (with a surprisingly interesting museum). The engaging pewter-smith will explain the story behind dozens of tiny figures while the soft metal sets in the moulds.

Sleeping

In its typically charming way, Amsterdam has hotels in wild and wonderful spaces: New life has been breathed into old buildings, from converted schools and industrial lofts to entire rows of canal houses. Many lodgings overlook gorgeous waterways or courtyards. But charm doesn't come cheap, and places fill fast – reserve far ahead, especially for summer and weekends.

Hotels

Any hotel with more than 20 rooms is considered large, and most rooms are on the snug side. A 'star' plaque on the front of every hotel indicates its rating (from one to five stars) according to the Hotelstars Union (www.hotelstars.eu). Its new criteria will take effect from 2020 and be in place from 2021; see the website for details.

Wi-fi is nearly universal across the spectrum, but air-conditioning and lifts (elevators) are not.

BUDGET

Other than hostels, lodgings in the lowest price bracket, with furnishings that are, at best, cheap and cheerful, are thin on the ground. Rates often include a simple breakfast.

Some basic budget lodgings welcome party guests as well as pot smokers (in smoking lounges, not in rooms). Check whether smoking marijuana is permitted when booking. Many hotels have strict no-drugs policies.

MIDRANGE

Most of these properties are low on formality. Not many midrange hotels of more than two storeys have lifts, and their narrow, ladder-like staircases can take some getting used to, especially with luggage. Increasingly, breakfast costs extra.

TOP-END

Expect lifts, minibars and room service. The most luxurious have air-conditioning and fitness centres. Breakfast is rarely included.

B&Bs & Houseboats

Most B&Bs don't have exterior signage, with access by reservation only. Several are on houseboats. Despite the name, many B&Bs don't serve breakfast.

Hostels

Jeugdherbergen (youth hostels) are plentiful. The Netherlands hostel association goes by the name Stayokay (www.stayokay.com) and is affiliated with Hostelling International (HI; www.hihostels.com). Independent luxury hostels are prevalent, too.

Apartment Rentals

Amsterdam's authorities have ruled that private properties (including Airbnb listings) can only be rented by up to four people at a time for a maximum of 30 days per year in total (and only direct from the owner; sublets aren't allowed). Council checks regularly take place; guests in illegally rented properties can be removed. Apartment rentals can be expensive; serviced-apartment complexes, such as Yays (www.yays.com), or a hotel may work out cheaper.

A great alternative is **SWEETS Hotel** (☐020-740 10 10; www.sweetshotel.amsterdam; d from €160; ☎), comprising 28 of the city's canal-bridge houses, which have been converted into two-person apartments. They're equipped with fridges, cutlery, crockery and water views; two have kitchenettes. You're emailed a password for a Bluetooth app to gain access. Guests must be over 21.

NEED TO KNOW

Price Ranges
The following price ranges are for an en-suite double room in high season (excluding breakfast).

€	less than €100
€€	€100–€180
€€€	more than €180

Useful Websites
➡ **Lonely Planet** (lonely planet.com/the-nether lands/amsterdam/hotels) Recommendations and bookings.

➡ **I Amsterdam** (www. iamsterdam.com) Wide range of options from the city's official website.

Reservations
➡ Book as far ahead as possible, especially for festival, summer and weekend visits.

➡ Many hotels offer discounts if you book directly via their websites.

➡ There's often a minimum stay of two or three nights, especially at weekends and during major events.

Tipping
Tipping is not expected, though at larger hotels the porter often receives a euro or two, and the room cleaner gets a few euros for a job well done.

Tax
Properties often include the 7% *toeristenbelasting* (tourist tax) in quoted rates, but ask before booking. If you're paying by credit card, some hotels add a surcharge of up to 5%.

Lonely Planet's Top Choices

Hotel Not Hotel (p225) Students from Eindhoven's Design Academy designed these wildly artistic spaces.

Volkshotel (p228) Designer hotel in a former newspaper building with a fabulous rooftop bar.

Sir Albert Hotel (p227) Diamond factory converted to sparkly design hotel.

Ambassade Hotel (p222) Golden Age canal houses shelter this exquisite hotel with original CoBrA art on the walls.

Best by Budget

€
Cocomama (p222) Red-curtained boutique hostel in a former brothel.

Generator Amsterdam (p228) Designer hostel overlooking Oosterpark.

St Christopher's at the Winston (p220) Buzzing Red Light District hangout with an on-site nightclub.

Christian Youth Hostel 'The Shelter Jordan' (p224) An oasis of sobriety.

€€
Hotel Fita (p225) Sweet little family-owned hotel a stone's throw from the Museumplein.

Hotel V (p223) Retro-chic hotel facing lush Frederiksplein.

Conscious Hotel Westerpark (p224) Eco innovations include recycled materials at this Westerpark hotel inside a national monument.

€€€
Hotel Okura Amsterdam (p227) Rare-for-Amsterdam elevated views and four Michelin stars in the building.

Toren (p222) Blends 17th-century opulence with a sensual decadence.

Pillows Anna van den Vondel (p226) Gorgeous boutique hotel in a trio of 19th-century mansions.

Best Canal Views

Seven Bridges (p223) One of the city's most exquisite little hotels on one of its loveliest canals.

Linden Hotel (p224) A Jordaan gem.

Hotel Estheréa (p221) Olde-worlde grandeur in Golden Age canal houses.

Best Only in Amsterdam

SWEETS Hotel (p217) Live like Amsterdam's bridge keepers once did in one of 28 converted canal-bridge houses.

Faralda Crane Hotel (p228) Inside a crane in Amsterdam Noord.

Mr Jordaan (p224) Design elements include bedheads shaped like gabled Amsterdam canal houses.

De Dageraad (p221) Boutique B&B houseboat moored in the Eastern Docklands.

Best Design Savvy

Hotel Notting Hill (p223) A lobby wall of vintage suitcases is among designer Wim Hoopman's touches.

Hotel Not Hotel (p225) Design academy students put together rooms that are eye-popping art installations.

Andaz Amsterdam (p222) A wonderland envisioned by iconic Dutch designer Marcel Wanders.

Sir Adam (p228) Designer rooms inside the A'DAM Tower.

Where to Stay

NEIGHBOURHOOD	FOR	AGAINST
Medieval Centre & Red Light District	In the thick of the action; close to sights, nightlife, theatres and transport.	Can be noisy, touristy and seedy; not great value for money.
Nieuwmarkt, Plantage & the Eastern Islands	Nieuwmarkt is near the action, but slightly more low-key than the Medieval Centre. Plantage hotels are amid quiet greenery.	Parts of Nieuwmarkt are close enough to the Red Light District to get rowdy spillover. Plantage and especially Eastern Islands lodgings can be a hike from the major sights, requiring a tram or bike ride.
Western Canal Ring	Tree-lined canals; charming boutiques and cafes. Within walking distance of Amsterdam's most popular sights.	Given all the positives, rooms book out early and are invariably pricey.
Southern Canal Ring	Swanky hotels, central location, handy for the restaurants of Utrechtsestraat.	Can be loud, crowded, pricey and touristy, especially around the high-traffic nightlife areas of Leidseplein and Rembrandtplein
Jordaan & the West	Cosy cafes, quirky shops and charming village character.	Sleeping options are few, due in part to the paucity of big-name sights close by.
Vondelpark & the South	Genteel, leafy streets; often walking distance to Museumplein; small, gracious properties; lots of midrange options and cool design hotels.	Limited nightlife in the South; prices around the Vondelpark often high end.
De Pijp	Ongoing explosion of dining/drinking venues; located near Museumplein and the Southern Canal Ring; fast metro access to the centre.	Options are fairly limited.
Oosterpark & East of the Amstel	Lower prices due to remote location (albeit just a short tram/metro ride from the Medieval Centre); quiet area amid locals.	Fewer options for dining and drinking.
Amsterdam Noord	Some truly unique properties; burgeoning drinking, dining and creative scene.	Transport limited in some areas.

🛏 Medieval Centre & Red Light District

ST CHRISTOPHER'S AT THE WINSTON
HOSTEL €

Map p290 (☑020-623 13 80; www.st-christo phers.co.uk; Warmoesstraat 129; dm/s/d from €32/97/121; @ 🛜; 🚊4/14/24 Dam) This place hops 24/7 with rock 'n' roll rooms, a busy nightclub (p80) with live bands nightly, a bar and restaurant, a beer garden and a smoking deck downstairs. En-suite dorms sleep up to eight. Local artists were given free rein on the rooms; results range from super-edgy (entirely stainless steel) to questionably raunchy. Rates include breakfast (and earplugs!).

FLYING PIG DOWNTOWN HOSTEL
HOSTEL €

Map p290 (☑020-420 68 22; www.flyingpig.nl; Nieuwendijk 100; dm €35-64, d from €137; @ 🛜; 🚊2/4/11/12/13/14/17/24/26 Centraal Station) Hang out with hundreds of young dope-smoking backpackers at this very relaxed, massive 250-bed hostel. It's a bit grungy, but no one seems to mind, especially when there's so much fun to be had in the throbbing lobby bar. There are also full kitchen facilities and a cushion-lined basement nicknamed the 'happy room'. Weekend bookings require a minimum three-night stay.

HOTEL THE EXCHANGE
DESIGN HOTEL €€

Map p290 (☑020-523 00 80; www.hotelthe exchange.com; Damrak 50; d from €147; @ 🛜; 🚊2/4/11/12/13/14/17/24/26 Centraal Station) Opposite the former stock exchange (hence the hotel's name), these 61 rooms have been dressed 'like models' in eye-popping style by students from the Amsterdam Fashion Institute. Anything goes, from oversized-button-adorned walls to a Marie Antoinette dress tented over the bed. Its one- to five-star rooms range from small and viewless to sprawling sanctums, but all have en-suite bathrooms.

A-TRAIN HOTEL
HOTEL €€

Map p290 (☑020-624 19 42; www.atrain hotel.nl; Prins Hendrikkade 23; s/d/tr/f from €110/160/188/300; @ 🛜; 🚊2/4/11/12/13/14/17/24/26 Centraal Station) Reflecting its unbeatable location facing Centraal Station, the train theme at this old-fashioned, family-run hotel extends from the clocks, photographs and memorabilia at reception

to the train-track-painted floor leading to the breakfast room with railway-carriage-style booths (rates include continental breakfast). Its 34 dark-timber-furnished rooms include two four-person family rooms with kitchenettes.

HOTEL RÉSIDENCE LE COIN
APARTMENT €€

Map p294 (☑020-524 68 00; www.lecoin.nl; Nieuwe Doelenstraat 5; apt from €175; 🛜; Ⓜ Rokin) Owned by the University of Amsterdam, Hotel Résidence Le Coin has 42 high-class (albeit small) apartments spread over seven historical buildings, all equipped with designer furniture, wood floors, fast wi-fi and kitchenettes – and all reachable by lift. It's superbly located just a five-minute stroll to pretty Nieuwmarkt.

HOTEL LUXER
HOTEL €€

Map p290 (☑020-330 32 05; www.hotelluxer.nl; Warmoesstraat 11; d/tr from €150/225; ✳🛜; 🚊2/4/11/12/13/14/17/24/26 Centraal Station) A pleasant surprise, this smart little number offers some of the best value for money in the thick of the Red Light District. Its 47 rooms are small but well equipped (air-con!), and at night the breakfast area becomes a chic little bar. Breakfast costs €9 if you book in advance (otherwise it's €12.50).

⭐ HOTEL V NESPLEIN
DESIGN HOTEL €€€

Map p294 (☑020-662 32 33; www.hotelvnes plein.nl; Nes 49; d/ste from €196/279; ✳🛜; Ⓜ Rokin, 🚊4/14/24 Rokin) Vintage and designer furniture fills the public areas and rooms of this hotel in a fantastic location on theatre-lined Nes. Spacious rooms start at 18 sq metres and have wooden floors, exposed-brick walls and rain showers in the sleek bathrooms (some also have bathtubs). Its industrial-styled restaurant, the Lobby, serves creative modern Dutch cuisine.

INK HOTEL AMSTERDAM
DESIGN HOTEL €€€

Map p290 (☑020-627 59 00; www.accorhotels. com; Nieuwezijds Voorburgwal 67; d/ste from €190/322; ✳🛜; 🚊2/11/12/13/17 Nieuwezijds Kolk) Occupying the 1904 to 1986 premises of Dutch Catholic newspaper (and later magazine) *De Tijd* (*The Time*), Ink honours its journalistic heritage with printing plates, old typewriters and vintage editions on the walls of its bar-restaurant, the Pressroom. Leading Amsterdam architectural firm Concrete designed its 149 rooms with features such as blackboard-style murals. The basement gym opens 24 hours.

★ W AMSTERDAM
DESIGN HOTEL €€€

Map p294 (📞020-811 25 00; www.marriott.com; Spuistraat 175; d/ste from €358/508; ❊@🛜❊; 🚇2/11/12/13/17 Dam) Designer hotel chain W's Amsterdam premises occupy two landmark buildings, the Royal Dutch Post's former telephone exchange, and a former bank – part of which now houses Dutch design mega-store X Bank (p84). Its 238 rooms (including connecting family rooms and 28 suites) combine design and vintage elements; there's a state-of-the-art spa, a gym, an amazing rooftop lap pool, restaurants and bars.

HOTEL TWENTY SEVEN
LUXURY HOTEL €€€

Map p294 (📞020-218 21 80; www.hoteltwenty seven.com; Dam 27; ste from €595; ❊🛜; 🚇4/14/24 Dam) In a monumental 1916 building on the Dam overlooking the Royal Palace, this ultra-luxury hotel opened in 2018. Starting at 40 sq metres and stretching up to 219 sq metres, its 16 sumptuous suites have oak floors, Nepalese carpets, handwoven Italian fabrics and original CoBrA art, as well as a personal butler. Downstairs is a Michelin-starred restaurant and cocktail bar.

HOTEL ESTHERÉA
HOTEL €€€

Map p294 (📞020-624 51 46; www.estherea.nl; Singel 303-309; d/f/ste from €255/355/425; 🅿❊🛜; 🚇2/11/12 Spui) Olde-worlde grandeur reigns at this hotel spread over several Golden Age canal houses. Each of its 91 rooms is unique, with mahogany panelling, chandeliers, and richly patterned fabrics and wallpapers. Some have canal views and others overlook the leafy courtyard; ground-floor suites have patios and Jacuzzis. There's a gym, library and 24-hour bar. Parking costs €55; breakfast is €18.

🛏 Nieuwmarkt, Plantage & the Eastern Islands

CHRISTIAN YOUTH HOSTEL 'THE SHELTER CITY'
HOSTEL €

Map p296 (📞020-625 32 30; www.shelter hostelamsterdam.com; Barndesteeg 21; dm €22.90-27.40; @🛜; Ⓜ Nieuwmarkt) Extremely convenient for central Amsterdam, this rambling Christian-run hostel is just outside the Red Light District, but a world away, powered by religious zeal and operating a no-drugs-or-alcohol policy. If you can handle this, the payback is spick-and-span

single-sex dorms (two to 20 beds, some with in-room bathrooms), free breakfasts, and a peaceful cafe and garden courtyard.

★ LLOYD HOTEL
BOUTIQUE HOTEL €€

Map p298 (📞020-561 36 07; www.lloydhotel.com; Oostelijke Handelskade 34; d/ste from €140/218; @🛜; 🚇26 Rietlandpark) Magnificent waterside Lloyd was a hotel for emigrants from the Netherlands, who stayed here before setting sail, back in 1921. Many original fixtures remain, alongside contemporary art installations and design. The one- to five-star rooms range from budget with shared bathrooms to racquetball-court-sized top-end extravaganzas with unique features (foldaway bathrooms, a giant bed for seven, a grand piano etc).

DE DAGERAAD
HOUSEBOAT €€

Map p298 (http://bedbreakfastdedageraad.nl; Ertskade 2; d €125-165; 🛜; 🚇26 Rietlandpark) This two-bedroom boutique B&B houseboat, dating from 1929, is moored on the easternmost tip of Zeeburg. The homely place has beautifully decorated white-walled cabins, both with en suite, sundeck, underfloor heating and TV, and a communal kitchenette with fridge and microwave. Breakfast is included in the price.

HOTEL REMBRANDT
HOTEL €€

Map p298 (📞020-627 27 14; www.hotelrem brandt.nl; Plantage Middenlaan 17; s/d from €135/150; 🛜; 🚇14 Plantage Kerklaan) Built for a 19th-century merchant, the sumptuous Rembrandt Hotel has an impressive red and white facade. Rooms are all different, but are generally light and bright, with colourful curtains or design touches and prints on the walls. Room 8 has a nearly life-sized mural of *The Night Watch;* three rooms have a balcony or garden terrace, and one a sauna.

★ MISC EATDRINKSLEEP
BOUTIQUE HOTEL €€€

Map p296 (📞020-330 62 41; www.misceatdrink sleep.com; Kloveniersburgwal 20; d from €175; ❊🛜; Ⓜ Nieuwmarkt) Steps from the Nieuwmarkt, the Misc has six charming rooms, all individually decorated, from the lanterns and bed canopy of the Wonders Room to the Design Room's bright and modern stylings. Choose between garden-and canal-view rooms; the latter have air-conditioning and cost more, but all rooms are light and bright. There's a filling breakfast included in the price.

🛏 Western Canal Ring

BANK HOTEL　　　　　BOUTIQUE HOTEL €€
Map p300 (📞020-667 80 86; www.thebankhotel amsterdam.nl; Haarlemmerstraat 120; s/d/tr/ste from €145/165/195/255; ❄🖥; 🚋18/21/22 Buiten Brouwersstraat) Built in the 1920s to headquarter the Amsterdamsche Bank, this art deco brick beauty 700m west of Centraal Station has been transformed into a contemporary hotel. Its 20 rooms have natural-stone bathrooms; one double has a balcony, while the penthouse suite takes in sweeping views of Amsterdam's skyline. The restaurant serves gastropub fare by day and high-end Dutch cuisine at night.

⭐**AMBASSADE HOTEL**　　BOUTIQUE HOTEL €€€
Map p302 (📞020-555 02 22; www.ambas sade-hotel.nl; Herengracht 341; d/tr/ste from €260/360/450; ❄🖥; 🚋2/12 Spui) Rambling across 10 Golden Age canal houses on the Herengracht, these 56 unique rooms and suites of varying sizes have period furnishings, antique furniture, gilded mirrors, chandeliers and art from the hotel's extensive collection from the CoBrA movement; many have romantic canal views. On-site are a library with thousands of books and a bar, and a French brasserie.

⭐**'T HOTEL**　　　　　BOUTIQUE HOTEL €€€
Map p300 (📞020-422 27 41; www.thotel.nl; Leliegracht 18; d/f from €209/379; ❄🖥; 🚋13/17 Westermarkt) Named for Amsterdam's waterways, the eight rooms in this charming 17th-century canal house are individually decorated with black-and-white sketches of old Dutch scenes, printed cushions and shower curtains, and patterned wallpapers by interior-print designer Katarina Stupavska, whose family owns the hotel. Dazzling blue-and-white Delftware designs line the family room, which has a loft sleeping area reached by a ladder.

⭐**HOTEL IX**　　　　　BOUTIQUE HOTEL €€€
Map p300 (📞020-845 84 51; www.hotelixam sterdam.com; Hartenstraat 8; d from €187; 🖥; 🚋13/17 Westermarkt) In the heart of the delightful Negen Straatjes shopping district, IX has five super-stylish suites (sleeping up to four) named for the area's 'Nine Streets', with black-and-white murals and complimentary minibars. The pick is the Berenstraat suite, with its own roof terrace. Note

there's no on-site reception (entry is via digicodes sent prior to arrival), no breakfast and no lift.

DYLAN　　　　　BOUTIQUE HOTEL €€€
Map p302 (📞020-530 20 10; www.dylanam sterdam.com; Keizersgracht 384; d/ste from €370/655; ❄@🖥; 🚋2/11/12 Spui) Exquisite boutique hotel the Dylan occupies an 18th-century Keizersgracht canal house that is set around a herringbone-paved, topiary-filled inner courtyard. Bespoke furniture such as silver-leaf and mother-of-pearl drinks cabinets adorn its 40 individually decorated rooms and suites (some duplex). Its Michelin-starred Restaurant Vinkeles also hosts private chef's tables aboard its boat, the *Muze*, as it cruises the canals.

ANDAZ AMSTERDAM　　DESIGN HOTEL €€€
Map p302 (📞020-523 12 34; www.hyatt.com; Prinsengracht 587; d/ste from €375/775; ❄@🖥; 🚋2/11/12 Prinsengracht) Visionary Dutch designer Marcel Wanders transformed Amsterdam's former public library into this fantasy of giant gold and silver cutlery, fish murals, Delftware-inspired carpets, library-book pages writ large on the walls and other flights of imagination. The 122 rooms and suites have Geneva sound systems, king-size beds, and complimentary snacks and non-alcoholic drinks. Guests get free bike hire.

TOREN　　　　　BOUTIQUE HOTEL €€€
Map p300 (📞020-622 60 33; www.thetoren.nl; Keizersgracht 164; s/d/ste from €203/237/339; ❄🖥; 🚋13/17 Westermarkt) A title holder for room size and personal service, the Toren's communal areas have a 17th-century opulence, with gilded mirrors, fireplaces and magnificent chandeliers. The 38 guestrooms are elegantly furnished and come with facilities such as Nespresso coffee machines.

🛏 Southern Canal Ring

⭐**COCOMAMA**　　　　　　HOSTEL €
Map p304 (📞020-627 24 54; www.cocomama hostel.com; Westeinde 18; dm/d from €42/120, minimum 2-night stay; 🖥; 🚋4 Stadhouderskade) Once a high-end brothel, this boutique hostel's doubles and dorms are light, bright and decorated with flair, with white walls and quirky designer Delftware or windmill

themes. Amenities are way above typical hostel standard, with en-suite bathrooms, in-room wi-fi, a relaxing back garden, a well-equipped kitchen, a book exchange and a super-comfy lounge open 24 hours. Breakfast is included.

★ HOTEL V
FREDERIKSPLEIN
BOUTIQUE HOTEL €€

Map p304 (☑020-662 32 33; www.hotelvfrederiksplein.nl; Weteringschans 136; d €99-219; ☎; ☒1/7/19/24 Frederiksplein) With soothing, leafy views over lush Frederiksplein, but only a quick shimmy from the bars and restaurants of Utrechtsestraat, Hotel V exudes a style that's well above its price bracket. Its 48 rooms have cool design cred with touches such as funky wall stencils and mid-century leather armchairs.

SEVEN BRIDGES
BOUTIQUE HOTEL €€

Map p304 (☑020-623 13 29; www.sevenbridges hotel.nl; Reguliersgracht 31; d €135-280; ☎; ☒4 Keizersgracht) Beautifully set on one of Amsterdam's loveliest canals, the Seven Bridges will immerse you in aristocratic opulence. Rooms are sumptuously decorated with oriental rugs and polished antiques. The urge to sightsee may fade once breakfast (€10), served on fine china, is delivered to your room.

HOTEL FREELAND
BOUTIQUE HOTEL €€

Map p304 (☑020-622 75 11; www.hotel freeland.com; Marnixstraat 386; s/d/tr from €80/130/150, s without bathroom from €70; ☀☎; ☒1/2/5/7/11/12/19 Leidseplein) In a prime canal-side location, the Freeland has 15 simple, nicely old-fashioned rooms with tiled walls; each has a floral theme (tulips, roses and sunflowers). Add in a tasty breakfast and it pretty much kills the Leidseplein competition. The hotel is LGBT-friendly and all-welcoming. Breakfast costs €8 per person.

HOTEL KAP
HOTEL €€

Map p304 (☑020-624 59 08; Den Texstraat 5b; d/tr/q from 120/170/210; ☎; ☒Vijzelgracht, ☒1/7/19/24 Vijzelgracht) In a 19th-century building with an old-fashioned feel, this boutique hotel boasts a good location and courteous, LGBT-friendly owners. There are steep stairs and no lift, but the rooms are bright and modern after renovations completed in 2018, including new bathrooms, floors and TVs hooked up to Netflix.

HOTEL LA BOHEME
HOTEL €€

Map p304 (☑020-624 28 28; www.la-boheme-amsterdam.com; Marnixstraat 415; d/tr €150/210; ☎; ☒1/2/5/7/11/12/19 Leidseplein) Hotel La Boheme's rooms are clean, simple and in demand thanks to its central location; booking well in advance is a must. On weekends, a minimum stay of three nights is required. Breakfast is included.

HOTEL ADOLESCE
BOUTIQUE HOTEL €€

Map p304 (☑020-626 39 59; www.en.adolesce.nl; Nieuwe Keizersgracht 26; s/d €90/160, with shared bathroom €85/125; ☎; ☒Waterlooplein, ☒14 Waterlooplein) In a canal house just across from the Hermitage Museum, this little family-owned hotel has lots of comforting old-fashioned charm. Steep steps lead to 10 spotless rooms of all shapes and sizes; all are decorated with bright modern prints. Breakfast is included, and available all day.

★ SEVEN ONE SEVEN
BOUTIQUE HOTEL €€€

Map p304 (☑020-427 07 17; www.717hotel.nl; Prinsengracht 717; d from €400; ☀☎; ☒2/11/12 Prinsengracht) With looks straight from the pages of a style magazine, the exquisitely decorated rooms here come with that all-too-rare luxury: space. It'll be hard to tear yourself away from these rooms, all of which have soaring ceilings, vast sofas, striking use of colour and contemporary-meets-antique decorations.

HOTEL NOTTING HILL
DESIGN HOTEL €€€

Map p304 (☑020-523 10 35; www.hotelnotting hill.nl; Westeinde 26; d from €250; ☀☎; ☒4 Stadhouderskade) Decorated with flair by Dutch designer Wim Hoopman of Hoopman Interior Projects (aptly abbreviated to HIP), this office-block-turned-boutique features outsized contemporary art and 71 sleek, calm rooms with lots of feature wallpaper. Higher-priced rooms have canal views. It's in a bulls-eye location between Utrechtsestraat and De Pijp.

BANKS MANSION
HOTEL €€€

Map p304 (☑020-420 00 55; www.carlton.nl/banksmansion; Herengracht 519-525; s/d from €250/350, s/d ste €400/600; ☀☎; ☒2/11/12 Keizersgracht) This swish, renovated hotel has plush, comfortable art-deco-style rooms and a stylish Frank Lloyd Wright–inspired lobby. Bathrooms feature a huge rain shower. You'll pay around €40 more for a canal view, though rooms on the side get a glimpse for free. All drinks, minibar and breakfasts (buffet and cooked) are included in the price.

🛏 Jordaan & the West

CHRISTIAN YOUTH HOSTEL
'THE SHELTER JORDAN' HOSTEL €
Map p310 (☑020-624 47 17; www.shelterhostel amsterdam.com; Bloemstraat 179; dm €33-41; @🛜; 🚊5/13/17/19 Marnixstraat) Putting up with the 'no everything' (drinking, smoking, partying) policy at this 96-bed hostel isn't hard, because it's such a gem. Single-sex dorms are quiet and clean, there's a piano, a courtyard garden and the breakfasts – especially the fluffy pancakes – are great. The cafe serves cheap meals the rest of the day.

★CONSCIOUS HOTEL
WESTERPARK BOUTIQUE HOTEL €€
Map p303 (☑020-820 33 33; www.conscious hotels.com; Haarlemmerweg 10; d/tr from €134/142; 🛜; 🚊5 Van Limburg Stirumstraat) 🌱 Opened in 2018 in the magnificent brick Stadsdeelkantoor, built in 1885 and now a national monument, this addition to Amsterdam's Conscious Hotels group has 89 rooms incorporating recycled materials, down to coat hangers made from radiator parts. Wind provides electricity, and aquaponic walls grow the cafe's vegetables and herbs (rates include an all-organic breakfast); toiletries and soaps are also organic.

★HOUSEBOAT MS LUCTOR B&B €€
Map p303 (☑06 2268 9506; www.boatbed andbreakfast.nl; Westerdok 103; d from €140; 🛜; 🚊48 Westerdoksdijk) 🌱 A brimming organic breakfast basket (included in the rate) is delivered to you each morning at this metal-hulled, mahogany-panelled 1913 houseboat, moored in a quiet waterway 10 minutes' walk from Centraal Station (five from the Jordaan). Eco initiatives include solar power, two bikes to borrow and a canoe for canal explorations. Minimum stay is two nights.

LINDEN HOTEL BOUTIQUE HOTEL €€
Map p308 (☑020-622 14 60; www.lindenhotel. nl; Lindengracht 251; d from €150; 🛜; 🚊3/5 Marnixplein) In a peaceful canal-side location footsteps from some of the Jordaan's best restaurants and markets, the Linden has small but beautifully furnished rooms with jade-green feature walls, iridescent shell-

pink cushions, swirl-patterned carpets and scented candles. Free tea, coffee and water infusions are available in the lobby. There's a tiny lift; staff couldn't be friendlier or more helpful.

BACKSTAGE HOTEL HOTEL €€
Map p310 (☑020-624 40 44; www.backstage hotel.com; Leidsegracht 114; s shared bathroom from €85, d with bathroom/shared bathroom from €159/125; 🛜; 🚊5/7/19 Leidseplein) Seriously fun, this music-themed hotel is a favourite among musicians jamming at nearby Melkweg and Paradiso, as evidenced by the lobby bar's band-signature-covered piano and pool table. Gig posters (many signed) line the corridors, and rooms are neo-retro black and white, with music stations and drum-kit overhead lights. You can borrow guitars or turntables and vinyl for your room.

HOTEL DE WINDKETEL APARTMENT €€
Map p303 (www.windketel.nl; Watertorenplein 8; d from €160; 🛜; 🚊5 Van Hallstraat) In the middle of a pedestrianised square, this diminutive octagonal water tower was constructed in 1897 as part of Amsterdam's waterworks and salvaged by local residents to share with visitors. Dutch design graces the ground-floor kitchen and dining room, 1st-floor living room, and top-floor bathroom and skylit bedroom beneath the original slatted-timber ceiling. Minimum three-night stay; no kids under 12.

★MR JORDAAN DESIGN HOTEL €€€
Map p308 (☑020-626 58 01; www.mrjordaan. nl; Bloemgracht 102; s/d/tr from €129/220/285; 🛜; 🚊13/17 Westermarkt) Wooden bedheads shaped like a row of gabled canal houses, bedside cacti, and lighting made from plumbing pipes – along with vintage fixtures in public spaces such as 1960s TVs, battered suitcases and typewriters – are just some of the unexpected design elements at this super-cool, refreshingly irreverent hotel in the heart of the Jordaan.

MORGAN & MEES BOUTIQUE HOTEL €€€
Map p310 (☑020-233 49 30; www.morganand mees.com; 2e Hugo de Grootstraat 2-6; d/ste from €187/238; ❄🛜; 🚊3 Hugo de Grootplein) It's all about comfort and cool at this stylish little hotel at the Jordaan's edge. Nine crisp white rooms with Coco-Mat queen- or king-size beds, rain showers and big TVs sit on top of Morgan & Mees' slick bar and restau-

rant. The easy-going staff make you feel at home, and the off-the-beaten-path location also lends an intimate vibe.

ROOM MATE AITANA   DESIGN HOTEL €€€
Map p303 (☑020-891 48 00; www.room-mate hotels.com; IJdok 6; d/tr/ste from €260/305/340; 🅿✳@🛜; 🚋48 Westerdoksdijk) Built from glittering glass, with interiors by architect Tomas Alia, this striking property overlooks the Western Islands and IJ River. State-of-the-art rooms in varying sizes and decor – from bold reds and pinks to abstract cut-outs of canal houses – are framed by floor-to-ceiling windows. There's a 24-hour gym, restaurant, bar, sunny waterside terrace and (if you arrive by boat) guest moorings.

🛌 Vondelpark & the South

STAYOKAY AMSTERDAM VONDELPARK   HOSTEL €
Map p312 (☑020-589 89 96; www.stayokay. com; Zandpad 5; dm €20-65, tw from €100; 🛜; 🚋1/3/11 1e Constantijn Huygensstraat) Practically in the Vondelpark, this HI-affiliated 536-bed hostel attracts a mix of international backpackers, families and groups. Renovated in 2018, it offers private rooms and fresh mixed, female- and male-only dorms sleeping from two to nine, sporting lockers, private bathrooms and well-spaced bunks. Breakfast is a cut above most hostels and there's a plant-filled spacious lobby bar-cafe with workspaces and quiet nooks.

CITYHUB AMSTERDAM   HOSTEL €
Map p312 (www.cityhub.com/amsterdam; Bellamystraat 3; hub from €85; ✳🛜; 🚋7/17 Ten Katestraat) Close to De Hallen (p165), this high-tech hostel has Japanese-style capsules or 'hubs' – don't expect to spread out too much – with colourful lighting and inbuilt speakers controlled by an app. Pop on

your wristband, which acts as your room key and allows access to the self-serve bar. Bathrooms are spotless, the staff are friendly and there are lockers for your luggage.

⭐**HOTEL NOT HOTEL**   DESIGN HOTEL €€
Map p312 (☑020-820 45 38; www.hotelnothotel. com; Piri Reisplein 34; d with/without bathroom from €139/60; ✳🛜; 🚋7/17 Witte de Withstraat) Stay in a work of art at this out-there collection of installations. Sleep inside Amsterdam Tram 965 (in a king-size bed), cosy into a cute blue-and-white VW van, bed down behind a secret bookcase, escape the daily grind in the Crisis Free Zone framed by Transylvanian-inspired woodcarvings to deter evil spirits, or climb a ladder to a crow's nest.

⭐**HOTEL FITA**   HOTEL €€
Map p312 (☑020-679 09 76; www.fita.nl; Jan Luijkenstraat 37; s/d from €125/159; 🛜; 🚋2/3/5/12 Van Baerlestraat) Family-owned Fita, on a quiet street close to Museum Quarter, has 20 light-filled rooms with Nespresso machines and smart bathrooms; a bountiful free breakfast of eggs, pancakes, cheeses and breads; and a lift. The friendly young owner keeps the property in mint condition, and service is attentive. It's one of the neighbourhood's best-value digs, and tends to book up fast.

COLLECTOR   B&B €€
Map p312 (☑020-673 67 79; www.the-collector. nl; De Lairessestraat 46; d €120-150; @🛜; 🚋3/5/12 Museumplein) This lovely B&B has two immaculate, spacious rooms with large windows, each furnished with its own museum-style display of clocks, wooden clogs and antiques collected by the owner, Karel. Each room also features a balcony and TV, and the kitchen is well stocked for guests to prepare breakfast (the eggs come from Karel's hens in the garden).

ALL ABOARD!
At the laid-back hostel **Train Lodge** (☑020-684 92 24; www.trainlodge.com; Changiweg 121; dm from €30, 3-/6-bed private compartments from €93.50/182; ✳🛜; MSloterdijk) on Sloterdijk Station's tracks, decommissioned Zürich–Rome sleeper carriages now contain 132 beds in three- and six-berth compartments (some female only). Compartments have washbasins; shared showers and toilets are in the corridors. Although it's outside the city centre, it's just a six-minute metro ride to Centraal Station. Breakfast costs €6.50.

CONSCIOUS HOTEL
MUSEUM SQUARE
BOUTIQUE HOTEL €€

Map p312 (☎020-820 33 33; www.conscioushotels.com; De Lairessestraat 7; d/f from €135/166; @🛜; 🚊3/5/12 Museumplein) 🏊 Renovated in 2019, this is the most intimate of the Conscious Hotels group, and closest to the major Amsterdam museums. It has a lush garden terrace and eco- and design-conscious rooms, featuring furniture made from recycled materials. Enjoy a complimentary glass of wine during Free Wine Hour at 6pm each evening, and organic breakfasts in the morning (extra €16).

SWEETS HOTEL
OVERTOOMSESLUIS
RENTAL HOUSE €€

Map p312 (☎020-740 10 10; www.sweetshotel.amsterdam; Overtoomsesluis; ste from €140; ❄🛜) One of 28 historic bridge houses around the city converted into hotel suites by a team of architects, designers and builders, this unique house is sandwiched between Vondelpark and Rembrandtpark, with easy access to all of the area's restaurants and nightlife. It's decked out with hip furniture, a cosy bed nook and kitchen facilities.

CONSCIOUS HOTEL
THE TIRE STATION
HOTEL €€

Map p312 (☎020-820 33 33; www.conscioushotels.com; Amstelveenseweg 5; d €100-180; P🛜; 🚊1 Rhijnvis Feithstraat) 🏊 Located in the former Michelin tyre station, doors away from its sister Conscious Hotel Vondelpark (there are four Conscious hotels in total), this hotel is popular with travellers for its sleek yet ecofriendly rooms. Comfy beds are backed by cork pin boards and decorated with quirky pictures, while smallish bathrooms have good showers and an encouraging 'Get Naked' sign.

OWL HOTEL
HOTEL €€

Map p312 (☎020-618 94 84; www.owl-hotel.nl; Roemer Visscherstraat 1; s/d €125/165; 🛜; 🚊1/3/11 1e Constantijn Huygensstraat) Well located near Vondelpark, this hotel is a little old-fashioned but rooms are bright and quiet, and staff are warm and welcoming. The owl figurines in reception have been sent by former guests from all over the world to add to the hotel's collection. Family rooms are available and the buffet breakfast is served in a bright, garden-side room.

CONSCIOUS HOTEL
VONDELPARK
BOUTIQUE HOTEL €€

Map p312 (☎020-820 33 33; www.conscioushotels.com; Overtoom 519; d/tr from €90/121.50; ❄🛜; 🚊1 Rhijnvis Feithstraat) 🏊 The 81-room Vondelpark branch of this enviro-conscious group is a friendly place to stay, close to Overtoom restaurants and green Vondelpark. It wears its eco-heart on its sleeve, with a plant wall in the lobby, self-sustaining pot plants in the rooms, huge floral murals, and recycled materials made into artful furnishings (including pressed-cardboard bathroom bench tops). The organic breakfast buffet costs €16.

NEIGHBOUR'S MAGNOLIA
HOTEL €€

Map p312 (☎020-676 93 21; www.magnoliahotelamsterdam.com; Willemsparkweg 205; s/d from €100/125; 🛜; 🚊2 Emmastraat) Offering excellent value in the Old South (Amsterdam's wealthiest district, just south of Vondelpark), this is a good choice, with helpful staff, rooms with colourful touches and lovely outlooks, and a peaceful location. Those at the rear have balconies overlooking a quiet, flower-filled courtyard (and, yes, there's a magnolia tree). Breakfast costs €12.50.

FLYNT B&B
B&B €€

Map p312 (☎020-618 46 14; www.flyntbedandbreakfast.nl; 1e Helmersstraat 34; d €90-140; @🛜; 🚊1 1e Constantijn Huygensstraat) In a great location near Museum Quarter, this two-room B&B has a friendly owner, creatively decorated rooms (complete with a bike hanging on the wall of the bike-themed room, of course) and a cosy breakfast nook (with breakfast goodies available around the clock).

⭐PILLOWS ANNA
VAN DEN VONDEL
BOUTIQUE HOTEL €€€

Map p312 (☎020-683 30 13; www.pillowshotels.nl; Anna van den Vondelstraat 6; d from €300; ❄🛜; 🚊1/11 1 Jan Pieter Heijestraat) This grown-up boutique hotel with exemplary service, housed in a row of three grand, red-and-white-striped 19th-century mansions, has rooms with views over its private tranquil English garden. Beds are clothed in soft, white linen, walls are gentle dove-grey, and chairs have a mid-century look and pale-blue crushed-velvet upholstery. A bedside device makes ordering room service a breeze. Breakfast costs €26.

HILTON AMSTERDAM HISTORIC HOTEL €€€
Map p312 (☑020-710 60 00; www.hilton.com; Apollolaan 13; d from €220; ✳🤏; 🚌2 Cornelius Schuytstraat) Famous as the place that John and Yoko staged their 'bed-in for peace' in 1969, this Hilton classic is close to Vondelpark in the lush Old South district, with canal-side lawns and all the five-star accoutrements. You can even stay in a piece of history in the 'John & Yoko' suite, with fabulous views through its huge windows, plus a balcony.

CONSERVATORIUM HOTEL DESIGN HOTEL €€€
Map p312 (☑020-570 00 00; www.conservatoriumhotel.com; Van Baerlestraat 27; d from €470; ✳🤏; 🚌3/5/12 Van Baerlestraat) Opposite the Concertgebouw, this palatial neo-Gothic building was originally a bank, then the city's conservatorium of music. Its most recent incarnation sees it stunningly converted into an eight-storey, five-star hotel with impressive public spaces – especially the huge covered courtyard, where soaring glass and steel connect the 19th-century brickwork – and contemporary rooms with neutral hues and designer furnishings.

HOTEL DE HALLEN DESIGN HOTEL €€€
Map p312 (☑020-515 04 53; www.hoteldehallen.com; Bellamyplein 47; d €190-280; ✳🤏; 🚌7/17 Ten Katestraat) Part of the De Hallen cultural centre (p165), housed in what were once tram sheds, this designer hotel has cool features, from a swing in the lobby to the industrial-chic 57 rooms, all of which have Coco-Mat mattresses, Nespresso machines and minibars. Sleek public spaces include restaurant Remise47, lounge areas, a bar and a wraparound, sun-shaded terrace. Breakfast costs €20.

🛏 De Pijp

BICYCLE HOTEL AMSTERDAM HOTEL €€
Map p316 (☑020-679 34 52; www.bicyclehotel.com; Van Ostadestraat 123; d/tr/f from €100/150/160, s/d/tr shared bathroom from €65/85/105; @🤏; Ⓜ De Pijp, 🚌3/4 2e Van der Helststraat) 🌿 With solar panels on the roof providing power, Marjolein and Clemens' green-minded hotel has rooms that are comfy and familiar. It also hires bikes (per day €8) and serves a killer organic breakfast (included in the rate). Look for the bikes mounted on the brick exterior.

LITTLE AMSTEL B&B €€
Map p316 (☑06 1532 1577; www.littleamstel.com; Amsteldijk 700; d from €125; 🤏; 🚌4 Stadhouderskade) Windows in these two cabin-style rooms aboard a houseboat look directly over the Amstel, the river that gave Amsterdam its name. The 'basic' room has one east-facing window, while the 'standard' has a double aspect. Both have private entrances, as well as en-suite bathrooms, small fridges and tea- and coffee-making facilities. Breakfast (€5 to €15) can be delivered.

NINE(T)TEEN B&B €€
Map p316 (☑020-233 32 19; www.nine-t-teen.nl; Hemonystraat 10; d/ste from €134/274; 🤏; 🚌4 Stadhouderskade) Brilliantly situated in De Pijp's northeastern corner near the Southern Canal Ring, this B&B has 19 en-suite rooms across four townhouses. Basement rooms have small windows; other rooms and suites open to balconies or terraces. All come with Nespresso machines and a small fridge; breakfast costs an extra €9.50.

★SIR ALBERT HOTEL DESIGN HOTEL €€
Map p316 (☑020-710 72 58; www.sirhotels.com/albert; Albert Cuypstraat 2-6; d/ste from €170/320; ✳@🤏; Ⓜ De Pijp, 🚌3/12/24 De Pijp) A 19th-century diamond factory houses this glitzy design hotel. Its 90 creative rooms and suites have high ceilings and large windows, with custom-made linens and Illy espresso machines; iPads are available for use in the Persian-rug-floored study. Energetic staff are helpful and professional. Of the 10 balcony rooms, west-facing 336, 337 and 338 have sunset views over the canal.

HOTEL OKURA AMSTERDAM HOTEL €€€
Map p316 (☑020-678 71 11; www.okura.nl; Ferdinand Bolstraat 333; d/ste from €198/255; ✳@🤏🏊; 🚌4/12 Cornelis Troostplein) Rare-for-Amsterdam attributes that elevate this business-oriented hotel way above the competition include panoramic city views (particularly from higher-priced north-facing rooms), four Michelin stars on the premises – two at top-floor Ciel Bleu (p185), one at ground-floor Japanese restaurant Yamazato and one at ground-floor teppanyaki restaurant Sazanka – and a health club with an 18m-long jet-stream swimming pool. Bountiful breakfast buffets cost €32.

🛏 Oosterpark & East of the Amstel

GENERATOR AMSTERDAM   HOSTEL €
Map p318 (📱020-708 56 00; www.generatorho
stels.com; Mauritskade 57; dm €43, d & q €120-
200; 🛜; 🚊14 Alexanderplein) Part of a cool
designer hostel chain, Generator occupies
a century-old zoological university building with large windows overlooking lush
Oosterpark, in a rapidly gentrifying area.
Twin and quad rooms are bright and smart-
ly decorated, all with en-suite bathrooms.
Sociable areas include a cafe with terrace
overlooking the park and a bar carved from
the old lecture hall.

STAYOKAY AMSTERDAM OOST   HOSTEL €
Map p318 (📱020-551 31 90; www.stayokay.com;
Timorplein 21; dm €20-65, tw from €80; @🛜;
🚊14 Zeeburgerdijk) Renovated in 2018, this
branch of Stayokay hostels is impressive,
with over 600 beds spread over three floors
in a large, handsome red-brick building.
Most of the spick-and-span rooms are four-,
six-, or eight-bed dorms, all light and bright
with en-suite bathroom. Private rooms for
two to six people are also available. Linens
are free, but towels cost €4.50.

★VOLKSHOTEL   HOTEL €€
Map p318 (📱020-261 21 00; www.volkshotel.
nl; Wibautstraat 150; r €120-250; 🛜; Ⓜ Wibautstraat) Ignore the drab exterior: 'People's
Hotel' has the vibe of an uber-cool media
company, with glass-box meeting rooms
and lots of bright young things on laptops
in the work space. The quirky rooms vary,
but all feature designer touches and bold
colours. There are hot tubs with fabulous
views on the rooftop, and Canvas (p195)
roof-terrace bar is a city hotspot.

🛏 Amsterdam Noord

★CLINKNOORD   HOSTEL €
Map p319 (📱020-214 97 30; www.clinkhostels.
com; Badhuiskade 3; dm/s/d from €28/90/135;
❄🛜; 🚊Buiksloterweg) Clink is a designer
hostel chain with other branches in London, and here occupies a 1920s laboratory
on the IJ riverbank, by the Buiksloterweg
ferry terminal – a free, five-minute ferry
ride from Centraal Station (ferries run
24/7). Dorms are done up in minimalist-

industrial style, with four to 14 beds and
en-suite facilities.

CAMPING VLIEGENBOS   CAMPGROUND €
Map p319 (📱020-636 88 55; Meeuwenlaan 138;
2-person tent site €18-22, cabins €75-100; ☺Apr-
Oct; 🛜; 🚊IJplein, Ⓜ Noorderpark) Less than
2km from the IJplein ferry stop, this camp-
ground in woodland is small and gets busy,
but it's very leafy and feels rural considering it's so close to the city. There are some
basic cabins with bunks, and tipis if you
don't have your own tent. Staff are helpful
and friendly and there's a cafe-bar and bike
hire (€12 per day).

SWEETS HOTEL
GERBEN WAGENAARBRUG   RENTAL HOUSE €€
Map p319 (📱020-740 10 10; www.sweetshotel.
amsterdam; Kraaienplein; ste from €140; 🛜;
🚊IJplein, Ⓜ Noorderpark) The largest of 28
historic bridge houses around the city that
have been transformed into hotel suites by
a team of architects, designers and builders, this three-storey house is a short walk
from some of Amsterdam Noord's bars, restaurants and cafes, and overlooks the boats
bobbing in the Noordhollandsch Kanaal.
The interior pops with bright colours and
comes equipped with everything you need.

★FARALDA
CRANE HOTEL   DESIGN HOTEL €€€
Map p319 (📱020-760 61 61; www.faralda.com;
NDSM-plein 78; ste from €975; ❄🛜; 🚊NDSM-
werf) What's that imposing industrial crane
rising up at NDSM-werf? It's a hotel. The
three fantasy-world suites perched at varying heights – Free Spirit, Secret and Mystique – have looks worthy of a drug baron's
hideout, with free-standing baths, bold
objets d'art and vertiginous views. On the
crane's rooftop, you can soak in the heated
bubbling outdoor hot tub, with astounding
views across to central Amsterdam.

★SIR ADAM   DESIGN HOTEL €€€
Map p319 (📱020-215 95 10; www.sirhotels.com;
Overhoeksplein 7; d/ste from €210/450; ❄@🛜;
🚊Buiksloterweg) This cool design hotel is a
perfect fit for hip Amsterdam Noord, with
its mammoth, view-framing plate-glass windows, pillow menu, rainfall shower, Illy coffee
machine and Crosley Cruiser record player in
the rooms. Part of the Sir Hotel group, it's
located in the A'DAM Tower (p200), so you
have a choice of bars, clubs and restaurants
on site, including Moon (p202).

Understand
Amsterdam

Amsterdam Today

Amsterdam is expanding on every level. The city's population is growing rapidly, with grand-scale urban projects rising up, merging Golden Age charm with hyper-modernity. Below ground, new infrastructure and facilities are being built beneath the city's streets and canals. Yet this go-getting city is something of a victim of its own success, with significant steps now being taken to combat overtourism and ensure sustainability.

Best on Film

The Fault in Our Stars (2014) Based on the John Green novel, this story of two cancer-stricken young lovers travelling to Amsterdam is sad yet uplifting.
The Paradise Suite (2015) A Bulgarian woman forced into prostitution, a Swedish piano prodigy, a Serbian war criminal and other troubled characters cross paths in Amsterdam.
Tulip Fever (2017) Based on the 1999 novel by Deborah Moggach, this love story takes place in 17th-century Amsterdam during the heady days of tulip mania.

Best in Print

The Diary of Anne Frank (Anne Frank; 1952) A moving account of a young girl's thoughts and yearnings while in hiding from the Nazis in Amsterdam. The book has been translated into 60 languages.
After the Silence (Jake Woodhouse; 2014) Noir novel in which Inspector Jap Rykel, an Amsterdam detective, hunts down a murderer in the city's tangled streets. It's book one of a four-part series.
The Miniaturist (Jessie Burton; 2014) Golden Age–set novel centred on Petronella Oortman, owner of an intricate dollhouse. The title character is an artist who helps Nella furnish it.

Crowd Control

Amsterdam's visitor numbers are skyrocketing, with 19 million tourists in 2018 alone – an astonishing figure given the city's 866,737-strong population.

Quantity isn't the only concern; quality is an issue too, with throngs of hard-partying visitors disturbing residential neighbourhoods, short-term apartment rentals driving rents and property prices up, and local shops and community services being displaced by lucrative souvenir and snack vendors.

The city has taken the drastic step of no longer actively promoting Amsterdam as a tourist destination. But it still welcomes visitors and is introducing measures to manage the crowds.

From 2020, guided Red Light District tours are banned, as are free guided tours city-wide, and all tour companies must have permits and comply with stringent rules. Digital fences at nightlife hotspots like Leidseplein and Rembrandtplein will send notifications via social media to remind visitors to treat the area and residents respectfully.

Diverting budget airlines to Lelystad Airport (50km east of Amsterdam) from 2020 frees up Schiphol International Airport to handle greater passenger numbers, and directs visitors to explore the capital's surrounds.

Socially minded initiatives like 'marrying' a local for a day and fishing plastic from the city's waterways while cruising them in boats made from the recycled waste also aim to integrate locals with visitors, and encourage travel as a force for good.

Building Up

Amsterdam's cityscape has been a work-in-progress from the outset. During the Golden Age, 400-plus years ago, forward-thinking planners built the Canal Ring to drain and reclaim waterlogged land to accommodate the exploding population. Today it's a similar story. Amsterdam is running out of room for its growing number of denizens – the city's population is increasing at a rate of 11,000 per year, and it's expected to hit one million by the 2030s. Urban planners are using visionary architecture to make room for the newcomers.

The shores along IJ River are seeing swooping modern developments transform industrial areas such as the Eastern and Western Docklands (on either side of Centraal Station). A vast new residential hub is springing up around the latter, with the construction of the Houthavens ('lumber ports') neighbourhood on seven artificial islands. Across the water, the once industrial Amsterdam Noord area is rapidly expanding.

Further east is IJburg, an archipelago of 10 artificial islands in the IJmeer (IJ lake). Seven islands are now inhabited; construction on the last three commenced in 2019, with completion set for 2026.

Digging Deep

The city's premium on space has also driven builders underground. The Noord/Zuidlijn (North–South metro line), linking Amsterdam Noord with the World Trade Centre in the south has been a resounding success since opening in 2018. Public transport company GVB is now calling for the Noord/Zuidlijn to be extended to Schiphol Airport, and for the construction of an East–West cross-city metro line (Oost/Westlijn) from IJburg to Schiphol.

The 600-space Albert Cuyp underground parking station below the Ruysdaelkade canal in De Pijp saw the removal of 300 car spaces from the streets above to allow better access for pedestrians and, especially, cyclists (the garage itself has 60 bike spaces).

Bicycle spaces have long been an issue in this bike-oriented city. The bike-parking garage at Centraal Station is gaining a 5th level and an additional 1500 places in 2021. Work has started on a 7000-capacity underground bicycle garage beneath IJ River on Centraal Station's northern side, and on two floating platforms adjacent to the ferry terminals, accommodating 4000 bikes. Both will be completed by 2025.

Ultimately, the goal is to build 50km of tunnels below the city centre with parking stations, sports facilities such as swimming pools, cinemas and supermarkets. Upon leaving Amsterdam's ring road, the A10, all traffic would be diverted underground.

Sustainable City

Amsterdam plans to be completely climate-proof by 2050, reducing current carbon-dioxide emissions by 95%. Only emission-free vehicles will be allowed within the ring road by 2025. By 2040, all buildings will be free of natural gas; the city will create 25 new parks; and green rooftops will be increased by 50,000 sq metres to help with water run-off, biodiversity and pollution mitigation.

if Amsterdam were 100 people

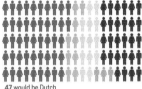

47 would be Dutch
9 would be Moroccan
8 would be Surinamese
5 would be Turkish
3 would be Indonesian
28 would be other

belief systems
(% of population)

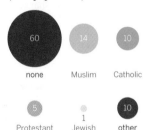

60 none — 14 Muslim — 10 Catholic — 5 Protestant — 1 Jewish — 10 other

population per sq km

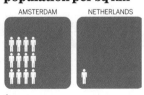

AMSTERDAM — NETHERLANDS

≈ 420 people

History

Amsterdam may have spawned one of the world's great trading empires, but this area was once an inhospitable patchwork of lakes, swamps and peat, at or below sea level; its contours shifted with the autumn storms and floods. The oldest archaeological finds here date from Roman times, when the IJ River lay along the northern border of the Roman Empire. Maritime trading, egalitarian attitudes and engineering ingenuity all paved the way for the modern city today.

From the Beginning

The mighty Romans – who had conquered the lands now known as the Netherlands in the 1st century – left behind no colosseums or magnificent tombs. In uncharacteristic style, they left practically no evidence, much less any grand gestures, of settlement. While the swampy, sea-level topography made the construction of grand edifices challenging, the Romans had been known to bypass such challenges before in other regions. In the end, they simply had other more important lands south of the Low Countries to inhabit and rule.

Around 1200, a fishing community known as Aemstelredamme ('the dam built across the Amstel') emerged at what is now the Dam, and the name Amsterdam was coined.

The city's symbol, XXX, appears on its coat of arms, flag (two horizontal red stripes with a central black stripe with three diagonal white St Andrew's crosses), municipal buildings and merchandising everywhere. It originated in 1505 when Amsterdam was a fishing town (St Andrew is the patron saint of fisherman).

Early Trade

Farming was tricky on the marshland and with the sea on the doorstep, early residents turned to fishing. But it was commercial trade that would flourish. While powerful city-states focused on overland trade with Flanders and northern Italy, Amsterdam shrewdly levelled its sights on the maritime routes. The big prizes? The North and Baltic Seas, which were in the backyard of the powerful Hanseatic League, a group of German trading cities.

Ignoring the league's intimidating reputation, Amsterdam's clever *vrijbuiters* (buccaneers) sailed right into the Baltic, their holds full of cloth and salt to exchange for grain and timber. It was nothing short of

TIMELINE	1150–1300	1275	1345
	Dams are built to retain the IJ River between the Zuiderzee and Haarlem. A tiny community of herring fishermen settles on the banks of the Amstel river.	Amsterdam is founded after toll-free status is granted to residents along the Amstel. The city gains direct access to the ocean via the Zuiderzee, now the IJsselmeer.	The 'Miracle of Amsterdam' occurs and the city becomes an important place of pilgrimage, causing its population to grow considerably.

a coup. By the late 1400s the vast majority of ships sailing to and from the Baltic Sea were based in Amsterdam.

By this time sailors, merchants, artisans and opportunists from the Low Countries (roughly present-day Netherlands, Belgium and Luxembourg) made their living here.

At the time, Amsterdam was unfettered by the key structures of other European societies. With no tradition of Church-sanctioned feudal relationships, no distinction between nobility and serfs, and hardly any taxation, a society of individualism and capitalism took root. The modern idea of Amsterdam – free, open, progressive and flush with opportunity – was born.

Independent Republic

The Protestant Reformation wasn't just a matter of religion; it was also a classic power struggle between the 'new money' (an emerging class of merchants and artisans) and the 'old money' (the land-owning, aristocratic order sanctioned by the established Catholic Church).

The Protestantism that took hold in the Low Countries was its most radically moralistic stream, known as Calvinism. It stressed the might of God and treated humans as sinful creatures whose duty in life was sobriety and hard work. The ascetic Calvinists stood for local decision-making and had a disdain for the top-down hierarchy of the Catholic Church.

Calvinism was key to the struggle for independence by King Philip II of Spain. The deeply unpopular Philip, a fanatically devout Catholic, had acquired the Low Countries in something of a horse trade with Austria. His efforts to introduce the Spanish Inquisition, centralise government and levy taxes enraged his subjects and awoke a sense of national pride.

In 1579 the seven northern provinces, with mighty Amsterdam on their side, declared themselves to be an independent republic, led by William of Orange: the seed that grew into today's royal family. William was famously dubbed 'the Silent' because he wisely refused to enter into religious debate. To this day, he remains the uncontested founder – and father – of the Netherlands.

Golden Age (1580–1700)

In 1588, Den Haag was established as the seat of the Dutch Republic, but Amsterdam grew rapidly to become the largest and most influential city in the Netherlands.

By 1600 Dutch ships controlled the sea trade between England, France, Spain and the Baltic, and had a virtual monopoly on North

The Miniaturist (2014), by Jessie Burton, is a Golden Age–set novel centred on Petronella Oortman, owner of the intricate dollhouse that's now a big Rijksmuseum draw. The title character is an enigmatic artist who helps Nella furnish it precisely to scale... and may hold the key to her family's future.

1380	1452	1519	1543
Canals of the present-day Medieval Centre are dug. Amsterdam flourishes, winning control over the sea trade in Scandinavia and later gaining free access to the Baltic.	Following the second 15th-century fire to devastate the city, laws decree that brick and tile are the only building materials that can be used in the city.	Spain's Charles V is crowned Holy Roman Emperor. Treaties and dynastic marriages make Amsterdam part of the Spanish Empire, with Catholicism the main faith.	Charles V unites the Low Countries (roughly the area covering what is now the Netherlands, Belgium and Luxembourg) and establishes Brussels as the region's capital.

Sea fishing and Arctic whaling. Jewish refugees taught Dutch mariners about trade routes, giving rise to the legendary Dutch East India and Dutch West India Companies. For a while, the Dutch ran rings around the fleets of great powers, which were too slow or cumbersome to react. In the absence of an overriding religion, ethnic background or political entity, money reigned supreme.

Two decades on, Dutch traders had gone global, exploring the far corners of the earth, and by the mid-17th century the Dutch had more seagoing merchant vessels than England and France combined. Half of all ships sailing between Europe and Asia belonged to the Dutch, and

THE CURIOUS HISTORY OF TULIPMANIA

The Dutch tulip craze of 1636–37 ranks alongside the greatest economic booms and busts in history.

Tulips originated as wildflowers in Central Asia and were first cultivated by the Turks, who filled their courts with these beautiful spring blooms (the word tulip derives from 'turban' due to the petals' resemblance to the headwear). In the mid-1500s the Habsburg ambassador to Istanbul brought some bulbs back to Vienna, where the imperial botanist, Carolus Clusius, learned how to propagate them. In 1590 Clusius became director of the Hortus Botanicus in Leiden – one of Europe's oldest botanical gardens – and had great success growing and cross-breeding tulips in the Netherlands' cool, damp climate and fertile delta soil.

The more exotic specimens of tulip featured frilly petals and 'flamed' streaks of colour, which attracted the attention of wealthy merchants, who put them in their living rooms and hallways to impress visitors. Trickle-down wealth and savings stoked the taste for exotica in general, and tulip growers arose to service the demand.

A speculative frenzy ensued, and people paid top florin for the finest bulbs, many of which changed hands time and again before they sprouted. Bidding often took place in taverns and was fuelled by alcohol.

Of course, this bonanza couldn't last, and when several bulb traders in Haarlem failed to fetch their expected prices in February 1637, the bottom fell out of the market. Within weeks many of the country's wealthiest merchants went bankrupt and many more people of humbler origins lost everything.

Love of the unusual tulip endured, however, and cooler-headed growers perfected their craft. To this day, the Dutch continue to be the world leaders in tulip cultivation and supply most of the bulbs planted in Europe and North America. They also excel in other bulbs such as daffodils, hyacinths and crocuses. The flamed, frilly tulips are now known as Rembrandt tulips because of their depiction in so many 17th-century paintings.

For an informative read about the era, pick up a copy of *Tulipomania: The Story of the World's Most Coveted Flower* by Mike Dash.

1578	1580	1600s	1602
Amsterdam is captured in a bloodless coup. A Dutch Republic made up of seven provinces is declared a year later, led by Willem the Silent.	The Protestant Reformation picks up steam and Catholicism is outlawed, with clandestine worship permitted.	The Golden Age places Amsterdam firmly on the cultural map. While Rembrandt paints in his atelier, the grand inner ring of canals is constructed. The city's population surges to 200,000.	Amsterdam becomes the site of the world's first stock exchange when the offices of the Dutch East India Company trade their own shares.

exotic products – coffee, tea, spices, tobacco, cotton, silk and porcelain – became commodities. Amsterdam became home to Europe's largest shipbuilding industry, and the city was veritably buzzing with prosperity and innovation.

In 1651, England passed the first of several Navigation Acts that posed a serious threat to Dutch trade, leading to several thorny, inconclusive wars on the seas. Competitors sussed out Dutch trade secrets, regrouped and reconquered the sea routes. In 1664 the British captured the colony of New Netherland, including the provincial capital New Amsterdam (now New York City) from the Dutch. After the ensuing Second Anglo-Dutch War (1665–67), the 1667 Treaty of Breda saw the British retain New Netherland and the Dutch retain Suriname in South America (governed by the Dutch until 1954). The British also lost their claim on the eastern Indonesian spice island of Run (governed by the Dutch until 1949), a good deal for the Dutch for many years due to the high trading value of spices, particularly prized nutmeg grown on Run.

Louis XIV of France seized the opportunity to invade the Low Countries two decades later, and the period of prosperity known as the Golden Age ended. While the city hardly went into decay or ruin, the embattled economy would take more than a century to regain its full strength.

Historical Reads: Non-Fiction

....

Amsterdam: A History of the World's Most Liberal City (Russell Shorto)

....

The Embarrassment of Riches (Simon Schama)

....

Amsterdam: The Brief Life of a City (Geert Mak)

HISTORY WEALTHY DECLINE (1700–1814)

Wealthy Decline (1700–1814)

While the Dutch Republic didn't have the resources to fight France and England head on, it had Amsterdam's money to buy them off and ensure freedom of the seas.

As the costs mounted, Amsterdam went from being a place where everything (profitable) was possible, to a lethargic community where wealth creation was a matter of interest rates. Gone were the daring sea voyages, the achievements in art, science and technology, and the innovations of government and finance. Ports such as London and Hamburg became powerful rivals.

The decline in trade brought poverty, and exceptionally cold winters hampered transport and led to serious food shortages. The winters of 1740 and 1763 were so severe that some residents froze to death.

Amsterdam's support of the American War of Independence (1776) resulted in a British blockade of the Dutch coast, followed by British conquests of Dutch trading posts around the world, forcing the closure of the Dutch West and East India Companies.

Enter the French: in 1794 French revolutionary troops invaded the Low Countries. In a convenient act of nepotism, the Dutch Republic

Historical Reads: Fiction

....

Tulip Fever (Deborah Moggach)

....

Max Havelaar (Eduard Douwes Dekker)

....

The Coffee Trader (David Liss)

....

Rembrandt's Whore (Sylvie Matton)

1618	1636–37	1664–67	1688
World's first weekly broadsheet newspaper, the *Courante uyt Italien, Duytslandt, &c.*, is printed in Amsterdam. Catholicism is outlawed, with clandestine worship permitted.	Tulipmania sweeps the nation, when the flower bulbs are more valuable than a canal house. Tulip speculators get rich fast, but the market crashes and many are left bankrupt.	The British capture the Dutch colony of New Netherland, including New Amsterdam (now New York); the resulting 1667 Treaty of Breda sees the Dutch claim the spice island of Run.	William III of Orange repels the French with the help of Austria, Spain and Brandenburg. William then invades England, where he and his wife are proclaimed king and queen.

became a monarchy in 1806, when Napoleon installed his brother Louis Napoleon as king.

After Napoleon's defeat in 1813, Amsterdam's trade with the world recovered only slowly; domination of the seas now belonged to the British.

During his early-19th-century reign, Louis Napoleon's attempts to learn Dutch were appreciated if not always successful, notably when he stated that he was the *Konijn van 'Olland* (Rabbit of 'Olland), instead of the *Koning van Holland* (King of Holland).

New Infrastructure (1814–1918)

In the first half of the 19th century, Amsterdam was a gloomy, uninspiring place. Its harbour had been neglected and the sandbanks in the IJ River proved too great a barrier for modern ships. Rotterdam was set to become the country's premier port.

Things began to look up as the country's first railway, between Amsterdam and Haarlem, opened in 1839. Trade with the East Indies was the backbone of Amsterdam's economy, and a canal, later extended to the Rhine, helped the city to benefit from the Industrial Revolution underway in Europe.

Amsterdam again attracted immigrants, and its population doubled in the second half of the 19th century. Speculators hastily erected new housing beyond the Canal Ring – dreary, shoddily built tenement blocks.

The Netherlands remained neutral in WWI, but Amsterdam's trade with the East Indies suffered from naval blockades. Food shortages brought riots, and an attempt to bring the socialist revolution to the Netherlands was put down by loyalist troops.

Boom & Depression (1918–1940)

After WWI, Amsterdam remained the country's industrial centre. The Dutch Shipbuilding Company operated the world's second-largest wharf and helped carry a large steel and diesel-motor industry. The harbour handled tropical produce that was processed locally, such as tobacco and cocoa (Amsterdam remains the world's biggest cocoa importer).

The 1920s were boom years. In 1920 KLM (Koninklijke Luchtvaart Maatschappij; Royal Aviation Company) began the world's first regular passenger air service between Amsterdam and London from an airstrip south of the city, and bought many of its planes from Anthony Fokker's factory north of the IJ River. There were two huge breweries, a sizable clothing industry and even a local car factory. The city hosted the Olympic Games in 1928.

The world Depression in the 1930s hit Amsterdam hard. Make-work projects did little to defuse the mounting tensions between socialists, communists and a small but vocal party of Dutch fascists. The city took

1795	1806	1813–14	1830
French troops occupy the Netherlands and install the Batavian Republic. The fragmented United Provinces become a centralised state, with Amsterdam as its capital.	The Dutch Republic becomes a monarchy when Napoleon installs his brother Louis Napoleon as king.	The French are overthrown and William VI of Orange is crowned as Dutch King William I.	With French help, the southern provinces secede to form the Kingdom of Belgium. The country is not formally recognised by the Dutch government until 1839.

in 25,000 Jewish refugees fleeing Germany; many were turned back at the border because of the country's neutrality policy.

WWII (1940–45)

The Netherlands attempted to remain neutral in WWII, but Germany invaded in May 1940. For the first time in almost 400 years, Amsterdammers experienced war first-hand. Few wanted to believe that things would turn really nasty – the Germans, after all, had trumpeted that the Dutch were of the 'Aryan brotherhood'.

In February 1941, dockworkers led a protest strike over the treatment of Jews, commemorated as the 'February Strike'. By then, however, it was already too late.

The Dutch Resistance, set up by an unlikely alliance of Calvinists and communists, only became large-scale when the increasingly desperate Germans began to round up able-bodied men to work in Germany.

FROM OUD AMSTERDAM TO NIEUW AMSTERDAM

One of the wall plaques on the Schreierstoren (p71), in the Red Light District, explains that the English captain Henry Hudson set sail from here in 1609 in his ship, the *Halve Maen (Half Moon)*. The Dutch East India Company had enlisted him to find a northern passage to the East Indies, but instead he ended up exploring the North American river that now bears his name. On the return voyage his ship was seized in England and he was forbidden to sail again to a foreign nation.

The maverick Hudson disregarded the order. Commissioned by powerful private investors from Britain and Russia, he sailed to America in search of the elusive Northwest Passage. Though an accomplished navigator, the headstrong Hudson hardly endeared himself to his crew, who mutinied in the summer of 1611. Hudson, his son and a handful of others were set adrift in a row boat in what's now known as Hudson Bay, where they are presumed to have died.

In any event, Hudson's reports about the island at the mouth of the Hudson River made it back to base. The Dutch soon established a fort on an island called Manhattan that flowered into a settlement called Nieuw Amsterdam; in 1626 an agent of the recently established Dutch West India Company purchased the island from Native Americans for 60 guilders (the equivalent, at the time, of US$24). In 1664 the Dutch West India Company's local governor, the imperious Calvinist Pieter Stuyvesant, surrendered the town to the British, who promptly renamed it New York. Stuyvesant retired to the Lower Manhattan market garden called Bouwerij, now known as the Bowery.

Interestingly, Manhattan's Wall St, now one of the centres of world finance, was originally the site of a fortified wall erected by the Dutch to keep out the British.

1865–76	1885	1889	1914–20
Rapid economic and social change sees the North Sea Canal dug, the Dutch railway system expanded and socialist principles of government established.	The Rijksmuseum opens its doors in its current location, 87 years after it was founded in Den Haag.	Centraal Station makes its grand debut, and – in an instant – Amsterdam is connected by rail to the rest of Europe.	The Netherlands remains neutral in WWI. Food shortages cripple the country, leading to strikes, unrest and growing support for the Dutch Communist Party.

Towards the end of the war, the situation in Amsterdam was dire. Coal shipments ceased; many men aged between 17 and 50 had gone into hiding or to work in Germany; public utilities were halted; and the Germans began to plunder anything that could assist their war effort. Thousands of lives were lost to severe cold and famine. Canadian troops finally liberated the city in May 1945 in the final days of the war in Europe.

Postwar Growth (1945–62)

The city's growth resumed after the war, with US aid through the Marshall Plan.

Massive apartment blocks arose in areas annexed west of the city to meet the continuing demand for housing, made more acute by the demographic shift away from extended families. The massive Bijlmermeer housing project (now called De Bijlmer) southeast of the city, begun in the mid-1960s and finished in the 1970s, was built in a similar vein.

Cultural Revolution (1962–82)

For nearly a century leading up to the 1960s, Dutch society had become characterised by *verzuiling* (pillarisation), a social order in which each religion and political persuasion achieved the right to do its own thing, with its own institutions. Each persuasion represented a pillar that supported the status quo in a general 'agreement to disagree'. In the 1960s the old divisions were increasingly irrelevant and the pillars came tumbling down, but not the philosophy they spawned.

Amsterdam became Europe's *magisch centrum* ('magic centre'): hippies smoked dope on the Dam, camped in the Vondelpark and tripped at clubs such as the Melkweg, an abandoned dairy barn. In 1972 the first coffeeshop opened and in 1976 marijuana was decriminalised to free up police resources for combating hard drugs. With soaring housing prices, squatters began to occupy buildings left empty by speculators. In the process, they helped save several notable historical structures from demolition.

Since 2010, squatting has been illegal, and some former squats have become legitimate cultural centres.

New Consensus (1982–2000)

Twenty years after the cultural revolution began, a new consensus emphasised a decentralised government. Neighbourhood councils were established with the goal of creating a more livable city, through integration of work, schools and shops within walking or cycling distance;

Hans Brinker, who supposedly stuck his finger in a dyke and saved the Netherlands from a flood, is an American invention and unknown in the Netherlands. He starred in a 19th-century children's book.

Jewish inhabitants gave the city its nickname, Mokum, from the Yiddish for 'town' (derived from the Hebrew *makom*, meaning 'place'). The term is widely used today, and Amsterdam natives are known as Mokummers.

1928	1939	1940	1944–45
Amsterdam hosts the Olympic Games during the 1920s boom years. The Olympic flame is lit for the first time since ancient Greece.	The Dutch government establishes Westerbork as an internment camp to house Jewish refugees.	Germany invades the Netherlands. Rotterdam is destroyed by the Luftwaffe, but Amsterdam suffers only minor damage before capitulating.	The Allies liberate the southern Netherlands, but the north and west of the country are cut off from supplies. Thousands of Dutch perish in the bitter 'Hunger Winter'.

decreased traffic; renovation rather than demolition; friendly neighbourhood police; a practical, non-moralistic approach towards drugs; and legal recognition of homosexual couples.

By the early 1990s, the families and small manufacturers that had dominated inner-city neighbourhoods in the early 1960s had been replaced by professionals and a service industry of pubs, coffeeshops, restaurants and hotels. The city's success in attracting large foreign businesses resulted in an influx of high-income expats.

JEWISH AMSTERDAM

It's hard to overstate the role Jewish people have played in the evolution of civic and commercial life in Amsterdam. The first documented Jewish presence goes back to the 12th century, but it was expulsion from Spain and Portugal in the 1580s that brought a large number of Sephardic (Jews of Spanish, Middle Eastern or North African heritage) refugees.

As in much of Europe, Jews in Amsterdam were barred from many professions. Monopolistic guilds kept most trades firmly closed. But some Sephardim were diamond cutters, for which there was no guild. Other Sephardic Jews introduced printing and tobacco processing, or worked in unrestricted trades such as retail, finance, medicine and the garment industry. The majority, however, eked out a meagre living as labourers and small-time traders. They lived in the Nieuwmarkt area, which developed into the Jewish quarter.

Amsterdam's Jewish people did have some human rights unheard of elsewhere in Europe. They were not confined to a ghetto and, with some restrictions, could buy property. Although the Protestant establishment sought to impose restrictions, civic authorities were reluctant to restrict such productive members of society.

The 17th century saw more Jewish refugees arrive, this time Ashkenazim (Jews from Europe outside of Iberia), fleeing pogroms in Central and Eastern Europe. Amsterdam became the largest Jewish centre in Europe – some 10,000 strong by Napoleonic times. The guilds and all remaining restrictions on Jews were abolished during the French occupation, and Amsterdam's Jewish community thrived in the 19th century.

All that came to an end, however, with WWII. The Nazis brought about the near-complete annihilation of Amsterdam's Jewish community. Before the war about 140,000 Jews lived in the Netherlands, of whom about 90,000 lived in Amsterdam (comprising 13% of the city's population). Only about 5500 of Amsterdam's Jews survived the war, barely one in 16, the lowest proportion of anywhere in Western Europe.

Today there are approximately 30,000 Jews in the Netherlands, some half of whom live in Amsterdam.

1966	1976	1980	2001
Crown Princess Beatrix marries German-born Claus von Amsberg (1926–2002). Despite violent protests on their wedding day he ultimately becomes one of the most popular Dutch royals.	The Netherlands' drug laws distinguish soft from hard drugs; possession of small amounts of marijuana is decriminalised.	Queen Beatrix' investiture in Amsterdam is disrupted by smoke bombs and riots instigated by squatters reacting against the lack of affordable housing.	The Netherlands becomes the first country in the world to legalise same-sex marriage. Numerous nations follow suit in the years after.

New Millennium (2000–Present)

Ups and downs have characterised the 21st century for Amsterdam. Debate erupted over the Netherlands' policy towards newcomers, which quickly led to a tightening of immigration laws. Pim Fortuyn, a right-wing politician, declared the country 'full' before he was assassinated in 2002.

The number of people leaving the country reached a 50-year high, although most departed for economic and family reasons. Tensions flared in 2004, when filmmaker Theo van Gogh – known for his anti-Muslim views – was murdered on an Amsterdam street. The leading political parties in the Netherlands responded with a big shift to the right. In 2006 the government passed a controversial immigration law requiring newcomers – except those from countries with reciprocal arrangements or pre-existing treaties – to have competency in the Dutch language and culture before they could get a residency permit. Immigration from non-Western countries subsequently slowed considerably after the law was enacted, later ticking upward again given the many refugees fleeing conflict in the Middle East.

Immigration overall has been on the rise since 2008, and Amsterdam's population continues to grow rapidly due in part to its thriving tech industries.

In 2008, the Dutch government announced plans to reduce the number of coffeeshops and legal brothels. The legal age of sex trade workers was raised from 18 to 21 in 2013, and rules went into effect in 2014 to shut down coffeeshops operating near schools. Amsterdam's authorities are often at odds with the national government when it comes to such policies, especially those involving coffeeshops, and the city is loath to enforce the issue. Nonetheless, a number of coffeeshops have closed, as have many Red Light District's windows.

HISTORY NEW MILLENNIUM (2000–PRESENT)

Amsterdam is the official (constitutional) capital of the Netherlands, but Den Haag is the seat of government and the site of the royal family's residence, Huis ten Bosch. All embassies are located in Den Haag, although some countries also have consulates general in Amsterdam.

SIGHTS FOR HISTORY BUFFS

➡ **Amsterdam Museum** (p70) Lift the veil on the city's storied past.

➡ **Stadsarchief** (p121) Plumb the city's rich archives.

➡ **Anne Frank Huis** (p106) See the annexe where the Frank family hid, and pages from Anne's poignant diary.

➡ **Verzetsmuseum** (p94) Learn about Dutch Resistance efforts during WWII.

➡ **West-Indisch Huis** (p108) Ponder the 17th-century building where the Dutch West India Company's governors authorised establishing New Amsterdam (now New York City).

2002	2004	2008	2010
Pim Fortuyn, a hard-line politician on immigration and integration, is assassinated. The ruling Dutch parties shift to the right after suffering major losses in the national election.	Activist filmmaker Theo van Gogh, a fierce critic of Islam, is murdered, touching off intense debate over the limits of Dutch multicultural society.	The city announces Project 1012. The goal is to clean up the Red Light District and close prostitution windows and coffeeshops believed to be controlled by organised crime.	Members of the Dutch government officially apologise to the Jewish community for failing to protect the Jewish population from genocide.

A budget crisis over austerity measures as a result of the global financial crisis led to the fall of the Dutch government in 2012. Subsequent elections saw Prime Minister Mark Rutte retain the position of de-facto head of government and form a new coalition government with his liberal People's Party for Freedom and Democracy (VVD) and the centre-left Labour party. The latter was the faction of Eberhard van der Laan, who was mayor of Amsterdam from 2010 until his death in office in 2017.

At the Royal Palace, Queen Beatrix stepped down after 33 years, abdicating in favour of her eldest son Willem-Alexander, who became king on 30 April 2013. He is the first male to accede to the Dutch throne since 1890.

In the 2017 Dutch general election, Mark Rutte's VVD party defeated controversial far-right politician Geert Wilders' Party for Freedom (PVV), gaining 33 seats to the PVV's 20. The next general election will take place in 2021.

In July 2018, Femke Halsema became Amsterdam's first-ever female mayor and the first from the left-wing Green political party GroenLinks, after it prevailed at the local elections in March the same year. The next municipal elections will be held in 2022.

It was revealed in 2017 that King Willem-Alexander, a qualified pilot, had been flying twice a month as a 'guest pilot' for Dutch airline KLM (and prior to that, Martinair) for 21 years. He has since stepped down from the part-time job.

HISTORY NEW MILLENNIUM (2000–PRESENT)

2013	2015	2017	2018
After a 33-year reign, Queen Beatrix abdicates in favour of her eldest son, Willem-Alexander, who becomes the Netherlands' first king in 123 years.	Scores of sex workers and their supporters take to the streets to protest the closure of roughly one-fifth of the Red Light District's windows.	Prime Minister Mark Rutte's People's Party for Freedom and Democracy (VVD) defeats Geert Wilders' Party for Freedom (PVV) in the national elections.	Femke Halsema becomes Amsterdam's inaugural female mayor and the first mayor from the left-wing Green political party GroenLinks.

Dutch Painting

They don't call them the Dutch Masters for nothing. The line-up includes Rembrandt, Frans Hals and Jan Vermeer – these iconic artists are some of the world's most revered and celebrated painters. And then, of course, there's Vincent van Gogh, who toiled in ignominy while supported by his loving brother Theo, and 20th-century artists including De Stijl proponent Piet Mondrian and graphic genius MC Escher. Understanding these quintessential Dutch artists requires a journey back into history.

15th & 16th Centuries (Flemish & Dutch Schools)

Above: *The Merry Family* (p246), Jan Steen

Prior to the late 16th century, when Belgium was still part of the Low Countries, art focused on the Flemish cities of Ghent, Bruges and Antwerp. Paintings of the Flemish School featured biblical and allegorical subject matter popular with the Church, the court and (to a lesser extent) the nobility, who, after all, paid the bills and called the shots.

Among the most famous names of the era are Jan van Eyck (c 1385–1441), the founder of the Flemish School and one of the earliest artists to use oils in detailed panel painting; Rogier van der Weyden (1400–64), whose religious portraits showed the personalities of his subjects; and Hieronymus (aka Jeroen) Bosch (1450–1516), with his macabre allegorical paintings full of religious topics. Pieter Bruegel the Elder (1525–69) used Flemish landscapes and peasant life in his allegorical scenes.

In the northern Low Countries, painters began to develop a style of their own. Although the artists of the day never achieved the level of recognition of their Flemish counterparts, the Dutch School, as it came to be called, was known for favouring realism over allegory. Haarlem, just west of Amsterdam, was the centre of this movement, with artists such as Jan Mostaert (1475–1555), Lucas van Leyden (1494–1533) and Jan van Scorel (1495–1562). Painters in the city of Utrecht were famous for using chiaroscuro (deep contrast of light and shade), a technique associated with the Italian master Caravaggio.

17th Century (Golden Age)

When the Spanish were expelled from the Low Countries, the character of the art market changed. There was no longer the Church to buy artworks and no court to speak of, so art became a business, and artists were forced to survive in a free market. In place of Church and court emerged a new, bourgeois society of merchants, artisans and shopkeepers who didn't mind spending money to brighten up their houses and workplaces. The key: they had to be pictures the buyers could relate to.

Painters became entrepreneurs in their own right, churning out banal works, copies and masterpieces in factory-like studios. Paintings were mass-produced and sold at markets alongside furniture and chickens. Soon the wealthiest households were covered in paintings from top to bottom. Foreign visitors commented that even bakeries and butcher shops seemed to have a painting or two on the wall. Most painters specialised in one of the main genres of the day.

Rembrandt van Rijn

The 17th century's greatest artist, Rembrandt van Rijn (1606–69), grew up a miller's son in Leiden, but had become an accomplished painter by his early 20s.

In 1631 he went to Amsterdam to run the painting studio of the wealthy art-dealer Hendrick van Uylenburgh. Portraits were the studio's cash cow, and Rembrandt and his staff (or 'pupils') churned out scores of them, including group portraits such as *The Anatomy Lesson of Dr Tulp*. In 1634 he married Van Uylenburgh's niece, Saskia, who often modelled for him.

Rembrandt fell out with his boss, but his wife's capital helped him buy the sumptuous house next door to Van Uylenburgh's studio (the current Museum het Rembrandthuis, p89). There Rembrandt set up his own studio, with staff who worked in a warehouse in the Jordaan. These were happy years: his paintings were a success and his studio became the largest in Holland, though his gruff manner and open agnosticism didn't win him dinner-party invitations from the elite.

Rembrandt became one of the city's biggest art collectors. He was a master manipulator, and not only of images: the painter was also known to have his own pictures bid up at auctions. He often sketched and painted for himself, urging his staff to do likewise. Residents of the surrounding Jewish quarter provided perfect material for his dramatic biblical scenes.

DUTCH PAINTING 17TH CENTURY (GOLDEN AGE)

Female painters during the Dutch Golden Age were rare. Judith Leyster (1609–60) was the only woman registered with the artists' guild during the time. She trained with Frans Hals, and his influence is seen in her fluid portraits. The Rijksmuseum has some of her works.

Great Rembrandt Paintings

The Night Watch (1642; Rijksmuseum)

The Denial of St Peter (1660; Rijksmuseum)

Self Portrait (1628; Rijksmuseum)

The Merry Drinker, Frans Hals

Night Watch

In 1642, a year after the birth of their son Titus, Saskia died and business went downhill. Although Rembrandt's majestic group portrait *The Night Watch* (1642) was hailed by art critics (it's now the Rijksmuseum's prize exhibit, and there's a life-size bronze sculpture re-creation on Rembrandtplein), some of the influential people he depicted were not pleased. Each subject had paid 100 guilders, and some were unhappy at being shoved to the background. In response, Rembrandt told them where they could shove their complaints. Suddenly he received far fewer orders.

Rembrandt began an affair with his son's governess, but kicked her out a few years later when he fell for the new maid, Hendrickje Stoffels, who bore him a daughter. The public didn't take kindly to the man's lifestyle and his spiralling debts, and in 1656 he went bankrupt. His house and rich art collection were sold and he moved to the Rozengracht in the Jordaan.

Jan Steen was also a tavern keeper, and his depictions of domestic chaos led to the Dutch expression 'a Jan Steen household'.

Etchings

No longer the darling of the wealthy, Rembrandt continued to paint, draw and etch – his etchings on display in the Museum het Rembrandthuis are some of the finest ever produced. He also received the occasional commission, including the monumental *Conspiracy of Claudius Civilis* (1661) for the city hall, although authorities disliked it and had it removed. In 1662 he completed the *Staalmeesters* (The Syndics) for the drapers' guild and ensured that everybody remained clearly visible, though it ended up being his last group portrait.

Later Works

The works of his later period show that Rembrandt had lost none of his touch. No longer constrained by the wishes of clients, he enjoyed new-

The Damrak, George Hendrik Breitner (p246)

found freedom. His works became more unconventional, yet showed an ever-stronger empathy with their subject matter, as in *The Jewish Bride* (1667). The many portraits of Titus and Hendrickje, and his ever-gloomier self-portraits, are among the most stirring in the history of art.

A plague epidemic between 1663 and 1666 killed one in seven Amsterdammers, including Hendrickje. Titus died in 1668, aged 27 and just married; Rembrandt died a year later, a broken man.

Frans Hals

Another great painter of this period, Frans Hals (c 1582–1666), was born in Antwerp but lived in Haarlem. He devoted most of his career to portraits, dabbling in occasional genre scenes with dramatic chiaroscuro. His ability to capture his subjects' expressions was equal to Rembrandt's, though he didn't explore their characters as much. Both masters used the same expressive, unpolished brush strokes and their styles went from bright exuberance in their early careers to dark and solemn later on. His *Merry Drinker* (1628–30), in the Rijksmuseum's collection, with its bold brush strokes, could almost have been painted by an Impressionist.

Group Portraits

Hals also specialised in group portraits, in which the participants were depicted in almost natural poses, unlike the rigid line-ups produced by lesser contemporaries – though he wasn't as cavalier as Rembrandt in subordinating faces to the composition. A good example is the pair of paintings known collectively as *The Regents & the Regentesses of the Old Men's Almshouses* (1664) in the Frans Hals Museum in Haarlem. The museum is a space Hals knew intimately; he spent his final years in the almshouse.

Great Frans Hals Paintings

The Merry Drinker (1628–30; Rijksmuseum)

Wedding Portrait (1622; Rijksmuseum)

Meagre Company (1637; Rijksmuseum)

Johannes Vermeer

The grand trio of 17th-century masters is completed by Johannes (also known as Jan) Vermeer (1632–75) of Delft. He produced only 35 meticulously crafted paintings in his career and died poor with 10 children; his baker accepted two paintings from his wife as payment for a debt of more than 600 guilders. Yet Vermeer mastered genre painting like no other artist. His paintings include historical and biblical scenes from his earlier career, his famous *View of Delft* (1661) in the Mauritshuis in Den Haag, and some tender portraits of unknown women, such as the stunningly beautiful *Girl with a Pearl Earring* (c 1665), also hanging in the Mauritshuis.

To comprehend Vermeer's use of perspective, study *The Love Letter* (1670) in the Rijksmuseum (p153). *The Little Street* (1658) in the Rijksmuseum's collection is Vermeer's only street scene.

Great Vermeer Paintings

Kitchen Maid (c 1660; Rijksmuseum)

Woman in Blue Reading a Letter (c 1663; Rijksmuseum)

Girl with a Pearl Earring (c 1665; Mauritshuis, Den Haag)

Other Golden Age Painters

Around the middle of the century, the focus on mood and subtle play of light began to make way for the splendour of the baroque. Jacob van Ruysdael (c 1628–82) went for dramatic skies, while Albert Cuyp (1620–91) painted Italianate landscapes. Van Ruysdael's pupil Meindert Hobbema (1638–1709) preferred less heroic, more playful scenes, full of detail.

The genre paintings of Jan Steen (1626–79) show the almost frivolous aspect of baroque. A good example is the animated revelry of *The Merry Family* (1668) in the Rijksmuseum; it shows adults having a good time around the dinner table, oblivious to the children in the foreground pouring themselves a drink.

18th Century

Vermeer's work is known for serene light pouring through tall windows. The calm, spiritual effect is enhanced by dark blues, deep reds, warm yellows and supremely balanced composition. Good examples include the Rijksmuseum's *Kitchen Maid* (aka *The Milkmaid*) and *Woman in Blue Reading a Letter.*

The Golden Age of Dutch painting ended almost as suddenly as it began when the French invaded the Low Countries in 1672. The economy collapsed and the market for paintings went south with it. Painters who stayed in business concentrated on 'safe' works that repeated earlier successes. In the 18th century they copied French styles, pandering to the fashion for anything French.

Cornelis Troost (1696–1750) was one of the best genre painters, and is sometimes compared to the British artist William Hogarth (1697–1764) for his satirical as well as sensitive portraits of ordinary people; Troost, too, introduced scenes of domestic revelry into his pastels.

Gerard de Lairesse (1641–1711) and Jacob de Wit (1695–1754) specialised in decorating the walls and ceilings of buildings – De Wit's trompe l'oeil decorations (painted illusions that look real) in the Bijbels Museum (p108) are worth seeing.

19th Century

The late 18th century and most of the 19th century produced little of note, save for the landscapes and seascapes of Johan Barthold Jongkind (1819–91), the gritty, almost photographic Amsterdam scenes of George Hendrik Breitner (1857–1923) and – of course – the works of Vincent van Gogh (1853–90).

Jongkind and Breitner appear to have inspired French Impressionists, many of whom visited Amsterdam. They reinvented 17th-century realism and influenced the Hague School of the last decades of the 19th century. Painters such as Hendrik Mesdag (1831–1915), Jozef Israels (1824–1911) and the three Maris brothers (Jacob, Matthijs and Willem) created landscapes, seascapes and genre works, including Mesdag's impressive *Panorama Mesdag* (1881; located in Den Haag), a gigantic, 360-degree cylindrical painting of the seaside town of Scheveningen.

Top: *Self Protrait*,
Vincent van Gogh
Right: Johannes
Vermeer's *Milkmaid*
(p153) at the Rijks-
museum

Vincent Van Gogh

Without a doubt, the greatest 19th-century Dutch painter was Vincent van Gogh (1853–90), whose convulsive patterns and furious colours were in a world of their own and still defy comfortable categorisation. (A post-Impressionist? A forerunner of expressionism?)

While the Dutch Masters were known for their dark, brooding paintings, it was Van Gogh who created an identity of suffering as an art form, with a morbid style all his own. Even today, he epitomises the epic struggle of the artist: the wrenching poverty; the lack of public acclaim; the reliance upon a patron – in his case, his faithful brother Theo; the mental instability; the untimely death by suicide; and, of course, one of the most iconic images of an artist's self-destruction, the severed ear.

The Artist's Legend

Vincent van Gogh may have been poor – he sold only one painting in his lifetime – but he wasn't old. It's easy to forget from his self-portraits, in which he appears much older (partly the effects of his poverty), that he was only 37 when he died. But his short life continues to influence art to this day.

Born in Zundert in 1853, the Dutch painter lived in Paris with his younger brother Theo, an art dealer, who financially supported him from his modest income. In Paris he became acquainted with seminal artists including Edgar Degas, Camille Pissarro, Henri de Toulouse-Lautrec and Paul Gauguin.

Van Gogh moved south to Arles, Provence, in 1888. Revelling in its intense light and bright colours, he painted sunflowers, irises and other vivid subjects with a burning fervour. He sent paintings to Theo in Paris to sell, and dreamed of founding an artists colony in Provence, but only Gauguin followed up his invitation. Their differing artistic approaches – Gauguin believed in painting from imagination, Van Gogh painting what he saw – and their artistic temperaments, fuelled by absinthe, came to a head with the argument that led to Van Gogh lopping his ear (which he gave to a sex worker acquaintance) and his subsequent committal in Arles.

In May 1889, Van Gogh voluntarily entered an asylum in St-Rémy de Provence, where he painted prolifically during his one-year, one-week and one-day confinement, including masterpieces like *Irises* and *Starry Night*. While there, Theo sent him a positive French newspaper critique of his work. The following month, Anna Boch, sister of his friend Eugène Boch, bought *The Red Vines* (or *The Red Vineyard;* 1888) for 400 francs (less than €100 today). It now hangs in Moscow's Pushkin Museum.

Legacy of a Tortured Genius

On 16 May 1890 Van Gogh moved to Auvers-sur-Oise, just outside Paris, to be closer to Theo, but on 27 July that year he shot himself, possibly to avoid further financial burden on his brother, whose wife had just had a baby son, named Vincent, and who was also supporting their ailing mother. Van Gogh died two days later with Theo at his side. Theo subsequently had a breakdown, was also committed, and succumbed to physical illness. He died, aged 33, just six months after Van Gogh.

It would be less than a decade before Van Gogh's talent would start to achieve wide recognition, and by the early 1950s, he had become a household name. In 1990 he broke the record for a single painting *(A Portrait of Doctor Gachet)* at Christie's, which fetched US$82.5 million. Accounting for inflation, it's still one of the highest prices paid at a public auction for art to this day.

Even Van Gogh's last words ring with the kind of excruciating, melancholic beauty that his best paintings express. With Theo at his side, two days after he shot himself in the chest, he's said to have uttered in French *'la tristesse durera toujours'* (the sadness will last forever).

Van Gogh produced an astonishing output of art during his 10-year artistic career, of which 864 paintings and almost 1200 drawings and prints have survived.

20th Century & Beyond

During the 20th century, the standout De Stijl movement was a major influence on the arts, while abstract expressionism also made waves. In the 21st century, artistic endeavours have focused on Dutch design and tech innovations, but the works of up-and-coming Amsterdam artists can be seen in galleries and studios throughout the city.

De Stijl

De Stijl (The Style), also known as neoplasticism, was a Dutch design movement that aimed to harmonise all the arts by bringing artistic expressions back to their essence. Its advocate was the magazine of the same name, first published in 1917 by Theo van Doesburg (1883–1931).

A major proponent of De Stijl was Piet Mondrian (originally Mondriaan; 1872–1944), who initially painted in the Hague School tradition. After flirting with cubism, he began working with bold rectangular patterns, using only the three primary colours (yellow, blue and red) set against the three neutrals (white, grey and black). He named this style neoplasticism and viewed it as an undistorted expression of reality in pure form and pure colour. His *Composition in Red, Black, Blue, Yellow & Grey* (1920), in the Stedelijk Museum's (p158) collection, is an elaborate example.

Mondrian's later works were more stark (or 'pure') and became dynamic again when he moved to New York in 1940. The world's largest collection of his paintings resides in the Gemeentemuseum (Municipal Museum) in his native Den Haag.

Throughout the 1920s and 1930s, De Stijl also attracted sculptors, poets, architects and designers. One of these was Gerrit Rietveld (1888–1964), designer of the Van Gogh Museum and several other buildings, but best known internationally for his furniture, such as the Red Blue Chair (1918) and his range of uncomfortable zigzag seats that, viewed side-on, formed a 'z' with a backrest.

MC Escher

One of the most remarkable graphic artists of the 20th century was Maurits Cornelis Escher (1898–1972). His drawings, lithographs and woodcuts of blatantly impossible images continue to fascinate mathematicians: a waterfall feeds itself; people go up and down a staircase that ends where it starts; a pair of hands draw each other. You can see his work at Stedelijk Museum (p158), and at the dedicated Escher in het Paleis in Den Haag.

CoBrA

After WWII, artists rebelled against artistic conventions and vented their rage in abstract expressionism. In Amsterdam, Karel Appel (1921–2006) and Constant (Constant Nieuwenhuys; 1920–2005) drew on styles pioneered by Paul Klee and Joan Miró, and exploited bright colours and 'uncorrupted' children's art to produce lively works that leapt off the canvas. In Paris in 1945 they met up with the Danish Asger Jorn (1914–73) and the Belgian Corneille (Cornelis van Beverloo; 1922–2010), and together with several other artists and writers formed a group known as CoBrA (Copenhagen, Brussels, Amsterdam). It has been called the last great avant-garde movement.

Their first major exhibition, in the Stedelijk Museum in 1949, aroused a storm of protest (with comments such as 'my child paints like that, too'). Still, the CoBrA artists exerted a strong influence in their respective countries, even after they disbanded in 1951. The Cobra Museum (p160) in Amstelveen, south of central Amsterdam, displays a good range of their works, including colourful ceramics.

DUTCH PAINTING 20TH CENTURY & BEYOND

Van Gogh Museum's Famous Five

Sunflowers (1889)

Wheatfield with Crows (1890)

Self Portrait with Felt Hat (1886–87)

Almond Blossom (1890)

The Bedroom (1888)

MC Escher's work was greatly influenced by his visit to the Alhambra, the 14th-century Moorish palace in Granada, Spain. The repetitive, interlocking geometric patterns sculpted into the structure's walls and ceilings provided inspiration for his own designs.

Architecture in Amsterdam

The lovely canalscapes depicted in centuries-old paintings of Amsterdam remain remarkably unchanged. The city was spared from wartime destruction, and it has been careful about preserving its core from ham-fisted developers. In fact, the enchanting old centre contains no fewer than 7000 historical monuments interspersed between its humpback bridges and profusion of trees including leafy elms, plane trees, lime trees, poplars and willows along the canal banks.

A City Built on Freedom

Above: Centraal
Station (p69)

Unlike many capitals, Amsterdam has few grand edifices to trumpet. There is hardly the space for a Louvre or a Westminster Abbey, which would be out of keeping with Calvinist modesty anyway. But you'll be pressed to find another city with such a wealth of residential architecture, and with an appeal that owes more to understated elegance than to power and pomp.

Amsterdam's beauty was built on freedoms – of trade, religion and aesthetics. Many of its gabled mansions and warehouses were erected by merchants in the Golden Age, with little meddling by city officials. Thus its leading citizens determined the look of the city, in what amounted to an early urban experiment.

Dutch architecture today is one of the country's most successful exports, with names such as Rem Koolhaas and Lars Spuybroek popping up on blueprints from Beijing to Seattle. Back home, rivalry can be intensely local as talents in Amsterdam and Rotterdam jostle for a spot in the architectural pantheon.

Middle Ages

Around the year 1200, Amsterdam was a muddy little trading post on the Amstel river. The soft marshland couldn't support brick, so the earliest houses were made of timber, often with clay and thatched roofs (similar to ones still standing in Amsterdam Noord today), but even these modest abodes would list into the soggy ground.

Two fires burned down much of the city centre in 1421 and 1452, and wood was subsequently outlawed as a main building material. There was plenty of clay to make brick, but this was too heavy, as was stone.

Engineers solved the problem by driving piles into the peat. Timber gave way to heavier brick, and thatched roofs were replaced by sturdier tile. Brick and sandstone became de rigueur for most structures.

Dutch Renaissance

As the Italian Renaissance filtered north, Dutch architects developed a rich ornamental style that merged the classical and the traditional with their own brand of subtle humour. They inserted mock columns, known as pilasters, into facades and replaced old spout gables with step gables. Sculptures, columns and little obelisks suddenly appeared all over the Canal Ring. Red brick and horizontal bands of white were all the rage, too.

Without a doubt, the best-known talent of this period was Hendrick de Keyser (1565–1621), the city sculptor. He worked with Hendrick Staets, a canal ring planner, and Cornelis Danckerts, the city bricklayer, to produce some of Amsterdam's finest masterpieces, including magnificent canal architecture such as the Bartolotti House (Map p300) at Herengracht 170-172. De Keyser also designed several of Amsterdam's churches. His Zuiderkerk (p90), Noorderkerk (p139) and Westerkerk (p108) show off the style of the day with ornate steeples and layouts, and florid details enlivening the walls and roof lines.

One of the city's signature buildings and a Rembrandt favourite, the Montelbaanstoren (p91) was built as a defensive tower in 1516. Its octagonal steeple was designed by master architect Hendrick de Keyser in 1606 to house a clock that's still in use today.

ARCHITECTURE IN AMSTERDAM A CITY BUILT ON FREEDOM

Must-See Canal Buildings

Bartolotti House
(Western Canal Ring)

Entrepotdok
(Plantage)

Museum
Willet-Holthuysen
(Southern Canal Ring)

Huis Met de
Hoofden (Western
Canal Ring)

GABLES

Among Amsterdam's great architectural treasures are its magnificent gables – the roof-level facades that adorn the elegant houses along the canals. The gable hid the roof from public view, and helped to identify the house, until the French occupiers introduced house numbers in 1795. Gables then became more of a fashion accessory.

There are four main types of gable: the simple spout gable, with diagonal outline and semicircular windows or shutters, that was used mainly for warehouses from the 1580s to the early 1700s; the step gable, a late-Gothic design favoured by Dutch Renaissance architects; the neck gable, also known as the bottle gable, a durable design introduced in the 1640s; and the bell gable, which appeared in the 1660s and became popular in the 18th century.

NEMO Science Museum (p94) by architect Renzo Piano

Dutch Classicism

During the Golden Age of art in the 17th century, architects such as Jacob van Campen and brothers Philips and Justus Vingboons decided to stick to Greek and Roman classical design, dropping many of De Keyser's playful decorations.

Influenced by Italian architects, the Dutch made facades look like temples and pilasters like columns. All revolved around clever deception. Neck gables with decorative scrolls came into fashion, often crowned by a temple-like roof. Garlands appeared under windows, and red brick, which was prone to crumbling, was hardened with dark paint.

The Vingboons designed the Bijbels Museum (p108) and the fine example at Keizersgracht 319 (Map p302). Don't miss Justus Vingboons' Trippenhuis (p92): it's about as austere as it gets. It was built between 1660 and 1664 for the wealthy Trip brothers, who made their fortune in metals, artillery and ammunition. The most striking hallmarks are up at roof level – chimneys shaped like mortars.

The most impressive example of Dutch Classicism is Jacob van Campen's town hall (now the Royal Palace). It was the largest town hall in Europe, and was given a precious shell of Bentham sandstone, and a marble interior inspired by the Roman palaces.

18th-Century 'Louis Styles'

The Gallic-culture craze proved a godsend for architect and designer Daniel Marot, a Huguenot refugee who introduced matching French interiors and exteriors to Amsterdam. Living areas with white stuccoed ceilings were bathed in light that streamed in through sash windows. As the elegant bell gable became a must, many architects opted for the next big thing: a horizontal cornice.

Canal houses with different kinds of gables (p251)

The dignified facades and statuary of the Louis XIV style hung on until about 1750. In rapid succession it was followed by Louis XV style – rococo rocks, swirls and waves – and Louis XVI designs, with pilasters and pillars making a comeback. The late-Louis-style Felix Meritis (p114), with its enormous Corinthian half-columns, is an exemplar of the genre.

19th-Century Neo-styles

After the Napoleonic era, the Dutch economy stagnated, merchants closed their pocketbooks and fine architecture ground to a halt. Seen as safe and sellable, neoclassicism held sway until the more prosperous 1860s, when planners again felt free to rediscover the past.

The late 19th century was all about the neo-Gothic, harking back to the grand Gothic cathedrals, and the neo-Renaissance. It was around this time that Catholics regained their freedom to worship openly, and built churches like mad in neo-Gothic style.

A leading architect of the period was Pierre Cuypers, known for his skilful design of several neo-Gothic churches. Cuypers also designed two of Amsterdam's most iconic buildings: Centraal Station (p262) and the Rijksmuseum (p153), both of which display Gothic forms and Dutch Renaissance brickwork. A similar melange is CH Peters' General Post Office, now the Magna Plaza (p85) shopping centre.

Around the turn of the century, the neo-Goths suddenly fell out of favour as art nouveau spread its curvy plant-like shapes across Europe. Gorgeous relics of the era include the Amsterdam American Hotel (p125) and the riotous Pathé Tuschinskitheater (p132).

Notable Historic Buildings

Oude Kerk (Old Church; Red Light District)

Nieuwe Kerk (New Church; Medieval Centre)

Royal Palace (Medieval Centre)

Amsterdam American Hotel (Southern Canal Ring)

Rijksmuseum (the South)

Berlage & the Amsterdam School

The father of modern Dutch architecture was Hendrik Petrus Berlage (1856–1934). He criticised the lavish neo-styles and their reliance on the past, instead favouring simplicity and a rational use of materials.

In Berlage's view, residential blocks were a holistic concept rather than a collection of individual homes. Not always popular with city elders, Berlage influenced what became known as the Amsterdamse School (Amsterdam School) and its leading exponents Michel de Klerk, Piet Kramer and Johan van der Mey.

The titans of the Amsterdam School designed buildings of 'Plan South', an ambitious project mapped out by Berlage. It was a productive period: the Beurs van Berlage (p71) displayed the master's ideals to the full, with exposed inner struts and striking but simple brick accents.

Johan van der Mey's remarkable Scheepvaarthuis (p90) was the first building in the Amsterdam School style. It draws on the street layout to reproduce a ship's bow.

De Klerk's Het Schip (p140) and Kramer's De Dageraad (p177) are like fairy-tale fortresses rendered in a Dutch version of art deco. Their eccentric details are charming, but the 'form over function' ethic meant these places weren't always great to live in.

> The Amsterdam School ushered in a new philosophy of city planning, given a boost by the 1928 Olympic Games held in Amsterdam. Humble housing blocks became brick sculptures with curved corners, odd windows and rocket-shaped towers, to the marvel (or disgust) of traditionalists.

Functionalism

As the Amsterdam School flourished, a new generation began to rebel against the movement's impractical and expensive methods. In 1927 they formed a group called 'de 8', influenced by the German Bauhaus school, America's Frank Lloyd Wright and France's Le Corbusier.

Architects such as Ben Merkelbach and Gerrit Rietveld believed that form should follow function and advocated steel, glass and concrete. The Committee of Aesthetics Control didn't agree, however, which is why you'll see little functionalism in the Canal Ring.

After WWII, entire suburbs, such as the sprawling Bijlmermeer in Amsterdam-Zuidoost, were designed along functionalist lines. By the late 1960s, however, resistance had grown against such impersonal, large-scale projects.

Rietveld left Amsterdam the Van Gogh Museum (p156), where the minimalist, open space allows the artist's works to shine.

> **Notable Contemporary Buildings**
>
> NEMO Science Museum (Eastern Islands)
>
> EYE Film Institute (Amsterdam Noord)
>
> Muziekgebouw aan 't IJ (Eastern Islands)
>
> OBA: Centrale Bibliotheek Amsterdam (Eastern Islands)

The Present

On the shores of the IJ River just east of Centraal Station stands the Oosterdokseiland, a row of landmark buildings that includes the OBA: Centrale Bibliotheek Amsterdam (p95) and features a high-density mix of shops, restaurants, offices, apartments and a music conservatorium.

Looking southeast from Centraal Station, you can't miss the green copper snout of NEMO (p94), a science museum designed by Renzo Piano that resembles the prow of a ship. The cube-like glass shell of the

---

HOISTS & HOUSES THAT TIP

Many canal houses deliberately tip forward. Given the narrowness of staircases, owners needed an easy way to move large goods and furniture to the upper floors. The solution: a hoist built into the gable, to lift objects up and in through the windows. The tilt allowed loading without bumping into the house front. Some houses even have huge hoist-wheels in the attic with a rope and hook that run through the hoist beam.

The forward lean also makes the houses seem larger, which makes it easier to admire the facade and gable – a fortunate coincidence for everyone.

Top: Westerkerk bell
tower (p108)
Right: Entrepotdok (p92)

Kraanspoor (p201) by OTH Architecten

Muziekgebouw aan 't IJ (p101) stands not far to the north, on the IJ waterfront. In the Plantage district, a must-see is the huge Entrepotdok (p93). Sprawling half a kilometre along a former loading dock, the shipping warehouses have been recast as desirable apartments, studios and commercial spaces.

Heading east, the Eastern Islands and docklands were full of derelict industrial buildings until the 1980s and early '90s, when they got a new lease of life. Borneo, Java and KNSM islands are home to innovative residential projects as well as stylishly repurposed buildings.

Further east is the IJburg neighbourhood, on a string of artificial islands 10km from the city centre. Some 45,000 residents are predicted to inhabit the islands upon completion. The curvaceous Enneüs Heerma Brug, dubbed 'Dolly Parton Bridge' by locals, links it to the mainland.

Northwest of Centraal Station and also on the IJ, you'll find a flurry of construction in the Houthavens ('lumber ports') area, whose seven artificial islands are transforming into a new residential hub. One of the most striking sites in the area is the REM Eiland (p141), a 22m-high former pirate-broadcasting rig now housing a restaurant and bar.

Multistorey residential and commercial buildings are also mushrooming on the Amstel's upper eastern side.

Across the IJ River in Amsterdam Noord, housing blocks and office towers are springing up on a former industrial estate at the Overhoeks development, where the architectural centrepieces are the EYE Film Institute (p201) and A'DAM Tower (p200), along with the glass-box-topped craneway, the Kraanspoor (p201).

Based in Amsterdam, influential architecture firm Concrete has designed projects around the globe, from London's Spice Market to Seoul's Hyundai finance outlets and New Jersey's Harborside Plaza skyscrapers. Locally, Concrete designed REM Eiland and the Van Gogh Museum's central hall, among many, many other buildings.

Top: Bartolotti House (p251)
Right: EYE Film Institute (p201) by Delugan Meissl Associated Architects

Dutch Design

Contemporary Dutch design has a reputation for minimalist, creative approaches to everyday furniture and homewares, mixed with vintage twists and tongue-in-cheek humour to keep it fresh. What started out as a few innovators accelerated to become a movement that put the Netherlands at the forefront of the industry. Dutch fashion is also reaching far beyond the country's borders, with designs that are vibrant and imaginative, yet practical, too.

The Beginning of a Movement

The Dutch design movement today can be traced back to a handful of designers working in different materials and mediums around the same time, who started gaining respect at home and abroad.

Providing a key platform was Droog (p102), established in 1993. This design collective works with a community of designers to help produce its works and sell them to the world, with the partners to make it happen and the connections to facilitate collaborations with big brands. Signature Droog designs employ surreal wit, such as a chandelier made of 80-plus light bulbs clustered like fish eggs, or an off-centre umbrella inspired by the country's blustery weather.

Design Pioneers

Dutch Design Events

....

Amsterdam Fashion Week (www. fashionweek. nl) Twice-yearly runway shows.

....

Design Icons (www. design-icons.com) Weekend-long festival in early April.

....

vt wonen&design beurs (www.vt wonen.nl) Six-day interior design fair in early October.

Among the contemporary pioneers was Marcel Wanders, who first drew international acclaim for his iconic Knotted Chair, produced by Droog in 1996. Made from a knotted aramid-and-carbon-fibre thread and resin, Wanders' air drying technique meant it was ultimately shaped by gravity. It's now in the permanent collection of the Museum of Modern Art in New York. Wanders founded Moooi (p149) in 2001 – the name is a play on the Dutch word for 'beautiful', with an additional 'o' symbolising extra beauty and uniqueness. Now a world-leading design label, Moooi also showcases other pioneering designers such as Maarten Baas (best known for his Smoke series of charred timber furniture) and Studio Job (Job Smeets and Nynke Tynagel's neo-Gothic decorative arts).

Other pioneering designers include Droog designer Jurgen Bey, who has strong architectural links, working with interior and public-space design; Hella Jongerius, whose designs include porcelain plates and tiles using new printing techniques; Piet Hein Eek, who works with reclaimed wood; sculptor Hans van Bentem, who produces dazzling chandeliers; and Ineke Hans, whose celebrated recyclable plastic Ahrend 380 chair incorporates a table.

Furniture, product and interior designer Richard Hutten has been involved with Droog since its foundation. Famed for his 'no sign of design' humorous, functional furniture, his works have been exhibited worldwide and are held in the permanent collections of museums including Amsterdam's Stedelijk Museum (p158).

Gaining Momentum

The momentum that Wanders, Bey, Hutten and others generated inspired a new wave of young designers. This second generation focused not just on concept and function, but also on aesthetics. Often starting with traditional influences, their works tend to mix vintage and reclaimed materials, colour and form, resulting in something totally unique. Renowned second-wave makers include Wieki Somers, awarded for designs such as her Merry-go-round Coat Rack and rowboat-shaped Bathboat tub and Marloes Hoedeman, who designed the interiors of retailer Scotch & Soda and who has since segued into fashion design, with her lingerie and swimwear brand Love Stories.

The Future of Dutch Design

Dutch designers to watch out for include: Lex Pott, working with raw materials including wood, stone and metal; Mae Engelgeer, a designer who incorporates tufts of colour and texture into towels, rugs and other textiles at her studio in the Eastern Islands; Dirk Vander Kooij, who uses 3D printing to create furniture and lighting; and Floris Wubben, who makes furniture from die-cast clay.

The waves of intrepid designers have also triggered an explosion of new design stores stocking innovative pieces by established and emerging artists, which continues to feed the industry. Not simply places to view the artistic designs, gain inspiration, or pick up products for your own home or workplace (although they are all that), these accessible galleries frequently incorporate cafes where you can browse design magazines amid the wares (and where, often, even the chair you're sitting on is for sale).

Design & Fashion

As the Dutch furniture, product and interior designers were taking flight, so too was a generation of cutting-edge fashion designers.

Amsterdam fashion house Viktor & Rolf, founded by Viktor Horsting and Rolf Snoeren, enjoys huge international success. From haute couture to ready-to-wear collections, their range now spans men's and women's apparel, shoes, accessories including eyewear, and fragrances. Collaborations such as with retail giant H&M have broadened their appeal.

Dutch retail brands making a global impact include Amsterdam success story Scotch & Soda (www.scotch-soda.com), selling its own-label affordable designs for men, women and children, as well as the Amsterdams Blauw denim line and a vintage furniture collection. Amsterdam brand Denham the Jeanmaker (p115) is also making a name for itself in denim wear, both in the city and as far afield as Japan.

Lingerie label Undressed by Marlies Dekkers (p117) was hailed as a new approach in lingerie design; her spin-off lines include Undressed Men, Undressed Secrets (her vintage lingerie collection), Sundressed (beachwear and sunglasses) and Nightdressed (evening wear). Launched in 2014, Marloes Hoedeman's lingerie and swimwear label Love Stories (p115) has been a runaway success that has seen her open boutiques across Europe and beyond.

Shoe and accessory designer Hester van Eeghen (p117) creates eye-catching leather shoes and handbags in bright colours, fur, suede, and geometric patterns and prints.

Headed up by Anja Klappe, Agna K (www.agnak.com) teams up with changing young designers to build its classic, well-cut womenswear collections.

Best Dutch Design Stores

Hôtel Droog (Nieuwmarkt)

Moooi (Jordaan)

Frozen Fountain (Western Canal Ring)

Hutspot (De Pijp)

X Bank (Medieval Centre)

Best Boutiques for Dutch Fashion

Locals (Medieval Centre)

Johnny at the Spot (Vondelpark)

VLVT (the South)

Tenue de Nîmes (Western Canal Ring)

Vanilia (Western Canal Ring)

Other designers to keep an eye on include Daisy Kroon, who produces brightly coloured, minimally cut womenswear, and Jivika Biervliet, who seeks out and subverts boundaries in her conceptual, wearable menswear lines. Renowned stylist to the stars Danie Bles is earning recognition with ByDanie, her line of bohemian, retro-tinged clothing and accessories for women. Amsterdam footwear label EIJK, founded by Jolanda van Eijk, handcrafts classical and contemporary high-heeled shoes and boots. Jenny from the Block (Janna Meijer) digitally designs jewellery, then 3D-prints it in precious metals.

Designer Hotels

Dutch design has now moved beyond furnishings and fashion to become a lifestyle. This is evident at several hotels that have opened in recent years, where design is implicit to the brand.

Take Droog, the trailblazing collective. It expanded its concept to Hôtel Droog (p102), a complex that houses the Droog store, along with a gallery and cafe, and a guest room (really an apartment, complete with a kitchen and separate bedroom) on the top floor.

Another inspired hotel intersecting the design and fashion spheres is the independent Hotel The Exchange (p220) in Amsterdam's former stock exchange. Created by Otto Nan and Suzanne Oxenaar, who also worked on Amsterdam's Lloyd Hotel (p221), Hotel The Exchange's 61 rooms are dressed 'like models' by young designers from the Amsterdam Fashion Institute. Decor ranges from details such as buttons or embroidery hoops on the walls to eye-popping whole-room concepts such as a gigantic knitted jumper or Rembrandt-esque collar.

Marcel Wanders put his talents to work on the Hyatt's fantastical Andaz Amsterdam (p222), in the city's former public library. Students from Eindhoven's Design Academy let their imaginations run wild creating the rooms at Hotel Not Hotel (p225).

Dutch design is at the heart of Mr Jordaan (p224) hotel, and the new W Amsterdam (p221), inside a former telephone exchange and bank that also incorporates immense design emporium X Bank (p84).

Amsterdam architectural firm Space & Matter renovated 28 of the city's canal-bridge houses, where bridge keepers once resided, to create unique short-stay apartments collectively known as SWEETS Hotel (p217).

Dutch Design Online

Dutch Design Daily (www.dutchdesigndaily.com) Highlights a new idea daily.

Dutch Profiles (http://dutchdesign.submarinechannel.com) Short videos explain design concepts.

Amsterdam Next (www.amsterdamnext.com) Guide to local interior design.

Survival Guide

Transport

ARRIVING IN AMSTERDAM

Schiphol International Airport

Situated 18km southwest of the city centre, **Schiphol International Airport** (AMS; www.schiphol.nl; Schiphol Blvd) has ATMs, currency exchanges, tourist information, car hire, train-ticket sales counters, luggage storage, food and free wi-fi. It's linked to the city centre by train.

Train

Trains run to Amsterdam's Centraal Station (€4.50 one way, 15 minutes) 24 hours a day. From 6am to 12.30am they go every 10 minutes or so; hourly in the wee hours. The rail platform is inside the terminal, down the escalator.

Shuttle Bus

A shuttle van is run by **Connexxion** (www.schipholhotel shuttle.nl; one way/return €18.50/29.50), every 30 minutes from 6.30am to 9pm, from the airport to many hotels. Look for the Connexxion desk by Arrival Hall 4.

Bus

Connexxion Bus 397/Amsterdam Airport Express from 5.11am to 12.44am or Connexxion Bus N97 from 1.15am to 4.44am (both services €6.50 one way, 25 minutes) is the quickest way to places by Museumplein and Leidseplein. Buses depart outside the arrivals hall door. Buy a ticket from the driver (credit/debit cards only, no cash).

Taxi

Taxis take 30 to 45 minutes to the centre (longer in heavy traffic), costing around €39. The taxi stand is just outside the arrivals hall door.

Lelystad Airport

Lelystad Airport (☑0320-284 770; www.lelystadairport.nl; Emoeweg 7), 50km east of Amsterdam, is undergoing a large expansion project due to be completed in 2020 that will see it take over many budget airline and freight flights from Schiphol International Airport, with newly created transport links to/from Amsterdam. Check the airport website for updates.

Centraal Train Station

Centraal Station (Map p290; Stationsplein; ☑2/4/11/12/13/14/17/24/26 Centraal Station) is in the city centre, with easy onward connections. The station has ATMs, currency exchanges, tourist information, restaurants, shops, luggage storage

---

CLIMATE CHANGE & TRAVEL

Every form of transport that relies on carbon-based fuel generates CO_2, the main cause of human-induced climate change. Modern travel is dependent on aeroplanes, which might use less fuel per kilometre per person than most cars but travel much greater distances. The altitude at which aircraft emit gases (including CO_2) and particles also contributes to their climate change impact. Many websites offer 'carbon calculators' that allow people to estimate the carbon emissions generated by their journey and, for those who wish to do so, to offset the impact of the greenhouse gases emitted with contributions to portfolios of climate-friendly initiatives throughout the world. Lonely Planet offsets the carbon footprint of all staff and author travel.

TRAIN TRIPS FROM AMSTERDAM

NS (www.ns.nl), aka Dutch Railways, runs the nation's rail service. Trains are frequent from Centraal Station and serve domestic destinations such as Haarlem, Leiden and Delft several times per hour, making for easy day trips.

The main service centre to buy tickets for both national and international trains is on the station's west side.

Domestic Tickets

➡ Tickets can be bought at the NS service desk windows or at ticketing machines. The ticket windows are easiest to use, though there is often a queue.

➡ Pay with cash, debit or credit card. Visa and MasterCard are accepted, though there is a €0.50 surcharge to use them, and they must have chip-and-PIN technology.

➡ There is a €1 surcharge for buying a single-use disposable ticket. Locals typically use a personalised, rechargeable plastic chip card (OV-Chipkaart), which exempts them from the fee.

➡ Visitors can get a non-personalised rechargeable OV-Chipkaart at NS windows or at GVB public transport offices. It costs €7.50 (non-refundable) and has a €20 minimum balance.

➡ If you want to use a ticketing machine and pay cash, bear in mind that they accept coins only (no paper bills). The machines have instructions in English.

➡ There's little difference in comfort between 1st and 2nd class, but if the train is crowded there are usually more seats in 1st class.

➡ There are two types of domestic train: Intercity (faster, with fewer stops) and Sprinter (slower, stops at each station).

➡ Taking your bike on board costs €6.90. Bikes are only accepted on off-peak Sprinter services.

➡ Check both in *and* out with your ticket/card. Tap it against the card reader in the gates or free-standing posts. You'll hear one beep to enter, and two beeps when departing.

International Tickets

➡ NS International (www.nsinternational.nl) has separate windows to buy international tickets. Queues can be long. Upon entering, take a numbered ticket. When your number is called, you can proceed to the window.

➡ Unless you have a credit card with chip-and-PIN technology (even then, not all foreign chip-enabled cards will work), you'll need to use cash to buy your ticket on-site. There's a €7.50 to €22.50 booking charge for on-site purchases.

➡ An alternative is to buy tickets online at www.b-europe.com, which accepts foreign cards. You may need to print the tickets out.

➡ Be sure to reserve in advance during peak periods.

(€7 to €10 per day), and national and international train ticket sales.

Transport Options

Metro Lines 51, 52, 53 and 54 serve Centraal Station.

Tram Of Amsterdam's 15 tram lines, 8 stop at Centraal Station, and then fan out to the rest of the city. For trams 4, 14, 24 and 26, head far to the left (east) when you come out the station's main entrance; look for the 'A' sign. For trams 2, 12, 13 and 17, head to the right (west) and look for the 'B' sign.

Taxi Taxis queue near the front station entrance toward the west side. Fares are meter-based. It should be €15 to €20 for destinations in the centre, canal ring or Jordaan.

Bus Stations

Buses operated by Eurolines (www.eurolines.com) and FlixBus (www.flixbus.com) connect Amsterdam with all major European capitals and numerous smaller destinations. Book tickets online.

Eurolines buses use **Duivendrecht station** (Stationsplein 3; Ⓜ Duivendrecht), south of the centre, which has an

COMMON TRAM ROUTES

Medieval Centre	Tram 2, 4, 11, 12, 13, 14, 17, 24
Jordaan & Western Canal Ring	Tram 3, 5, 13, 17, 19
Southern Canal Ring	Tram 1, 2, 5, 7, 11, 12, 19 for Leidseplein; 4, 7, 14, 24 for Rembrandtplein
Vondelpark & the South	Tram 1, 2, 3, 5, 11, 12, 24
De Pijp	Tram 3, 4, 12, 24
Nieuwmarkt & Plantage	Tram 1, 3, 7, 14, 19, 26

easy metro link to Centraal Station (about a 20-minute trip via metros 50 or 54).

FlixBus runs to/from Sloterdijk train station, west of the centre, which is linked to Centraal Station by metros 50 or 51 (a six-minute trip).

Car

If you're arriving by car, it's best to leave your vehicle in a park-and-ride lot near the edge of town. A nominal parking fee (around €8 for the first 24 hours and €1 per day thereafter) also gets you discounted public transport tickets. For more info see www.iamsterdam.com.

GETTING AROUND

Central Amsterdam is relatively compact and best seen on foot or by bicycle. The GVB (www.gvb.nl; Stationsplein 10; ☺7am-9pm Mon-Fri, 8am-9pm Sat, 9am-9pm Sun; 🚋2/4/11/12/13/14/17/24/26 Centraal Station) operates the public transport system, a mix of tram, bus, metro and ferry.

The excellent 9292 Journey Planner (www.9292.nl) calculates routes, costs and travel times, and will get you for door to door wherever you're going in the city.

Bicycle

The vast majority of Amsterdammers get around town on their *fietsen* (bikes). Cy-

cling is a big deal here. Bike-hire companies are located all over the city (p29).

Bus

The GVB offers unlimited-ride passes for one to seven days (€8.50 to €36.50), valid on trams, some buses and the metro.

➡ Alternatively, buy a disposable OV-chipkaart (www.ov-chipkaart.nl; one hour €3.20) from the **GVB information office** (www.gvb.nl; Stationsplein 10; ☺7am-9pm Mon-Fri, 8am-9pm Sat, 9am-9pm Sun; 🚋2/4/11/12/13/14/17/24/26 Centraal Station).

➡ *Nachtbussen* (night buses) run after other transport stops (from 1am to 6am, every hour). A ticket costs €4.50.

➡ Note that Connexxion buses (which depart from Centraal Station and are useful to reach sights in southern Amsterdam) and the No 397 airport bus are not part of the GVB system. They cost more (around €6.50).

Train

Trains run by NS (www.ns.nl) serve the outer suburbs and, aside from travelling to/from the airport, most visitors to Amsterdam will rarely need to use them unless undertaking trips further afield. You must top up OV-chipkaarts

at NS machines to use NS trains.

Metro lines, which also serve outer suburbs as well as some inner-city stations, are operated by **GVB** (www.gvb.nl; Stationsplein 10; ☺7am-9pm Mon-Fri, 8am-9pm Sat, 9am-9pm Sun; 🚋2/4/11/12/13/14/17/24/26 Centraal Station) and use GVB's integrated ticketing system. If you're travelling between two neighbourhoods served by metro, it can be much faster than taking a tram, especially in heavy traffic.

Tram

➡ Most public transport within the city is by tram. The vehicles are fast, frequent and ubiquitous, operating between 6am and 12.30am.

➡ Tickets are sold on board by credit/debit card only (cash not accepted). Buy a disposable OV-chipkaart (www.ov-chipkaart.nl; one hour €3.20) or a day pass (one to seven days €8.50 to €36.50) from the **GVB information office** (www.gvb.nl; Stationsplein 10; ☺7am-9pm Mon-Fri, 8am-9pm Sat, 9am-9pm Sun; 🚋2/4/11/12/13/14/17/24/26 Centraal Station).

➡ When you enter *and* exit, wave your card at the machine to 'check in' and 'check out'.

Boat

From late March to early November, the **Canal Bus** (🕿020-217 05 00; www.stromma.nl; day pass €24.50, cruises €11.50-14.50, pedalos €10; ☺9am-6pm Mon-Wed, to 8pm Thu-Sun; 🚭) offers a unique hop-on, hop-off service between its docks around the city and near big museums.

Free ferries to Amsterdam Noord depart from piers behind Centraal Station.

Car

Amsterdam's narrow streets, unfenced canals and hundreds of thousands of cyclists mean driving is *not* recommended.

Parking

➡ Pay-parking applies in the central zone from 6am to midnight Monday to Saturday, and noon to midnight on Sunday. To use the parking machines you need a Dutch credit card; alternatively, go online at www.3377.nl to pay.

➡ Costs are around €7.50/55 per hour/day in most of the city centre and Canal Ring, and around €6/30 in the Jordaan, Museumplein area and around. Prices ease as you move away from the centre.

➡ Clampings are common and fines are steep.

➡ Parking garages include locations at Centraal Station, Damrak, near Leidseplein and under Museumplein and the Stopera, but they're often full and generally cost more than street parking.

➡ A park-and-ride deal near the edge of town is a much better bet.

Road Rules

➡ Drive on the right-hand side of the road.

➡ Seat belts are required for everyone in a vehicle.

➡ Children under 12 must ride in the back if there's room.

➡ Be alert for bicycles, and if you are trying to turn right, be aware that bikes going straight ahead have priority.

➡ Trams always have right of way.

➡ On roundabouts (traffic circles), approaching vehicles have right of way, unless there are traffic signs indicating otherwise.

➡ The blood-alcohol limit when driving is 0.05%.

Car Hire

Requirements for hiring a car in the Netherlands:

➡ Be able to show a valid driving licence from your home country.

➡ Be at least 23 years of age (some companies levy a small surcharge for drivers under 25).

➡ Have a major credit card.

RENTAL AGENTS

Note that most cars have manual transmission. If you need an automatic car, request it well in advance and be prepared for a hefty surcharge.

All the big multinational rental companies are here; many have offices on Overtoom, near the Vondelpark. Rentals at Centraal Station and at Schiphol International Airport incur a surcharge. Companies include the following:

Avis (www.avis.nl)

Enterprise (www.enterprise.nl)

Europcar (www.europcar.nl)

Hertz (www.hertz.nl)

Sixt (www.sixt.nl)

AUTOMOBILE ASSOCIATION

The ANWB (www.anwb.nl) is the Netherlands' auto association. Members of auto associations in their home countries (the AAA, CAA etc) can get assistance, free maps, discounts and more.

Taxi

➡ Taxis are expensive and not very speedy given Amsterdam's maze of streets.

➡ You don't hail taxis on the road. Instead, find them at stands at Centraal Station, Leidseplein and other busy spots around town. You needn't take the first car in the queue.

TRAVEL PASSES

➡ Travel passes are extremely handy and provide substantial savings over per-ride ticket purchases.

➡ The GVB offers unlimited-ride passes for one to seven days (€8.50 to €36.50), valid on trams, some buses and the metro.

➡ Passes are available at the GVB information office and I Amsterdam Visitor Centres (p271), but not on board.

➡ The I Amsterdam Card (www.iamsterdam.com; per 24/48/72/96/120 hours €60/80/95/105/115) includes a GVB travel pass in its fee.

➡ A wider-ranging option is the Amsterdam & Region Day Ticket (€19.50), which goes beyond the tram/metro system, adding on night buses, airport buses, Connexxion buses and regional EBS buses that go to towns such as Haarlem, Muiden and Zaanse Schans. The pass is available at the GVB office and at visitor centres.

➡ Another choice is the Amsterdam Travel Ticket (per one/two/three days €17/22.50/28). It's basically a GVB unlimited-ride pass with an airport train ticket added on. Buy it at the airport (at the NS ticket window) or GVB office.

➡ Another method is to book a taxi by phone. **Taxicentrale Amsterdam** (TCA; ☏020-777 77 77; www.tcataxi.nl) is the most reliable company.

➡ Fares are meter-based. The meter starts at €3.19, then it's €2.35 per kilometre thereafter. A ride from Leidseplein to the Dam costs about €16; from Centraal Station to Jordaan is €13 to €19.

➡ Ride-share service Uber (www.uber.com) operates in Amsterdam; rates vary according to demand.

TOURS

Guided tours are a great way to get to grips with the city, especially if you're short on time.

Walking tours abound, including themed tours covering subjects such as history, architecture or food. Cycling tours and boat tours are also ubiquitous.

Be aware that, as of 2020, city authorities have banned guided tours along sex workers' windows in the Red Light District. Beyond the Red Light District, paying guided tours are still permitted provided tour guides have a permit and follow strict rules.

Free tours and tour touts anywhere in the city are no longer allowed. All tour participants will need to pay a VMR (tourist tax).

★**Plastic Whale** (☏020-737 30 49; www.plasticwhale.com; 2½hr guided tour €39.50; ☺by reservation) Help clean up Amsterdam's waterways while touring them with this pioneering 'plastic-fishing' operator (the world's first). You're

provided with nets to fish out plastic waste from the rivers, harbours and canals; materials collected are recycled to make furniture and even the nine-seat electric boats in which the trips take place. Departs daily year-round from several locations around Amsterdam.

★**Rederij Lampedusa** (Map p298; http://rederij lampedusa.nl/en; Dijksgracht 6; 2hr canal tour €19; ☺canal tours 11am & 1.30pm Sat May-Sep; 🚊26 Muziekgebouw) Take a two-hour canal-boat tour around Amsterdam harbour in former refugee boats, brought from Lampedusa (Italy) by Dutch founder Tuen. The tours are full of heart and offer a fascinating insight, not only into stories of contemporary migration, but also about how immigration shaped Amsterdam's history – especially the canal tour. Departs from next to Mediamatic.

Who is Amsterdam Tours (☏06 4204 2506; www.whois amsterdamtours.com; €59; ☺by reservation 10.30am Thu-Sun) Who is Amsterdam offers an altogether more personal approach than your average walking tour. You'll discover the people behind the city and gain insight into the lives of real Amsterdammers as their stories are passionately told by tour guide Alexandra. Tours last 3½ hours and include 'the best apple pie in Amsterdam' and a glass of local craft beer.

Mee in Mokum (Map p294; www.gildeamsterdam.nl; Gedempte Begijnensloot; tours

adult/child €10/5; ☺11am & 2pm Tue-Sun; 🚊2/11/12 Spui) Mee in Mokum's walkabouts are led by volunteers of all ages who often have personal anecdotes to add. Tours last between two and three hours and depart from the cafe in the Amsterdam Museum (p70). Reserve at least a day in advance and pay cash on the day.

Architectuur Tours (Map p296;☏06 3014 0945; www.architectuurtoursamsterdam.nl; Dijkstraat 55; standard tours €12.50-25; Ⓜ Nieuwmarkt) Architectural historian Alex Hendriksen offers highly recommended tours, including walking tours that explore the buildings of Nieuwmarkt and boat tours along the IJ River, which fascinatingly expose the layers of history and development. Check online for available spots on the English-language Open Tours throughout the year. Standard tours have a minimum of eight people, but customised private tours are also available.

Hungry Birds Street Food Tours (www.hungry birds.nl; 5hr day/night tour per person €89/95; ☺by reservation) Guides take you 'off the eaten track' to chow on Dutch and ethnic specialities. Its range of tours lasting five hours (or so) visit local hotspots from street vendors to family run premises across several neighbourhoods; there are also three-hour daytime tours in De Pijp (€79). Prices include all food. The meet-up location is given after you make reservations.

Directory A–Z

Accessible Travel

➡ Travellers with reduced mobility will find Amsterdam moderately equipped to meet their needs.

➡ Most offices and museums have lifts and/or ramps and toilets for visitors with disabilities.

➡ A large number of budget and midrange hotels have limited accessibility, as they occupy old buildings with steep stairs and no lifts.

➡ Restaurants tend to be on ground floors, though 'ground' sometimes includes a few steps.

➡ Most buses are wheelchair accessible, as are metro stations. Trams are becoming more accessible as new equipment is added. Many lines have elevated stops for wheelchair users. The GVB website (www. gvb.nl) denotes which stops are wheelchair accessible.

➡ Accessible Travel Netherlands publishes a downloadable guide (www.accessibletravelnl. com) to restaurants, sights, transport and routes in Amsterdam for those with limited mobility.

➡ Check the accessibility guide at Accessible Amsterdam (www. toegankelijkamsterdam.nl).

➡ Download Lonely Planet's free Accessible Travel guides from http://lptravel.to/ AccessibleTravel.

Customs Regulations

For visitors from EU countries, limits only apply for excessive amounts. Log on to www.belastingdienst.nl for details.

Residents of non-EU countries are limited to the following:

Alcohol 1L of spirits, 2L of wine or 16L of beer.

Coffee 500g of coffee, or 200g of coffee extracts or coffee essences.

Perfume Up to €430 in value.

Tea 100g of tea, or 40g of tea extracts or tea essences.

Tobacco 200 cigarettes, or 250g of tobacco (shag or pipe tobacco), or 100 cigarillos, or 50 cigars.

Discount Cards

Visitors of various professions, including artists, journalists, museum conservators and teachers, may get discounts at some venues if they show accreditation.

Students regularly get a few euro off museum admission; bring ID.

Seniors over 65, and their partners of 60 or older, benefit from reductions on public transport, museum admissions, concerts and more. You may look younger, so bring your passport.

I Amsterdam Card (www. iamsterdam.com; per 24/48/72/96/120 hours €60/80/95/105/115) Provides admission to more than 30 museums, a canal cruise, and discounts at shops, entertainment venues and restaurants. Also includes a GVB transit pass. Useful for quick visits to the city. Available at I Amsterdam Visitor Centres and some hotels.

Museumkaart (www.museum kaart.nl; adult/child €64.90/ 32.45, plus one-time registration €5) Free and discounted entry to some 400 museums all over the country for one year. Purchase it at participating museum ticket counters. You initially receive a temporary card valid for 31 days (maximum five museums); you can then register it online and receive a permanent card sent to a Dutch address, such as your hotel, within three to five working days.

Holland Pass (www.holland pass.com; three/four/six attractions from €45/60/75) Similar to the I Amsterdam Card, but without the rush for usage; you can visit sights over a month. Prices are based on the number of attractions, which you pick from tiers (the most popular/expensive sights are gold tier). Also includes a train ticket from the airport to the city, and a canal cruise. Purchase it online; pick-up locations include Schiphol Airport and the city centre.

Electricity

Type C
220V/50Hz

Type F
230V/50Hz

Emergency

Police, fire, ambulance ☑112

Internet Access

➡ Free wi-fi is common in lodgings across the price spectrum; many places also have a computer or tablet on-site for you to use.

➡ Hotels will usually print boarding passes and tickets for guests on request.

➡ Most bars, *cafés* (pubs) and coffeeshops have free wi-fi. You may need to ask for the code.

➡ For free wi-fi hotspots around the city, check www.wifi-amsterdam.nl.

Legal Matters

Amsterdam *politie* (police) are pretty relaxed and helpful unless you do something clearly wrong, such as littering or smoking a joint right under their noses.

Police can hold offenders for up to six hours for questioning (plus another six hours if they can't establish your identity, or 24 hours if they consider the matter serious). You won't have the right to a phone call, but you can request that they notify your consulate. You're presumed innocent until proven guilty.

Drugs

➡ Technically, marijuana is illegal. However, possession of soft drugs (eg cannabis) up to 5g is tolerated. Larger amounts are subject to prosecution.

➡ Don't light up in an establishment other than a coffeeshop without checking that it's OK.

➡ Hard drugs are treated as a serious crime.

➡ Never buy drugs of any kind on the street; deaths can and do occur.

ID Papers

Anyone over 14 years of age is required by law to carry ID. Foreigners should carry a passport or a photocopy of the relevant data pages; a driver's licence isn't sufficient.

Prostitution

Prostitution is legal in the Netherlands. The industry is protected by law, and sex workers pay tax. Much of this open policy stems from a desire to undermine the role of pimps and the underworld in the sex industry.

In Amsterdam's Red Light District the streets are well-policed, but the back alleys are more dubious.

LGBT+ Travellers

The Netherlands was the first country to legalise same-sex marriage (in 2001), and Amsterdam's LGBT scene is among the world's largest.

Warmoesstraat, Zeedijk, Rembrandtplein, Leidseplein and Reguliersdwarsstraat are the main hubs.

Top festivals include the music-rocking **Milkshake Festival** (www.milkshake festival.com) in late July, and **Pride Amsterdam** (www.pride.amsterdam) from late July to early August.

Resources:

Gay Amsterdam (www.gay amsterdam.com) Lists hotels, shops and clubs, and provides maps.

Pink Point (Map p300; ☑020-428 10 70; www.pinkpoint.nl; Westermarkt; ☉10.30am-6pm Mon-Sat, noon-6pm Sun; ☒13/17 Westermarkt) Located behind the Westerkerk, Pink Point is part LGBT information kiosk, part souvenir shop. It's a good place to pick up news about parties, events and social groups.

Reguliers (www.reguliers.net) Info on the Reguliersdwarsstraat scene, including current club openings and closings.

Gay & Lesbian Information and News Center (www.gaylinc.nl) Lists hotels, restaurants, nightlife and 'sexciting' events around town.

Medical Services

➡ If you're a citizen of the EU, Switzerland, Iceland, Norway or Liechtenstein, a European Health Insurance Card (EHIC) covers you for most medical care. If you qualify, make sure you arrange the paperwork in your home country prior to travelling to the Netherlands. You still might have to pay on the spot for medical services, but you should be able to claim it back at home.

➡ The Netherlands also has reciprocal health arrangements with Australia. Australian citizens will need to obtain a certificate of eligibility, known as an A111; see www.humanservices. gov.au, which also details the process for obtaining refunds.

➡ Citizens of other countries are advised to take out travel insurance that covers health insurance.

➡ Worldwide travel insurance is available at www.lonelyplanet. com/travel-insurance. You can buy, extend and claim online anytime – even if you're already on the road.

Emergency Rooms

A number of hospitals have 24-hour emergency facilities, including:

Onze Lieve Vrouwe Gasthuis (☑020-599 91 11; www.olvg.nl; Oosterpark 9; ☺24hr; 🚊1/3 Beukenweg) At Oosterpark, near the Tropenmuseum. It's the closest public hospital to the centre of town.

Amsterdam UMC (☑020-444 44 44; www.vumc.com; De Boelelaan 1117; ☺24hr; 🚊16/24 VU Medisch Centrum) University hospital in the city's south.

Pharmacies

Forget about buying flu tablets and antacids at supermarkets; for anything stronger than toothpaste you'll have to go to a pharmacy.

After hours, call **Informatie Dienstdoende Apotheken** (☑020-592 33 15; ☺24hr) to find out which pharmacies are open nearest to you.

Referrals

Contact the Centrale Doktersdiensten (Central Doctors Service; www.doktersdiensten.nl) for doctor, dentist or pharmacy referrals day or night.

Money

The Netherlands uses the euro (€). Denominations of the currency are €5, €10, €20, €50, €100, €200 and €500 notes, and €0.05, €0.10, €0.20, €0.50, €1 and €2 coins (amounts under €1 are called cents). Unlike many eurozone countries, one- and two-cent coins aren't used in the Netherlands.

ATMs

Automatic teller machines can be found outside most banks, at the airport and at Centraal Station. Most accept credit cards such as Visa and MasterCard, as well as cash cards that access the Cirrus and Plus networks. Check with your home bank for service charges before leaving.

In the city centre and at the airport, ATMs often have queues or run out of cash on weekends.

Cash

A surprising number of businesses do not accept credit cards, so it's wise to have cash on hand. (Conversely, many places only accept cards.)

Changing Money

Generally your best bet for exchanging money is to use GWK Travelex (www.gwk.nl), which has several branches around town:

GWK Travelex Centraal Station (☑020-627 27 31; Stationsplein 13f; ☺10am-5pm; 🚊2/4/11/12/13/14/17/24/26 Centraal Station)

GWK Travelex Leidseplein (☑020-622 14 25; Leidsestraat 103; ☺9am-9pm Mon-Fri, from 10am Sat, 10am-8pm Sun; 🚊1/2/5/7/11/12/19 Leidseplein)

GWK Travelex Schiphol Airport (☑020-653 51 21; Arrival Hall 3; ☺6am-10pm)

Credit Cards

All the major international credit cards are recognised, and most hotels and large stores accept them. But a fair number of shops, restaurants and other businesses, such as some

---

PRIOPASS

Priopass (www.priopass.com) is offered by many hotels. The pass – either a printed piece of paper or an electronic version on your mobile phone – provides fast-track entry to most attractions. It's not a discount card – you pay normal rates for museums and tours. But many visitors like it because it's convenient for queue-skipping, there's no deadline for use (so you don't have to scurry around and see several museums in a day to get your money's worth), and you only end up paying for what you use (ie it's not bundled with transit passes, canal cruises etc). The pass itself is free; you link it to your credit card and get charged as you go along.

PRACTICALITIES

➜ **Weights & measures** The metric system is used.

➜ **Smoking** Forbidden inside all hotel rooms, bars and restaurants by law, but permitted outdoors on venues' terraces.

➜ **Dutch newspapers** *De Telegraaf,* the Netherlands' biggest seller; and *Het Parool,* Amsterdam's paper, with the scoop on what's happening around town.

➜ **English newspapers** The *New York Times International Edition* and the *Guardian,* and weeklies such as the *Economist* and *Time,* are commonly available on newsstands.

➜ **Listings magazines** *Uitkrant* is free and widely available around town.

supermarkets, do not accept credit cards, or only accept debit cards with chip-and-PIN technology. Be aware that foreign-issued cards (even chip-and-PIN-enabled foreign credit or debit cards) aren't always accepted (including in some ticket machines), so check first.

Some establishments levy a 5% surcharge (or more) on credit cards to offset the commissions charged by card providers. Always ask beforehand.

Tipping

Bars Not expected.

Hotels Tip €1 to €2 per bag for porters; cleaning staff get a few euros for a job well done.

Restaurants Leave 5% to 10% for a cafe snack (if your bill comes to €9.50, you might round up to €10), 10% or so for a restaurant meal.

Taxis Tip 5% to 10%, or round up to the nearest euro.

Opening Hours

Opening hours sometimes decrease during off-peak months (October to Easter).

Cafés (pubs), bars & coffeeshops Open noon (exact hours vary); most close 1am Sunday to Thursday, 3am Friday and Saturday

General office hours 8.30am–5pm Monday to Friday

Museums 10am–5pm, though some close Monday

Restaurants 11am–2.30pm and 6–10pm

Shops 9am/10am–6pm Monday to Saturday, noon-6pm Sunday. Smaller shops may keep shorter hours and/or close Monday. Many shops stay open late (to 9pm) Thursday.

Supermarkets 8am–8pm; in the city centre some stay open until 9pm or 10pm

Post

The national post office in the Netherlands is privatised and has gone through various name changes. The current operator is PostNL (www.postnl.nl). It has closed most city post offices and to mail a letter or package you'll need to go to a postal service shop, which may be a supermarket or tobacco shop or something else. Use the website (available in English) to find a location near you.

Public Holidays

Most museums adopt Sunday hours on public holidays (except Christmas and New Year, when they close), even if they fall on a day when the place would otherwise be closed, such as Monday.

Nieuwjaarsdag (New Year's Day) 1 January

Goede Vrijdag (Good Friday) March/April

Eerste Paasdag (Easter Sunday) March/April

Tweede Paasdag (Easter Monday) March/April

Koningsdag (King's Day) 27 April (26 April if 27 April is a Sunday)

Dodenherdenking (Remembrance Day) 4 May (unofficial)

Bevrijdingsdag (Liberation Day) 5 May (unofficially celebrated annually; officially every five years, next in 2020)

Hemelvaartsdag (Ascension Day) 40th day after Easter Sunday

Eerste Pinksterdag (Whit Sunday; Pentecost) 50th day after Easter Sunday

Tweede Pinksterdag (Whit Monday) 50th day after Easter Monday

Eerste Kerstdag (Christmas Day) 25 December

Tweede Kerstdag (Second Christmas Day; Boxing Day) 26 December

Taxes & Refunds

Value-added tax (BTW in Dutch) is levied on most goods and services at 6% for restaurants, hotels, books, transport, medicines and museum admissions, and 21% for most other items. It should already be included in stated prices.

Non-EU residents may be able to claim a refund on a minimum €50 spent per shop per day. The website www.belastingdienst.nl has details.

Telephone

The Dutch phone network, KPN (www.kpn.com), is efficient, and prices are reasonable by European standards.

Mobile Phones

Ask your provider about an international plan or buy a local prepaid SIM card, which can be used in most unlocked phones. The EU has abolished international roaming costs; beware of high roaming charges from other countries.

Phone Codes

Drop the leading 0 on numbers if you're calling from outside the Netherlands.

Netherlands country code 31

Amsterdam city code 020

Free calls 0800

Mobile numbers 06

Paid information calls 0900, cost varies

Time

Amsterdam is in the Central European time zone (GMT/UTC plus one hour). Currently it also observes daylight saving hours: clocks go forward one hour at 2am on the last Sunday in March and back again at 3am on the last Sunday in October. In 2019, the European Parliament voted to scrap daylight saving time. Although the law had yet to be finalised at the time of research, the practice is expected to end in 2021.

Be aware that the Dutch use 'half' to indicate 'half before' the hour. If you say 'half eight' (8.30pm in many forms of English), a Dutch person will take this to mean 7.30pm.

Toilets

➡ Public toilets are not a widespread facility on Dutch streets, apart from the free-standing public urinals for men in places such as the Red Light District.

➡ Many people duck into a *café* (ask first!) or department store.

➡ The standard fee for toilet attendants is €0.50.

➡ The app HogeNood (High Need; www.hogenood.nu) maps the nearest toilets based on your location.

Tourist Information

I Amsterdam Visitor Centre (Map p290; 020-702 60 00; www.iamsterdam.com; Stationsplein 10; ⊙9am-6pm; 2/4/11/12/13/14/17/24/26 Centraal Station) Main branch; located in front of Centraal Station. Sells discount cards, theatre and museum tickets, maps and public-transit passes.

Visas

Until 2021, visas for stays of up to 90 days are not required for citizens of the EU, the EEA (European Economic Area) and Switzerland, much of Eastern Europe, Israel, USA, Canada, the majority of Central and South American nations, Japan, Malaysia, Singapore, Australia and New Zealand. All other nationalities, including nationals of China, Russia and South Africa, require a visa.

The Netherlands is part of the Schengen agreement, which includes all EU states (minus Britain and Ireland) and a handful of European countries including Switzerland. In general, a visa issued by one Schengen country is good for all of the other member countries.

The Netherlands Foreign Affairs Ministry (www.government.nl) lists consulates and embassies around the world. Visas and extensions are handled by the Immigratie en Naturalisatiedienst (Immigration & Naturalisation Service; www.ind.nl). Study visas must be applied for via your college or university in the Netherlands.

From 2021, non-EU nationals who don't require a visa for entry to the Schengen area will need prior authorisation to enter under the new European Travel Information and Authorisation System (ETIAS). Travellers can apply online; the cost will be €7 for a three-year, multi-entry authorisation. Visit www.etias.com for more information.

Women Travellers

In terms of safety, Amsterdam is probably as secure as it gets in Europe's major cities. There's little street harassment, even in the Red Light District, although it's best to walk with a friend to minimise unwelcome attention.

Language

Dutch has around 20 million speakers world-wide. As a member of the Germanic language family, Dutch has many similarities with English.

The pronunciation of Dutch is fairly straight-forward. It distinguishes between long and short vowels, which can affect the meaning of words, for example, *man* (man) and *maan* (moon). Also note that aw is pronounced as in 'law', eu as the 'u' in 'nurse', ew as the 'ee' in 'see' (with rounded lips), oh as the 'o' in 'note', öy as the 'er y' (without the 'r') in 'her year', and uh as in 'ago'.

The consonants are pretty simple to pro-nounce too. Note that kh is a throaty sound, similar to the 'ch' in the Scottish *loch*, r is trilled and zh is pronounced as the 's' in 'pleasure'. This said, if you read our coloured pronuncia-tion guides as if they were English, you'll be understood just fine. The stressed syllables are indicated with italics.

Where relevant, both polite and informal op-tions in Dutch are included, indicated with 'pol' and 'inf' respectively.

BASICS

Hello.	*Dag./Hallo.*	dakh/ha·*loh*
Goodbye.	*Dag.*	dakh
Yes./No.	*Ja./Nee.*	yaa/ney
Please.	*Alstublieft.* (pol)	al·stew·*bleeft*
	Alsjeblieft. (inf)	a·shuh·*bleeft*
Thank you.	*Dank u/je.* (pol/inf)	dangk ew/yuh

WANT MORE?

For in-depth language information and handy phrases, check out Lonely Planet's *Dutch phrasebook*. You'll find it at **shop. lonelyplanet.com**, or you can buy Lonely Planet's iPhone phrasebooks at the Apple App Store.

You're welcome.	*Graag gedaan.*	khraakh khuh·*daan*
Excuse me.	*Excuseer mij.*	eks·kew·zeyr mey

How are you?
Hoe gaat het met u/jou? (pol/inf)	hoo khaat het met ew/yaw

Fine. And you?
Goed.	khoot
En met u/jou? (pol/inf)	en met ew/yaw

What's your name?
Hoe heet u/je? (pol/inf)	hoo heyt ew/yuh

My name is ...
Ik heet ...	ik heyt ...

Do you speak English?
Spreekt u Engels?	spreykt ew *eng*·uhls

I don't understand.
Ik begrijp het niet.	ik buh·*khreyp* het neet

ACCOMMODATION

Do you have a ... room?	*Heeft u een ...?*	heyft ew uhn ...
single	*éénpersoons-kamer*	eyn·puhr·sohns·kaa·muhr
double	*tweepersoons-kamer met een dubbel bed*	twey·puhr·sohns·kaa·muhr met uhn du·buhl bet
twin	*tweepersoons-kamer met lits jumeaux*	twey·puhr·sohns·kaa·muhr met lee zhew·*moh*
How much is it per ...?	*Hoeveel kost het per ...?*	hoo·*veyl* kost het puhr ...
night	*nacht*	nakht
person	*persoon*	puhr·*sohn*

Is breakfast included?
Is het ontbijt inbegrepen?	is het ont·*beyt* in·buh·khrey·puhn

bathroom	badkamer	bat·kaa·muhr
bed and breakfast	gasten- kamer	khas·tuhn- kaa·muhr
campsite	camping	kem·ping
guesthouse	pension	pen·syon
hotel	hotel	hoh·tel
window	raam	raam
youth hostel	jeugdherberg	yeukht·her·berkh

DIRECTIONS

Where's the ...?
Waar is ...?　　waar is ...

How far is it?
Hoe ver is het?　　hoo ver is het

What's the address?
Wat is het adres?　　wat is het a·dres

Can you please write it down?
Kunt u dat alstublieft opschrijven?
kunt ew dat al·stew·bleeft op·skhrey·vuhn

Can you show me (on the map)?
Kunt u het mij tonen (op de kaart)?
kunt ew het mey toh·nuhn (op duh kaart)

at the corner	op de hoek	op duh hook
at the traffic lights	bij de verkeers- lichten	bey duh vuhr·keyrs· likh·tuhn
behind	achter	akh·tuhr
in front of	voor	vohr
left	links	lingks
near (to)	dicht bij	dikht bey
next to	naast	naast
opposite	tegenover	tey·khuhn·oh·vuhr
straight ahead	rechtdoor	rekh·dohr
right	rechts	rekhs

EATING & DRINKING

What would you recommend?
Wat kan u aanbevelen?
wat kan ew aan·buh·vey·luhn

What's in that dish?
Wat zit er in dat gerecht?
wat zit uhr in dat khuh·rekht

I'd like the menu, please.
Ik wil graag een menu.　　ik wil khraakh uhn me·new

Delicious!
Heerlijk/Lekker!　　heyr·luhk/le·kuhr

Cheers!
Proost!　　prohst

Please bring the bill.
Mag ik de rekening alstublieft?
makh ik duh rey·kuh·ning al·stew·bleeft

KEY PATTERNS

To get by in Dutch, mix and match these simple patterns with words of your choice:

When's (the next bus)?
Hoe laat gaat (de volgende bus)?
hoo laat khaat (duh vol·khun·duh bus)

Where's (the station)?
Waar is (het station)?　　waar is (het sta·syon)

I'm looking for (a hotel).
Ik ben op zoek naar (een hotel).
ik ben op zook naar (uhn hoh·tel)

Do you have (a map)?
Heeft u (een kaart)?　　heyft ew (uhn kaart)

Is there (a toilet)?
Is er (een toilet)?　　is uhr (uhn twa·let)

I'd like (the menu).
Ik wil graag (een menu).
ik wil khraakh (uhn me·new)

I'd like to (hire a car).
Ik wil graag (een auto huren).
ik wil khraakh (uhn aw·toh hew·ruhn)

Can I (enter)?
Kan ik (binnengaan)?　　kan ik (bi·nuhn·khaan)

Could you please (help me)?
Kunt u alstublieft (helpen)?
kunt ew al·stew·bleeft (hel·puhn)

Do I have to (get a visa)?
Moet ik (een visum hebben)?
moot ik (uhn vee·zum he·buhn)

I'd like to reserve a table for ...	Ik wil graag een tafel voor ... reserveren.	ik wil khraakh uhn taa·fuhl vohr ... rey·ser·vey·ruhn
(two) people	(twee) personen	(twey) puhr·soh·nuhn
(eight) o'clock	(acht) uur	(akht) ewr
I don't eat ...	Ik eet geen ...	ik eyt kheyn ...
eggs	eieren	ey·yuh·ruhn
fish	vis	vis
(red) meat	(rood) vlees	(roht) vleys
nuts	noten	noh·tuhn

Key Words

bar	bar	bar
bottle	fles	fles
breakfast	ontbijt	ont·beyt
cafe	café	ka·fey
cold	koud	kawt
dinner	avondmaal	aa·vont·maal

drink list	*drankkaart*	*drang*·kaart
fork	*vork*	vork
glass	*glas*	khlas
grocery store	*kruidenier*	kröy·duh·*neer*
hot	*heet*	heyt
knife	*mes*	mes
lunch	*middagmaal*	*mi*·dakh·maal
market	*markt*	markt
menu	*menu*	me·*new*
plate	*bord*	bort
pub	*kroeg*	krookh
restaurant	*restaurant*	res·toh·*rant*
spicy	*pikant*	pee·*kant*
spoon	*lepel*	*ley*·puhl
vegetarian (food)	*vegetarisch*	vey·khey·*taa*·ris
with/without	*met/zonder*	met/*zon*·duhr

Meat & Fish

beef	*rundvlees*	*runt*·vleys
chicken	*kip*	kip
duck	*eend*	eynt
fish	*vis*	vis
herring	*haring*	*haa*·ring
lamb	*lamsvlees*	*lams*·vleys
lobster	*kreeft*	kreyft
meat	*vlees*	vleys
mussels	*mosselen*	*mo*·suh·luhn
oysters	*oester*	*oos*·tuhr
pork	*varkensvlees*	*var*·kuhns·vleys
prawn	*steurgarnaal*	*steur*·khar·naal
salmon	*zalm*	zalm
scallops	*kammosselen*	*ka*·mo·suh·luhn
shrimps	*garnalen*	khar·*naa*·luhn
squid	*inktvis*	*ingkt*·vis
trout	*forel*	fo·*rel*
tuna	*tonijn*	toh·*neyn*
turkey	*kalkoen*	kal·*koon*
veal	*kalfsvlees*	*kalfs*·vleys

QUESTION WORDS

How?	*Hoe?*	hoo
What?	*Wat?*	wat
When?	*Wanneer?*	wa·*neyr*
Where?	*Waar?*	waar
Who?	*Wie?*	wee
Why?	*Waarom?*	waa·*rom*

Fruit & Vegetables

apple	*appel*	*a*·puhl
banana	*banaan*	ba·*naan*
beans	*bonen*	*boh*·nuhm
berries	*bessen*	*be*·suhn
cabbage	*kool*	kohl
capsicum	*paprika*	*pa*·pree·ka
carrot	*wortel*	*wor*·tuhl
cauliflower	*bloemkool*	*bloom*·kohl
cucumber	*komkommer*	kom·*ko*·muhr
fruit	*fruit*	fröyt
grapes	*druiven*	*dröy*·vuhn
lemon	*citroen*	see·*troon*
lentils	*linzen*	*lin*·zuhn
mushrooms	*paddestoelen*	*pa*·duh·stoo·luhn
nuts	*noten*	*noh*·tuhn
onions	*uien*	*öy*·yuhn
orange	*sinaasappel*	see·*naas*·a·puhl
peach	*perzik*	*per*·zik
peas	*erwtjes*	*erw*·chus
pineapple	*ananas*	*a*·na·nas
plums	*pruimen*	*pröy*·muhn
potatoes	*aardappels*	*aart*·a·puhls
spinach	*spinazie*	spee·*naa*·zee
tomatoes	*tomaten*	toh·*maa*·tuhn
vegetables	*groenten*	*khroon*·tuhn

Other

bread	*brood*	broht
butter	*boter*	*boh*·tuhr
cheese	*kaas*	kaas
eggs	*eieren*	*ey*·yuh·ruhn
honey	*honing*	*hoh*·ning
ice	*ijs*	eys
jam	*jam*	zhem
noodles	*noedels*	*noo*·duhls
oil	*olie*	*oh*·lee
pastry	*gebak*	khuh·*bak*
pepper	*peper*	*pey*·puhr
rice	*rijst*	reyst
salt	*zout*	zawt
soup	*soep*	soop
soy sauce	*sojasaus*	*soh*·ya·saws
sugar	*suiker*	*söy*·kuhr
vinegar	*azijn*	a·*zeyn*

Drinks

beer	*bier*	beer
coffee	*koffie*	ko·fee
juice	*sap*	sap
milk	*melk*	melk
red wine	*rode wijn*	roh·duh weyn
soft drink	*frisdrank*	fris·drangk
tea	*thee*	tey
water	*water*	waa·tuhr
white wine	*witte wijn*	wi·tuh weyn

EMERGENCIES

Help!
Help!   help

Leave me alone!
Laat me met rust!   laat muh met rust

Call a doctor!
Bel een dokter!   bel uhn dok·tuhr

Call the police!
Bel de politie!   bel duh poh·leet·see

There's been an accident.
Er is een ongeluk gebeurd.   uhr is uhn on·khuh·luk khuh·beurt

I'm lost.
Ik ben verdwaald.   ik ben vuhr·dwaalt

I'm sick.
Ik ben ziek.   ik ben zeek

It hurts here.
Hier doet het pijn.   heer doot het peyn

Where are the toilets?
Waar zijn de toiletten?   waar zeyn duh twa·le·tuhn

I'm allergic to (antibiotics).
Ik ben allergisch voor (antibiotica).   ik ben a·ler·khees vohr (an·tee·bee·yoh·tee·ka)

SHOPPING & SERVICES

I'd like to buy ...
Ik wil graag ... kopen.   ik wil khraakh ... koh·puhn

I'm just looking.
Ik kijk alleen maar.   ik keyk a·leyn maar

Can I look at it?
Kan ik het even zien?   kan ik het ey·vuhn zeen

Do you have any others?
Heeft u nog andere?   heyft ew nokh an·duh·ruh

How much is it?
Hoeveel kost het?   hoo·veyl kost het

That's too expensive.
Dat is te duur.   dat is tuh dewr

Can you lower the price?
Kunt u wat van de prijs afdoen?   kunt ew wat van duh preys af·doon

SIGNS

Ingang	Entrance
Uitgang	Exit
Open	Open
Gesloten	Closed
Inlichtingen	Information
Verboden	Prohibited
Toiletten	Toilets
Heren	Men
Dames	Women

There's a mistake in the bill.
Er zit een fout in de rekening.   uhr zit uhn fawt in duh rey·kuh·ning

ATM	*pin-automaat*	pin·aw·toh·maat
foreign exchange	*wisselkantoor*	wi·suhl·kan·tohr
post office	*postkantoor*	post·kan·tohr
shopping centre	*winkel-centrum*	wing·kuhl·sen·trum
tourist office	*VVV*	vey·vey·vey

TIME & DATES

What time is it?
Hoe laat is het?   hoo laat is het

It's (10) o'clock.
Het is (tien) uur.   het is (teen) ewr

Half past (10).
Half (elf).   half (elf)
(lit: half eleven)

am (morning)	*'s ochtends*	sokh·tuhns
pm (afternoon)	*'s middags*	smi·dakhs
pm (evening)	*'s avonds*	saa·vonts

yesterday	*gisteren*	khis·tuh·ruhn
today	*vandaag*	van·daakh
tomorrow	*morgen*	mor·khuhn

Monday	*maandag*	maan·dakh
Tuesday	*dinsdag*	dins·dakh
Wednesday	*woensdag*	woons·dakh
Thursday	*donderdag*	don·duhr·dakh
Friday	*vrijdag*	vrey·dakh
Saturday	*zaterdag*	zaa·tuhr·dakh
Sunday	*zondag*	zon·dakh

January	januari	ya·new·waa·ree
February	februari	fey·brew·waa·ree
March	maart	maart
April	april	a·pril
May	mei	mey
June	juni	yew·nee
July	juli	yew·lee
August	augustus	aw·khus·tus
September	september	sep·tem·buhr
October	oktober	ok·toh·buhr
November	november	noh·vem·buhr
December	december	dey·sem·buhr

TRANSPORT

Public Transport

Is this the ... to (the left bank)?	Is dit de ... naar (de linker-oever)?	is dit duh ... naar (duh ling·kuhr-oo·vuhr)
ferry	veerboot	veyr·boht
metro	metro	mey·troh
tram	tram	trem
platform	perron	pe·ron
timetable	dienstregeling	deenst·rey·khuh·ling

NUMBERS

1	één	eyn
2	twee	twey
3	drie	dree
4	vier	veer
5	vijf	veyf
6	zes	zes
7	zeven	zey·vuhn
8	acht	akht
9	negen	ney·khuhn
10	tien	teen
20	twintig	twin·tikh
30	dertig	der·tikh
40	veertig	feyr·tikh
50	vijftig	feyf·tikh
60	zestig	ses·tikh
70	zeventig	sey·vuhn·tikh
80	tachtig	takh·tikh
90	negentig	ney·khuhn·tikh
100	honderd	hon·duhrt
1000	duizend	döy·zuhnt

When's the ... (bus)?	Hoe laat gaat de ... (bus)?	hoo laat khaat duh ... (bus)
first	eerste	eyr·stuh
last	laatste	laat·stuh
next	volgende	vol·khun·duh

A ticket to ..., please.
Een kaartje naar ... graag. — uhn kaar·chuh naar ... khraakh

What time does it leave?
Hoe laat vertrekt het? — hoo laat vuhr·trekt het

Does it stop at ...?
Stopt het in ...? — stopt het in ...

What's the next stop?
Welk is de volgende halte? — welk is duh vol·khun·duh hal·tuh

I'd like to get off at ...
Ik wil graag in ... uitstappen. — ik wil khraak in ... öyt·sta·puhn

Is this taxi available?
Is deze taxi vrij? — is dey·zuh tak·see vrey

Please take me to ...
Breng me alstublieft naar ... — breng muh al·stew·bleeft naar ...

Cycling

I'd like ...	Ik wil graag ...	ik wil khraakh ...
my bicycle repaired	mijn fiets laten herstellen	meyn feets laa·tuhn her·ste·luhn
to hire a bicycle	een fiets huren	uhn feets hew·ruhn

I'd like to hire a ...	Ik wil graag een ... huren.	ik wil khraakh uhn ... hew·ruhn
basket	mandje	man·chuh
child seat	kinderzitje	kin·duhr·zi·chuh
helmet	helm	helm

Do you have bicycle parking?
Heeft u parking voor fietsen? — heyft ew par·king vohr feet·suhn

Can we get there by bike?
Kunnen we er met de fiets heen? — ku·nuhn wuh uhr met duh feets heyn

I have a puncture.
Ik heb een lekke band. — ik hep uhn le·kuh bant

bicycle path	fietspad	feets·pat
bicycle pump	fietspomp	feets·pomp
bicycle repairman	fietsenmaker	feet·suhn·maa·kuhr
bicycle stand	fietsenrek	feet·suhn·rek

GLOSSARY

bibliotheek – library

bier – beer

biertje– glass of beer

bitterballen – small, round meat croquettes

broodje – bread roll (with filling)

bruin café – brown cafe; traditional Dutch pub

café – pub, bar; also known as *kroeg*

coffeeshop (also spelt *koffieshop* in Dutch) – cafe authorised to sell cannabis

CS – Centraal Station

drop – salted or sweet liquorice

dwarsstraat – street connecting two (former) canals

eetcafé – *café* serving meals

fiets – bicycle

frites – French fries; also known as *patat*

gezellig – convivial, cosy

gezelligheid – conviviality/ cosiness

gracht – canal

Grachtengordel – Canal Ring

GVB – Gemeentevervoerbedrijf; Amsterdam municipal transport authority

GWK – Grenswisselkantoor; official currency exchanges

hof – courtyard

hofje – almshouse or series of buildings around a small courtyard or garden, such as the Begijnhof

jenever – Dutch gin; also spelled *genever*

kaas – cheese

kade – quay

kerk – church

koffiehuis – coffee house (distinct from a *coffeeshop*)

koninklijk – royal

kroketten – croquettes

markt – town square, market

NS – Nederlandse Spoorwegen; Dutch railway company

OV-chipkaart – fare card for Dutch public transit

pannenkoeken – pancakes

paleis – palace

plein – square

proeflokaal – tasting house

Randstad – literally 'rim city'; the urban agglomeration including Amsterdam, Utrecht, Rotterdam and Den Haag

stamppot – potatoes mashed with another vegetable (eg sauerkraut or kale), served with bacon bits and a smoked sausage

stedelijk – civic, municipal

steeg – alley, lane

straat – street

stroopwafel – thin, syrup-filled waffle

toren – tower

VVV – tourist office

waag – old weigh house

De Wallen – Red Light District

zaal – hall

Behind the Scenes

SEND US YOUR FEEDBACK

We love to hear from travellers – your comments keep us on our toes and help make our books better. Our well-travelled team reads every word on what you loved or loathed about this book. Although we cannot reply individually to your submissions, we always guarantee that your feedback goes straight to the appropriate authors, in time for the next edition. Each person who sends us information is thanked in the next edition – the most useful submissions are rewarded with a selection of digital PDF chapters.

Visit **lonelyplanet.com/contact** to submit your updates and suggestions or to ask for help. Our award-winning website also features inspirational travel stories, news and discussions.

Note: We may edit, reproduce and incorporate your comments in Lonely Planet products such as guidebooks, websites and digital products, so let us know if you don't want your comments reproduced or your name acknowledged. For a copy of our privacy policy visit lonelyplanet.com/privacy.

OUR READERS

Many thanks to the travellers who used the last edition and wrote to us with helpful hints, useful advice and interesting anecdotes:

Becca Williams, Emma Wilding, Imogen Lockyer, Noni May, Véronique Baar, Viktoria Pohl

WRITER THANKS

Catherine Le Nevez

Hartelijk bedankt first and foremost to Julian, and to everyone in Amsterdam and throughout the Netherlands who provided insights, inspiration and good times during this update and over the years. Huge thanks too to my Amsterdam co-authors Kate and Barbara, and to Matt Phillips, Dan Fahey and everyone at LP. As ever, *merci encore* to my parents, brother, *belle-sœur, neveu* and *nièce*.

Kate Morgan

A big thank you to Destination Editor Matt Phillips for commissioning me to work on this fantastic city. Thank you to Christa Doorhof and all of the staff at I Amsterdam for your assistance, and to the many people in Amsterdam who provided assistance and gave me local tips along the way. Finally, a huge thanks to my partner Trent for travelling with me and for all of your support.

Barbara Woolsey

A big heartfelt thanks to all those who have helped in my career along the way, leading to this dream of completing my first Lonely Planet project (in no particular order): Clair Woolsey, Remy Woolsey, René Frank, Marlene Dow and family, Debby Harris, Dixie Michie, Brenda Woolsey-Hartford, Bhec Fernandez, Alyssa Gabrielle and Allexa Scarlet Masongsong, Nolan Janssen, Marc Linneweber, Alexa Kaminsky, Garth and Gloria Pickard, Andrea Schulte-Peevers and Nicola Williams.

ACKNOWLEDGEMENTS

Cover photograph: Zuiderkerk at night, little-wormy/Getty Images ©

Amsterdam Transport Network Map © GVB Amsterdam. Map designed by Carto Studio, Amsterdam

THIS BOOK

This 12th edition of Lonely Planet's *Amsterdam* guidebook was researched and written by Catherine Le Nevez, Kate Morgan and Barbara Woolsey. The previous edition was also written by Catherine, with Abigail Blasi. This guidebook was produced by the following:

Destination Editors Daniel Fahey, Matt Phillips
Senior Product Editors Sandie Kestell, Genna Patterson
Regional Senior Cartographer Mark Griffiths
Product Editor Barbara Delissen
Book Designer Jessica Rose

Assisting Editors James Bainbridge, Michelle Bennett, Gemma Graham, Lorna Parkes, Tamara Sheward, Simon Williamson
Cartographers Hunor Csutoros, Mick Garrett
Cover Researcher Meri Blazevski
Thanks to Sasha Drew, Paul Harding, Gabrielle Stefanos

See also separate subindexes for:

🍴 **EATING P283**

🍷 **DRINKING & NIGHTLIFE P285**

☆ **ENTERTAINMENT P286**

🔒 **SHOPPING P286**

🛏 **SLEEPING P287**

🏃 **SPORTS & ACTIVITIES P287**

Index

Sights 000
Map Pages **000**
Photo Pages **000**

Sights 000
Map Pages **000**
Photo Pages **000**

Amsterdam Maps

Sights
- Beach
- Bird Sanctuary
- Buddhist
- Castle/Palace
- Christian
- Confucian
- Hindu
- Islamic
- Jain
- Jewish
- Monument
- Museum/Gallery/Historic Building
- Ruin
- Shinto
- Sikh
- Taoist
- Winery/Vineyard
- Zoo/Wildlife Sanctuary
- Other Sight

Activities, Courses & Tours
- Bodysurfing
- Diving
- Canoeing/Kayaking
- Course/Tour
- Sento Hot Baths/Onsen
- Skiing
- Snorkelling
- Surfing
- Swimming/Pool
- Walking
- Windsurfing
- Other Activity

Sleeping
- Sleeping
- Camping
- Hut/Shelter

Eating
- Eating

Drinking & Nightlife
- Drinking & Nightlife
- Cafe

Entertainment
- Entertainment

Shopping
- Shopping

Information
- Bank
- Embassy/Consulate
- Hospital/Medical
- Internet
- Police
- Post Office
- Telephone
- Toilet
- Tourist Information
- Other Information

Geographic
- Beach
- Gate
- Hut/Shelter
- Lighthouse
- Lookout
- Mountain/Volcano
- Oasis
- Park
- Pass
- Picnic Area
- Waterfall

Population
- Capital (National)
- Capital (State/Province)
- City/Large Town
- Town/Village

Transport
- Airport
- Border crossing
- Bus
- Cable car/Funicular
- Cycling
- Ferry
- Metro station
- Monorail
- Parking
- Petrol station
- S-Bahn/Subway station
- Taxi
- T-bane/Tunnelbana station
- Train station/Railway
- Tram
- U-Bahn/Underground station
- Other Transport

Routes
- Tollway
- Freeway
- Primary
- Secondary
- Tertiary
- Lane
- Unsealed road
- Road under construction
- Plaza/Mall
- Steps
- Tunnel
- Pedestrian overpass
- Walking Tour
- Walking Tour detour
- Path/Walking Trail

Boundaries
- International
- State/Province
- Disputed
- Regional/Suburb
- Marine Park
- Cliff
- Wall

Hydrography
- River, Creek
- Intermittent River
- Canal
- Water
- Dry/Salt/Intermittent Lake
- Reef

Areas
- Airport/Runway
- Beach/Desert
- Cemetery (Christian)
- Cemetery (Other)
- Glacier
- Mudflat
- Park/Forest
- Sight (Building)
- Sportsground
- Swamp/Mangrove

Note: Not all symbols displayed above appear on the maps in this book

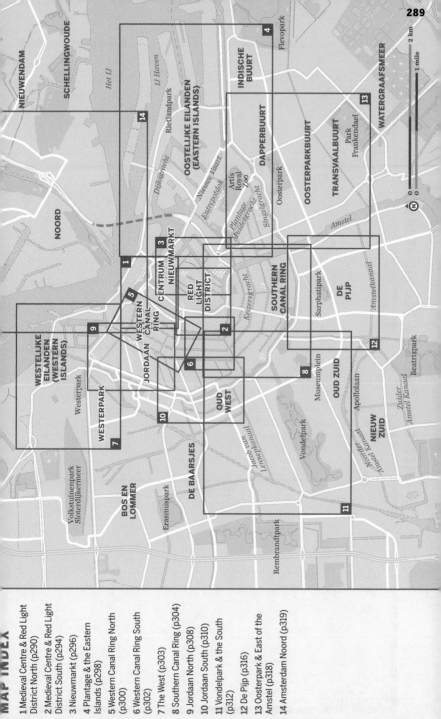

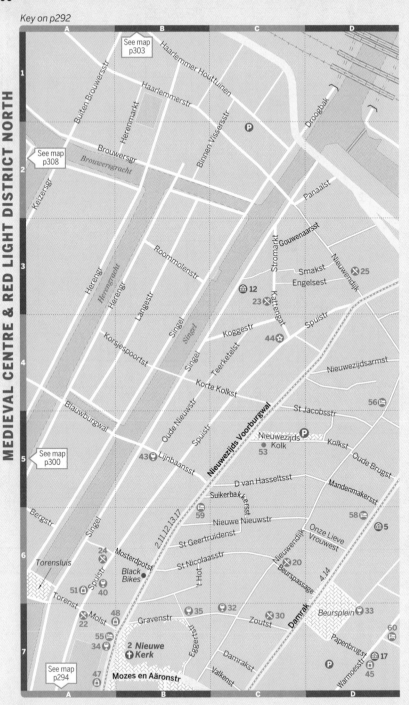

MEDIEVAL CENTRE & RED LIGHT DISTRICT NORTH

See map p303

See map p308

See map p300

See map p294

Buten Brouwersstr
Haarlemmer Houttuinen
Haarlemmerstr
Herenmarkt
Binnen Vissersstr
Brouwersgr
Brouwersgracht
Keizersgr
Herengr
Herengracht
Herengr
Roommolenstr
Langestr
Korsjespoortst
Singel
Singel
Singel
Koggestr
Teerketelst
Koggestr
Korte Kolkst
Blauwburgwal
Oude Nieuwstr
Spuistr
Lijnbaansst
Panaalst
Stromarkt
Gouwenaarsst
Smakst
Engelsest
Kattengat
Spuistr
Nieuwendijk
Nieuwezijdsarmst
St Jacobsstr
Nieuwezijds Voorburgwal
Nieuwezijds Kolk
Kolkst
Oude Brugst
Mandenmakersst
D van Hasseltsst
Suikerbakkersst
2,11,12,13,17
Nieuwe Nieuwstr
St Geertruidenst
St Nicolaasstr
Nieuwendijk
Onze Lieve Vrouwest
Beurspassage
Droogbak
Bergstr
Singel
Torensluis
Mosterdpotst
Black Bikes
Spuistr
Torenst
Molst
Gravenstr
Zoutst
Beursplein
Damrak
Beursplein
Papenbrugst
2 Nieuwe Kerk
Eggertstr
Damrakst
Valkenst
Mozes en Aäronstr
Warmoesstr

P
P
P
P

12
23
25
44
56
53
43
59
58
5
24
51
40
48
22
55
34
35
32
30
33
60
20
17
45
47

2

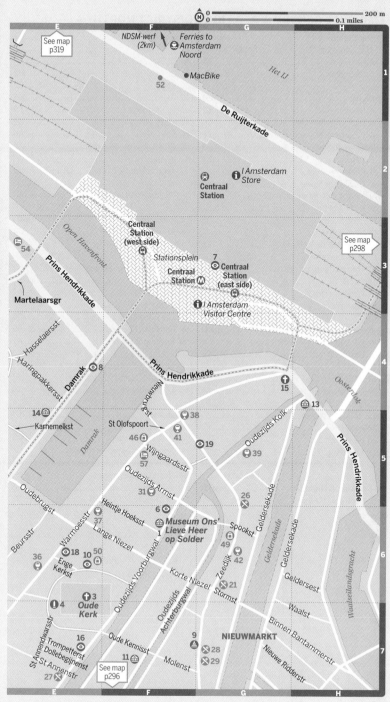

0
0
200 m
0.1 miles

See map
p319

NDSM-werf
(2km)

Ferries to
Amsterdam
Noord

MacBike

52

De Ruijterkade

Het IJ

i Amsterdam
Store

Centraal
Station

Open Havenfront

54

Prins Hendrikkade

Centraal
Station
(west side)

Stationsplein

7
Centraal
Station
(east side)

Centraal
Station M

See map
p298

Martelaarsgr

i Amsterdam
Visitor Centre

Hasselaersst

Haringpakkersst

Damrak

8

Prins Hendrikkade

Nieuwendijk

15

Oosterdok

Prins Hendrikkade

14

Karnemelkst

Damrak

St Olofspoort

38

41

46

19

Oudezijds Kolk

13

39

Wijngaardsst

57

Oudezijds Armst

31

Oudebrugst

Beursstr

Heintje Hoeksst

Warmoesstr

37

Lange Niezel

6

Museum Ons'
Lieve Heer
op Solder

26

Gelderskade

Gelderskade

Waalseilandsgracht

Spookst

49

42

36

18

10

50

Enge
Kerkst

Korte Niezel

Oudezijds Voorburgwal

Zeedijk

21

Stormst

Gelderskade

Gelderst

Waalst

Binnen Bantammerstr

4

3
Oude
Kerk

Oudezijds Achterburgwal

Oude Kennisst

9

NIEUWMARKT

Nieuwe Ridderstr

St Annendwarsst

16

Trompetterst

Dollebegijnenst

St Annenstr

27

11

Molenst

28

29

See map
p296

MEDIEVAL CENTRE & RED LIGHT DISTRICT NORTH *Map on p290*

MEDIEVAL CENTRE & RED LIGHT DISTRICT NORTH

MEDIEVAL CENTRE & RED LIGHT DISTRICT SOUTH *Map on p294*

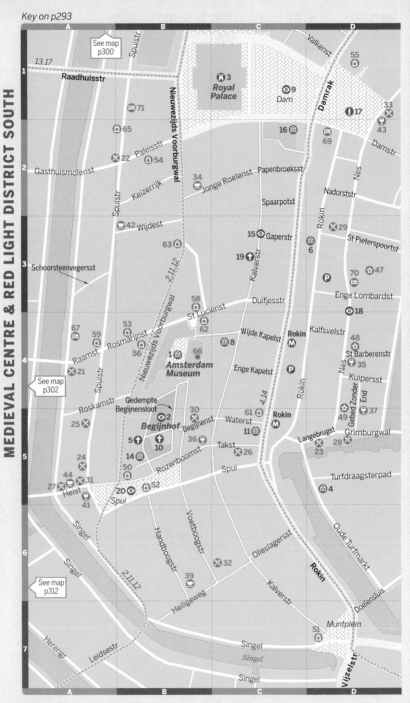

MEDIEVAL CENTRE & RED LIGHT DISTRICT SOUTH

See map p300

13,17

Raadhuisstr

Spuistr

Nieuwezijds Voorburgwal

3
Royal
Palace

9
Dam

Valkenst

Damrak

55

33
43

17

71

65

Paleisstr

22

54

Gasthuismolenst

Spuistr

Keizerrijk

16

69

Damstr

34

Jonge Roelenst

Papenbroeksst

Spaarpotst

Nes

Nadorststr

42

Wijdest

63

58

St Lucienst

62

Schoorsteenvegersst

2,11,12

Nieuwezijds Voorburgwal

Duifjesstr

Wijde Kapelst

Enge Kapelst

15

Gaperstr

19

Kalverstr

Rokin

6

29

St Pieterspoortst

70

47

Enge Lombardst

18

Rokin

M

Kalfsvelstr

48

St Barberenstr

35

Nes

Kuiperss

49

Gebed Zonder End

37

67

59

Rosmarijnst

53

56

8

1
Amsterdam
Museum

66

Raamst

Spuistr

Roskamstr

21

Gedempte
Begijnensloot

2

Begijnhof

30

Begijnenst

Waterst

61

Rokin

M

Langebrugst

28

Grimburgwal

25

5

10

36

11

Takst

26

23

4,14

14

50

Rozenboomst

20

52

Spui

Turfdraagsterpad

4

24

44

31

27

41

Heist

Spui

Singel

Singel

Handboogstr

Voetboogstr

2,11,12

32

39

Heiligeweg

Olieslagersst

Kalverstr

Rokin

Oude Turfmarkt

Muntplein

51

Doelensluis

Herengr

Leidsestr

Singel

Singel

Singel

Vijzelstr

See map p302

See map p312

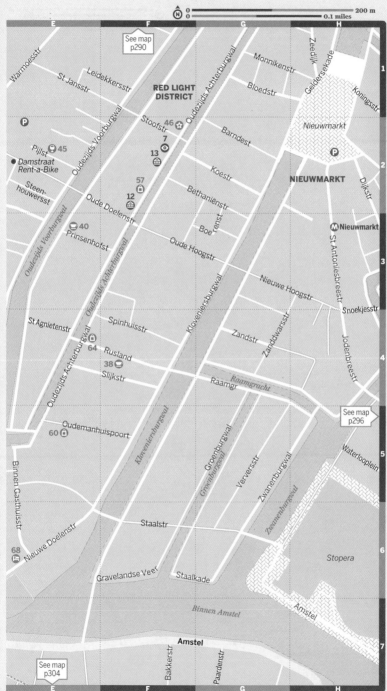

See map p290

See map p296

See map p304

RED LIGHT DISTRICT

NIEUWMARKT

Stopera

NIEUWMARKT

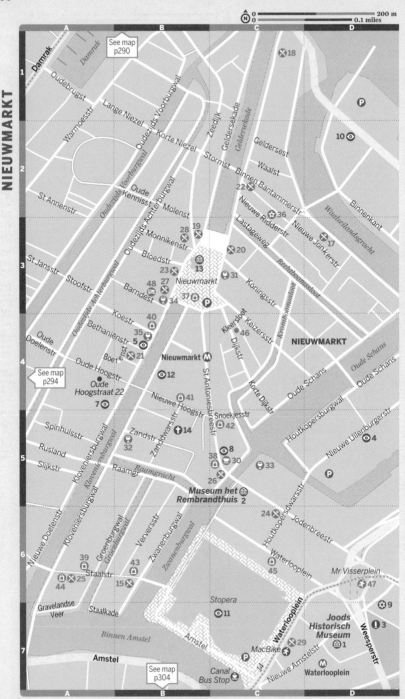

See map p290

N 0 ——————— 200 m
0 ——————— 0.1 miles

Damrak

Damrak

Oudebrugst

Warmoesstr

Lange Niezel

Korte Niezel

Oudezijds Voorburgwal

Zeedijk

Geldersekade

Geldersekade

Stormst

Geldersest

Waalst

Binnen Bantammerstr

Binnenkant

Waalseilandsgracht

St Annenstr

Oude Kennisst

Oudezijds Voorburgwal

Oude

Molenst

Oudezijds Achterburgwal

Monnikenstr

Nieuwe Ridderstr

Lastageweg

Nieuwe Jonkerstr

Recht Boomssloot

St Jansstr

Stoofstr

Oudezijds Achterburgwal

Bloedstr

Barndest

Koningsstr

Kromboomssloot

Koestr

Bethaniënstr

Boerenst

Oude Doelenstr

Oude Hoogstr

Oude Hoogstraat 22

Nieuwmarkt

Nieuwe Hoogstr

St Antoniesbreestr

Snoekjesstr

Dijkstr

Kleersloot

Keizersstr

Korte Dijkstr

Oude Schans

Oude Schans

Oude Schans

NIEUWMARKT

Houtkopersburgwal

Nieuwe Uilenburgerstr

Spinhuisstr

Rusland

Slijkstr

Kloveniersburgwal

Kloveniersburgwal

Zandstr

Zanddwarsstr

Raamgr

Raamgracht

Groenburgwal

Groenburgwal

Verversstr

Zwanenburgwal

Zwanenburgwal

Museum het
Rembrandthuis

Houtkopersdwarsstr

Jodenbreestr

Nieuwe Doelenstr

Staalstr

Gravelandse Veer

Staalkade

Binnen Amstel

Amstel

Waterlooplein

Waterlooplein

Waterlooplein

Mr Visserplein

Joods
Historisch
Museum

Weesperstr

Stopera

Amstel

MacBike

Nieuwe Amstelstr

Canal
Bus Stop

See map p304

See map p294

18
10
22
36
17
28 19
20
23
13
31
48 27
34 37
40
35
5
21
12
41
14
32
42
8
38 30
26
33
2
24
39
43
44 25
15
45
47
9
3
11
29
1
46
7
16

PLANTAGE & THE EASTERN ISLANDS

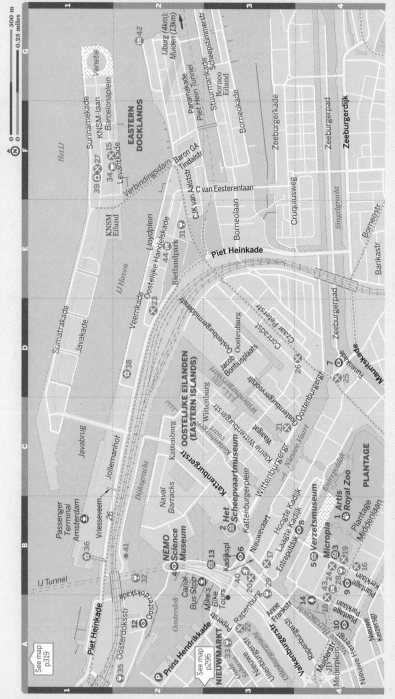

N

0   500 m
0   0.25 miles

See map p319

See map p296

IJ Tunnel

Piet Heinkade

Het IJ

Sumatrakade

Javakade

IJ Haven

KNSM
Eiland

Surinamekade
KNSM-laan
Barcelonaplein

Venetie

EASTERN
DOCKLANDS

Levantkade

Verbindingsdam

Baron GA
Tindalstr

CJK van Aalststr

C van Eesterenlaan

Panamakade
Piet Hein Tunnel
Stuurmankade

Borneo
Eiland

Borneokade

Borneolaan

Zeeburgerkade

Cruquiusweg

Zeeburgerpad

Zeeburgerdijk

Singelgracht

Borneostr

Bankastr

Ijburg (4km);
Muiden (13km)

Lloydplein

Oostelijke Handelskade

Rietlandpark

Piet Heinkade

Veemkade

Zeeburgerpad

Mauritskade

Funenkade

Czaar Peterstr

Conradstr

Oostenburg
Jacob
Bontiusplaats

Oostenburgervoorstr

Oostenburgergr

Oostenburgerstr

Kattenburg

Kattenburgerstr

Kleine Wittenburgerstr

Grote Wittenburgerstr

Wittenburgerstr

Wittenburg

Kattenburgerstr

OOSTELIJKE EILANDEN
(EASTERN ISLANDS)

Dijksgracht

Naval
Barracks

Kattenburgerplein

Jollemanhof

Javabrug

Passenger
Terminal
Amsterdam

Viesseveem

Oosterdoksstr

Oosterdok

Canal
Bus Stop

Mike's
Bike
Tours

Pepstr

Kadijkspl

Nieuwevaart

Hoogte Kadijk

Laagte Kadijk

Entrepotdok

Nieuwe Vaart

Waalgat

PLANTAGE

Artis
Royal Zoo

Plantage
Middenlaan

Prins Hendrikkade

NIEUWMARKT

Valkenburgerstr

Uilenburgerstr

Nieuwe Uilenburgerstr

Rapenburg

Anne
Frankstr

Rapenburg

Rapenburgerstr

NEMO
Science
Museum

Het
Scheepvaartmuseum

Micropia

Verzetsmuseum

Plantage
Kerklaan

Plantage
Parklaan

Nieuwe Herengracht

Nieuwe Herengracht

Muiderstr

Plantage
Middenlaan

Metjenplein
Jn

Plantage
Kerklaan

Nieuwe
Keizersgr

1
2
3
4
5
6
7
8
9
10
12
13
14
16
18
19
20
21
22
23
24
25
26
27
28
29
31
32
33
34
35
36
38
39
40
41
42
44

PLANTAGE & THE EASTERN ISLANDS

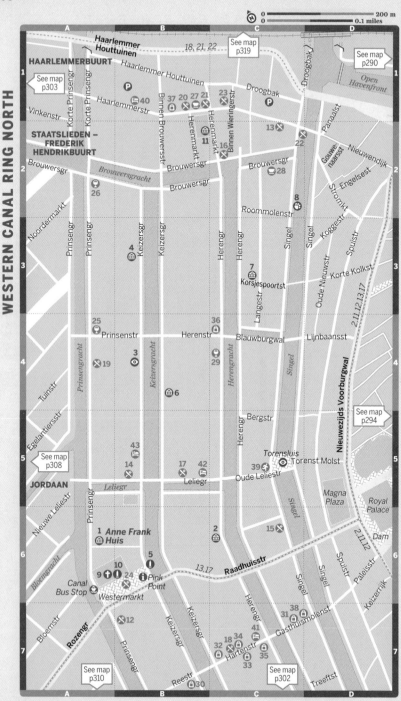

0 | 200 m
0 | 0.1 miles

See map p319
See map p290
See map p303
See map p308
See map p294
See map p310
See map p302

HAARLEMMERBUURT

Haarlemmer Houttuinen

18, 21, 22

Haarlemmer Houttuinen

Droogbak

Open Havenfront

Vinkenstr

Korte Prinsengr

Korte Prinsengr

Haarlemmerstr

40

37 20 27 21

23

Droogbak

Panaalst

STAATSLIEDEN – FREDERIK HENDRIKBUURT

Herenmarkt

11

Binnen Wieringerstr

13

22

Nieuwendijk

Brouwersgr

Brouwersgracht

Brouwersgr

Brouwersgr

16

28

Roommolenstr

8

Gouwe naarsst

Engelsest

Stromkt

Singel

Koggestr

Spuistr

26

4

7

Korsjespoortst

Herengr

Herengr

Oude Nieuwstr

Korte Kolkst

2,11,12,13,17

Noordermarkt

Prinsengr

Prinsengr

Keizersgr

Keizersgr

36

Herenstr

Blauwburgwal

Lijnbaanstr

Nieuwezijds Voorburgwal

25

Prinsenstr

3

19

6

29

Herengracht

Langestr

Singel

Tuinstr

Egelantiersstr

43

14

17 42

Leliegr

Bergstr

Herengr

Torensluis

39

Torenst Molst

Magna Plaza

Royal Palace

JORDAAN

Leliegr

Oude Leliestr

15

2,11,12

Dam

Nieuwe Leliestr

Prinsengr

1 Anne Frank Huis

2

5

13,17

Raadhuisstr

Singel

Spuistr

Paleisstr

Keizerrijk

Bloemgracht

Canal Bus Stop

9 10 24

Pink Point

Westermarkt

12

Bloemstr

Rozengr

Prinsengr

Keizersgr

Keizersgr

Reestr

30

Herengr

31 38

Gasthuismolenst

41

18 34

32 33 35

Hartenstr

Singel

Singel

Treeftst

WESTERN CANAL RING NORTH

WESTERN CANAL RING NORTH

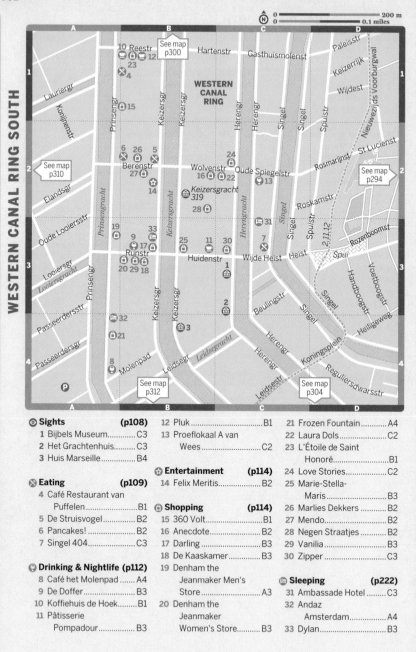

WESTERN CANAL RING SOUTH

THE WEST

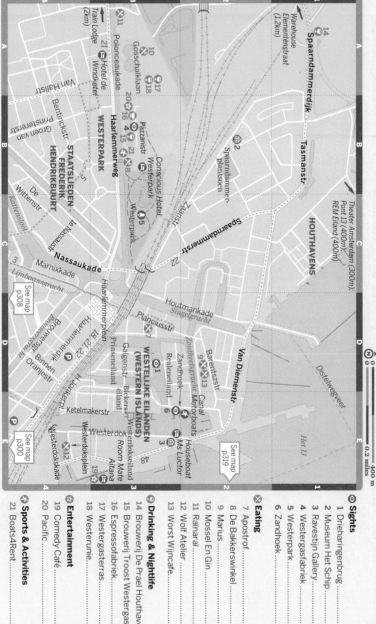

SOUTHERN CANAL RING

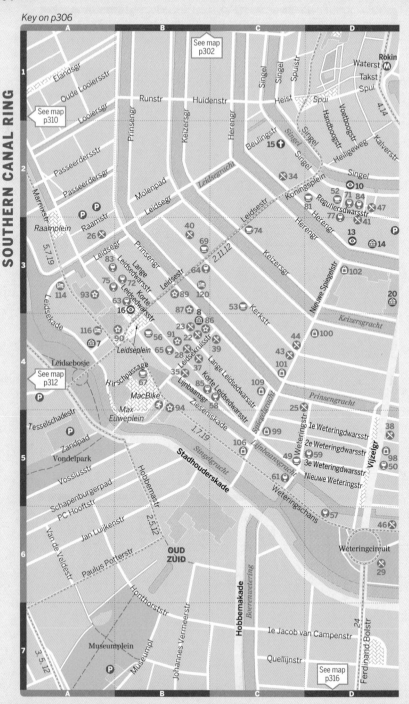

See map
p302

See map
p310

See map
p312

See map
p316

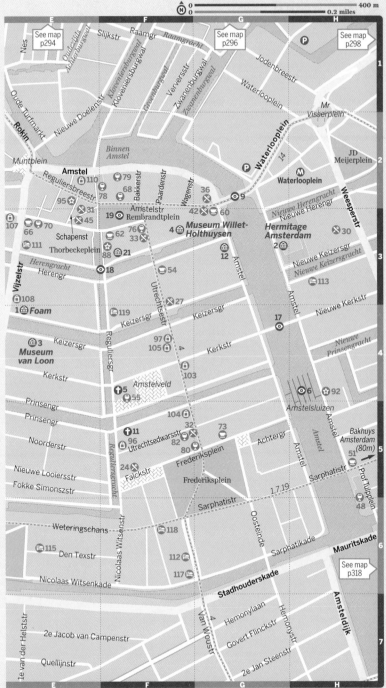

SOUTHERN CANAL RING *Map on p304*

SOUTHERN CANAL RING

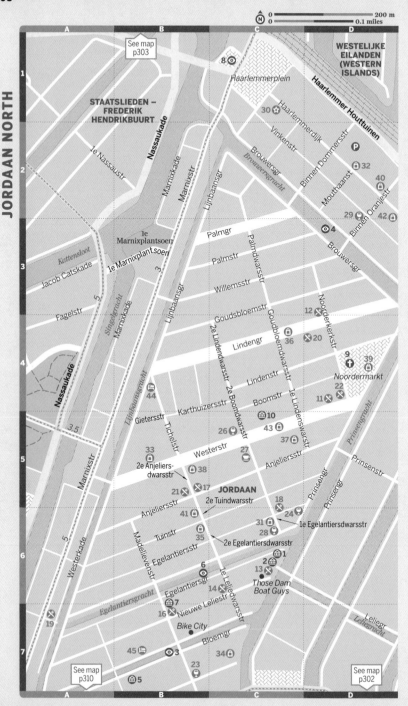

JORDAAN NORTH

See map p303

WESTELIJKE
EILANDEN
(WESTERN
ISLANDS)

Haarlemmerplein

8

Haarlemmer Houttuinen

STAATSLIEDEN –
FREDERIK
HENDRIKBUURT

30

Haarlemmerdijk

Nassaukade

1e Nassaustr

Marnixkade

Marnixstr

Lijnbaansgr

Vinkenstr

Binnen Dommerssstr

Mouthaanstr

Binnen Oranjestr

P

32

40

29

42

Brouwersgr

Brouwersgracht

1e
Marnixplantsoen

1e Marnixplantsoen

Palmgr

Palmstr

Palmdwarsstr

Brouwersgr

4

Kattensloot

Jacob Catskade

Willemsstr

Goudsbloemstr

Goudsbloemdwarsstr

Noorderkerkstr

12

Fagelstr

Singelgracht

Marnixkade

Lindengr

Lindenstr

36

20

9

39

Noordermarkt

Nassaukade

2e Lindendwarsstr

2e Boomdwarsstr

1e Lindenswarsstr

Prinsengracht

22

11

44

Karthuizersstr

Boomstr

10

Gietersstr

Tichelstr

26

43

37

Marnixstr

33

Westerstr

27

2e Anjeliers-
dwarsstr

38

Anjeliersstr

5

Westerkade

21

17

JORDAAN

2e Tuindwarsstr

41

18

24

Prinsengr

Prinsengr

Prinsenstr

Madelievenstr

Tuinstr

35

2e Egelantiersdwarsstr

31

1e Egelantiersdwarsstr

28

Egelantiersstr

1

6

2

13

Those Dam
Boat Guys

Egelantiersgr

14

1e Leliedwarsstr

19

7

Nieuwe Leliestr

16

Bike City

Leliegr

Lelieghracht

Bloemgr

45

3

34

23

See map p310

5

See map p302

0   200 m
0   0.1 miles

N

JORDAAN NORTH

JORDAAN SOUTH

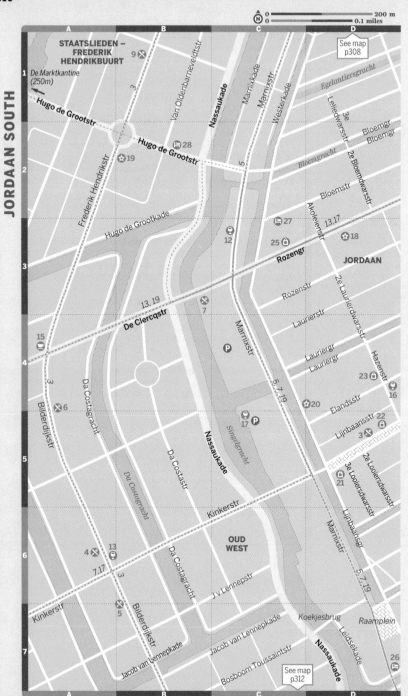

0 ———— 200 m
0 ———— 0.1 miles

See map p308

STAATSLIEDEN –
FREDERIK
HENDRIKBUURT

De Marktkantine
(250m)

Hugo de Grootstr

Van Oldenbarneveldtstr

Nassaukade

Marnixkade

Marnixstr

Westerkade

Egelantiersgracht

Hugo de Grootstr

9

28

19

Hugo de Grootkade

3e Leliedwarsstr

Bloemgr
Bloemgr

Bloemgracht

2e Bloemdwarsstr

Bloemstr

Bloemstr

Akoleienstr

13, 17

27

12

25

18

Rozengr

JORDAAN

Rozenstr

Rozenstr

2e Laurierdwarsstr

De Clercqstr

13, 19

7

Laurierstr

Laurierstr

Laurierstr

Laurierstr

Hazenstr

15

Marnixstr

Da Costagracht

23

16

3

6

Bilderdijkstr

Da Costastr

Elandsstr

20

5, 7, 19

Lijnbaansstr

22

17

3

Nassaukade

Singelgracht

3e Loolerstwarsstr

21

2e Looierstwarsstr

Kinkerstr

OUD
WEST

Da Costagracht

Da Costastr

Lijnbaangr

Marnixstr

5, 7, 19

4

13

J v Lennepstr

Kinkerstr

7, 17

3

Koekjesbrug

Raamplein

5

Bilderdijkstr

Jacob van Lennepkade

Jacob van Lennepkade

Bosboom Toussaintstr

Leidsekade

Nassaukade

26

See map p312

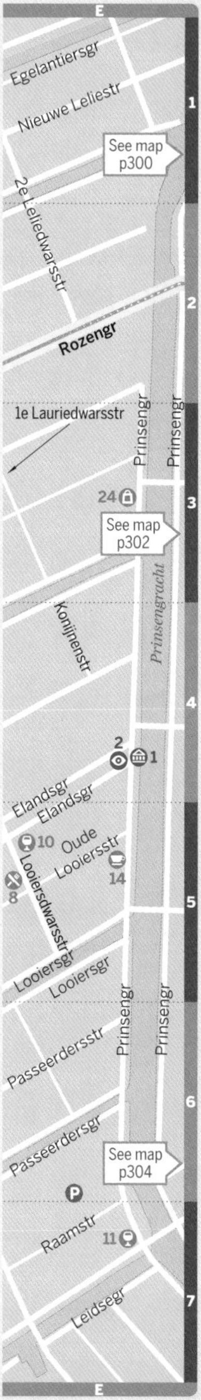

JORDAAN SOUTH

Egelantiersgr
Nieuwe Leliestr
2e Leliedwarsstr
Rozengr
1e Lauriedwarsstr
Konijnenstr
Elandsgr
Oude Looiersstr
Looiersdwarsstr
Looiersgr
Passeerdersstr
Passeerdersgr
Raamstr
Leidsegr
Prinsengr
Prinsengracht

See map p300
See map p302
See map p304

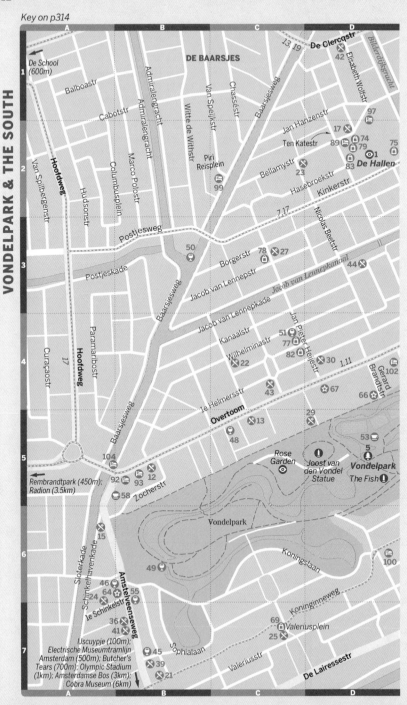

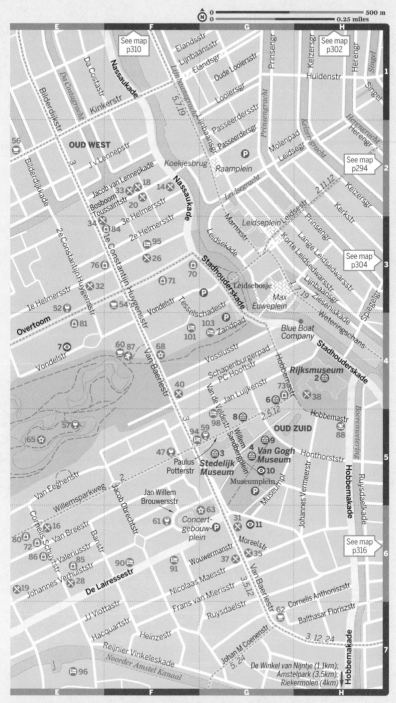

0   500 m
0   0.25 miles

See map p310

See map p302

See map p294

See map p304

See map p316

OUD WEST

OUD ZUID

Overtoom

De Lairessestr

Concertgebouwplein

Museumplein

Paulus Potterstr

Stedelijk Museum

Van Gogh Museum

Rijksmuseum

Blue Boat Company

Max Euweplein

Leidseplein

Raamplein

Koekjesbrug

Vondelstr

Van Baerlestr

Van Eeghenstr

Willemsparkweg

Jacob Obrechtstr

Nassaukade

Stadhouderskade

Stadhouderskade

Hobbemakade

Hobbemakade

Hobbemastr

Hobbemastr

Prinsengracht

Keizersgracht

Herengracht

Singel

Bilderdijkstr

Bilderdijkkade

Da Costastr

Da Costagracht

Kinkerstr

Nassaukade

2e Constantijn Huygensstr

1e Constantijn Huygensstr

1e Helmersstr

2e Helmersstr

2e Helmersstr

3e Helmersstr

Jacob van Lennepkade

J V Lennepstr

Bosboom Toussaintstr

Leidsekade

Leidsegracht

Leidsestr

Leidsegr

Lange Leidsedwarsstr

Korte Leidsedwarsstr

Korte Leidsedwarsstr

Lijnbaansgracht

Lijnbaansgr

Lijnbaansgr

Elandsstr

Elandsgr

Lijnbaanstr

Oude Looiersstr

Looiersgr

Passeerderstr

Passeerdersgr

Passeerdersgr

Molenpad

Leidsegr

Prinsengr

Huidenstr

Keizersgr

Kerkstr

Ziesenisskade

Weteringschans

Boerenwetering

Ruysdaelkade

Marnixstr

Tesselschadestr

Stadhouderskade

Zandpad

Vossiusstr

Schapenburgerpad

PC Hooftstr

Van de Veldestr

Jan Luijkenstr

Willem Sandbergplein

Honthorststr

Johannes Vermeerstr

Museumpl

Jan Willem Brouwersstr

Moreelsestr

Wouwermanstr

Nicolaas Maesstr

Frans van Mierisstr

Ruysdaelstr

Cornelis Anthoniszstr

Balthasar Floriszstr

Cornelis Schuytstr

Van Breestr

Bachstr

Valeriusstr

Johannes Verhulststr

JJ Viottastr

Hacquartstr

Heinzestr

Reijnier Vinkeleskade

Noorder Amstel Kanaal

De Lairessestr

Nicolaas Maesstr

Johan M Coenenstr

5, 24

3, 12, 24

3, 5, 12

2, 5, 12

2, 5, 12

1, 2, 11, 12

5, 7, 19

5, 7, 19

2, 7, 19

De Winkel van Nijntje (1.1km);
Amstelpark (3.5km);
Riekermolen (4km)

56

7

52

81

65

57

60 87

68

40

94

59

98

8

47

3

4

9

10

63

61

31

11

35

37

62

96

90

91

85

86

19

16

72

80

32

76

54

71

70

103

101

26

95

84

34

20

33 18

14

2

6 38

73

88

VONDELPARK & SOUTH *Map on p312*

VONDELPARK & THE SOUTH

DE PIJP *Map on p316*

DE PIJP

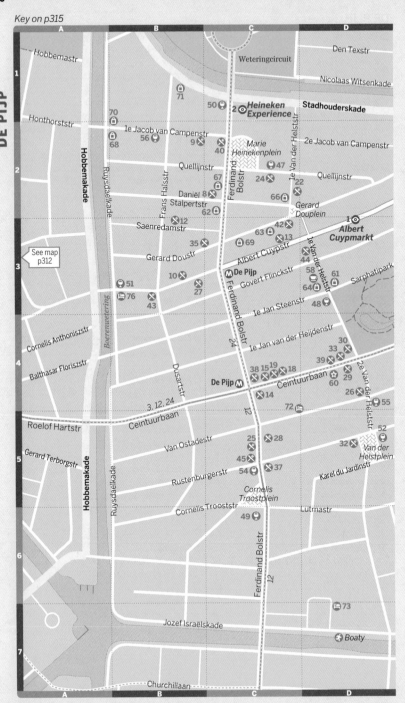

DE PIJP

Hobbemastr

Honthorststr

Hobbemakade

Ruysdaelkade

See map
p312

Boerenwetering

Cornelis Anthoniszstr

Balthasar Floriszstr

Hobbemakade

Ruysdaelkade

Gerard Terborgstr

Roelof Hartstr

Hobbemastr

71

70

1e Jacob van Campenstr

56

68

9

40

Quellijnstr

Frans Halsstr

Daniël
Stalpertstr 8

62

12

Saenredamstr

35

Gerard Doustr

10

27

51

76

43

Dusartstr

De Pijp

3, 12, 24

Ceintuurbaan

Van Ostadestr

Rustenburgerstr

45

54

25

37

Cornelis
Troostplein

Cornelis Trooststr

49

Jozef Israëlskade

Weteringcircuit

Den Texstr

Nicolaas Witsenkade

50

2

Heineken
Experience

Stadhouderskade

Marie
Heinekenplein

2e Jacob van Campenstr

47

24

66

67

Ferdinand Bolstr

1e Van der Helststr

22

Quellijnstr

Gerard
Douplein

63

69

42

13

1

Albert
Cuypmarkt

De Pijp

Govert Flinckstr

Albert Cuypstr

44

58

64

61

1e Van der Helststr

Sarphatipark

1e Jan Steenstr

48

Ferdinand Bolstr

24

1e Jan van der Heijdenstr

30

33

39

38 15 19 18

De Pijp

Ceintuurbaan

60

29

26

2e Van der Helststr

55

14

72

12

52

32

Van der
Helstplein

Karel du Jardinstr

12

Lutmastr

73

Boaty

Churchillaan

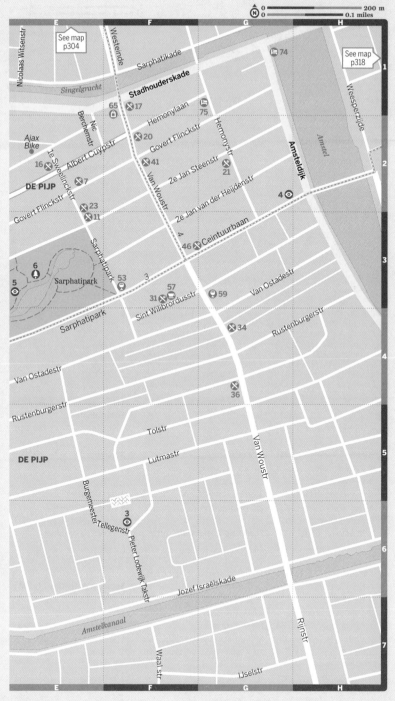

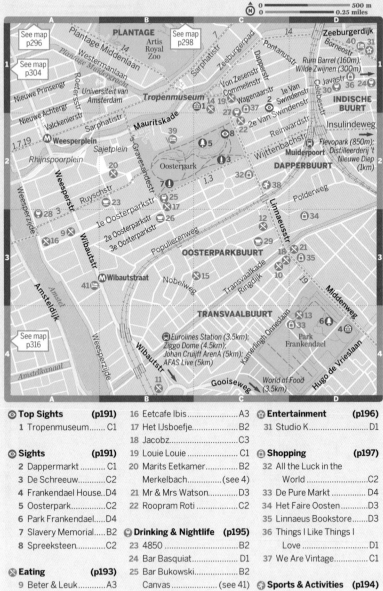

AMSTERDAM NOORD

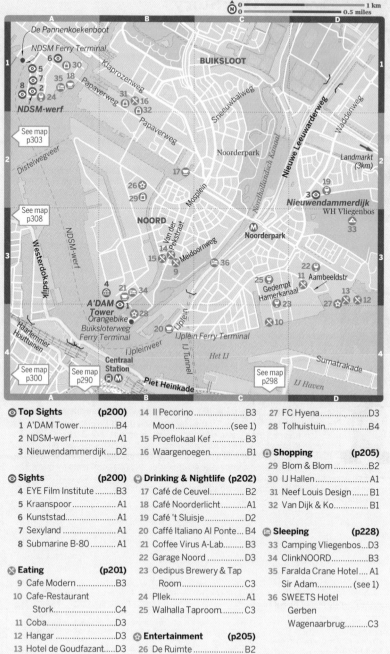

Our Story

A beat-up old car, a few dollars in the pocket and a sense of adventure. In 1972 that's all Tony and Maureen Wheeler needed for the trip of a lifetime – across Europe and Asia overland to Australia. It took several months, and at the end – broke but inspired – they sat at their kitchen table writing and stapling together their first travel guide, *Across Asia on the Cheap*. Within a week they'd sold 1500 copies. Lonely Planet was born.

Today, Lonely Planet has offices in Franklin, London, Melbourne, Oakland, Dublin, Beijing and Delhi, with more than 600 staff and writers. We share Tony's belief that 'a great guidebook should do three things: inform, educate and amuse'.

Our Writers

Catherine Le Nevez

De Pijp; Jordaan & the West; Medieval Centre & Red Light District; Western Canal Ring; Day Trips Catherine's wanderlust kicked in when she road-tripped across Europe from her Parisian base aged four, and she's been hitting the road at every opportunity since, travelling to some 60 countries and completing her Doctorate of Creative Arts in Writing, Masters in Professional Writing, and postgrad qualifications in Editing and Publishing along the way. Over the past decade-and-a-half she's written scores of Lonely Planet guides and articles covering Paris, France, Europe and far beyond. Her work has also appeared in numerous online and print publications. Topping Catherine's list of travel tips is to travel without any expectations. Catherine also wrote the Plan Your Trip, Understand and Survival sections.

Kate Morgan

Amsterdam Noord; Nieuwmarkt, Plantage & the Eastern Islands; Oosterpark & East of the Amstel; Vondelpark & the South Having worked for Lonely Planet for over a decade now, Kate has been fortunate enough to cover plenty of ground working as a travel writer on destinations such as Shanghai, Japan, India, Russia, Zimbabwe, the Philippines and Phuket. She has done stints living in London, Paris and Osaka but these days is based in one of her favourite regions in the world – Victoria, Australia. In between travelling the world and writing about it, Kate enjoys spending time at home working as a freelance editor.

Barbara Woolsey

Southern Canal Ring Barbara was born and raised on the Canadian prairies to a Filipino mother and Irish-Scottish father – and that third culture kid upbringing has fuelled a life's passion for cross-cultural storytelling. Barbara's career started in Bangkok working for Thailand's largest English-language newspaper, then travelling around Asia as a TV host for a Bangkok-based channel. Since then, she's voyaged across over 40 countries and five continents by plane, train and motorbike. In addition to writing for Lonely Planet, Barbara writes for newspapers, magazines and websites with readerships around the world. She spends most of her time in her adopted home of Berlin, Germany.

Published by Lonely Planet Global Limited
CRN 554153
12th edition – May 2020
ISBN 978 1 78701 519 7
© Lonely Planet 2020   Photographs © as indicated 2020
10 9 8 7 6 5 4 3 2 1
Printed in Malaysia